Assessment and Treatment
of Sex Offenders

Assessment and Treatment of Sex Offenders: A Handbook

Edited by

Anthony R. Beech, Leam A. Craig and Kevin D. Browne

WILEY-BLACKWELL

A John Wiley & Sons, Ltd., Publication

This edition first published 2009
© 2009 John Wiley & Sons Ltd.

Wiley-Blackwell is an imprint of John Wiley & Sons, formed by the merger of Wiley's global Scientific, Technical, and Medical business with Blackwell Publishing.

Registered Office
John Wiley & Sons Ltd, The Atrium, Southern Gate, Chichester, West Sussex, PO19 8SQ, UK

Editorial Offices
The Atrium, Southern Gate, Chichester, West Sussex, PO19 8SQ, UK
9600 Garsington Road, Oxford, OX4 2DQ, UK
350 Main Street, Malden, MA 02148-5020, USA

For details of our global editorial offices, for customer services, and for information about how to apply for permission to reuse the copyright material in this book please see our website at www.wiley.com/wiley-blackwell.

The right of the editors to be identified as the authors of the editorial material in this work has been asserted in accordance with the Copyright, Designs and Patents Act 1988.

Library of Congress Cataloging-in-Publication Data

Assessment and treatment of sex offenders : a handbook / [edited by]
Anthony R. Beech, Leam A. Craig & Kevin D. Browne.
    p. cm.
    Includes bibliographical references and index.
    ISBN 978-0-470-01899-6 chbks   ISBN 978-0-470-01900-9   (pbk. : alk. paper)
  1. Sex offenders.   2. Sex offenders–Rehabilitation.   3. Sex offenders–Psychology.   4. Criminal behavior,
Prediction of.   5. Risk assessment.   I. Beech, Anthony R. II. Craig, Leam.   III. Browne, Kevin.
    HV6556.A77 2009
    365'.661–dc22

                                                                                                    2008022819

British Library Cataloguing in Publication Data
  A catalogue record for this book is available from the British Library

Typeset in 11/13pt Times New Roman by Thomson Digital
Printed and bound in Singapore by Markono Print Media Pte Ltd
1   2009

Dedication

Anthony Beech: *For Dawn and Jake, with all my love, who have to endure many hours without me to enable projects like this to see the light of day.*

Leam Craig: *For my parents and Nola, for their never-ending love and support, and for Rohan's future.*

Kevin Browne: *For my children; I hope the time I have invested in this project at their expense will be compensated by their better protection as a result of this book.*

Acknowledgements

We would like to thank all those at Wiley (especially Gillian Lesley and Claire Rushton) for allowing us the opportunity to produce this book. We would also like to give a special thank you to Gill Whitley for all her hard work in copyediting the manuscript.
Anthony Beech, Leam Craig and Kevin Browne
Spring 2008

Contents

About the Editors   xi

List of Contributors   xiii

Foreword   xxv

INTRODUCTION

1. Overview   1
    Anthony R. Beech, Leam A. Craig and Kevin D. Browne

2. Attachment Problems and Sex Offending   13
    Jackie Craissati

PART ONE: RISK ASSESSMENT

3. Factors Associated with Sexual Recidivism   39
    Franca Cortoni

4. The Predictive Accuracy of Risk Factors and Frameworks   53
    Leam A. Craig, Anthony R. Beech and Leigh Harkins

PART TWO: APPROACHES TO OFFENDER ASSESSMENT

5. Sex Offender Risk-Based Case Formulation   77
    Douglas P. Boer, Jo Thakker and Tony Ward

6. Psychometric Assessment of Sexual Deviance   89
    Leam A. Craig and Anthony R. Beech

7. Measuring Sexual Deviance: Attention-Based Measures   109
    Carmen L.Z. Gress and D. Richard Laws

8. The Standardisation of Phallometry   129
    Yolanda Fernandez

9. Using the Polygraph to Manage Risk in Sex Offenders   145
    Don Grubin

10. Assessment of Sexual Addiction   163
    Liam E. Marshall and Matt D. O'Brien

PART THREE: ASSESSMENTS FOR SPECIFIC POPULATIONS

11. Decision Making During the Offending Process: An Assessment
    Among Subtypes of Sexual Aggressors of Women   181
    Jean Proulx and Eric Beauregard

12. Internet Sex Offenders   199
    David Middleton

13. The Assessment of Treatment-Related Issues and Risk in Sex Offenders
    and Abusers with Intellectual Disability   217
    William R. Lindsay and John L. Taylor

14. The Peaks: Assessing Sex Offenders in a Dangerous and Severe
    Personality Disorders Unit   237
    Todd E. Hogue

15. Predicting Risk of Sexual Recidivism in Juveniles: Predictive
    Validity of the J-SOAP-II   265
    *Robert A. Prentky, Ann Pimental, Deborah J. Cavanaugh
    and Sue Righthand*

PART FOUR: INTERVENTIONS

16. Models of Offender Rehabilitation: The Good Lives Model and the
    Risk-Need-Responsivity Model   293
    Tony Ward, Rachael M. Collie and Patrice Bourke

17. Modifying Sexual Preferences   311
    William. L. Marshall, Matt D. O'Brien and Liam E. Marshall

18. Advances in the Treatment of Adult Incarcerated Sex
    Offenders   329
    Ruth E. Mann and William L. Marshall

19. A Community Residential Treatment Approach for Sexual Abusers:
    A Description of the Lucy Faithfull Foundation's Wolvercote Clinic
    and Related Projects   349
    Hilary Eldridge and Donald Findlater

PART FIVE: ISSUES/INTERVENTIONS FOR SPECIFIC POPULATIONS

20. Treatment for Men with Intellectual Disabilities and Sexually
    Abusive Behaviour   369
    Glynis Murphy and Neil Sinclair

21. Interventions with Sex Offenders with Mental Illness   393
    Tanya Garrett and Brian Thomas-Peter

22. Working with Sex Offenders with Personality Disorder
    Diagnoses   409
    Lawrence Jones

23. Understanding the Complexities and Needs of Adolescent
    Sex Offenders   431
    Phil Rich

24. Multisystemic Therapy for Youth with Problem Sexual
    Behaviors   453
    *Elizabeth J. Letourneau, Charles M. Borduin and
    Cindy M. Schaeffer*

25. Female Sex Offenders: Issues and Considerations in Working
    with this Population   473
    Hannah J. Ford

PART SIX: POLICY AND PRACTICE

26. Working to Prevent Sexual Abuse in the Family   491
    Kevin D. Browne

27. Police Work with Sex Offenders: Detection, Management
    and Assessment   515
    Kevin D. Browne

28.   Community Strategies for Managing High-Risk Offenders: The
      Contribution of Multi-Agency Public Protection Arrangements   535
      Hazel Kemshall and Jason Wood

29.   Actuarial Risk Assessments in USA Courtrooms   551
      Dennis M. Doren

Index   **567**

About the Editors

Anthony R. Beech, DPhil, BSc, FBPsS, C.Psychol (Forensic) is Professor of Criminological Psychology, at the Centre for Forensic and Criminological Psychology, University of Birmingham, UK. He has published widely on the assessment and treatment of sexual offenders and is the principal researcher on the Sex Offender Treatment Evaluation Project (STEP) team that has examined the effectiveness of treatment for sex offenders provided in UK prisons and probation services. His work is regarded as having a major influence on assessment and treatment in the UK. He has recently completed an authored book with Professor Tony Ward and Dr Devon Polaschek entitled *Theories of Sexual Offending* and an edited book with Dr Theresa Gannon, Professor Tony Ward and Dr Dawn Fisher entitled *Aggressive Offenders' Cognition: Theory, Research and Practice* both in the Wiley Series in Forensic Clinical Psychology. Email: a.r.beech@bham.ac.uk

Leam A. Craig, PhD, MSc, BA (Hons), C.Sci, AFBPsS, EuroPsy, C.Psychol (Forensic) is a consultant forensic psychologist and Partner of Forensic Psychology Practice Ltd. He is the holder of the European Certificate in Psychology. His current practice includes direct services to forensic NHS Adult Mental Health Trusts and consultancy to Prison and Probation Services. He acts as an expert witness to civil and criminal courts in the assessment of sexual and violent offenders. He coordinates community-based treatment programmes for sexual offenders with learning disabilities in NHS and probation settings. His doctoral research investigated the assessment, treatment and management of sex offenders and he has published numerous research articles and chapters in a range of research and professional journals. He has recently completed an authored book with Professors Anthony Beech and Kevin Browne entitled *Assessing Risk in Sex Offenders: A Practitioner's Guide*: Wiley (2008), and is currently working on *Assessment and Treatment of Sexual Offenders with Intellectual Disabilities: A Handbook*: Wiley (with Professors Kevin Browne and William Lindsay). He is an Honorary Senior Research Fellow at the Centre for Forensic and Family Psychology, University of Birmingham, UK. Email: leamcraig@forensicpsychology.co.uk

Professor Kevin D. Browne, BSc, MSc, PhD, MEd, C.Biol, C.Psychol (Forensic) is both a chartered biologist and chartered psychologist employed by the University of Liverpool as Chair of Forensic and Child Psychology. He has been researching family violence and child maltreatment for 30 years and has published extensively on the prevention of violence to children. After 12 years as an Executive Councillor of the International Society for the Prevention of Child Abuse and Neglect (ISPCAN), he is currently consultant to the European Commission, UNICEF and heads the World Health Organization Collaborating Centre on Child Care and Protection based in the UK. His research interests are concerned with the development of aggression, antisocial and criminal behaviour in children and teenagers, in particular the role of family violence, child abuse and neglect. His most recent policy publications are a chapter on 'Violence against the child in the home and family' contributed to the UN Secretary General's World Report on Violence to Children (October 2006) and a policy briefing to the World Health Organization (August 2007) on *Preventing Child Maltreatment in Europe: A Public Health Approach*. Email: kevin.browne@liverpool.ac.uk

List of Contributors

Eric Beauregard, PhD is an Assistant Professor in the School of Criminology at Simon Fraser University. Before coming to Simon Fraser University, he worked for six years in the Correctional Service of Canada where he was responsible for the assessment of sex offenders. He received his PhD from the University of Montreal and has published a number of papers and book chapters on sexual homicide and the offending patterns of sexual offenders. His current research interests include the analysis of the criminal event, the decision making of sexual offenders, geographic and offender profiling.

Anthony R. Beech, DPhil, FBPsS is Professor of Criminological Psychology, in the Centre for Forensic and Criminological Psychology, School of Psychology, University of Birmingham and a Fellow of the British Psychological Society. See 'About the Editors' section for more information about this author/ editor.

Douglas P. Boer, PhD, RClinPsych (Canada and New Zealand) is an Associate Professor in the Department of Psychology at The University of Waikato, Hamilton, New Zealand and an Adjunct Professor of the Royal Melbourne Institute of Technology, Melbourne, Australia. Prior to coming to New Zealand in 2006, he worked for 15 years in the Correctional Service of Canada in a variety of roles, including: sex offender programme therapist, sex offender programme director and supervising/regional psychologist. He currently is the Director of the Clinical Psychology Programme at The University of Waikato, New Zealand. He also provides community-based treatment programmes for sexual offenders with intellectual disabilities and acts as an expert witness for criminal courts in Canada and the USA in the assessment of violent and sexual offenders. Dr Boer is an Associate Editor for the journal *Sex Offender Treatment* and the New Zealand Editor for the *Sexual Abuse in Australia and New Zealand: An Interdisciplinary Journal* (SAANZ). Finally, he has authored or co-authored a number of publications in the field of forensic correctional psychology including the Sexual Violence Risk–20.

Charles M. Borduin, PhD is Professor of Psychology at the University of Missouri-Columbia and Director of the Missouri Delinquency Project. He received his doctorate in clinical psychology from the University of Memphis and interned at Rutgers Medical School. Dr Borduin is the co-developer of Multisystemic Therapy, a family-based therapeutic approach that has been identified as an effective treatment for violence and other serious antisocial behaviours in adolescents. His research has been funded by various federal agencies, including the National Institute of Mental Health and the National Institute on Alcohol Abuse and Alcoholism. Dr Borduin has published more than 100 journal articles, book chapters and books on the development and validation of effective mental health services for youth with complex clinical problems, and has served as a national and international consultant to government and private agencies on the reform of children's mental health services.

Patrice Bourke, MSc has a master's degree in Investigative Psychology from the University of Liverpool, and is completing a PhD degree in forensic psychology at Victoria University of Wellington. Her research investigates offence-related competency and expertise in the area of child sexual offending. She has worked in residential facilities with juvenile offenders (including juvenile sex offenders) and has been a member/contributor on a variety of research teams both in the UK and in New Zealand.

Professor Kevin D. Browne, PhD, MEd is both a chartered biologist and chartered psychologist, and is Chair of Forensic and Child Psychology at the University of Liverpool. See 'About the Editors' section for more information about this author/editor.

Deborah J. Cavanaugh, MA received her BA and MA degree in Clinical Psychology from Bridgewater State College. Her first research project involved an examination of the relationship between childhood conduct disorder, ADHD and handedness in adult sex offenders. This study was conducted at the Massachusetts Treatment Center for Sexually Dangerous Persons under the guidance of Dr Robert Prentky and Dr Martin Kafka. As a result, she was awarded the first 'Theo Seghorn Memorial Scholarship for most Promising Graduate Student' in the field of sexual abusers, from the Massachusetts Chapter of the Association for Treatment of Sexual Abusers (MATSA) in 2002. She currently works as the Program Coordinator and Data Analyst for Justice Resource Institute's Research and Clinical Practice Program. Her current clinical interests include trauma and the impact on the developing brain, and treating psychiatric disorders in juveniles with sexually abusive behaviours.

Rachael M. Collie, MA, DipClinPsyc is a clinical psychologist who has worked in the clinical forensic field since 1996. She currently teaches in clinical forensic psychology at Victoria University of Wellington, New Zealand, and maintains a small clinical forensic psychology practice. She is completing her PhD in the area of personality and sexual offending.

Franca Cortoni, PhD is an Assistant Professor in the School of Criminology at the University of Montreal. Before coming to the University of Montreal, she worked for several years in the Correctional Service of Canada where she most recently was the Director of Programming Research. She received her PhD in Clinical Forensic Psychology from Queen's University in Kingston, Ontario, Canada. Since 1989, she has worked with and conducted research on male and female offenders in penitentiary and community settings. She has provided consultancy and training services in the assessment and treatment of sexual and violent offenders to mental health professionals, correctional workers, members of parole boards, and Criminal Court judges in Australia, Canada, the UK, and the USA. Her research interests include both male and female violent and sexual offenders.

Leam A. Craig, PhD, EuroPsy is a consultant forensic psychologist and a Partner of Forensic Psychology Practice Ltd. See 'About the Editors' section for more information about this author/editor.

Jackie Craissati, PhD is a consultant clinical and forensic psychologist and Head of Forensic Psychology Services for Oxleas Foundation NHS Trust in South-East London. She has a special interest in the community management of high risk sexual, violent and personality disordered offenders and has published three books and a number of research articles in this area of work. She runs – in partnership with the probation service and social care providers – a number of community projects including a therapeutic residential service for personality disordered offenders, funded by the Home Office and the Department of Health.

Dennis M. Doren, PhD is the Evaluation Director at the Sand Ridge Secure Treatment Center in Wisconsin. He received his PhD in Clinical Psychology with a subspecialty in Crime and Delinquency Studies from the Florida State University in 1983. Since mid-1994, he has conducted and testified about sex offender civil commitment evaluations, served as a consultant, and/or done training on risk assessment of sex offenders in all but 2 of the 20 jurisdictions with active sex offender civil commitment laws, as well as other places where civil commitments were not the main issue. His second book, published in 2002, was entitled *Evaluating sex offenders: A manual for civil commitments and beyond.* His other publications concerning sex offender assessments include dozens of articles in professional periodicals and book chapters. Dr Doren has presented at various national and international conferences on topics related to the diagnostic and risk assessment of sexual offenders.

Hilary Eldridge, Dip. SW, CQSW is Chief Executive of the Lucy Faithfull Foundation, a child protection charity specialising in child sexual abuse. She began working with sex offenders and their families after qualifying as a probation officer in 1975. In 1988 she co-founded a residential assessment and treatment centre for sex offenders, which was superseded by the Lucy Faithfull Foundation, established in 1993. She co-authors and monitors the charity's assessment and treatment programmes for adult male and female offenders and for young people who engage in sexually harmful behaviours. She consults to probation and prisons and is an international speaker. Hilary was a member of the Joint Prison and Probation Accreditation Panel from

1999 to 2002, and of the Nolan Committee reviewing child protection in the Catholic Church. She is a member of HM Government's Sexual Violence Stakeholder Advisory Group and a specialist adviser on the Department of Health and NIMHE Victims of Violence and Abuse Prevention Programme. She is an Honorary Lecturer in the Centre for Forensic and Family Psychology at the University of Birmingham.

Yolanda Fernandez, PhD graduated in Clinical/Forensic Psychology in 2001 from Queen's University in Kingston, Ontario. As a registered psychologist she currently holds the position of Chief Psychologist, Regional Coordinator of Sexual Offender Treatment Programs within the Correctional Service of Canada. Additionally, she spent 14 months in the position of Chief Psychologist at Millhaven Institution, a maximum security correctional facility. Yolanda has also worked as the Clinical Director of Rockwood Psychological Services, and the Clinical Director of the Sexual Offender Treatment Program located at Bath Institution (a medium security federal penitentiary). In 1999 Yolanda designed a training package to teach effective therapist skills to clinicians working with sexual offenders. She has provided this training within Canada, the United States and several European countries. In addition to her clinical work Yolanda is an active researcher who currently has several presentations at international conferences and over 20 publications. Her publications include an edited book, two co-authored books and three co-edited books. Yolanda's research interests include therapeutic process in sexual offender treatment, empathy deficits in sexual offenders, and phallometric testing with sexual offenders. She has been an active member of the Association for the Treatment of Sexual Abusers since 1996, including spending two years as the Student Representative to the Board of Directors.

Donald Findlater, FRSA, is Director of Research and Development with the Lucy Faithfull Foundation, a child protection charity working across the UK. He left a career in the Probation Service to manage the Foundation's Wolvercote Clinic, the UK's only residential assessment and treatment centre for men with allegations of or convictions for sexual offences against children. Following closure of the Clinic, he has helped pioneer developments in sex offender treatment, management and support and in child sexual abuse prevention using public health models. These developments include Circles of Support and Accountability and Stop it Now! UK and Ireland and its Helpline for people concerned about their own behaviour or that of others. Donald is often called upon by the media to comment upon sex offender risk, assessment and management, as well as upon child sexual abuse prevention. He sits on the Board of the Independent Safeguarding Authority.

Hannah J. Ford, MPhil, ClinPsyD is a clinical psychologist working in the West Midlands with young people in care, including those who are involved in offending. Before moving to this role, Hannah worked for the Lucy Faithfull Foundation, contributing to the assessment and treatment of perpetrators of sexual offences against children, and completing a Home Office commissioned evaluation of national need for residential treatment provision for sex offenders (with Anthony Beech). She has a particular interest in women who commit sexual offences and has written a book about this topic, published in 2006 by Wiley, entitled *Women Who Sexually Abuse Children*. She also has an interest in sex offenders with intellectual disabilities and has recently undertaken research in this area, which is currently being prepared for publication.

Tanya Garrett, PhD has completed postgraduate training in clinical psychology (MSc University of Birmingham, 1989) and psychotherapy (MSc University of Warwick, 1992). She is an honorary senior lecturer at the University of Birmingham, and a chartered clinical and forensic psychologist and chartered scientist. She has worked in both forensic and generic mental health services, both with adults and children, and currently manages the psychology service at a forensic CAMHS inpatient facility. She has served on the Investigatory Panel of the British Psychological Society's Investigatory Committee, and the Investigatory Committee itself. Her PhD was in the field of sexual contact with patients/boundary violations. She has undertaken research in a variety of fields, including ethical issues in therapy, sexual contact between therapists and patients, inappropriate behaviour between trainers and trainees, Asian sexual offenders, and sexual offender treatment and evaluation. Her clinical interests include risk assessment of parents in childcare/abuse cases, and therapy with offenders, particularly those with personality disorder and sexual offenders.

Carmen L.Z. Gress PhD is a researcher and consultant on issues related to offender assessment, risk management, treatment, and program evaluation. She received her Ph.D. in Educational Psychology in 2007 from the University of Victoria, BC and completed a postdoctoral position at Simon Fraser University, Burnaby BC. She has worked with a variety of professionals such as psychologists, psychiatrists, probation officers and case managers as well as adult and youth offenders, including sexual offenders, mentally ill offenders, and violent offenders. Her research interests include the assessment and promotion of self- and group-regulatory processes, assessment of characteristics that indicate failure or dysfunction in self-regulation, and attention-based assessments of sexual interest. In 2003, Dr. Gress received the ATSA Student Research Grant (Falconer Grant): Children or Adolescents Who Sexually Offend. As of September 2008 she is the Director of Research Planning and Offender Programming in the Community Corrections and Corporate Programs Branch of the Ministry of Public Safety and Solicitor General, British Columbia, Canada.

Don Grubin, MD is the Professor of Forensic Psychiatry at Newcastle University and (Hon) Consultant Forensic Psychiatrist in Northumberland, Tyne & Wear NHS Trust. He trained at the Maudsley and Broadmoor Hospitals, and at the Institute of Psychiatry in London. Amongst a number of clinical initiatives and research studies involving sex offenders, he has been closely involved in the introduction and evaluation of polygraphy in the supervision and treatment of sex offenders in England. He has been in Newcastle since 1994.

Leigh Harkins, PhD is a lecturer in the School of Psychology at the University of Birmingham. Her PhD has examined the effectiveness of sexual offender treatment. Leigh has published manuscripts in peer-reviewed journals in the area of sex offender treatment and has presented her research at international conferences. Leigh's research interests include examining 'what works' in sex offender treatment, risk assessment in sexual offenders, and process issues in sex offender treatment.

Todd E. Hogue, PhD is currently Professor of Forensic Psychology at the University of Lincoln. He has worked in a range of prison-, community- and health-based forensic settings mainly with sexual offenders and personality disordered individuals. Since 1995 he has been involved in the development of specialist services for personality disordered offenders requiring care in a high security hospital, including being Lead Psychologist to the development of the Peaks (DSPD) Unit at Rampton Hospital. His research interests are: personality disorder and risk, evaluating forensic clinical practice, phallometric and cognitive assessments of sexual interest, and the effect of staff attitudes towards sexual and/or personality disordered offenders.

Lawrence Jones, MSc., AFBPsS is Lead Psychologist at the Peaks Dangerous and Severe Personality Disorder Unit, Rampton Hospital, Nottinghamshire Healthcare Trust UK, and is a chartered consultant clinical and forensic psychologist. He has worked with offenders in community, prison and healthcare settings. He is a former Chair of the Division of Forensic Psychology of the British Psychological Society. His interests include: making use of the milieu, personality disorder, sexual offending, offence paralleling behaviour, motivation and engagement, substance misuse, strengths-based interventions and case formulation.

Hazel Kemshall, PhD is currently Professor of Community and Criminal Justice at De Montfort University, Leicester. Her research interests are in high-risk offenders, public protection, and multi-agency approaches to risk management. She has published extensively on risk in social care and in criminal justice, including *Understanding Risk in Criminal Justice* (2003), Open University Press. She has carried out numerous evaluations of risk practice, including projects sponsored by the ESRC, Scottish Executive and Home Office.

D. Richard Laws, PhD is currently Co-Director of the Pacific Psychological Assessment Corp. (PPAC), which markets visual stimuli for assessment and training manuals for use in forensic psychology. He is additionally the Director of Pacific Design Research, which serves as a development arm of PPAC. Dr Laws holds adjunct faculty appointments at Simon Fraser University and the University of Birmingham (UK). He received his PhD in Educational Psychology in 1959 from Southern Illinois University-Carbondale. He currently serves on the editorial boards of *Sexual Abuse: A Journal of Research and Treatment; Journal of Sexual Aggression* (as Associate Editor); *Journal of Interpersonal Violence*, and *Legal and Criminological Psychology*. He is the author of numerous journal articles, book chapters and scholarly essays, and co-editor/-author of a number of books and manuals. Dr Laws is the recipient of the Significant Achievement Award (1989) and Service Award (1998) of the Association for the Treatment of Sexual Abusers (ATSA) and has served as President of that organisation (1992–93).

Elizabeth J. Letourneau, PhD is Associate Professor, Family Services Research Center, Medical University of South Carolina. She received her doctorate in clinical psychology from Northern Illinois University and interned at the Medical University of South Carolina. Her research has focused on treatment effectiveness of clinical (e.g., Multisystemic Therapy) and legal interventions with juvenile sex offenders and other juvenile delinquents. She is currently adapting Multisystemic Therapy for use with HIV positive adolescents who engage in risky sexual behaviours. Her research has been funded by various federal agencies, including the Centers for Disease Control and Prevention, the National Institute of Mental Health, and the National Institute of Justice. Dr Letourneau has been active in the Association for the Treatment of Sexual Abusers since 1991.

William R. Lindsay, PhD, FBPS, FIASSID, is Consultant Psychologist and Lead Clinician in Scotland for Castlebeck Care. He was previously Head of Psychology (LD) in NHS Tayside and a consultant with the State Hospital. He is Professor of Learning Disabilities and Forensic Psychology at the University of Abertay, Dundee and Visiting Professor at the University of Northumbria, Newcastle. He has published over 200 research articles and book chapters and given many presentations and workshops on cognitive therapy and the assessment and treatment of offenders with intellectual disability.

Ruth E. Mann, PhD is a chartered forensic psychologist and is responsible for the assessment and treatment of sexual offenders within HM Prison Service England and Wales. She has worked for HM Prison Service for over 20 years, first as a treatment provider and then as a treatment manager before taking up her current operational policy position. Her areas of particular interest include the role of cognition in sexual offending, and the development of reliable and valid measures of dynamic risk factors.

William L. Marshall OC, PhD, FRSC is currently an Emeritus Professor of Psychology and Psychiatry at Queen's University and Director of Rockwood Psychological Services, which provides treatment for sexual offenders in Canadian federal prisons. Bill is also Head of the Sexual Offenders' Unit and Director of Programs at the St Lawrence Valley Correctional and Treatment Centre's Secure Treatment Facility. He has over 340 publications including 17 books and has been, or still is, on the Editorial Board of 17 international journals. Bill was President of the Association for the Treatment of Sexual Abusers in 1999–2000. In 1999 Bill was awarded the Santiago Grisolia Prize from the Queen Sophia Centre in Spain which is given for worldwide contributions to the reduction of violence, and in 2000 he was elected a Fellow of the

Royal Society of Canada. Bill was appointed an Officer of the Order of Canada by the Governor General of Canada in 2006.

Liam E. Marshall, MA has worked directly with sexual offenders in correctional settings for more than 10 years. He has been a therapist for Preparatory, Moderate-Intensity, Deniers and Maintenance Programs delivered by Rockwood Psychological Services in Canada. Liam's current position is co-chair of research and assistant unit director of a facility for psychiatrically disturbed offenders at the Brockville Psychiatric Hospital. Liam has trained therapists in the delivery of sexual offender programming for prison services in the UK, Canada, Australia, the United States and New Zealand. He is on the editorial board of the journal *Sexual Addiction and Compulsivity*, has authored a number of journal articles and book chapters, is a co-editor and co-author of two books: *Treating Sexual Offenders: An Integrated Approach*: Routledge, and *Controversial Issues in Research and the Treatment of Sexual Offenders*: Wiley, and has made numerous presentations on a wide range of sexual offender issues. Liam's publications, presentations and research interests include: elderly sexual offenders, sexual addiction, attachment, empathy, coping, mood, phallometry, and the therapeutic process. He is currently completing his doctoral thesis.

David Middleton is Visiting Professor in Community and Criminal Justice at De Montfort University and Honorary Research Fellow in Forensic Psychology at Birmingham University. During a 30-year career in probation, David has specialised in sex offender treatment and risk management. He developed the first accredited community-based sex offender treatment programme (C-SOGP) and later co-developed the first accredited treatment programme for Internet sex offenders (i-SOTP). He joined the Home Office to oversee the implementation of all accredited community sex offender treatment programmes in England and Wales, leaving in December 2006. He now runs his own consultancy, training and research organisation specialising in risk assessment and management of sexual offenders. He was a member of the List 99 Experts Panel in the Department for Children, Schools and Families, and internationally has been the UK representative on the Council of Europe Committee of Experts on the Treatment of Sexual Offending, Visiting Expert to the United Nations Asia and Far East Institute, and consultant to the Ministry of Justice of Japan.

Professor Glynis Murphy, PhD, FBPsS is Chair of Clinical Psychology and Learning Disability at the University of Kent. She is a chartered clinical and forensic psychologist, Fellow of the British Psychological Society and President of the International Association of the Scientific Study of Intellectual Disabilities (IASSID). She is co-editor of *Journal of Applied Research in Intellectual Disabilities* and now works at the Tizard Centre, University of Kent. For many years, she has had research interests in challenging behaviour, abuse, forensic issues and the law in learning disabilities, and she has published widely on these topics. Amongst other activities, she is currently running a multi-site trial of cognitive behavioural treatment for people with learning disabilities at risk of sexual offending.

Matt D. O'Brien, MSc received his master's degree in Criminology from Keele University in 1994 and his master's degree in Applied Criminological Psychology from the University of London in 1997. Matt has worked with sexual offenders in correctional settings for 10 years. In the English and Welsh Prison Service he was a therapist for sexual offender programmes addressing the treatment needs of high-, medium- and low-risk offenders. He worked at the Prison Service HQ running national training courses, assessing the quality of programme delivery, providing clinical advice to treatment managers, developing a new assessment measure, and designing a new programme. More recently Matt has been a therapist for Preparatory, Maintenance and Deniers programs in Federal Institutions in Ontario, Canada. Matt has trained therapists in the delivery of sexual offender programming for Prison Services in England and Wales, Scotland, Northern Ireland and the United States. He has made a number of presentations on a range of sexual offender issues and co-authored a number of journal articles and book chapters.

Ann Pimental, MSCJ/MHC has been employed by Justice Resource Institute (JRI) since 1997 when she began working at the Massachusetts Treatment Center for Sexually Dangerous Persons under the direction of Dr Robert Prentky. In 2001, she became the project manager for JRI's Research Department. In 2002, she received her master's degrees from Suffolk University in Criminal Justice and Mental Health Counselling. Ann has managed several research projects from both state and federal funding sources. She also oversees the clinical aspects of the newly expanded Research & Clinical Practice Program of JRI and has experience in counselling survivors of domestic violence and sexual assault. In addition, she has several years of experience scoring and writing up the J-SOAP-II.

Robert A. Prentky, PhD teaches in the Department of Psychology at Fairleigh Dickinson University and is Director of the MA Program in Forensic Psychology. He has practiced as a forensic psychologist for the past 25 years, and in that capacity assessed or supervised the assessment of over 2,000 sexual offenders and paraphilics. He has been the principal or co-principal investigator on 14 state and federal grants and has served as an ad hoc reviewer for 17 professional journals. He chaired two conferences on sexual offenders for the New York Academy of Sciences (1988 and 2002). He has presented several hundred times in the USA, Europe, Canada and Israel, and published 80+ papers/chapters and five books. He was elected a Fellow of the American Psychological Association (2003) and the Association for Psychological Science (2006).

Jean Proulx, PhD is a Professor and Director of the School of Criminology at the University of Montreal. In addition, since 1987, he is working as a clinical psychologist at the Philippe Pinel Institute of Montreal. He has published over 100 papers or book chapters in the field of sexual aggression. His current research interests include the offending process of sexual aggressors, sexual murderers and sexual sadism, and treatment compliance.

School of Criminology, University of Montreal, C.P. 6128, Succursale Centre-Ville, Montreal (Quebec), Canada, H3C 3J7.

Phil Rich, EdD, MSW is the Clinical Director of the Stetson School, a 111-bed long-term residential treatment program for sexually reactive children and juvenile sexual offenders in Massachusetts, where he supervises a clinical team of 18 clinicians and 8 case managers. Phil is the author of *Understanding Juvenile Sexual Offenders: Assessment, Treatment, and Rehabilitation*, and *Attachment and Sexual Offending: Understanding and Applying Attachment Theory to the Treatment of Juvenile Sexual Offenders*, and is currently writing *A Comprehensive Risk Evaluation of Juvenile Sexual Offenders: Understanding and Assessing Risk*, due for publication in late 2008.

Sue Righthand, PhD is a clinical psychologist in independent practice. She provides clinical and programme consultation, programme development and evaluation as well as psychotherapy, forensic assessment and training. Dr Righthand provides consultation to the Maine Departments of Corrections and Health and Human Service as well as the Maine District Court. She has extensive experience working with juveniles and adults who commit sex offences. Her publications include *Juveniles Who Have Sexually Offended: A Review of the Professional Literature* (Righthand & Welch, 2001), the *Juveniles Sex Offender Protocol II* (Prentky & Righthand, 2003), and *Child Maltreatment Risk Assessments: An Evaluation Guide* (Righthand, Kerr & Drach, 2003).

Cindy M. Schaeffer, PhD received her doctorate in child clinical psychology from the University of Missouri-Columbia. During her graduate training she specialised in family-based treatments for juvenile offenders and served as a Multisystemic Therapy (MST) therapist for three years. Her dissertation research examined the long-term effectiveness of MST in reducing criminal recidivism over a 13-year follow-up period with a sample of serious and violent juvenile offenders. Dr Schaeffer completed a post-doctoral fellowship in Prevention Science at the Johns Hopkins Bloomberg School of Public Health, where she focused on the development of antisocial behaviour across childhood and adolescence. Dr Schaeffer is now an Associate Professor in the Department of Psychiatry and Behavioral Sciences at the Medical University of South Carolina and a member of the Family Services Research Center faculty. Her work involves improving outcomes for juvenile offenders receiving MST by incorporating vocational skills training, and adapting MST for families in which there is substantiated child abuse or neglect and caregiver substance abuse.

Neil Sinclair, MAppPsych is a consultant clinical psychologist in private practice in West Malling, Kent. He qualified as a clinical psychologist in 1982 in Perth, Western

Australia and worked in university, government and private sectors for people with intellectual disability in Australia from 1982 to 1995. He has worked in the UK as a clinical psychologist since 1996 where he has held posts including Head of Greenwich Learning Disability Psychology Service, Consultant Psychologist in West Kent, Head of Psychology at Cedar House in Kent until 2007, and Corporate Psychology Adviser for Care Principles Ltd. He has developed and implemented a risk assessment approach for clients with an intellectual disability at risk of offending, and contributed to the dissemination of the SOTSEC-ID sex offender treatment model for offenders with a learning disability in the UK over the last 10 years. He has presented at a number of national and international conferences and is in the final stages of a PhD supervised by Professor Glynis Murphy.

John L. Taylor, DPsychol is Professor of Developmental Disability Psychology at Northumbria University and Consultant Clinical Psychologist and Psychological Services Professional Lead with Northumberland, Tyne & Wear NHS Trust.

Jo Thakker, PhD is a clinical psychologist and senior lecturer in psychology at the University of Waikato, New Zealand. Her primary research areas are correctional and theoretical psychology, and substance use and abuse.

Brian Thomas-Peter, PhD is a chartered clinical forensic psychologist working at Reaside Clinic and Birmingham University. He has international experience of service provision, postgraduate training, management and consultancy work. Until recently he was Chief Supervisor in Forensic Psychology to the BPS, and in 2004 became an Accredited Behavioural Investigative Advisor to the Police National Crime and Operations Faculty.

Tony Ward, PhD, MA (Hons), DipClinPsyc is Professor of Clinical Psychology and Clinical Director at Victoria University of Wellington, New Zealand. He was previously director of the Kia Marama Programme for sexual offenders at Rolleston Prison, Christchurch, New Zealand and has taught clinical and forensic psychology at Canterbury and Melbourne Universities. His research interests include the offence process in offenders, ethical aspects of practice, cognitive distortions and models of rehabilitation. He has published over 235 research articles, chapters and books. These include: *Issues and controversies*: Sage (with Richard Laws and Steve Hudson, 2003); *Theories of sexual offending*: Wiley (with Devon Polaschek and Anthony Beech, 2006); *Rehabilitation: Beyond the risk paradigm*: Routledge (with Shadd Maruna, 2007); and *Morals, rights, and practice in human services*: Jessica Kingsley (with Marie Connolly, 2007).

Jason Wood is a senior lecturer in the Faculty of Health and Life Sciences at De Montfort University. He has research interests and expertise in the community management of high-risk offenders, including the effectiveness of strategies used to involve the public. In 2005, he evaluated the implementation of Multi-Agency Public Protection Arrangements (MAPPA) with Kemshall and Mackenzie, for the Home Office (Kemshall *et al.*, 2005). He also led an investigation into MAPPA work with high-risk sex offenders (with Kemshall, Maguire, Hudson and Mackenzie) commissioned by the Home Secretary in 2006 for the Child Sex Offender Review (Wood & Kemshall, 2007).

Foreword

This is an important and timely book. It captures part of what is needed in attempting to understand sexual offending. First, however, one needs to recognise two different discourses which currently operate in relation to sex crime. At the public level there is an explicit focus on regulation and control. Sex offenders have become the beasts in our midst. In control terms beasts need to be separated from the herd and hence, there is an exclusionary tendency – something akin to criminal apartheid for those who have committed sexual offences. The apotheosis of the regulatory focus was heralded, in the United Kingdom at least, by the passing of the Sex Offenders Act 1997 whereby sex offenders had to register after being convicted or cautioned. In short, while there are variations, many countries have tried to confront the considerable societal concern about the phenomenon of sexual offending by regulation and control.

Meanwhile, there has been a less public but equally fervent discourse, which centres on the importance of the assessment and treatment of sexual offenders. Of course, in the final analysis, this parallel discourse cannot or should not be totally separate from the discourse of regulation and control, but currently the discourse of assessment and control operates at a more subterranean level, for it is seen – perhaps largely by politicians – as something which is less enthusiastically embraced by members of the public. This may or may not be true for sometimes the public is less punitive than politicians believe. Indeed, the public may appreciate the futility and impossibility of addressing the issue of sex offending simply by regulation and control.

Anyway, the discourse of assessment and treatment is pivotal to this book. There has been a burgeoning interest in the assessment and treatment of sexual offenders over the past two decades and this development has coincided with a challenge to the previous, almost monopolistic stance of forensic psychiatrists in this area. Now there are a variety of professional voices espousing an interest in forensic mental health (Rogers & Soothill, 2008) in general and sexual offending in particular. Psychologists, especially since the early 1990s, have been crucial in pioneering new ways of assessing and treating sex offenders. But how new and how different? Here the work also needs to be seen within an historical context.

This book provides an opportunity to showcase some of the remarkable developments over the past two decades, which have provided new insights into ways of conceptualising sexual offenders. Appropriate assessment and treatment follow from this. But how does all this link with past endeavours in this field?

Following the numerous chapters in this book there are approaching two thousand references cited of which over one-half refer to articles, books and reports published in this still incomplete first decade of the 21st century. Its 'up-to-dateness' certainly cannot be challenged. A further 30 percent of the references cite work from the 1990s, yet a further 15 percent of the references refer to work published in the 1970s and 1980s. However, there are just 32 pieces of work which relate to work published before 1970. This was a surprise.

Only two of these publications overlap, that is, are cited in at least two of the chapters. In fact, these two pieces were probably cited twice because the two chapters had a co-author in common. Of the 30 distinct pieces of work cited, the chronological first is Bayes' famous essay published in 1764 relating to 'solving a problem in the doctrine of chance', while the second is G.S. Hall's pioneering text on *Adolescence* published in 1904. In fact, of the 30 pieces cited, only 10 could be considered to have a direct focus on sexual offending of which the first is Kurt Freund's paper, 'Diagnostika homosexuality u muszu' published in *Ceskoslovak Medicine* in 1957.

What all this seems to mean is that the assessment and treatment of sexual offending does not have a 'classic' history which is routinely cited. However, this is in some ways curious, for the 1950s, for instance, was an era when the two discourses mentioned earlier were for a while less separate.

Sexual offenders have always had the possibility of provoking outrage and condemnation rather than attracting sympathy and assistance. Moral panics are sometimes fuelled by a supposed sexual component – in fact, the infamous Jack the Ripper offences committed in the late 1880s continue to titillate. However, in the specific area of *non-consensual* sex crime there have been some massive shifts – from the Victorian era when the alleged sex offender was more likely to be acquitted than not, to the 1950s when sex offenders were more likely to be awarded a non-custodial sentence rather than a custodial sentence or to be acquitted. Certainly for a while in the 1950s and early 1960s, in the criminal justice field, the public world of control and regulation began to coalesce with the subterranean efforts of practitioners in trying to offer something more positive to sexual offenders. Reports in local newspapers heralded this implicit optimism by indicating that treatment – such as probation with a condition of treatment – was being awarded to convicted sex offenders. The emphasis was on trying to do something which might alleviate suffering while, at the same time, recognising that a crime had been committed. Curiously, of course, in terms of *consensual* sex crime, the attempt to shift the label of homosexuality from being a crime to a sickness may have contributed to another kind of suffering.

Less than a decade later, the enthusiasm to treat began to wane and definitions began to shift. In truth, the results, while limited in scientific terms, were not impressive and the death knell was marked by the dire philosophy that 'nothing works'.

However, a new enthusiasm emerged in the 1990s which was underpinned by a more optimistic 'philosophy' seeking to understand 'what works?'. The present book is partly a crucial stock-taking exercise, identifying what has been achieved, while not being hesitant to recognise that much more needs to be done in trying to identify 'what works'. So will the present endeavours have the same sad outcome of the 1950s?

I think not. The current efforts, so well represented in this book, are not simply the output of some dedicated but often isolated individuals. The base is now much wider than that, calling upon theoretical perspectives which resonate and have a pedigree in parent disciplines. Perhaps more importantly, it is much more of a scientific enterprise whereby both successes and failures in theory and in practice can be more readily identified and documented.

All science eventually has human implications. However, a scientific focus on sexual offending is more direct than most. The suffering caused by sexual offending is very real with its impact much more long-lasting than previously appreciated. It is thus important that an appropriate 'body of knowledge' in relation to sexual offending continues to develop and this present volume provides a very useful foundation stone towards this end.

Keith Soothill

Emeritus Professor of Social Research, Lancaster University, UK

April 2008

REFERENCES

Bayes, T. (1764). An essay towards solving a problem in the doctrine of chances. *Philosophical Transactions of the Royal Society of London*, 53, 370–418.

Freund, K. (1957). Diagnostika homosexuality u muszu. *Ceskoslovak Medicine*, 53, 382–393.

Hall, G.S. (1904). *Adolescence: Its psychology and its relations to physiology, anthropology, sociology, sex, crime, religion, and education (Vols. I & II)*. New York: D. Appleton & Co.

Rogers, P. & Soothill, K. (2008). Understanding forensic mental health and the variety of professional voices. In K. Soothill, P. Rogers & M. Dolan (Eds), *Handbook of forensic mental health*. (pp. 3–18) Cullompton: Willan.

1

Overview

ANTHONY R. BEECH

LEAM A. CRAIG

KEVIN D. BROWNE

Sexual offending is a worldwide phenomenon, for example in England and Wales the latest statistics, from Jansson, Povey and Kaiza (2007) for the years 2006–2007, report that the police recorded 57,542 sexual offences (which is just under 1% of all of the recorded crime for this period). Of these reported crimes, just over three-quarters (43,755) are classified as serious sexual offences, i.e., rape, sexual assault and sexual activity with children. The other (less serious) sexual offences consist of unlawful sexual activity with mostly 'consenting' adults such as exploitation of prostitution and soliciting. The number of male offenders convicted of sexual offences in the UK has increased over the past 20 years. In 1996 the Home Office reported an increase in prison population in 1994 of 161% for convicted rapists and 93% for those convicted of other sexual offences between 1984 and 1994. The number of convictions for rape increased by 84% between 1992 and 2002 (Councell, 2003). From a statistical review of the prison population in 2002, it can be calculated that the total number of male prisoners serving a sentence for sexual offences in the UK has risen by an average of 68% from 3,146 in 1992 to 5,283 in 2002. In October 2007 the Ministry of Justice recorded the prison population in England and Wales as 81,812 (a 2% rise on 2006), of which 7,428 had been convicted of committing sexual offences (Ministry of Justice, 2007). Compared to the number of prisoners convicted of committing sexual offences in 2006 (6,855), this represents an increase of 8.4%, a rise greater than that of the general prison population. Craig, Browne, Stringer and Hogue (2008) recently estimated the UK sexual reconviction rate (16 follow-up studies, $n = 7,189$) as 5.8% at a two-year follow-up, 6.9% up to four years, and 17.4% at six years or more of follow-up. Sexual reconviction rates have been shown to differ between those who received a custodial sentence compared to those who did not receive a custodial

Assessment and Treatment of Sex Offenders: A Handbook. Edited by Anthony Beech, Leam Craig and Kevin Browne. © John Wiley & Sons Ltd, 2009.

sentence but were sentenced to probation or community supervision for committing sexual offences. Essentially, those sentenced to imprisonment would be expected to have committed more serious offences than those who received probation orders. For the prison sample ($n = 5,915$), the UK sexual reconviction rate showed an average of 6.0% up to a two-year follow-up (range 1.2 to 10.3%), 7.8% up to a four-year follow-up (range 4.3 to 12%), and 19.5% for six or more years of follow-up (range 8.5 to 25%) (Craig *et al.*, 2008). The UK sexual reconviction rate for the non-custodial samples ($n = 1,274$) showed an average of 5.7% up to a two-year follow-up (range 4 to 7.1%), 5.9% up to four years (range 2 to 5.5%), and 15.5% at six years or more follow-up. The trend was for those sentenced to prison to exhibit a higher sexual reconviction rate than those supervised in the community (Craig *et al.*, 2008).

Sexual offenders are a heterogeneous group with a number of subgroups including adolescent offenders, female offenders, offenders with learning disabilities, and offenders with mental health problems. While the vast majority of sex offences are committed by adult male perpetrators (Ministry of Justice, 2007), Lovell (2002) estimates that around a third of all sexual offences are committed by juveniles. Adolescent sex offenders are defined as adolescents from age 13 to 17 years who commit illegal sexual behaviour. Research in this area has risen dramatically over the last decade and it has been recognised that adolescents accounted for nearly 16% of all forcible rapes and 17% of all other sex offences in 1995 (Righthand & Welch, 2001). Approximately one-third of sexual offences against children are committed by teenagers and those offences against children under 12 years of age are typically committed by boys aged between 12 and 15 years (Snyder & Sickmund, 1999). In the United States in 1995, 16,100 adolescents were arrested for sexual offences (excluding rape and prostitution) and approximately 18 adolescents per 100,000 were arrested for forcible rape (Sickmund, Snyder & Poe-Yamagata, 1997). In England and Wales in 2007, of the young adults (20 years and below) sentenced to imprisonment (7,444), 334 had been convicted of committing sexual offences (Ministry of Justice, 2007).

Although sexual offences are most often committed by male perpetrators, evidence does exist for the presence of a small number of female sex offenders. Currently female sexual offenders account for less than 1% of sex offenders in prison, (Jansson *et al.*, 2007); however, this figure can be regarded as a severe underestimate of the actual number of women who sexually abuse. This is illustrated by figures from ChildLine, from April 2002 to March 2003, which indicate that those children calling about being abused sexually by a female was 12%. As for sexual offenders who have mental health problems, the latest published figures reported by Lockmuller, Beech and Fisher (2008), were 94 individuals admitted to a psychiatric hospital in 2004, with 403 (12% of the total psychiatric population) detained patients at end of December 2004.

An additional subgroup of sexual offenders is the intellectually disabled (ID) sex offender. It is only in recent years that this subgroup of sexual offenders has been the focus of research which has led to the development of a range of psychometric measures for this client group (see Craig, Stringer & Hutchinson, in press). Although the true prevalence rate of sexual offending by men with ID is difficult to establish (Murphy, 2007), McBrien, Hodgetts and Gregory (2003) found that 41% of a sample of adults with ID referred to a local authority engaged in challenging behaviours defined as 'sex-related', of which 17% had police contact and 4% were convicted of sexual offences. After reviewing the literature on sexual reconviction rates for sexual offenders with ID, Craig and Hutchinson (2005) estimate the reconviction rate for sex offenders with ID to be 6.8 times that of non-ID sex offenders at two years, and 3.5 times that at four years follow-up. While there is a great deal of overlap between ID and non-ID sex offenders, there are also some important differences between these two groups. Like mainstream sex offenders, sex offenders with ID display deviant sexual arousal and cognitive distortions (Broxholme & Lindsay, 2003) and are often deficient in sexual knowledge and skills (Craig, Stringer & Moss, 2006). Other issues, however, are more idiosyncratic to the ID population such as limited knowledge of laws relating to sexual behaviour having implications for the assessment of risk of sexual recidivism (Craig, in press).

When describing sexual offenders we are actually describing an extremely diverse group; ranging from people who as far as we know have confined themselves to downloaded abusive images from the Internet to individuals who have carried out contact sexual offences against children and/or adults, to those who have killed as part of a sexual assault. Table 1.1 describes the most well-known types of sexual offender,

Table 1.1 Types of sexual offenders and suggested potential motivations (from Lockmuller, Beech & Fisher, 2008 reprinted by kind permission of Willan Publishing)

Offence Type	Victim	Motivation (examples only)
Child Abuse (can be non-contact through to penetrative)	Child, related or unrelated, male or female, age specific. Some offenders 'cross over' between sex, age and relatedness	- Primary or fixated sexual interest in children (paedophilia) - Preferred partner is not available - Belief in entitlement to sex
Rape	Adult, male or female, who does not give permission to commit penetrative sexual acts	- Sexual - Anger - Sadistic (or a combination of above)
Sexual Murder	Anyone who is murdered during commission of sexual offence	- Murdering to prevent disclosure of sexual offence - Find murder arousing
Internet Offences (there may be different types of Internet offenders but it is unclear at this time)	Most commonly children – content of illegal sexual material downloaded from the Internet 'child pornography'	- Direct contact offences – motivation to sexually offend but have not done so yet

(Continued)

Table 1.1 Continued

Offence Type	Victim	Motivation (examples only)
Exhibitionism (non-contact offence)	Anyone who is exposed to the offender's genitals from a distance	- Compulsively drawn to collect indecent images of children with no intention of engaging in contact offences - Need for but fear of intimacy - Stress relief - Can influence the degree of risk of more serious contact offences presented by the offender

most of which are described in the book, and the putative motivations for why such individuals carry out these types of offences.

In terms of work with sex offenders, the practitioner is often required to assess the risk they present or provide effective interventions. Hence, the aim of this book is to gather together in one place recent thinking regarding the assessment and treatment of these diverse groups of sexual offenders from a number of leading researchers and practitioners in the field, with the specific aim of providing workers in the field with an overview of up-to-date assessment and treatment approaches.

However, this is not a 'how-to-do' book on assessment and treatment as such, for that we would recommend our companion book entitled *Assessing Risk in Sex Offenders: A Practitioner's Guide* by Leam Craig, Kevin Browne and Anthony Beech (2008) also published by Wiley. What we hope to have achieved in gathering together the chapters in this volume, is to add further information to those already well versed in assessment and treatment approaches, as well as acting as a starting-off point for those new to the field who want to get an idea of what assessment and treatment of sexual offenders is all about.

STRUCTURE OF THE BOOK

The book itself is divided into a number of sections as follows:

Introduction

The second chapter in the introductory section of this book is by Jackie Craissati on attachment theory. We have included this chapter because we think that this concept is incredibly important when thinking about the aetiology of sexual offending behaviours as well as about attachment styles and implications for treatment, as an individual's attachment style can be seen as a set of enduring characteristics for making sense of one's life experiences and interactions with others (Young, Klosko & Weisharr, 2003). Ward, Hudson and Marshall (1996) argue that this is how expectations are developed about interpersonal relationships in that individuals may see themselves as worthy and deserving of another's attention, or conversely as worthless and undeserving of anybody's attention. Secure attachments give rise to internal working models of others as safe, helpful and supportive (Baldwin, 2005), while insecure attachment causes the individual to become highly socially ranked, and is especially focused on the power of others to control or reject them (Gilbert, 2005). Therefore, attachment difficulties may represent a key determinant in explaining why some forms of interpersonal violence and abuse occur, as well as thinking about effective treatments for abusers. The remainder of the book is structured as follows:

Part One: Risk Assessment

This part of the book deals with current risk assessment frameworks. In Chapter 3 Franca Cortoni examines factors associated with sexual recidivism. Here, she outlines those historical (static risk) factors that have been identified as being predictive of future offending, together with an outline of some of the better known actuarial risk assessment instruments (i.e., the Sex Offender Risk Appraisal Guide (SORAG; Quinsey et al., 2008), the Rapid Risk Assessment for Sexual Offence Recidivism (RRASOR; Hanson, 1997), and Static-99 (Hanson & Thornton, 2000)), that combine these items into scales that can usefully assess sexual offenders' level of problems. She also outlines the latest thinking about both the assessment of psychological problems related to future offending (i.e., dynamic risk assessment) and the importance of assessing situational and contextual risk factors (acute dynamic risk factors). The other chapter (Chapter 4) in this section, by Leam Craig, Anthony Beech and Leigh Harkins, examines these ideas in more detail as well as looking at the limitations of risk instruments, and posing the question of whether risk assessment needs to be put on a firmer theoretical footing from the work of Beech and Ward (2004), and Ward and Beech (2004), with the answer that this would, in our opinion, certainly advance thinking in the field.

Part Two: Approaches to Offender Assessment

This part of the book deals with specific assessment approaches. First, in Chapter 5 Douglas Boer, Jo Thakker and Tony Ward look at case formulation as has been informed by theory, and the risk assessment concepts outlined in Part One of the book. The following chapters cover in greater detail assessment using psychometrics, attentional-based measures, the penile plethysmograph and the polygraph. In Chapter 6 Leam Craig and Anthony Beech specifically examine how psychometric measures can assess psychological problems (dynamic risk), i.e., the deviant sexual interests, pro-offending attitudes, socio-affective difficulties and self-regulation sets of problems identified by Thornton (2002). The concept of psychological deviance is also outlined, as originally defined by Beech (1998), and broadened by Thornton (2002). Expanding on this we also consider the risk assessment properties and accuracy in predicting sexual reconviction using the psychological deviance index as an indicator of risk. In Chapter 7 Carmen Gress and Richard Laws outline exciting developments in the assessment of sexual interests using attentional-based methodologies. While in Chapter 8 Yolanda Fernandez reports up-to-date information and casts a critical eye over that old warhorse of assessment, the penile plethysmograph (PPG). In Chapter 9 Don Grubin describes the use of the polygraph to manage risk in sexual offenders. The polygraph itself has been around for a long time like the PPG, however, it is fair to say that it is mainly through Don Grubin's work that the polygraph is starting to be considered seriously as a tool to manage risk in the UK. Finally in this section, in Chapter 10 Liam Marshall and Matt O'Brien examine the measurement of sexual addiction with particular emphasis on examining sexual addiction in those who use the Internet for sexual purposes.

Part Three: Assessments for Specific Populations

It is fair to say that much of the theorising on assessment that has been developed, has been around those who commit contact sexual offences against children, hence in Part Three we have aimed to provide an overview of assessments for differing client groups such as: rapists and sexual murderers, Internet sexual offenders, intellectually disabled sexual offenders; sexual offenders with a coexisting personality disorder, and juvenile sexual offenders. In Chapter 11 Jean Proulx and Eric Beauregard report a motivational typology of sexual aggressors of women. Here, they note the evidence, which has also been reported elsewhere (Beech, Fisher & Ward, 2005; Beech, Ward & Fisher, 2006; Fisher & Beech, 2007), of three basic types of this kind of offender: sadistic, angry, and opportunistic, that cut across the categories rapist or sexual murderer. These findings are incredibly important both for assessment purposes and also because they have implications of what to do about treating offenders with different motivations. For example, sexual offenders with a sadistic motivation to their offending could be problematic on standard treatment programmes where a major component of therapy is making offenders aware of the distress caused to their victims. For offenders who are anger motivated, these, and other, data would suggest that offence-focused work may be better targeted towards anger and hostility problems, as well as schema-focused work around these men's long-standing grievance schemas about women. While, for sexually motivated offenders there is a willingness to undertake sexual assaults to satisfy their sexual urges and a general failure to control such deviant sexual thoughts and behaviours, schema-focused work related to getting the offender to control his actions would seem to be useful.

In Chapter 12 David Middleton describes current approaches to the assessment of those who use the Internet for sexual purposes. This chapter is particularly interesting in that it not only describes how such an assessment can be carried out, but also examines whether ideas from Ward and Siegert (2002) regarding the aetiological pathways of contact sexual offending can be applied to Internet offenders (which David Middleton argues clearly can be); and whether there is clear evidence of crossover from viewing images to the commission of contact sexual offences (which is not so clear). In Chapter 13 Bill Lindsay and John Taylor describe the assessment of risk in intellectually disabled sexual offenders with particular regard to the static and dynamic risk assessment described in Chapter 3. In Chapter 14 Todd Hogue describes the assessment of sexual offenders with a dangerous and severe personality disorder in the Peaks Unit at Rampton Hospital. Here, he describes the assessment of this type of sexual offender with particular interest being paid to the relationship of personality disorder and risk. Following this, in Chapter 15 Robert Prentky, Ann Pimental, Deborah Cavanaugh and Sue Righthand describe risk assessment procedures when working with juvenile sexual offenders with particular regard to the Juvenile Sex Offender Assessment Protocol-II [J-SOAP-II] (Prentky & Righthand, 2003) which is a risk assessment procedure that contains scales measuring the dynamic risk areas of *Sexual Drive/Preoccupation* and *Impulsive/Antisocial Behaviour*, as well as an *Intervention* scale; and a putative strengths factor of *Community Stability*.

Part Four: Interventions

This part of the book contains four chapters that describe interventions with sexual offenders. In Chapter 16 Tony Ward, Rachael Collie and Patrice Bourke provide an overview of current models of offender rehabilitation with particular regard to the 'What Works' (Andrews & Bonta, 2003; McGuire, 1995) risk, need, responsivity model that has been the dominant paradigm in work with sexual offenders since the early 1990s; and the more recent 'Good Lives' model developed by Tony Ward and colleagues (e.g., Ward & Gannon, 2006; Ward & Mann, 2004; Ward, Mann & Gannon, 2007) which is more of a strengths-based approach to treatment than the *What Works* approach and may be the way forward in terms of the future of interventions; it is certainly starting to take in work with offenders in the UK. In Chapter 17 Bill Marshall, Matt O'Brien and Liam Marshall describe interventions to modify sexual deviance. This area is of course very important when working with sexual offenders, as it has been found that sexual deviance (typically measured by the penile plethysmograph, see Chapter 8) is the strongest dynamic risk predictor of future sexual recidivism (Hanson & Bussière, 1998; Hanson & Morton-Bourgon, 2005). Hence, the importance that must be placed on the modification of deviant sexual preferences in sexual offenders. In Chapter 18 Ruth Mann and Bill Marshall describe the most up-to-date advances in treatment of sexual offenders. Here, they particularly focus on the areas of pro-offending thinking (cognitive distortions), victim empathy work, relapse prevention, treatment style and therapeutic processes, risk assessment and treatment planning, and what would be the recommended content for a comprehensive treatment package for sexual offenders. While in the final chapter of this section (Chapter 19), Hilary Eldridge and Donald Findlater describe a community-based approach to working with sexual offenders. They also briefly describe the innovative Stop it Now! public education campaign targeting: offenders and potential offenders; friends and family of offenders and potential offenders; parents and carers of young people with sexually worrying behaviour, in order to give adults the sound information they need to recognise worrying thoughts, attitudes and behaviour in themselves or others and enabling them to take steps that will protect a child.

Part Five: Interventions for Specific Populations

In this section we have gathered together a number of authors who describe treatment approaches for working with specific populations. In Chapter 20 Glynis Murphy and Neil Sinclair describe community interventions for intellectually disabled sexual offenders, in particular describing the Sex Offender Treatment Services Collaborative in Intellectual Disabilities (SOTSEC-ID) approach to treatment. Glynis and Neil report the results of one of the first attempts to develop and standardise a treatment protocol designed for sexual offenders with ID in the UK. Although this client group has been previously neglected in the literature, the SOTSEC-ID model does appear to be a promising model of treatment for men with ID and sexually abusive behaviour.

In Chapter 21 Tanya Garrett and Brian Thomas-Peter describe interventions with sexual offenders with mental illness. They begin by considering the prevalence of this client group and go on to describe the therapy interfering behaviours typically encountered. They draw attention to the limitations of using a standard treatment model with sexual offenders with mental illness and describe an alternative 'modular' programme for psychiatric patients who have a history of sexual offending.

Continuing with the theme of working with special populations, in Chapter 22 Lawrence Jones offers a detailed examination of the strategies and pitfalls when working with personality disordered sexual offenders. Lawrence reminds us that because of the heterogeneity and complexity in this population, formulation-based interventions need to be informed by a wide range of theoretical perspectives and are inevitably complex. He begins by exploring the differing personality features associated with different sexual offences (e.g., rape, sexual homicide, child abuse, psychopathic sexual offending and sadistic offending) and goes onto to consider a number of treatment approaches when working with sexual offenders with personality disorders. He outlines the threats to effective treatment and describes the successes of a number of intervention approaches that he has been involved in, including the development of Therapeutic Communities.

Both Chapters 23 and 24 describe working with adolescent sexual offenders. Phil Rich notes, and goes into detail about, the complexities and needs of this group. He begins by highlighting the need to understand sexually reactive children and sexually abusive adolescents compared to adult sexual offenders, and the ways that we actually define and provide treatment for these different populations. He distinguishes between adolescent and adult sexual offenders and considers how the development of adult behaviour, psychopathology and personality disorder can help us to understand sexually abusive behaviour in adolescents. In developing an effective treatment programme, he considers adolescent brain development and maturation which he links to the development of empathy and morality. These, he argues, form the basis of an integrated and multifaceted model of treatment approach. Continuing with the theme of juvenile sexual offenders, in Chapter 24 Elizabeth Letourneau, Charles Borduin and Cindy Schaeffer describe a multisystemic therapeutic (MST) approach to the treatment of problematic sexual behaviours. Before reviewing the treatment outcome literature, they present an overview of the correlates of problem sexual behaviour in youths and go on to describe an alternative, ecologically-based intervention for youth with criminal and non-criminal sexual behaviour problems. They suggest that adolescent sexual offenders are embedded in multiple systems relating to family problems, peer relationships and academic difficulties in school and the goals of MST are to empower parents with the skills and resources needed to independently address the difficulties in raising adolescents and empower adolescents to cope with familial and non-familial problems. In support of this approach, they describe the results of two clinical trials with encouraging results.

While, in the final chapter of this section (Chapter 25), Hannah Ford describes both the assessment and the treatment of female sexual offenders, a commonly overlooked group of sexual offenders. She aims to outline some of the potentially broad-ranging needs of these women and questions whether directly applying assessment procedures for male offenders to females is appropriate. She describes the characteristics of female sexual offenders and pays particular attention to the assessment of risk and factors associated with sexual recidivism. She goes on to describe the identification of treatment needs in this client group and reviews the associated difficulties often reported by female sexual offenders including childhood victimisation, relationship and mental health difficulties and how these impact on risk and treatment need. She questions whether certain features of treatment programmes can potentially repeat negative aspects of women offenders' lives and how this might be attended to.

Part Six: Policy and Practice

The final section of the book describes important policies and practices in working with sexual offenders. It begins with Chapter 26, by Kevin Browne, who describes strategies to prevent sexual abuse in the family. Identified as a global phenomenon, the extent, detection, assessment and management of sexual offences committed in the family home, and their prevention is also considered. Here, the following are considered: (1) the sexual abuse of children by parents, siblings and relatives, as well as sexual assault on intimate adult partners; (2) educational approaches targeting vulnerable families and offenders with known risk factors; (3) working with sexually abusing families through assessment, separation, rehabilitation or transition to a new family. Browne concludes that the treatment of offenders is perhaps the most effective way of protecting children on a long-term basis.

Reports to the police of sexual assault in the UK have more than doubled over the last 20 years. Therefore, in Chapter 27 Kevin Browne continues by reviewing police work with sex offenders, particularly detection, management and assessment. He describes how the police deal with cases of sexual assault, false allegations, corroboration of witness statements and child protection referrals. The work of specialist units and strategies for proactive intelligence gathering is also described, together with ways in which known sex offenders are managed in the community. Recent developments of police involvement in Multi-Agency Public Protection Arrangements (MAPPA) are reviewed, in terms of their activities in public protection panels, risk assessment, management, disclosure and notification. The limitations of current policies are that they focus selectively on known or convicted sex offenders. He concludes that there is a necessity to collect and maintain intelligence on alleged sex offenders, as well those cautioned or convicted, for the prevention and detection of sexual assaults on children and adults.

Despite the limitations that only one in ten alleged sex offenders is convicted of a sex offence, it is important to consider the community strategies for managing high-risk offenders and the contribution of MAPPA as a small number of offenders ('the critical few') can harm a large number of victims. Hence, in Chapter 28 Hazel Kemshall and Jason Wood critically describe the development of MAPPA and their associated legislation in the UK. Improvements are identified in the allocation of offenders to the appropriate level of risk management; the full completion of risk assessment tools in all cases; clearer mechanisms for recording risk assessments and risk management decisions, a case review system that is matched to the risk management plans and dedicated resources for the coordination and administration of MAPPA. They conclude that current risk management strategies have provided effective and consistent partnership working practices across agencies for the prevention of recidivism in high-risk sex offenders.

Finally, Dennis Doren in the last chapter of the book (Chapter 29) describes how actuarial risk assessments are used in USA courtrooms, and how they have been incorporated into the legal and justice systems. The chapter begins by describing actuarial risk assessment instruments relevant to the courtroom and the circumstances in which they are considered of relevance to the courts. Issues around the judicial consideration of actuarial information are examined, and these issues are discussed in detail. In conclusion, Doren offers some comments concerning the future utility of actuarial information in the courts.

REFERENCES

Andrews, D.A. & Bonta, J. (2003). *The psychology of criminal conduct* (3rd edn). Cincinnati, OH: Anderson.

Baldwin, M.W. (2005). *Interpersonal cognition*. New York: Guilford.

Beech, A.R. (1998). A psychometric typology of child abusers. *International Journal of Offender Therapy and, Comparative Criminology, 42*, 319–339.

Beech, A., Fisher, D. & Ward, T. (2005). Sexual murderers' implicit theories. *Journal of Interpersonal Violence, 20*, 1366–1389.

Beech, A.R. & Ward, T. (2004). The integration of etiology and risk in sexual offenders: A theoretical framework. *Aggression and Violent Behavior, 10*, 31–63.

Beech, A., Ward, T. & Fisher, D. (2006). The identification of sexual and violent motivations in men who assault women: Implications for treatment. *Journal of Interpersonal Violence, 21*, 1635–1653.

Broxholme, S.L. & Lindsay, W.R. (2003). Development and preliminary evaluation of a questionnaire on cognitions related to sex offending for use with individuals who have mild intellectual disabilities. *Journal of Intellectual Disability Research, 47*, 472–482.

Councell, R. (2003). The prison population in 2002: A statistical review. Research Development and Statistics Directorate: Findings Report 228, Home Office. Available from: The Research Development and Statistics Directorate, Communication Development Unit, Room 264, Home Office, 50 Queen Anne's Gate, London, SW1H 9AT, UK. Available electronically from: http://www.homeoffice.gov.uk/rds/pdfs2/r228.pdf

Craig, L.A. (in press). Controversies in assessing risk and deviancy in sex offenders with intellectual disabilities. *Psychology, Crime and Law*.

Craig, L., Browne, K.D. & Beech, A.R. (2008). *Assessing risk in sex offenders: A practitioner's guide*. Chichester: John Wiley & Sons, Ltd.

Craig, L.A., Browne, K.D., Stringer, I. & Hogue, T.E. (2008). Sexual reconviction rates in the United Kingdom and actuarial estimates. *Child Abuse and Neglect, 32*, 121–138.

Craig, L.A. & Hutchinson, R. (2005). Sexual offenders with learning disabilities: Risk, recidivism and treatment. *Journal of Sexual Aggression, 11*, 3, 289–304.

Craig, L.A., Stringer, I. & Hutchinson, R. (in press). Core assessment of adult sex offenders with a learning disability. In M. Calder (Ed.), *The complete guide to sexual abuse assessments* (2nd edn). Willan.

Craig, L.A., Stringer, I. & Moss, T. (2006). Treating sexual offenders with learning disabilities in the community: A critical review. *International Journal of Offender Therapy and, Comparative Criminology, 50*, 369–390.

Fisher, D. & Beech, A.R. (2007). Identification of motivations for sexual murder. In J. Proulx & M. Cusson (Eds), *Sexual murderers: A comparative analysis and new perspectives* (pp. 175–190). Chichester: John Wiley & Sons, Ltd.

Gilbert, P. (2005). Compassion and cruelty: A biopsychosocial approach. In P. Gilbert (Ed.), *Compassion: Conceptualisations, research and use in psychotherapy* (pp. 9–74). London: Routledge.

Hanson, R.K. (1997). *The development of a brief actuarial risk scale for sexual offence recidivism.* (User Report 1997–04.) Ottawa: Department of the Solicitor General of Canada. Available electronically from: www.sgc.gc.ca/epub/corr/e199704/e199704.htm.

Hanson, R.K. & Bussière, M.T. (1998). Predicting relapse: A meta-analysis of sexual offender recidivism studies. *Journal of Consulting and Clinical Psychology, 66*(2), 348–362.

Hanson, R.K. & Morton-Bourgon, K.E. (2005). The characteristics of persistent sexual offenders: A meta-analysis of recidivism studies. *Journal of Consulting and Clinical Psychology, 73*, 1154–1163.

Hanson, R.K. & Thornton, D. (2000). Improving risk assessment for sex offenders: A comparison of three actuarial scales. *Law and Human Behavior, 24*, 1, 119–136.

Jansson, K., Povey, D. & Kaiza, P. (2007). Violent and sexual crime. In S. Nicholas, C. Kershaw & A. Walker (Eds), *Crime in England and Wales 2006/07* (4th edn) (pp. 49–65). London: Home Office.

Lockmuller, M., Fisher, D. & Beech, A.R. (2008). Sexual offenders with mental health problems: epidemiology, assessment and treatment. In K. Soothill, M. Dolan & P. Rogers (Eds), *Handbook of forensic mental health* (pp. 442–475). Uffculme, Devon: Willan.

Lovell, E. (2002). Children and young people who display sexually harmful behaviour. London: NSPCC.

McBrien, J., Hodgetts, A. & Gregory, J. (2003). Offending behaviour in services for people with learning disabilities in one local authority. *Journal of Forensic Psychiatry & Psychology, 14*(2), 280–297.

McGuire, J. (Ed.) (1995). *What works: Reducing offending – Guidelines from research and practice.* Chichester, UK: John Wiley & Sons, Ltd.

Ministry of Justice (2007). Population in custody: Monthly tables October 2007 England and Wales. Available electronically from: http://www.justice.gov.uk/docs/population-in-custody-oct07.pdf

Murphy, G.H. (2007). Intellectual disabilities, sexual abuse and sexual offending. In A. Carr, J. McEvoy, P. Noonan-Walsh & G. O'Reilly (Eds), *Handbook of intellectual disability and clinical psychology practice* (pp. 831–866). London: Routledge.

Prentky, R.A. & Righthand, S. (2003). Juvenile Sex Offender Assessment Protocol-II (J-SOAP-II) Manual. Bridgewater, MA: Justice Resource Institute.

Quinsey, V.L., Harris, G.T., Rice, M.E. & Cormier, C. (1998). *Violent offenders: Appraising and managing risk*. Washington DC: American Psychological Association.

Righthand, S. & Welch, C. (2001). Juveniles who have sexually offended: a review of the professional literature. US Department of Justice, Office of Juvenile Justice and Delinquency Prevention. Retrieved from: http://www.ncjrs.org/html/ojjdp/report_juvsex_offend/.

Sickmund, M., Snyder, H. & Poe-Yamagata, E. (1997). *Juvenile offenders and victims: 1997 update on violence*. Washington, DC: Office of Juvenile Justice and Delinquency Prevention.

Snyder, H.N. & Sickmund, M. (1999). *Juvenile offenders and victims: 1999 national report*. Washington, DC: Office of Juvenile Justice and Delinquency Prevention.

Thornton, D. (2002). Constructing and testing a framework for dynamic risk assessment. *Sexual Abuse: A Journal of Research and, Treatment, 14*(2), 139–153.

Ward, T. & Beech, A.R. (2004). The etiology of risk: A preliminary model. *Sexual Abuse: A Journal of Research and, Treatment, 16*, 271–284.

Ward, T. & Gannon, T. (2006). Rehabilitation, etiology, and self-regulation: The comprehensive good lives model of treatment for sexual offenders. *Aggression and Violent Behavior, 11*, 77–94.

Ward, T., Hudson, S.M. & Marshall, W.L. (1996). Attachment style in sex offenders: A Preliminary Study. *Journal of Sex Research, 33*, 17–26.

Ward, T. & Mann, R. (2004). Good lives and the rehabilitation of offenders. A positivist approach to sex offender treatment. In P.A. Linley & S. Joseph (Eds), *Positive psychology in practice* (pp. 598–616). Chichester: John Wiley & Sons, Ltd.

Ward, T., Mann, R. & Gannon, T.A. (2007). The good lives model of rehabilitation: Clinical implications. *Aggression and Violent Behavior, 12*, 2, 208–228.

Ward, T. & Siegert, R.J. (2002). Toward a comprehensive theory of child sexual abuse: A theory knitting perspective. *Psychology, Crime and Law, 8*, 319–351.

Young, J.E., Klosko, J.S. & Weisharr, M.E. (2003). *Schema therapy: A practitioner's guide*. London: Guilford Press.

2

Attachment Problems and Sex Offending

JACKIE CRAISSATI

INTRODUCTION

Sexual offending is an interpersonal crime, there is always a perpetrator and a victim, and their relationship – however fleeting and distorted – is central to any understanding of the crime. Such a relationship may be purely symbolic, held in the perpetrator's mind within or outside of conscious awareness (Doctor, 2003). For example, an indecent exposer may hold expectations of the victim's response, perhaps hoping for an expression of shock mutating into fascination and admiration, a fantasy of potential seduction which is most unlikely to have any bearing on the reality of the situation. The offence relationship may have an objective reality, with a clear targeting of the victim based on his or her characteristics. This can sometimes be seen in incestuous abuse, in which the offending commenced with an emotional closeness and identification between the perpetrator and child victim which is controlled and distorted by the former transforming the relationship into sexualised contact and abuse. Alternatively, the offence relationship may represent – for the perpetrator – a displacement of painful emotional states such as fear of abandonment, rage and humiliation, that have their origin in actual experiences originating in early life or in failed adult romantic relationships; the offence may represent an attempt by the perpetrator to regain control and self-esteem by reversing and re-enacting such experiences (Rosen, 1979). Thus, whatever the nature of the sexual offending, the offence always represents a failure of the perpetrator to achieve intimacy – integrating both emotional and sexual needs – in pro-social ways. This presupposes that any understanding of sexual offending needs to trace the pattern of relationships within the perpetrator's life, with a particular understanding of the cognitive and affective states of mind which relate to interpersonal functioning.

Assessment and Treatment of Sex Offenders: A Handbook. Edited by Anthony Beech, Leam Craig and Kevin Browne. © John Wiley & Sons Ltd, 2009.

This chapter therefore aims to consider the relevance of attachment theory to the development of adult relationship patterns, considering the current state of knowledge regarding the development of early attachment in childhood and adolescence, its link to romantic or courtship behaviours, and the implications for antisocial behaviour – sexual offending in particular. There is no intention to provide a complete theoretical model for sexual offending – which is clearly understood to encompass an extraordinarily diverse group of offenders, behaviours, motivations and risks – but rather to provide a core grounding in key ideas which have applicability to the assessment of aetiology, risk, and treatment approaches in this group of offenders. Indeed, attachment theory has enormous popularity as a model because of its accessibility of ideas, and its integrative nature – combining a biological, social and cognitive understanding of human behaviour – which is compatible with a wide variety of theoretical perspectives.

The chapter inevitably restricts itself to an overview of the subject, with reference to the evidence base where it is available and of central relevance. The literature, to date, is almost exclusively focused on mainstream western societies, and may or may not be relevant to more culturally diverse populations of sex offenders where there are significant differences to expectations of parenting practices, adolescent rites and romantic attachments. Furthermore the attachment literature for sex offenders makes little reference to specific findings for female or learning disabled sex offenders, which also fall beyond the scope of this chapter. For the interested reader, there are key texts which are highly informative. These include: Felicity de Zulueta's (2006) updated book, *From Pain to Violence*; Phil Rich's (2006) book on *Attachment and sexual offending* in juvenile sexual offenders; Beech and Mitchell's (2005) paper on neurobiological perspectives on attachment problems in sexual offenders; and Stephen Smallbone's chapter (2006, pp. 93–108) on an attachment revision of Marshall and Barbaree's integrated theory on the aetiology of sexual offending.

ATTACHMENT THEORY

Definition

It is perhaps appropriate to commence with a consideration of the term 'attachment' and the potential for confusion in the way that it is used (Rich, 2006). Attachment theory is based on a very specific and unique relationship: the attachment relationship and attachment bond between a child and primary caregiver (Bowlby, 1969). All other close relationships are referred to as affiliative relationships (Rich, 2006). However, attachment is also used to describe a sense of social connection that one individual has to another and the sense of social relatedness or belonging that an individual has to a larger reference group (Rich, 2006). This definition includes the child – caregiver relationship, but also friendships and other affiliative bonds (and the wider society), as well as later romantic attachments and relationships with one's own children (Bartholomew & Horowitz, 1991).

Infant Attachment

Any consideration of attachment theory must start with Bowlby (1969, 1973, 1980) who postulated that the primary function of early object relationships is to provide the infant with a sense of security in environments that induce fear. Bowlby believed that infants are genetically predisposed to form attachments at a critical point in their first year of life in order to increase their chance of survival. Since the attachment relationship is not present at birth, evolutionary processes favoured the development of behaviours in the infant – smiling and crying – which attract a positive response from the caregiver. The infant needs to explore and learn from the environment while seeking out and maintaining protective proximity to the attachment figure during times of danger, thus protecting the infant from physical and psychological harm. Threat (when the baby is alarmed or anxious) activates the attachment system. Bowlby proposed that the quality of attachment was dependent upon the appropriateness and promptness of the adult's response to these contact-seeking signals of the infant, that is, infants become securely attached to caregivers who consistently and appropriately respond to their attachment behaviours. On the basis of these interactions between the infant and caregiver, self – other representations develop, which he termed 'internal working models', which reflect the child's cumulative experience of sensitivity on the part of that caregiver. Bowlby assumed that this attachment system remained a central organiser of interpersonal behaviour throughout the life span.

These ideas were developed still further by Bowlby's colleague, Mary Ainsworth (e.g., Ainsworth *et al.*, 1978) who observed that insensitively parented one-year-olds tended either to avoid the caregiver after a brief period of separation ('anxious-avoidant'), or refuse to be comforted by her on her return ('anxious-resistant'). In contrast, sensitively parented children sought comfort from the caregiver following brief separation. That is, insensitive parenting (usually mothering in early research studies) did not lead to no attachment at all, but to an insecure attachment to the caregiver. These observations formed the basis of the Strange Situation Test, a laboratory procedure to assess infant attachment around 12 months of age, which produced levels of stress in the infant sufficient to activate the infant's attachment behavioural system. In non-clinical samples, around two-thirds of infants are placed in the secure category, 22% are classified as anxious-avoidant, and 12% as anxious-ambivalent (Ainsworth *et al.*, 1978).

When maternal patterns of caregiving behaviour and infant patterns of attachment were explored (Ainsworth *et al.*, 1978), mothers of securely attached infants were found to be sensitive and responsive, with the infant's needs being met promptly and appropriately. These maternal attributes were elaborated further, to include six characteristics:

- Sensitivity-insensitivity
- Acceptance-rejection
- Cooperation-interference
- Accessibility-ignoring

- Emotional expression
- Maternal rigidity.

Mothers of anxious-avoidant infants tend to be more rejecting, angry and intrusively over-involved. Mothers of anxious-ambivalent infants are characterised by being withdrawn, uninvolved, and inconsistent in their parent style. The infant responses to these categorisations are shown in Table 2.1.

A disorganised category was developed later by Main and Solomon (1990) to distinguish a group of insecurely attached infants who did not appear to have a coherent attachment strategy and demonstrated extremely disturbed and disorganised behaviour in relation to the attachment figure, which comprised alternating approach/avoidance behaviours, prolonged freezing, apprehensiveness, helplessness, and depressive behaviours. The caregivers of such children are perceived to be frightened (as a result of unresolved experiences of loss or trauma in parental development), or to behave in a frightening and threatening manner, thus creating a seemingly unresolvable conflict for the child, as the parent is simultaneously a source of distress and a source of comfort (described in Burk & Burkhart, 2003). Disorganised/disorientated attachment styles are associated with persistence of disturbance in internal mental states, and the development of interactional behaviours characterised by control and lack of social reciprocity.

An important component of secure attachment is the development of reflective functioning (Fonagy, 1999). The caregiver demonstrates reflective functioning by the capacity of giving meaning to the infant's experiences, sharing and predicting his or her behaviour; the persistent failure of the caregiver to recognise the child's subjective state in infancy impairs their reflective functioning. As Fonagy explains, the initial representation of the self is dependent on "my caregiver thinks of me as thinking, therefore I exist as a thinker". This developmental acquisition enables people to understand each other in terms of mental states and intentions, and it is the key to developing a sense of agency and continuity as well as enabling us to interact successfully with others (de Zulueta, 2006). Insecure attachment styles – particularly disorganised type – are associated with significant impairments in reflective functioning.

Subsequent researchers have pointed to the role of the infant in the formation of attachment, specifically investigating infant temperament and its influence on the quality of attachment. The findings have been mixed, and it is probably reasonable to conclude that the attachment relationship is a bidirectional process, with the mother (and other central caregivers) exerting the most influence, and infants responding in a way that serves to maintain the mother's behaviour (Crittenden, 1988).

Psychobiological Processes

Having described the basis of attachment theory in terms of cognitive and social psychological processes, it is important to pause at this stage to consider the psychobiological underpinnings of this theory. Brain function is a highly complex and

Table 2.1 Categorisations of attachment

Infant Strange Situation behaviour	Adult Attachment Interview: adult states of mind	Bartholomew & Horowitz (1991): close relationships	Brennan, Clark & Shaver (1998): adult romantic attachment
Secure Explores room and toys with interest in pre-separation episodes. Shows signs of missing parent during separation, often crying by the second separation. Obvious preference for parent over stranger. Greets parent actively, usually initiating physical contact. Usually some contact maintaining by second reunion, but then settles and returns to play.	*Secure/autonomous (F)* Coherent, collaborative discourse. Valuing of attachment, but seems objective regarding any particular relationship. Description and evaluation of attachment-related experiences are favourable or unfavourable.	*Secure (A)* It is easy for me to become emotionally close to others. I am comfortable depending on others and having others depend on me. I don't worry about being alone or having others not accept me.	*Secure* Low on avoidance (not avoiding intimacy, comfortable with closeness & not overly self-reliant), and low on anxiety (little preoccupation, jealousy or fear of abandonment, little fear of rejection). Use touch to express affection, endorses affectionate sexual behaviours, experiences positive emotions following sex.
Avoidant (A) Fails to cry on separation from parent. Actively avoids and ignores parent on reunion. Little or no proximity or contact seeking, no distress, and no anger. Response to parent appears to be unemotional. Focuses on toys or environment throughout procedure.	*Dismissing (Ds)* Not coherent. Dismissing of attachment-related experiences and relationships. Normalising ("excellent, very normal mother"), with generalised representations of history unsupported or actively contradicted by episodes recounted. Transcripts also tend to be excessively brief.	*Dismissing (D)* I am comfortable without close emotional relationships. It is very important to me to feel independent and self-sufficient, and I prefer not to depend on others or have others depend on me.	*Dismissing-avoidant* Highly avoidant but low levels of anxiety in intimate relationships. Compulsively self-reliant, avoiding touch in relationships, low levels of negative emotions following sex, most likely to endorse promiscuous sexual behaviours.

(Continued)

Table 2.1 Continued

Infant Strange Situation behaviour	Adult Attachment Interview: adult states of mind	Bartholomew & Horowitz (1991): close relationships	Brennan, Clark & Shaver (1998): adult romantic attachment
Resistant or ambivalent (C) May be wary or distressed even prior to separation, with little exploration. Preoccupied with parent throughout procedure, may seem angry or passive. Fails to settle and take comfort in parent or reunion, and usually continues to focus on parent and cry. Fails to return to exploration after reunion.	*Preoccupied (E)* Not coherent. Preoccupied with or by past attachment experiences/relationships, speaker appears angry, passive or fearful. Sentences often long, grammatically entangled, or filled with vague usages ("and that"). Transcripts often excessively long.	*Preoccupied (C)* I want to be completely emotionally intimate with others, but I often find that others are reluctant to get as close as I would like. I am uncomfortable being without close relationships, but I sometimes worry that others don't value me as much as I value them.	*Preoccupied (ambivalent)* Low levels of avoidance but high levels of anxiety in intimate relationships. Use touch to express emotion and seek care, but desires more touch than receives. Endorses affectionate sexual behaviours, but some negative emotions following sex.
Disorganised, disoriented (D) Displays disorganised and/or disoriented behaviours in the parent's presence, suggesting a temporary collapse of behavioural strategies (e.g., freezing or clinging whilst leaning away with gaze averted). Infant will ordinarily otherwise fit A, B or C.	*Unresolved, disorganised (U/d)* During discussions of loss/abuse, individual shows striking lapse in the monitoring of reasoning or discourse, e.g., may briefly indicate a belief that a dead person was killed by a childhood thought. Individual may lapse into prolonged silence or eulogistic speech. Otherwise fits D, E or F.	*Fearful (B)* I am uncomfortable getting close to others. I want emotionally close relationships, but I find it difficult to trust others completely, or to depend on them. I worry that I will be hurt if I allow myself to become too close to others.	*Fearful-avoidant* Highly avoidant (avoiding intimacy, discomfort with closeness, self-reliant) and highly anxious (preoccupied, jealous, fearful of abandonment & rejection) in intimate relationships. A lack of touch in relationships, and high levels of negative emotions after sex.

Comments:

Comments:

Comments:
Based on semi-structured interview & multiple measures of attachment.

Four short statements, as forced-choice, and Likert rating of four statements.

Can rate close, romantic, or specific relationships.

Continuous ratings on two dimensional model of positive/negative self & other model.

Comments:
36 item self-report, Likert scale, questionnaire (ECR) based on romantic attachments.

Two dimensions of high/low avoidance and high/low anxiety.

Four clusters associated with different attitudes to touch and sex within relationships.

specialised area, but a broad summary of current thinking can be derived from de Zulueta (2006) and Beech and Mitchell (2005). Infants are not born with the capability of regulating their arousal and emotional reactions, soothing or comforting themselves, or maintaining psychophysiological homeostatis; it is the caregiver's response to the infant's distress signals – holding, caressing, smiling, feeding and giving meaning – which enables attunement to take place, enabling the modulation and reduction of cortisol levels in relation to specific stressors. Cortisol levels are used as a measure of adrenocortical activation, which is a traditional measurement of stress (de Zulueta, 2006). The neuropeptides – oxytocin and vasopressin – are also implicated, in their actions both as hormones and as neurotransmitters (Beech & Mitchell, 2005). Cortisol levels are raised in the infant when separated briefly (that is, the infant is stressed) and endogenous opiates are involved in the development of secure attachments to the caregiver. If attachment theory is understood, biologically, as a regulatory theory, then the orbitofrontal area – close to the limbic system, connected to the autonomic system, and largely located in the right hemisphere – is the focus for the acquisition of specific forms of knowledge which can regulate interpersonal behaviour, modulating and regulating social and emotional behaviours (particularly the perception of internal emotional states and the emotional states of others. Thus secure attachment can be understood as providing a neurobiological buffer against stress, as well as promoting the development of attunement with others, a capacity for reflection and empathic perception (Fonagy, 1999).

Insecure attachment – particularly disorganised attachment – but also chronic childhood abuse, is associated with two separate psychobiological response patterns – hyperarousal (the fight or flight response activated by the sympathetic component of the autonomic nervous system) and dissociation (freezing activated by the parasympathetic component) (Van Ijzendoorn, Schuengel & Bakermans-Kranenberg, 1999). In traumatic states of helplessness, endogenous opiates are released to produce numbing of pain (Lyons-Ruth & Jacobvitz, 2003). With no caregiver to restore equilibrium, these chronic stress states can cause severe damage to the right hemisphere cortical limbic circuits, which in turn, are associated with other alterations in brain function, resulting in long-term problems with the regulation of emotions, capacity to play and fantasise, and to form future attachments. Low cortisol in particular, as a consequence of chronic stress, is associated with emotional withdrawal states in general (Beech & Mitchell, 2005).

This model would suggest that the neurobiological consequences of insecure attachment in early life renders the individual more vulnerable to the effects of later experiences of abuse – including sexual abuse – resulting in greater difficulties in resolving post traumatic stress responses (de Zulueta, 2006).

Stability of Attachment over the Lifespan

Researchers have also investigated the predictive stability of early attachment categorisations (Fonagy et al., 1997; Green & Goldwyn, 2002). Follow-up studies showed that early insecure relations preceded moodiness, depression and aggression in preschool years, and primary school. However, even securely attached infants could develop behavioural problems if the interactional patterns between mother and child were unsupportive, inconsistent, uninvolved and confused at three and a half years; and conversely insecurely attached infants were less likely to develop subsequent behavioural problems if their interactions with their mother were warm, supportive and appropriate. Thus subsequent variations in the parent – child relationship, and family circumstances, appear to be critical in determining whether the developmental pathway is continued, diluted or abandoned (Fonagy *et al.*, 1997). These findings support some of the criticisms of attachment theory, that is, it overemphasises early relationships, oversimplifies the complexities of attachment categorisation, pays insufficient attention to interactional maintaining factors which influence continuity (and discontinuity), and does not account for the important influence of secondary attachment figures (Brown & Wright, 2001).

Brown and Wright (2001) suggest that insecure attachment is neither a necessary, nor a sufficient cause of later pathology, rather attachment should be conceptualised within a risk/vulnerability model for psychopathology. Although insecure attachment proved to be a risk factor for the later development of psychopathology, its high base rate in the normal population has reduced its predictive value (Green & Goldwyn, 2002). For example, it has been suggested that attachment history should be considered alongside child characteristics, parental management style and family ecology. Nevertheless, research suggests that avoidant attachment patterns tend to be associated with later antisocial and externalising problems; ambivalent patterns with social withdrawal in middle childhood and anxiety disorders in late adolescence (summarised in Green & Goldwyn, 2002). Disorganised attachment is associated with a wide range of specific later effects, including poor peer interactions and behavioural difficulties (particularly oppositional behaviour).

Adolescence is characterised by biological, mental and social change, and is therefore a time when the self – other dialect is particularly strong. Puberty is the final period of rapid neurological change in human development, and predominant attachment patterns in the adolescent become sexualised (Brown & Wright, 2001), marking a period of sensual physical closeness with another which has not been experienced since the mother – infant dyad over a decade previously. This idea is developed in the section on attachment and sex offending below. Cognitive maturation results in many young people changing their understanding of themselves, their parents and the world generally, and experimenting with alternative ideas and behaviours, thus adolescence is a time when internal working models are transferred to peers (social group functioning) and social institutions. This is a period of consolidation in attachment when insecure patterns can be reversed or become entrenched (Brown & Wright, 2001). Insecurely attached adolescents are less able to integrate and reorganise models because information is selectively attended to with the defensive exclusion of information, or considered unreliable, so discrepancies in the model being used are not identified, preventing integration taking place.

By adulthood, internal working models have been adjusted and modified, but essentially they are likely to be self-perpetuating because of the biasing effect on incoming information and the tendency for individuals to both select and create environments that confirm their existing beliefs. The work on romantic bonds in adulthood has been based on the premise: that there will be similar attachment patterns among adults as among children; that these romantic relationships will function in similar ways, in terms of mate selection, secure base and safe haven behaviour, avoidant attachment and defence mechanisms; and that attachment patterns are stable from infancy to adulthood. Researchers have found a correspondence between infant attachment styles and the categorisation of adult romantic attachments (Hazan & Shaver, 1987, 1994) with around two-thirds of adults being classified as securely attached. These adult classifications are moderately stable, but may change in response to changes in personal circumstances, such as losing a partner, or experiencing a supportive and loving relationship (Hazan & Shaver, 1994). Hazan and Shaver (1987) – and subsequently Bartholomew and Horowitz (1991) – developed models of adult attachment which are based on a dimension of anxiety and avoidance, and positive and negative internal models of self and other, respectively. These models are described further in the section on measuring attachment, and are represented in relation to the Strange Situation and adult attachment categorisations, in Table 2.1.

THE RELATIONSHIP OF ATTACHMENT TO EXPERIENCES OF ABUSE AND TRAUMA

It is important to distinguish experiences of abuse, that are perpetrated by primary caregivers, in infancy (neglect and emotional abuse) and are therefore integral to the formation of insecure attachment bonds, from later childhood experiences of abuse perpetrated by a primary caregiver (usually the father) who was not abusive at the time that early attachment bonds were formed in infancy. This complicated structure is not adequately addressed in the literature, and there is little or no data on the attachment patterns found in children who have been physically or sexually abused. However, there is a body of work on trauma experiences in personality disorder, particularly borderline type (e.g., Bateman & Fonagy, 2004). Both physical and sexual abuse are reported more commonly than normal subjects in personality disordered populations, but only borderline patients consistently report high levels of sexual abuse (well over two-thirds of most samples) (Bateman & Fonagy, 2004).

The relationship between secure attachment (as a buffer) and insecure attachment (as a vulnerability/risk factor) has already been described in relation to later abuse (in the section on stability of attachment over the lifespan). Both biologically and psychologically, the impact of insecure attachment is to predispose the older child and adult to post traumatic stress responses to later trauma. It is not necessarily the traumatic event itself, which cannot be overcome, but the impact of associated features such as the personal meaning of the event, the ability to disclose and be believed or validated, to activate effective social support mechanisms. Trauma leads to a partial collapse of interpersonal interpretive function, disorganisation of attention, poor stress regulation, and reduces the capacity for reflective function (Fonagy, 1999).

With regard to offenders – and sexual offenders in particular – the research evidence seems to suggest that the family backgrounds of violent and sexual offenders are characterised by neglect, violence and disruption, although it has been difficult to find clear and consistent distinctions between rapists and violent offenders, both of whom tend to be comparable in terms of physical and sexual abuse experiences, and in terms of more behavioural maladjustment at school (Haapasalo & Kankkonen, 1997). Child molesters tend to report the highest levels of sexual victimisation in childhood, and these are associated with poor family relations (Dhawan & Marshall, 1996). Sexual victimisation is also associated with sex offenders who began their sexually coercive behaviour in adolescence rather than as adults, and similarly with earlier onset of masturbation (Smallbone & McCabe, 2003).

Craissati and colleagues (Craissati, McClurg & Browne, 2002b; Craissati & Beech, 2004, 2006) explored the role of key adverse developmental experiences in sex offenders in a series of studies across London. They found that around half of all child molesters (and a quarter of rapists) reported sexual victimisation, although this figure dropped when the methodology was based on probation file information rather than clinical interview. They also found that sexually victimised sex offenders were significantly more likely to engage in a range of psychosexually disturbed behaviour in adulthood. Sexually abused offenders were also much more likely to report emotional abuse in childhood (92% versus 43%) and behavioural disturbance (73% versus 33%).

Furthermore, when childhood attachment experiences were measured, using the Parental Bonding Instrument (Parker, Tupling & Brown, 1979, see below), child molesters reported high levels of maternal affectionless control (low care and high overprotection) associated with developmental experiences of sexual, emotional or physical abuse; the only significant finding with rapists was that both maternal and paternal affectionless control was associated with behavioural disturbance in childhood (Craissati, McClurg & Browne, 2002a). Overall, levels of emotional and physical abuse, and childhood behavioural disturbance ranged between 30–50% with similarities between rapists and child molesters. All forms of abuse – but emotional abuse and behavioural disturbance in particular – were associated with a diagnosis of personality disorder in adulthood (Craissati, Webb & Keen, 2008). The researchers found that higher scores on a number of risk prediction instruments were associated with emotional abuse, behavioural disturbance, or any one type of abusive experience in childhood; and these key developmental variables could enhance the accuracy of risk prediction when considered together with a static risk prediction tool (Craissati & Beech, 2006).

MEASURING ATTACHMENT

Inevitably, there are an enormous number of attachment-related assessment measures, too numerous to mention (e.g., Bartholomew & Shaver, 1998). Closer scrutiny, however, reveals that many have similarities, and are based on the original classificatory systems of Ainsworth and Main & Solomon's original attachment model. The choice of assessment approach largely depends on the task and its purpose: whether some form of 'objective' picture is required regarding the nature of the attachment between parent and child or between a couple; or whether it is important to assess an individual's perception of his/her attachment to a caregiver, whether or not it has become a distorted and selective set of memories. It may also be interesting to administer a psychometric assessment measure of attachment which can be applied pre- and post-treatment, based on the premise that conscious perceptions of attachment and bonding may become more accurate, balanced or realistic as a result of therapeutic change.

For many situations, clinically-based approaches will suffice, with attention paid throughout the interview to patterns of attachment in the offender's background, encompassing early experiences and adolescence, adult relationships and the relational aspects of the offending behaviour. Observational approaches are most common in child-centred services, where parent – child interactions can be assessed; clearly the Strange Situation is the most famous example of a standardised observational approach which has been adapted for research purposes. However, interviews with couples, and attention to the dynamics of the patient – therapist relationship, can also provide key attachment-related observational material.

Psychometric Assessment

Psychometric measures fall into two categories: the semi-structured interview approaches, and self-report questionnaire. The most commonly used of the former, includes the Adult Attachment Interview (AAI; George, Kaplan & Main, 1987). A comparison of classificatory systems is outlined in Table 2.1. Semi-structured interview approaches are sometimes thought to be superior to self-report questionnaires on the basis that they may search out more detailed qualitative information which allows for a more robust rating of attachment, not simply predicated on the respondent's conscious appraisal of his attachment relationships (Ward, Hudson & Marshall, 1996). However, they do require more time and expertise to administer and score, which is not always available to a wide range of practitioners.

The Relationships Questionnaire (RSQ; Bartholomew & Horowitz, 1991) is a single item measure made up of four short paragraphs, each describing a prototypical attachment pattern as it applies in close adult peer relationships. Participants are then asked to rate their degree of correspondence to each prototype on a seven-point scale. This then provides a profile of an individual's attachment feelings and behaviour. The RSQ has some flexibility as it can be worked in terms of general orientations to close relationships, or to a specific relationship, or romantic relationships. The ratings provide a continuous profile although it can also be used to categorise participants (see Table 2.1) on the basis of a model of self – positive or negative – and a model of the other – positive or negative. The validation of this instrument relies on ratings obtained from the Peer Attachment Interview, and subsequent validation of the attachment dimensions were based on multiple measures of attachment (Brennan, Clark & Shaver, 1998). Therefore, although the instrument can be used as self-report, it is more likely to be valid when used to summarise a broader based attachment assessment.

The Adult Attachment Interview (AAI) is a one-hour structured semi-clinical interview which focuses on early attachment experiences and their effects. Subjects are asked for five adjectives to describe their relationship to each parent during childhood, and then for memories which support the choice of each adjective. They are asked whether they felt closer to one parent, or rejected during childhood, whether parents had been threatening with them and why parents may have behaved as they did during childhood; and how these experiences may have affected the development of their personality. The interview is transcribed verbatim, and the assessment is rated from the discourse record. The assessment is based on a set of nine-point rating scales which address: childhood experience with each parent, the client's current state of mind in relation to this experience, and the overall coherence of the transcript and any lapse in reasoning. Rational discourse is considered to be high in quality (evidenced), quantity (succinct yet complete), relevant, and clear and orderly. Four final classifications are possible, as described in Table 2.1.

The AAI has been widely used and validated (Fonagy, Steele & Steele, 1991), and although there are criticisms of it, it does appear to show a high concordance with observational studies. For example, in as many as 80% of cases, infant attachment classification can be predicted on the basis of adult attachment classification made before the birth of the child (Fonagy, 1999). It has been used with offending populations, property offenders being found to be dismissing or preoccupied in their classification, whilst violent offenders were more likely to be unresolved or cannot classify categorisation (Fonagy *et al.*, 1997).

Of the numerous self-report measures, perhaps one of the more commonly used in adolescents and adults to rate their perception of the bonding experiences as children with their parents, is the *Parental Bonding Instrument* (Parker, Tupling & Brown, 1979). The PBI comprises 25 self-report questions scored in two dimensions: *care* ranges from affection and empathy to indifference and emotional coldness; *control/overprotection* ranges between intrusion and prevention of independence to independence and autonomy. Participants can then be classified into one type of four attachment bonds, as reported for each parent: optimal bonding (high care, low protection), affectionate constraint (high care, high protection), affectionless control (low care, high protection), and weak bonding (low care, low protection)

The PBI has been used with sexual offenders by Craissati, McClurg and Browne (2002a), who compared child molesters and rapists finding that the affectionless control style of parental bonding was highly prevalent in child molesters; a subsequent comparison study with normal controls and a violent, non-sexual group of offenders, reported by Craissati (2003), found that rapists were almost as likely to rate their parents as providing optimum bonding as the control group – particularly for their mothers – and that there was a lack of significant differences between groups overall. This may represent expected distortions in the self-report style of rapists and child molesters, or suggest some problems with the psychometric properties of the PBI, or difficulties with the study sample. However, it would indicate that although the PBI provides interesting results, it should be used with caution for the time being.

The *Inventory of Parent and Peer Attachment* (IPPA; Armsden & Greenberg, 1987) is the most commonly used of the adolescent attachment self-report instruments, and is based on the conceptual framework of attachment theory. It comprises three sets of 25 questions, in 'mother', 'father', and 'peer' categories, regarding how well each of these figures serves as a source of psychological security. Subscale scores are available for trust (degree of mutual trust), communication (quality of communication), and alienation (extent of anger and alienation), with a total attachment score for either high or low security. The authors of the IPPA conclude that self-esteem and satisfaction with life are highly related to the quality of parent and peer relationships, and adolescents classified as high security appear well adjusted. As yet, there is no normative data reported for the IPPA with adolescents, as compared with juvenile sex offenders (Rich, 2006), although Rich notes that there are studies underway to compare juvenile sex offenders with non-sexual juvenile delinquents on the IPPA.

Perhaps the most commonly recommended scale for assessing romantic attachment is the *Experiences in Close Relationships* (ECR; Brennan, Clark & Shaver, 1998). This is a 36 item self-report questionnaire which is based on two subscales: avoidance (or discomfort with closeness and discomfort depending on others) and anxiety (or fear of rejection and abandonment). The two dimensions yield four types of classification which are closely allied to Bartholomew and Horowitz's categories, which are in turn, linked to the AAI categories (see Table 2.1). The psychometric properties of the ECR appear to be somewhat more robust than those for the RQ, perhaps because it relies on a wide range of questions drawn from numerous romantic attachment questionnaires to underpin its two-dimensional structure. Interestingly, the original report on the ECR examined the association between the attachment categories and two subscales for touch (51 items, four constructs – using touch to express affectionate proximity, desiring more physical contact, touch aversion, and using touch to assure a haven of safety) and sex (47 items relating to sexual behaviour and emotions following sexual activities). These findings are of particular relevance to sexual offenders, and are detailed briefly in Table 2.1.

ATTACHMENT AND ITS LINK WITH ANTISOCIAL BEHAVIOUR AND ADULT OFFENDING

There is now a strong body of evidence identifying the link between childhood disruptive behaviour problems (conduct disorder), adolescent delinquency and later antisocial behaviour in adulthood, although this trajectory is by no means predetermined and many behaviourally disordered children (and delinquent adolescents) do not progress to adult antisocial acts (Fonagy *et al.*, 1997). Continuity of such behaviours over the lifespan has been shown to be related to poor parental attachment (Fergusson & Lynskey, 1998); Le Blanc (1992) explored the complex relationship between family bonding, structural socio-economic family factors, later delinquency and adult offending. He found that structural factors determined the quality of family bonding which was, in turn, a central cause of delinquency in terms of the acceptance, or rebuttal, of constraints (regulations, supervision and discipline); family functioning and delinquent behaviour during the second part of adolescence was essential to an explanation of adult criminality.

Chapple (2003) explored the model of the intergenerational transmission of violence – a widely accepted causal explanation for the connection between parental violence and adolescent violence. In particular she explored the difference between poor attachment to parents and a lack of parental control. She defined attachment as connectedness and found in her study that: adolescent 'dating' violence was far higher for those who were weakly attached to their violent parents; delinquency was lowest in those children who were securely attached to conventional parents (exerting parental controls); and parental attachment had a negative effect on the perceived likelihood of dating violence regardless of whether the respondent witnessed inter-parental violence or not.

Fonagy (1999) also proposed that a disorganised attachment system – coupled with a history of abuse in childhood and an absent male parental figure – provided an explanatory model for relationship violence in adulthood. Reder and Duncan (2001) suggest that anxiously attached men tend to enter partnerships with equally anxiously attached women, and together they enact recurrent cycles of proximity-seeking followed by aggressive distancing behaviour. They conceptualise these difficulties as unresolved care and control conflicts, and suggest that some aspects of parental child abuse may relate to crisis interactions between the parent and child, in which the child's crying infers a need for extra comforting but he/she rejects the parent's efforts, and the child's need for care is experienced as demanding and controlling of the parent.

It is also important to note, as described above, that there is an established link between early attachment problems and vulnerability to subsequent abusive experiences in childhood; and a link between childhood abuse and later criminality. Thus, what is the nature of the relationship between the development of attachment in early life and later antisocial – particularly violent – behaviour? Bowlby (1944) postulated from early on that psychopathy, violence and crime were primarily related to disorders of attachment and represented distorted attempts at interpersonal emotional exchanges. Insecure attachment in childhood – particularly detached or disorganised types – is associated with unresponsive, rejecting parenting, such that the infant internalises working models in which relationships are generally viewed as characterised by anger, mistrust, chaos and insecurity; disruptive behaviours emerge as strategies to maximise parental attention; normal self-protective infant and toddler expressions of anger turn to aggression when parental insensitivity is pervasive, and are clearly dysfunctional as aggression threatens to break apart the attachment bond. Thus anger and aggression lie at the root of all insecure attachment. Fonagy et al. (1997) suggest that the attachment system may be involved in both predatory and affective acts of violence; whereas in the former case the individual seeks the object, and the purpose of such proximity seeking is primarily destructive, in the latter case, proximity triggers an intense defensive reaction of a violent kind.

For the delinquent adolescent, the early absence of a strong attachment to the parent may have been masked by the adult's physical capacity to control the child, and the absence of parental control through emotional ties may not become clear until early adolescence, when the life task is to transfer bonds to peers and social institutions (such as school), and there is a need for strongly internalised controls through morality, empathy, caring and commitment (Fonagy *et al.*, 1997). It has already been established (see above) that insecure early attachments are associated with poor empathy and perspective-taking ability, and it may be that a key component of crimes against the person is that awareness of the mental state of the other (the potential victim) must be blocked in order to inflict harm; thus mentalising ability is a prerequisite to socialisation.

ATTACHMENT IN SEXUAL OFFENDERS

There has been a flurry of research in the last 10 years exploring the nature of attachment in sexual offenders, with attempts to delineate pathways from attachment experiences in early life, through to adult intimacy and linking these to broad typologies of sexual offending behaviour. Some broadly consistent findings have emerged, although there continues to be some complex and contradictory evidence which would urge caution in oversimplifying the model.

As outlined in the introduction, all sexual offending necessitates an understanding of issues of emotional loneliness (when intimate relationships are ultimately emotionally unfulfilling), poor self-esteem, and fear of intimacy (in which adult relationships themselves or emotional commitment to relationships are avoided) (Marshall, 1993). More recent developments in theoretical perspectives include additional general themes within relationships of difficulties with emotional regulation and personality dysfunction, self-definition and perspective taking (Burk & Burkhart, 2003); work by Baker and Beech (2004) and Baker, Beech and Tyson (2006) has examined the relevance of disorganised attachment styles and their relationship to dissociation and early maladaptive schemas in sex offenders.

The role of the internal working model is to act as a bridge between early attachment experience and these adult intimacy problems. Studies of attachment styles in sex offenders – when compared to violent and non-violent offenders – tend to show both general and specific links (Smallbone and colleagues, 1998, 2000, 2001, 2003), that is, all offenders report greater levels of insecure attachments than non-offender controls; sexual and violent offenders report greater levels of insecure attachments than other offenders; coercive sexual behaviour in non-offenders is associated with greater levels of insecure childhood attachment, even when antisociality and aggression are controlled for, as well as greater levels of adult attachment avoidance. If we then explore differences within sex offender groups, there is evidence that rapists tend to endorse emotional and behavioural patterns consistent with avoidant or dismissive attachment, to report idealised versions of parental experiences; and are more likely to have been physically abused by a family member than were child molesters; while child molesters tend to endorse emotional and behavioural patterns consistent with preoccupied or fearful patterns of attachment, to report dependent and problematic relationships with their mothers, and are more likely to have been victims of childhood sexual assault than rapists (Burk & Burkhart, 2003; Craissati, McClurg & Browne, 2002a, 2002b; Ward, Hudson & Marshall, 1996).

These findings are underpinned by Smallbone's (2006) theoretical model which builds on Bowlby's premise that attachment, sexuality and parenting are the three most important social behavioural systems for species survival. Here, Smallbone places a particular emphasis on the pathway to sexual offending, identifying the way in which sexual drive, sexual attraction and mate selection have evolved to direct mating, reproduction and parenting. *Sexual drive* motivates humans to seek sexual contact with non-specific others, that is, humans are biologically prepared to respond sexually to a very broad range of potential sexual stimuli (Fisher *et al.*, 2002). *Sexual attraction* (romantic passion) has the purpose of directing sexual drive toward a more restricted range of objects, that is, it provides for courtship behaviour to be focused on specific kinds of individuals. *Mate selection* is thought to have evolved for the purpose of cooperating with reproductive mates to ensure the survival of offspring, but has the additional benefits of promoting personal benefits including mutual support, happiness and intimacy.

In psychosocial terms, the task of organising the three systems presents significant developmental and social challenges. Early problematic attachment environments tend to be associated with early-onset puberty, opportunistic or coercive sexual behaviour, many short-term unstable pair bonds, and low levels of parental investment (Smallbone, 2006). His attachment conceptualisation of sexual offending emphasises problems in the development of capacities for behavioural restraint, with a reduced capacity for empathy and perspective taking, difficulties in emotional self-regulation and the development of a coercive interpersonal style – all of which should act as deterrents for the reining in of powerful emotions of distress, sexual drive and sexual attraction. In this way a distressed male may direct his own attachment behaviour toward a child, bringing him into a more intense emotional interaction and a more physical interaction with the child; in turn this may cue cognitive, affective and sensory sexual responses which, if not restrained, may in turn precipitate overt sexual behaviour.

Ward *et al.* (1995) develop a theoretical perspective with an emphasis on attachment styles and associated features of sexual offending behaviour. They suggest that anxious/ambivalently attached sex offenders – who lack self-confidence and tend to seek the approval of others – seek attachments with individuals who they can control and who admire them (vulnerable women and children), but their inability to satisfy their intimacy needs in adult relationships will make them likely to become emotionally dependent upon their relationships with children. Such offenders would be unlikely to be aggressive or use coercion because of their concerns for the victim's enjoyment.

Fearful/avoidantly attached sex offenders – who desire emotional contact with others but are so afraid of rejection that they avoid establishing emotionally intimate relationships with adults – develop significant intimacy and social skills deficits which then makes it very difficult to develop romantic adult relationships, even if so desired. Sexual activity then becomes an indirect means of making contact with others, and they will seek impersonal sexual contacts with others. Such sex offenders are more likely to be very self-focused during their offending, to have poor victim empathy, to involve minimal personal contact with the victim, and to use coercive (but not aggressive) behaviours if necessary to achieve their sexual goals (the child/adult's cooperation). (See also Baker & Beech, 2004; Baker, Beech & Tyson, 2006).

Dismissing/avoidantly attached sex offenders – primarily driven by a desire to maintain a sense of autonomy and independence – are likely to seek relationships or social contacts that involve minimal levels of emotional or personal disclosure. Therefore, although they also seek impersonal sex, it is more likely to be characterised by a degree of hostility, in order to maintain a distance and aloofness from others. Tending to blame others for their lack of intimacy, they may well direct their hostility towards the gender of their preferred adult partners and to be profoundly uninterested in the feelings of others. Their offences are likely to be characterised by the expression of non-instrumental aggression, often seen in rape offences.

IMPLICATIONS FOR THE MANAGEMENT AND TREATMENT OF SEX OFFENDERS

The theme of attachment will be alluded to repeatedly throughout this book, whether in a discussion of dynamic risk factors (see Chapters 3 & 4) or in considering treatment. However, some general observations can be made here, which clearly emerge from the above discussion.

Sex offenders who are managed in the community in England and Wales necessarily form a relationship with their local public protection agencies in the form of the Multi-Agency Public Protection Arrangements (MAPPA; National Probation Service, 2003); see Chapter 28. For, subject to lifelong registration under the Sex Offenders Register (1997 Sex Offender Act), this is inevitably an enduring relationship over time, despite inevitable changes of personnel within the agencies. It is reasonable to assume that attachment patterns – established in early life and relevant to their offending – will be replicated within their relationship to the MAPPA. Insecure patterns may result in excessive dependency on professionals, an expectation of rejection with associated selective attention to perceived rejection or slights, or conversely dismissive, non-compliant attitudes in which the offender resorts to habitual strategies of secretive and manipulative behaviours for survival. Anticipating and understanding these core features of an offender will inform the management plan, and without such an understanding, the MAPPA is vulnerable to being drawn into the offender's inner world, unconsciously re-enacting the role of collusive or abusive parental figure.

The central question regarding attachment as it relates to sex offender interventions/programmes is that of responsiveness to treatment (treatability) that is, should attachment be understood as a static factor, firmly established in early life and something which needs to be managed in adulthood; or should attachment be understood as a rather more dynamic factor, open to permutation as a result of adult life experiences and treatment interventions. The more recent work on treatment approaches for personality disordered individuals – including offenders (Dowsett & Craissati, 2008) – would suggest that attachment and its implications are central to mainstream approaches. Furthermore, as suggested in the introduction to this chapter, attachment models transcend particular theoretical approaches, integrating key ideas emerging from traditional psychoanalytical but also cognitive behavioural approaches. For example, attending to the patient – therapist relationship is a core feature of schema focused therapy (Young, Klosko & Weisharr, 2003), an important component of Dialectical Behaviour Therapy (Linehan, 1993), and a fundamental pre-requisite of formal psychoanalysis.

The relevance of attachment models to sex offender treatment falls broadly into two areas: process and content. In terms of process, there is good evidence to suggest that non-specific characteristics of therapists are crucial to the positive outcome of treatment; with sex offenders, Beech and Fordham (1997) found that successful treatment groups (associated with greater positive pre-post treatment change) were more cohesive, well organised, encouraged the open expression of feelings, produced a sense of group responsibility, and instilled a sense of hope in the group members brought about by good leadership style. Subsequently Marshall *et al.* (2003) found that empathy, warmth, directiveness and reward, were key features of successful therapists with sex offenders. This would suggest that attention to ideas of good enough parenting – consistency, positive empathic regard, modelling reflection and flexibility, adherence to safe boundaries, and interest in the offender's individual path to developing a pro-social sense of self – are all ways in which problems with the early formation of attachment patterns can be revisited and repaired. This is supported by wider evidence that internal representational models of attachment can be altered and repaired by the repeated and consistent experience of exposure to positive caregiving (Morton & Browne, 1998), and, for example, that the experience of therapy in insecurely attached mothers was central to their ability to break the cycle of abuse with their own children (Morton & Browne, 1998).

In terms of content, there is an established evidence-base that identified higher risk and/or more 'deviant' sexual offenders (see Chapter 6) have greater treatment need. This is reflected in the development of programmes – such as the Extended Sex Offender Treatment Programme within the England and Wales criminal justice system (Mann, 2004) – which attends to developmental experiences and core beliefs (schema), as well as more pervasive adult traits such as emotional regulation and perspective taking which are impaired as a result of attachment problems. The aim is to engage sex offenders in the task of achieving insight into the development of their attachment difficulties, improving their 'reflective functioning', and enabling them to develop skills in improving their capacity for forming and maintaining adult relationships, and/or broadening the range of ways in which meaningful interpersonal bonds can be created without a narrow focus on sexual gratification (Ward & Marshall, 2004).

Finally, there is growing interest in the potential for medication – specifically SSRIs (selective serotonin re-uptake inhibitors) which raise synaptic 5HT levels, with a range of beneficial effects. These include improvements in feelings of emotional isolation and low mood, a diminution of sexual appetitive behaviour, and a reduction in impulsivity, but also may increase brain plasticity with an associated increased capacity for behaviour to be modified (if applied in conjunction with psychological treatment interventions) (Beech & Mitchell, 2005).

CONCLUSIONS

The current resurgence of interest in attachment theory is associated with a compelling body of research, which has been reviewed in this chapter. Furthermore, it is no surprise to find that attachment problems are central to an understanding of sex offenders and their offending behaviour. The model provides continuity between early childhood experiences, the traumatic impact of later abusive events, difficulties in achieving stable, emotionally fulfilling romantic relationships, and proposes a general pathway to sexual offending which is compatible with the theory. There are implications for attachment problems and sexual offending, in terms of providing an accessible conceptual framework within which practitioners and agencies can enhance the effectiveness of their treatment and management interventions.

REFERENCES

Ainsworth, M., Blehar, M., Waters, E. & Wall, S. (1978). *Patterns of attachment*. Hillsdale, NJ: Erlbaum.

Armsden, G.C. & Greenberg, M.T. (1987). The inventory of parent and peer attachment: Relationships to well-being in adolescence. *Journal of Youth and Adolescence, 16*, 427–454.

Baker, E. & Beech, A. (2004). Dissociation and variability of adult attachment dimensions and early maladaptive schemas in sexual and violent offenders. *Journal of Interpersonal Violence, 20*, 1–18.

Baker, E., Beech, A. & Tyson, M. (2006). Attachment disorganization and its relevance to sexual offending. *Journal of Family Violence, 21*, 221–231.

Bartholomew, K. & Horowitz, L.M. (1991). Attachment styles among young adults: A test of a four-category model. *Journal of Personality and Social Psychology, 61*, 226–244.

Bartholomew, K. & Shaver, P. (1998). Methods of assessing adult attachment: Do they converge? In J.A. Simpson & W.S. Rholes (Eds), *Attachment Theory and Close Relationships* (pp. 46–76). New York: Guilford Press.

Bateman, A. & Fonagy, P. (2004). *Psychotherapy for borderline personality disorder: Mentalization-based treatment*. Oxford: Oxford University Press.

Beech, A.R. & Fordham, A. (1997). Therapeutic climate of sexual offender treatment programs. *Sexual Abuse: A Journal of Research and Treatment, 9*, 219–237.

Beech, A.R. & Mitchell, I.J. (2005). A neurobiological perspective on attachment problems in sexual offenders and the role of selective serotonin re-uptake inhibitors in the treatment of such problems. *Clinical Psychology Review, 25*, 153–182.

Bowlby, J. (1944). Forty-four juvenile thieves: Their characters and home lives. *International Journal of Psychoanalysis, 25*, 19–52.

Bowlby, J. (1969). *Attachment and loss. Volume I: Attachment*. London: Hogarth Press.

Bowlby, J. (1973). *Attachment and loss. Volume II: Separation: Anxiety and anger*. London: Hogarth Press.

Bowlby, J. (1980). *Attachment and loss. Volume III: Loss, sadness and depression*. New York: Basic Books.

Brennan, K.A., Clark, C.L. & Shaver, P.R. (1998). Self-report measurement of adult attachment: An integrative overview. In J.A. Simpson& W.S. Rholes (Eds), *Attachment theory and close relationships* (pp. 46–76). New York: Guilford Press.

Brown, L.S. & Wright, J. (2001). Attachment theory in adolescence and its relevance to developmental psychopathology. *Clinical Psychology and Psychotherapy, 8*, 15–32.

Burk, L.R. & Burkhart, B.R. (2003). Disorganized attachment as a diathesis for sexual deviance. Developmental experience and the motivation for sexual offending. *Aggression and Violent Behavior, 8*, 487–511.

Chapple, C.L. (2003). Examining intergenerational violence: Violent role modeling or weak parental controls? *Violence and Victims, 18*, 143–161.

Craissati, J. (2003). *Risk, Reconviction and their relationship to key developmental variables in a complete urban sample of child molesters and rapists*. PhD Thesis. University of Birmingham, UK.

Craissati, J. & Beech, A. (2004). The characteristics of a geographical sample of convicted rapists: sexual victimization and compliance in comparison to child molesters. *Journal of Interpersonal Violence, 19*, 225–240.

Craissati, J. & Beech, A. (2006). The role of key developmental variables in identifying sex offenders likely to fail in the community: An enhanced risk prediction model. *Child Abuse and Neglect, 30*, 327–339.

Craissati, J., McClurg, G. & Browne, K. (2002a). The parental bonding experiences of sex offenders: A comparison between child molesters and rapists. *Child Abuse and Neglect, 26*, 909–921.

Craissati, J., McClurg, G. & Browne, K. (2002b). Characteristics of perpetrators of child sexual abuse who have been sexually victimised as children. *Sexual Abuse: A Journal of Research and Treatment, 14*(3), 225–240.

Craissati, J., Webb, L. & Keen, S. (2008). The relationship between developmental variables, personality disorder and risk in an urban community sample of child molesters and rapists. *Sexual Abuse: A Journal of Research and Treatment*. In press.

Crittenden, P. (1988). Relationships at risk. In J. Belsky& T. Nezworski (Eds), *Clinical Implications of Attachment* (pp. 136–174). Hillsdale, NJ: Lawrence Erlbaum Associates.

de Zulueta, F. (2006). *From Pain to Violence* (2nd edn). Chichester: John Wiley & Sons, Ltd.

Dhawan, S. & Marshall, W.L. (1996). Sexual abuse histories of sexual offenders. *Sexual Abuse: A Journal of Research and Treatment, 8*, 7–15.

Doctor, R. (2003) (Ed.). *Dangerous patients: A psychodynamic approach to risk assessment and management*. London: Karnac.

Dowsett, J. & Craissati, J. (2008). *Managing personality disordered offenders in the community: A psychological approach*. Hove, UK: Routledge.

Fergusson, D.M. & Lynskey, M.T. (1998). Conduct problems in childhood and psychosocial outcomes in young adulthood: A prospective study. *Journal of Emotional and Behavioral Disorders, 6*, 2–18.

Fisher, H.E., Aron, A., Mashek, D. *et al.* (2002). Defining the brain systems of lust, romantic attraction and attachment. *Archives of Sexual Behavior, 31*, 413–419.

Fonagy, P. (1999). Male perpetrators of violence against women: An attachment theory perspective. *Journal of Applied Psychoanalytic Studies, 1*, 7–27.

Fonagy, P., Steele, M. & Steele, H. (1991). Maternal representations of attachment during pregnancy predicts the organization of infant–mother attachment at one year of age. *Child Development, 62*, 891–905.

Fonagy, P., Target, M., Steele, M. & Steele, H. (1997). The development of violence and crime as it relates to security of attachment. In J. Osojsky (Ed.), *Children in a violent society* (pp. 150–177). New York: Guilford Press.

George, C., Kaplan, N. & Main, M. (1987). *The Attachment Interview*. Unpublished manuscript, University of California, Berkeley.

Green, J. & Goldwyn, R. (2002). Attachment disorganisation and psychopathology: new findings in attachment research and their potential implications for developmental psychopathology in childhood. *Journal of Child Psychology and Psychiatry, 43*, 835–846.

Haapasalo, J. & Kankkonen, M. (1997). Self-reported childhood abuse among sex and violent offenders. *Archives of Sexual Behavior, 26*, 421–431.

Hazan, C. & Shaver, P. (1987). Romantic love conceptualized as an attachment process. *Journal of Personality and Social Psychology, 52*, 511–524.

Hazan, C. & Shaver, P. (1994). Attachment as an organizational framework for research on close relationships. *Psychological Inquiry, 5*, 1–22.

Le Blanc, M. (1992). Family dynamics, adolescent delinquency, and adult criminality. *Psychiatry, 55*, 336–353.

Linehan, M.M. (1993). *Cognitive-behavioral treatment of borderline personality disorder*. New York: Guilford Press.

Lyons-Ruth, K. & Jacobvitz, D. (2003). Attachment disorganization: Unresolved loss, relational violence, and lapses in behavioral and attentional strategies. In J. Cassady & P.R. Shaver (Eds), *Handbook of attachment: Theory, research and clinical applications* (pp. 520–554). New York: Guilford Press.

Main, M. & Solomon, J. (1990). Procedures for identifying infants as disorganised/disoriented during Ainsworth strange situations. In M.T. Greenberg, D. Cicchetti & E.M. Cummings (Eds), *Attachment in the pre-school years: Theory, research and intervention* (pp. 121–160). Chicago: University of Chicago Press.

Mann, R. (2004). Innovations in sex offender treatment. *Journal of Sexual Aggression, 10*, 141–152.

Marshall, W.L. (1993). The role of attachments, intimacy, and loneliness in the etiology and maintenance of sexual offending. *Sexual and Marital Therapy, 8*, 109–121.

Marshall, W.L., Fernandez, Y., Serran, G.A. *et al.* (2003). Process issues in the treatment of sexual offenders: A review of the relevant literature. *Aggression and Violent Behavior, 8*, 205–234.

Morton, N. & Browne, K.D. (1998). Theory and observation of attachment and its relation to child maltreatment: A review. *Child Abuse and Neglect, 22*, 1093–1104.

Parker, G., Tupling, H. & Brown, L.B. (1979). A parental bonding instrument. *British Journal of Medical Psychology, 52*, 1–10.

Reder, P. & Duncan, S. (2001). Abusive relationships, care and control conflicts and insecure attachments. *Child Abuse Review, 10*, 411–427.

Rich, P. (2006). *Attachment and sexual offending*. Chichester: John Wiley & Sons, Ltd.

Rosen, I. (1979). The general psychoanalytical theory of perversion: a critical and clinical case study. In I. Rosen (Ed.), *Sexual deviation* (2nd edn) (pp. 65–78). Oxford: Oxford University Press.

Smallbone, S.W. (2006). An attachment-theoretical revision of Marshall and Barbaree's Integrated theory of the etiology of sexual offending. In W.L. Marshall, Y.M. Fernandez, L.E. Marshall & G.A. Serran (Eds), *Sexual offender treatment: Controversial issues* (pp. 93–108). Chichester: John Wiley & Sons, Ltd.

Smallbone, S.W. & Dadds, M.R. (1998). Childhood attachment and adult attachment in incarcerated adult male sex offenders. *Journal of Interpersonal Violence, 13*, 555–573.

Smallbone, S.W. & Dadds, M.R. (2000). Attachment and coercive sexual behavior. *Sexual Abuse: A Journal of Research and Treatment, 12*, 3–15.

Smallbone, S.W. & Dadds, M.R. (2001). Further evidence for a relationship between attachment insecurity and coercive sexual behavior in nonoffenders. *Journal of Interpersonal Violence, 16*, 22–35.

Smallbone, S.W. & McCabe, B. (2003). Childhood attachment, childhood sexual abuse, and onset of masturbation among adult sexual offenders. *Sexual Abuse: A Journal of Research and Treatment, 15*, 1–9.

Van Ijzendoorn, M.H., Schuengel, C. & Bakermans-Kranenberg, M.J. (1999). Disorganized attachment in early childhood: Meta-analysis of precursors, concomitants, and sequelae. *Development and Psychopathology, 11*, 225–250.

Ward, T., Hudson, S. & Marshall, W.L. (1996). Attachment style in sex offenders: A preliminary study. *The Journal of Sex Research, 33*, 17–26.

Ward, T., Hudson, S.M., Marshall, W.L. & Siegert, R. (1995). Attachment style and intimacy deficits in sexual offenders: A theoretical framework. *Sexual Abuse: A Journal of Research and Treatment, 7*, 317–335.

Ward, T. & Marshall, W. (2004). Good lives, aetiology and the rehabilitation of sex offenders: A bridging theory. *Journal of Sexual Aggression, 17*, 153–169.

Young, J.E., Klosko, J.S. & Weishaar, M.E. (2003). *Schema therapy: A practitioner's guide*. New York: Guilford Press.

PART ONE

Risk Assessment

3

Factors Associated with Sexual Recidivism

FRANCA CORTONI

INTRODUCTION

Risk assessment is the central feature that influences all aspects of the management of sexual offenders (Andrews & Bonta, 2003; Hanson, 2006). Professionals tasked with evaluating risk need to consider what factors were related to the offending behaviour in order to determine the likelihood of future offending. This entails having an understanding of the factors associated with risk. Assessments of risk using unstructured clinical judgement based on a traditional model of psychopathology yields predictions that are little or no better than chance (Andrews & Bonta, 2003; Hanson & Bussière, 1998; Quinsey et al., 2006). Research has shown that major mental illnesses and psychological problems such as anxiety and depression are unrelated to recidivism (Bonta, Law & Hanson, 1998; Hanson & Bussière, 1998; Quinsey et al., 2006). Other factors also traditionally considered as being related to risk such as the degree of force used in the sexual offence, the degree of victim injury, and the level of intrusiveness (e.g., intercourse versus fondling), were also found to be unrelated to sexual recidivism (Hanson & Bussière, 1998). So what then needs to be taken into consideration to assess risk? The assessment of risk needs to consider the individual characteristics of the offender that increase or decrease the probability of recidivism and our understanding of these characteristics is based on empirical evidence that has demonstrated the relationship between these factors and sexual recidivism.

No single study is sufficient to determine what is or is not a risk factor. Cumulative knowledge from independent studies is necessary before a characteristic can be established as a risk factor, and the strongest evidence comes from follow-up studies (Hanson, 1997a). Likely due to the increased societal attention to sexual crimes (Hart, Laws & Kropp, 2003), follow-up studies of sexual recidivism have proliferated in more recent years. In their initial meta-analyses of 61 follow-up studies of sexual

Assessment and Treatment of Sex Offenders: A Handbook. Edited by Anthony Beech, Leam Craig and Kevin Browne. © John Wiley & Sons Ltd, 2009.

offenders between 1943 and 1995, Hanson and Bussière (1998) noted that half of these studies had been produced after 1989. In their updated meta-analysis, Hanson and Morton-Bourgon (2005) located 37 additional studies conducted between 1995 and 2003 as well as 10 updates to the studies included in their 1998 work, thereby providing increased confidence in our current knowledge of the risk factors for sexual recidivism. There are two types of risk factors: static and dynamic. Static risk factors are unchangeable aspects in the offender's history that are related to recidivism, while dynamic factors are those aspects of the offender that are amenable to change, and may identify when an offender is most at risk (Hanson, 1997a). This chapter provides a review of these factors.

STATIC RISK FACTORS

Our understanding of the static factors related to sexual and non-sexual recidivism is well established. Research on the prediction of recidivism has a long history (Andrews & Bonta, 2003; Quinsey *et al.*, 2006) and has demonstrated that the predictors of recidivism are virtually the same for prison and forensic populations (Bonta, Law & Hanson, 1998). Likely the most influential research that specifically examined the risk factors for recidivism among sexual offenders is Hanson and Bussière's (1998) meta-analysis. In their study, they examined the results of 61 studies that contained information on a total of 28,972 sexual offenders. Their study supported existing evidence that sexual offenders share many characteristics with other offenders, while also possessing additional unique features.

Static predictors of risk for general and violent (non-sexual) recidivism include: being at a younger age and being single; and having a history of lifestyle instability, of rule violations, of alcohol and drug abuse, of antisocial behaviour, and of violent crimes (Gendreau, Little & Goggin, 1996; Hanson & Bussière, 1998). Generally, these characteristics demonstrate the presence of antisocial traits and personality, factors which have a consistent and strong relationship with recidivism (Andrews & Bonta, 2003; Quinsey *et al.*, 2006). In their updated meta-analysis, Hanson and Morton-Bourgon (2005) confirmed that the major predictor of general and violent recidivism among sexual offenders was an antisocial orientation, demonstrated by antisocial traits and personality and a history of rule violations. Any assessment of risk of sexual offenders therefore must take into account the presence and extent of antisociality in the offender's history.

History of Sexual Offending

Although there are commonalities in static risk factors between sexual and non-sexual offenders, there are also some features that are uniquely related to sexual recidivism. Just as a history of general criminal behaviour is predictive of any recidivism, a history of sexual offending has consistently been shown to relate to further sexual offending, while the higher the number of offences and the more varied the history of sexual offending, the more likely the offender is to continue in his offending behaviour (Hanson & Bussière, 1998; Quinsey *et al.*, 2006). Further, the type of victim is also related to risk. Offenders who strictly engage in father–daughter incest tend to show the lowest rates of recidivism, while offenders who have male victims, or victims unrelated to them tend to show the highest rates (Hanson & Thornton, 1999). Similarly, offenders who engage in a variety of contact and non-contact sexual offences also demonstrate higher rates of recidivism (Hanson & Thornton, 1999).

The details related to the offending history may simply reflect an enduring interest in deviant sexual activity. However, not all men who commit sexually deviant acts demonstrate an enduring preference for these behaviours (Marshall, 2001). Rather, an enduring propensity for sexual offending appears to additionally require, among other factors, a willingness to disregard the rights of others, a characteristic of antisociality. This feature further demonstrates the importance of assessing antisocial character-istics of sexual offenders. Taken together, the combination of an interest in deviant sexual activity and antisociality are the best predictors of sexual recidivism (Hanson & Morton-Bourgon, 2005; Roberts, Doren & Thornton, 2002), and any assessment of risk of sexual offenders must take into account these two categories of predictors.

Assessing Static Risk Factors

The assessment of static risk factors is best conducted using one of the many tools established for that purpose. Likely the best known and established tools for the assessment of sexual recidivism are the Sex Offender Risk Appraisal Guide (SORAG; Quinsey *et al.*, 2006), the Rapid Risk Assessment for Sexual Offence Recidivism (RRASOR; Hanson, 1997b), and the Static-99 (Hanson & Thornton, 1999). Such tools have the advantage of having strong empirical support and transparency as well as providing high inter-rater reliability (Hart, Laws & Kropp, 2003). Risk assessments based strictly on static risk factors however do not provide information on areas related to sexual recidivism that may predict the onset of the offending behaviour. This is the focus of the next section.

DYNAMIC RISK FACTORS

The major limitation of static factors is their non-changeable nature. While an assess-ment based strictly on static factors provides a clear level of risk that can be linked to a probability of reoffending (Hanson & Thornton, 1999; Quinsey *et al.*, 2006), it does not provide any information regarding the factors that may impact on the management of offenders. Given that risk of reoffending is not a static state, dynamic factors add an important dimension as they improve the accuracy of risk prediction as well as provide focused avenues for the management of that risk (Hanson & Harris, 1998; Quinsey *et al.*, 2006; Thornton, 2002). Dynamic risk factors are changeable characteristics of the offender that have a demonstrated empirical relationship with sexual offending behaviour and that, when reduced, lead to reductions in recidivism (Hanson, 2006; Hanson & Harris, 2001).

Our current knowledge of the dynamic risk factors of sexual offenders stem from three major sources of work. Beech, Fisher and Beckett (1999) developed the Sexual Offender Treatment Evaluation Project (STEP) and found, based on the deviancy index from Beech (1998), that child molesters can be categorised into high and low deviancy groups. High deviancy child molesters are characterised by high levels of distorted cognitions about children, high levels of sexual preoccupation and high levels of sexual arousal to children. They tend to emotionally identify with children and have more problems establishing emotionally satisfying relationships with adults. Not surprisingly, these offenders tended to have more intra- and extra-familial victims, and more male victims. Conversely, low deviancy child molesters show very low levels of these characteristics, and demonstrate more social competence. Beech, Friendship, Erikson and Hanson (2002) further demonstrated that this categorisation of dynamic factors into high and low deviancy added utility to the prediction of sexual recidivism.

Thornton (2002) developed the Initial Deviance Assessment (IDA) in which the dynamic risk factors of sexual offenders fall within four domains that include sexual interest, distorted attitudes, socio-affective functioning, and self-management. He tested three aspects of his model (information on sexual interests was unavailable for his research) with a sample of child molesters and confirmed that recidivist child molesters exhibited more distorted attitudes not only about child sexual abuse but also about rape. They also demonstrated more socio-affective dysfunctions such as feelings of inadequacy, emotional identification with children, emotional loneliness, and a high tendency to dwell on negative emotional states. These offenders also showed poor self-management abilities, marked particularly by an impulsive lifestyle. Thornton (2002) replicated his results with a separate group of sexual offenders comprised of both child molesters and rapists, providing support for the position that these dynamic factors are applicable to both types of offenders. Further, his results showed that the dynamic risk factors tested in his model were predictive of sexual reoffending independent of static factors, providing additional evidence of the importance of dynamic risk factors in the prediction of recidivism.

Hanson and Harris (1998, 2000) conducted a comparison of recidivists and non-recidivists child molesters and rapists with the aims of establishing dynamic risk factors for sexual recidivism, and developing a plausible approach to their assessment. Their work resulted in the development of the Sex Offender Need Assessment Rating (SONAR). They have since evolved this instrument into the STABLE and ACUTE scales, and established the *Dynamic Supervision Project*, a three and a half year prospective study of sexual offenders under community supervision across Canada, and the US states of Alaska and Iowa to determine their predictive utility.

In their original 1998 study, offenders' files were reviewed for static risk factors, and a list of dynamic risk factors was generated from theoretical review, review of previous research, including the Hanson and Bussière (1998) meta-analysis, and interviews with community supervisors of the sexual offenders in the study. Dynamic factors were divided into stable and acute categories (Hanson & Harris, 1998). Stable dynamic risk factors were defined as relatively enduring characteristics related to sexual recidivism that are amenable to change (Hanson & Harris, 2001). These risk factors have alternatively been described as criminogenic needs (Andrews & Bonta, 2003) or causal psychological risk factors (Beech & Ward, 2004). Hanson and Harris' stable factors include sexual self-regulation, cognitions supportive of sexual offending, intimacy deficits, social influences, and self-regulation and cooperation with supervision. While the exact way to combine these dynamic factors in a risk assessment remains an empirical question (Hanson, 2006; Hart, Laws & Kropp, 2003; Quinsey *et al.*, 2006), research has demonstrated a convergence in the main dynamic domains related to sexual recidivism (Beech, Fisher & Thornton, 2003; Hanson & Harris, 2001; Hanson & Morton-Bourgon, 2005; Thornton, 2002, 2005). Acute dynamic risk factors are those factors useful in identifying *when* an offender is at most risk of reoffending, although they may not necessarily relate to the long-term potential of recidivism (Hanson & Harris, 1998). Acute factors can be viewed as short-term states that create conditions for sexual offending.

STABLE DYNAMIC RISK FACTORS

Sexual Interests and Sexual Self-Regulation

Sexual deviance is an important feature of future risk (Hanson & Morton-Bourgon, 2005). Sexual deviance refers to the presence of arousal to deviant sexual stimuli such as children or violence. The presence of deviant sexual interests and arousal has long been established as a powerful predictor of sexual recidivism, particularly when combined with high levels of psychopathy (Quinsey *et al.*, 2006). Typically, a physiological assessment is the best method to establish sexual deviance, although such tests are not without their limitations (Laws, 2003). Many offenders fail to demonstrate arousal under assessment conditions and this lack of arousal does not mean that an individual is automatically at lower risk of offending. Many factors influence whether sexual arousal occurs during a physiological assessment, including the ability to suppress arousal (see Laws, 2003, for a review). When a physiological assessment of arousal is not possible, sexual deviance can be inferred from an examination of the history of sexual offending, or through the use of various psychometric instruments (Beech, Fisher & Thornton, 2003; Craig *et al.*, 2007; Seto *et al.*, 2004).

The strong relationship between deviant arousal and offending has tended to obscure the fact that beside deviant sexual interests, the extent to which an offender is generally preoccupied with sex is related to sexual reoffending (Hanson & Bussière, 1998; Hanson & Morton-Bourgon, 2005). Sexual offenders tend to give sex an exaggerated importance in their lives, and tend to believe they have stronger sexual urges and needs than most people (Hanson & Harris, 1998). Indicators of sexual preoccupation include the frequency in which offenders engage in any type of sexual activity such as masturbation, and the use of pornography or other similar sex-related activities such as attending strip bars or prostitutes. The presence of paraphilias such as fetishism, particularly if they are related to the offending behaviour, provides another indication of sexual preoccupation (Thornton, 2005).

The relationship between mood and sexual activity is also of importance. In the traditional relapse prevention model as applied to sexual offenders, negative emotional states such as anxiety and depression have traditionally been posited as high risk factors related to sexual offending (Laws, 1989). Again, however, research has failed to empirically establish these factors (Hanson & Bussière, 1998; Hanson & Morton-Bourgon, 2005). While negative moods themselves are not related to recidivism, the mechanisms utilised by sexual offenders to regulate their moods and deal with difficulties in their lives are a central feature related to future sexual offending.

When sexual offenders experience interpersonal conflict, anger, loneliness and humiliation, there are marked increases in their deviant sexual fantasies and accompanying masturbation (Looman, 1995; McKibben, Proulx & Lusignan, 1994; Proulx, McKibben & Lusignan, 1996). Further, sexual offenders also utilise sex as a coping mechanism to deal with life stressors (Cortoni & Marshall, 2001). The focus of the assessment therefore should be on the determination of the sexual self-regulation methods typically used by the offender when they experience conflict or negative emotional states.

Attitudes Supportive of Sexual Offending

Attitudes are described as representations of past experiences which guide, bias, or otherwise influence behaviour (Ajzen & Fishbein, 1977). As a dynamic risk factor related to sexual offending, attitudes refer to a general cognitive disposition that facilitates sexual offending behaviour (Hanson & Harris, 2001; Mann & Beech, 2003). Research has long established that antisocial cognitions are predictive of general criminal behaviour (Andrews & Bonta, 2003), and within the sexual offender area, cognitive distortions that justify or minimise the offending behaviour (e.g., Abel et al., 1989; Barbaree, 1991; Bumby, 1996), and attitudes supportive of sexual aggression (e.g., Burt, 1980) are considered to be core features of sexually aggressive behaviour. Research with both adjudicated sexual offenders and community samples continues to show that cognitive components that support sexual offending are related to sexually offending behaviour (Bumby, 1996; Burt, 1980; Hudson et al., 2002; Thornton, 2002).

While much work remains to be done to understand the specific nature of the distorted cognitions that are related to sexual offending, there is consistent evidence that an overall predisposition to be tolerant of sexual offending is related to sexual recidivism (Hanson & Harris, 2001; Hanson & Morton-Bourgon, 2005). The measurement of such a predisposition, however, continues to be fraught with difficulties, particularly regarding rape-related cognitive distortions (Feelgood, Cortoni & Thompson, 2005; Ward et al., 1997). A number of psychometric instruments were developed for the assessment of pro-offending attitudes and cognitive distortions (e.g., Abel, Becker & Cunningham-Rathner, 1984; Bumby, 1996; Check, 1984), and higher scores on these scales tend to be related to persistence in sexual offending (Hudson et al., 2002). Hanson and Harris (2001) have also demonstrated that these distorted views about sexual offending are easily evaluated during an interview. The areas of importance include attitudes that excuse, permit, or condone sexual offending and attitudes that indicate a sense of entitlement to sex, and maladaptive beliefs about relationships, gender roles and children (Thornton, 2002).

More recently, Mann and Beech (2003) proposed a schema-based model in efforts to address the lack of clarity in the construct of cognitive distortions as applied to sexual offenders and to provide a theoretical foundation to explain the role of cognitions in sexual offending. Specifically, they posited that sexual aggressors adhere to stereotypical, hostile, or distorted views of women, children and sex. They also posited that these offenders have core beliefs about themselves and the world that predispose them to interpret ambiguous or threatening information in a hostile fashion. These two types of schemas interact with other factors such as deviant arousal or impulsivity to lead to sexual offending.

The empirical verification of this model is still in its infancy and preliminary evidence suggests that these types of schemas may be more related to interpersonal violence in general as opposed to strictly sexual offending (Milner & Webster, 2005). An additional complication in this work is that the assessment of schemas is difficult since they may not be directly assessed via paper-and-pencil measures. Until innovative evaluative methods are established (e.g., Nunes, Firestone & Baldwin, 2007), these schemas could be assessed through autobiographies ('Life Maps') or in-depth analyses of every day events (Mann & Shingler, 2006; Milner & Webster, 2005).

The discussion on the cognitive components linked to sexual offending cannot conclude without addressing denial of the offending behaviour and lack of empathy for victims. Denial and minimisation of the offending behaviour has long been viewed as such a crucial factor related to future risk of recidivism that virtually all treatment programmes address this issue (Marshall *et al.*, 1998). Research, however, has failed to demonstrate a link between denial or admittance and risk of recidivism (Hanson & Bussière, 1998; Hanson & Morton-Bourgon, 2005), and treatment programmes for categorical deniers have now emerged (Marshall *et al.*, 2001). Similarly, despite the traditional prominence of victim empathy work in the treatment of sexual offenders, research has failed to establish a predictive relationship between this factor and sexual offending (Hanson & Morton-Bourgon, 2005). There are suggestions that the mechanisms underlying denial and lack of empathy may actually be related to offence evaluations and expectations on the part of the offender (Ward *et al.*, 1998), and serve to mitigate anxiety, guilt, and shame (Bumby, 2000). It is therefore not surprising that the evidence points to the importance of generalised distorted attitudes and beliefs as predictive of risk as opposed to denial and minimisation of the offending behaviour and a lack of empathy towards one's own victim.

Significant Social Influences

The presence of criminal associates is one of the strongest predictors of recidivism in general (Andrews & Bonta, 2003). Criminal associates promote antisocial attitudes and an antisocial lifestyle, providing strong support for continued criminal activities.

Within the area of sexual offending, associates who also engage in sexually offending behaviour may serve as social support for further offending, and when offenders are involved in pro-paedophilic organisations, the support for sexual offending is explicit (Hanson & Harris, 2001).

In some cases, however, the social influences in the offender's life are not antisocial or pro-sexual offending, but they can still have an impact on the offender's potential for reoffending. Specifically, significant others who support the offender's views that he is no longer at risk, generate conflict in the offender's life, provide access to victims because they do not believe the offender poses a risk, or interfere with supervision orders or with self-management efforts on the part of the offender all constitute negative influences that are linked to a reoccurrence of sexual offending. These negative social influences contribute to sexual recidivism, and Hanson and Harris (1998, 2001) suggest that if the balance of negative influences outweighs positive influences by two or more in the offender's life, this factor is likely to contribute to an increased risk of reoffending.

Intimacy Difficulties

The general ways in which sexual offenders relate to people and the specific ways in which they engage in intimate relationships are related to sexual recidivism (Thornton, 2002). Inherent in the interpersonal difficulties exhibited by sexual offenders is a lack of intimacy in relationships. Marshall (1989) was the first to introduce the concept of intimacy deficits as being an important part of the dynamics of sexual offending behaviour. In this seminal paper, he posited that sexual offenders have difficulties establishing emotionally satisfying relationships and consequently experience emotional loneliness as a result of insecure attachment with caregivers during childhood. In a number of studies, he and colleagues demonstrated that low intimacy and high emotional loneliness were features commonly found in sexual offenders (Cortoni & Marshall, 2001; Marshall *et al.*, 1997; Seidman *et al.*, 1994; Ward, McCormack & Hudson, 1997).

Difficulties with establishing emotionally satisfying relationships lead to little breadth and depth of intimacy in relationships. These features tend to manifest themselves as avoidance of adult intimacy, and conflicted or uncommitted relationships. Both a lack of intimate partners and the presence of conflicts within an existing intimate relationship are predictive of sexual reoffending (Hanson & Bussière, 1998; Hanson & Morton-Bourgon, 2005). For rapists, difficulties in intimate relationships may be related to their experiences of adversarial or impersonal relationships with family and peers, thereby leading to a general lack of concern for others (Hanson, 2006). For child molesters, their difficulties with adult intimate relationships may stem from the emotional congruence with children that characterises them (Wilson, 1999). The importance of this factor cannot be underestimated. Hanson and Morton-Bourgon (2005) found that emotional congruence with children was a powerful predictor of sexual recidivism among child molesters.

Self-Regulation and Cooperation with Supervision

As previously mentioned, deviant sexual interests and an antisocial orientation are the major predictors of sexual recidivism (Hanson & Morton-Bourgon, 2005; Quinsey *et al.*, 2006). Individuals who possess antisocial characteristics tend to demonstrate problematic self-regulatory skills, including high levels of impulsivity, and poor problem-solving skills (Andrew & Bonta, 2003). Self-regulation refers to the offender's ability to self-monitor and to inhibit impulsive, irresponsible and rule-breaking decisions (Thornton, 2005). The literature on criminogenic factors shows that all types of offenders demonstrate a pattern of lifestyle instability and a history of rule violations, with low adherence to social conventions such as educational and work pursuits (Andrews & Bonta, 2003). These offenders tend to show no evidence of analyses of their problems, or any anticipation of the consequences of their responses to their problems (Zamble & Quinsey, 1997). Furthermore, they tend to use problem-solving strategies that actually increase rather than solve their problems, although they believe that their solutions are effective (Zamble & Quinsey, 1997). Among sexual offenders, just like with any other type of offender, evidence of lifestyle instability and low frustration levels are indicative of difficulties in anticipating consequences of one's actions and in establishing and working towards long-term goals (Thornton, 2002), leading to poor life choices, including engaging in offending behaviour.

Rule violations and a lack of cooperation with supervision are particularly predictive of sexual recidivism (Hanson & Morton-Bourgon, 2004), and sexual offenders who demonstrate general antisocial tendencies would be expected to have particular difficulties in this area (Hanson & Harris, 2001). Generally, these offenders tend to break their conditions of community supervision and fail to meet other commitments such as work or treatment demands. They also minimise their risk, and fail to engage in identified strategies to prevent a return to offending behaviour, including dropping out of treatment (Hanson & Morton-Bourgon, 2004). While the effectiveness of treatment in reducing sexual recidivism is a hotly debated topic (Quinsey *et al.*, 2006), the evidence is clear regarding drop-outs: the failure to complete treatment is an important marker of lack of cooperation with supervision that is related to sexual recidivism (Hanson & Bussière, 1998).

It is not surprising that problems in self-regulations and a pattern of rule violations are related to sexual recidivism. Research has provided indications that criminogenic models are at the root of sexual offending patterns (Lussier, 2005). In his research examining developmental pathways to sexual offending, Lussier found that antisocial tendencies were common developmental precursors to both rapists and child molesters. Interestingly, though, assessment and treatment efforts have traditionally focused on the factors unique to sexual offenders such as deviant sexual interests and intimacy deficits (Ward & Marshall, 2004) and have mostly neglected to consider the antisocial characteristics of these offenders (Cortoni, 2005). Hanson and Morton-Bourgon (2005) pointed out that "the prototypical sexual recidivist is not upset or lonely; instead he leads an unstable, antisocial lifestyle and ruminates on sexually deviant themes"

(p. 1158). Consequently, failure to attend to these antisocial characteristics entails that an important component of risk of sexual recidivism is being ignored.

ACUTE DYNAMIC RISK FACTORS

Hanson and Harris (1998) introduced the notion of 'acuteness' of risk factors for sexual recidivism following their research which showed that the imminence of sexual offending could be linked to observable behaviours. Their research indicated that acute risk factors include emotional collapse and increased hostility; substance abuse; sexual preoccupation; collapse of social support; victim access; and rejection of supervision (Hanson, 2005). In their integration of risk factors within an aetiological framework, Beech and Ward (2004) argue that these acute factors are better viewed as contextual risk factors or triggering events that interact with stable trait-like factors to lead to sexual offending. In their review of Hanson and Harris's (2001) acute factors, Beech and Ward (2004) identified sexual preoccupation as an acute risk factor in its own right, and grouped the remaining factors into behavioural and affective events that trigger sexual offending.

Emotional collapse refers to a sudden increase in negative emotional states such as anxiety, depression, frustration, feelings of stress. This collapse may also take the form of increased hostility toward others when unwarranted. As previously noted, the baseline level of emotional states is not predictive of sexual reoffending. Rather it is the way in which an offender deals with these emotional states that is related to sexual offending (Hanson, 2000). Beside noticeable mood changes, offenders may also demonstrate a return to alcohol or drug use, or a return to a pattern of sexual preoccupation, particularly when this preoccupation is tied to everyday coping mechanisms.

A collapse of support networks leads to a reduction in behavioural controls for the offender. This collapse could be outside the control of the offender (e.g., an important support moves away due to work) or the offender may start to avoid prosocial activities or reduce his ties with his support network. Access to victims may increase, either because the support network is no longer vigilant, or because the offender himself is creating opportunities for access to victims. Finally, a negative change in the offender's community functioning is likely indicative of rapidly increasing risk. This change is typically demonstrated via absences at scheduled events, missed appointments, and failure to show up at work or to attend treatment. Even if the offender does attend work or treatment, there is a noticeable lack of investment in treatment or work, and a lack of adherence to community supervision conditions.

As mentioned above, in 2001, Hanson established the *Dynamic Supervision Project*, a longitudinal study of sexual offenders under community supervision, to validate dynamic risk factors. The most recent results from this study indicate that while all acute factors were related to reoffending, the most predictive proximal factors were *access to a victim*, *rejection of supervision*, and *sexual preoccupation* (Hanson, 2005). This ongoing research demonstrates the importance of keeping up to date with this rapidly evolving field. Further, and perhaps more importantly, Hanson's research continues to show that acute factors are behavioural cues that are readily observable by properly trained staff, indicating the importance of monitoring sexual offenders in the community for these signals of increased risk.

CONCLUSION

It must be noted that this review of static and dynamic risk factors applies only to adult male sexual offenders. Much less is known about the risk factors of juvenile sexual offenders and of adult female sexual offenders. While the research on risk factors for sexual recidivism among juvenile sexual offenders is ongoing (e.g., Worling, 2001), only one study to date has attempted to determine the static factors related to sexual recidivism among female sexual offenders (Williams & Nicholaichuk, 2001). Further, it is only recently that an attempt has been made to establish the recidivism rates of these women (Cortoni & Hanson, 2005). Evaluators must proceed with extreme caution when they are tasked with evaluating risk in these two populations.

Risk assessment remains an inexact science. While static factors are well established as powerful predictors of risk, the evidence presented here shows that dynamic risk factors do add incremental validity to risk assessments. Research on dynamic risk factors is still incomplete, and much remains to be understood (Hanson, 2006). Improving our understanding of these factors, and how change on these factors impacts on risk continues to be a seminal line of inquiry to improve our ability to assess and manage sexual offending behaviour. Despite these limitations, it is incumbent upon risk evaluators to ensure they have a thorough understanding of the empirical evidence for the static and dynamic factors related to sexual recidivism, and apply this understanding in the analyses of their cases to maximise the validity of their risk assessment.

REFERENCES

Abel, G.G., Becker, J.B. & Cunningham-Rathner, J. (1984). Complications, consent, and cognitions in sex between children and adults. *International Journal of Law and Psychiatry*, 7, 89–103.

Abel, G.G., Gore, D.K., Holland, C.L. *et al.* (1989). The measurement of the cognitive distortions of child molesters. *Annals of Sex Research*, 2, 135–153.

Ajzen, I. & Fishbein, M. (1977). Attitude-behavior relations: A theoretical analysis and review of empirical research. *Psychological Bulletin*, 84, 888–918.

Andrews, D.A. & Bonta J. (2003). *The psychology of criminal conduct* (3rd edn). Cincinnati, Ohio: Anderson.

Barbaree, H. (1991). Denial and minimization among sex offenders: Assessment and treatment outcome. *Forum on Corrections Research*, 3, 30–33.

Beech, A.R. (1998). A psychometric typology of child abusers. *International Journal of Offender Therapy and Comparative Criminology*, 42, 319–339.

Beech, A.R., Fisher, D. & Beckett, R.C. (1999). *An evaluation of the Prison Sex Offender Treatment Programme.* UK Home Office Occasional Report. Available from Home Office Publications Unit, 50 Queen Anne's Gate, London, SW1 9AT, England. Available electronically from: www.homeoffice.gov.uk/rds/pdfs/occ-step3.pdf.

Beech, A.R., Fisher, D.D. & Thornton, D. (2003). Risk assessment of sex offenders. *Professional Psychology: Research and Practice, 34*, 339–352.

Beech, A., Friendship, C., Erikson, M. & Hanson, R.K. (2002). The relationship between static and dynamic risk factors and reconvictions in a sample of UK child abusers. *Sexual Abuse: A Journal of Research and Treatment, 14*, 155–167.

Beech, A.R. & Ward, T. (2004). The integration of etiology and risk in sexual offenders: A theoretical framework. *Aggression and Violent Behavior, 10*, 31–63.

Bonta, J., Law, M. & Hanson, R.K. (1998). The prediction of criminal and violent recidivism among mentally disordered offenders: A meta-analysis. *Canadian Journal of Criminology, 39*, 127–144.

Bumby, K.M. (1996). Assessing the cognitive distortions of child molesters and rapists: development and validation of the MOLEST and RAPE scales. *Sexual Abuse: A Journal of Research and Treatment, 8*, 37–54.

Bumby, K.M. (2000). Empathy inhibition, intimacy deficits, and attachment difficulties in sex offenders. In D.R. Laws, S.M. Hudson & T. Wards (Eds), *Remaking relapse prevention with sex offenders* (pp. 143–166). Thousand Oaks, CA: Sage Publications.

Burt, M.R. (1980). Cultural myths and supports for rape. *Journal of Personality and Social Psychology, 38*, 217–230.

Check, J.V.P. (1984). *The Hostility Towards Women Scale*. Unpublished doctoral dissertation. University of Manitoba, Manitoba, Canada.

Cortoni, F. (2005). *Criminal career pathways of sexual offenders: Clinical implications*. Paper presented at the 24th Research and Treatment Conference of the Association for the Treatment of Sexual Abusers, Salt Lake City, Utah, November.

Cortoni, F. & Hanson, R.K. (2005). A review of recidivism rates of adult female sexual offenders. (Research Report No. R-169.) Ottawa: Research Branch, Correctional Service Canada.

Cortoni, F.A. & Marshall, W.L. (2001). Sex as a Coping Strategy and its Relationship to Juvenile Sexual History and Intimacy in Sexual Offenders. *Sexual Abuse: A Journal of Research and Treatment, 13*, 27–43.

Craig, L.A., Thornton, D., Beech, A. & Browne, K.D. (2007). The relationship of statistical and psychological risk markers to sexual reconviction in child molesters. *Criminal Justice and Behavior, 34*, 314–329.

Feelgood, F., Cortoni, F. & Thompson, A. (2005). Sexual coping, general coping and cognitive distortions in incarcerated rapists and child molesters. *Journal of Sexual Aggression, 11*, 157–170.

Gendreau, P., Little, T. & Goggin, C. (1996). A meta-analysis of the predictors of adult offender recidivism: What works! *Criminology, 34*, 575–607.

Hanson, R.K. (1997a). Sex offender risk assessment. In C.R. Hollin (Ed), *Handbook of offender assessment and treatment* (pp. 85–96). Chichester, UK: John Wiley & Sons, Ltd.

Hanson, R.K. (1997b). *The development of a brief actuarial risk scale for sexual offence recidivism*. (User Report No. 97–04.) Ottawa: Corrections Research, Department of the Solicitor General of Canada.

Hanson, R.K. (2000). What is so special about relapse prevention? In D.R. Laws, S.M. Hudson & T. Wards (Eds), *Remaking relapse prevention with sex offenders* (pp. 27–38). Thousand Oaks, CA: Sage Publications.

Hanson, R.K. (2005). The assessment of criminogenic needs of sexual offenders by community supervision officers: Reliability and Validity. Paper presented at the 66th Annual Conference of the Canadian Association of Psychology, Montréal, Québec, Canada, June 2005.

Hanson, R.K. (2006). Stability and changes: dynamic risk factors for sexual offenders. In W.L. Marshall, Y.M. Fernandez, L.E. Marshall & G.A. Serran (Eds), *Sexual offender treatment: Controversial issues* (pp. 17–31). Chichester, UK: John Wiley & Sons, Ltd.

Hanson, R.K. & Bussière, M.T. (1998). Predicting Relapse: A meta-analysis of sexual offender recidivism studies. *Journal of Consulting and Clinical Psychology, 66*, 348–362.

Hanson, R.K. & Harris, A. (1998). *Dynamic predictors of sexual recidivism*. (User Report No. 98–01.) Ottawa: Corrections Research, Department of the Solicitor General Canada.

Hanson, R.K. & Harris, A. (2000). Where should we intervene: Dynamic predictors of sexual offence recidivism. *Criminal Justice and Behavior, 27*, 6–35.

Hanson, R.K. & Harris, J.R. (2001). A structured approach to evaluating change among sexual offenders. *Sexual Abuse: A Journal of Research and Treatment, 13*, 105–122.

Hanson, R.K. & Morton-Bourgon, K.E. (2004). *Recidivism risk factors for sexual offenders: An updated meta-analysis.* (User Report No. 2004–02.) Ottawa: Corrections Research, Public Safety and Emergency Preparedness Canada.

Hanson, R.K. & Morton-Bourgon, K.E. (2005). The characteristics of persistent sexual offenders: A meta-analysis of recidivism studies. *Journal of Consulting and Clinical Psychology, 73*, 1154–1163.

Hanson, R.K. & Thornton, D. (1999). *Static 99: Improving actuarial risk assessment for sex offenders.* (User Report No. 99–02.) Ottawa: Corrections Research, Department of the Solicitor General of Canada.

Hart, S., Laws, D.R. & Kropp, P.R. (2003). The promise and the peril of sex offender risk assessment. In T. Ward, D.R. Laws & S.M. Hudson (Eds), *Sexual deviance: Issues and controversies* (pp. 207–243). Thousand Oaks, CA: Sage Publications.

Hudson, S.M., Wales, D.S., Bakker, L. & Ward, T. (2002). Dynamic risk factors: The Kia Marama evaluation. *Sexual Abuse: A Journal of Research and Treatment, 14*, 101–117.

Laws, D.R. (1989). *Relapse prevention procedures with sexual offenders.* New York: Guilford Press.

Laws, D.R. (2003). Behavioral economic approaches to the assessment and treatment of sexual deviation. In T. Ward, D.R. Laws & S.M. Hudson (Eds), *Sexual deviance: Issues and controversies* (pp. 65–81). Thousand Oaks, CA: Sage Publications.

Looman, J. (1995). Sexual fantasies of child molesters. *Canadian Journal of Behavioural Science, 27*, 321–332.

Lussier, P. (2005). *Developmental pathways to sexual offending.* Paper presented at the 24th Research and Treatment Conference of the Association for the Treatment of Sexual Abusers, Salt Lake City, Utah, November 2005.

Mann, R.E. & Beech, A.R. (2003). Cognitive distortions, schemas, and implicit theories. In T. Ward, D.R. Laws & S.M. Hudson (Eds), *Sexual deviance: Issues and controversies* (pp. 135–153). Thousand Oaks, CA: Sage Publications.

Mann, R.E. & Shingler, J. (2006). Schema-driven cognition in sexual offenders: theory, assessment and treatment. In W.L. Marshall, Y.M. Fernandez, L.E. Marshall & G.A. Serran (Eds), *Sexual offender treatment: Controversial Issues* (pp. 173–185). Chichester, UK: John Wiley & Sons, Ltd.

Marshall, W.L. (1989). Intimacy, loneliness and sexual offenders. *Behavioural Research and Therapy, 27*, 491–503.

Marshall, W.L. (2001). Adult sexual offenders against women. In C.R. Hollin (Ed.), *Handbook of offender assessment and treatment* (pp. 333–348). Chichester: John Wiley & Sons, Ltd.

Marshall, W.L., Champagne, F., Sturgeon, C. & Bryce, P. (1997). Increasing the self-esteem of child molesters. *Sexual Abuse: A Journal of Research and Treatment, 9*, 321–333.

Marshall, W.L., Fernandez, Y.M., Hudson, S.M. & Ward, T. (1998). *The sourcebook of sex offender treatment programs.* New York, Plenum Press.

Marshall, W.L., Thornton, D., Marshall, L.E. *et al.* (2001). Treatment of sexual offenders who are in categorical denial: A pilot project. *Sexual Abuse: A Journal of Research and Treatment, 13*, 205–216.

McKibben, A., Proulx, J. & Lusignan, R. (1994). Relationships between conflict, affect and deviant sexual behaviors in rapists and pedophiles. *Behaviour Research and Therapy, 13*, 571–575.

Milner, R.J. & Webster, S.D. (2005). Identifying schemas in child molesters, rapists and violent offenders. *Sexual Abuse: A Journal of Research and Treatment, 17*, 425–439.

Nunes, K.L., Firestone, P. & Baldwin, M.W. (2007). Indirect assessment of cognitions of child sexual abusers with the Implicit Association Test. *Criminal Justice and Behavior, 34*, 454–475.

Proulx, J., McKibben, A. & Lusignan, R. (1996). Relationships between affective components and sexual behaviors in sexual aggressors. *Sexual Abuse: A Journal of Research and Treatment, 8*, 279–289.

Quinsey, V.L., Harris, G.T., Rice, M.E. & Quinsey, V.L. (2006). *Violent offenders: Appraising and managing risk*. Washington, DC: American Psychological Association.

Roberts, C.F., Doren, D.M. & Thornton, D. (2002). Dimensions associated with assessments of sex offender recidivism risk. *Criminal Justice and Behavior*, *29*, 569–589.

Seidman, B.T., Marshall, W.L., Hudson, S.M. & Robertson, P.J. (1994). An examination of intimacy and loneliness in sex offenders. *Journal of Interpersonal Violence*, *9*, 518–534.

Seto, M.C., Harris, G.T., Rice, M.E. & Barbaree, H.E. (2004). The Screening Scale for Pedophilic Interests and recidivism among adult sex offenders with child victims. *Archives of Sexual Behavior*, *33*, 455–466.

Thornton, D. (2002). Constructing and testing a framework for dynamic risk assessment. *Sexual Abuse: A Journal of Research and Treatment*, *14*, 137–151.

Thornton, D. (2005). *Evaluating risk factor domain and clusters*. Paper presented at the 24th Research and Treatment Conference of the Association for the Treatment of Sexual Abusers, Salt Lake City, Utah, November 2005.

Ward, T., Fon, C., Hudson, S.M. & McCormack, J. (1998). A descriptive model of dysfunctional cognitions in child molesters. *Journal of Interpersonal Violence*, *13*, 129–155.

Ward, T., Hudson, S.M., Johnson, L. & Marshall, W.L. (1997). Cognitive distortions in sex offenders: An integrative review. *Clinical Psychology Review*, *17*, 479–507.

Ward, T., McCormack, J. & Hudson, S.M. (1997). Sexual offenders' perceptions of their intimate relationships. *Sexual Abuse: A Journal of Research and Treatment*, *9*, 57–73.

Williams, S.M. & Nicholaichuk, T. (2001, November). *Assessing static risk factors in adult female sex offenders under federal jurisdiction*. Paper presented at the 21st Research and Treatment Conference of the Association for the Treatment of Sexual Abusers, San Antonio, TX, November 2001.

Wilson, R.J. (1999). Emotional congruence in sexual offenders against children. *Sexual Abuse: A Journal of Research and Treatment*, *11*, 33–47.

Worling, J.A. (2001). Personality-based typology of adolescent male sexual offenders: Differences in recidivism rates, victim-selection characteristics, and personal victimization histories. *Sexual Abuse: A Journal of Research and Treatment*, *13*, 149–166.

Zamble, E. & Quinsey, V.L. (1997). *The criminal recidivism process*. Cambridge, UK: Cambridge University Press.

4

The Predictive Accuracy of Risk Factors and Frameworks

LEAM A. CRAIG

ANTHONY R. BEECH

LEIGH HARKINS

INTRODUCTION

The identification of the risks posed by sexual offenders and the factors associated with their recidivism are crucial to an understanding of appropriate and effective interventions to prevent the sexual assault of children. Therefore, professionals working with sex offenders are often called on to assess the risk they present. These assessments are normally concerned either with the risk of further sexual offences or with the risk of future violence of any kind. To carry out this task the professional typically uses a combination of actuarial scales and clinical judgement. Although it should be noted that actuarial scales typically outperform unguided clinical judgement (e.g., Bengtson & Långström, 2007; Grove *et al.*, 2000; Grubin, 1999).

Most actuarial scales primarily use static risk factors (i.e., historical factors that by their very nature are unchangeable such as previous history of sexual offending). However, while static risk factors are good for measuring long-term risk, they say little of what needs to change to decrease a person's risk of recidivism. Therefore, actuarial risk scales can be criticised for being heavily reliant on static factors, that is to say historical incidents in someone's life (such as a serious of sexual convictions), that by their very nature are not amenable to change. This observation is illustrated in the results of a review of 22 studies (N = 32,733), by Craig *et al.* (2004c), who reported data on 12 risk scales, where they found that 10 scales predominately used static risk factors, while only 5 considered treatment effects.

Assessment and Treatment of Sex Offenders: A Handbook. Edited by Anthony Beech, Leam Craig and Kevin Browne. © John Wiley & Sons Ltd, 2009.

In contrast, clinical judgement may allow a decision to be made at an ideographic level, but until recently has been less well informed by research. Although a new generation of guided clinical judgement measures in the offender literature, such as the Sexual Violence Risk-20 (Boer *et al.*, 1997), are now available for clinicians to aid their judgements.

In the last few years very real attempts have been made to draw these approaches together, both in general (i.e., Andrews & Bonta, 2006), and sexual offender (Beech *et al.*, 2002; Thornton, 2002) literatures.

The aim of this chapter is to look at these approaches to assessment, specifically examining the predictive accuracy of risk factors, and risk frameworks, in assessing sexual recidivism risk; and to consider the application of risk assessment measures commonly used in criminal justice settings.

ASSESSING THE ACCURACY OF RISK FRAMEWORKS

The predictive accuracy of a method of risk assessment is best indexed through the Receiver Operating Characteristics analysis' Area Under the Curve (AUC) statistic (Hanley & McNeil, 1982; Mossman, 1994; Rice & Harris, 1997; Quinsey *et al.*, 1998). This index has the advantage that it is not distorted by variations in the base rate of recidivism. The AUC itself is the plot of the 'hit rate' or *sensitivity* (the percentage of reoffenders correctly identified as high risk on assessment) against the 'false alarm rate' or *specificity* (the percentage of those correctly identified as low risk who did not go on to reoffend) for each score on the scale in question based on the contingency table design (Figure 4.1).

The higher the value of the AUC the better the assessment measure, with .5 (meaning no predictive accuracy) to 1.0 (meaning perfect predictive accuracy). Typically a value of .7 or above is considered to be an indication that the instrument in question has significant predictive power. See Figure 4.2 for an example of an AUC curve.

Having set the scene for assessing the efficacy of risk assessment approaches, we will now examine some common approaches in the field in more detail.

APPROACHES TO RISK ASSESSMENT

There are a number of different methodologies for carrying out risk assessments (as shown in Table 4.1), but these generally fall into actuarial risk scale and clinical approaches (typically assessing dynamic measures of sexual offenders' problems).

We will now examine these approaches in more detail.

The Actuarial Risk Assessment Approach

The actuarial approach statistically identifies relevant risk factors predictive of sexual reconviction from which a numerical risk score can be calculated. This score translates

Table 4.1 Approaches to assessing risk of reoffending

Actuarial assessment	Actuarial risk scales utilise statistical techniques to generate reliable risk predictors which are designed to predict the likelihood of a future behaviour. The items are selected, empirically derived and often scored dichotomously (present or absent). The sum scores of these items are translated into a level of risk of sexual reconviction (e.g., low, medium or high).
Unguided clinical judgement	A clinician reviews case materials without any significant a priori list or theory to prioritise the relative importance of the data obtained but judgements are made.
Structured clinical judgement	This process starts from an a priori set of ideas of what is important, but this list is based on the clinician's own experiences and theories without support from research results.
Anamnestic approach	This approach has a limited degree of structure and considers a series of personal and situational factors, conditions and events that resulted in past sexual violence and assumes that those same factors will lead to future offending. However, there is no empirical support for such an approach, which assumes that offending patterns are static.
Research-guided clinical judgement	This consists of an a priori set of risk factors developed from a research-supported list. Risk assessment guidelines define what information to consider, how to identify risk factors and how to synthesize risk items into an estimate of risk.
Clinically adjusted actuarial approach	This approach initially uses one or more actuarial instruments followed by potential adjustments to the actuarial results based on clinical judgements. However, an adjustment based on a clinician's own judgement away from empirically derived risk scales may limit the predictive utility of the scale (Hart, Laws & Kropp, 2003). This approach is currently being empirically tested.

into a risk descriptor of *low, medium,* or *high* risk of sexual reconviction. Advocates of the actuarial approach contend that accurate risk appraisal demands the use of statistically based models where clinical judgement is omitted (Quinsey *et al.*, 1998).

However, these measures tend to be heavily reliant on static factors. This observation is illustrated by Craig, Browne and Stringer (2003), in a review of the predictive accuracy of 12 sex offender risk assessment measures, who found that 10 predominately used static (historical, non-changing) risk factors, 7 did not consider

OUTCOME

		Non-recidivists	Recidivists
PREDICTION	Low Risk	True Negative D	False Negative C
	High Risk	False Positive B	True Positive A

- **Positive predictive accuracy** (PPA) = a/(a + b): the percentage of the high-risk group who subsequently reoffended.

- **Negative predictive accuracy** (NPA) = d/(c+ d): the percentage of the non-high-risk group who did not subsequently reoffend.

- **Sensitivity** = a/(a + c): the percentage ofthose reoffenders who were correctly identified as being high risk.

- **Specificity** = d/(b + c): the percentage of the non-offending group who were correctly identified as not being high risk.

Figure 4.1 Contingency table for predictive studies using a cohort design

treatment effects, and 10 were better at distinguishing general rather than sexual recidivism. Factors such as a diagnosis of psychopathy, deviant sexual interests and offence history are consistently associated with sex offender recidivism (Olver & Wong, 2006; Quinsey, Rice & Harris, 1995; Serin, Mailloux & Malcolm, 2001). While

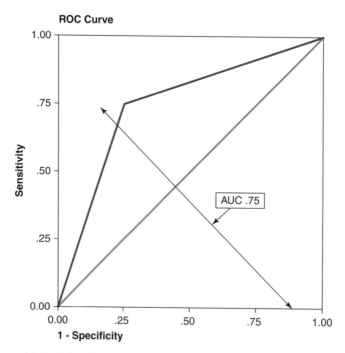

Figure 4.2 Relative Operating Characteristic: Area Under the Curve = .75

psychopathy, a form of severe and often dangerous personality disorder, combined with measures of sexual deviance is especially predictive of sexual recidivism (Hildebrand, de Ruiter & de Vogel, 2004; Olver & Wong, 2006; Rice & Harris, 1997; Serin, Mailloux & Malcolm, 2001). See Chapter 3 for a fuller discussion of static risk factors.

Due to their ease of use, the literature has witnessed an increase in the number of actuarial risk scales that are available. The following is a brief description of some of the better known risk scales developed for adult male offenders in the UK and North America.[1]

Structured Anchored Clinical Judgement (SACJ-Min; reported in Grubin, 1998; Hanson & Thornton, 2000)

This scale was developed by David Thornton based on data from HM Prison Service in the UK. SACJ-Min assesses risk of sexual and violent recidivism. It is made up of three stages; the first stage involves five items, which cover current and past criminal history and grade the offender into a risk category (low, medium or high). The second stage has eight items which are referred to as 'aggravating factors' and the presence of two or more of these raises the risk category by one level. The third stage assesses current behaviour and response to treatment and can reduce the risk category. Hanson and Thornton (2000) reported SACJ-Min correlations of $r = .23$ (AUC $=$ .67) with sexual offence recidivism, and $r = .22$ (AUC $= .64$) with any violent recidivism.

Rapid Risk Assessment for Sexual Offence Recidivism (RRASOR; Hanson, 1997)

RRASOR contains four items, each of which have been found by Hanson (1997) to be related to sexual reconviction. These items are: past sexual offences, age at commencement of risk, extra-familial victims and male victims. Offenders are allocated points according to the presence of these and given a risk categorisation on this basis. In a validation study, RRASOR was found to significantly correlate with sexual offence recidivism ($r = .28$; AUC $= .68$), and with any violent recidivism ($r = .22$; AUC $= .64$) (Hanson & Thornton, 2000).

Static-99 (Hanson & Thornton, 2000)/Static-2002 (Hanson & Thornton, 2003)

Hanson and Thornton developed Static-99 from items from SACJ and RRASOR. It consists of 10 items: prior sex offences, prior sentencing occasions, convictions for

---

[1] To be able to use the scales the authors of each will need to be contacted to obtain all the necessary information and scoring guides. In some instances there is also a training requirement.

non-contact sex offences, index non-sexual violence, prior non-sexual violence, unrelated victims, stranger victims, male victims, lack of a long-term intimate relationship and if the offender is aged under 25 on release (or now, if the offender is in the community). For the prediction of sex offence recidivism, Static-99 (AUC $= .71, r = .33$) was more accurate than the RRASOR or SACJ-Min. Static-99 also showed moderate predictive accuracy for violent (including sexual) offence recidivism (AUC $= .69$, $r = .32$). A number of studies have shown the Static-99 to have reasonable to good levels of predictive accuracy for sexual recidivism use AUC analysis from .63 (Langton *et al.*, 2007; Looman, 2006), to .76 (Sjöstedt & Långström, 2001). The latest meta-analysis reported by Hanson and Morton-Bourgon (2007) found that Static-99 has moderate predictive accuracy of Cohen's $d^2 = .70$ in 42 samples consisting of 13,288 offenders.

Craissati and Beech (2006) suggest that the predictive accuracy of Static-99 can be improved by adding *Sexual Risk Behaviours* (i.e., new offence with a sexual element, the targeting of victims and any behaviour associated with the index offence) and different historical risk factors for rapists and child molesters (i.e., physical abuse during childhood and a history of two or more childhood disturbances for rapists, and victim of child sexual abuse for child molesters). It was found that *Sexual Risk Behaviours* factors improved the predictive accuracy for rapists, but not for child abusers; and that historical factors improved predictive accuracy for child molesters, but not for rapists.

Static-2002 was developed to improve the consistency of the scoring criteria of Static-99, and increase its predictive validity. It consists of 13 items: age at release; number of sentencing occasions for sexual offences; any arrest as a juvenile for a sexual offence along with a conviction as an adult for a separate offence; high rate of sexual offending; any conviction for non-contact sex offences; any male victims; two or more victims under 12 years of age, one unrelated; any unrelated victims; any stranger victims; number of prior arrest/sentencing occasions; any breach of conditional release; number of years free prior to index offence; any convictions for non-sexual violence.

Several studies have provided support for the predictive validity of Static-2002 (Hanson & Thornton, 2003; Langton *et al.*, 2007). Hanson and Thornton (2003) found that for those cases with five or fewer items missing, the scale had an AUC of .71 for sexual recidivism. Haag (2005) found an AUC of .76 in predicting sexual recidivism among 461 sexual offenders who completed treatment programmes in Canada. Langton *et al.* (2007) found an overall AUC value of .71 for their sample of 464 treated sexual offenders.

---

[2]Cohen's d is commonly used in meta-analyses and is an effect size indicator which is derived by (M1–M2)/S_w where M1 is the mean of the deviant group, M2 is the mean of the non-deviant group, and S_w is the pooled within standard deviation (Hasselblad & Hedges, 1995).

Risk Matrix 2000 (RM2000; Thornton et al., 2003)

This scale has separate indicators for risk of sexual recidivism (RM2000-Sexual, RMS) and overall violence (RM2000-Violent, RMV). The Prison, Probation and Police Services in England and Wales have adopted the scale nationally. Scoring of RMS is a two-stage process. The first stage involves the rating of three static items: age at commencement of risk, sexual appearances and total criminal appearances. Points are awarded and the offender placed in one of four categories (low, medium, high or very high). The second stage of RMS contains four aggravating factors: male victim, stranger victim, non-contact sexual offences and lack of a long-term intimate relationship. If two aggravating factors are present the risk category is raised one level and if all four are present the risk is raised two levels. Validated on treated ($n = 647$) and untreated ($n = 429$) sex offenders, RMS obtained AUCs of .77 and .75 respectively (Thornton et al., 2003).

RMV variables, which were selected on a priori grounds, include: age on release, amount of prior violence and a history of burglary. Validated on two samples followed up over 10 years ($n = 311$) and between 16–19 years ($n = 429$) RMV obtained AUCs of .78 and .80 respectively (Thornton et al., 2003).

Craig, Beech and Browne (2006) report that four other historical risk factors (not considered in RM2000 or Static-99) positively correlated with sex and violent reconviction. These were: history of foster care, history of substance abuse, history of employment problems/instability, and history of school maladjustment. Factoring the four risk items increased the strength of correlation between RMS and RMV, and Static-99 scales and sexual/violent or general reconviction across the 10-year follow-up period. However, there was little effect on the predictive accuracy associated with sexual non-violent offences.

Sex Offence Risk Appraisal Guide (SORAG; Quinsey et al., 1998)

The SORAG was developed in Canada. It was designed to predict violence committed by sexual offenders. SORAG has 14 items which cover: living with both biological parents until age 16, school maladjustment, alcohol problems, evidence of a sustained intimate relationship, non-violent criminality, violent criminality, previous sexual contact convictions, convictions against girls under 14 only, failure on prior conditional release, age at index offence, evidence of personality disorder, schizophrenia, evidence of deviant sexual preferences and psychopathy (as defined by the Psychopathy Checklist-Revised, Hare, 1991). Hanson, Morton and Harris (2003), averaging five findings, reported that this scale had an average predictive accuracy a little better than RRASOR and a little worse than Static-99. The scale may, however, have particular advantages in samples where personality disorder and strong deviant sexual preferences vary independently of prior sexual convictions.

Minnesota Sex Offender Screening Tool-Revised (Epperson, Kaul & Hesselton, 1998)

Developed by the Minnesota Department of Corrections, this is a 16-item scale. This covers: number of sexual convictions, length of sex offending history, whether the offender was under any supervision when a sex offence was committed, any sex offence committed in a public place, use or threat of force, multiple acts on a single victim, different age groups of victim, offended against a 13–15 year old and being at least five years older than the victim, stranger victims, antisocial behaviour as an adolescent, substance abuse, employment history, discipline history while incarcerated, chemical dependency while incarcerated, sex offender treatment while incarcerated, age at release.

It can be seen that this scale has been developed for use with prisoners and covers a broader range of items than many of the other scales. It is, however, notably harder to score than scales like RRASOR, Static-99, and RM2000 and makes assumptions about the availability and nature of sexual offender treatment and chemical dependency treatment that may not apply outside Minnesota. The scale performed well (AUC = .76) when tested in Minnesota by its authors (Epperson, 2000) but rather less well when cross-validated by independent researchers in a Canadian sample. In the latter sample, however, its predictive accuracy was still significant, AUC = .70 (Langton *et al.*, 2002).

Sexual Violence Risk-20 (SVR-20; Boer et al., 1997)

Developed in Canada, this scale is different from other risk predictors in that it does not use the final score to place an individual within a probability of reconviction range but rather leaves it to the assessor to make a judgement regarding risk level. It is therefore more of a 'judgment after review' instrument than a true actuarial risk predictor, and contains a number of dynamic items (see below). The scale is intended to provide a list of items that have been shown by research to be indicative of reconviction. This allows the assessor to weight items in accordance with each individual situation. This of course means that the instrument's accuracy will vary depending on the judgement of the clinician applying it.

The SVR-20 has 20 items, which cover psychosocial adjustment, sexual offences and future plans, these are: deviant sexual preference, victim of child abuse, level of psychopathy, major mental illness, substance abuse, suicidal or homicidal ideation, relationship problems, employment problems, violent non-sexual offences, general criminality, supervision failure, high frequency of sex offences, range of sex offences, physical harm to victim, use of weapons, escalation in frequency or severity of sex offences, extreme denial or minimisation of sex offences, pro-offending attitudes, lacks realistic plans, and negative attitude towards intervention. The SVR-20 framework also allows for the addition of three extra acute dynamic risk items: acute mental disorder, recent loss of social support network and frequent contact with potential victims.

Table 4.2 allows comparisons to be made of the predictive accuracy of these risk scales.

LIMITATIONS OF CURRENT RISK ASSESSMENT SCALES

As noted above, the accuracy of prediction of a risk instrument depends on a comparison of *sensitivity* or 'hit rate' with the 'false alarm rate' or *specificity*. However, the probability that a positive result is true varies with the base rate of the group to which the test is being applied. With rare conditions, even the most accurate test will produce many *false positives*, and the large number outside the condition serves to magnify even small errors in the test (Janus & Meehl, 1997). Indeed, with a base rate of 4.3%, Hood *et al.* (2002) reported Static-99 over-estimated risk in 49 out of 50 cases. While Craissati (2003) reports that with a base rate of 2%, Static-99 over-predicted risk 29 times out of 30.

The implications of over-estimating risk may mean an offender is denied parole or may be required to undergo extended supervision and participate in sex offender treatment programmes unnecessarily (Mailloux *et al.*, 2003). However, this observation has to be balanced against the potential risk of false negatives (assessing somebody as not being risky when in fact they then go on to commit further sexual assaults).

Risk can also vary depending upon the risk scale used, in a comparison of settings (i.e., those offenders from hospital or prison settings), Craig, Browne and Stringer (2004) considered the application of six risk assessment measures on a sample of 139 sex offenders (51 non-incarcerated and 88 incarcerated). The measures employed were SACJ-Min, RRASOR, Static-99, RM 2000 (RM/Sexual and RM/Violence) and the SVR-20. In the incarcerated sample between 1% and 42% were classified as low risk, compared with 1% and 66% who were classified as high risk based on the scale used. In the community sample 8%–43% as low risk, and 4%–70% as high risk, again depending upon the scale used. This variability between different risk scales may, in part, be due to a systemic flaw, commonly known as the *statistical fallacy* effect (Dingwall, 1989).

This effect describes the process of comparing a single individual to the group data. The actuarial method compares similarities of an individual's profile to the aggregated knowledge of past events of convicted sexual offenders, in that an individual may share some, but not all, of the characteristics of the original sample. Using an actuarial scale on an individual who does not share all of the same risk characteristics can have the effect of reducing the predictive accuracy of the scale. For example, most risk classification instruments include the number of previous criminal convictions, prior sexual convictions and prior non-sexual violence. However, as Green, Gray and Willner (2002) found, sexual offenders with learning disabilities were more likely to be convicted of a sexual offence if they had targeted male children as victims. Therefore, those with female victims were less likely to have been convicted and, therefore, would not have a history of prior convictions. Under these conditions, actuarial measures may underestimate the risk of sexual reconviction for sexual offenders with learning disabilities.

Table 4.2 The predictive accuracy of sex offender risk assessment measures

Risk Scale	Author	n	Recidivism (AUC)		
			Sexual	Violent*	Any**
SACJ-Min	Craig, Beech & Browne (2006)	85(so)	0.52	0.58 (NSV)	0.57
		131 (s/v)	0.54	0.59 (NSV)	0.59
RRASOR	Hanson & Thornton (2000)	1208	0.67	0.64	0.60
	Barbaree et al. (2001)	215	0.76	0.65	
	Bartosh et al. (2003)	186	0.63	0.73	
	Craig, Beech & Browne (2006)	85 (so)	0.48	0.71 (NSV)	0.55
		131 (s/v)	0.57	0.55 (NSV)	0.51
	Hanson (1997)	2,592	0.71		
	Hanson & Morton-Bourgon (2004)	5,266	0.59d	0.34d	0.26d
	Hanson & Thornton (2000)	1208	0.68	0.64	
	Harris, Rice et al. (2003)	396	0.59	0.56	
	Harris & Rice (2003)	combined	0.71		
	Långström (2004)	1,303	0.73	0.59 (NSV)	
	Sjöstedt & Grann (2002)	1,288	0.73		
	Sjöstedt & Långström (2000)	1,400	0.72		
	Sjöstedt & Långström (2002)	51	0.73	0.62	
	Thornton et al. (2003)	429	0.70		
Static-99	Barbaree et al. (2001)	215	0.70	0.70	0.71
	Bartosh et al. (2003)	186	0.63	0.72	0.69
	Beech et al. (2000)	53	0.73		
	Craig, Beech & Browne (2006)	85 (so)	0.52	0.69	0.57
		131 (s/v)	0.50	0.66	0.62
	Craig, Browne et al. (2004a)	121 (s/v)	0.59	0.59 (NSV)	0.55
	Craig, Browne et al. (2006a)	119	0.67		
	Craig, Thornton et al. (2007)	119	0.66		
	Friendship, Mann & Beech (2003)	2,557	0.70	0.70	
	Hanson & Thornton, (2000)	1,208	0.71	0.69	
	Hanson & Morton-Bourgon (2004)	5,103	0.63d	0.57d	0.52d

Study	n			
Harris & Rice (2003)	combined	0.80		
Harris, Rice et al. (2003)	396	0.63	0.62	
Långström (2004)	1,303	0.75	0.72 (NSV)	
Looman (2006)	258	0.63	0.56	
Nunes et al. (2002)	258	0.70	0.69	
Sjöstedt & Grann (2002)	1,273	0.75		
Sjöstedt & Långström (2000)	1,400	0.76	0.74	
Thornton (2002)	117	0.92		
Thornton & Beech (2002)	121	0.91		
	53	0.75		
RMS Thornton et al. (2003)	429	0.73		
Craig, Beech & Browne (2006)	85 (so)	0.59	0.64	0.61
	131 (s/v)	0.55	0.68	0.66
Craig, Browne et al. (2004a)	121 (s/v)	0.56	0.55 (NSV)	0.60
	429 (u/t)	0.75		
	647(t)	0.77		
RMV Thornton et al. (2003)			0.86	
Craig, Beech & Browne (2006)	85 (so)	0.65	0.84	0.75
	131 (s/v)	0.53	0.68 (NSV)	0.76
Craig, Browne et al. (2004a)	121 (s/v)	0.55	0.85	0.70
Thornton et al. (2003)	647 (t)		0.80	
	429 (u/t)		0.78	
SORAG Barbaree et al. (2001)	311	0.70	0.73	0.76
Bartosh et al. (2003)	215	0.71	0.64	0.74
Bélanger & Earls (1996)	167	0.82		
Firestone et al. (1999)	57	0.65		
Harris et al. (2003)	558	0.66	0.73	
Harris & Rice (2003)	396	0.90		
Hartwell (2001)	51	0.67		0.70
Langton et al. (2007)	164		0.67	
Looman (2006)	269	0.69	0.69	
Nunes et al. (2002)	258	0.65	0.69	
	258			

(Continued)

Table 4.2 Continued

Risk Scale	Author	*n*	Recidivism (AUC)		
			Sexual	Violent*	Any**
	Rice & Harris (2002)	82	0.81	0.76	
	Quinsey et al. (1998)	618	0.62		
SVR-20	Craig, Beech & Browne (2006)	85 (so)	0.46	0.57	0.65
		131 (s/v)	0.47	0.54	0.62
	Craig, Browne et al. (2006b)	139 (s/v)	0.48	0.56	0.60
	Hanson & Morton-Bourgon (2004)	819	0.77*d*		0.52*d*
	Sjöstedt & Långström (2002)	51	0.49	0.64	

NOTE:

*Including sexual offences

**Including sexual, sexual violent, non-sexual violent, non-sexual non-violent

AUC: Area under the Curve of the Receiver Operating Characteristic

t: Treated sample

u/t: Untreated sample

so: Sex offender only sample

s/v: Sex and violent offender samples combined

NSV: Non-sex violence

d: Effect size values: According to Cohen (1998) *d* values of .20 (AUC = .56) are considered small, those of 0.50 (AUC = .62) medium, and those of .80 (AUC = .72) large.

Bartosh *et al.* (2003) investigated the validity of Static-99, RRASOR, MnSOST-R and SORAG in predicting recidivism, and found that the effectiveness of each instrument varied depending on offender type. For example, when examining extra-familial child abusers, Static-99 and SORAG were both significantly predictive of sexual and/or violent reoffending. Although the RRASOR was significant in predicting sexual recidivism for the group as a whole, it was less consistent than the Static-99 in reaching statistically significant ROC values for the specific offender types. In terms of extra-familial molesters, the RRASOR did not establish significance for sexual recidivism. However, when incest offenders were considered, the RRASOR neared significance in terms of sexual recidivism (ROC $= .727$, $p = .07$) and sexual and/or violent recidivism (ROC $= .843$, $p = .05$) but was not significant in terms of violent or any reoffence. For intra-familial (incest) offenders, all four instruments were at least moderately predictive of sexual recidivism, but only the Static-99 and the SORAG were highly predictive of violent recidivism. None of the four instruments established consistent predictive validity in regard to rapists or non-contact sexual offenders. Only the MnSOST-R failed to illustrate significant ROC values in regard to either sexual or violent reoffending. When the MnSOST-R was confined to extra-familial offenders, the scale was significant only in predicting any recidivism (ROC $= .688$, $p < .01$). Similarly, for rape offenders and non-contact offenders, the MnSOST-R neared predictive validity only in terms of any recidivism (ROC $= .671$, $p = .05$; and $.705$, $p = .08$) and did not establish significance in terms of any other categories of recidivism. Despite the fact that ROC analysis is relatively unaffected by base rates.

As to the more general limitations of actuarial instruments:

(a) Actuarial scales yield a probability in a sample of individuals (i.e., 40% probability means that the instrument predicts 40 out of 100 men with a particular risk score will recidivate, not a single person has a 40% chance of being reconvicted.

(b) As actuarial risk assessment instruments have been developed around official recidivism events (reconvictions), the probabilities associated with each risk category inevitably under-estimate true reoffence rates. Falshaw *et al.* (2003), for example, compared differences in offending base rates between official (using the Home Office Offenders Index (OI) and Police National Computer (PNC)) and unofficial sources (a community-based sexual offender treatment programme). They found that the unofficial sexual recidivism rate was 5.3 times greater than the reconviction rate calculated from the OI, and 1.8 times greater than that calculated from the PNC.

(c) Actuarial estimates of risk may be misleading for unusual individuals with characteristics that were not well represented in the samples used to construct or test the actuarial instruments. For example, the sexual reconviction rate of sexual offenders with learning disabilities was found to be 6.8 times and 3.5 times that of non-learning disabled sexual offenders at two-year and four-year follow-up in a study reported by Craig and Hutchinson (2005). Base rate may also differ dependent on setting (e.g., hospital or prison populations) (Rogers, 2000), or ethnicity (Långström, 2004).

(d) Actuarial instruments seek to estimate long-term risk and take no account of acute risk factors that might indicate imminent reoffending.

(e) Actuarial instruments do not indicate which factors need to be addressed in treatment for risk to be reduced and fail to consider mediating factors (Rogers, 2000).

(f) We would further add that actuarial risk scales are often viewed with suspicion by some clinicians for being too mechanistic when compared to clinical approaches to risk assessment.

Despite these limitations, Beech, Fisher and Thornton (2003) note that static actuarial instruments presently represent the most cost-effective way of dividing convicted offenders into groups that differ in overall long-term risk, and hence in their need for custodial, supervision, or treatment resources to manage that risk. It is also now widely acknowledged that actuarial risk measures outperform clinical judgement (Hanson & Morton-Bourgon, 2005) when predicting sexual reconviction. For example, Bengtson and Långström (2007) found that unguided clinical judgement performed little better than chance in a sample of 121 offenders followed up for 18 years in Denmark, while Static-99 was highly predictive of sexual, severe sexual and violent reconvictions[3] (AUC = .62, .72, .71), as was Static-2002 (AUC = .67, .69, .71).

Other authors have also argued that risk assessment models may be enhanced by adding idiographic (person-specific) risk factors. Idiographic risk factors would include clinically determined criminogenic factors, facilitators and inhibitors of risk. One example of this approach is the Multiaxial Risk Appraisal (MARA; Craig *et al.*, 2004b). The MARA framework seeks to provide a more global assessment of risk by adding idiographic (personal-specific) identification of risk factors to the kind of nomothetic model described here. Idiographic risk factors would include clinically determined criminogenic factors, facilitators and inhibitors of risk, and psychometric assessments of psychopathology and deviance (see Craig and Beech, Chapter 6 this volume), while the nomothetic approach compares risk to large group norms. It is, however, not yet known whether adding idiographic factors actually enhances or undermines predictive accuracy. Even where the idiographic method correctly identifies a personally-relevant risk factor there is still the problem of knowing how heavily to weight this factor (as for example in the SVR-20). Over-weighting of idiographic factors would be expected to lead to a decline in overall predictive accuracy.

DYNAMIC ASSESSMENT

Dynamic Factors

Dynamic risk factors are enduring risk factors linked to the likelihood of offending that can nevertheless be changed following intervention. Dynamic factors can be subdivided into *stable* and *acute* factors.

---

[3] Sexual or non-sexual.

Stable dynamic risk factors are those factors which are relatively persistent characteristics of the offender but which are subject to change over a long period of time such as: social and emotional problems; general problems in emotional/behavioural regulation; attitudes legitimising sexual assault (cognitive distortions); and sexual interests (in children or coercive sex with adults). Hanson and Bussière (1998), in a meta-analytical review of 61 studies ($n = 28,972$), found that the strongest stable dynamic predictor of sexual recidivism in child molesters was, unsurprisingly, sexual arousal to children as measured by the penile plethysmograph (see Chapter 7 for a review of this instrument). This result has also been found in a more recent meta-analysis by Hanson and Morton-Bourgon (2004).

Acute dynamic risk factors are rapidly changing triggering/situational risk factors such as substance misuse, isolation, and collapse of social supports that will typically occur around the time of offending, allowing the extreme expression of stable dynamic risk problems, i.e., need for intimacy, positive/negative emotional states, deviant thoughts and fantasies and sexual arousal (Beech & Ward, 2004).

An example of the interaction between *stable* and *acute* risk factors is reported by Hanson and Harris (1998), who explored stable dynamic and acute dynamic predictors of risk in 200 recidivists and 201 non-recidivists sexual offenders (rapists, child abusers with male victims, and child abusers with female victims); where they found that the recidivists in the sample, in comparison to non-recidivists, were more sexually deviant, had more paraphilias, were more likely to have a lifestyle congruent with sexual deviance, were more likely to have dropped out of treatment, or were considered treatment failures, and/or had substance abuse problems. Measures of remorse, sexual offence justification, feeling that some women deserved to be raped, having attitudes that sexualised children and feeling that the offender was entitled to express their strong sexual drive differentiated recidivists from the non-recidivists. Not surprisingly, the recidivists tended to view themselves as posing little risk of committing new sexual offences and took fewer precautions to avoid high-risk situations. The social environment of non-recidivists, in comparison to the recidivists, tended to be more positive.

Dynamic Frameworks

A framework that uses dynamic risk factors can be seen in the Structured Risk Assessment (SRA; Thornton, 2002; Webster *et al.*, 2006) model. The SRA is a research guided multi-step framework for assessing the risk presented by a sex offender and provides a systematic way of going beyond static risk classification that provides information around dynamic psychological and behavioural domains: *sexual interests, distorted attitudes, social and emotional functioning* and *self-management,* in what Thornton terms an *Initial Deviance Assessment* (IDA). Thornton argues that combining the psychological factors identified in the IDA with a static assessment allows better predictive accuracy than using static assessment alone. As a predictor of sexual recidivism the Number of Dysfunctional Domains (0 to 4) obtained a large

AUC indices ranging from .83 to .85 compared with Static-99 (AUC ranging from .75 to .91) in a study reported by Thornton and Beech (2002). The measure and calculation of the degree of psychological deviance and its relationship to recidivism has been replicated by Craig *et al.* (2007).

Karl Hanson and Andrew Harris have developed a system with both stable and acute risk factors. Originally called SONAR (The Sex Offender Need Assessment Rating) this system has now been renamed in two parts: STABLE- and ACUTE-2000.

STABLE-2000 (Hanson & Harris, 2000a) assesses six stable dynamic dimensions: significant social influences, intimacy deficits, attitudes supportive of sexual assault, cooperation with supervision, sexual self-regulation (e.g., sex drive/pre-occupation, sex as a coping strategy and deviant sexual interests), and general self-regulation. Hence, STABLE-2000 factors are broadly consistent with the IDA. These items are scored, 0, 1, or 2, to produce a scale where those scoring 0 to 4 are considered low risk (n = 307), those scoring 5 to 8 as moderate risk (n = 333), and those scoring 9 to 12 as high risk (n = 86) (Hanson, 2005). The scale has been evaluated in a prospective study called the Dynamic Supervision Project (reported by Harris & Hanson, 2003; Hanson, 2005). This study running between years 2001 and 2006 followed over 1000 under community supervision, who have sexually offended against children or adults in all Canadian provinces, all three Canadian territories and the Correctional Service of Canada, Alaska and Iowa. STABLE-2000 factors were assessed every six months. Currently the inter-rater reliability of STABLE-2000 has been reported by Hanson (2005) as very good (ICC = .90), and the predictive accuracy as being reasonable (AUC = .76), for a sexual offence, and slightly better (AUC = .77) for any sexual offence or breach.

ACUTE-2000 (Hanson & Harris, 2000b) covers the following acute risk factors: victim access; emotional collapse (i.e., evidence of severe emotional disturbance/emotional crisis), collapse of social supports; hostility; substance abuse; sexual preoccupations and rejection of supervision. The final factor in this system is what Hanson and Harris term a 'unique factor' in that some offenders have unique characteristics that represent a real risk factor for that offender. The type of factors that could be important for an offender could be such events as: a specific date or event (i.e., an anniversary) that causes an emotional response, pain or discomfort – possibly triggering alcohol or drug abuse; homelessness, contact with a specified family member, health problems of a cyclical nature that may enter and leave the offender's situation with little warning, and being bothered by intrusive thoughts regarding their own victimisation. In evaluating the ACUTE-2000, static factors were also assessed at initial assessment while stable dynamic risk factors using STABLE-2000 were assessed every six months and acute factors were assessed after every supervision of the offender. The results so far indicate good reliability between supervising officers scoring ACUTE-2000 risk factors (ICC = .89) with reasonable predictive accuracy being for ACUTE-2000 (AUC = .74) for sexual offences (Hanson, 2005).

CAN THERE BE A THEORY OF RISK ASSESSMENT?

Although scale development is theory-driven, this development has arisen without the benefit of substantial theoretical foundations and the application of actuarial scales has been criticized for being atheoretical. One reason why dynamic factors have yet to be included in actuarial measures may lie in the definitions of dynamic risk factors. Beech and Ward (2004) recently postulated a model that attempts to redefine *dynamic* factors and to bridge the gap between empirical risk literature and current theorising. Having considered some of the major theories that have shaped current assessment and treatment approaches for sexual offenders, they developed a model of the offence process incorporating aetiological theories of sexual abuse and risk assessment systems.

They argue that developmental adversity can result in vulnerability to sexually abuse, and that stable dynamic or 'psychological vulnerability' (i.e., traits) factors and dispositional factors interact with triggering events (contextual factors) to produce acute dynamic risk factors. Redefined, stable factors are considered as 'trait' (i.e., dispositional) factors, and acute factors as 'state' (i.e., contextual) factors. They argue actuarial assessments really act as proxies for the psychological vulnerability factors and function as markers of dispositional sexual behaviours. Contextual or acute factors (i.e., access to the victim) interact with these vulnerabilities to produce acute mental states, leading to recidivism. This shares similarities with Hanson *et al.* (2003) who also suggest that many dynamic factors are actually proxies for enduring characteristics that are difficult, if not impossible, to change. For example, intimacy deficits can be seen as a symptom of personality disorder.

A promising direction for future development is the articulation of models that integrate aetiology and risk in sex offenders in a grounded theoretical framework. The Beech and Ward (2004) model seeks to bridge the gap between the empirically supported deviancy domains described in the Structured Risk Assessment model (Thornton, 2002) and the theoretical pathways to sexual offending described by Ward and Siegert (2002). Integrating aetiology and risk in a grounded theoretical framework is an area that has been neglected and is a promising feature of future risk assessment systems for sex offenders.

CONCLUSIONS

The assessment of risk of sexual reconviction in sexual offenders is an essential aspect of the prevention of sexual assault. Recent advances in risk assessment suggest that structuring information on risk factors for sexual offending is more useful for prediction than exclusively using clinical approaches and may have the potential to distinguish between sexual deviance and antisocial dimensions. The risk factors combined to form actuarial scales have been identified from meta-analytical techniques that have included both static and dynamic factors in the analyses and yet dynamic factors were not identified as predictive of recidivism. However, actuarial risk assessment systems are not without their critics. Questions now relate to the use of dynamic variables and their correlation to sexual recidivism. A structured approach to risk appraisal that includes both statistical risk assessment and clinical indicators of psychological vulnerabilities (and related historical risk factors) is likely to enhance the prediction of sexual recidivism. A more global assessment of risk includes a combination of risk assessment approaches (actuarial scales with research guided clinical judgement and clinically adjusted actuarial approaches) as part of a multi-axial approach to risk appraisal. As Hanson (2005) observes, the tone of the risk assessment literature has changed from the validity of carrying out risk assessments to debating the best method of risk assessment. While static factors are useful for long-term predictions, dynamic factors provide information on where and when to intervene.

REFERENCES

Andrews, D.A. & Bonta, J. (2006). *The psychology of criminal conduct* (4th edn). Cincinnati, OH: Anderson Publishing Company.

Barbaree, H.E., Seto, M.C., Langton, C.M. & Peacock, E.J. (2001). Evaluating the predictive accuracy of six risk assessment instruments for adult sex offenders. *Criminal Justice and Behavior, 28*, 490–521.

Bartosh, D.L., Garby, T., Lewis, D. & Gray, S. (2003). Differences in the predictive validity of actuarial risk assessments in relation to sex offender type. *International Journal of Offender Therapy and Comparative Criminology, 47*, 422–438.

Beech, A.R., Erikson, M., Friendship, C. & Ditchfield, J. (2001). A six year follow-up of men going through representative probation-based sex offender treatment programmes. *Home Office Research Findings, 144*. Available electronically from: http://www.homeoffice.gov.uk/rds/pdfs/r144.pdf

Beech, A.R., Erikson, M., Friendship, C. & Hanson, R.K. (2002). Static and dynamic predictors of reconviction. *Sexual Abuse: A Journal of Research and Treatment, 14*, 153–165.

Beech, A.R., Fisher, D. & Thornton, D. (2003). Risk assessment of sex offenders. *Professional Psychology, Research and Practice, 34*, 339–352.

Beech, A.R. & Ward, T. (2004). The integration of etiology and risk in sexual offenders: A theoretical framework. *Aggression and Violent Behavior, 10*, 31–63.

Bélanger, N. & Earls, C. (1996). Sex offender recidivism prediction. *Forum on Corrections Research, 8*, 2, 22–24.

Bengtson, S. & Långström, N. (2007). Unguided clinical and actuarial assessment of re-offending risk: A direct comparison with sex offenders in Denmark. *Sexual Abuse: A Journal of Research and Treatment, 19*, 135–154.

Boer, D.P., Hart, S.D., Kropp, P.R. & Webster, C.D. (1997). *Manual for the Sexual Violence Risk-20*. Obtainable from the Mental Health, Law, and Policy Institute, Simon Fraser University, Burnaby, British Columbia, Canada, V5 1S6. Website: www.sfu.ca/psychology/groups/mhlpi

Cohen, J. (1988). *Statistical power analysis for the behavioral sciences*. 2nd edition. Hillsdale, NJ: Erlbaum.

Craig, L.A., Beech, A.R. & Browne, K.D. (2006). A cross-validation of the Risk Matrix-2000 Scales. *Journal of Interpersonal Violence, 21*, 1–22.

Craig, L.A., Browne, K.D., Beech, A.R. & Stringer, I. (2004a). Personality characteristics associated with reconviction in sexual and violent offenders. *Journal of Forensic Psychiatry and Psychology, 15*, 532–551.

Craig, L.A., Browne, K.D., Beech, A.R. & Stringer, I. (2006a). Psychosexual characteristics of sexual offenders and the relationship to sexual reconviction. *Psychology, Crime and Law, 12*, 231–244.

Craig, L.A., Browne, K.D., Beech, A.R. & Stringer, I. (2006b). Differences in personality and risk characteristics in sexual, violent and general offenders. *Criminal Behaviour and Mental Health, 16,* 183–194.

Craig, L.A., Browne, K.D., Hogue, T.E. & Stringer, I. (2004b). New directions in assessing risk in sexual offenders. In G. Macpherson & J. Lawrence (Eds), *Clinical risk assessment and risk management: Issues in Forensic Psychology* (pp. 81–99). Leicester: The British Psychological Society Press.

Craig, L.A., Browne, K.D. & Stringer, I. (2003). Risk scales and factors predictive of sexual offence recidivism. *Trauma, Violence and Abuse: A Review Journal, 4,* 45–67.

Craig, L.A., Browne, K.D. & Stringer, I. (2004). Comparing sex offender risk assessment measures on a UK sample. *International Journal of Offender Therapy and Comparative Criminology, 48,* 7–27.

Craig, L.A., Browne, K.D., Stringer, I. & Beech, A. (2004c). Limitations in actuarial risk assessment of sexual offenders: A methodological note. *British Journal of Forensic Practice, 1,* 16–32.

Craig, L.A. & Hutchinson, R. (2005). Sexual offenders with learning disabilities: Risk, recidivism and treatment. *Journal of Sexual Aggression, 11,* 289–304.

Craig, L.A., Thornton, D., Beech, A.R. & Browne, K.D. (2007). The relationship of statistical and psychological risk markers to sexual reconviction. *Criminal Justice and Behavior, 34,* 314–329.

Craissati, J. (2003). Adjusting standard assessment and treatment models to meet the needs of sex offenders in the community. Paper presented at the 12th Annual Conference of the Division of Forensic Psychology, 26–28 March. Churchill College, Cambridge, UK.

Craissati, J. & Beech, A.R. (2006). The role of key developmental variables in identifying sex offenders likely to fail in the community: An enhanced risk prediction model. *Child Abuse and Neglect, 30,* 327–339.

Dingwall, R. (1989). Some problems about predicting child abuse and neglect, in O. Stevenson (Ed.), *Child abuse: Public policy and professional practice* (pp. 28–53). Hemel Hempstead: Harvester Wheatsheaf.

Epperson, D.L. (2000). *Minnesota Sex Offender Screening Tool – Revised.* Sinclair Seminars Conference on Sex Offender Re-Offense Risk Prediction in Madison, Wisconsin. Videotape available from: www.sinclairseminars.com

Epperson, D.L., Kaul, J.D. & Hesselton, D. (1998). *Final report on the development of the Minnesota Sex Offender Screening Tool-Revised (MnSOST-R).* Paper presented at the 17th Annual Conference of the Association for the Treatment of Sexual Abusers, Vancouver, Canada, October 1998.

Falshaw, L., Bates, A., Patel, V. *et al.* (2003). Assessing reconviction, re-offending and recidivism in a sample of UK sexual offenders. *Legal and Criminological Psychology, 8,* 207–215.

Firestone, P., Bradford, J.M., McCoy, M. *et al.* (1999). Prediction of recidivism in incest offenders. *Journal of Interpersonal Violence, 14,* 511–531.

Friendship, C., Mann, R.E. & Beech, A.R. (2003). Evaluation of a national prison-based treatment program for sexual offenders in England and Wales. *Journal of Interpersonal Violence, 18,* 744–759.

Green, G., Gray, N.S. & Willner, P. (2002). Factors associated with criminal convictions for sexually inappropriate behaviour in men with learning disabilities. *Journal of Forensic Psychiatry, 13,* 578–607.

Grove, W.M., Zald, D.H., Lebow, B.S. *et al.* (2000). Clinical versus mechanical prediction: A meta-analysis. *Psychological Assessment, 12,* 19–30.

Grubin, D. (1998). Sex offending against children: Understanding the risk. *Police Research Series, Paper 99.* Available from the Research and Statistics Directorate, Home Office, 50 Queen Anne's Gate, London, SW1H 9AT, England. Available electronically from: www.homeoffice.gov.uk/rds/prgpdfs/fprs99.pdf

Grubin, D. (1999). Actuarial and clinical assessment of risk in sex offenders. *Journal of Interpersonal Violence. 14,* 331–343.

Haag, A.M. (2005). Do psychological interventions impact on actuarial measures: An analysis of the predictive validity of the Static-99 and the Static-2002 on a reconviction measure of sexual recidivism. Unpublished doctoral dissertation, University of Calgary, Alberta, Canada.

Hanley, J.A. & McNeil, B.J. (1982). The meaning and use of the area under a Receiver Operating Characteristic (ROC) curve. *Radiology, 143,* 29–36.

Hanson, R.K. (1997). The development of a brief actuarial risk scale for sexual offence recidivism. (User Report No. 1997–04.) Ottawa: Department of the Solicitor General of Canada. http://www.sgc.gc.ca/epub/corr/e199704/e199704.htm

Hanson, R.K. (2005). The assessment of criminogenic needs of sexual offenders by community supervision officers: Reliability and validity. Paper presented at the Annual Conference of the Canadian Psychological Association, June 10th 2005, Montreal, Canada.

Hanson, R.K. & Bussière, M.T. (1998). Predicting relapse: A meta-analysis of sexual offender recidivism studies. *Journal of Consulting and Clinical Psychology, 66,* 348–362.

Hanson, R.K. & Harris. A.J.R. (1998). *Dynamic predictors of sexual recidivism.* Corrections Research Ottawa: Department of the Solicitor General Canada. Also available electronically from: http://www.sgc.gc.ca/epub/corr/e199801b/e199801b.htm

Hanson, R.K. & Harris, A.J.R. (2000a). *STABLE-2000.* Unpublished manuscript. Department of the Solicitor General Canada. Available from the authors: e-mail Andrew Harris at Andrew.Harris@PSEPC-SPPCC.GC.CA

Hanson, R.K. & Harris, A.J.R. (2000b). *ACUTE-2000.* Unpublished manuscript. Department of the Solicitor General Canada. Available from the authors: e-mail Andrew Harris at Andrew.Harris@PSEPC-SPPCC.GC.CA www.sgc.gc.ca/epub/corr/e200001a/e200001b/e200001b.htm

Hanson, R.K. & Morton-Bourgon, K. (2004). *Predictors of sexual recidivism: An updated meta-analysis.* Corrections Research, Public Safety and Emergency Preparedness Canada. Available electronically from: http://www.psepc-sppcc.gc.ca/publications/corrections/pdf/200402_e.pdf

Hanson, R.K. & Morton-Bourgon, K. (2005). The characteristics of persistent sexual offenders: A meta-analysis of recidivism studies. *Journal of Consulting and Clinical Psychology, 73,* 1154–1163.

Hanson, R.K. & Morton-Bourgon, K. (2007). *The accuracy of recidivism risk assessments for sexual offenders: A meta-analysis.* Public Safety and Emergency Preparedness Canada. Available electronically from: http://www.publicsafety.gc.ca/res/cor/rep/_fl/crp2007–01-en.pdf

Hanson, R.K., Morton, K.E. & Harris, A.J.R. (2003). Sexual offender recidivism: What we know and what we need to know. In R. Prentky, E. Janus, M. Seto & A.W. Burgess (Eds), Understanding and managing sexually coercive behavior. *Annals of the New York Academy of Sciences, 989,* 154–166.

Hanson, R.K. & Thornton, D. (2000). Improving risk assessment for sex offenders: A comparison of three actuarial scales. *Law and Human Behavior, 24,* 119–136.

Hanson, R.K. & Thornton, D. (2003). Notes on the development of Static-2002. Available online from: http://ww2.psepc-sppcc.gc.ca/publications/corrections/200301_Static_2002_e.asp

Hare, R. (1991). *Manual for the Psychopathy Checklist-Revised.* Toronto, Ontario: Multi-Health Systems, Inc.

Harris, A.J.R. & Hanson, R.K. (2003). The Dynamic Supervision Project: Improving the community supervision of sex offenders. *Corrections Today, 65,* 62–64.

Harris, G.T. & Rice, M. (2003). Actuarial assessment of risk among sex offenders. In R. Prentky, E. Janus, M. Seto & A.W. Burgess (Eds), Understanding and managing sexually coercive behavior. *Annals of the New York Academy of Sciences, 989,* 198–210.

Harris, G.T., Rice, M.E., Quinsey, V.L. *et al.* (2003). A multisite comparison of actuarial risk instruments for sex offenders. *Psychological Assessments, 15,* 413–425.

Hart, S., Laws, D.R. & Kropp, P.R. (2003). The promise and the peril of sex offender risk assessment. In T. Ward, D.R. Laws & S.M. Hudson (Eds), *Sexual deviance: Issues and controversies* (pp. 207–225). Thousand Oaks, CA: Sage Publications.

Hartwell, L.L. (2001). Sex Offender Risk Appraisal Guide: Validity and utility for Hawaii sex offender risk assessments. Unpublished Clinical Research Project, American School of Professional Psychology, Hawaii Campus.

Hasselblad, V. & Hedges, L.V. (1995). Meta-analysis of screening and diagnostic tests. *Psychological Bulletin, 117,* 167–178.

Hildebrand, M., de Ruiter, C. & de Vogel, V. (2004). Psychopathy and sexual deviance in treated rapists: Association with sexual and nonsexual recidivism. *Sexual Abuse: A Journal of Research and Treatment, 16*, 1–24.

Hood, R., Shute, S., Feilzer, M. & Wilcox, A. (2002). Sex offenders emerging from long-term imprisonment. A study of their long-term reconviction rates and of parole board members' judgments of their risk. *British Journal of Criminology, 42*, 371–394.

Janus, E.A. & Meehl, P.E. (1997). Assessing the legal standard for predictions of dangerousness in sex offender commitment proceedings. *Psychology, Public Policy and Law, 3*, 33–64.

Långström, N. (2004). Accuracy of actuarial procedures for assessment of sexual offender recidivism risk may vary across ethnicity. *Sexual Abuse: A Journal of Research and Treatment, 16*, 107–120.

Langton, C.M., Barbaree, H.E., Harkins, L. *et al.* (2002). Evaluating the predictive validity of seven risk assessment instruments for sex offenders. Paper presented at the 21st Annual Research and Treatment Conference of the Association for the Treatment of Sexual Abusers: Montreal, Canada, October 2002.

Langton, C.M., Barbaree, H.E., Seto, M.C. *et al.* (2007). Actuarial assessment of risk for reoffense among adult sex offenders: Evaluating the predictive accuracy of the Static-2002 and five other instruments. *Criminal Justice and Behavior, 34*, 37–59.

Looman, J. (2006). Comparison of two risk assessment instruments for sexual offenders. *Sexual Abuse: A Journal of Research and Treatment, 18*, 193–206.

Mailloux, D.L., Abracen, J., Serin, R. *et al.* (2003). Dosage of treatment to sexual offenders: Are we overprescribing? *International Journal of Offender Therapy and Comparative Criminology, 47*, 171–184.

Mossman, D. (1994). Assessing predictions of violence: being accurate about accuracy. *Journal of Consulting and Clinical Psychology, 62*, 783–792.

Nunes, K.L., Firestone, P., Bradford, J.M. *et al.* (2002). A comparison of modified versions of the Static-99 and the Sex Offender Risk Appraisal Guide. *Sexual Abuse: A Journal of Research and Treatment, 14*, 253–269.

Olver, M.E. & Wong, S.C.P. (2006). Psychopathy, sexual deviance, and recidivism among sex offenders. *Sexual Abuse: A Journal of Research and Treatment, 18*, 65–82.

Quinsey, V.L., Harris, G.T., Rice, M.E. & Cormier, C.A. (1998). *Violent offenders: Appraising and managing risk.* Washington DC: American Psychological Association.

Quinsey, V.L., Rice, M.E. & Harris, G.T. (1995). Actuarial prediction of sexual recidivism. *Journal of Interpersonal Violence, 10*, 85–105.

Rice, M.E. & Harris, G.T. (1997). Cross-validation and extension of the Violent Risk Appraisal Guide for child molesters and rapists. *Law and Human Behavior, 21*, 231–241.

Rice, M.E. & Harris, G.T. (2002). Men who molest their sexually immature daughters: Is a special explanation required? *Journal of Abnormal Psychology, 111*, 329–339.

Rogers, R. (2000). The uncritical acceptance of risk assessment in forensic practice. *Law and Human Behavior, 24*, 595–605.

Serin, R.C., Mailloux, D.L. & Malcolm, P.B. (2001). Psychopathy, deviant sexual arousal, and recidivism among sex offenders. *Journal of Interpersonal Violence, 16*, 234–246.

Sjöstedt, G. & Grann, M. (2002). Risk assessment: what is being predicted by actuarial prediction instruments? *International Journal of Forensic Mental Health, 1*, 179–183.

Sjöstedt, G. & Långström, N. (2000). Actuarial assessment of risk for criminal recidivism among sex offenders released from Swedish prisons 1993–1997. Poster presented at the 19th Annual Conference of the Association for the Treatment of Sexual Abusers, San Diego, CA, October 2000.

Sjöstedt, G. & Långström, N. (2001). Actuarial assessment of sex offender recidivism risk: A cross-validation of the RRASOR and the Static-99 in Sweden. *Law and Human Behavior, 25*, 629–645.

Sjöstedt, G. & Långström, N. (2002). Assessment of risk for criminal recidivism among rapists: A comparison of four different measures. *Psychology, Crime and Law, 8*, 25–40.

Thornton, D. (2002). Constructing and testing a framework for dynamic risk assessment. *Sexual Abuse: A Journal of Research and Treatment, 14*, 137–151.

Thornton, D. & Beech. A.R. (2002). Integrating statistical and psychological factors through the structured risk assessment model. Paper presented at the 21st Annual Conference of the Association of the Treatment of Sexual Abusers, Montreal, Canada, October 2002.

Thornton, D., Mann, R., Webster, S. *et al.* (2003). Distinguishing and combining risks for sexual and violent recidivism. In R. Prentky, E. Janus, M. Seto & A.W. Burgess (Eds), Understanding and managing sexually coercive behavior. *Annals of the New York Academy of Sciences, 989*, 225–235.

Ward, T. & Siegert, R.J. (2002). Toward a comprehensive theory of child sexual abuse: A theory knitting perspective. *Psychology, Crime and Law*, *8*, 319–351.

Webster, S.D., Mann, R.E., Carter, A.J. *et al.* (2006). Inter-rater reliability of dynamic risk assessment with sexual offenders. *Psychology, Crime and Law*, *12*, 439–452.

PART TWO

Approaches to Offender Assessment

5

Sex Offender Risk-Based Case Formulation

DOUGLAS P. BOER

JO THAKKER

TONY WARD

INTRODUCTION

There are many different ways of conceptualizing a sexual offender's risk of offending and associated treatment needs. While many of the offender's treatment needs could be described as dynamic risk factors (i.e., treatment needs that, if addressed, would decrease the offender's risk), certainly there may be treatment needs unrelated to risk. Thus there is no single approach that would be considered optimal across all types of sexual offenders. Given the complexity of human nature and human behaviour this is not at all surprising; formulating and predicting risk requires a process of piecing together a large amount of multifaceted information. Of course, the same can be said for psychological case formulation generally insofar as it is necessarily a complex task. Arguably, though, formulation in the field of pre-treatment risk and treatment needs assessment is especially demanding because of its emphasis on the assessment of the likelihood of a new offence and the nature of potential future offending by the individual offender. This assessment of risk may be used in a number of contexts, including the determination of an appropriate type and length of sentence, the development of appropriate parole conditions, and treatment planning. Hence, a pre-treatment risk and needs assessment is a very important clinical task.

In this chapter we review some of the key concepts and theories that have emerged in the field of sex offender treatment and relate these to case conceptualisation. The chapter pays closer attention to the sex offender treatment and risk assessment literature,

Assessment and Treatment of Sex Offenders: A Handbook. Edited by Anthony Beech, Leam Craig and Kevin Browne. © John Wiley & Sons Ltd, 2009.

than to the formulation literature as the latter is very broad and beyond the scope of this discussion.

RELAPSE PREVENTION

One of the most widely used approaches to understanding risk for reoffending is the Relapse Prevention (RP) model developed originally for use in the substance abuse field (as outlined by Marlatt and Gordon, 1985). The concept of relapse prevention (RP) arose out of the recognition that alcohol and other substance dependencies are difficult to treat because of the enduring nature of addictions. Rates of relapse vary considerably depending on a range of factors such as, the specific substance being used, the kind of treatment employed, the population sampled and the outcome measure that is utilised (e.g., see Gossop *et al.*, 2003; Miller, Walters & Bennett, 2001). However, generally, while many individuals do well in treatment in the short term there is typically a high rate of relapse. Hence the relapse prevention model was developed as a means of fortifying treatment so that the gains made during treatment could be maintained over time.

Though recognition of the importance of preventing relapse in addictive behaviours had probably been considered previously, it was not until the 1970s that investigators began to explore the issue of relapse in depth (Connors, Maisto & Donovan, 1996; Gerwe, 2000). One of the key goals of this exploration was to identify the range of factors that lead individuals to relapse. The most well known and most commonly utilised conceptualisation of relapse is that developed by Marlatt and colleagues (e.g., Marlatt, 1979, 1985; Marlatt & George, 1984; Marlatt & Gordon, 1980). This cognitive behavioural conceptualisation sees relapse as a process that unfolds over time and which has a number of key components. The process as outlined by Marlatt (1985) centres on the notion of high-risk situations which challenge the individual's ability to cope and therefore increase the probability of relapse. Thus, relapse is seen as a result of an individual's inability to cope with a high-risk situation which leads to a reoccurrence of the addictive behaviour.

Since its introduction over 20 years ago the RP model has been very influential in the treatment of substance abuse problems and it has also been adapted for use in a range of conditions in which impulse control issues play a prominent role.

For example, it has been widely applied in the conceptualisation and treatment of gambling (e.g., Echeburua, Fernandez-Montalvo & Baez, 2000) and, perhaps most notably, in the understanding and treatment of sexual offending (e.g., Laws, Hudson & Ward, 2000; Pithers, 1990; Ward & Stewart, 2003). One of the most important changes in the way that RP is applied is that it is now commonly used as an overarching framework for the instigation of treatment proper, rather than simply a model for maintenance of change (Laws, 1995). This is in part because the factors that are understood to contribute to relapse are the same factors that contribute to the development and maintenance of the problem.

The initial model outlined by Pithers (1990) which applied RP to the field of sexual offending was very similar to the original model developed for use in the substance abuse field; it presents relapse as a linear process in which an offender moves through a number of specific phases. In a nutshell this process is as follows: After the occurrence of one or more seemingly unimportant decisions (SUDS) the offender enters a high-risk situation. If the offender is unable to cope with this situation, a lapse occurs – such as viewing pornography – followed by the Abstinence Violation Effect (AVE). The AVE may include a number of phenomena, such as internal attributions and the Problem of Immediate Gratification (quaintly referred to as the PIG). At this point there are two possible scenarios: (1) an adaptive coping response which leads to avoidance of a relapse, or (2) a maladaptive coping response which leads to a relapse. One of the key tenets of this model is that relapse is a process rather than a spontaneous event, and, furthermore, this process is seen as having a number of contiguous steps which follow a fairly predictable linear course.

So, according to the RP model, an accurate conceptualization of risk of recidivism should include an analysis of the individual's offence chain (this being the sequence of events that unfolded during a previous offence). It is hypothesised, according to the RP model that if an offender is able to develop an understanding of the offence chain, and also to learn and implement adaptive coping strategies, that the risk for re-offending will be minimised. Thus, an RP approach to formulating risk requires that the risk assessor evaluate: (1) an individual's understanding of his or her previous offending (and in particular, the chain of events that led to it), and (2) an individual's skill acquisition (in particular coping skills that will allow for an adaptive coping response).

THE SELF-REGULATION MODEL

Ward and colleagues (Ward & Hudson, 1998, 2000; Ward, Hudson & Keenan, 1998) proposed a self-regulation model (for conceptualizing sex offending) which is essentially a modification of the original RP model. The key difference between this and the original model is that the self-regulation model proposes that there are a number of possible pathways to offending (rather than simply one general pathway). The self-regulation model also allows for both planned and unplanned offending, and takes into consideration the nature of an offender's affective experiences. Hence, arguably, the self-regulation model allows for a more detailed and sophisticated account of the relapse process.

'Self-regulation' is a complex term that refers to the control of (or lack of) a range of psychological phenomena, including behaviour, emotion and cognition. Also, as noted by Cochran and Tesser (1996), goals play an important role in self-regulation theory. Hence, the self is seen as being regulated in relation to an individual's intentions and objectives. For example, a person who wishes to consume an ice cream may have a range of specific thoughts and feelings which relate to this goal and these will impact on the sequence of behaviours that takes place in relation to acquiring the ice cream. Also, certain objects or events that are in some way desirable may (somewhat paradoxically) be avoided. For instance, an individual who is dieting may think about eating an ice cream but may nonetheless resist the temptation to acquire one. Thus according to the self-regulation model there are two general types of goals: *approach* goals and *avoidance* goals (Thakker, Ward & Tidmarsh, 2006). In terms of the ice-cream example, one may have the goal of acquiring and consuming an ice cream, or of avoiding ice cream consumption. It is important to note though, that either goal can lead to eating an ice cream.

As well as the distinction between approach and avoidance goals, the pathways are further differentiated yielding a total of four separate pathways; two of which are approach and two of which are avoidant. The four pathways are defined as follows:

- Avoidant-passive (under-regulation) – This pathway closely resembles the pathway in the original RP model. Situations and events challenge an individual's coping skills leading to negative affect and subsequently deviant sexual arousal. Covert planning combined with skill deficits lead to a high-risk situation and the problem of immediate gratification and ultimately a relapse.
- Avoidant-active (mis-regulation) – This pathway closely resembles the alternative route to relapse presented in the original RP model. Situations and events directly (rather than covertly) lead to a high-risk situation. Misregulation (i.e., faulty self-regulation) is seen as driving this process. In this pathway there is a commitment to restraint, however, faulty self-regulation strategies lead to the development of a high-risk situation and loss of control.
- Approach-automatic (under-regulation) – This pathway results in relapse through little or no planning. The offence is relatively spontaneous, occurring as a result of a chance encounter combined with the problem of immediate gratification.
- Approach-explicit (intact self-regulation) – This pathway captures those offences that occur through clear intent and explicit planning. These offenders are usually aware of their goals and set out to commit an offence, often with a well-organized plan.

The central idea is that sexual reoffending is a result of a complex process, in which self-regulation plays a key role. Furthermore, as detailed above, there are various forms of self-regulation, most of which involve some sort of dysfunction. In terms of risk assessment, this model is particularly useful because it allows a more fine-grained analysis of the relapse process. This, in turn, allows for the development of a more refined understanding of the nature and level of risk that an individual may pose in terms of recidivism. So, a risk assessment that uses the self-regulation model should: (1) determine the sort of pathway and type of self-regulation that best describes the individual's previous sexual offending behaviour; (2) examine the risk factors that contributed to the behaviour; (3) assess the individual's coping strategies, including past and current approaches; (4) determine the extent to which treatment may have addressed any problems with self-regulation or coping skills; and (5) make an overall assessment of the individual's self-regulation and use this information in assessing risk of recidivism.

While the self-regulation model of relapse was developed specifically for use in understanding sexual offending, it may also be useful for assessing risk of recidivism in other sorts of offending, as a variety of offending behaviours involve issues with self-regulation, in particular violent offending. With violent offences there may be similar problems with self-regulation, such as impulsivity, and it is likely that there are also various pathways to offending which may be similarly categorized with the terms *approach* and *avoidance*. Hence, it is proposed that the self-regulation model may be used more broadly than it was originally intended.

STATIC AND DYNAMIC FACTORS

Two of the most important concepts in the field of risk assessment are the terms *static* and *dynamic*. As outlined by Craig and colleagues (Craig *et al.*, 2005) static risk factors are factors that are unchangeable and typically historical (such as gender, age and offence history) whereas dynamic risk factors are variables that are susceptible to change. As noted by Craig and his colleagues, dynamic factors can be further divided into *stable* and *acute* factors wherein stable dynamic factors are reasonably consistent over time (such as personality), and acute dynamic factors are more readily malleable (such as drug use and emotional states such as anger and depression). Typically psychological formulations of risk are structured around this distinction; risk factors are categorized according to whether they are static or dynamic. Also, there is a range of psychometric instruments that are used to assess static and dynamic factors. Thus, this distinction plays a crucial role in most contemporary formulations of risk.

Traditionally, there has been an emphasis on the use of static factors in determining an offender's risk of recidivism as the link between these factors and reoffending has received more robust empirical support (Craissati & Beech, 2003). The view that static factors provide a more accurate picture of risk has led to the development of a range of psychometric tools that focus on these unchanging variables (Craig *et al.*, 2005). However, evidence suggests that dynamic variables also play an important role and there are now also a number of tests that either focus solely on dynamic variables, or include both static and dynamic variables. For example, research indicates that treatment is effective in reducing recidivism in sexual offenders (e.g., Hanson *et al.*, 2002) and therefore an accurate risk assessment ideally needs to have the ability to take such change into consideration. As noted by Hanson *et al.* (2002) research has demonstrated that combining the consideration of both static and dynamic factors in risk assessment leads to greater accuracy in the assessment of risk.

In their review of the role of dynamic factors in the prediction of risk of sexual reoffending, Craissati and Beech (2003) examined a number of approaches to the categorization of stable dynamic factors and propose that there are "five core dynamic domains". These are:

- Intimacy deficits/social competencies – This domain refers to difficulties in intimate relationships which are frequently indicated by an absence of lasting relationships or ongoing problems in relationships. Also, a general lack of understanding of the intricacies of interpersonal relationships leads to a tendency to misinterpret victims' wishes. Often there is a propensity to experience interpersonal conflict. There are also attachment difficulties that frequently date back to childhood relationships.

- Social influences – This domain refers to the quality of an individual's social network. It may be categorised as either positive, negative, or neutral. As noted by Craig and Beech, while this variable has been demonstrated to be very important in predicting risk of recidivism for general and violent offending, there is less evidence concerning its importance in sexual recidivism. However, it should be noted that sexual offenders are frequently ostracised by their communities which can be a significant stressor.

- Pro-offending attitudes – This domain refers to the presence of attitudes and beliefs that are supportive of offending behaviour. These beliefs may include seeing children as sexual beings, and assuming that women always want sexual interaction, even when they say no. Frequently there are beliefs of entitlement that revolve around the idea that if men want sex they should be able to have sex with anyone, anywhere, anytime.

- Sexual self-regulation – This domain refers to the presence of powerful thoughts and feelings about sexual activity and the desire to seek sexual gratification in an impulsive manner. Often there is a preoccupation with sex that dominates the individual's everyday life. Also, sex may be used as an emotional regulator; the offender will have sex in order to relieve his or her negative emotional states.

- General self-regulation – This domain essentially refers to more general self-control. It includes self-monitoring of thoughts, feelings and behaviours, and the ability to plan ahead and respond constructively to challenges. Often treatment focuses on the development of risk management plans; however, some offenders struggle with the implementation of these plans.

Also important in the assessment of dynamic factors are the more rapidly changing variables, typically referred to as acute dynamic factors. As outlined by Craissati and Beech these include: substance use and abuse, negative affective states (such as depression and anxiety), anger and hostility, and opportunities for contact with victims. Other research has also included non-cooperation with supervision in this list of factors (Beech, Fisher & Thornton, 2003).

FUNCTIONAL BEHAVIOURAL ANALYSIS

A sound risk assessment should also include a detailed functional analysis of an individual's offending behaviour (Beech, Fisher & Thornton, 2003). As noted by Beech *et al.*, a functional analysis usually follows the ABC model which requires a detailed examination of antecedents, behaviours and consequences. The general idea is to include scrutiny of thoughts and feelings in this analysis in order to gain an understanding of the function of the behaviour. For example, an offence may be more likely to occur when the offender is feeling depressed and a consequence of the behaviour may be the experience of a range of positive thoughts and emotions. One of the central goals of a functional analysis is to break the offence down into a series of steps and decisions so that both the clinician and the offender can gain an understanding of how the offence unfolded over time. This is very useful in terms of assessing risk as it allows for the identification of future manifestations of risk and also maladaptive coping strategies that may increase the likelihood of reoffending.

The traditional functional behavioural assessment (FBA) contains the following primary characteristics according to Tasse and Lie (2006):

- A specific operational definition of the target behaviour(s);
- A specification of the setting events for the target behaviour(s); that is, the situational context of the behaviour(s);
- A specification of the antecedents or precipitants of the target behaviour(s); that is, the regular precursors of the behaviour(s);
- A specification of the consequences of the target behaviour(s); that is, the events that regularly follow the performance of the behaviour(s);
- Whenever possible, an experimental design that allows the manipulation of the antecedents and consequences of the behaviour(s) to illustrate the causal relationship between these components of the target behaviour(s);
- Subsequent development of functional hypotheses in regard to the target behaviour(s) and the situation in which the behaviour(s) occurred, which may lead to possible interventions to stop or alleviate the behaviour(s);
- And finally, data collection to continuously assess and revise the FBA and associated interventions.

If we operationalise risk of offending from a functional analysis point of view, we need to develop an in-depth or 'micro' analysis of the offence process and its consequences. We also cannot afford the luxury of a single subject research design that requires manipulation of the antecedents, consequences and behaviour(s) in question: that would require reoffending. However, if care is taken in the specification of the situational context and the intra-personal variables affecting the individual offender, we may approach the rigour of a repeating single subject design – especially if the offender in question has offended a number of times or a thorough description of the single offence context is available.

FUNCTIONAL OFFENCE RISK ANALYSIS

By analogy to an FBA, a functional offence risk analysis (FORA) would contain the essential components that are important in the construction of a thorough FBA of an offender's antisocial behaviour. For example, it is obvious that a thorough analysis of the observable antecedents and consequences is crucial to determining the likelihood of a new offence. However, a FORA would also contain many issues in addition to the traditional components of an FBA described earlier. For example, we would argue that the function of the offending behaviour is multiply-determined by offender-specific dynamic risk factors and self-regulatory pathways that the individual offender generally engages in offending contexts and in pursuing other goals, not only those that are offensive in nature. We would describe such individual sets of risk factors (e.g., intimacy deficits, pro-offending attitudes, depression, sexual deviance) and the interaction of these risk factors with the person's usual self-regulatory pathway (e.g., avoidant-passive, approach-explicit) as the offender's intra-personal risk variables. Further, all interpersonal and situational cues (e.g., sexual attraction, social rejection, substances, locations), which we broadly label environmental cues, will further interact with the intra-personal risk variables to give us the individual offender's risk profile. Within that risk profile, each cue, intra-personal or environmental, will hold uniquely different degrees of relevance or 'valence' for initiating sexual behaviour, whether appropriate or offensive in nature.

For example, 'depression', an acute dynamic factor, is not very often a cue for sexual offending for most depressed people, but for those individuals who offend when depressed it can clearly serve as a risk increasing function. If some dynamic risk factor such as depression increases risk for an offender it has a 'positive valence' for that person. Similarly, if an offender who has pro-offending attitudes, and for whom alcohol disinhibits an approach-explicit pathway, then the unique combination of these factors, each with positive valences in terms of risk, would be part of the FORA for this offender.

Other Variables to Consider in a Functional Offence Risk Analysis

Generally the purpose of sexually offending behaviour would seem apparent – sexual contact – but there have been many other theoretical viewpoints as to why sexual offenders commit sexual offences. Taxonomic systems (e.g., Prentky & Knight, 1990) assume that different sorts of sexual offenders commit sexual offences for different reasons or motivations. Such taxonomies are based on group analyses and may not have much relevance to the individual case. In addition to the latter issue, the literature is weak in finding distinct motivations for sexual crimes and finds instead that sexual offenders are more often generalist offenders, often offending against a variety of victims as opposed to being the specialised offenders that the taxonomic analyses assume exist (e.g., Lussier, 2005; Miethe, Olson & Mitchell, 2006). Thus, we suggest that taxonomic or descriptive systems that do not provide further insights into the offence process should not be considered as essential components of a FORA. In contrast, the pathways described earlier in this chapter add to the FORA since these pathways provide some insight into the offender's approach or avoidance strategies in a descriptive manner. Plus, any one offender can use more than one offending pathway – the pathway analysis may be different from one offence to another, by the same offender.

Another set of variables that may be considered for inclusion in a FORA are standardised psychological test results. There are a number of psychological tests that may be relevant in this regard. For example, scores on the Psychopathy Checklist-Revised (PCL-R; Hare, 1991, 2003) have been shown in a plethora of studies on a wide variety of offenders, including sexual offenders (for a review see Hare, 2003) to have a robust, reliable and linear relationship with recidivism. Another widely used psychological test is the Multiphasic Sex Inventory (MSI; Nichols & Molinder, 1984). In contrast to the PCL-R, which is 20-item rating scale filled out by the clinician, the MSI is a self-report inventory regarding rationalisations and attributions for one's offending. Langton and Marshall (2000) suggested that the MSI and other self-report measures of cognitive distortions were of limited value as assessment instruments given the transparency of the items and the MSI's lack of discriminative validity. We would argue that any sort of psychological test, regardless of its relationship to risk or its discriminative validity, is of limited value in the individualised task of completing a FORA. Further, we would contend that any test which is based on group norms says very little about individual risk issues.

The final set of variables to consider including in a FORA is that of risk assessment test results. There are many tests designed explicitly for the purpose of risk assessment of sexual offenders. The Static-99 (Hanson & Thornton, 1999) and Sexual Violence Risk-20 (Boer *et al.*, 1997) are two of the most commonly used risk assessment measures in this regard and represent, respectively, the two most common types of risk assessment tests: actuarial and structured professional judgement (SPJ) measures. Actuarial tests are constructed using group data to find the most predictive set of variables to differentially describe an existing cohort of offenders (some recidivists, some not). SPJ measures, on the other hand, use both the empirical literature and the clinical practice literature to construct a set of items to be used as guidelines in the assessment of a particular type of offender. Actuarial tests seem more prone to the arguments used in the preceding paragraph against group-normed psychological tests, whereas SPJ instruments seem more prone to the arguments used against the usefulness of taxonomic systems – too general to be applied differentially across similar sorts of offenders.

While there are academic arguments as to the relative predictive accuracy of actuarial versus SPJ instruments (e.g., de Vogel *et al.*, 2004), Boer (2006) has suggested that perhaps the best strategy at the current time is to use the best of both types of tests to produce a 'convergent' estimate of risk. A convergent risk estimate would use the actuarial results to provide a 'risk baseline' of the likelihood of a new offence, and the SPJ measure to provide an overall risk estimate in terms of other risk issues (e.g., specificity, degree of harm, imminence). However valuable the resulting risk estimation information for assessing future risk potential, we would suggest that *neither* type of test actually adds much information to a FORA, since the latter is concerned with what has *already happened*, whereas the former is concerned about what *may happen*.

DISCUSSION

In this book chapter we have described the process of functional offence risk analysis (FORA) which can be used to integrate the main tenets of relapse prevention with sexual offenders, the self-regulation model of sexual offending, static and dynamic risk factors, and functional behavioural analysis (FBA). Each FORA would combine relapse prevention issues, self-regulatory processes, unique combinations of static and dynamic factors, and relate these variables to the individual offender's offence pattern. Particular factors could have differing valences depending on the importance of the factors to the degree that the variable potentiates offending. Much like traditional FBA, FORA would examine antecedents, behaviours and consequences, along with intra-personal and situational factors, to provide an analysis of the offenders from a functional viewpoint. We feel that such information would be complementary to that achieved through traditional risk assessment via actuarial or structured professional judgement instruments.

REFERENCES

Beech, A.R., Fisher, D.D. & Thornton, D. (2003). Risk assessment of sex offenders. *Professional Psychology: Research and Practice, 34,* 339–352.

Boer, D.P. (2006). Sexual offender risk assessment strategies: is there a convergence of opinion yet? *Sexual Offender Treatment, 1,* 1–4.

Boer, D.P., Hart, S.D., Kropp, P.R. & Webster, C.D. (1997). *Manual for the Sexual Violence Risk –20: Professional guidelines for assessing risk of sexual violence.* Vancouver, BC: The Mental Health, Law, and Policy Institute.

Cochran, W. & Tesser, A. (1996). The 'what the hell' effect: Some effects of goal proximity and goal framing on performance. In L.L. Martin & A. Tesser (Eds), *Striving and feeling: Interactions among goals, affect, and self-regulation.* New York: Lawrence Erlbaum.

Connors, G.J., Maisto, S.A. & Donovan, D.M. (1996). Conceptualizations of relapse: A summary of psychological and psychobiological models. *Addiction, 91,* s5–s13.

Craig, L.A., Browne, K.D., Stringer, I. & Beech, A. (2005). Sexual recidivism: A review of static, dynamic and actuarial predictors. *Journal of Sexual Aggression, 11,* 65–84.

Craissati, J. & Beech, A. (2003). A review of dynamic variables and their relationship to risk prediction in sex offenders. *Journal of Sexual Aggression, 9,* 41–55.

deVogel, V., de Ruiter, C., van Beek, D. & Mead, G. (2004). Predictive validity of the SVR-20 and Static-99 in a Dutch sample of treated sex offenders. *Law and Human Behavior, 28,* 235–251.

Echeburua, E., Fernandez-Montalvo, J. & Baez, C. (2000). Relapse prevention in the treatment of slot-machine pathological gambling: Long-term outcome. *Behavior Therapy, 31,* 351–364.

Gerwe, C.F. (2000). Chronic addiction relapse treatment: A study of the effectiveness of the high-risk identification and prediction treatment model. Part 1. *Journal of Substance Abuse Treatment, 19,* 415–427.

Gossop, M., Marsden, J., Stewart, D. & Kidd, T. (2003). The national treatment outcome research study (NTORS): 4–5year follow-up results. *Addiction, 98,* 291–303.

Hanson, R.K. & Thornton, D. (1999). *Static-99: Improving actuarial risk assessments for sex offenders.* (User report No.1999-02.) Ottawa: Department of the Solicitor General of Canada.

Hanson, R.K., Gordon, A., Harris, A.J.R. *et al.* (2002). First report of the collaborative outcome data project on the effectiveness of psychological treatment for sex offenders. *Sexual Abuse: A Journal of Research and Treatment, 14,* 169–194.

Hare, R.D. (1991). *Manual for the Hare Psychopathy Checklist-Revised.* Toronto, Ontario: Multi-Health Systems.

Hare, R.D. (2003). *Hare PCL-R* (2nd edn). New York: Multi-Health Systems.

Langton, C.M. & Marshall, W.L. (2000). The role of cognitive distortions in relapse prevention programs. In D.R. Laws, S.M. Hudson & T. Ward (Eds), *Remaking Relapse Prevention with Sex Offenders: A Sourcebook* (pp. 167–186). Thousand Oaks: Sage.

Laws, D.R. (1995). A theory of relapse prevention. In W. O'Donohue & L. Krasner (Eds), *Theories of behavior therapy: Exploring behavior change* (pp. 445–473). Washington DC: American Psychological Association.

Lussier, P. (2005). The criminal activity of sexual offenders in adulthood: revisiting the specialization debate. *Sexual Abuse: A Journal of Research and Treatment, 17,* 269–292.

Marlatt, G.A. (1979). Alcohol use and problem drinking: A cognitive behavioral analysis. In P.C. Kendall & S.D. Hollon (Eds), *Cognitive-behavioral interventions: Theory, research and procedures* (pp. 319–355). New York: Academic Press.

Marlatt, G.A. (1985). Relapse prevention: Theoretical rationale and overview of the model. In G.A. Marlatt & J.R. Gordon (Eds), *Relapse prevention: Maintenance strategies in the treatment of addictive behaviors* (pp. 3–70). New York: Guilford.

Marlatt, G.A. & George, W.H. (1984). Relapse prevention: Introduction and overview of the model. *British Journal of Addiction, 79,* 261–273.

Marlatt G.A. & Gordon, J.R. (1980). Determinants of relapse: Implications for the maintenance of behavior change. In P.O. Davidson & S.M. Davidson (Eds), *Behavioral medicine: Changing health lifestyles* (pp. 410–452). New York: Brunner/Mazel.

Marlatt, G.A. & Gordon, J.R. (1985). *Relapse prevention: Maintenance strategies in the treatment of addictive behaviors.* New York: Guilford.

Miethe, T.D., Olson, J. & Mitchell, O. (2006). Specialization and persistence in the arrest histories of sex offenders: a comparative analysis of alternative measures and offense types. *Journal of Research in Crime and Delinquency, 43,* 204–229.

Miller, W.R., Walters, S.T. & Bennett, M.E. (2001). How effective is alcoholism treatment in the United States? *Journal of Studies on Alcohol, 62,* 211–220.

Nichols, H.R. & Molinder, I. (1984). *Multi-phasic sex inventory.* Fircrest, WA: Nichols and Molinder Assessments.

Pithers, W.D. (1990). Relapse prevention with sexual aggressors: A method for maintaining therapeutic gain and enhancing external supervision. In M.L. Marshall, D.R. Laws & H.E. Barbaree (Eds), *Handbook of sexual assault: Issues, theories, and treatment of the offender* (pp. 343–361). New York, NY: Plenum Press.

Prentky, R.A. & Knight, R.A. (1990). Classifying sexual offenders: The development and corroboration of taxonomic models. In W.L. Marshall, D.R. Laws & H.E. Barbaree (Eds), *Handbook of sexual assault: Issues, theories, and treatment of the offender* (pp. 23–52). New York: Plenum.

Tasse, M.J. & Lie, D. (2006). Functional behavioural assessment in people with intellectual disabilities (mental retardation and developmental disorders). *Current Opinion in Psychiatry, 19,* 475–480.

Thakker, J., Ward, T. & Tidmarsh, P. (2006). A re-evaluation of relapse prevention theory in the treatment and risk management of adolescents who sexually offend: A good lives model. In H.E. Barbaree & W.L. Marshall (Eds), *The Juvenile Sex Offender* (pp. 313–335). New York: Guilford Press.

Ward, T. & Hudson, S.M. (1998). A model of the relapse process in sexual offenders. *Journal of Interpersonal Violence, 13,* 400–425.

Ward, T. & Hudson, S.M. (2000). A self-regulation model of relapse prevention. In D.R. Laws, S.M. Hudson & T. Ward (Eds), *Remaking relapse prevention with sex offenders: A sourcebook* (pp. 79–101). Thousand Oaks: Sage.

Ward, T., Hudson, S.M. & Keenan, T. (1998). A self-regulation model of the offense process. *Sexual Abuse: A Journal of Research and Treatment, 10,* 141–157.

Ward, T. & Stewart, C. (2003). The relationship between human needs and criminogenic needs. *Psychology, Crime and Law, 9,* 219–224.

6

Psychometric Assessment of Sexual Deviance

LEAM A. CRAIG

ANTHONY R. BEECH

INTRODUCTION

Psychometric measures are widely used to assess psychological constructs in sexual offenders; however, few of these measures have been empirically tested for their risk assessment and psychometric properties. For a psychological test to be useful it must have been standardised on the population it is to be used with and provide normative data by which an individual can be compared. This allows comparison between the subject and the study population so that judgements can be made as to how closely the subject's score relates to the mean. Standardisation has two elements: first the need to obtain information on the test scores of the general population by taking appropriate samples, and second the need to obtain a set of principles by which raw data from the test can be transformed to give a set of data which has a normal distribution. The latter becomes particularly important if the scores are to be subject to statistical analysis (Rust & Golombok, 1989). One of the difficulties in using many tests is that they frequently lack standardisation with appropriate norms which makes any comparisons questionable. Crucial to the process of standardising psychometric tests is the sample from which the norms are to be taken. However, many tests used to measure constructs in sexual offenders have been standardised on samples of college samples (for example, the Nowicki-Strickland Internal-External Locus of Control Scale; Nowicki, 1976). Fisher, Beech and Browne (1999) point out that apart from the problem of standardisation is the question of how valid a sample is. For example, to what extent can a sample of college students, as a normed sample, compare with a sample of sexual offenders, as the two samples may differ on social class, etc. A further consideration when using psychometric measures relates to the characteristics of the

Assessment and Treatment of Sex Offenders: A Handbook. Edited by Anthony Beech, Leam Craig and Kevin Browne. © John Wiley & Sons Ltd, 2009.

sample from which the test was standardised. Where specific groups are being sampled, a sample size of many hundreds is usually considered to be the norm (Kline, 1986).

Having normative data on measures used to assess attitudes, values and beliefs of sexual offenders is crucial to the assessment of treatment need and risk, and includes a wide range of psychological constructs. The purpose of this chapter is to review the different psychometric tests used to assess sexual offenders' problems and to examine to what extent such measures are useful in predicting risk and treatment need in sexual offenders.

PSYCHOMETRIC ASSESSMENT OF PSYCHOLOGICAL FUNCTIONING IN SEX OFFENDERS

A number of psychometric tests have been developed to measure various aspects of psychological functioning such as self-esteem, locus of control, emotional loneliness, empathy-taking skills and pro-sexual assault attitudes. However, a criticism of some of the measures is that they are too transparent (for example, the Abel and Becker Cognitive Distortions Scale; Abel *et al.*, 1984) and therefore raise the question as to whether it is possible to construct an unbiased scale (Langevin, 1991).

One of the more widely used psychometric measures used to assess psychosexual characteristics in sexual offenders is the Multiphasic Sex Inventory (MSI; Nichols & Molinder, 1984). The MSI is a psychometric measure specially designed to assess psychosexual characteristics of sexual offenders (rapists, child molesters, exhibitionists). The MSI provides information that is independent of personality and psychopathology tests and has been found to provide data that corroborates with physiological indices of arousal (Bernard *et al.*, 1989). It is used in more than 1,400 hospitals, clinics and agencies in the assessment of sexual offenders (Nichols & Molinder, 1984), across several different countries (Beech, Fisher & Beckett, 1999; Dowling *et al.*, 2000; Miner *et al.*, 1990). The MSI reflects Nichols and Molinder's (1984) conceptual framework of sexual offenders' motivations, appetites, interests and desires, and behavioural characteristics. The MSI is a 300-item self-report questionnaire that produces six types of scales:

1. **Validity Scales**
   Social/Sexual Desirability, which measures 'normal' sex drives and interests and identifies whether clients are responding in a socially desirable way;
   Sexual Obsession, which measures an offender's obsession with sex, and any tendency to exaggerate his problems; and
   Lie Scale, which measures the extent of denial and minimisation.
2. **Accountability Scales**
   Cognitive Distortions and Immaturity, which addresses the extent to which an offender adopts a victim stance in relationship to his present offence and measures levels of accountability accepted for offending behaviour;
   Justification (use of) which examines the various justifications sexual offenders may use to explain their offences; and

Attitude to Treatment, which measures the offender's attitudes to treatment for his sexual offending.

3. **Sexual Deviance Scales** (Child Molest – Gender, Rape and Exhibitionism) which assess the concept that a sex offender goes through an identifiable cognitive and behavioural progression leading up to a sexual offence. The sex offender's cognitions follow a path, beginning with the thought or fantasy of committing a sexual assault (antecedent thought), through a series of self-justifying positions on to planning and executing the assault. This scale assesses the style, magnitude and duration of sexually deviant behaviour.

4. **Paraphilias** (Atypical Sexual Outlet) **Scales** which comprise five subtests: 'fetishes', 'voyeurism', 'obscene call', 'bondage/discipline' and 'sado-masochistic' and measure the uniqueness and individuality of the offenders' sexuality and offending behaviour.

5. **Sexual Dysfunction Scales** which comprise four subtests: sexual inadequacies, premature ejaculation, physical disabilities and impotence.

6. **The Sex Knowledge and Beliefs Scale** which measure the offender's knowledge of sexual anatomy and physiology, but not reproductive systems. The protocol also considers sexual history of the offenders; Sex Deviance Development, Marriage Development, Gender Identity Development, Gender Orientation Development and Sex Assault Behaviour List.

The MSI scales have been shown to predict between 30% and 47% of treatment variance and are able to differentiate between treatment outcomes (success vs. failure) with 70% accuracy (Simkins *et al.*, 1989). Simkins *et al.* administered the MSI to 122 sex offenders and a factor analysis of the scale scores revealed four distinct factors: *Assault, Sexual Fantasy, Denial/Dysfunction* and *Normal*. The *Assault* factor was significantly correlated with all treatment outcome variables and also accounted for the largest proportion of variance when the MSI factor scores were entered into stepwise multiple regression analyses. However, the factors they extracted were not pure as many items loaded on more than one factor. That is to say, several scales were loaded onto more than one factor.

Few psychometric instruments have proved to be as reliable and accurate measures of psychosexual functioning as that of the MSI. Kalichman *et al.* (1992) found that only 30% of the variance in the MSI scales could be accounted for by the Minnesota Multiphasic Personality Inventory (MMPI), suggesting that many psychosexual characteristics are independent of personality. Kalichman *et al.* administered the MSI and MMPI to 248 rapists and found that the MSI Rape, Paraphilia and Cognitive Distortions and Immaturity scales distinguished between five empirically derived groups of rapists. Haywood *et al.* (1994) compared fake-good and fake-bad orientations on the MMPI with psychological distortion on the MSI in 59 alleged child abusers. They found that distortion on the MSI indices of minimisation and exaggeration was significantly associated with response-bias on the MMPI. Cognitive-distortion indices were highly influenced by response-bias where respondents attempt to present in favourable light minimising any negative psychological aspects. Geer *et al.* (2001) examined what factors increased the likelihood of treatment completion in sex offenders. Using the MSI-II (Nichols & Molinder, 2000), MMPI and the Abel and Becker Sexual Interest Card Sort, they found that it was possible to predict which sex offenders are likely to complete a prison-based sex offender treatment programme.

While the MSI is routinely used by sex offender treatment programmes to identify treatment need and assess cognitive shift, there are few studies in the literature that examine the risk assessment properties of the MSI in predicting sexual recidivism. Craig *et al.* (2006) administered the MSI to a 119 sexual offenders followed up to an average of 106 months. Here, sexual recidivists were compared to non-recidivists and it was found that the sexual recidivists obtained significantly higher scores on Sexual Social Desirability, Cognitive Distortions and Immaturity, Attitudes to Treatment and Rape interest scales compared to non-recidivists.

Craig *et al.* subjected the MSI to a confirmatory factor analysis Varimax rotated based on the resultant four-factor solution identified by Simkins *et al.* (1989). This revealed a four-factor structure of the MSI: *Sexual Deviance, Sexual Desirability, Dysfunction/Justification* and *Normal.* When the predictive accuracy of the MSI scales and factor structure was examined, Craig *et al.* found that the Sexual Obsessions (Area under the Curve (AUC)[1] = .85), Child Molest (AUC = .74), Rape (AUC = .74) and the Paraphilia (AUC = .74) scales obtained good predictive accuracy at two-year follow-up. The *Sexual Deviance* factor performed well in predicting sexual reconviction over a two-year period (AUC = .78). However, the *Normal* factor was a poor predictor of sexual reconviction and the *Justification* factor obtained moderate predictive results. As for comparing static and dynamic risk assessment (see Chapter 4), this study used the actuarial scale Static-99 (Hanson & Thornton, 2000) which obtained moderate effect in predicting sexual reconviction at two years (AUC = .67), with a non-significant effect at five (AUC = .61) and ten-year (AUC = .62) follow-up periods. The *Sexual Deviance* factor made a statistically significant contribution independent of Static-99 at both two years and five years follow-up.

PSYCHOMETRIC ASSESSMENT OF PERSONALITY TRAITS IN SEX OFFENDERS

Other psychometric measures that are routinely used in forensic settings include personality inventories (Blackburn, 1982; Quinnella & Bow, 2001). The use of such

---

[1]The Area Under the Curve (AUC) of the Receiver Operating Characteristic (ROC) analysis is the preferred analysis used to measure the predictive accuracy of a scale. This analysis plots the data points and compares the *sensitivity* or 'hit rate' (the percentage of reoffenders correctly identified as high risk on assessment) with *specificity* (the percentage of non-reoffenders correctly identified as low risk). A perfectly accurate test would yield a ROC hit rate of 1.0 (no overlap between recidivists and non-recidivists) and .50 indicating prediction no better than chance. Graphically represented, the 'curve' for a perfect test would travel up the vertical axis then along the top of the box until it reaches the top right-hand corner, where as a diagonal line (i.e., useless test) is .50.

inventories reflects higher prevalence of personality disorders in forensic (Metzner *et al.*, 1998) and psychiatric settings (Wise, 2001). Indeed, in a review of the literature, Metzner *et al.* (1998) reported the presence of personality disorders in prison ranged from 8% to 47% (M = 23%). Personality disorders associated with offending have been well established with particular regard to traits of antisocial personality disorder (Firestone *et al.*, 1998; Glover *et al.*, 2002) and psychopathy (Buffington-Vollum *et al.*, 2002; Hare *et al.*, 2000; Långström & Grann, 2002) as measured by the Psychopathy Checklist-Revised (PCL-R) (Hare, 1991).

A number of studies have found differences between sexual and non-sexual offenders in their personality and offence characteristics. Gudjonsson and Sigurdsson (2000) found that sexual offenders were significantly more introverted than violent offenders, tended to assault relatives and friends while violent offenders assaulted strangers, and obtained higher social desirability scores than the other groups. Rapists and violent offenders were more commonly intoxicated during the commission of the offence. Compared to violent offenders, sex offenders exhibited more schizoid, obsessive-compulsive and avoidant traits, and fewer antisocial traits (Fazel *et al.*, 2002).

Chantry and Craig (1994) reported that sexual offenders tended to be more passive, submissive and lacking in initiative than other offender groups, and aggressive offenders displayed more ego-centred, grandiose and narcissistic traits than did sexual offenders. Langevin *et al.* (1988), however, found that, although sex offenders showed more personality pathology compared to other offender groups, there were few differences within sex offender groups. Curnoe and Langevin (2002) divided 228 sex and non-sex offender controls into two groups, based on the presence or absence of deviant sexual fantasies. Using the Minnesota Multiphasic Personality Inventory-2 (MMPI-2), Butcher *et al.* (1989) found that those with deviant fantasies had more clinically significant scores on the F scale (used to help identify exaggeration of psychological problems in psychiatric, forensic and neuropsychological settings), Psychopathic Deviate, Masculinity-Femininity, Paranoia and Schizophrenia scales compared to those without deviant fantasies.

In contrast to the more traditionally used personality inventories, the Special Hospitals Assessment of Personality and Socialisation (SHAPS; Blackburn, 1982) has been subject to a few validation studies most of which have centred on assessments of mentally disordered offenders and psychopathy (Blackburn, 1986) in the UK. The SHAPS was designed for use with the English institutionalised populations and is drawn from the MMPI, the Buss-Durkee Hostility Inventory (BDHI; Buss & Durkee, 1957) and the Peterson-Quay-Cameron Psychopathy scale (PQC; Peterson, Quay & Cameron, 1959), and is a self-report assessment consisting of 213 items and is divided into 10 scales.

1. The *Lie* scale is one of the standard MMPI scales and while it measures defensive denial, it is not necessarily an indication of lying. High scores on this scale sometimes represent deliberate suppression of personal characteristics, lacking 'insight', lack of openness to experience or a coping style characterised by restricted reality testing and avoidance or distorting information. This scale is

theoretically part of the 'over-controlled' personality (Megargee, 1966). The test-retest reliability of this scale .76 (Blackburn, 1982).

2. The *Anxiety* scale was developed through factor analysis and items refer to worry, tension and proneness to dysphoric mood. The internal reliability (KR 20) of this scale is .92 and test-retest reliability of this scale .83 (Blackburn, 1982).

3. The MMPI *Extraversion* scale was derived empirically (Giedt & Downing, 1961). The scale splits into two independent clusters of social Extraversion and Impulsivity. The internal reliability and test-retest reliability of this scale .74 (Blackburn, 1982).

4. The *Hostility* scale reflects extra-punitive attitudes, mistrust of others, particularly authority figures, and beliefs in harmful influence by others. It also indicates a lack of self-criticism and a tendency to project blame. The internal reliability of this scale is .86 and test-retest reliability .83 (Blackburn, 1982).

5. The *Introversion* scale measures 'neurotic introversion' and is highly correlated with the MMPI Social Introversion scale. The test-retest reliability of this scale .88 (Blackburn, 1982).

6. The *Depression* scale relates to a proneness to apathy, dysphoric mood and depression. The test-retest reliability of this scale .74 (Blackburn, 1982).

7. Derived by Stein (1968) the *Tension* scale measures proneness to worry, and tension expressed somatically. The test-retest reliability of this scale .76 (Blackburn, 1982).

8. The *Psychopathic Deviate* scale is another standard MMPI scale and taps such aspects as family conflict, history of illegal or delinquent behaviour and lack of sensitivity to others, and paradoxically contains items relating to poor self-esteem and guilt. It has consistently been shown to discriminate between criminal and non-criminal populations. Blackburn considers this scale as a measure of undersocialisation or rejection of conventional standards. The test-retest reliability of this scale .62 (Blackburn, 1982).

9. The *Impulsivity* scale was derived from a factor analysis of MMPI items (Blackburn, 1971) and appears to measure attributes held to identify the psychopath (lack of affective control, easily aroused anger and thrill-seeking behaviour). It measures primarily awareness and acceptance of sexual and aggressive impulses rather than motor disinhibition. It correlates with unconventional values, sensation-seeking, interview ratings of psychopathy, history of aggressive offences and greater variety of offences (Blackburn, 1973), and has been shown to discriminate recidivists from first time offenders (Como, 1977). Internal reliability was shown to be .84 (Cronbach's alpha) in 238 adult males (Blackburn & Fawcett, 1999) and the test-retest reliability .72 (Blackburn, 1982).

10. The *Aggression* scale resulted from a factor analysis of several scales related to hostility and aggression (Blackburn, 1974) and reflects easily aroused anger, irritability, a tendency to engage in both verbal and physical aggression and a view of the self as dominant and rebellious (Blackburn, 1982). The test-retest reliability of this scale .67 (Blackburn, 1982).

Factor analysis of the SHAPS yielded two main factors (Blackburn, 1979): *Psychopathy* or *Antisocial Aggression* (measuring Impulsivity, Aggression, Hostility and Low Denial); and *Withdrawal* (measuring social Anxiety and proneness to Mood Disorder). In developing the SHAPS from the MMPI, Blackburn (1971) identified four clusters of antisocial/asocial personality; withdrawal and under-controlled personalities. He later categorised the four clusters displaying some of the traits of psychopathy (1975, 1986). *Primary* psychopaths (Type I) described as highly extroverted, lacking remorse, impulsive, aggressive and non-neurotic; *Secondary* (neurotic) psychopaths (Type II) described as withdrawn, anxious, introverted, impulsive, aggressive, resentful, under-socialised and prone to feelings of guilt; [Over] *Controlled* individuals (Type III) described as showing defensive characteristics indicating denial; and *Inhibited* individuals (Type IV) described as withdrawn, introverted, depressed with little aggression or impulsivity.

In one of the few studies to use the SHAPS with sexual offenders, Craig *et al.* (2004) administered the measure to 121 sexual and violent offenders followed up over two-, five- and ten-year periods. Of the sample, 15 (12%) offenders were reconvicted of a sexual offence, 16 (13%) reoffended violently and 25 (21%) reoffended in a general (non-sexual/non-violent) manner over the follow-up period. Over the follow-up periods, the SHAPS Impulsivity scale consistently obtained the highest AUC (.62, .70 and .71) for predicting general reconviction, and AUC of .65, .70 and .71 for violent reconviction over two-, five- and ten-year periods. However, it was found that none of the SHAPS scales predicted sexual reconviction. This is consistent with previous studies where it has been argued that sexual offending is independent of personality (Barbaree *et al.*, 2001; Sjöstedt & Långström, 2002).

ASSESSMENT OF THE CONSTRUCT OF 'SEXUAL DEVIANCY'

Common amongst sex offender treatment programmes are targets for change including pro-offending attitudes (e.g., perceiving children as sexual beings, lack of insight, cognitive distortions), and socio-affective deficits (e.g., under-assertiveness, low self-esteem and emotional loneliness). A number of psychometric measures and systems of assessment have been developed to assess targets for change in sexual offenders. Two systems in the UK have been developed that look at stable-dynamic, 'need' factors. The Sex Offender Treatment Evaluation Project (STEP) test battery (Beech *et al.*, 1999) used by the Probation Services in England and Wales to measure 'Deviancy' in child abusers and the Initial Deviance Assessment (IDA) from Thornton's (2002) Structured Risk Assessment model for use with sex offenders in the English and Welsh Prison Service. Although these systems were developed in the UK it can be argued that they have direct relevance to clinicians in other countries as they represent a significant advance in the development of more sophisticated risk assessment protocols (Beech *et al.*, 2003).

The deviancy construct in the STEP test battery was developed by Beech (1998) who classified child abusers according to their levels of problems on a battery of psychometric measures. The two main types of abusers identified using this system were termed *High Deviancy* and *Low Deviancy* in terms of the differences between groups on psychometric measures.

High Deviancy child abusers are defined as having a high level of treatment need as measured by high levels of pro-offending attitudes and social adequacy problems. In terms of pro-offending attitudes, Fisher *et al.* (1999) found that High Deviancy child abusers had significantly higher levels of distorted attitudes about children and sex than non-offenders. This group showed significantly poorer empathy for victims of sexual abuse than non-offenders. Other significant differences between high deviancy and non-offending men indicate that they report difficulty in forming intimate adult attachments, while perceiving their emotional needs could be better met by interacting with children than adults. The High Deviancy group were also found to be significantly more under-assertive and to have significantly lower levels of self-esteem than non-offenders. Beech (1998) reported that *Deviancy* tended to be associated with specific demographic factors. High deviancy offenders had, in general, many victims, were quite likely to have been convicted for a previous sexual offence(s), were more likely to have abused males or both males and females, and to have offended outside, or both inside and outside, the family.

Low Deviancy child abusers appear to have lower level treatment need than High Deviancy men. Although the Low Deviancy group show poor empathy for victims of sexual assault, they did not show globalised cognitive distortions about children nor did they show the high levels of emotional identification with children seen in High Deviancy offenders. Indeed, this emotional identification with children in this group was found to be significantly lower than non-offender controls (Fisher *et al.*, 1999). It was argued this result probably contributed, in part, to their denial about future risk to children. The Low Deviancy group also showed significantly higher levels of social adequacy problems than non-offenders, although this was not as marked as in the High Deviancy group. Beech (1998) found that low deviancy men were much more likely to have committed offences against one or two victims within the family.

These results indicate that not only did the psychometric responses differ between the two deviancy classifications but the groups also differed in terms of offence history. Compared to Low Deviancy men, High Deviancy offenders were found to have significantly more victims, were more likely to have a previous conviction for a sexual offence, were more likely to have committed offences outside the family, and were more likely to have committed offences against boys. In contrast, Low Deviancy men were found significantly more likely to be incest offenders and commit offences against girls. It has been argued that the High Deviancy/Low Deviancy distinction is simply a renaming of distinctions previously articulated in the literature i.e., fixated versus regressed (Groth, 1978); preferential versus situational (Howell, 1981); or high versus low fixation (Knight & Prentky, 1990). However, it should be noted that nearly a third of the men who would be identified as regressed or situational perpetrators in such classification (which would by definition be treated as low risk) were classified as High Deviancy. Further support for the psychological differences between the two deviancy classifications was reported by Beech *et al.* (1999) who found that High Deviancy child abusers require twice as many hours of treatment (160 hours) than do Low Deviancy child abusers (80 hours) to show 'treatment effect'.

Expanding on the Beech classification system, an alternative approach to structuring risk-related information in sexual offenders can be seen in the Structured Risk Assessment (SRA; Thornton, 2002) model. The SRA is a research-guided multi-step framework for assessing the risk presented by a sex offender and provides a systematic way of going beyond static risk classification. The full scheme covers static assessment and an Initial Deviance Assessment (IDA), an evaluation of progress based on treatment response, and risk management based on offence specialisation and acute risk factors. Thornton argues that combining the psychological factors identified in the IDA with static assessment allows better predictive accuracy than using static assessment alone. The Initial Deviancy Assessment (IDA) itself considers empirically derived dynamic psychological and behavioural factors. Deviance is defined in terms of the extent to which the offender's functioning is dominated by the psychological factors that contribute to his offending.

It is postulated the main dynamic risk factors fall into four domains: *Sexual Interests*, *Distorted Attitudes*, *Social and Emotional Functioning*, and *Self-Management* – here high deviancy means that the dynamic risk factors underlying offending are relatively intense and pervasive (Thornton, 2002). These are based on potentially changeable, but relatively stable psychological factors, organised into four domains, which are currently comprehensively assessed in the UK using the Structured Assessment of Risk and Need (SARN; Webster *et al.*, 2007) to assess a sexual offender's risk, need and progress in treatment (see Table 6.1). We will now briefly examine the thinking behind Thornton's ideas.

Domain 1 – Sexual Interests

This domain refers to both the direction and strength of sexual interests and considers offence-related sexual preferences and sexual preoccupation, both factors identified as predictive of sexual recidivism (Hanson & Bussière, 1998; Hanson & Morton-Bourgon, 2005; Pithers *et al.*, 1988; Proulx *et al.*, 1999).

Domain 2 – Distorted Attitudes

This domain refers to sets of beliefs about offences, sexuality or victims that can be used to justify sexual offending behaviour. Denial or minimisation of a particular offence is not considered relevant unless it can be linked to more general attitudes. Distorted beliefs in sexual offenders are well supported within the literature (Beech *et al.*, 1999; Hanson & Harris, 2000; Hanson & Scott, 1995; Pithers *et al.*, 1988; Ward *et al.*, 1995) as offence precursors consistent in both child abusers (Beech *et al.*, 1999; Hanson & Scott, 1995) and rapists (Hanson & Scott, 1995;

Table 6.1 Dynamic risk factors of SARN by domain

Domain/risk factor title	Brief description of risk factor
Sexual interests domain	
Sexual preoccupation	An obsession with sex so that sex is an unusually salient activity.
Sexual preference for children	A preference for sexual activity with pre-pubescent children over adults.
Sexualised violence	A preference for coerced sex rather than consenting sex.
Other offence-related sexual interest	Any other socially deviant sexual interest, which seemed to play a crucial role in committing the offence.
Distorted attitudes domain	
Adversarial sexual attitudes	A view of heterosexual relationships where the male is seen as dominant and the female as submissive.
Sexual entitlement	The egocentric belief that if a man desires sex, he is entitled to have it.
Child abuse supportive beliefs	Beliefs that justify sexual activity with children or minimise the seriousness of such offending.
Rape-supportive beliefs	Beliefs that justify or excuse rape of adult women.
Women are deceitful beliefs	Beliefs that women are deceptive, corruptive or exploitative.
Social and emotional functioning domain	
Inadequacy	Subjective feelings of loneliness, low self-esteem and an external locus of control.
Distorted intimacy balance	Preferring to meet emotional intimacy needs through relationships with children rather than adults.
Grievance thinking	A thinking style characterised by suspiciousness, anger, vengefulness and a failure to see others' point of view.
Lack of emotional intimacy	Failure to achieve emotionally intimate adult relationships, whether desired or not.
Self-management domain	
Lifestyle impulsiveness	A pattern of making impulsive and irresponsible decisions.
Poor problem solving	Failure to employ cognitive skills to solve life problems.
Poor emotional control	Uncontrolled outbursts of emotion.

Malamuth & Brown, 1994). Consistent with this, Hanson and Morton-Bourgon's (2005) meta-analysis found denial and minimisation unrelated to sexual recidivism, while more general attitudes tolerant of sexual crime were associated with sexual recidivism.

Domain 3 – Social and Emotional Functioning

This domain refers to the ways of relating to other people and to motivating emotions felt in the context of these interactions. Negative emotional states such as anxiety, depression and low self-esteem (Pithers *et al.*, 1988; Proulx *et al.*, 1999), and especially anger (Hanson & Harris, 2000), have been found to be offence precursors. Factors such as low self-esteem, loneliness and external locus of control seem to distinguish child abusers from comparison groups (Beech *et al.*, 1999). Meta-analytical results support the relevance of emotional congruence/emotional over-identification with children and to a lesser extent hostility as being important factors related to recidivism (Hanson & Morton-Bourgon, 2005).

Domain 4 – Self-Management

This domain refers to an individual's ability to plan, problem solve and regulate dysfunctional impulses that might otherwise lead to relapse (Pithers *et al.*, 1988; Ward, Hudson & Keenan, 1998). Antisocial behaviour and lifestyle impulsivity have been identified as precursors of sexual reoffending (Prentky & Knight, 1991). Thornton likens this construct to that of Factor 2 in the PCL-R (Hare, 1991) which has been found to predict sexual recidivism (Firestone *et al.*, 1999; Rice & Harris, 1997).

Beech *et al.* (2003) have suggested that a psychometric measure can be employed to assess each of Thornton's risk domains as shown in Table 6.2.

EXAMINING THE PREDICTIVE ACCURACY OF DEVIANCE DOMAINS

Thornton (2002) compared offenders with previous convictions for child abuse (*Repeat offenders*) against men who had been convicted for child sexual offences for the first time (*Current only*). *Repeat offenders* tended to score more highly on indicators of distorted attitudes, and obtained poorer scores on the socio-affective functioning and poorer self-management than the *Current only* group.

While Thornton and Beech (2002) examined the extent to which psychological deviance and sexual recidivism interact with Static-99 (Hanson & Thornton, 2000). They compared the accuracy of the deviancy assessments and Static-99 on two samples of sex offenders; 121 male adult sex offenders assessed prior to participating in a brief cognitive-behavioural prison programme in England and Wales (as reported by Thornton, 2002), and 53 male adult sex offenders assessed prior to participating in a brief community treatment programme (Beech *et al.*, 2002). Thornton and Beech combined psychometric data from the two samples to approximate the four deviancy domains reported in Table 6.1. They found the Number of Dysfunctional Domains obtained moderate accuracy in predicting sexual recidivism, (Area Under the Curve [AUC] ranging from .83 to .85) compared with Static-99 (AUC ranging

Table 6.2 Psychometric measures used to assess deviancy domains

Domains	Psychometric Measures
Sexual interests	The Sexual Obsessions Scale of the Multiphasic Sex Inventory (MSI; Nichols & Molinder, 1984)
Distorted attitudes	The Justifications Scale of the MSI The Abel and Becker Cognitions Scale (Abel *et al.*, 1984) The Bumby RAPE and MOLEST scales (Bumby, 1996) The Children and Sex: Cognitive Distortions Scale (Beckett, 1987) Burt Rape Scales (including rape myths, adversarial sexual attitudes, acceptance of interpersonal violence against women, sex role stereotyping) (Burt, 1980) Hostility towards women scale (Check, 1984)
Social and emotional functioning	The Children and Sex: Emotional Congruence Scale (Beckett, 1987) The UCLA Loneliness scale (Russell, Peplau & Cutrona, 1980) Thornton Self-Esteem Questionnaire (Thornton, 1989; Webster *et al.*, 2007) The Underassertivenss/Aggressiveness scales of the Social Response Inventory (Keltner, Marshall & Marshall, 1981) The Nowicki-Strickland Internal-External Locus of Control Scale (Nowicki, 1976) The Novaco Anger Scale (Novaco, 1975) The Dissipation-Rumination Scale (Caprara, 1986) Hypermasculinity Inventory (including calloused sexual attitudes (Mosher & Sirkin, 1984)
Self-management	The PCL-R (Hare, 1991) Factor 2 – which measures lifestyle impulsivity The Barratt Impulsivity Scale (BIS-II; Barratt, 1994) Emotion Control Questionnaire (Roger & Najarian, 1989) The Porteus Mazes (Porteus, 1955)

from .91 to .75). In both samples the number of dysfunctional domains made a statistically significant independent contribution to prediction over and above Static-99 risk category. Analysis of the combined samples confirmed that Static-99 and the Number of Dysfunctional Domains allowed better prediction than either factor alone.

Craig *et al.* (2007) recently considered the effectiveness of psychometric markers of risk in approximating the deviancy domains described in the SRA model and how these measures of dynamic risk could be used to predict sexual reconviction compared with actuarial risk scales. They administered the MSI and SHAPS to 119 sexual offenders. Four of the MSI scales and six of the SHAPS scales were selected on the basis of theoretical relevance to the four domains. The scales used to approximate the four domains were as follows:

1. Sexual Interests:	MSI Sexual Obsession
	MSI Paraphilia
2. Distorted Attitudes:	MSI Cognitive Distortions and Immaturity
	MSI Justifications
3. Social and Emotional Functioning:	SHAPS Anxiety
	SHAPS Hostility
	SHAPS Depression
	SHAPS Aggression
4. Self-Management:	SHAPS Psychopathic Deviate
	SHAPS Impulsivity

Of the sample of 119 sex offenders 7 (6%), 14 (12%) and 17 (14%) were reconvicted of a sexual offences over the two-, five- and ten-year follow-up periods respectively. The mean scores on the Deviancy domain scales were compared between recidivists and non-recidivists and it was found that recidivists obtained significantly higher scores on the MSI: Sexual Obsession and MSI: Cognitive Distortions and Immaturity scales than did the non-recidivists. Although not significant, the trend was for the recidivists to obtained higher scores on the SHAPS Hostility, Depression and Psychopathic Deviate scales.

In developing an integrated theory of risk assessment Beech and Ward (2004) examined to what extent actuarial risk scales corresponded with various aspects of psychological functioning as described in the four deviancy domains. To examine this empirically, Craig *et al.* (2007) reorganised Static-99 into three domains: *Sexual Deviance* (risk items – prior sexual convictions, male victims, non-contact sexual offences, non-relative and stranger victims); *General Criminality* (risk items – index non-sexual violence, prior non-sexual violence, and four or more sentencing occasions); and *Immaturity* (risk item – aged between 18–24 years). While the SHAPS and MSI scales were then combined with a principle component factorial procedure which produced a single factor for each domain. A *Psychological Deviance Index* (PDI) was calculated by standardising each of the scale scores for a domain (M = 0, SD = 1, i.e., z-scores), summed and divided by the number of scores. A domain was counted as dysfunctional if its average standard score was greater than zero. This means the number of dysfunctional domains index could be calculated running from 0 to 4.

It was found that these actuarial domains correlated with different aspects of the psychological risk factors. The *Sexual Interests* domain was significantly correlated with the Static-99 *Sexual Deviance* subscale and the Static-99 *Immaturity* subscale. The *Self-Management* domain was correlated with the Static-99 *General Criminality* and *Immaturity* subscales. As for the *Distorted Attitudes* domain, the MSI Cognitive Distortions and Immaturity scale was significantly correlated with both the Static-99 *Sexual Deviance* and *General Criminality* subscales, but the overall *Distorted Attitudes* domain was not. The *Social and Emotional Functioning* domain was significantly correlated with the Static-99 *Immaturity* subscale, as were the SHAPS scales Hostility and Aggression.

Table 6.3 Psychological Deviance Index and Sexual
Recidivism at five-year follow-up

PDI	Sexual Recidivism
0	3% of 29
1	10% of 19
2	8% of 26
3	14% of 21
4	26% of 23

When the rates of sexual recidivism were compared with the PDI, it was found that the increase in rates of sexual recidivism mirrored the increase in the degree of PDI (see Table 6.3).

However, it can also be seen from Table 6.3 that the rates of sexual reconviction and the PDI are not linear. However, when the PDI was grouped into Low (0), Moderate (1–2 domains) and High (3+ domains) categories, it was found that the degree of PDI and rates of reconviction were linear at 3%, 18% and 40% respectively. A logistic regression analysis revealed that the PDI made a statistically significant contribution to prediction of sexual reconviction independent of Static-99 at five-year follow-up.

Collectively, the studies outlined in this section suggest the integrated use of dynamic indicators combined with statistical estimates of risk allows for a better prediction of recidivism than that observed in statistical instruments alone. In contrast to Harris and Rice's (2003) observations, these studies demonstrate that the assessment of psychological factors has been shown to provide incremental predictive value to statistical instruments.

CONCLUSIONS

The use of psychometric measures used to approximate dynamic deviancy domains in predicting sexual reconviction challenges existing risk assessment procedures demonstrating that psychological trait factors provide unique information not captured by actuarial methods. Trait or psychological dispositional factors assessed at pre-release may also help to identify individuals exhibiting characteristics of psychological deviance who may require greater supervision. In addition to measuring the long-term risk potential of sex offenders using actuarial approaches, it has been demonstrated that psychometrically assessed information can have a significant contribution to the assessment of recidivism independent of actuarial systems. There appears to be a relationship between psychological and actuarial risk markers. Given the overlap between Static-99 subscales and the psychological risk markers, it may be that actuarial scales are best understood as being composed of historical markers for the past expression of the psychological risk factors. This is consistent with Beech and Ward (2004) who argue that actuarial assessments really act as proxies for the psychological vulnerability factors and function as markers of dispositional sexual behaviours. They suggest that developmental adversity can result in vulnerability to sexually abuse, and stable dynamic or 'psychological vulnerability' (i.e., traits) factors and dispositional factors that interact with triggering events (contextual factors) to produce acute dynamic risk factors. Psychometric indicators for the psychological risk factor domains on the other hand may reflect the more recent expression of these factors. The studies reported here support the use of psychometric measures of 'stable psychological vulnerability' (trait) markers in predicting sexual reconviction. The measure and integration of psychological vulnerability factors, or markers of deviance as additions to statistical systems of risk, are likely to further advance our understanding in predicting sexual reconviction.

REFERENCES

Abel, G.G., Becker, J.V. & Cunningham-Rathner, J. (1984). Complications, consent and cognitive distortions in sex between children and adults. *International Journal of Law and Psychiatry*, *7*, 89–103.

Barbaree, H.E., Seto, M.C., Langton, C.M. & Peacock, E.J. (2001). Evaluating the predictive accuracy of six risk assessment instruments for adult sex offenders. *Criminal Justice and Behavior*, *28*, 490–521.

Barratt, E.S. (1994). Impulsiveness and aggression. In J. Monahan & H.J. Steadman (Eds), *Violence and mental disorder: Developments in risk assessment* (pp. 21–79). Chicago, IL: University of Chicago.

Beckett, R.C. (1987). *The Children and Sex Questionnaire*. Available from: Richard Beckett, Room FF39, The Oxford Clinic, Littlemore Health Centre, Sandford Rd, Littlemore, Oxford, OX4 4XN, UK.

Beech, A.R. (1998). A psychometric typology of child abusers. *International Journal of Offender Therapy and Comparative Criminology*, *42*, 319–339.

Beech, A.R., Erikson, M, Friendship, C. & Hanson, R.K. (2002). Static and dynamic predictors of reconviction. *Sexual Abuse: A Journal of Research and Treatment*, *14*, 153–165.

Beech, A.R., Fisher, D. & Beckett, R.C. (1999). *An Evaluation of the Prison Sex Offender Treatment Programme*. UK Home Office Occasional Report. Home Office Publications Unit, 50 Queen Anne's Gate, London, SW1H 9AT, England. Available electronically from: www.homeoffice.gov.uk/rds/pdfs/occ-step3.pdf

Beech, A.R., Fisher, D. & Thornton, D. (2003). Risk assessment of sex offenders. *Professional Psychology, Research and Practice*, *34*, 339–352.

Beech, A.R. & Ward, T. (2004). The integration of etiology and risk in sex offenders: A theoretical model. *Aggression and Violent Behavior*, *10*, 31–63.

Bernard, G., Fuller, A., Robbins, L. & Shaw, T. (1989). *The child molester*. New York: Brunner/Mazel.

Blackburn, R. (1971). Personality types among abnormal homicides. *British Journal of Criminology*, *11*, 14–31.

Blackburn, R. (1973). A Study of impulsivity in abnormal offenders. Unpublished PhD Thesis, University of Southampton, UK.

Blackburn, R. (1974). Development and validation of scales to measure hostility and aggression. *Special Hospitals Research Reports*, No. 12. London: Special Hospitals Research Unit. Available from: Home Office, Special Hospitals Research Unit, 50 Queen Anne's Gate, London, SW1H 9AT, UK.

Blackburn, R. (1975). An empirical classification of psychopathic personality. *British Journal of Psychiatry*, *127*, 456–460.

Blackburn, R. (1979). Psychopathy and personality: The dimensionality of self report and behaviour rating data in abnormal offenders. *British Journal of Social and Clinical Psychology*, *18*, 111–119.

Blackburn, R. (1982). *The Special Hospital Assessment of Personality and Socialisation (SHAPS)*. Park Lane Hospital, UK. Unpublished manuscript.

Blackburn, R. (1986). Patterns of personality deviation among violent offenders: Replication and extension of an empirical taxonomy. *British Journal of Criminology*, *26*, 254–269.

Blackburn, R. & Fawcett, D.J. (1999). Manual for the antisocial personality questionnaire (APQ): An inventory for assessing personality deviation in offenders. *European Journal of Psychological Assessment*, *15*, 14–24.

Buffington-Vollum, J., Edens, J.F., Johnson, D.W. & Johnson, J.K. (2002). Psychopathy as a predictor of institutional misbehavior among sex offenders – A Prospective Replication. *Criminal Justice and Behavior*, *29*, 497–511.

Bumby, K. (1996). Assessing the cognitive distortions of child molesters and rapists. Development and validation of the RAPE and MOLEST scales. *Sexual Abuse: A Journal of Research and Treatment*, *8*, 37–54.

Burt, M. (1980). Cultural myths and support for rape. *Journal of Personality and Social Psychology*, *39*, 217–230.

Buss, A.H. & Durkee, A. (1957). An inventory for assessing different kinds of hostility. *Journal of Consulting Psychology*, *21*, 343–349.

Butcher, J., Dahlstrom, W., Graham, J. *et al.* (1989). *MMPI-2 manual for administration and scoring*. Minneapolis, MN: University of Minnesota Press.

Caprara, G.V. (1986). Indications of aggression: The dissipation-rumination scale. *Personality and Individual Differences*, *7*, 763–769.

Chantry, K. & Craig, R.J. (1994). Psychological screening of sexually violent offenders with the MCMI. *Journal of Clinical Psychology*, *50*, 430–435.

Check, J.V.P. (1984). The Hostility Towards Women Scale. Unpublished doctoral dissertation. University of Manitoba, Canada.

Como, P.G. (1977). The use of multiple personality variables to predict recidivism. MA Thesis. University of Texas.

Craig, L.A., Browne, K.D., Beech, A.R. & Stringer, I. (2004). Personality characteristics associated with reconviction in sexual and violent offenders. *Journal of Forensic Psychiatry and Psychology*, *15*, 532–551.

Craig, L.A., Browne, K.D., Beech, A.R. & Stringer, I. (2006). Psychosexual characteristics of sexual offenders and the relationship to sexual reconviction. *Psychology, Crime and Law*, *12*, 231–244.

Craig, L.A., Thornton, D., Beech. A.R. & Browne, K.D. (2007). The relationship of statistical and psychological risk markers to sexual reconviction in child molesters. *Criminal Justice and Behavior*, *34*, 314–329.

Curnoe, S. & Langevin, R. (2002). Personality and deviant sexual fantasies: An examination of the MMPIs of sex offenders. *Journal of Clinical Psychology*, *58*, 803–815.

Dowling, N., Smith, D., Proeve, M. & Lee, J.K.P. (2000). The Multiphasic Sex Inventory: A comparison of American and Australian samples of sexual offenders. *Australian Psychologist*, *35*, 244–248.

Fazel, S., Hope, T., O'Donnell, I. & Jacoby, R. (2002). Psychiatric, demographic and personality characteristics of elderly sex offenders. *Psychological Medicine*, *32*, 219–226.

Firestone, P., Bradford, J.M., McCoy, M. *et al.* (1998). Recidivism in convicted rapists. *Journal of the American Academy of Psychiatry and the Law*, *26*, 185–200.

Firestone, P., Bradford, J.M., McCoy, M. *et al.* (1999). Prediction of recidivism in incest offenders. *Journal of Interpersonal Violence*, *14*, 511–531.

Fisher, D., Beech, A.R. & Browne, K.D. (1999). Comparison of sex offenders to non-sex offenders on selected psychological measures. *International Journal of Offender Therapy and Comparative Criminology*, *43*, 473–491.

Geer, T.M., Becker, J.V., Gray, S.R. & Krauss, D. (2001). Predictors of treatment completion in a correctional sex offender treatment program. *International Journal of Offender Therapy and Comparative Criminology*, *45*, 302–313.

Giedt, F.H. & Downing, L. (1961). An extraversion scale for the MMPI. *Journal of Clinical Psychology*, *17*, 156–159.

Glover, A.J.J., Nicholson, D.E., Hemmati, T. *et al.* (2002). A comparison of predictors of general and violent recidivism among high-risk federal offenders. *Criminal Justice and Behavior*, *29*, 235–249.

Groth, A.N. (1978). Patterns of sexual assault against children and adolescents. In A. Burgess, L. Holstrom & S. Sgroi (Eds), *Sexual assault of children and adolescents* (pp. 3–24). Lanham, MD: Lexington Books.

Gudjonsson, G.H. & Sigurdsson, J.F. (2000). Differences and similarities between violent offenders and sex offenders. *Child Abuse and Neglect*, *24*, 363–372.

Hanson, R.K. & Bussière, M.T. (1998). Predicting relapse: A meta-analysis of sexual offender recidivism studies. *Journal of Consulting and Clinical Psychology*, *66*, 348–362.

Hanson, R.K. & Harris, A.J.R. (2000). Where should we intervene? Dynamic predictors of sexual offense recidivism. *Criminal Justice and Behavior*, *27*, 6–35.

Hanson, R.K. & Morton-Bourgon, K. (2005). The characteristics of persistent sexual offenders: A meta-analysis of recidivism studies. *Journal of Consulting and Clinical Psychology*, *73*, 1154–1163.

Hanson, R.K. & Scott, H. (1995). Assessing perspective-taking among sexual offenders, non-sexual criminal and non-offenders. *Sexual Abuse: A Journal of Research and Treatment*, *7*, 259–277.

Hanson, R.K. & Thornton, D. (2000). Improving risk assessment for sex offenders: A comparison of three actuarial scales. *Law and Human Behavior*, *24*, 119–136.

Hare, R.D. (1991). *Manual for the Psychopathy Checklist-Revised*. Toronto, Ontario: Multi-Health Systems, Inc.

Hare, R.D., Clark, D., Grann, M. & Thornton, D. (2000). Psychopathy and the predictive validity of the PCL-R: An international perspective. *Behavioral Sciences and the Law*, *18*, 623–645.

Harris, G.T. & Rice, M.E. (2003). Actuarial assessment of risk among sex offenders. In R.A. Prentky, E.S. Janus & M.C. Seto (Eds), *Sexually coercive Behaviour: Understanding and management*. Annals of the New York Academy of Sciences, *989*, 198–210.

Haywood, T.W., Grossman, L.S., Kravitz, H.M. & Wasyliw, O.E. (1994). Profiling psychological distortions in alleged child molesters. *Psychological Reports*, *75*, 915–927.

Kalichman, S.C., Henderson, M.C., Shealy, L.S. & Dwyer, M. (1992). Psychometric properties of the Multiphasic Sex Inventory in assessing sex offenders. *Criminal Justice and Behavior*, *19*, 384–396.

Keltner, A.A., Marshall, P.G. & Marshall, W.L. (1981). Measurement and correlation of assertiveness and social fear in a prison population. *Corrective and Social Psychiatry*, *27*, 41–47.

Kline, P. (1986). *A handbook of test construction*. New York: Methuen.

Knight, R.A. & Prentky, R.A. (1990). Classifying sexual offenders: The Development and corroboration of taxonomic models. In W.L. Marshall, D.R. Laws & H.E. Barbaree (Eds), *Handbook of sexual assault: Issues, theories and treatment of the offender* (pp. 23–53). New York: Plenum.

Langevin, R. (1991). A note on the problem of response set in measuring cognitive distortions. *Annals of Sex Research*, *4*, 288–292.

Langevin, R., Lang, R., Reynolds, R. *et al.* (1988). Personality and sexual anomalies: An examination of the Millon Clinical Multiaxial Inventory. *Annals of Sex Research*, *1*, 13–32.

Långström, N. & Grann, M. (2002). Psychopathy and violent recidivism among young criminal offenders. *Acta Psychiatrica Scandinavica*, *106*(Supplement 412), 86–92.

Malamuth, N.M. & Brown, L.M. (1994). Sexually aggressive men's perception of women's communication: Testing three explanations. *Journal of Personality and Social Psychology*, *67*, 699–712.

Megargee, E.I. (1966). Undercontrolled and overcontrolled personality types in extreme antisocial aggression. *Psychological Monographs*, *80*, 1–29.

Metzner, J., Cohen, F., Grossman, L. & Wettstein, R. (1998). Treatment in prison and jails. In R.M. Wettstein (Ed), *Treatment of offenders with mental disorders* (pp. 211–264). New York: Guilford Press.

Miner, M.H., Marques, J.K., Day, D.M. & Moeller, J.R. (1990). Impact of relapse prevention in treating sex offenders: Preliminary findings. *Annals of Sex Research, 3,* 165–185.

Mosher, D.L. & Sirkin, M. (1984). Measuring a macho personality constellation. *Journal of Personality, 18,* 150–163.

Nichols, H.R. & Molinder, I. (1984). *Multiphasic Sex Inventory.* Available from: Nichols and Molinder, 437 Bowes Drive, Tacoma, WA 98466, USA.

Nichols, H.R. & Molinder, I. (2000). *Multiphasic Sex Inventory-II* (Version 2). Available from: Nichols and Molinder, 437 Bowes Drive, Tacoma, WA 98466, USA.

Novaco, R. (1975). *Anger control: the Development and evaluation of an experimental treatment.* Lexington, MA: D.C. Heath.

Nowicki, S. (1976). *Adult Nowicki-Strickland Internal-External Locus of Control Scale.* Test manual available from: S. Nowicki, Jr, Department of Psychology, Emory University, Atlanta, GA 30322, USA.

Peterson, D.R., Quay, H.C. & Cameron, G.R. (1959). Personality and background factors in juvenile delinquency as inferred from questionnaire responses. *Journal of Consulting Psychology, 23,* 395–399.

Pithers, W.D., Kashima, K.M., Cumming, G.F. & Beal, L.S. (1988). Relapse prevention: A method of enhancing maintenance of change in sex offenders. In A.C. Salter (Ed), *Treating child sex offenders and victims: A practical guide* (pp. 131–170). Newbury Park, CA: Sage.

Porteus, S.D. (1955). *The maze test: Recent advances.* Palo Alto, CA: Pacific Books.

Prentky, R.A. & Knight, R.A. (1991). Identifying critical dimensions for discriminating among rapists. *Journal of Consulting and Clinical Psychology, 59,* 643–661.

Proulx, J., Pellerin, B., McKibben, A. *et al.* (1999). Recidivism in sexual aggressors: Static and dynamic predictors of recidivism in sexual aggressors. *Sexual Abuse: A Journal of Research and Treatment, 11,* 117–129.

Quinnella, F.A. & Bow, J.N. (2001). Psychological tests used in child custody evaluations. *Behavioral Sciences and the Law, 19,* 491–501.

Rice, M.E. & Harris, G.T. (1997). Cross-validation and extension of the violence risk appraisal guide for child molesters and rapists. *Law and Human Behavior, 21,* 231–241.

Roger, D. & Najarian, B. (1989). The construction and validation of a new scale for measuring emotion control. *Personality and Individual Differences, 10,* 845–853.

Russell, D., Peplau, L.A. & Cutrona, C.A. (1980). The revised UCLA Loneliness scale: Concurrent and discriminant validity evidence. *Journal of Personality and Social Psychology, 39,* 472–480.

Rust, J. & Golombok, S. (1989). *Modern psychometrics: The Science of psychological assessment.* London: Routledge.

Simkins, L., Ward, W., Bowman, S. & Rinck, C.M. (1989). The Multiphasic Sex Inventory: Diagnosis and prediction of treatment response in child sexual abuse. *Annals of Sex Research, 2,* 205–226.

Sjöstedt, G. & Långström, N. (2002). Assessment of risk for criminal recidivism among rapists: A comparison of four different measures. *Psychology, Crime & Law, 8,* 25–40.

Stein, K.B. (1968). The TSC Scale: The outcome of a cluster analysis of the 550 MMPI items. In P. McReynolds (Ed.), *Advances in psychological assessment,* (Vol. 1). Palo Alto: Science and Behaviour Books.

Thornton, D. (1989). Self-esteem scale. Unpublished manuscript. Available from: David Thornton, Sand Ridge Secure Treatment Center, Mauston, Wisconsin, USA.

Thornton, D. (2002). Constructing and testing a framework for dynamic risk assessment. *Sexual Abuse: A Journal of Research and Treatment, 14,* 137–151.

Thornton, D. & Beech. A.R. (2002). Integrating statistical and psychological factors through the structured risk assessment model. Paper presented at the 21st Annual Research and Treatment Conference, Association of the Treatment of Sexual Abusers, Montreal, Canada, October 2002.

Ward, T., Hudson, S.M. & Keenan, T. (1998). A self-regulation model of the sexual offence process. *Sexual Abuse: A Journal of Research and Treatment, 10*, 141–157.

Ward, T., Louden, K., Hudson, S.M. & Marshall, W.L. (1995). A descriptive model of the offence chain for child molesters. *Journal of Interpersonal Violence, 10*, 452–472.

Webster, S.D., Mann, R.E., Thornton, D. & Wakeling, H. (2007). Further validation of the short self-esteem scale with sexual offenders. *Legal and Criminological Psychology, 12*, 207–216.

Wise, E.A. (2001). The comparative validity of the MCMI-II and MMPI-2 personality disorder scales with forensic examinees. *Journal of Personality Disorders, 15*, 275–279.

7

Measuring Sexual Deviance: Attention-Based Measures

CARMEN L.Z. GRESS

D. RICHARD LAWS

INTRODUCTION

Why measure sexual interest in offenders? The answer is simple and straightforward. The nature of their sexual interests is what demarcates repetitive sexual offenders from both non-offenders and lower risk offenders (Hanson & Morton-Bourgon, 2005; Lalumière & Quinsey, 1994; Laws et al., 2000). Valid and effective technologies for measuring the sexual interests, thoughts and arousal patterns of sexual offenders are of critical value in the identification of treatment needs and the assessment of risk. Assessment data have the additional value in that sharing them with offenders may motivate them to accept and address their problem.

Since about 1971 a psychophysiological method called penile plethysmography (PPG), a direct measurement of circumferential or volumetric changes in the penis – has been used to assess sexual interest (Zuckerman, 1971). The procedure has, for the most part, proven to be an excellent technology for assessing sexual interest. However, it is expensive, invasive, labour intensive, limited to males, and ideally, like many psychological measures, requires a motivated and responsive subject (Laws, 2003). These problems do not render the procedure useless but they limit its utility and challenge its validity. In spite of these problems, a considerable literature has built up over the past three decades that more or less supports the use of PPG, as evident in Chapter 8 of this book (see for a review of the PPG). The search for a viable alternative to PPG has now been under way for more than a decade. In addition, concern over the reliance on self-report measures in assessing sexual offenders' perceptions, reasoning and judgement patterns has led some researchers to call for more research

Assessment and Treatment of Sex Offenders: A Handbook. Edited by Anthony Beech, Leam Craig and Kevin Browne. © John Wiley & Sons Ltd, 2009.

on measures less open to malingering or social desirability/impression management (Hanson & Morton-Bourgon, 2005; Hudson & Ward, 1997).

In this chapter, we review attention-based measures of sexual interest, implicit associations and motivational states (for information on self-report measures see Craig and Beech, this volume). This is not a comprehensive review of all measures associated with sexuality such as those found in the sexual health or the sexual dysfunction literatures. Instead, this chapter focuses on measures pertaining to sexual deviance, typically among males. In addition, because many of these measures are new to the field of sexual deviance, we include more detail on psychometric properties and methodologies than typically found in a book chapter, allowing a detailed comparison of methodologies. In the final discussion we highlight similarities and discrepancies among the methodologies, discuss clinical applicability and future directions.

ATTENTION-BASED MEASURES OF SEXUAL INTEREST

Researchers use measures of attention, specifically the performance associated with different aspects or processes of attention such as attention span, interference, selective attention, attention reflex, or attentional bias, to investigate complex behaviour patterns ranging from memory and emotion to the recent examinations of sexual interest (Geer, Estupinan & Manguno-Mire, 2000). The impetus for attention-based measures of sexual deviancy arose from studies demonstrating sexual information, such as images and text, is processed differently from neutral information (Geer & Melton, 1997), in that it can increase perception speed (Janssen *et al.*, 2000), introduce a hesitancy in decision making (Geer & Melton, 1997), or attenuate reflexive processes (Hecker, King & Scoular, 2006). Attention-based measures provide estimates of psychological constructs considered important to treatment and risk assessments without having to directly ask for them, making them in theory, less susceptible to socially desirable responding.

Currently, attention-based measures used in sexual offender research include (in alphabetical order): *choice reaction time* (Giotakis, 2005; Gress, 2006; Wright & Adams, 1994, 1999), *the Emotional Stroop* (Price, 2006; Smith & Waterman, 2004), The *Implicit Association Test* (Gray *et al.*, 2005; Nunes, Firestone & Baldwin, 2007), the *rapid serial visual presentation* task (Beech *et al.*, in press; Flak, Beech & Fisher, 2007), and *viewing time* paradigms (Abel *et al.*, 1998; Beech *et al.*, in press; Gress, 2005; Harris *et al.*, 1996; Letourneau, 2002). Although not yet applied to sexual offenders, the *startle probe reflex* approach may also be useful in assessment (Giargiari *et al.*, 2005; Hecker *et al.*, 2006).

Choice Reaction Time

Choice reaction time (CRT) is a simple method measuring how quickly and accurately an individual indicates to which category (there must be two or more from which to choose) the presented stimulus belongs. In general, research studies investigating the ability of CRT to assess sexual interest instruct a participant to view a variety of images on a computer screen, each image typically composed of a single person, and use specific keys on a keyboard or a like device to indicate the position of a white dot superimposed on the image. When the choice is made the software programme removes the two stimuli (image and dot) and presents the participant with two more. The location of the white dot, the image composition and the apparatus used to indicate location vary from study to study.

Wright and Adams (1994) investigated CRT's ability to non-intrusively measure Singer's aesthetic response. According to Singer (1984) sexual interest has three distinct stage-like responses: aesthetic, approach and genital. The *aesthetic response* is a hedonic or pleasurable feeling in response to visual or auditory stimuli that matches the individual's sexual interest. The *approach response* is the act of making physical movements toward the sexual interest in a desire to engage in touching, holding, caressing and so on. The *genital response* involves the autonomic change associated with physical arousal, such as tumescence. Wright and Adams (1994) hypothesised that: (a) an aesthetic response toward a sexually attractive individual should interfere or compete with other cognitive activity; and (b) incidental learning would be greater on preferred slides because there should be a correlation between length of time they viewed the slide and memory for the stimulus. They administered a CRT measure to 80 university undergraduate and local community participants, evenly categorised into four groups by sexual orientation (heterosexual and homosexual)[1] and biological sex. The measure contained 60 slides, comprised equally of commercially available nude males, nude females and neutral images from travel magazines, randomly presented with a three-second interval between presentations. The incidental learning task consisted of viewing the images a second time, without the white dot, and indicating the location of the dot (from memory) using the same device. Wright and Adams (1994) did not find any significant main effects, but they did find a significant triple interaction effect of orientation, stimulus type, and biological sex. Further analysis confirmed their expectations: (a) homosexual males were significant slower when indicating dot location on male slides than female or neutral slides; (b) heterosexual males were significant slower on female slides than male slides and neutrals; (c) heterosexual women were significant slower on male slides than female slides (but not neutral slides); and (d) homosexual women were significant slower on female and neutral slides. Results showed male participants made significantly more errors on the CRT task than female participants and more errors were made by both groups on male images. For the incidental learning task, males made significantly fewer errors than females. Regarding classification accuracy, the authors reported 76 of 80 subjects responded as predicted.

Wright and Adams (1999) repeated their experiment with a few adaptations. Eighty participants (same categories as above) viewed two series of 60 slides (a clothed set

---

[1]For clarity and consistency this chapter uses the terms heterosexual and homosexual to describe sexual orientation.

with pictures from fashion magazines and a nude set using the same images as the 1994 study), with an additional neutral set consisting of a solid blue background. Before engaging in the task, participants completed five practice trials with neutral slides. The subsequent learning task consisted of two sets of images: one from the CRT task and the second a new yet similar set. Administrators asked participants 'Did you see this before?' In this study, authors conducted internal consistency estimates and found their stimulus categories to be highly reliable with alphas above .90 for each category. Results provided partial confirmation of expectations. Homosexual males demonstrated significantly longer latencies when indicating dot location on male nude images than homosexual women (as expected), but not heterosexual men and no significant results were found between groups on clothed imagery. Heterosexual men demonstrated significantly longer latencies on female nude images than heterosexual women and homosexual men (as expected). Again, no significant results were found between groups on clothed images.

When examining within group latencies, the results were mixed. Each group took significantly longer to complete the task on their respective sexual interest image set than their non-interest group and neutral image set, except for heterosexual women who took longer on male and female images when compared to time taken on neutral images but their latencies on male images were not significantly longer than the latencies on female images. Heterosexual males had significantly longer latencies on female clothed images than male images but not neutral images. The authors also found participants made more errors on female and male images than neutral and more on nude images than clothed. In the learning task, participants were significantly more likely to correctly identify novel images as novel and each group demonstrated higher levels of recognition for their preferred category when the images were nude. There were no significant group differences for orientation, gender, or stimulus type. Classification accuracy was better overall with nude stimuli (100 for heterosexual men, homosexual men, and homosexual women but 50% for heterosexual women) but slightly better for heterosexual women when scoring with clothed stimuli (70%, 55%, 85%, and 90% respectively).

Giotakis (2005) investigated CRT and sexual interest in a similar study. The author administered 90 photos, 10 photos from 9 categories (violence [boxing, war, football], neutral, adult males, adolescent males, boys, adult females, adolescent females, girls and blank) to 135 participants, 58 of whom were sexual offenders (31 convicted for rape, 8 for intra-familial child molestation, 19 for extra-familial child molestation) and 53 males and 24 females as controls (staff from a nearby hospital). All images of people were clothed, non-sexual and commercially available. The author simplified the CRT task by having only two possible white dot locations, in either the right or left corner, with a two-second interval between slides. The incidental learning task repeated the 80 images and presented a second new but similar set of 80, with the task 'Do you recognise this picture?' Two main CRT results emerged: groups convicted for sexual offences demonstrated significantly longer overall reaction times than the control males and females and images of boys and of girls were viewed significantly less in relation to the other stimuli. There were no significant differences in error analyses. In the learning task, significant differences existed between groups (offenders vs. controls), stimulus types, with a significant interaction between the two. With novel stimuli, each group (even when delineated between offender types) were significantly more likely to correctly identify adolescents, with extra-familial offenders and female controls better at classifying female adolescents and all other groups better at classifying male adolescents. With the repeated stimuli, participants with convictions for rape and male controls were significantly more likely to correctly identify male adolescents, intra- and extra-familial offenders were better at classifying boys, and female controls were better at all female categories.

Santtila, Mokros and Viljanen (2006) replicated Wright and Adams (1994, 1999), with a few modifications, with 25 male university students (15 heterosexual and 10 homosexual). First, instead of using a plain blue background as the neutral stimulus, Santtila *et al.* used the same pictures in both sexual and neutral sets. The images, obtained from erotic Internet websites, consisted of 40 nude men and women. The authors modified the images in the neutral set by covering the torso with a solid rectangle. Second, the authors added a priming slide, sexual or neutral, before the target slide using the same images. The participants completed 480 prime target pairs (equally balanced between neutral and sexual stimuli) which consisted of a fixation point (on screen for 500 ms), a priming image (on screen for 13 ms), then the target images with a black dot superimposed in one of six locations (each corner, the middle, or all). For statistical analysis, the trials were split into three equal phases. In phase one both groups took significantly longer to respond to sexual stimuli matching their sexual interest than all other images. In phase two no significant differences were found. In phase three the priming slide modified results for heterosexual men: when the prime was sexual heterosexual men took significantly longer to respond to sexual female images but not when the prime was neutral. Homosexual men responded similarly for all images. An AUC[2] analysis predicting group membership from difference scores (latency to female images minus latencies to male images) produced estimates of .82 for phase one, .63 for phase two, and .60 for phase three, demonstrating that the test's performance diminished over trials.

Gress (2007) conducted an investigation of CRT and viewing time (VT). The author presented 40 clothed slides to 121 participants comprised of 40 youth non-sexual offenders, 50 university undergraduates and 22 adult sexual offenders, the majority of whom were heterosexual (88.5%). The slides consisted equally of male and female images in each of the five Tanner categories of physical development (toddlers, prepubescents, pubescents, adolescents and adults) (see Fuller *et al.*, 1988). There were four computer-modified image examples per category (see Laws & Gress, 2004 for further information) plus five neutral landscapes. Cronbach's alpha for each stimulus category (sex by age) ranged from .72 for female Tanner 3 (pubescent) images to .87 for female Tanner 1 (toddlers) images. Results indicated undergraduates demonstrated

---

[2]Area Under the Curve (AUC) analyses produce receiver operator characteristic or ROC curves, a graphical plot of the sensitivity vs. [1 − specificity] used to evaluate the binary group prediction.

significantly shorter response latencies than youth offenders but not adult sexual offenders. For female images, youth offenders and adult sexual offenders viewed Tanner 1 images longer than all other female images and undergraduates viewed Tanner 5 the longest. For male images, youth viewed Tanner 2 images longer than all others, undergraduates Tanner 5, and adult sexual offenders Tanner 1. Not surprisingly, given a predominantly heterosexual sample, average times for female images, regardless of age, were always longer than times for male images. An AUC analysis for total average time (collapsed across all categories) with sexual offenders as the target population (true positives; youth offenders and undergraduates as true negatives) was significant at 0.63. An AUC with all offenders as the target population was significant at 0.76.

Summary of CRT studies

CRT is a short and administratively simple method to assess sexual interest. It can reliably differentiate sexual interest for adult females from sexual interest in adult males, with longer latencies associated with sexual interest. This straightforward procedure takes approximately 30 minutes and as demonstrated does not require nude photographs to produce significant results. To ready this tool for clinical settings, studies evaluating CRT's potential to differentiate age preference, specifically a sexual preference for children, as well as scoring methods and individual applicability are required.

Emotional Stroop

The Emotional Stroop task is a modification of the Stroop colour-naming task which requires participants to read a list of colour words printed in different colours (Stroop, 1935). The Stroop effect occurs when respondents are slower to name font colours of words printed in a colour that does not match word meaning. The Emotional Stroop is a modification theorised to assess attentional bias, a focus on one or two aspects of a situation while unsuspectingly ignoring the rest (Williams, Mathews & MacLeod, 1996). A number of studies have demonstrated that participants with clinical anxiety disorders generally take longer to identify the colour of words with threatening themes when compared to control subjects (Williams et al., 1996). In addition, individuals demonstrating high trait anger demonstrated the Stroop effect when responding to anger words (Eckhardt & Cohen, 1997) and threat words (Van Honk et al., 2001).[3] Smith and Waterman administered the Emotional Stroop to sexual offenders to determine if the offenders' emotional response latencies to offence-specific words would

---

[3]Although beyond the scope of this chapter, it is important to note that controversy exists about whether the Emotional Stroop actually measures the Stroop effect. See Algom, Chajut and Lev (2004); Chajut, Lev and Algom (2005); and Dalgliesh (2005) for more information.

be significantly different from their responses to non-offence-specific words as well as to the responses of non-sexual offenders.

Smith and Waterman (2004) investigated the Emotional Stroop with 43 participants (10 sexual offenders, 10 violent offenders, 10 non-violent offenders and 13 university undergraduates). The authors administered 150 experimental trials consisting of 25 words in each of the following themed categories: aggression, sexuality, positive emotion, negative emotion, neutral words and colour words (always incongruent with font colour). The task consisted of a fixation 'x' appearing for 500 ms in the centre of the screen followed by a word. After 10 practice trials, participants were instructed to quickly and accurately name the colour in which the word was printed (red, green, blue, or yellow). Both sexual and violent offenders bias scores, calculated by subtracting the mean CRT to neutral word presentations from each of the mean CRTs to stimulus word conditions (sexual, aggression, positive, negative and colour) were significantly slower than the undergraduate sample. In addition, sexual offenders demonstrated the largest interference bias (i.e., they produced the longest reaction times to colour-naming sexual words compared to neutral words). Results should be interpreted with caution, however, as the authors found significant correlations between reaction times and depression among sexual offenders and violent offenders.

Price (2006) conducted two successive studies, separated by a vocabulary test, with 75 participants (15 sexual offenders [rape], 15 sexual offenders [child molestation], 15 violent offenders, 15 non-violent offenders and 15 community participants). The first was a replication of Smith and Waterman (2004). In the second study the author separated the sexually themed words into two categories, rape and child molestation, to determine if different types of sexual offending (for example, child molestation vs. rape) demonstrated attentional bias to corresponding words, rather than sexually themed words in general. In addition, a third category of intimacy was added as sexual offenders in general are believed by many to lack intimacy skills. Price hypothesised this may result in shorter latencies for that category of words. Administration and scoring practices were the same as Smith and Waterman (2004). Results of Study 1 demonstrated sexual offenders with convictions for rape were significantly slower to colour name sexually themed words when compared to the community sample, and were slower, but not significantly slower than the child molesters, violent offenders and non-violent non-sexual offenders. Sexual offenders with convictions for child molestation were significantly slower than the community and non-violent non-sexual offender groups when naming colour words (regular Stroop test). Unfortunately, no significant differences for any word categories were found in Study 2.

Summary of Emotional Stroop studies

The Emotional Stroop is simple, easy to administer and score, and has a long-established history in cognitive psychology. Although these studies used voice-activated software, the measure can be administered via paper and pencil, making it the most flexible and portable of all the attention-based measures. Its introduction to the field of sexual offender treatment is recent and research is limited but shows promise. The measure requires further examination to determine its usefulness in sex offender research, assessment and treatment.

Implicit Association Tests

Implicit association tests (IAT) assess the strength of unspoken or hidden relations between two separate concepts such as *child* and *adult* and two contrary attributions such as *pleasant* and *unpleasant*. In general the tasks begin with participants classifying concepts then attributes into specific categories predetermined by the researcher. Then participants view pairs of words and use (a) a specific key on the right-hand side of the keyboard to quickly and accurately indicate whether the pair of words on screen match one type of predetermined concept-attribution pairing (e.g., *child* and *pleasant*), and (b) a key on the left if the words match the other type of group pairing (e.g., *adult* and *unpleasant*). Participants then repeat this task with either the concept or attribute reversed (e.g., *child* and *unpleasant*, *adult* and *pleasant*). The number of exemplars per condition range from three to eight (Brown, Gray & Snowden, in press). The strength of the association between specific concept-attribute pairings is inferred from the response latencies on the tasks (i.e., participants respond quicker to pairings that match already established associations).

Gray *et al.* (2005) designed an IAT to assess associations between the concepts *children* and *adults* and the attribute *sex*. The authors administered the IAT to 78 male participants. Eighteen had sexually offended against children and 60 had committed other serious offences, including violent and sexual assault of adults. The IAT consists of five stages:

1. Participants classified attribute words as either *sex* or *not sex*;
2. Participants classified concept target words (exemplars) as either *child* or *adult*;
3. Half of the participants identified pairs assumed to be congruent (e.g., *adult* and *sex*, *child* and *non-sex*) and the other half identified non-congruent pairs (e.g., *adult* and *non-sex*, *child* and *sex*);
4. The same task as stage 3 but the buttons were reversed;
5. A repeat of stage 3 with reverse conditions.

Gray *et al.* (2005) found that child abusers responded significantly more slowly on trials in which *adult* and *sex* were paired than on the trials in which *child* and *sex* were paired, indicating these participants were more likely to associate sexual behaviours with children rather than adults. Non-sexual offenders demonstrated the opposite pattern. The comparison produced a large effect size ($d = 0.84$) between the two groups.

To examine three specific implicit theories (children as sexual beings, uncontrollability of sexuality and sexual entitlement) Mihailides, Devilly and Ward (2004) compared 25 sexual offenders with convictions for child abuse to 25 non-sexual offenders, 25 male university students and 25 female university students. Each participant completed three IATs each with five stages (same as Gray *et al.*, 2005 above). Significant differences emerged between the sexual offender and the comparison groups for each implicit theory. Sexual offenders took significantly less time to classify words *about children* when paired with *sexual* attributes, *sexual* attributes when paired with *losing control*, *mine* concept words when paired with *sexual* attributes, and *not-mine* words with *not-sexual* attributes. Further analysis by the authors demonstrated no differences among samples in IAT as a result of handedness (indicating the dominant hand is not faster or slower than the non-dominant hand when categorising the words), age, or general response times.

Nunes, Firestone and Baldwin (2007) compared 27 convicted child abusers with 29 non-sexual offenders to examine cognitions regarding self and children. Specifically, the authors assessed three attributes (pleasant, social power and sexual attractiveness) as related to children and adults. Each participant completed six IATs (one for each match between the three attributes and two concepts), each with five stages (same as Gray *et al.*, 2005 above). Results demonstrated sexual offenders took significantly longer time than non-sexual offenders to classify *children* with *sexually attractive*. No other IAT results were significant.

Summary of IAT studies

Perhaps the most promising and ready to implement of the attention-based measures, the IAT is a slightly more complex measure than the CRT, or Emotional Stroop, but computer software makes it easy to administer and score. The IAT reliably discriminates between those who offend against children and non-offenders. Importantly, it can do this without using images of children, although research demonstrates pictures can be used, extending its use to populations with learning disabilities or low reading levels. In addition, the IAT informs clinicians of offenders' maladaptive schemas providing a clear starting point for treatment. Further research comparing sexual offenders with various offences (child molestation, rape, exhibitionism, etc.) and evaluating its applicability to youth offenders would be of great benefit to this field.

Rapid Serial Visual Presentation (RSVP)

Rapid serial visual presentation (RSVP), a brief display of information (generally text) in a limited space in sequential order (Potter & Levy, 1969), is a method commonly used in perceptual and cognitive psychology. It provides an opportunity to observe attentional blink, when an individual can detect one target stimulus in a group of distractor stimuli but fails to or takes longer to detect a second different target presented within half a second of the first target (Raymond, Shapiro & Arnell, 1992; Shapiro & Raymond, 1994). The 'attentional blink' is believed to be the time taken to select and process stimuli from visual short-term memory (VSTM; Jolicoeur, 2002), and is affected by manipulations in visual similarity between targets and distractors and conceptual similarities, for example, when the first target stimulus is more salient to the viewer (Kyllingsbaek, Schneider & Bundesen, 2001).

Beech *et al*. (in press) used the RSVP method to determine if sexual offenders with child victims would have significantly more errors identifying Target 2 after correctly identifying Target 1 as a child. The authors presented two conditions each with 216 sequences of 11 images to 35 adult male sexual offenders with offences against children (16 intra-familial and 18 extra-familial) and 20 non-offenders. The sequences were counter-balanced and separated into four presentation blocks. The images consisted of clothed children and animals for Target 1 and trains and chairs (half facing left, half facing right) for Target 2. Each image was displayed for 100 seconds with no breaks between images. The interval between Target 1 and Target 2 was 100 ms, 200 ms, or 300 ms. In the first condition participants used a keyboard to report Target 1 (object) and Target 2 (object and direction). In the second condition participants reported Target 2 only, to determine if an interference effect could be detected without identifying Target 1. Beech *et al*. (in press) determined that participants exhibited the attentional blink effect as participants were significantly more accurate in the second condition when they did not report Target 1, than in the first condition. Results indicated that sexual offenders, both intra-familial and extra-familial, made significantly more errors than non-offenders when reporting Target 2 objects after correctly identifying the Target 1 object as a child. The authors also examined the ability of an outcome score (total Child Category Target 2 score minus total Animal Category Target 2 score in the first condition, contingent upon Target 1 accuracy) to classify sexual offenders from non-offenders. An Area Under the Curve (AUC) analysis produced a significant AUC of .75, suggesting a value of .5 SD above the mean of the outcome score for the non-offender sample as a cut-off, was sensitive enough to correctly identified 74% of the sexual offender sample while indicating 30% in the non-offender sample as false positives.

Summary of RSVP studies

The RSVP, a newcomer to sexual offender research, is another promising tool to reliably discriminate between sexual offenders and non-offenders. Like other attention-based tools, it demonstrates that many sexual offenders have different attentional triggers from non-offenders, which provides invaluable information to treatment and risk assessments.

Viewing Time

Viewing time (VT) measures of sexual interest assess how long an individual takes to view an image of a single person which may indicate the sexual attractiveness of the stimulus. This methodology, also reported as 'visual reaction time' (Abel *et al*., 1998; Abel *et al*., 2004) uses real or computer-modified images typically comprised of males and females at various ages and in various poses ranging from non-sexual to erotic. Although VT research is similar to reaction time research, i.e., there is a specific task to complete within a structured environment, in VT there is no correct answer as in traditional reaction time research, nor are there instructions regarding speed or accuracy. Therefore, participants are not 'reacting' but rather responding to an inquiry at their own pace (Maletzky, 2003). As there are other established reviews of VT, this chapter only presents more recent research.

Letourneau (2002) examined VT and sexual interest with 59 offenders convicted for hands-on sexual offences from a Level III military prison (terms of 5 years or more or status as an officer). In addition to PPG and the Multiphasic Sex Inventory (MSI; Nichols & Molinder, 1984), the author administered the *Abel Assessment for Sexual Interest* (AASI; Abel *et al.*, 2001) which is composed of 22 stimulus categories, 7 slides per category. In this study, the author used only 18 of the 22 images for statistical analysis: Caucasian and African-American women and men over 22 years, Caucasian and African-American girls and boys ages 2–4, 8–10, and 14–17 years, and sadism against women and men (there are only Caucasian stimuli in the two sadism categories). All images were clothed. The participants viewed each slide twice, the first to familiarise themselves with the images and the second to rate the sexual attractiveness. Cronbach alphas on untrimmed[4] VTs ranged from .60 to .90. To assess validity, four true[5] categories of sexual interest were created based on age and gender of the participants' victims: young girls, young boys, adolescent girls and adult women. Results indicated significant correlations between untrimmed and trimmed VTs for young males and female adolescents and applicable true sexual interest categories. VTs and PPG scores for young males, young females and adult females were significant correlated, the latter with untrimmed VTs only.

In addition, Letourneau (2002) examined clinical accuracy. In clinical settings, clinicians use the rule-of-thirds method for the AASI on the eight trimmed z-scores consistent with the client's ethnicity. "Clinicians are to isolate the space between the lowest score and the highest adolescent or adult score. They are to then divide that space into thirds and consider any child category score VT that crosses the first third as a category that represents probable deviant sexual interest" (Fischer & Smith, 1999, p. 199). Using this method, the author found the AASI statistically able to identify sexual offenders with young male victims but not other groups.

Abel and colleagues (Abel *et al.*, 2004) examined the VTs from 16 categories of slides (from a larger stimulus set), divided equally between clothed Caucasian and African-American males and females, and ages 2–4, 8–10, 14–17, over 21. Participants were selected from a database of adolescent clients who completed the AASI between 1994 and March 2003. The authors grouped the adolescent offenders into two categories: those who admitted to sexually assaulting someone five years younger (1,704 participants) and those who did not admit, were not accused, and whose therapist did not believe they sexually assaulted someone five years their junior (534

---

[4]Trimmed latencies were collapsed into categories, excluding for each participant his highest time per category.
[5]In this study, the authors noted that 'true' sexual interest is difficult to assess considering sexual offenders are not always honest about their sexual interests.

participants). The participants, after viewing a set of practice images, viewed each slide once to rate the sexual attractiveness of each image (VTs were the length of time taken to rate and advance the slide). The authors found that mean viewing times to slides of children differed significantly between those who had at least one victim five years younger than them and those who did not. The authors reported an AUC of .64 when discriminating the two participant samples.

Gress (2005) investigated classification schemes produced by viewing time scores and past sexual behaviour. The author presented 64 computer-modified images comprised of clothed and unclothed males and females of various ages (5, 9, 13, and adult) to 26 adult male sexual offenders referred to an adult community outpatient clinic for treatment. The images were randomly ordered and displayed 10 times each, each one with a different question, for a total of 640 slides. The slides were presented in 8 blocks of 80 with a minimum of a two-minute break between each block. Questions included ratings of sexual attractiveness, friendship, and if the client would like to have sex with the person portrayed on the slide. The author calculated VT scores by collapsing each VT into category means determined by age, gender and appearance. For all categories except ages 13 (13 female clothed, 13 male clothed, 13 female nude and 13 male nude) category VT means more than one standard deviation above the grand mean were considered indications of sexual interest. For the age 13 categories, the author used a stricter cut-off point of 1.2 standard deviations above the grand mean. Gress (2005) found VT correctly classified 16 out of 19 or 84% of sexual offenders with child victims, 4 out of 7 or 57% of sexual offenders with adult victims. Three out of seven or 43% were incorrectly classified as having a sexual interest in children (false positives). In addition, VT correctly classified 16 out of 17 or 94% as heterosexual and 5 out of 9 as bisexual.

Worling (2006) investigated VT with *Affinity 1.0*, (currently the *Affinity 2.5*), a VT measure initially developed to assess sexual interest among learning disabled offenders (Glasgow, Osborne & Croxen, 2003). The author administered *Affinity* to 78 adolescent males 52 of whom committed offences against someone younger than 12. *Affinity 1.0* displays in a fixed random order clothed images of 28 females and 28 males in four age categories: toddlers, pre-adolescents, adolescents and adults. Participants rate the sexual attractiveness of each image using a mouse and on-screen slider. Raw scores are collapsed into categories then converted to z-scores. A deviance index is calculated by dividing the VT z-score for child images by the VT z-score for the adult images. Cronbach alphas estimating internal reliability of the categories ranged from .62 for female adolescents to .82 for female toddlers and male pre-adolescents. Similar to Letourneau's (2002) results, *Affinity*'s deviance index was capable of statistically discriminating adolescents with a male child victim from adolescents with victims from all other age/gender groups.

Gress (2007) investigated the relationship between VT and CRT (see details for CRT above) and sexual interest. The author presented 80 slides (half clothed and half nude) to 121 participants, 40 youth offenders, 50 university undergraduates and 22 adult sexual offenders, the majority of who were heterosexual. The slides consisted equally of male and female images in each of the five Tanner categories of physical development (see Fuller *et al.*, 1988). There were four computer-modified image examples per category (see Laws & Gress, 2004), plus five neutral landscapes. Each image was presented five times, each time with one of five questions (for example, 'How old is this person?' or 'Do you find this person sexually attractive?'), for a total of 400 slides. Participants indicated their response to each question by pressing a number on the keypad that matched the Likert scale presented on screen at all times. The author examined the latencies to the clothed images and neutral images only, for a total of 225 slides. Cronbach's alpha for each stimulus category (sex by age) ranged from .72 for male Tanner 5 images to .85 for male Tanner 2 images, with two exceptions: male Tanner 3 (.44) and male Tanner 4 (.69). Results indicated significant differences between the adult sexual offenders and the youth non-sexual offenders but not between the youth non-sexual offenders and the university students, with indication of influence by age or education. In addition, the VT measure demonstrated excellent clinical utility in its ability to differentiate adult heterosexual sexual offenders from non-sexual offenders (for example, AUC = 0.87 female mature images, 0.88 male child images).

Summary of VT studies

Perhaps the most researched attention-based tool with sexual offenders, VT reliably identifies sexual interest (orientation and age preference) and like research on CRT, it informs us that the use of response latencies as an indication of sexual interest may be gender specific (cleaner patterns for males than females, at least in the VT's current format). VT shows promise in clinical applicability, as it reliably differentiates sexual offenders with young male victims from other sexual offenders accomplished via clothed and/or computer-modified stimuli. Nonetheless, investigations into standard, clearly detailed and evidence-based scoring methods, such as those currently underway by Fischer and colleagues (Fischer & Morgan, 2006) are urgently required.

Startle Probe Reflex

The startle eye-blink phenomenon, also known as the eye startle blink reflex, acoustic startle response and startle probe reflexes, is an autonomic response, resulting from primary neural pathways associated with approach and avoidance behaviours, to an intense stimulus (Cornwell, Echiverri & Grillon, 2006). Although there are no published investigations on sexually deviant behaviours using this methodology, a brief review is appropriate as research in this area is ongoing (Hecker *et al.*, 2006). The startle blink reflex examines motivational states (e.g., approach vs. avoidance) via the magnitude of the blink (typically assessed via EMG electrodes placed under the lower eyelid) and its latency. These variables vary as a function of the person's emotional valiance toward the attended to stimulus (Koukounas & Over, 2000). Specifically, a person attending to a pleasant or positive visual or auditory stimulus will demonstrate attenuated (less magnitude and slower) eye-blink responses when presented with an intense and unexpected stimulus (e.g., blast of white noise). On the other hand, they will demonstrate an augmented (increased magnitude and faster) eye-blink response when startled while attending to a stimulus they find aversive or negative (Hecker *et al.*, 2006). For example, Koukounas and McCabe (2001a) found significant startle probe reflex differences for both males and females between neutral and violent film segments, with startle reflexes significantly stronger for violent films, and significant differences between genders, with females demonstrating significantly higher startle probe reflexes to violent films then men.

Koukounas and Over (2000) demonstrated that repeated viewings of erotic films become less physically arousing and decreased pleasant or positive motivation states. The authors found eye blink startle responses augmented significantly across trials of the same erotic film indicating a decrease in positive sensations associated with the film with repeated exposure. Participants' startle reflexes attenuated, i.e., decreased in magnitude to two novel erotic films and then increased again when the original film was reinstated. Koukouna and McCabe (2001b) found participants to exhibit a diminished startle reflex when viewing erotic films participants found attractive compared to those they found aversive.

Giargiari *et al.* (2005) examined startle probe reflexes, pre-pulse inhibition (the inhibition of the startle reflex, caused by a preceding weak stimulus) of the startle probe reflex, and self-reported sexual desire for 36 photos, 24 of which were sexually provocative (equally balanced for males and females) and 12 neutral. The participants (76 heterosexual men and 77 heterosexual women) displayed significantly lower startle magnitudes when viewing opposite-sex stimuli compared to neutral stimuli. In addition, participants with higher self-reported sexual desire showed greater decreases while viewing opposite-sex stimuli as compared to neutral stimuli than did participants with lower sexual desire. Finally, the authors found a significant association between PPI and sexual desire for both sexual stimulus categories.

Hecker, King and Scoular (2006) examined three research questions using the startle probe reflex: (a) will startle probe reflexes attenuate when viewing sexual attractive images? (b) does the startle probe reflex vary when viewing images portraying a variety of potential sexual partners (including deviant partners)? and (c) can the startle probe reflex be voluntarily suppressed? Using various erotic, aversive and neutral slides, the authors found that participants (a) demonstrated significantly increased intensity of eye blink startle reflexes to aversive stimuli in comparison to neutral or sexual images, (b) demonstrated significantly attenuated eye-blink reflexes while viewing photographs of sexually mature females and tasked to imagine sexual activity with them, relative to the magnitudes of their eye-blink reflexes while engaged in the same activity with photos of non-preferred sexual targets, and (c) were unable to suppress their sexual interest even when instructed.

Summary of the startle probe reflex research

The startle probe reflex is an intriguing measure deserving a further look. As research by Hecker *et al.* (2006) and Koukounas and colleagues (2001a, 2000) demonstrates, the startle probe differentiates sexual interest in adult females from sexual interest in adult males and appears resistant to individual manipulation, an important element missing from the other studies reviewed above. Further research is required to investigate the place of startle probes in sex offender research and treatment and fine tune its ability to differentiate arousal to sexual and aversive stimuli.

CONCLUSIONS

Are some cognitions hard-wired and immutable or can treatment professionals aid clients in adjusting maladaptive thoughts and reactions via psychological and phar-maceutical treatments? Attention-based measures can answer these types of questions and as evidenced by this review, there has been a significant boom in researching attention-based measures and sexual deviance. Many studies cited above describe valid and reliable methods investigating individual differences in sexual offenders' cognitions, such as implicit associations and sexual interests. These constructs are essential to skilled assessments and treatment of sexual offenders. Currently in clin-ical settings, the *AASI* and Affinity 2.5 are the only alternatives or augmentations to self-report and PPG. This review suggests that situation will soon change.

Benefits of This Approach

Attention-based measures are quick, easily standardised, non-intrusive, non-invasive and strongly supported by decades of cognitive research. Many are easy to admin-ister and score (especially if computerised), may be resistant to manipulation, and may be useful with unmotivated clients. These measures enhance assessments and inform comprehensive treatment by objectively capturing information offenders may or may not consciously know about themselves or be willing to admit, such as deviant sexual interests, motivation states and implicit or unknown associations. In addition, attention-based measures provide valuable research tools to investigate the etiology and development of sexual offending. For example, to inform treatment offenders' deviant thoughts are important to identify, regardless of whether these thoughts are formed before or after offending For prevention, however, the timing of formation is critical, i.e., if inappropriate associations form before offending occurs, are they associated with an increased risk to offend and if addressed does that decrease risk? Similarly, are sexual thoughts and experiences a precursor to demonstrating attentional bias for sexually preferred material, or in some cases, could the bias be a pre-existing physical condition? If the latter, could individuals who experience strong attentional bias for specific sexual stimuli develop obsessive thinking patterns resulting in sexually inappropriate behaviours? Research questions such as these are more easily addressed with attention-based measures as they require less time, are easy to administer, and may be used with youth and other vulnerable populations.

Cautions When Using Attentional-Based Tasks

Attention-based research, like all psychological studies, is not without problems. Difficulties include data reduction methods (very few studies above mentioned methods for outlier analysis), results biased in their cultural and ethnic generalisability (most participants were Caucasian), and possible effects of volunteer biases common to sex research (see Strassburg & Lowe, 1995; Wolchik, Braver & Jensen, 1985 for discussion on significant differences between volunteers and non-volunteers in studies on sexuality). One study reviewed above did acknowledge and take steps to reduce volunteer bias by providing no information about the nature of the study prior to arrival at the laboratory (a step many institutional review boards or ethics committees may not permit) and administered all measures in a single session (Giargiari et al., 2005).

Known confounds of response latencies include age and intelligence, typically negatively and positively correlated respectively. The relationship between age and latency is not always linear, however, as demonstrated in Gress' (2006a) study where the University sample (average age 19.95, SD = 3.07) produced the shortest latencies (mean = 1.34, SD = .06), the youth offenders (average age 16.5, SD = 1.60) the longest latencies (mean = 1.07, SD = .08), and sexual offenders (average age 41.11, SD = 10.46) were in the middle (mean = 1.44, SD = .14). A significant advantage of IAT is its apparent immunity to the effects of age when scored in a particular manner (Gray et al., 2005).

Typically, studies utilising any of the above measures cite many of the other methods as evidence of applicability and appropriateness, perhaps because the application of attention-based measures to sexual offender research is relatively new and support was scarce. Although all these measures provide strong evidence in general for attention-based measures in sex offender research and application, the measures assess different cognitive processes and should therefore not be seen as interchangeable. As the focus on attention-based measures grows, to build a diverse and strong body of research supporting attention-based methodologies with sexual offenders, the field would benefit from stricter adherence to the theoretical underpinnings of each method.

Clinical Applicability of Attentional-Based Tasks

The application of attentional-based measures to clinical settings requires clear and empirically validated procedures and scoring methods. Of all the measures reviewed above, IAT, the Emotional Stroop, and the RSVP appear most capable. Although more complex than CRT or Emotional Stroop, IAT is a well-defined methodology which appears to reliably identify specific thought patterns, such as associating children with sexual behaviours, key to informing comprehensive treatments. With similar evidence from larger and more diversified studies, this tool will be an essential component of all sexual offender assessments.

The Emotional Stroop like the CRT is a simple and elegant method to investigate sexual interests and deviancy and it may prove to be the briefest and most accessible attentional-based method for clinical settings. Although both studies used voice-activated software, Stroop methods do not require computers, only a couple of worksheets and a timer. The scoring procedures are well researched and documented. Similarly, the scoring method of RSVP appears to be clear and effective. Unfortunately there is only one study investigating its applicability to sexual offenders. Research thus far suggests further investigations of both measures would be worthwhile, but a significant amount of research on these instruments is required before stating these measures inform clinical practice.

Despite a number of studies investigating VT, convincing evidence for clinical applicability remains elusive due to scoring difficulties. For example, only one published study evaluated the AASI clinical scoring methods (Letourneau, 2002) and unfortunately, the results did not provide strong support for its current use in clinical settings. Ongoing investigations on ipsative and normative standardised VT scoring procedures hope to address this situation (Fischer & Morgan, 2006; Gress, 2006b).

FUTURE DIRECTIONS

We should seek to develop cognitive or attention-based assessment procedures that can be used with sexual deviants but are not limited to that clientele. Ideally these procedures are:

- Entirely portable and usable in any setting;
- Relatively inexpensive, easy to implement and use;
- Easy to score and interpret;
- Non-intrusive and resistant to manipulation or lack of motivation;
- Useable with males and females of any age, and importantly,
- Completely open to psychometric evaluation, and
- Admissible in legal settings, an important goal considering this is a forensic population.

The cognitive psychology literature, exclusive of the sexual deviance literature, has for decades reported the testing of procedures that meet those criteria.

REFERENCES

Abel, G.G., Huffman, J., Warberg, B. & Holland, C.L. (1998). Visual reaction time and plethysmography as measures of sexual interest in child molesters. *Sexual Abuse: Journal of Research and Treatment*, *10*, 81–95.

Abel, G.G., Jordan, A., Hand, C.G. *et al.* (2001). Classification models of child molesters utilizing the Abel Assessment for Sexual Interest. *Child Abuse & Neglect*, *25*, 703–718.

Abel, G.G., Jordan, A., Rouleau, J.L. *et al.* (2004). Use of visual reaction time to assess male adolescents who molest children. *Sexual Abuse: Journal of Research and Treatment*, *16*, 255–265.

Algom, D., Chajut, E. & Lev, S. (2004). A rational look at the Emotional Stroop phenomenon: A generic slowdown, not a Stroop effect. *Journal of Experimental Psychology: General*, *133*, 323.

Beech, A., Kalmus, E., Tipper, S.T. *et al.* (in press). Children induce an enhanced attentional blink in child molesters: An objective measure of sexual interest. *Psychological Assessment.*

Brown, A.S., Gray, N.S. & Snowden, R.J. (in press). Developing an implicit association test for forensic use. *Personality and Social Psychology Bulletin.*

Chajut, E., Lev, S. & Algom, D. (2005). Vicissitudes of a misnomer: Reply to Dalgleish (2005). *Journal of Experimental Psychology: General, 4.*

Cornwell, B.R., Echiverri, A.M. & Grillon, C. (2006). Attentional blink and prepulse inhibition of startle are positively correlated. *Psychophysiology, 43,* 504–510.

Dalgliesh, T. (2005). Putting some feeling into it – the conceptual and empirical relationships between the classic and Emotional Stroop tasks: Comment on Algom, Chajut and Lev (2004). *Journal of Experimental Psychology: General, 134,* 585–591.

Eckhardt, C.I. & Cohen, D.J. (1997). Attention to anger-relevant and irrelevant stimuli following naturalistic insult. *Personality and Individual Differences, 23,* 619–629.

Fischer, L. & Morgan, D. (2006). *Norm referenced clinical decision-making with Affinity viewing-time.* Paper presented at the Association for the Treatment of Sexual Abusers, Chicago, IL.

Fischer, L. & Smith, G. (1999). Statistical adequacy of the Abel Assessment for Interest in Paraphilias. *Sexual Abuse: Journal of Research & Treatment, 11,* 195–205.

Flak, V., Beech, A. & Fisher, D. (2007). Forensic assessment of sexual interests: The current position. *Issues in Forensic Psychology, 6,* 70–83.

Fuller, A.K., Barnard, G., Robbins, L. & Spears, H. (1988). Sexual maturity as a criterion for classification of phallometric stimulus slides. *Archives of Sexual Behavior, 17,* 271–276.

Geer, J.H., Estupinan, L.A. & Manguno-Mire, G.M. (2000). Empathy, social skills, and other relevant cognitive processes in rapists and child molesters. *Aggression and Violent Behavior, 5,* 99–126.

Geer, J.H. & Melton, J.S. (1997). Sexual content-induced delay with double-entendre words. *Archives of Sexual Behavior, 26,* 295–316.

Giargiari, T.D., Mahaffey, A.L., Craighead, W.E. & Hutchison, K.E. (2005). Appetitive responses to sexual stimuli are attenuated in individuals with low levels of sexual desire. *Archives of Sexual Behavior, 34,* 547–556.

Giotakis, O. (2005). A combination of viewing reaction time and incidental learning task in child molesters, rapists, and control males and females. *European Journal of Sexology; Sexologies, 54,* 13–22.

Glasgow, D.V., Osborne, A. & Croxen, J. (2003). An assessment tool for investigating paedophile sexual interest using viewing time: An application of single case methodology. *British Journal of Learning Disabilities, 31,* 96–102.

Gray, N.S., Brown, A.S., MacCulloch, M.J. *et al.* (2005). An implicit test of the associations between children and sex in pedophiles. *Journal of Abnormal Psychology, 114,* 304.

Gress, C.L.Z. (2005). Viewing time measures and sexual interest: Another piece of the puzzle. *Journal of Sexual Aggression, 11,* 117–125.

Gress, C. L. Z. (2006a). *Delays in cognitive processing when viewing sexual material: An investigation of two response latency measures.* Paper presented at the 2nd International Summer Conference: Research in Forensic Psychiatry, Regensburg, Germany.

Gress, C. L. Z. (2006b). *Delays in cognitive processing when viewing sexual material: An investigation of two response latency measures.* Unpublished doctoral thesis, University of Victoria, Victoria, BC.

Gress, C.L.Z. (2007). *Delays in attentional processing when viewing sexual imagery: The development and comparison of two measures.* Unpublished dissertation, University of Victoria, Victoria, BC.

Hanson, R.K. & Morton-Bourgon, K.E. (2005). The characteristics of persistent sexual offenders: A meta-analysis of recidivism studies. *Journal of Consulting and Clinical Psychology, 73,* 1154–1163.

Harris, G.T., Rice, M.E., Quinsey, V.L. & Chaplin, T.C. (1996). Viewing time as a measure of sexual interest among child molesters and normal heterosexual men. *Behaviour Research & Therapy, 34,* 389–394.

Hecker, J.E., King, M.W. & Scoular, R.J. (2006). *Startle eye-blink: Preliminary support for a promising method of measuring sexual interest.* Paper presented at the American Psychology & Law Society, St. Petersburg, FL.

Hudson, S.M. & Ward, T. (1997). Intimacy, loneliness, and attachment style in sexual offenders. *Journal of Interpersonal Violence, 12,* 323.

Janssen, E., Everaerd, W., Spiering, M. & Janssen, J. (2000). Automatic processes and the appraisal of sexual stimuli: Toward an information processing model of sexual arousal. *Journal of Sex Research, 37,* 8–23.

Jolicoeur, P. (2002). From perception to action: Making the connection. In W. Prinz & B. Hommel (Eds), *Common mechanisms in perception and action* (pp. 558–586). Oxford, UK: Oxford University Press.

Koukounas, E. & McCabe, M.P. (2001a). Emotional responses to filmed violence and the eye blink startle response. *Journal of Interpersonal Violence, 16,* 476–499.

Koukounas, E. & McCabe, M.P. (2001b). Sexual and emotional variables influencing sexual response to erotica: A psychophysiological investigation. *Archives of Sexual Behavior, 30,* 393–408.

Koukounas, E. & Over, R. (2000). Changes in the magnitude of the eye blink startle response during habituation of sexual arousal. *Behavior Research & Therapy, 38,* 573–594.

Kyllingsbaek, S., Schneider, W.X. & Bundesen, C. (2001). Automatic attraction of attention to former targets in visual displays of letters. *Perception and Psychophysics, 63,* 85–98.

Lalumière, M.L. & Quinsey, V.L. (1994). The discriminability of rapists from non-sex offenders using phallometric measures: A meta-analysis. *Criminal Justice and Behavior, 21,* 150.

Laws, D.R. (2003). Penile plethysmography: Will we ever get it right? In T. Ward, D.R. Laws & S.M. Hudson (Eds), *Sexual deviance: Issues and controversies* (pp. 82–102). Thousand Oaks, CA: Sage.

Laws, D.R. & Gress, C.L.Z. (2004). Seeing things differently: The viewing time alternative to penile plethysmography. *Legal and Criminological Psychology, 9,* 183–196.

Laws, D.R., Hanson, R.K., Osborn, C.A. & Greenbaum, P.E. (2000). Classification of child molesters by plethysmographic assessment of sexual arousal and a self-report measure of sexual preference. *Journal of Interpersonal Violence, 15,* 1297–1312.

Letourneau, E.J. (2002). A comparison of objective measures of sexual arousal and interest: Visual reaction time and penile plethysmography. *Sexual Abuse: Journal of Research and Treatment, 14,* 207–223.

Maletzky, B.M. (2003). Letter to the editor. *Sexual Abuse: Journal of Research & Treatment, 15,* 393.

Mihailides, S., Devilly, G.J. & Ward, T. (2004). Implicit cognitive distortions and sexual offending. *Sexual Abuse: A Journal of Research and Treatment, 16,* 333–350.

Nichols, H.R. & Molinder, I. (1984). Multiphasic Sex Inventory Manual: Available from: Nichols & Molinder, 437 Bowes Drive, Tacoma, WA 98466, USA.

Nunes, K.L., Firestone, P. & Baldwin, M.W. (2007). Indirect assessment of cognitions of child sexual abusers with the implicit association test. *Criminal Justice and Behavior, 34,* 454–475.

Potter, M.C. & Levy, E.I. (1969). Recognition memory for a rapid sequence of pictures. *Journal of Experimental Psychology, 81,* 10–15.

Price, S. (2006). *A Stroop replication study measuring the automatic processing of sexual information.* Paper presented at the American Psychology & Law Society, St. Petersburg, FL, March.

Raymond, J.E., Shapiro, K.L. & Arnell, K.A. (1992). Temporary suppression of visual processing in an RSVP task: An attentional blink? *Journal of Experimental Psychology: Human Perception and Performance, 18,* 849–860.

Santtila, P., Mokros, A. & Viljanen, K. (2006). *Using the choice reaction time task to detect sexual interest: A feasibility study using gay and straight men.* Paper presented at the 2nd International Summer Conference: Research in Forensic Psychiatry, Regensburg, Germany.

Shapiro, K.L. & Raymond, J.E. (1994). Temporal allocation of visual attention: Inhibition or interference? In D. Dagenbach & T. Carr (Eds), *Inhibitory processes in attention, memory and language* (pp. 327–358). London, UK: Academic Press.

Singer, B. (1984). Conceptualizing sexual arousal and attraction. *Journal of Sex Research, 20,* 230–240.

Smith, P. & Waterman, M. (2004). Processing bias for sexual material: The Emotional Stroop and sexual offenders. *Sexual Abuse: Journal of Research and Treatment, 16,* 163–171.

Strassburg, D.S. & Lowe, K. (1995). Volunteer bias in sexuality research. *Archives of Sexual Behavior, 24,* 369–382.

Stroop, J.R. (1935). Studies of interference in serial-verbal reaction. *Journal of Experimental Psychology: General, 18,* 643–662.

Van Honk, J., Tuiten, A., de Haan, E. *et al.* (2001). Attentional biases for angry faces: Relationships to trait anger and anxiety. *Cognition and Emotion, 15,* 279–297.

Williams, J.M.G., Mathews, A. & MacLeod, C. (1996). The Emotional Stroop task and psychopathology. *Psychological Bulletin, 120,* 3–24.

Wolchik, S.A., Braver, S.L. & Jensen, K. (1985). Volunteer bias in erotica research: Effects of intrusiveness of measure and sexual background. *Archives of Sexual Behavior, 14,* 93–106.

Worling, J. (2006). Assessing sexual arousal with adolescent males who have offended sexually: Self-report and unobtrusively measured viewing time. *Sexual Abuse: A Journal of Research and Treatment, 18,* 383–400.

Wright, L.W. Jr & Adams, H.E. (1994). Assessment of sexual preference using a choice reaction time task. *Journal of Psychopathology and Behavioral Assessment, 16,* 221–231.

Wright, L.W. Jr & Adams, H.E. (1999). The effects of stimuli that vary in erotic content on cognitive processes. *The Journal of Sex Research, 36,* 145–151.

Zuckerman, M. (1971). Physiological measures of sexual arousal in the human. *Psychological Bulletin, 75,* 297–329.

8

The Standardisation of Phallometry

YOLANDA FERNANDEZ

INTRODUCTION

Despite a lengthy history of debate over the use of penile plethysmography (also known as phallometric testing or phallometry) it remains one of the most contentious issues in literature on the evaluation of sexual offenders (Gazan, 2002; Laws, 2003). In fact, critics of phallometric testing have identified such a wide range of problems that it is impossible to provide an exhaustive account in any one article. Issues identified have ranged from the ecological validity of laboratory-assessed sexual preferences (Blader & Marshall, 1989) to the ability of subjects to fake responses during testing (Card & Farrall, 1990; Freund, 1967b; Henson & Rubin, 1971; Laws & Rubin, 1969), to ethical problems with the collection of and use of deviant stimuli (Krueger & Kaplan, 2002). However, the most serious obstacle to a broad acceptance of phallometric testing with sexual offenders is likely the lack of any agreed upon standardised methodology. There is a consensus among reviewers that the standardisation of penile plethysmography is in an unacceptable state (Barker & Howell, 1992; Howes, 1995; Lalumière & Harris, 1998; Laws, 2003; Marshall & Fernandez, 2000, 2003; Simon & Schouten, 1993; Walter & Schouten, 1993) and there is some scepticism that this will ever be resolved satisfactorily (Laws, 2003). Laws (2003) goes as far as to describe the use of the penile plethysmograph as 'an art' rather than a science because of the lack of agreed upon standards for performing assessments.

If phallometry is to serve as a satisfactory measure of sexual arousal it must, like any test, meet particular criteria. Psychometric principles require that any test must be: (1) reasonably standardised; (2) reliable; (3) valid; and (4) predict future behaviour. The lack of adherence to the first criteria (standardisation) necessarily makes it more difficult to establish the second and third criteria, namely the basic psychometric properties of reliability and validity. This is because meaningful comparisons between studies

---

Assessment and Treatment of Sex Offenders: A Handbook. Edited by Anthony Beech, Leam Craig and Kevin Browne. © John Wiley & Sons Ltd, 2009.

that have used widely varying procedures are difficult, if not impossible, to make. Studies that use significantly different methodologies should expect to have conflicting findings regarding the reliability and validity of any given test. It should therefore not be surprising that this is what has been found in the literature on phallometric testing. Several earlier articles have provided thorough reviews of the variability in procedures between studies addressing the psychometric properties of phallometric testing (Laws, 2003; Marshall & Fernandez, 2003; O'Donohue & Letourneau, 1992); however, some of the most pertinent differences in the literature that clearly illustrate the difficulties a lack of standardisation in methodology creates, are outlined below.

MEASURING DEVICES

The two major techniques for measuring penile tumescence are the volumetric and circumferential methods. The volumetric assessment of sexual arousal uses a tube-like device that encloses the entire penis and is sealed at the base of the penis by a cuff-like device. As the penis engorges during an erection air within the tube is displaced and measured to provide an estimate of the magnitude of penile erection. Circumferential approaches may use either a flexible metal gauge (Barlow *et al.*, 1970), or a thin rubber tube filled with mercury or indium-gallium that operates as a strain gauge (Bancroft, Jones & Pullen, 1966). The metal band gauge is considered reliable and durable but tends to be expensive. Laws (1977) reported that the two types of circumferential gauges produced approximately equivalent results but noted the metal band tended to displace while the subject detumesces. Although the metal-in-rubber strain gauge is somewhat less durable it tends to be less expensive to purchase and is the more commonly used measurement apparatus for circumferential measures.

The issue of volumetric versus circumferential measurement or erectile responses remains controversial. Proponents of the volumetric method claim that the two approaches are not equivalent. It has been suggested that volumetric methods are more accurate (Langevin, 1989; McConaghy, 1999) and require shorter durations of exposure to the stimuli providing the subjects with less time to distort their responses (McConaghy, 1999). McConaghy (1999) suggests that circumferential methods of assessment require longer exposure to stimuli because during the initial stages of the erectile response the blood flow into the penis cannot maintain circumference while increasing length. Indeed, it has been empirically demonstrated that as the length of the penis increases the circumference initially decreases (Earls & Marshall, 1982). In order for circumferential measures to register an increase in arousal, time must be allowed for the penis to first lengthen and then increase in circumference. Kuban, Barbaree and Blanchard (1999) overcame many of the problems associated with using volumetric devices and demonstrated that the volumetric device detected small changes in the penis while circumferential measures were valid only after arousal exceeded 10% full erection.

In contrast to the claims made by McConaghy (1999), proponents of circumferential methods have suggested that the similarities between the methods are greater than the differences by noting the high correlations between the outputs of the two measures. Both McAnulty and Adams (1992) and Wheeler and Rubin (1987) concluded that volumetric assessments are technically more difficult, display more artefacts, and are no more sensitive than circumferential methods. Langevin (1989) pointed out that volumetric assessments are cumbersome and require extensive training while circumferential methods are more durable and easier to use and, as a result, circumferential methods appear to be the more commonly used apparatus in phallometric testing.

STIMULUS DIFFERENCES

Stimuli are generally presented in three forms: slides projected onto a screen, videotaped clips, or audiotapes. Videotapes present ethical problems akin to those generated by slide stimuli (see discussion below) and they also generate such high arousal that discrimination between different categories of stimuli is reduced (Marshall & Fernandez, 2000).

Slide presentations generally consist of still pictures of nude male and female stimuli of varying ages. The stimuli can vary along a variety of dimensions (black and white vs. colour, presence or absence of background, single vs. two or more figures, and the presence or absence of sexual activity). There has been no attempt in the literature to match stimuli for psychophysical properties despite evidence that responses to stimuli are significantly controlled by variations in such properties (Gescheider, 1976; Stevens, 1975). Responses to visual stimuli have been shown to vary according to brightness and hue, and as a function of the relative distribution of these dimensions among the elements of a stimulus (Sekuler & Blake, 1994). The same is true for auditory stimuli with loudness and pitch (Stevens, 1951).

Slides are thought to be best suited to assess subjects' age and gender preferences (Lalumière & Harris, 1998). Interestingly, it has been found that the responses of men to pictures of post-pubertal adolescents are indistinguishable from responses to pictures of young adults (Harris & Rice, 1996).

Despite its popularity, there are several major concerns with using slide stimuli to assess sexual preferences. It has been noted that it is difficult to obtain high levels of arousal using slides (Abel *et al.*, 1975) and consequently subjects may not discriminate between appropriate and inappropriate stimuli, making interpretation of profiles troublesome. There are also serious ethical questions regarding the use of nude photographs of children. Informed consent from the children in the photographs or from their parents is likely impossible to obtain, particularly if the photographs were seized by the police from alleged child molesters; some people believe these children are re-victimised every time the stimulus set is shown (Launay, 1994). The use of such stimuli has not only generated controversy among clinicians and researchers (Card & Olsen, 1996; Laws 1996), their use has been banned in several states of the USA (Murphy, 2001). An alternative approach is to use composite pictures, which are the result of combining photographs of different models (Cohen, 1988), or computer-generated pictures of children (Konopasky & Konopasky, 2000). Researchers have begun to produce such stimulus sets and are in the process of validating them, but at present such stimulus sets are not widely utilised. Although computer-generated or composite photographs might address the issue of informed consent for slide stimuli, this type of solution does not necessarily circumvent the ethical issue of showing naked children.

AUDIOTAPES

The audio presentation of stimuli includes descriptions of adult sexual interactions and sexual activity between an adult and a child or verbal descriptions of adult – adult sexual interactions including: consensual sexual activity, sexual assault, non-sexual violence and neutral (neither sexual nor violent) interactions.

It has been claimed that audiotaped stimuli have the advantage of being able to present cues that, for technical and ethical reasons, cannot be presented in other ways (Abel & Blanchard, 1976). For example, violent sexual assaults on children cannot ethically be presented visually and the dynamics of these acts cannot be captured by still slides but they may be described vividly on an audiotape. In addition, audio-taped stimuli may be tailored to the unique interests of the subject by varying the parameters of the stimuli such as age of the victim, use of violence and other relevant features. However, Walter and Schouten (1993) point out that such variety may influence subjects' responses in ways that are difficult to determine. Subjects presented with complex stimuli may respond to other erotic cues such as the description of the situation or the type of sexual activity rather than the attributes of the target of interest in the stimuli (e.g., description of pre-pubescent features). Abel et al. (1975) demonstrated that different homosexual subjects responded differentially to the various elements in their sexual stimuli and both Laws (1984) and Barbaree (1990) found the same idiosyncratic responding in sexual offenders. To date, research on stimulus modality and content has been limited and has generally focused on one or two characteristics of the stimuli rather than possible interactions between various aspects included in complex stimuli.

Additional differences between stimuli used in various studies are the number of exemplars presented for each category (e.g., adult females, children, rape) and the duration of the stimulus presentation. Studies using circumferential measures tend to present stimuli for longer periods (2 to 4 minutes) whereas studies using volumetric measures present stimuli for approximately 30 seconds (Murphy & Barbaree, 1994). As noted previously this may be because volumetric measures are more sensitive to the early part of the erectile response. Avery-Clark and Laws (1984) demonstrated that at least three minutes of exposure to auditory stimuli was necessary to reach maximum discrimination levels.

Along the same lines the presence, duration and temporal location of the sexual elements in auditory stimuli may vary among studies. It is reasonable to consider that different sexual activities (e.g., oral sex, genital sex, anal sex) might produce different, and likely idiosyncratic, responding in subjects. In addition to stimuli variations of gender, age, and sexual activity, stimuli also vary in terms of elements such as humiliation, forcefulness, brutality and sexual intrusiveness. Marshall and Fernandez (2003) note that no attempts have been made to empirically determine the most 'sexually significant' elements in auditory stimuli and create stimuli with comparable presence, temporal location and duration of these elements despite the fact that some researchers claim the different findings across phallometric studies are due to differing stimulus content (Lalumière & Quinsey, 1994).

Finally, the presence or absence of 'warm-up' stimuli varies between studies. Warm-up stimuli are used to familiarise subjects with the procedures before assessing their arousal. Although some researchers have indicated in studies whether or not they use warm-up stimuli they do not always elaborate on the features contained in such stimuli.

Lalumière and Harris (1998) suggest aural stimuli are best for identifying preferences for coercive sex with children or women. They claim that graphic depictions of violent coercive sex are the most valid stimuli. However, practitioners vary in their degree of comfort with such graphic material and may choose to utilise more conservative stimuli for ethical reasons (Launay, 1994).

SCORING

Raw Scores and Transformations

Phallometric results may be represented as raw scores in the form of either millimetre change in the circumference of the penis, voltage changes, or volume changes.

Other scoring methods include transforming raw scores to either percentage of full erection or standard scores (z-scores). Transforming scores reduces inter-subject variability due to penis size or responsiveness and allows for comparisons of responses both within and between subjects (Howes, 1995). Transforming scores has also been promoted in an attempt to deal with the issue of low arousal among numerous subjects during phallometric testing (Howes, 2003).

In order to express change as a percentage of full erection, it is necessary to obtain a measure of the subject's full erection. This can be done either by estimating the size of a full erection or, when measuring the erectile response to an arousing stimulus, by having the subject self-report when he has a full erection. Unfortunately, subjects are not always accurate in estimating their full erection (Launay, 1994). Additional problems that have been identified with transforming scores to percent of full erection are that subjects may not actually attain a full erection (Walter & Schouten, 1993), estimates of full erection may not be satisfactorily accurate because of differences in penis size and responsivity (Lalumière & Harris, 1998), and normative estimates of full erection may increase classification errors (Howes, 1995, 2003). Definitions of what constitutes a full erection have been remarkably inconsistent in the research literature. Estimates of average circumferential change have ranged from 7 mm to 3 cm from a flaccid state to full erection (Becker *et al.*, 1992; Furr, 1991; Hunter & Goodwin, 1992; Launay, 1994; Proulx *et al.*, 1997). In a more recent study Howes

(2003) noted that the large number of idiosyncratic calculation methods for a full erection currently in existence in the research literature does "not reflect well on the state of the literature". In an attempt to provide some standardisation for estimating full erection Howes reported a mean of 32.6 mm change with a standard deviation of 8.8 mm change in study with a sample size of 724 subjects and was able to provide confidence intervals for estimating a full erection.

Due to the disadvantages noted with transforming scores to percent full erection, some researchers feel that transforming data to z-scores (ipsative method) is the best alternative. This method provides a single 'standard' scale of measurement such that all distributions under consideration are converted to a single scale for comparison. Standard scores have useful descriptive properties and are easy to interpret as each score specifies how many standard deviations an individual is above or below the mean. In a comparison of raw data, percent full erection, and z-score methods, Earls, Quinsey and Castonguay (1987) concluded that z-scores accounted for more of the variance and produced similar criterion validity to the other two scoring methods. On the other hand, practitioners point to several disadvantages of using z-scores over percent full erection. Among the problems identified have been that z-scores do not provide a measure of the magnitude of the erectile response (Launay, 1994), that phallometric responses in individuals are rarely normally distributed and that z-scores are not robust in such circumstances (Howes, 2003), and that z-scores are susceptible to accentuating small differences within subjects (Earls, Quinsey & Castonguary, 1987; Hall, 1990; Simon & Shouten, 1992). Barbaree and Mewhort (1994) demonstrated that when arousal to all stimuli was either very low or very high, z-score transformations exaggerated the relative differences in responding to the deviant and appropriate stimuli. Consequently, group results become distorted because the small differences evident in subjects with low or high levels of responding are given as much weight as those who discriminate strongly between stimuli (Hall, 1990; Launay, 1994).

Deviance Indices

Erectile responses may also be described by using indices of deviant arousal such as ratio and difference scores. Ratio scores are calculated by dividing the average (or peak) response to an inappropriate category (e.g., rape stimuli) by the average (or peak) response to an appropriate category (e.g., consenting sex). According to Lalumière and Harris (1998), a ratio score of 1.00 or more is considered a deviant profile. In this case the subject's response to the inappropriate category is at least as strong or stronger than his response to an appropriate category. Difference scores are calculated by subtracting the average (or peak) response to an inappropriate category (e.g., pre-pubescent female) from the average (or peak) response to an appropriate category (e.g., adult female). Lalumière and Harris (1998) suggest a difference score of 0.0 or less should be considered a deviant profile.

Lalumière and Harris (1998) maintain that cut-off scores of 1.0 for ratios and 0.0 for difference scores are fairly conservative limits resulting in few non-deviant subjects being classified as deviant. Marshall and Eccles (1991) propose a less conservative ratio of .80 as the cut-off for deviance. They also recommend that practitioners pay attention to the absolute value of a subject's arousal to stimuli in addition to relative indices, or valuable information may be lost. Marshall and Eccles note that, regardless of the relationship with non-deviant stimuli, if the absolute level of arousal to inappropriate stimuli is greater than 30% of full erection, the profile should be considered deviant. Finally, Walter and Schouten (1993) suggest that how indices function may depend on the stimulus set used. Without standardised stimulus sets, indices may vary in unexpected ways making comparisons between studies of dubious value.

Low Responders

There is little consensus in the literature as to how to deal with low responders despite studies which have indicated as many as 20% of known sexual offenders may show no arousal to any sexual stimuli during phallometric testing (Farrall & Card, 1988; Marshall, Barbaree & Christophe, 1986; Marshall & Fernandez, 2003; Proulx *et al.*, 1994). Some clinicians believe that responses of less than 15% of full erection are clinically useful because such low responses are below the level of awareness and are, therefore, difficult to control or fake (Launay, 1994). Quinsey, Chaplin and Varney (1981) have recommended that a valid profile is one in which the subject demonstrates higher responses to sexual stimuli than to neutral stimuli regardless of the absolute level of responding. In contrast, other researchers have indicated that a minimum level of arousal must be attained to reliably determine the meaning of the resultant pattern. Marshall and Eccles (1991) suggest that a minimum response of 10% full erection is required for a valid profile, whereas other researchers have suggested using cut-offs of 20% full erection (Howes, 1995; Murphy, Hanes & Worley, 1991) and 30% full erection (Davidson & Malcolm, 1985). While some researchers have routinely excluded low responders from research studies (Freund & Blanchard, 1989; Looman *et al.*, 1998; Malcolm, Andrews & Quinsey, 1993), others have reported that including low response subjects did not affect the sensitivity of their phallometric assessments (Harris *et al.*, 1992). Still other researchers have failed to mention in their studies whether or not they excluded low responders. Interestingly, Howes (2003) posits that pressure on researchers to use "more sanitized and less explicit" stimuli, particularly in the United States, is likely to increase the problem of low arousal during phallometric testing leading to difficulties in interpreting data.

Differences in Instructions

Most studies fail to describe in detail instructions provided to subjects about the procedure of phallometric testing. Differences in instructions can range from differences in the descriptions of the stimuli to what the subject should expect or do in terms of responding. Some subjects may be told to 'go with the flow' and that some arousal is expected, while others may be told nothing about their possible responding. There is evidence to suggest that instructional sets can impact responding. A number of studies have supported the suggestion that instructing subjects to suppress all responding may maximise discrimination between rapists and non-rapists (Abel *et al.*, 1978; Murphy *et al.*, 1985; Wormith *et al.*, 1988).

Subject Differences

Whether or not we can accurately use phallometry to differentiate populations whose sexual behaviours differ is not a straightforward question. Past research has typically compared sexual offenders to men who are presumed to be non-offenders. Unfortunately, it is not a simple task to identify a 'pure' sample of non-offenders for the comparison group. Studies have shown that among university males 17% admit to having sexually molested a child as an adult (Briere & Runtz, 1989; Finkelhor, 1979) and substantial numbers of 'normal' males indicate some likelihood that they would, or have, raped a woman (Koss, Gidycz & Wisniewski, 1987). In addition, Langevin (1988) reported that it is common for presumed non-offenders to show sexual arousal to quite young children at phallometric testing. Screening procedures of 'normal' males volunteering for phallometric studies have regularly led to the exclusion of 35–45%, and on one occasion 62%, of these volunteers on the basis of them indicating deviant tendencies (Marshall & Fernandez, 2000). These procedures, of course, rely on the subjects' honesty so it is likely that some men with deviant tendencies escape detection and are included in the 'non-offender' samples. An even more serious problem is suggested by studies by Freund and colleagues who showed that accused men who deny committing a sexual offence are likely to show normal responses at phallometric assessment (Freund & Blanchard, 1989; Freund, Chan & Coulthard, 1979).

Given these problems with identifying non-deviant groups, Marshall and Fernandez (2000) suggested that an alternative approach might be to compare responses of identified sexual offenders of one type with the responses of another type of sexual offender. Harris *et al.* (1992) and Hall, Shondrick and Hirshman (1993) have also suggested that it is just as important to discriminate among subgroups of sexual offenders, as it is to discriminate offenders from non-offenders. Finally, Frenzel and Lang (1989) indicated that one of the main tasks of forensic psychologists working in this area is to "determine the nature of erotic preferences among subgroups of child sexual abusers" (p. 257). However, there is still little consensus in the literature as to the best comparison group when studying sexual preferences in sexual offenders.

THE CURRENT STATE OF STANDARDISATION IN PHALLOMETRY

The lack of a standardised approach to phallometric testing is hardly a new issue. O'Donahue and Letourneu (1992) identified no less than 17 potential sources of procedural variation in the assessment of child molesters using phallometric testing, several of which were confirmed in Howes' (1995) survey of laboratories across Canada and the United States. Howes concluded that centres using phallometric testing utilise an unacceptably wide range of stimuli, have no standard procedure for assessment, have little, if any, normative data, often use questionable methodology and demonstrate limited agreement as to how to analyse and interpret results. Several years later the Marshall, Serran and Yates' (2003b) survey of phallometric testing in Canadian and American sex offender programmes suggested little improvement in standardisation in phallometry. The survey confirmed that many of the areas of potential procedural variation identified by O'Donohue and Letourneau continue to be a problem among sites. Interestingly, however, 70% of Canadian respondent sites and 55% of American respondent sites noted that they have concerns about the lack of standardisation in phallometric testing.

Issues relevant to standardisation of phallometric testing queried in the Marshall *et al.* (2003b) survey included questions about the types of stimuli and apparatus used, instructions to subjects, data collection, data transformation, dealing with faking, training of technicians, and characteristics (gender) of the technician. Among the American sites 95% reported using auditory stimuli while only 35% indicated they used visual (mainly slide) stimuli. Approximately 25% reported using video stimuli. All but three (9%) of the Canadian sites indicated they used both auditory and visual (slide) stimuli while 21% stated they also used videos. Stimulus sets in use also varied, particularly by country. American sites used mostly the ATSA (Association for the Treatment of Sexual Abusers) stimulus set (44%) or the Monarch set (42%) while the majority of Canadian laboratories used stimuli developed by Quinsey's (50%) or Barbaree's (30%) groups. Other stimulus sets less reported among sites in both countries included those developed by Farrall, Limestone, Broadmoor, Laws, Konapasky, Becker, Eccles, Freund, and the CSC Ontario Region Standardized Slide Set. All sites reported providing subjects with instructions, although some used instructions provided during training (e.g., Monarch/BTI) and some simply provided information regarding the purpose of the assessment and instructions on how to use the equipment.

Although circumferential devices were the most commonly reported measurement method for both countries, some sites preferred the metal band gauge while others indicated they used mercury-in-rubber or indium-gallium strain gauges. A small number of respondents reported using volumetric methods during phallometric testing. Calibration of instruments ranged from before and after each use to monthly recalibration. Additionally, while the majority of respondents indicated they collected data as millimetre change, only about half of the American sites reported transforming data, mostly to percent full erection and some to z-scores. Only about one-third of the American sites calculated deviance indices (ratio or difference scores). In contrast the vast majority (94%) of Canadian sites transformed data and calculated deviance indices.

Responses to how sites dealt with the issue of faking during phallometric testing were also inconsistent. Some sites reported doing nothing to control faking. Other sites described various methods including having clients describe stimuli, using attention cues, visual monitoring of clients, discussing faking with clients and suggesting that it will be obvious, tracking GSIR and respiration, BTI protocol (tone and star), polygraphy and examining the data profile.

Among both Canadian and American sites technicians of both genders were reported and a wide variety of training for technicians, both formal and informal, was identified. Training approaches included such informal approaches as on-site training (e.g., observing laboratory assessments and conducting assessments under supervision), literature reviews, mentoring/apprenticeships and university courses that focused on phallometrics. Formal approaches included specialised workshops at conferences or workshops provided by identified experts in phallometry (e.g., Monarch/BTI, Farrall Institute, Steve Jensen, ATSA, John Bradford, and William Pithers). However, the results of this survey were certainly more comforting than Howes' (1995) survey of 48 centres using phallometry that noted 18% of technicians reported having no training in phallometric procedures at all.

THE FUTURE OF PHALLOMETRY

In order to evaluate the adequacy of phallometry as a psychophysiological test, it is necessary to identify the standards against which the procedure is to be assessed. For a test to be of worth it must be standardised and shown to be both reliable and valid (Kline, 1993). Two attempts have been made to generate a standardised protocol (same stimuli, procedures, instructions to subjects and response transformations) for phallometric testing. A multi-site study, across five sites in the United States and three sites in Canada, was launched in the late 1980s (Abel *et al.*, 1989). The study of the age and gender assessment for child molesters focused on standardising the characteristics of research participants, individual slides, characteristics of the slide set, calibration of the equipment, the procedure, consent and handling of data. Unfortunately, however, only one site actually collected and reported data (Laws, Gulayets & Frenzel, 1995). This attempt at a multi-site evaluation of a standardised protocol was never finished.

On a more positive note, another proposal for a multi-site standardisation study was put forward by Marshall and colleagues (Marshall, Marshall & Yates, 2003). The study proposes collecting phallometric data across nine sites associated with the Correctional Service of Canada and 10 sites within the HM Prison Service in England and Wales over a two-year period. Apparently several sites from the United States and Europe have also agreed to participate. The proposal estimates that data on over 1000 sexual offender subjects and 200 normative subjects will be collected during the course of the study. The standardised stimulus sets proposed for the study are updated versions of the audiotaped Child Sexual Violence (Quinsey & Chaplin, 1988) and Female Sexual Violence (Quinsey, Chaplin & Varney, 1981) stimulus sets. Additionally, Marshall, Marshall and Yates (2003) have created standardised instructional sets and consent forms for the assessment process. All sites are to report data in an identical manner (i.e., as both raw scores and z-score transformations) to a central coordinating office. Analyses of the data will focus on the internal consistency, test – retest reliability and criterion validity of the phallometric assessment data.

Ultimately a distribution of normal scores for the normal group is to be determined. This study will do much to address many of the standardisation problems identified to date and provides some optimism for the future of phallometric testing. At last contact it appeared that approval had been obtained at all sites except the Correctional Service of Canada, where approval was still pending (W.L. Marshall, personal communication, July 2006).

So why does phallometric testing remain as widely used as it is? The driving force behind the popularity of phallometry at the present time is likely the research generated during the past several years that has demonstrated some predictive validity for phallometric testing. The sexually violent recidivism of child molesters in particular may be statistically predicted by phallometric responses measured prior to treatment (Hanson & Bussière, 1998, 2001; Rice, Harris & Quinsey, 1990; Rice, Quinsey & Harris, 1991). Phallometric testing has further gained legitimacy through endorsements by associations such as the Association for the Treatment of Sexual Abusers, which promotes the use of phallometry to corroborate self-reports regarding sexual arousal patterns during assessments of sexual offenders (ATSA, 2005). Additionally, the manual generated by HM Prison Service to train technicians on the penile plethysmograph states that the empirical relationship between deviance assessed through phallometric testing and sexual offence recidivism is the primary justification for use of the penile plethysmograph in their sex offender treatment programme assessment battery (HM Prison Service, 2005). In a similar vein, the majority of respondents in the Marshall, Serran and Yates (2003) survey reported finding phallometrics to be a valuable tool for risk assessments, and evaluation of sexual preferences, arousal and treatment planning and progress.

Prior to an unqualified acceptance of phallometric testing for use in the assessment and treatment of sexual offenders much more work needs to be done to create a standardised assessment tool that will, in turn, contribute to more consistent research on the psychometric properties of this testing technique. The researchers who originally designed phallometric testing did not adhere to accepted standards for the development of psychological tests (American Educational Research Association, 1999), consequently, improvements in phallometric testing may require beginning again with such standards in mind. Unlike other psychological tests (e.g., intelligence tests) research on phallometry did not begin with studies of non-deviant or 'normal' populations (Freund, 1957, 1967a). Until a standardised protocol has been agreed upon, and the results of phallometric testing are more clearly understood, users should exercise caution in interpreting such results. In particular caution should be used in making decisions based on phallometric results. Hopefully, in the not too distant future, researchers will provide a more substantive basis for phallometric testing.

REFERENCES

Abel, G.G. & Blanchard, E.G. (1976). The measurement and generation of sexual arousal in male sexual deviates. *Progressive Behavior Modification*, 2, 99–136.

Abel, G.G., Becker, J.V., Card, R.D. *et al.* (1989). *The stimulus standardisation study of the Multisite Assessment Group*. Paper presented at the First International Conference on the Treatment of Sex Offenders, Minneapolis, May 1989.

Abel, G.G., Blanchard, E.B., Barlow, D.H., & Mavissakalian, M. (1975). Identifying the specific erotic cues in sexual deviation by audiotaped descriptions. *Journal of Applied Behavior Analysis, 8*, 247–260.

Abel, G.G., Blanchard, E.B., Becker, J.V. & Djenderedjian, A. (1978). Differentiating sexual aggressives with penile measures. *Criminal Justice and Behavior, 5*, 315–322.

American Educational Research Association (1999). *Standards for educational and psychological testing*. Washington, DC: American Psychological Association.

Association for the Treatment of Sexual Abusers (ATSA) (2005). *Practice standards and guidelines for members of the Association for the Treatment of Sexual Abusers*. Beaverton, OR: Author.

Avery-Clark, C. & Laws, D.R. (1984). Differential erection response patterns of sexual child abusers to stimuli describing activities with children. *Behavior Therapy, 15*, 71–83.

Bancroft, J., Jones, H.G. & Pullen, B.R. (1966). A simple transducer for measuring penile erection, with comments on its use in the treatment of sexual disorders. *Behavior Research and Therapy, 4*, 239–241.

Barbaree, H.E. (1990). Stimulus control of sexual arousal. In W.L. Marshall, D.R. Laws, & H.E. Barbaree (Eds), *Handbook of sexual assault: Issues, theories, and treatment of the offender* (pp. 115–142). New York: Plenum Press.

Barbaree, H.E. & Mewhort, D.J.K. (1994). The effects of the z-score transformation on measures of relative erectile response strengths: A re-appraisal. *Behavior Research and Therapy, 32*, 547–558.

Barker, J.G. & Howell, R.J. (1992). The plethysmograph: A review of recent literature. *Bulletin of the American Academy of Psychiatry and the Law, 2*, 13–25.

Barlow, D.H., Becker, R., Leitenberg, H. & Agras, W.S. (1970). A mechanical strain gauge for recording penile circumference change. *Journal of Applied Behaviour Analysis, 3*, 73–76.

Becker, J.V., Stein, R.M., Kaplan, M.S. & Cunningham-Rathner, J. (1992). Erection response characteristics of adolescent sex offenders. *Annals of Sex Research, 5*, 81–86.

Blader, J.C. & Marshall, W.L. (1989). Is the assessment of sexual arousal in rapists worthwhile? A critique of current methods and the development of a response compatibility approach. *Clinical Psychology Review, 9*, 569–587.

Briere, J. & Runtz, M. (1989). University males' sexual interest in children: Predicting potential indices of paedophilia in a nonforensic sample. *Child Abuse and Neglect, 13*, 65–75.

Card, R.D. & Farrall, W. (1990). Detecting faked responses to erotic stimuli: A comparison of stimulus condition and response measures. *Annals of Sex Research, 3*, 381–396.

Card, R.D. & Olsen, S.E. (1996). Visual plethysmograph stimuli involving children: Rethinking some quasi-logical issues. *Sexual Abuse: A Journal of Research and Treatment, 8*, 267–271.

Cohen, F. (1988). Therapeutic uses of sexually explicit photographs. In B.K. Schwartz & H.R. Cellini (Eds), *A practitioners' guide to treating the incarcerated male sex offender* (pp. 183–186). Washington, DC: US Department of Justice, National Institute of Corrections.

Davidson, P.R. & Malcolm, P.B. (1985). The reliability of the rape index: A rapist sample. *Behavioral Assessment, 7*, 283–292.

Earls, C.M. & Marshall, W.L. (1982). The simultaneous and independent measurement of penile circumference and length. *Behavior Research Methods and Instrumentation, 14*, 447–450.

Earls, C.M., Quinsey, V.L. & Castonguay, L.G (1987). A comparison of three methods of scoring penile circumference changes. *Archives of Sexual Behavior, 16*, 493–500.

Farrall, W.R. & Card, R.D. (1988). Advancements in physiological evaluation of assessment and treatment in the sexual aggressor. In R. Prentky & V.L. Quinsey (Eds), *Human sexual aggression: Current perspectives* (pp. 261–273). New York: New York Academy of Sciences.

Finkelhor, D. (1979). *Sexually victimized children*. New York: Free Press.

Frenzel, R.R. & Lang, R.A. (1989). Identifying sexual preferences in intrafamilial and extrafamilial child sexual abusers. *Annals of Sex Research, 2*, 255–275.

Freund, K. (1957). Diagnostika homosexuality u muszu. *Ceskoslovak Medicine, 53*, 382–393.

Freund, K. (1967a). Diagnosing homo or heterosexuality and erotic age-preference by means of a psychophysiological test. *Behavior Research and Therapy, 5,* 209–228.

Freund, K. (1967b). Erotic preference in pedophilia. *Behavior Research and Therapy, 5,* 339–348.

Freund, K. & Blanchard, R. (1989). Phallometric diagnosis of pedophilia. *Journal of Consulting and Clinical Psychology, 57,* 1–6.

Freund, K, Chan, S. & Coulthard, R. (1979). Phallometric diagnoses with 'nonadmitters'. *Behavior Research and Therapy, 17,* 451–457.

Furr, K.D. (1991). Penis size and magnitude of erectile change as spurious factors in estimating sexual arousal. *Annals of Sex Research, 4,* 265–279.

Gazan, F. (2002). Penile Plethysmography before the European Court of Human Rights. *Sexual Abuse: A Journal of Research and Treatment, 14,* 89–93.

Gescheider, G.A. (1976). *Psychophysics: Methods and theories.* Hillsdale, NJ: Lawrence Erlbaum.

Hall, G.C.N. (1990). Validity of physiological measures of pedophilic sexual arousal in a sexual offender population: A reply to Quinsey and Laws. *Journal of Consulting and Clinical Psychology, 58,* 889–891.

Hall, G.C.N., Shondrick, D.D. & Hirshman, R. (1993). The role of sexual arousal in sexually aggressive behavior: A meta-analysis. *Journal of Consulting and Clinical Psychology, 61,* 1091–1095.

Hanson, R.K. & Bussière, M.T. (1998). *Predictors of sexual offender recidivism: A meta-analysis.* (User Report No. 1994-04.) Ottawa: Department of the Solicitor General of Canada.

Harris, G. T. & Rice, M.E. (1996). The science in phallometric measurement of male sexual interest. *Current Directions in Psychological Science: A Journal of the American Psychological Society, 5,* 156–160.

Harris, G.T., Rice, M.E., Quinsey, V.L. *et al.* (1992). Maximizing the discriminant validity of phallometric assessment. *Psychological Assessment, 4,* 502–511.

Henson, D.E. & Rubin, H.B. (1971). Voluntary control of eroticism. *Journal of Applied Behavior Analysis, 4,* 38–44.

HM Prison Service, Offending Behaviour Programmes Unit (2005). *Draft administration manual for penile plethysmograph.* Unpublished manuscript.

Howes, R.J. (1995). A survey of plethysmographic assessment in North America. *Sexual Abuse: A Journal of Research and Treatment, 7,* 9–24.

Howes, R.J. (2003). Circumferential change scores in phallometric assessment: Normative data. *Sexual Abuse: A Journal of Research and Treatment, 15,* 365–375.

Hunter, J.A. & Goodwin, D.W. (1992). The clinical utility of satiation therapy with juvenile sexual offenders: Variations and efficacy. *Annals of Sex Research, 5,* 71–80.

Kline, P. (1993). *The handbook of psychological testing.* New York: Routledge.

Konopasky, R.J. & Konopasky, A.W.B (2000). Remaking penile plethysmography. In D.R. Laws, S.M. Hudson & T. Ward (Eds), *Remaking relapse prevention with sex offenders* (pp. 257–284). Thousand Oaks, CA: Sage Publications.

Koss, M.P., Gidycz, C.A. & Wisniewski, N. (1987). The scope of rape: Incidence and prevalence of sexual aggression and victimization in a national sample of higher education students. *Journal of Consulting and Clinical Psychology, 55,* 162–170.

Krueger, R.B. & Kaplan, M.S. (2002). Behavioral and Psychopharmacological Treatment of the Paraphilic and Hypersexual Disorders. *Journal of Psychiatric Practice, 8,* 21–32.

Kuban, M., Barbaree, H.E. & Blanchard, R. (1999). A comparison of volume and circumference phallometry: Response magnitude and method agreement. *Archives of Sexual Behavior, 28,* 345–359.

Lalumière, M.L. & Harris, G.T. (1998). Common questions regarding the use of phallometric testing with sexual offenders. *Sexual Abuse: A Journal of Research and Treatment, 10,* 227–237.

Lalumière, M.L. & Quinsey, V.L. (1994). The discriminability of rapists from non-sex offenders using phallometric measures: A meta-analysis. *Criminal Justice and Behavior, 21,* 150–175.

Langevin, R. (1988). Defensiveness in sex offenders. In R. Rogers,(Ed.), *Clinical assessment of malingering and deception* (pp. 269–290). New York: Guilford Press.

Langevin, R. (1989). *Sexual preference testing.* Toronto: Juniper Press.

Launay, G. (1994). The phallometric assessment of sex offenders. *Criminal Behavior and Mental Health*, *4*, 48–70.

Laws, D.R. (1977). A comparison of two circumferential penile transducers. *Archives of Sexual Behavior*, *6*, 45–51.

Laws, D.R. (1984). The assessment of dangerous sexual behaviour in males. *Medicine and Law*, *3*, 127–140.

Laws, D.R. (1996). Marching into the past: A critique of Card and Olsen. *Sexual Abuse: A Journal of Research and Treatment*, *8*, 273–278.

Laws, D.R. (2003). Penile plethysmography: Will we ever get it right? In T. Ward, D.R. Laws & S.M. Hudson (Eds), *Sexual deviance: Issues and controversies*. Thousand Oaks, CA: Sage Publications.

Laws, D.R. & Rubin, H.B. (1969). Instructional control of an autonomic sexual response. *Journal of Applied Behavior Analysis*, *2*, 93–99.

Laws, D.R., Gulayets, M.J. & Frenzel, R.R. (1995). Assessment of sex offenders using standardized slide stimuli and procedures: A multi-site study. *Sexual Abuse: A Journal of Research and Treatment*, *7*, 155–166.

Looman, J., Abracen, J., Maillet, G. & Di Fazio, R. (1998). Phallometric non-responding in sexual offenders. *Sexual Abuse: A Journal of Research and Treatment*, *10*, 325–336.

Malcolm, P.B., Andrews, D.A. & Quinsey, V.L. (1993). Discriminant and predictive validity of phallometrically measured sexual age and gender preference. *Journal of Interpersonal Violence*, *8*, 486–501.

Marshall, W.L., Barbaree, H.E. & Christophe, D. (1986). Sexual offenders against female children: Sexual preferences for age of victims and type of behaviour. *Canadian Journal of Behavioural Science*, *18*, 424–439.

Marshall, W.L. & Eccles, A. (1991). Issues in clinical practice with sex offenders. *Journal of Interpersonal Violence*, *6*, 68–93.

Marshall, W.L. & Fernandez, Y.M. (2000). Phallometric testing with sexual offenders: Limits to its value. *Clinical Psychology Review*, *20*, 807–822.

Marshall, W.L. & Fernandez, Y.M. (2003). *Phallometric testing with sexual offenders: Theory, Research and Practice*. Brandon, VT: Safer Society Press.

Marshall, W.L., Marshall, L.E. & Yates, P. (2003). *A proposal for a multi-site standardisation study of phallometric testing*. Unpublished document.

Marshall, W.L., Serran, G.A. & Yates, P. (2003). *Survey of Canadian and United States treatment programs' use of phallometry*. Unpublished report. Sexual Offenders Program Unit, Correctional Services of Canada, Ottawa.

McAnulty, R.D. & Adams, H.E. (1992). Validity and ethics of penile circumference measures of sexual arousal: A reply to McConaghy. *Archives of Sexual Behavior*, *21*, 177–186.

McConaghy, N. (1999). Unresolved issues in scientific sexology. *Archives of Sexual Behavior*, *28*, 285–318.

Murphy, W.D. (2001). Psychophysiology and risk assessment. In C.R. Hollin, (Ed.). *Handbook of offender assessment and treatment* (pp. 97–109). Chichester, UK: John Wiley & Sons, Ltd.

Murphy, W.D. & Barbaree, H.E. (1994). *Assessments of sex offenders by measures of erectile response: Psychometric properties and decision making*. Brandon, VT: The Safer Society Press.

Murphy, W.D., Haynes, M.R. & Worley, P.J. (1991). Assessment of adult sexual interest. In C.R. Hollin & K. Howells (Eds), *Clinical approaches to sex offenders and their victims* (pp. 77–92). Chichester, UK: John Wiley & Sons, Ltd.

Murphy, W.D., Haynes, M.R., Coleman, E.M. & Flanagan, B. (1985). Sexual responding of 'nonrapists' to aggressive sexual themes: Normative data. *Journal of Psychopathology and Behavioral Assessment*, *7*, 37–47.

O'Donohue, W. & Letourneau, E. (1992). The psychometric properties of the penile tumescence assessment of child molesters. *Journal of Psychopathology and Behavioral Assessment*, *14*, 123–174.

Proulx, J., Aubut, J., McKibben, A. & Cote, M. (1994). Penile response of rapists and non-rapists to rape stimuli involving physical violence of humiliation. *Archives of Sexual Behavior*, *23*, 295–310.

Proulx, J., Pellerin, B., McKibben, A. *et al.* (1997). Penile responses of rapists and non-rapists to rape stimuli involving physical violence or humiliation. *Archives of Sexual Behavior, 23*, 295–310.

Quinsey, V.L. & Chaplin, T.C. (1988). Preventing faking in phallometric assessments of sexual preference. In R.A. Prentky & V.L. Quinsey (Eds), *Human sexual aggression: Current perspectives* (pp. 49–59). New York: Annals of the New York Academy of Sciences.

Quinsey, V.L., Chaplin, T.C. & Varney, G. (1981). A comparison of rapists and non-sex offenders' sexual preferences for mutually consenting sex, rape and physical abuse of women. *Behavioral Assessment, 3*, 137–135.

Rice, M.E., Harris, G.T. & Quinsey, V.L. (1990). A follow-up of rapists assessed in a maximum security psychiatric facility. *Journal of Interpersonal Violence, 5*, 435–448.

Rice, M.E., Quinsey, V.L. & Harris, G.T. (1991). Sexual recidivism among child molesters released from a maximum security psychiatric institution. *Journal of Consulting and Clinical Psychology, 59*, 381–386.

Sekular, R. & Blake, R. (1994). *Perception* (3rd edn). New York: McGraw-Hill.

Simon, W.T. & Schouten, P.G.W. (1992). Problems in sexual preference testing in child sexual abuse cases: A legal and community perspective. *Journal of Interpersonal Violence, 7*, 503–516.

Simon, W.T. & Schouten, P.G.W. (1993). The plethysmograph reconsidered comments on Barker and Howell. *Bulletin of the American Academy of Psychiatry and the Law, 21*, 505–512.

Stevens, S.S. (1951). Mathematics measurement and psychophysics. In S.S. Stevens,(Ed.), *Handbook of experimental psychology* (pp. 1–49). New York: John Wiley & Sons, Inc.

Stevens, S.S. (1975). *Psychophysics: Introduction to its perceptual, neural, and social prospects.* New York: John Wiley & Sons, Inc.

Walter, T.S. & Schouten, P.G.W. (1993). The plethysmograph reconsidered: Comments on Barker and Howell. *Bulletin of the American Academy of Psychiatry and the Law, 21*, 505–512.

Wheeler, D. & Rubin, H.B. (1987). A comparison of volumetric and circumferential measures of penile erection. *Archives of Sexual Behavior, 16*, 289–299.

Wormith, J.S., Bradford, J.M.W., Pawlak, A. *et al.* (1988). The assessment of deviant sexual arousal as a function of intelligence, instructional set and alcohol ingestion. *Canadian Journal of Psychiatry, 33*, 800–808.

9

Using the Polygraph to Manage Risk in Sex Offenders

DON GRUBIN

INTRODUCTION

Polygraphy, often referred to misleadingly as lie detection, was first used as an adjunct to the supervision of offenders in the late 1960s by two American judges who, independent of each other, introduced post-conviction testing of probationers on an informal basis. Their aim was both to deter criminal activity and to identify reoffending when it occurred (Holden, 2000). Although the evaluation of these initiatives was limited in design and scope, it was concluded that polygraphy had a marked impact on recidivism, and also led to the recovery of a considerable amount of stolen property (Teuscher, 1978). Similarly, Abrams and Ogard (1986) reported that over a two-year period 69% of probationers who were required to take periodic polygraph examinations remained offence free, compared with 26% of probationers who were not tested.

In the 1990s post-conviction testing began to be applied to the treatment and supervision of sex offenders, and by the end of the decade it was estimated that probation and parole agencies in up to 35 States were employing polygraphy in this capacity (English *et al.*, 2000a; Holden, 2000), with polygraphy either being made a condition of a sex offender's probation or parole, or constituting a required component of his treatment programme.

Proponents of post-conviction polygraph testing argue enthusiastically that it assists in overcoming denial, provides important information necessary for risk assessment and helps to monitor adherence to supervision conditions. Research reports describe big increases in self-disclosures regarding past number and types of victims, types of offences, age of onset of sexually deviant behaviour, continued masturbation to deviant fantasies and engagement in high risk behaviours (Ahlmeyer *et al.*, 2000; English *et al.*, 2000b; Grubin *et al.*, 2004). Yet critics continue to view post-conviction

Assessment and Treatment of Sex Offenders: A Handbook. Edited by Anthony Beech, Leam Craig and Kevin Browne. © John Wiley & Sons Ltd, 2009.

polygraph testing with scepticism, raising questions regarding its utility, accuracy, regulation, the way in which examination results are interpreted, and linked to all these points, the absence of a robust empirical foundation (British Psychological Society, 1986; Cross & Saxe, 2001; Fiedler, Schmid & Stahl, 2002). This may explain why, in spite of its widespread use with sex offenders in the United States and its emergence in this capacity in England and Wales, polygraphy does not tend to feature in textbooks aimed at those who treat or supervise sex offenders.

There are a number of contributing factors to the controversy regarding post-conviction sex offender testing (PCSOT). Critics often confuse post-conviction testing with other applications where its use can be more problematic (such as pre-employment screening or security vetting), they do not always appreciate how polygraphy is intended to integrate with treatment and supervision as a whole, they believe it can have a negative effect on therapeutic relationships or an offender's self-esteem, they are concerned about abuses that have occurred in other settings, and they point to the lack of well-designed studies demonstrating efficacy (Cross & Saxe, 2001). Proponents, on the other hand, not infrequently overstate the impact of polygraphy, ignore difficult issues such as the effects of variables like personality, intelligence or testing history on accuracy, and they may overlook the significant gaps in the PCSOT evidence base (English *et al.*, 2000a).

The aim of this chapter is to place these issues regarding PCSOT in context, clarifying the role it has to play in sex offender treatment and supervision.

BACKGROUND

The polygraph does not measure lies. Instead, it is based on the notion that the act of deception is associated with an arousal response in the automatic nervous system (a part of the central nervous system that regulates the body's internal environment, for example, temperature, cardiovascular tone and gut activity, and which is largely outside conscious control). Whether this arousal is caused by the fear of deception, orientation to an issue of emotional salience and 'threat' to the individual, the increased cognitive processing required for deception, or some other mechanism is unclear. The notion that polygraphy is dependent on the anxiety associated with lying is a great oversimplification.

Polygraphy gets its name from the original analogue instruments that were developed in the first part of the 20th century in which blood pressure, pulse, respiration rate and electrodermal (i.e., sweat gland) activity were simultaneously recorded with pens writing on a moving sheet of paper – hence 'many writings'. Modern polygraphs, although digitalised and computerised, still typically record these same measures, that is, they measure physiological activity in the cardiovascular and respiratory systems and in the sweat glands (via skin conductance). In the context of a polygraph examination, changes in breathing, pulse rate, blood pressure and sweating that occur in response to emotionally salient questions are measured using scoring procedures that determine whether the examinee's responses are indicative of deception. The polygraph examination is composed of three parts:

- a pre-examination interview in which a range of issues are explored and the questions to be asked when the examinee is attached to the instrument are agreed;
- a testing phase in which the examinee's responses to a small number of questions (typically no more than four) that can be answered 'yes' or 'no' are recorded while he or she is attached to the instrument, with the question set repeated a number of times to exclude 'rogue' responses; no discussion takes place during the test itself;
- a post-test 'debrief' interview that takes place after the polygraph charts have been evaluated and the examiner has reached an opinion regarding whether or not the examinee has been deceptive (an inconclusive finding is also possible), giving the examinee an opportunity to explain any deceptive findings.

THE BASICS OF PCSOT

Unlike investigative polygraph examinations carried out in the criminal justice system or the intelligence community where the emphasis is on whether an individual 'passes' or 'fails' the test per se, the aim of PCSOT is primarily to facilitate the disclosure of information, with repeated testing over time the norm. Although a passed polygraph examination can provide useful confirmation and reassurance regarding an offender's behaviour, and a failed one in the absence of disclosure may be an indicator of problematic behaviour, the focus is on helping the offender modify his behaviour and to prevent reoffending, rather than to detect an offence that has already occurred.

There are four types of test that are commonly employed in PCSOT:

- *Sex history disclosure:* this test is designed to explore an offender's sexual background, in particular his history of sexually deviant behaviour. Its aim is to produce a more accurate understanding of his sexual behaviour that will be of use in risk assessment, treatment and supervision. A questionnaire covering a range of behaviours, ideally completed beforehand by the offender with his therapist or supervising probation officer, usually forms the core of the pre-test interview.
- *Maintenance:* this test asks about behaviours associated with an offender's licence conditions or relapse prevention plan. Maintenance testing is a form of screening test intended to uncover risky behaviours, allowing intervention to take place before an offence can occur.
- *Specific issue offence:* this test asks about circumstances associated with the index offence. It may relate to whether or not an offence was committed at all, as in the case of an offender who absolutely denies the charge on which he was convicted, or it might focus on a limited aspect of the offence about which there appears to be significant denial, or where the offender claims memory loss. The aim is to assist

the offender to provide a more reliable offence description, helping to overcome denial and enhancing engagement.

- *Monitoring:* this test focuses on a single issue about which there is current concern, often to help determine whether a reoffence has occurred.

It is claimed that when used in the treatment and supervision of sex offenders, polygraph testing results in more reliable sexual histories (especially in respect to the onset and extent of deviant sexual behaviour), fuller accounts of offence behaviour with decreased denial, increased reporting of high-risk behaviours, and reductions in reoffending, either because of early intervention or through offenders modifying their behaviour (Grubin *et al.*, 2004), although the number of well-designed studies that support these assertions are few. It is certainly the case, however, that many accept the capacity of PCSOT to elicit disclosures from offenders, to the extent that a number of legal cases in the United States have focused on the need to balance self-incrimination associated with polygraph disclosures and public protection concerns (for example, *Carswell* v. *Indiana*, 1999; *United States* v. *Antelope*, 2005).

It is important to emphasise that PCSOT does not take place in isolation, but is incorporated within the wider management of offenders. English and colleagues (English, 1998; English *et al.*, 2000b) have described a model they call the "containment approach" which is a good illustration of this. In the containment approach, a 'triangle' comprising the supervising probation officer, the treatment provider and the polygraph examiner is formed, with good communication between the three ensuring that new information about an offender is used appropriately in risk management. Thus, for example, a supervising officer's loosely formed concerns about an offender can be explored in a polygraph examination, with the outcome followed up in treatment. Used in this manner, it is probably better not to consider polygraphy as a 'test' per se, but rather as a *treatment tool* to be used in conjunction with other tools (Williams, 1995).

UTILITY OF PCSOT

The Rationale for PCSOT

Effective risk assessment and risk management (which includes treatment) requires information – information regarding an offender's history, his attitudes and beliefs, his self-management skills, his current behaviour and a range of other matters. This information comes from a range of sources and methods, including interview, observation, documentation, psychometric testing, measures of sexual arousal, but it is the combination of a range of methods, each providing something that is sometimes new, sometimes complementary to what is already known, that provides the most comprehensive evaluation of an offender (Beech, Fisher & Thornton, 2003). Indeed, any aetiological understanding of an offender's risk, for example of the type advocated by Beech and Ward (2004), is dependent on a rich tapestry of historical, dynamic and psychological factors.

Even if one focuses narrowly on relapse prevention type models, where the emphasis is on the sequence of cognitive and behavioural steps that result in a sexual reoffence, it is necessary to have an accurate grasp of an offender's 'risk' factors. Community supervision aims to monitor and restrict the offender's identified risk behaviours, thereby in theory lowering the risk of reoffending. The problem is, these can include behaviours such as masturbating to deviant fantasies, accessing the Internet, or visiting a park where there are children (Mann, 2004), all of which may be difficult or impossible to observe, or appear relatively benign to others.

One of the best sources of information, and at times the only source, is the offender himself. Unfortunately, offenders for a variety of reasons frequently fail to provide accurate accounts. Sometimes this is due to a lack of insight or understanding, sometimes to cognitive distortions that allow the offender to convince himself or others that what he did is not so bad, and sometimes to outright lying. For instance, although perhaps at the more extreme end of the spectrum, Maletzky (1991) reported that 87% of the offenders in his programme denied all or parts of their crimes, while Barbaree (1991) similarly observed that 54% of rapists and 66% of child molesters completely denied their offences, and 98% of all the sexual offenders in his sample minimised their offences to some extent. Offenders, however, can also tell the truth, but it can be difficult to know when this is the case.

Even with modern approaches such as 'tagging' and 'intensive supervision', we are left with limited information. Tagging, for example, provides information only about an offender's location, not about what he is doing while there. Round the clock supervision for all community-based sex offenders is simply not feasible, particularly where risk is judged, perhaps wrongly, as not being high. Furthermore, the deterrence associated with an offender believing his supervisor will know what he is doing is impossible if he is able to keep his behaviour secret.

PCSOT is intended to help fill this information gap by facilitating disclosure, and by making it more likely that problematic behaviour will be uncovered, providing additional motivation for offenders to control their behaviour. Although much of the published evidence for this is either theoretical or anecdotal in nature (e.g., Blasingame, 1998; English et al., 2000b; Kokish, 2003), what research there is has been generally supportive.

STUDIES INTO THE UTILITY OF PCSOT

Sex History Disclosures

In one of the earliest published studies on post-conviction polygraphy, Emerick and Dutton (1993) compared the sex offence history (i.e., number of victims and offences) of adolescent offenders on three occasions: when file information was collected, at the intake interview, and following a polygraph examination. They reported an increase in mean number of victims from 1.5 to 1.9 to 2.8, and in undetected offences from 20.6

to 27 to 76.6. They also described gaining additional information about pornography use and number of paraphilic interests.

Subsequent research has produced similar findings. Ahlmeyer *et al.* (2000), for example, reported that 35 inmates in their study admitted to a mean of 83 victims and 394 offences after completing a sexual history questionnaire, but disclosed 183 victims and 528 offences after polygraph testing; parolees also reported more victims and offences, albeit the increase was much less pronounced. Heil, Ahlmeyer, & Simons (2003), looking at 'crossover offending' (i.e., where victims come from different age, gender and relationship categories) in the same sample, reported much more crossover than had previously been known; for instance the proportion of inmates who had offended against both children and adults increased from 7% to 70%.

In addition to obtaining information regarding offence history, other studies have also reported increases in the number of deviant interests reported by offenders, decreases in the age at which they admitted to first engaging in sexually deviant behaviour, and a decrease in self-reported histories of the offenders themselves having been sexually victimised (Hindman & Peters, 2001; Wilcox *et al.*, 2005).

Although indicative, these studies suffer from not having true comparison groups, with offenders acting as their own controls. The data is also confounded by the fact that offenders are typically taking part in treatment programmes, and it is difficult to tease out what might be the effect of polygraphy from what is the result of therapy. Finally, they do not tend to make clear the extent to which disclosures made using polygraphy were dealt with more leniently than disclosures made in other settings, making it more likely that admissions will be made. These shortcomings, of course, do not mean that the findings are not valid, only that they should not be treated as definitive until more rigorously designed trials are carried out.

Modifying Behaviour

A number of studies have asked offenders about the impact of polygraphy on their behaviour. Harrison and Kirkpatrick (2000), for example, in a small sample of sex offenders (n = 28), found that just over half reported a general decrease in risk behaviours, such as masturbating to deviant fantasies and having contact with potential victims, that they attributed to polygraphy. In a larger study involving 95 sex offenders who were mandated to take periodic polygraph tests in California, Kokish, Levenson, & Blasingham (2005) found that 72% reported that periodic polygraph helped them avoid high-risk behaviours and reoffending. Finally, Grubin and Madsen (unpublished) asked 114 sex offenders who were required to take biannual polygraph tests whether the polygraph affected their behaviour; just over half reported that polygraphy was 'moderately' to 'extremely' helpful in assisting them to remain offence-free, and two-thirds that it was useful in assisting them to avoid engaging in risk behaviours (33% claimed that they were less likely to masturbate to deviant fantasies, 31% that they were less likely to have contact with children, and 25% that they were less likely to use or buy pornography).

Taken together, the results from these studies provide some support for the view that PCSOT results in at least some offenders modifying their behaviour. However, they are self-report studies with no means to validate what the offenders claim. Another approach to the question of whether PCSOT brings about behaviour modification was taken in a prospective study carried out in England, which set out to test whether polygraphy would reduce the likelihood of offenders engaging in high-risk behaviours (Grubin *et al.*, 2004). A small sample of sex offenders (32 out of the 115 who were originally approached to take part in the trial) were seen on three occasions; all were thought to be well engaged in treatment and probation officers had few concerns about them, making it unlikely that any findings would be distorted by treatment effects. On the first occasion, up to four high-risk behaviours were identified. Offenders were then placed into one of two conditions: a 'polygraph aware' group was told to expect a polygraph test focusing on their specified high-risk behaviours, while men in a second, 'polygraph unaware' group were simply told that their behaviour would be reviewed. On the second occasion, three months later, participants were again interviewed about their identified behaviours, but all, regardless of the group they were in, were asked to submit to a polygraph test. The hypothesis was that the polygraph aware group would report having engaged in fewer of their risk behaviours.

When polygraphed three months after their first interview, 31 of the men disclosed information of direct relevance to their therapy or supervision, which only one had previously disclosed to his probation officer. Over 80% of the offenders admitted to ongoing offence-relevant fantasies in spite of denying this in treatment, but more worrying were disclosures made by a third of the offenders regarding high-risk behaviours such as having unsupervised contact with children or going to places where they might encounter potential victims; one man disclosed prowling public toilets with a knife in search of young boys, another to over 50 incidents of frottage involving young girls on public transport, and a third to regular unsupervised 'dates' with his previous 13-year-old victim. There was no difference in the number of behaviours reported by men in the polygraph aware (M = 2.4, SD = 1.6) and the polygraph unaware groups (M = 2.7, SD = 1.9), suggesting that knowledge of the polygraph test had not acted as a deterrent for engaging in risk behaviour.

However, 21 of these offenders agreed to be retested 3 months later. On this second occasion, it was found that disclosures of high-risk behaviour decreased in frequency and number (29% reported no risk behaviour and passed their polygraph tests, while of the remainder 60% had already disclosed the relevant information to their supervisors), and the behaviours themselves were rated as being less serious (Madsen, Parsons & Grubin, 2004); in addition, more offenders passed the polygraph examination itself (at the first exam, two-thirds of offenders 'failed' the polygraph, while 78% 'passed' the second test). Grubin *et al.* (2004) also examined when in the procedure offenders disclosed risk behaviours: during the first polygraph test, only 37% disclosed all their risk behaviour during the initial or pre-test interviews (suggesting that it was the polygraph test itself, and not just the systematic polygraph interview, that was responsible for the disclosures), but this increased to 80% of those polygraphed a second time.

It appeared from this study that the polygraph did result in a modification of behaviour, but only after offenders had experience of a polygraph test, even though the nature of the study meant that the polygraph examinations themselves were not integrated into the treatment and supervision process.

Again, generalisations from this study need to be made cautiously. The attrition rate was high, with just 21 offenders completing the study (representing only 42% of the original sample who agreed to take part, and 18% of the offenders who were eligible to do so). In addition, the improved outcome at the time of the second polygraph examination could have been the result of offenders learning how to 'beat' the polygraphy, or them becoming habituated to testing. So, although this study adds further support to the claim that polygraphy facilitates disclosures, like the disclosure research described above further confirmatory studies are needed to increase confidence in the results.

Comparison Studies

As referred to above, most PCSOT studies typically lack comparison groups, and their findings may be confounded by the effects of treatment. In an attempt to overcome this problem, English et al. (2000) retrospectively compared sex offender treatment programmes that either did or did not incorporate polygraph testing. They found that offenders in the polygraph programmes were more likely to have reported offending against both male and female victims, and against both juveniles and adults, as well as having disclosed greater amounts of sexually deviant activity generally than offenders who were not required to complete a polygraph examination.

A more direct attempt to incorporate a comparison sample was made by us in a large, prospective trial of polygraphy carried out in England. In this study, polygraphy was introduced on a voluntary basis to the sex offender treatment programmes of 10 probation areas, with polygraphed offenders compared with sex offenders in four probation areas where polygraphy was not introduced (http://www.probation.justice.gov.uk/files/pdf/Polygraph%20Pilot%20Report%20%20July%202006.pdf). Outcome was based on a range of measures, including the number of clinically relevant disclosures made, changes in risk assessment and impact on management.

Over a two-year period, 347 sex offenders attended for testing, 33% of whom (n = 116) were tested on two or more occasions; in total, 483 polygraph examinations were carried out. The testing uptake rate was 43%, and the retest rate 47%. Feedback from probation officers was received in respect of just over two-thirds of all the tests that were carried out. The comparison sample comprised 180 offenders, representing about 60% of sex offenders in treatment programmes in the comparison sites; supervising officers for the comparison offenders who provided data were surveyed again 6 to 12 months later (Time 2) regarding the same offender in order to form a subgroup with which to compare the polygraphed offenders who were retested. Information for Time 2 was received in relation to 36% of the offenders from the original comparison group.

About 40% of the tests carried out in the trial were sex history disclosure examinations, another 40% were maintenance tests, with the remainder specific issue tests relating to either the index offence or monitoring.

Disclosures Regarding Current Behaviour

Based on their knowledge of a case from probation records and discussions with probation officers, examiners reported that new disclosures relevant to treatment and supervision were made in nearly 80% of all tests, regardless of whether the test was 'passed', 'failed', or 'inconclusive'. Nearly 30% of these disclosures took place in the post-test interview that followed the offender having been questioned while attached to the polygraph – in other words, after being challenged with the result of the test, suggesting that they were not the result of offenders simply believing that the polygraph would detect them if they lied (the so-called 'bogus pipeline' effect).

When supervising officers of polygraphed offenders were asked about new disclosures relevant to their supervision, they reported that these were made in 70% of the first tests (this did not match the examiners' estimate because the reports from supervising officers related to only a proportion of the tests that were carried out); this compared with 14% of supervising officers of non-polygraphed offenders reporting new disclosures over the previous months. Similarly, supervising officers of polygraphed offenders reported new disclosures in two-thirds of retests, compared with 13% reported by supervising officers of the non-polygraphed offenders at Time 2 (Table 9.1).

The odds of a polygraphed offender making a disclosure relevant to his treatment or supervision were 14 times greater than they were for a non-polygraphed offender making such a disclosure. Because offenders in both groups were in various but similar

Table 9.1 Clinically relevant new disclosures reported by supervising officers of polygraphed offenders after first tests and retests, and by supervising officers of non-polygraphed offenders at comparable times (95% confidence intervals)

	Supervising Officers Polygraph	Supervising Officers Non-polygraph	Significance
New Disclosure	First test	Time 1	
Yes	128 (70%)	25 (14%)	$p < 0001$
No	55 (30%)	155 (86%)	odds ratio $= 14.4$ (C.I. 8.5–24.4)
Total	183	180	
New Disclosure	Retest	Time 2	
Yes	36 (67%)	8 (13%)	$p < 0001$
No	18 (33%)	56 (87%)	odds ratio $= 14.0$, (C.I. 5.6–35.0)
Total	54	64	

stages of treatment, it is unlikely that the increased disclosures related to progress in treatment; likewise, offenders in both groups would, apart from polygraphy, have been supervised in a similar manner.

Seriousness of Disclosures

Probation officers were asked to rate the seriousness of the disclosures made by offenders, using the following definitions:

- low: passive types of behaviour, such as masturbating to deviant fantasies
- medium: possible preludes to reoffending (e.g., going to places where there might be potential victims
- high: specific breaches or actual offending.

In cases where supervising officers reported that disclosures were made, 25% indicated that the disclosures were in the *medium* category, and 19% were rated as *high* (this was of the same order as reported by Grubin *et al.*, 2004). Disclosures that took place in sexual history or specific issue offence examinations tended to relate to past actions rather than to current behaviours of concern, but maintenance and other specific issue (monitoring) examinations focused on *current* behaviour, and were thus of particular relevance for the supervising officer. Of the 95 maintenance and monitoring examinations for which we had feedback from supervising officers, 26% resulted in disclosures that were rated as being of *medium* severity, and 7% were of *high* severity, amounting to a third of these examinations.

Risk Assessment and Intervention

The feedback forms completed by polygraph supervising officers requested information about revisions to risk assessment and changes in intervention that they attributed to the polygraph examination. For comparison purposes, non-polygraph supervising officers were asked about changes in risk or intervention that had taken place over the preceding three to six months. While both polygraph and non-polygraph supervising officers reported making revisions in risk assessment with similar frequency (in about 20% of cases), there was a significant difference in the direction of change: non-polygraph supervising officers typically *reduced* risk, with 55% of their changes in risk being downwards, while 81% of the risk modifications made by polygraph supervising officers were to increase risk. It should be noted, of course, that the research design did not allow for a determination of the extent to which these increases in risk assessment were justified.

Overall, it was found that changes in risk assessment, supervision, treatment, or the initiation of a new intervention were reported more frequently by the supervising officers of polygraphed offenders compared with those supervising non-polygraph offenders: change in one of these variables was reported for 41% of the polygraphed offenders, compared with 27% of those who were not polygraphed ($p < 01$, odds ratio 1.9, confidence interval 1.2–2.9).

Other Effects

Apart from actual changes in risk assessment, treatment and supervision, probation officers were asked whether the polygraph examination had any other effect on their interaction with the offender. These 'other effects' related to qualitative aspects of a probation officer's work with sex offenders, and included such things as confirmation of an existing risk assessment, improved cooperation with supervision, progress in overcoming denial, increased engagement in treatment, or obtaining information that was passed on to child protection agencies or public protection meetings, and were reported after nearly one-half of tests. The three case examples below, taken from the study, provide an illustration of how PCSOT impacted on engagement in treatment, identifying new treatment targets, and risk management:

A 30-year-old man with no previous offending history was convicted of the indecent assault of his 10-year-old stepdaughter. He claimed he had only ever touched her on one occasion, on her breasts and over her pyjamas, in spite of the girl's statement of digital penetration of her vagina. After a 'deception indicated' polygraph test, he admitted to sexual arousal to 13- and 14-year-old girls, and to having masturbated to fantasies of his stepdaughter prior to the offence. The treatment facilitator commented, "He is now able to view his offending behaviour in the context of sexual abuse as a result of disclosing inappropriate sexual fantasies towards his victim. Motivation has improved, denial and minimisation has decreased".

A 56-year-old man with no previous sex offending history was convicted of Internet-related offences. In a sex history examination he admitted to stealing knickers from his sister's house a few years previously, to sexual fantasies regarding schoolgirls, and to sitting in a cinema car park in order to watch young girls. Based on this and other information he disclosed about his sexual fantasies, probation officers identified "a new target around dealing with inappropriate fantasies and possible fantasy modification work".

A 24-year-old man was on parole having been convicted of unlawful sexual intercourse with a 14-year-old girl. His probation officer believed he was maintaining a sexual relationship with his victim, but this was persistently denied by the offender. His monitoring included a tag and a curfew at night, with which he was compliant. He denied any wrongdoing during the pre-test interview, but the outcome of the test was 'deception indicated'. In the post-test interview he admitted to ongoing regular contact with his former victim, and to some sexual activity with her (in his home after his curfew, so not detected by the tag). The probation officer passed this information to the police and Social Services, and the offender was arrested. When interviewed by the police the girl reported spending one night a week in the offender's home, where in addition to the sexual activity described by him she said they also engaged in sexual intercourse. In his feedback the probation officer commented, "Hugely beneficial to my assessment and intervention. Developed a closer relationship with other agencies [in managing the case]".

Overall Impact on Assessment, Supervision, Interventions and Treatment

When the 'other effects' referred to above are taken into account, supervising officers reported that the polygraph examination had an impact on their treatment or supervision in 65% of the tests for which we had feedback. Even where there was no direct impact, overall they rated polygraphy as being *Somewhat* or *Very helpful* in over 90% of cases. Very few tests were considered by probation officers to have had either no or a negative impact.

Some time has been taken in describing the results of this study as to date it is the largest of its kind. Even so, its conclusions are indicative rather than definitive. The polygraphed and non-polygraphed offenders were not randomised nor were they explicitly matched, and though they appeared to be similar in terms of offence characteristics and level of risk there may have been differences between them that influenced the findings. This was particularly relevant given the voluntary nature of the study, as it is possible that offenders who volunteer for polygraph testing may differ from sex offenders on probation generally. Nevertheless, it provides further evidence in support of those who argue that PCSOT can make an important contribution to the treatment and supervision of sex offenders on probation, allowing probation officers to better monitor risk and to bring about more effective and timely interventions.

ACCURACY OF PSCOT

Regardless of its utility, if PCSOT is not reasonably accurate then its long-term value as a treatment and supervision tool is debateable, as offenders would come to see polygraphy as a toothless dog. Because the physiological activity measured by the polygraph is not uniquely (or even always) associated with deception, and because of variations in technique, examiner experience and skill, there is ample opportunity for error when the polygraph is used to determine an individual's veracity. A definitive review undertaken by the National Academy of Sciences (National Research Council, 2003) concluded that polygraph accuracy is probably in the region of 81–91%. The review concluded that this level of accuracy was not sufficiently robust for it to be used in security applications where the base rate of deception is likely to be low (and the number of false positives would therefore be unacceptably high), but it also stated that polygraphy becomes more viable in settings where the expected base rate of deception is greater, putting the threshold at about 10% – a level that is almost certainly met in PCSOT.

However, the National Academy of Sciences review also noted that specific issue testing (where just one issue is the focus of the examination) is more accurate than tests where a number of issues are included. The latter is usually the case in screening tests, and in PCSOT.

It is difficult to know how accurate polygraphy is in the context of PCSOT as relevant studies are difficult to design. Kokish *et al.* (2005), in an anonymous survey, simply asked offenders about the accuracy of the polygraph tests they had completed whilst on probation. Although it was not possible to match offender responses with their actual tests, they found that 95 offenders reported polygraphy to have accurately identified truth-telling 92%, and deception 82%, of the time in 405 tests. Grubin and Madsen (2006), using a similar design, obtained comparable results: they found that 121 offenders who had taken 263 tests claimed that polygraphy had accurately identified deception in 84% of cases, and truth-telling 85% of the time. Because of the relatively low number of failed tests in these samples, however, the positive predictive value (the likelihood that an offender said to have failed a test has actually lied) was relatively low; on the other hand, the negative predictive value (the likelihood that someone who is said to have passed a test is telling the truth) was high.

In an experimental study where sex offenders were asked about illicit drug use as part of a multi-issue test, and both their responses and the results of polygraphy were compared with hair analysis, Madsen and Grubin (unpublished) found that the polygraph, when scored by 'blind' examiners, was 80% accurate in identifying truth-telling and 100% accurate in detecting deception, but the numbers of those who tested positive for drugs was very low. It was of note that the examiners themselves, as opposed to the blind examiners who viewed the charts later, were less accurate. Again, the positive predictive value was low, and the negative predictive value high.

Although limited, these studies suggest that PCSOT is likely to fall within the 80–90% accuracy band suggested by the National Academy of Sciences review, albeit probably at the lower end of this range. The question, then, is whether 80% accuracy is accurate enough for sex offender applications. Provided that no action is taken simply on the basis of a passed or failed polygraph test on its own, most of those involved in PCSOT argue that it is – the consequences of a mistaken outcome are not great (no one is deprived of a job, convicted of an offence, or should be sent to jail), disclosures can be of great use regardless of test outcome, and 80% accuracy is after all much better than chance. Problems arise, however, when too much emphasis is placed on test results in isolation, particularly in jurisdictions where repeatedly failing a test can result in breach of probation or parole licence.

ETHICS OF PSCOT

Some therapists argue that PCSOT has the potential to do more harm than good. They are concerned that the challenge and implicit distrust associated with polygraphy may harm their therapeutic relationship with the offender, and the test itself will have a negative impact on an offender's self-esteem, decreasing his engagement and increasing his risk. However, there is no evidence to demonstrate such effects. On the contrary, what evidence there is suggests that offenders by and large find polygraphy to be helpful, and therapists generally report positive effects on treatment (Harrison &

Kirkpatrick, 2000; Kokish *et al.*, 2005; Grubin & Madsen, unpublished; the English National Probation Service study described above).

The British Psychological Society (2004) raised a number of concerns about polygraphy in general, and some about PCSOT in particular. It commented, for example, that in the absence of a firm evidence base the use of mandatory polygraph testing, with negative consequences for failing to comply, may be unethical, although it could be pointed out that the same might be said of mandatory sex offender treatment. The BPS quite rightly observed that it would be wrong to assume that a person who refuses to take a polygraph test has something to hide, but again, in a post-conviction context, a failure to cooperate with any aspect of supervision is a well-described potential indicator of risk (Hanson & Harris, 2000).

The BPS was also concerned that because of polygraphy's error rate the use of the polygraph may be an infringement of an individual's civil liberties, although it is not clear whether this related to polygraph testing in post-conviction applications as well as in respect to employee screening and security vetting. It argues that polygraphy testing should only be carried out when informed consent is freely given, based on full and valid explanations, with which most examiners would agree. Whether such consent can be given in a criminal justice setting, however, is not straightforward, nor is the issue of balancing the need for offender consent with the counterbalancing issue of public safety.

Finally, there is the issue of the invasion of privacy associated with polygraph testing. In this respect, it should be noted that the European Court has ruled that penile plethysmography (PPG), which most would consider considerably more 'invasive' than polygraphy, can be made a compulsory part of sex offender treatment on the grounds of public safety (Gazan, 2002), and that refusal to take a PPG is grounds for prolonged detention (one wonders about the status of informed consent in this context). It should be remembered that the questions asked during a polygraph examination are asked anyway, but with polygraphy offenders are challenged more effectively regarding their answers. If the information relating to risk obtained during polygraph examination adds significantly to what would be known otherwise, the ethics of not using it must also be considered.

False Disclosures

A particularly problematic issue for PCSOT is the possibility of offenders making false disclosures in order to explain a deceptive result, to please the examiner or probation officer (sometimes referred to as 'defensive lying'), or even to obscure the actual reason for a failed test (Cross & Saxe, 2001). It is certainly the case that in other interrogative type settings some individuals are particularly prone to making false confessions (Gudjonsson *et al.*, 2004). In the Kokish *et al.* (2005) survey of 95 sexual offenders referred to above, 5% reported making false disclosures after having failed a polygraph examination. The Madsen *et al.* (2004) survey had similar findings, while Grubin and Madsen (unpublished) recorded a rate of 9%, observing that those who claimed to have made false disclosures were more impulsive than other offenders in their study.

While the incidence of false disclosure does not seem to be high, it is high enough to be of relevance; it is similar to the 12% incidence reported among prison inmates (Sigurdsson & Gudjonsson, 1996a, 1996b). Individuals with personality disorder are particularly vulnerable to making false confessions, which is a concern given the high prevalence of personality disorder amongst sex offenders (Abel, Mittleman, & Becker, 1985). Other groups with whom caution must be shown are younger offenders (in the United States offenders as young as 12 are tested), and those with learning disability – not only is the theoretical risk of false disclosure greater in these groups, but testing may also be less accurate in them (National Research Council, 2003).

CONCLUSIONS

When used by well-trained examiners and in conjunction with other techniques, PCSOT appears to have an important contribution to make to the treatment and supervision of sex offenders. Further research, however, needs to be carried out to clarify and confirm the extent of this contribution. In addition, there are a number of nuts and bolts type issues not covered in this chapter that need to be addressed, such as better standardisation of PCSOT, examiner training (few examiners have experience of working with sex offenders before they become involved in PCSOT), and regulation of examiners. Factors such as the impact of repeated testing, the effect of personality characteristics on test outcome, and the influence of IQ also require better understanding. But overall, rather than needing to justify PCSOT, the stage has probably now been reached where those who do not use polygraphy in managing sex offender risk should be thinking about the justification of their positions.

REFERENCES

Abel, G.G., Mittleman, M.S. & Becker, J.V. (1985). Sex offenders: Results of assessment and recommendations for treatment. In M.H. Ben-Aron, S.J. Hucker & C.D. Webster (Eds), *Clinical criminology: The assessment and treatment of criminal behavior* (pp. 207–220). Toronto, Canada: M & M Graphics.

Abrams, S. & Ogard, E. (1986). Polygraph surveillance of probationers. *Polygraph, 15*, 174–182.

Ahlmeyer, S., Heil, P., McKee, B. & English, K. (2000). The impact of polygraphy on admissions of victims and offenses in adult sexual offenders. *Sexual Abuse: A Journal of Research and Treatment, 12*, 123–139.

Barbaree, H.E. (1991). Denial and minimization among sex offenders: Assessment and treatment outcome. *Forum on Corrections Research, 3*, 30–33.

Beech, A.R., Fisher, D. & Thornton, D. (2003). Risk assessment of sex offenders. *Professional Psychology: Research and Practice, 34*, 339–352.

Beech, A.R. & Ward, T. (2004). The integration of etiology and risk in sex offenders: A theoretical model. *Aggression and Violent Behavior, 10*, 31–63.

Blasingame, G.D. (1998). Suggested clinical uses of polygraphy in community-based sexual offender treatment programs. *Sexual Abuse: A Journal of Research and Treatment, 10*, 37–45.

British Psychological Society (1986). Report of the working group on the use of the polygraph in criminal investigation and personnel screening. *Bulletin of the British Psychological Society, 39*, 81–94.

British Psychological Society (2004). *A review of the current scientific status and fields of application of polygraphic deception detection*. Final report from the BPS Working Party. Available from: http://www .bps.org.uk/downloadfile.cfm?file_uuid=9081F97A-306E-1C7F-B65E-570A3444FF4D&ext=pdf

Cross, T.P. & Saxe, L. (2001). Polygraph testing and sexual abuse: The lure of the magic lasso. *Child Maltreatment, 6*, 195–206.

Emerick, R.L. & Dutton, W.A. (1993). The effect of polygraphy on the self-report of adolescent sex offenders: implications for risk assessment. *Annals of Sex Research, 6*, 83–103.

English, K. (1998). The containment approach: An aggressive strategy for the community management of adult sex offenders. *Psychology, Public Policy, & Law Special Issue: Sex Offenders; Scientific, Legal, and Policy Perspectives, 4*, 218–235.

English, K., Jones, L., Pasini-Hill, D. & Cooley-Towell, S. (2000a). *The value of polygraph testing in sex offender management*. Research report submitted to the National Institute of Justice. Colorado: Colorado Department of Public Safety.

English, K., Jones, L., Patrick, D. *et al.* (2000b). We need you to become experts in the post-conviction polygraph. *Polygraph, 29*, 44–62.

Fiedler, K., Schmid, J. & Stahl, T. (2002). What is the current truth about polygraph lie detection? *Basic and Applied Social Psychology, 24*, 313–324.

Gazan, F. (2002). Penile plethysmography before the European Court of Human Rights. *Sexual Abuse: A Journal of Research and Treatment, 14*, 89–93.

Grubin, D. & Madsen, L. (2006). The utility and accuracy of post-conviction polygraph testing with sex offenders. *British Journal of Psychiatry, 188*, 479–483.

Grubin, D., Madsen, L., Parsons, S. *et al.* (2004). A prospective study of the impact of polygraphy on high risk behaviors in adult sex offenders. *Sexual Abuse: A Journal of Research and Treatment, 16*, 209–222.

Gudjonsson, G.H., Sigurdsson, J.F., Bragason, O.O. *et al.* (2004). Confessions and denials and the relationship with personality. *Legal and Criminological Psychology, 9*, 121–133.

Hanson, R.K. & Harris, A.J.R. (2000). Where should we intervene? Dynamic predictors of sexual offence recidivism. *Criminal Justice and Behavior, 27*, 6–35.

Harrison, J.S. & Kirkpatrick, B. (2000). Polygraph testing and behavioral change with sex offenders in an outpatient setting: An exploratory study. *Polygraph, 29*, 20–25.

Heil, P., Ahlmeyer, S. & Simons, D. (2003). Crossover sexual offences. *Sexual Abuse: A Journal of Research and Treatment, 15*, 221–236.

Hindman, J. & Peters, J.M. (2001). Polygraph testing leads to better understanding adult and juvenile sex offenders. *Federal Probation, 65*, 8–15.

Holden, E.J. (2000). Pre- and post-conviction polygraph: building blocks for the future – procedures, principles, and practices. *Polygraph, 29*, 69–97.

Kokish, R. (2003). The current role of post-conviction sex offenders polygraph testing in sex offender treatment. *Journal of Child Sexual Abuse, 12*, 175–194.

Kokish, R., Levenson, J.S. & Blasingham, G. (2005). Post-conviction sex offender polygraph examination: Client-reported perceptions of utility and accuracy. *Sexual Abuse: A Journal of Research and Treatment, 17*, 211–221.

Madsen, L., Parsons, S. & Grubin, D. (2004). A preliminary study of the contribution of periodic polygraph testing to the treatment and supervision of sex offenders. *British Journal of Forensic Psychiatry and Psychology, 15*, 682–695.

Maletzky, B.M. (1991). *Treating the sexual offender*. Newbury Park, CA: Sage Publications.

Mann, R.E. (2004). Innovations in sex offender treatment. *Journal of Sexual Aggression, 10*, 141–152.

National Research Council (2003). *The Polygraph and Lie Detection*. Committee to Review the Scientific Evidence on the Polygraph. Division of Behavioral and Social Sciences and Education. Washington, DC: The National Academies Press.

Sigurdsson, J.F. & Gudjonsson, G.H. (1996a). The psychological characteristics of 'false confessors'. A study among Icelandic prison inmates and juvenile offenders. *Personality and Individual Differences*, *20*, 321–329.

Sigurdsson, J.F. & Gudjonsson, G.H. (1996b). The relationship between types of claimed false confession and the reasons why suspects confess to the police according to Gudjonsson Confession Questionnaire (GCQ). *Legal and Criminological Psychology*, *1*, 259–269.

Teuscher, T. (1978). The polygraph and probation. *Polygraph*, *7*, 1–4.

Wilcox, D., Sosnowski, D., Warberg, B. & Beech, A. (2005). Sexual history disclosure using the polygraph in a sample of British Sex Offenders in treatment. *Polygraph*, *34*, 171–183.

Williams, V.L. (1995). Response to Cross and Saxe's "A critique of the validity of polygraph testing in children sexual abuse cases". *Journal of Child Sexual Abuse*, *4*, 55–71.

COURT CASES

Carswell v. *Indiana*, 721 N.E.2d 1255. (Ind. Ct. App. 1999)

United States v. *Antelope*, 395 F.3d 1128 (2005)

10

Assessment of Sexual Addiction

LIAM E. MARSHALL

MATT D. O'BRIEN

INTRODUCTION

In our treatment programmes in two Canadian federal prisons, some sexual offenders exhibit behaviours that can be described as being indicative of sexual addiction. For example, some offenders are so preoccupied with sexual thoughts that they have difficulty interacting appropriately with prison staff members. Indeed, some sexual offender clients report being plagued with inappropriate sexual fantasies or appear to enjoy the offence details of other group participants even after they receive feedback indicating that their behaviour is inappropriate. Some of our sexual offender clients also self-report being sexually addicted, some of whom report having attended a community sexual addiction programme.

Various authors have described sexual addiction as a sexual desire which stretches the capacity or desire to control behaviour and that these behaviours persist despite significant harmful consequences (Carnes, 1983, 1989; Goodman, 1998). There has been controversy about the use of the term sexual addiction as the descriptor for the cluster of behaviours associated with problematic sexual behaviour. Under Section 320.90, of the DSM III-R (1987) there is an example of a Sexual Disorder Not Otherwise Specified as "distress about a pattern of repeated sexual conquests or other forms of nonparaphilic *sexual addiction*, involving a succession of people who exist only as things to be used" (p. 296, italics added). Subsequent editions of the DSM have made no reference to sexual addiction which is due at least in part to a lack of empirical research and politics surrounding sexual issues (Smith, 1994).

Other authors have used various different terms for similar symptoms dependent on their personal preference, usually reflecting preferred treatment method. *Sexually compulsive* (Coleman, 1987), *sexually impulsive* (Barth & Kinder, 1987), *hypersexual* (Kafka, 1997; Kafka & Hennen, 1999), *sexually excessive* (Manley & Koehler, 2001),

Assessment and Treatment of Sex Offenders: A Handbook. Edited by Anthony Beech, Leam Craig and Kevin Browne. © John Wiley & Sons Ltd, 2009.

or a variant of obsessive-compulsive disorder (Coleman, 1990; Leedes, 2001) are all terms describing sexual behaviour problems that are similar to Carnes' (1983) notion of sexual addiction. All these points of view agree that the sexual desires of some individuals over-rides their capacity or desire to control their behaviour and that these behaviours persist despite significant harmful consequences. For some of these 'sexual addicts' their problematic behaviour reflects increased rates of overt sexual contacts, excessive masturbation, or habitual use of the Internet to access sexual sites including pornography.

There has been some effort to reach consensus among sexual addiction theorists and researchers on the nosology of sexual addiction; see the journal *Sexual Addiction and Compulsivity, Volume 8* (2001) for the papers presented at this symposium. This led to the creation of a research project meant to develop both a standardised measure and give information on the nosology of sexual addiction; however, there has been nothing published to date.

There are many features of sexual addiction that could have relevance for the treatment of sexual offenders, such as the lack of desire (or inability) to control sexual behaviour and the persistence of these behaviours, despite negative consequences (for the offender, but even more importantly for victims). Indeed, as shown in Table 10.1, there are many features of sexual addiction that have already been demonstrated to be relevant to sexual offenders. Consequently, in 1997 a research programme examining

Table 10.1 Brief review of research demonstrating a relationship between sexual offending and features of sexual addiction

Features of sexual addiction; from Carnes (1981, 1989)	Examples from research on sexual offenders
Comorbidity: Substance abuse	• Hanson & Harris, 2000 • Abracen, Looman & Anderson, 2000
Comorbidity: Eating disorders	• McElroy *et al.*, 1999
Having experienced childhood or adolescent sexual abuse	• Dhawan & Marshall, 1996
Sexual preoccupation	• Hanson & Morton-Bourgon, 2004 • Hanson & Harris, 2000 • Knight, Carter & Prentky, 1989
Coping using sex	• Cortoni & Marshall, 2001 • Marshall, Serran & Cortoni, 2000
Shame	• Sparks *et al.*, 2003
Intimacy deficits	• Seidman *et al.*, 1994
Cognitive distortions	• Barbaree, 1991
Experience acute mood changes	• Hanson & Morton-Bourgon, 2004
Low self-esteem	• Marshall *et al.*, 1997
Continue problematic behaviour despite severe consequences	• Hanson, Gordon *et al.*, 2002
High religiosity	• Eshuys & Smallbone, 2006
Family history of emotional abuse	• Bass & Levant, 1992

the features and relevance of sexual addiction in incarcerated sexual offenders was initiated by Marshall and colleagues (Marshall & Marshall, 1998, 2001, 2006; Marshall, Marshall & Moulden, 2000; Marshall *et al.*, 2004). Little other research on sexual addiction in sexual offenders is available. Only three other published papers could be found (Blanchard, 1990, 1991, 1995) and problems with methodology in these studies casts doubt on the ability to generalise the findings beyond the sample used.

The aim of this chapter is to report data on sexual addiction from our studies. The findings will be presented in the following order: first we will report on the psychometric properties of the measures of sexual addiction. Next, we will report the observed prevalence of sexual addiction in incarcerated sexual offenders and socio-economically-matched community comparison groups. We will then report on our findings based on Carnes' (1989) hypothesis that sexual addiction is co-morbid with other addictions. A hallmark of sexual addiction is out of control sexual behaviour therefore we next examine the link between sexual addiction and history of sexual outlets and propensity to use sex as a coping strategy. Finally, we will report our findings on the possible relationship between sexual addiction and psychopathy. Because sexual addiction to the Internet is becoming a growing problem (Delmonico, Griffin & Carnes, 2002), we will also examine the currently available evidence and any links to other forms of sexual addiction, such as risky sexual behaviours, etc.

MEASURES OF SEXUAL ADDICTION

There currently exist a number of measures of sexual addiction, such as the *Sexual Addiction Screening Test* (SAST) (Carnes, 1989) and the *Sexual Dependence Inventory-Revised* (SDI-R) (Delmonico, Bubenzer & West, 1998). There are also a number of other measures of sexually addictive-like behaviour, such as the *Compulsive Sexual Behavior Inventory* (Miner *et al.*, 2005), the *Sexual Outlet Inventory* (Kafka, 1991) and the *Sexual Compulsivity Scale* (Kalichman *et al.*, 1994). However, no study, to date, has examined differences and similarities between these measures and the measures of sexual addiction. Because Carnes is viewed as the father of the sexual addiction model and his measure is modelled on his theory of sexual addiction, we chose to use the *Sexual Addiction Screening Test* (SAST) (Carnes, 1989).

In our studies, the *Sexual Addiction Screening Test* (SAST) (Carnes, 1989) demonstrated good internal consistency with alphas ranging from .89 to .93. We subjected the SAST to both an exploratory factor analysis, using principal axis factoring, and then a confirmatory factor analysis using the maximum likelihood method with promax rotation. Three, two and one factor solutions were tested for improvement of fit using *Root Mean Square Error of Approximation* (RMSEA; Steiger & Lind, 1980) and the *Proportional Reduction in Error* (PRE) method. These analyses revealed a one factor solution, accounting for 39% of the variance in SAST scores, to be the most satisfactory representation of our data. The SAST appears to be measuring a single latent factor, which Carnes (1989) calls *sexual addiction*. Consequently any relationships found in our research ought to be indicative of sexual addiction, as defined by Carnes

(1989), and its correlates. Carnes (1989) reports that scores on the SAST are unrelated to the degree of consequences for both the addict and others; that is, scores on the SAST do not predict dangerousness. Consequently, any over-representation of sexual offenders as sexual addicts will be a function of their responses to the SAST and not because they have committed an offence.

PREVALENCE OF SEXUAL ADDICTION

The prevalence of sexual addiction in a middle-class community is estimated to be between 3% and 6% (Carnes, 1989). Unfortunately, few empirical papers have addressed important questions about sexual addiction such as prevalence rates in the general community and the prevalence of sexual addiction in special populations. In their study on sexual addiction using the *Sexual Dependency Inventory-Revised* (SDI-R) Delmonico, Bubenzer and West (1998) report 33 (19.4%) of 170 respondents to be sexually addicted. This study included self-identified sexual addicts (N = 73, 43%), sexual offenders (N = 55, 32%), and a comparison group who were not identified as sexual offenders or sexual addicts (N = 42, 25%). Unfortunately, the distribution of sexual addicts among the three groups was not reported. However, it is worth noting that fewer subjects (19.4%) were classified as being sexual addicts by the SDI-R than self-reported being a sexual addict (43%). This finding reinforces our use of the SAST rather than the SDI as the measure of sexual addiction in our research.

In our studies (Marshall & Marshall, 1998, 2001, 2006; Marshall, Marshall & Moulden, 2000; Marshall *et al.*, 2004) sexual offenders reported greater rates of sexual addiction (35%–43%) than matched, community samples (12%–15%). Clearly, the behaviours described in the SAST are a greater problem for incarcerated sexual offenders than non-offenders. However, what is also interesting about these findings is the high rate of sexual addiction in this lower-socio-economic comparison group. Up to 15% of non-offenders were found to meet criteria for sexual addiction which is substantially higher than Carnes' estimate (3%–6%) of the rate of sexual addiction in the community. It is unknown whether this reflects an underestimate by Carnes, or a socio-economic cohort difference.

CO-MORBID ADDICTIONS

Carnes (1989) hypothesised that sexual addiction is likely to be co-morbid with other addictive behaviours, such as alcohol and drug addiction, and Schneider and Schneider (1991) found that sexual addicts did indeed exhibit co-morbidity problems; sexual addicts were found to be at greater risk for an eating disorder and pathological gambling. In our studies on co-morbidity we did not find support for sexual addiction being co-morbid with alcohol or drug problems. The measures of drug (*Drug Abuse Screening Test* [DAST]; Skinner, 1982, 1998) and alcohol (*Michigan Alcoholism Screening Test* [MAST]; Selzer, 1971) problems were always highly correlated with each other; however, they were never significantly related to sexual addiction. This was particularly surprising since other researchers have reported greater alcohol problems in sexual offenders than non-sexual offenders and comparison groups (Abracen, Looman & Anderson, 2000; Looman *et al.*, 2004). In our studies community respondents reported greater problems with drugs than did incarcerated sexual offenders and Abracen *et al.* (2000) and Looman *et al.* (2004) also found greater problems with drugs for non-sexual offender groups than sexual offenders.

SEXUAL BEHAVIOURS OF ADDICTS

If sexual addicts are unable or unwilling to control their behaviour it seems reasonable to believe that they might engage in a higher frequency of sexual behaviours than non-addicts. Oddly, we found no significant differences in frequency, age of onset, or diversity of sexual behaviours between sexual addicts and non-addicts. It appears that although sexual addicts report an inability to control their sexual desires, their overt sexual behaviour does not significantly differ from non-addicts. This seems to suggest that sexual addicts may be plagued by urges and fantasies but that this increased sexual desire does not necessarily translate into increased overt sexual acts. These unresolved urges and fantasies may lead to attempts to meet needs in inappropriate ways. This hypothesis is further supported by our observation of significant differences between sexual addicts and non-addicts, on self-reported sexual urges. Although, sexual addicts were significantly more likely to report unconventional thoughts, fantasies and urges, they were no more likely to report engaging in these behaviours. In fact, sexual addicts were less likely to engage in conventional sex with a partner, but more likely to masturbate to fantasies of unconventional sex, than non-addicts. These results would seem to suggest that for those sexual addicts who become sexual offenders it is their withdrawal from appropriate sexual relationships and engagement in deviant sexual behaviours that is problematic and this may be leading some sexual addicts to offend. Sexual offenders may fantasize about their previous sexual behaviours when under duress and as a result develop a sexual addiction. Research on sexual offenders has shown an increase in deviant fantasizing when coping with distress (Looman, 1995; McKibben, Proulx & Lusignan, 1996; Proulx, McKibben & Lusignan, 1996).

SEXUAL ADDICTION AND COPING USING SEX

Cortoni and Marshall (2001) report research which they claim demonstrates that sexual activity functions as a coping strategy for sexual offenders. That is, when under stress, sexual offenders will use sexual activity, either consenting or non-consenting, as a way to cope. This finding is supported by research (Looman, 1995; McKibben, Proulx & Lusignan, 1994; Proulx, McKibben & Lusignan, 1996) which demonstrated that sexual offenders were more likely to engage in deviant sexual fantasizing while in a negative mood. Therefore, sexual offender sexual addicts may be more likely to use sex as a coping strategy. In our research sexual offender sexual addicts were more likely to self-report using sex as a coping strategy than sexual offender non-addicts. This seems to offer support for our earlier finding that sexual addicts do not actually engage in overt sexual behaviours at a greater frequency than non-addicts.

SEXUAL ADDICTION AND PSYCHOPATHY

Psychopathy has been a widely examined issue in the field of offending and also has relevance for sexual offenders. It is generally examined under Hare's two-factor model (Hare, 1991): antisocial personality traits and social deviance (Harpur, Hare & Hakstian, 1989). There are many aspects of psychopathy that may be related to sexual addiction, for example, poor behavioural control, impulsivity, failure to accept responsibility for own actions. However, in our research we failed to find any relationship between psychopathy and sexual addiction (Marshall et al., 2004). Interestingly, higher psychopathy was found to be related to greater engagement in unconventional sex, highest number of orgasms in one week, and lower ability to resist engaging in inappropriate sex. All of which were unrelated to the measure of sexual addiction. From our limited research on sexual addiction and psychopathy in incarcerated sexual offenders, there does not appear to be any overlap between these two concepts.

SUMMARY OF OUR RESEARCH

The results of our research appears to suggest that sexual addiction is a significant problem for incarcerated sexual offenders, with more than one-third of our sexual offenders being classified as sexual addicts. A central argument to the use of sexual addiction to describe the problem is the likely presence of co-morbid addictions. We did not find support for this hypothesis when examining the relationship of sexual addiction to alcohol or drug addiction. Sexual addicts were also not found to have greater sexual behaviour problems than non-addicts. However, they did appear to be plagued by more sexual thoughts, urges and fantasies. When we examined our factor analyses of the sexual addiction measure (SAST) the items that loaded most heavily on the underlying single factor of the SAST were items that appear to be related to thoughts about sexual behaviour, in particular, to feelings of shame and guilt about sexual behaviour. Although it is speculative, but arguably supported by our findings, incarcerated sexual offender sexual addicts may have had difficulties around their interpretation of their sexual desires such that the more they try to not think about sex, the more it plagues them. They may act on these thoughts when in a vulnerable state (see Marshall & Marshall, 2000, for a description of vulnerability in sexual offenders) and then interpret their behaviour as being out of their control as both an explanation and a rationalisation for their behaviour.

ONLINE SEXUAL BEHAVIOUR PROBLEMS

In this section we review the literature on the development of the Internet as an outlet for sexual activity and interest, the consequences of online sexual compulsivity, and the relationship between sexual preoccupation and offending. For a review of the literature on the characteristics and assessment of those who have been convicted of the possession, making and distribution of indecent images of children please refer to Chapter 12 in this book by David Middleton.

The advent of easily available pornography on the Internet appears to be a problem for some sexual offenders. Some of our sexual offender clients have been incarcerated because they accessed illegal material online. Others have problems because their use/overuse of the Internet impairs other areas of functioning. Examples of functional impairment are: clients who chat or engage in sexual activities online with others while essentially ignoring people in their immediate environment causing disruptions to supportive relationships; using the Internet at work – the most common time for accessing the Internet for sexual purposes is 9am and 5pm (Carnes, 2001a; Cooper *et al.*, 2001b) – may cause difficulties at work, including the possibility of losing a job.

Sex has been a major factor in the development of activity on, and interest in, the Internet (Cooper, 1997; Cooper *et al.*, 1999a). So much so that an estimated 20% of Internet users engage in some form of online sexual activity (Cooper, Delmonico & Burg, 2000), and according to Carr (2000) this number is rapidly increasing. This is not a surprise because since its inception sexuality has been a significant financial engine driving the growth of the Internet (Hapgood, 1996; Stefanac, 1993). It has been suggested that sexual pursuits may account for almost 70% of money spent online (Sprenger, 1999). The speed and capabilities of the Internet when combined with sexuality have produced an effect so dramatic that it has been said that it is catalyzing the next 'sexual revolution' (Cooper *et al.*, 1999a). Figures taken from www .sexual-addict.com (Johnson, 2007) indicate that there are 4.2 million pornographic websites (12% of the total number), and that there are 68 million daily pornographic search engine requests (25% of the total). The Internet has clearly presented an unprecedented opportunity for individuals to have anonymous, cost-effective and unfettered access to an essentially unlimited range of sexual stimuli, an opportunity of which many are taking advantage.

While many people are engaging in online sexual activity, Cooper and his colleagues (Cooper *et al.*, 1999a, 1999c) and Greenfield (1999) assure us that the majority of people who visit sexual sites on the Internet do so in moderation for recreational purposes and do not suffer any negative consequences. Research by Cooper, Delmonico and Burg (2000) found that nearly 83% of all users of sexual sites on the Internet did not report any difficulties in their life as a result of their online behaviour.

However, the National Council on Sexual Addiction and Compulsivity (NCSAC, 2000) claims that two million Internet users are sexually addicted. This is possibly a relatively small percentage of those who use the Internet, but a large total number of people. Cooper *et al.*, (1999c), in the first large-scale study of online sexual activity, reported that only 8.3% of those who used the Internet for sexual purposes 11 hours or more per week experienced difficulties in other areas of their lives. Cooper, Delmonico and Burg (2000) used an online survey with a measure of compulsivity to better understand the characteristics and usage patterns of those who had employed the Internet for sexual purposes. Using a sample of 9,265 respondents, the authors report that 13% of respondents showed signs of moderate to severe problems of compulsivity and distress. In his study, Carnes (2001) found that about 6% of Internet users have concerns about their use of the Internet for sex.

CATEGORISATION OF ONLINE SEXUAL BEHAVIOUR PROBLEMS

Cooper *et al.* (2001b) showed support for the existence of three subtypes of online sexual compulsivity. The first is the *Stress-Reactive* user who uses sex on the Internet as a way of relieving high levels of stress. The second is the *Depressive* user who uses sex on the Internet as an escape from depression in their lives. The last type of user acknowledges that Internet sex allows for an escape from the daily routine of life into a world of *Fiction and Fantasy* that fulfils one's sexual desires.

According to Schneider (2000) the behaviour users of online sexual material can rapidly accelerate in severity. A common theme in her study was that certain types of pornography were initially accessed out of curiosity and then quickly became the focus of the user's interest. Patients frequently reported that they were now doing things sexually, or obsessing about things, that were never a part of their sexual repertoire prior to accessing online sexual material.

AETIOLOGY OF ONLINE SEXUAL BEHAVIOUR PROBLEMS

In Griffiths' (2000) study of five cases of excessive sexual computer usage it was concluded that use was symptomatic, and highlighted the way the subjects used the Internet to counteract other deficiencies. Those with psychological problems may use the Internet to hide behind rather than to face their social or sexual fears and conflicts. Walther, Anderson and Park (1994) and Young and Rogers (1998) showed higher levels of Internet usage to be related to increased levels of depression. One of the possible consequences of depression may be that certain Internet users become vulnerable to the sexually addictive use of the Internet (Reed, 1994).

CONSEQUENCES OF ONLINE SEXUAL COMPULSIVITY

In her study, Schneider (2000) reports that some of the adverse consequences of online sexual compulsivity include depression, social isolation, and decreased job performance or job loss and abandonment of other social activities. One key consequence was reported to be a loss of interest in 'ordinary' sex with one's usual partner. Similarly, sexual offender sexual addicts in our research reported engaging in conventional sex with a partner less, and masturbating to unconventional fantasies more, than non-sexual addicts. As online sexual activity becomes more widespread some have expressed a concern that it will give more people unrealistic expectations of their love lives and threaten relationships, fearing that long-term exposure to sexually explicit material may decrease attraction to one's primary partner or increase the desire for emotionally uncommitted sexual involvement (Greenfield, 1999; Kraut *et al.*, 1998).

Carnes (1999), in an important study of nearly 1,000 persons who engaged in online sexual compulsivity, found that "by far the biggest losses recorded were in the workplace" (p. 87). The main loss was time. Most reported not being able to work up to their potential, with 80% reporting a loss of productivity and 86% reportedly acting out sexually in some way in the workplace. In a study which involved surveying almost 40,000 adults, 20% reported going online for sexual activities at work (Cooper, Scherer & Mathy, 2001a). For compulsive users who have access at work, upwards of 2.5 hours per day may be spent engaged in online sexual activity at work (Cooper *et al.*, 2001a). Interestingly it has been found that 70% of all adult content Internet traffic occurs during the 9 to 5 workday (Carnes, 2001).

RELATIONSHIP TO OFFENDING

For at least some who go online for sexual stimulation the need for sexual satiation can become an obsession that has the potential to escalate into a criminal act. There is evidence that at least some men who access child pornography sites on the Internet are led there by earlier access to other adult-oriented sites (Cooper *et al.*, 1999b; Cooper, Delmonico & Burg, 2000; Greenfield, 1999; Schneider, 2000). According to Zwicke (2000) the distribution of what is frequently termed 'child pornography' online is rapidly increasing; Wyre (2003) reported that in a six-month period in 2001 there was a 345% increase in sites containing child abusive images on the Internet.

In addition, sexual preoccupation in general has been linked to recidivism (Hanson & Harris, 2000; Hanson & Morton-Bourgon, 2004). In Hanson and Morton-Bourgon's (2004) metanalysis of dynamic risk variables (see Chapter 4) sexual preoccupation was one of the strongest predictors of sexual recidivism and was also strongly related to violent recidivism (sexual and non-sexual). These authors offered a potential explanation for how sexual preoccupation may be relevant to sexual recidivism: a general lack of self-control (common among young people and general criminals), specific problems controlling sexual impulses, and a tendency to over-value sex in the pursuit of happiness. It is also likely that for some, sexual activity on the Internet will not constitute illegal behaviour but will seriously interfere with the development or maintenance of a satisfying lifestyle, and possibly relate to future acts of criminality.

THE FUTURE

This field is clearly young. Internet growth over the last 15 years has required researchers and clinicians to examine paradigms that never before existed, and Cooper (1998) appears to be correct in his assertion that the helping professions have been slow to respond to these phenomena. Continued research will need to be provided to fully understand, evaluate and treat those with online sexual behaviour problems. Once the problems are better understood, future research should focus on the development of valid and reliable protocols to assist with accurate evaluation and treatment of problematic online behaviours. One driver in this ought to be the inevitability that the Internet sexuality of the future is likely to be even more engaging, have a greater impact and be potentially more dangerous and widespread than it is at the present time.

INVOLVEMENT BY WOMEN AND CHILDREN

There is emerging evidence that women are over-represented among those with online sexual compulsivity (Cooper, Delmonico & Burg, 2000). According to Nielsen NetRatings the number of women in the UK downloading Internet pornography has soared 30% to 1.4 million. Scientific research and information regarding children, teens and sexual activity on the Internet is just now emerging. We are uncertain about the potential for youth to become sexual compulsives if they engage in online sexual activities. However, there is some evidence that the largest consumers of Internet pornography come from the 12–17 year age groups (Internet Filter Review [IFR], 2003), and according to Nielsen NetRatings more than half of all children have viewed adult images "while looking for something else". According to IFR the average age of people in the USA who are first exposed to Internet pornographic images is 11 years.

Longo, Brown and Orcutt (2002) point out that we should be cautious about children's exposure to large amounts of inappropriate sexual materials on the Internet given that the American Psychological Association has determined that exposure to excessive amounts of television violence is impacting children and their aggressive behaviours in negative ways. Boies (2002) reports that 3.5% of his sample of college students viewed sexually explicit material online and masturbated to it at least once a day, which suggests potential compulsivity in this subgroup. Whether this will lead to sexual offending is unknown at this time.

CONCLUSIONS

Sexual addiction, as described by Carnes (1983, 1989) and outlined in the *Sexual Addiction Screening Test*, appears to be a greater problem for sexual offenders than community comparison groups. From our research it appears that sexual offender sexual addicts are plagued by sexual preoccupation and, oddly, that this has the effect of reducing the number of conventional sexual outlets and increasing the rate of masturbation to unconventional sexual outlets. This hypothesis was also supported by the findings on sexual addicts who have problems with online sexual activities. Specifically, greater time spent online accessing sexual materials resulted in less interest in 'ordinary' sexual behaviours with a partner.

From the research we reported and reviewed, it seems that sexual addiction/compulsion/preoccupation is sought out to cope with deficits in other areas of functioning which has the effect of isolating the addict from others. This then further escalates problem areas resulting in a greater need to cope, which can lead to a greater use of sex to alleviate negative affect.

The sexual offender field has been reluctant to consider sexual addiction in sexual offenders. This is most likely due to the association of addiction to 12-step treatment programmes where part of the goal is to have the addict admit to powerlessness to control their behaviour. Most current approaches to sexual offender treatment require at least some degree of acceptance of responsibility for behaviour by offenders (see Marshall *et al.*, 2006) and this appears to be in conflict with 12-step programmes. Given our findings, however, it would seem prudent for sexual offender researchers to consider examining the features of sexual addiction in sexual offenders.

The sexual offender respondents in our research come from our treatment programme setting, a medium-security federal prison in Canada, and our treatment outcome data offer hope for the effective reduction of risk for recidivism, both sexual and non-sexual, in sexual offender sexual addicts. In addition our sexual offender clients include a growing number of men convicted of using the Internet to access child pornography. Sexual preoccupation has been found to be a predictor of sexual recidivism (Hanson & Harris, 2000) and more than one-third of the sexual offender respondents in our research were classified as sexual addicts. Our observed recidivism rate in 534 treated sexual offenders released for a mean of 5.5 years is just 3.2% which is a marked decrease in recidivism from the expected rate (16.9%) based on actuarial measures (see Marshall *et al.*, 2006, for a description of our treatment programme and a summary of our outcome data). If our samples are representative of the group in our outcome data, then the theoretical approach we use may shed some light on the treatment of sexual addiction more generally.

REFERENCES

Abracen, J., Looman, J. & Anderson, D. (2000). Alcohol and drug abuse in sexual and nonsexual violent offenders. *Sexual Abuse: Journal of Research and Treatment, 12,* 263–274.

Barbaree, H.E. (1991). Denial and minimization among sex offenders: Assessment and treatment outcome. *Forum on Corrections Research, 3,* 30–33.

Barth, R.J. & Kinder, B.N. (1987). The mislabeling of sexual impulsivity. *Journal of Sexual and Marital Therapy, 13,* 15–23.

Bass, B.A. & Levant, M.D. (1992). Family perception of rapists and pedophiles. *Psychological reports, 71,* 211–214.

Blanchard, G.T. (1990). Differential diagnosis of sexual offenders: Distinguishing characteristics of the Sex Addict. *American Journal of Preventative Psychiatry and Neurology, 2,* 45–47.

174 ASSESSMENT AND TREATMENT OF SEX OFFENDERS

Blanchard, G.T. (1991). The role of sexual addiction in the sexual exploitation of patients by male psychiatrists. *American Journal of Preventative Psychiatry and Neurology, 3*, 24–27.

Blanchard, G.T. (1995). Sexually addicted lust murderers. *Sexual Addiction & Compulsivity, 2*(1), 62–71.

Boies, S.C. (2002). University students' uses of and reactions to online sexual information and entertainment: Links to online and offline sexual behaviour. *The Canadian Journal of Human Sexuality, 11*, 77–89.

Carnes, P. (1983). *Out of the shadows: Understanding sexual addiction.* Minneapolis, MN: CompCare.

Carnes, P. (1989). *Contrary to love: Helping the sexual addict.* Minneapolis, MN: CompCare.

Carnes, P.J. (1999). Editorial: Cybersex, sexual health, and the transformation of culture. *Sexual Addiction and Compulsivity, 6*, 77–78.

Carnes, P.J. (2001). Cybersex, courtship, and escalating arousal: Factors in addictive sexual desire. *Sexual Addiction and Compulsivity, 8*, 45–78.

Carr, L. (2000). Sizing up virtual vice: Porn and gambling are making more money than ever. http://thestandard.com/article/display/0,1151,1754900.html

Coleman, E. (1987). Sexual compulsivity: Definition, etiology, and treatment considerations. *Journal of Chemical Dependency Treatment, 1*, 189–204.

Coleman, E. (1990). Toward a synthetic understanding of sexual orientation. In D.P. McWhirter & S.A. Sanders (Eds), *Homosexuality/heterosexuality: Concepts of sexual orientation.* (pp. 267–276). Oxford: Oxford University Press.

Cooper, A. (1997). The Internet and sexuality: Into the new millennium. *Journal of Sex Education and Therapy, 22*, 5–6.

Cooper, A. (1998). Sexuality and the Internet: Surfing into the new millennium. *CyberPsychology and Behavior, 1*, 187–193.

Cooper, A., Boies, S., Maheu, M. & Greenfield, D. (1999a). Sexuality and the Internet: The next sexual revolution. In F. Muscarella & L. Szuchman (Eds), *The psychological science of sexuality: A research based approach* (pp. 519–545). New York: John Wiley & Sons, Inc.

Cooper, A., Delmonico, D.L. & Burg, R. (2000). Cybersex users, abusers, and compulsives: New findings and implications. *Sexual Addiction and Compulsivity, 7*, 5–29.

Cooper, A., Griffin-Shelley, E., Delmonico, D.L. & Mathy, R.M. (2001b). Online sexual problems: Assessment and predictive variables. *Sexual Addiction and Compulsivity, Special Issue: Preparing for DSM-V, 8*, 267–285.

Cooper, A., Putnam, D.E., Planchon, L.A. & Boies, S.C. (1999b). Online sexual compulsivity: Getting tangled in the net. *Sexual Addiction and Compulsivity, 6*, 79–104.

Cooper, A., Scherer, C., Boies, S.C. & Gordon, B. (1999c). Sexuality on the Internet: from sexual exploration to pathological expression. *Professional Psychology: Research and Practice, 30*, 154–64.

Cooper, A., Scherer, C. & Mathy, R. (2001a). Overcoming methodological concerns in the investigation of online sexual activities. *Cyberpsychology and Behavior, 4*, 437–448.

Cortoni, F. & Marshall, W.L. (2001). Sex as a coping strategy and its relationship to juvenile sexual history and intimacy in sexual offenders. *Sexual Abuse: A Journal of Research and Treatment, 13*, 27–44.

Delmonico, D.L., Bubenzer, D.L. & West, J.D. (1998). Assessing sexual addiction using the Sexual Dependency Inventory-Revised. *Sexual Addiction and Compulsivity, 5*, 179–187.

Delmonico, D.L., Griffin, E. & Carnes, P.J. (2002). *Treating online compulsive sexual behavior: When cybersex is the drug of choice.* New York, NY: Brunner-Routledge.

Dhawan, S. & Marshall, W.L. (1996). Sexual abuse histories of sexual offenders. *Sexual Abuse: A Journal of Research and Treatment, 8*, 7–15.

Eshuys, D. & Smallbone, S. (2006). Religious affiliations among adult sexual offenders. *Sexual Abuse: A Journal of Research and Treatment, 18*, 279–288.

Goodman, A. (1998). *Sexual addiction: An integrated approach.* Madison, WI: International Universities Press.

Greenfield, D.N. (1999). *Virtual addiction: Help for netheads, cyberfreaks, and those who love them.* Oakland, CA: New Harbinger Publications.

Griffiths, M. (2000). Excessive Internet use: Implications for sexual behavior. *Cyberpsychology and Behavior, 3,* 537–552.

Hanson, R.K. & Harris, A.J.R. (2000). Where should we intervene? Dynamic predictors of sex offence recidivism. *Criminal Justice and Behavior, 21,* 187–202.

Hanson, R.K. & Morton-Bourgon, K. (2004). Predictors of sexual recidivism: An updated meta-analysis. Public Safety and Emergency Preparedness Canada: Report 2004: 02.

Hanson, R.K., Gordon, A., Harris, A.J.R. *et al.* (2002). First report of the collaborative outcome data project on the effectiveness of psychological treatment for sex offenders. *Sexual Abuse: A Journal of Research and Treatment, 14,* 169–194.

Hapgood, F. (1996). Sex sells, Inc. *Technology, 4,* 45–51.

Hare, R.D. (1991). *Manual for the Hare Psychopathy Checklist-Revised.* Toronto: Multi-Health Systems.

Harpur, T.J., Hare, R.D. & Hakstian, A.R. (1989). Two-factor conceptualization of psychopathy: Construct validity and assessment implications. *Psychological Assessment, 1,* 6–17.

Johnson, M. (2007). Internet Pornography Statistics. Retrieved November 2007 from: http://www.sexual-addict.com/learn-PornFacts.htm

Kafka, M.P. (1991). Successful antidepressant treatment of nonparaphilic sexual addictions and paraphilias in men. *Journal of Clinical Psychiatry, 52,* 60–65.

Kafka, M.P. (1997). Hypersexual desire in males: An operational definition and clinical implications for men with paraphilias and paraphilia-related disorders. *Archives of Sexual Behavior, 26,* 505–526.

Kafka, M.P. & Hennen, J. (1999). The paraphilia-related disorders: An empirical investigation of non-paraphilic hypersexuality disorders in outpatient males. *Journal of Sex and Marital Therapy, 25,* 305–319.

Kalichman, S.C., Adair, V., Rompa, D. *et al.* (1994). Sexual sensation seeking: Scale development and predicting AIDS-risk behaviour among homosexually active men. *Journal of Personality Assessment, 62,* 385–397.

Knight, R.A., Carter, D.L. & Prentky, R.A. (1989). A system for the classification of child molesters: Reliability and application. *Journal of Interpersonal Violence, 4,* 3–23.

Kraut, R., Lundmark, V., Patterson, M. *et al.* (1998). Internet Paradox: A social technology that reduces social involvement and psychological well-being? *American Psychologist, 53,* 1017–1031.

Leedes, R. (2001). The three most important criteria in diagnosing sexual addiction unerringly – obsession, obsession, and obsession. Paper presented at the AFAR/Vanderbilt Symposium, Nashville, TN, March 2001.

Longo, R.E., Brown, S.M. & Orcutt, D.P. (2002). Effects of Internet Sexuality on Children and Adolescents. In A. Cooper (Ed), *Sex and the Internet: A Guidebook for Clinicians.* New York: Brunner-Routledge.

Looman, J. (1995). Sexual fantasies of child molesters. *Canadian Journal of Behavioural Science, 27,* 321–332.

Looman, J., Abracen, J., DiFazio, R. & Maillet, G. (2004). Alcohol and drug abuse among sexual and nonsexual offenders: Relationship to intimacy deficits and coping strategy. *Sexual Abuse: A Journal of Research & Treatment, 16,* 177–189.

Manley, G. & Koehler, J.D. (2001). Proposed diagnostic features of sexual behaviour disorder. Paper presented at the AFAR/Vanderbilt Symposium, Nashville, TN, March 2001.

Marshall, L.E. & Marshall, W.L. (1998). Sexual addiction and substance abuse in sexual offenders. Paper presented at the 17th Annual Treatment and Research Conference of the Association for the Treatment of Sexual Abusers, Vancouver, Canada, October 1998.

Marshall, W.L. & Marshall, L.E. (2000). The origins of sexual offending. *Trauma, Violence, and Abuse: A Review Journal, 1,* 250–263.

Marshall, L.E. & Marshall W.L. (2001). Excessive sexual desire disorder among sexual offenders: The development of a research project. *Sexual Addiction and Compulsivity: The Journal of Treatment and Prevention, 8,* 301–307.

Marshall, L.E. & Marshall, W.L. (2006). Sexual addiction in incarcerated sexual offenders. *Sexual Addiction and Compulsivity: The Journal of Treatment and Prevention, 13,* 377–390.

Marshall, L.E., Marshall, W.L. & Moulden, H. (2000). *Sexual addiction, substance abuse, coping, and sexual history in sexual offenders.* Paper presented at the 19th Annual Treatment and Research Conference of the Association for the Treatment of Sexual Abusers, San Diego, USA, November 2000.

Marshall, W.L., Serran, G.A. & Cortoni, F.A. (2000). Childhood attachments, sexual abuse, and their relationship to adult coping in child molesters. *Sexual Abuse: A Journal of Research and Treatment, 12,* 17–26.

Marshall, W.L., Champagne, F., Brown, C. & Miller, S. (1997). Empathy, intimacy, loneliness, and self-esteem in nonfamilial child molesters. *Journal of Child Sexual Abuse, 6,* 87–97.

Marshall, L.E., Moulden, H.M., Serran, G.A. & Marshall, W.L. (2004). *Sexual addiction and psychopathy in incarcerated sexual offenders.* Paper presented at the 23rd Annual Treatment and Research Conference of the Association for the Treatment of Sexual Abusers, Albuquerque, USA, October 2004.

Marshall, W.L., Marshall, L.E., Serran. G.A. & Fernandez, Y.M. (2006). *Treating sexual offenders: An integrated approach.* New York: Routledge.

McElroy, S.L., Soutullo, C.A., Taylor, P.J. *et al.* (1999). Psychiatric features of 36 men convicted of sexual offenses. *Journal of Clinical Psychiatry, 60,* 414–420.

McKibben, A., Proulx, J. & Lusignan, R. (1996). Relationships between conflict, affect and deviant sexual behaviours in rapists and pedophiles. *Behaviour Research and Therapy, 32,* 571–575.

Miner, M.H., Coleman, E., Center, B.A. *et al.* (2005). The compulsive sexual behaviour inventory: psychometric properties. *Archives of Sexual Behavior, 36,* 579–587.

National Council on Sexual Addiction and Compulsivity (NCSAC) (2000). *Cybersex and sexual addiction.* Retrieved April13, 2000 from National Council on Sexual Addiction and Compulsivity website: http//:www.ncsac.org/cybersex.htm

Proulx, J., McKibben, A. & Lusignan, R. (1996). Relationships between affective components and sexual behaviours in sexual aggressors. *Sexual Abuse: A Journal of Research and Treatment, 8,* 279–290.

Reed, M.D. (1994). Pornography addiction and compulsive sexual behavior. In D. Zillmann, J. Bryant & A.C. Huston (Eds), *Media, children, and the family: Social scientific, psychodynamic, and clinical perspectives* (pp. 249–269). Hillsdale, NJ: Lawrence Erlbaum Associates.

Schneider, J.P. (2000). Effects of cybersex addiction on the family: results of a survey. *Sexual Addiction and Compulsivity, 7,* 31–58.

Schneider, J.P. & Schneider, B. (1991). *Sex, lies, and forgiveness: Couples speaking out on healing from sex addiction.* New York: HarperCollins.

Seidman, B.T., Marshall, W.L., Hudson, S.M. & Robertson, P.J. (1994). An examination of intimacy and loneliness in sex offenders. *Journal of Interpersonal Violence, 9,* 518–534.

Selzer, M.L. (1971). The Michigan Alcoholism Screening Test (MAST): The quest for a new diagnostic instrument. *American Journal of Psychiatry, 127,* 1653–1658.

Skinner, H.A. (1982). The Drug Abuse Screening Test. *Addictive Behaviors, 7,* 363–371.

Skinner, H.A. (1998). *The Drug Abuse Screening Test (DAST): Guidelines for Administration and Scoring.* Toronto, Canada: Addiction Research Foundation.

Smith, D.E. (1994). Response to Schneider. *Sexual Addiction and Compulsivity, 1,* 45.

Sparks, J., Bailey, W., Marshall, W.L. & Marshall, L.E. (2003). *Shame and Guilt in Sexual Offenders.* Paper presented at the 22nd Annual Treatment and Research Conference of the Association for the Treatment of Sexual Abusers, St Louis, USA.

Sprenger, P. (1999, September 30). The porn pioneers. The Guardian (Online), pp. 2–3.

Stefanac, S. (1993). Sex and the new media. *NewMedia, 3,* 38–45.

Steiger, J.H. & Lind, J.C. (1980, May). Statistically-based tests for the number of common factors. Paper presented at the May annual meeting of the Psychometric Society, Iowa City, IA.

Walther, J.B., Anderson, J.F. & Park, D.W. (1994). Interpersonal effects in computer-mediated interaction: A meta-analysis of social and antisocial communication. *Communication Research, 21,* 460–487.

Wyre, R. (2003). Child Porn. *Community Care,* September, 11–17.

Young, K.S. & Rogers, R.C. (1998). The relationship between depression and Internet addiction. *CyberPsychology and Behavior, 1,* 25–28.

Zwicke, L. (2000). *Crime on the Superhighway: A Guide to Online Safety.* Retrieved March, 2007 from: http://www.geocities.com/CapitolHill/6647/

PART THREE

Assessments for Specific Populations

11

Decision Making During the Offending Process: An Assessment Among Subtypes of Sexual Aggressors of Women

JEAN PROULX

ERIC BEAUREGARD

INTRODUCTION

Over the last few decades, a number of typologies of sexual aggressors of women (rapists and sexual murderers) have been developed (e.g. Beauregard & Proulx, 2002; Beech, Fisher & Ward, 2005; Gebhard *et al.*, 1965; Groth & Birnbaum, 1979; Knight, 1999; Knight & Prentky, 1990; Polaschek *et al.*, 2001; Proulx *et al.*, 1999; Ressler, Burgess & Douglas, 1988; Revitch & Schlesinger, 1981, 1989). While a variety of taxometric approaches (e.g., theoretical, clinical, multivariate, qualitative) have been used to identify types of sexual aggressors (Beauregard, Proulx & St-Yves, 2007), number of types is small, namely sadistic, angry, opportunistic and compensatory, and relatively consistently observed in all typologies. Hence the question is: why have the types of sexual aggressors of women exhibited such stability across typologies?

To answer this question, we will use the rational choice perspective theoretical framework from criminology. First, we will outline the core concepts of this perspective. Second, we will describe the main types of sexual aggressors of women. Third, we will present the results of the taxometric analyses we performed using correspondence analysis (Greenacre & Blasius, 1994). Finally, we will discuss the internal logic of the offending processes associated with each type identified in our taxometric study

Assessment and Treatment of Sex Offenders: A Handbook. Edited by Anthony Beech, Leam Craig and Kevin Browne. © John Wiley & Sons Ltd, 2009.

of sexual aggressors of women. This discussion of the types of sexual aggressors of women will be based on a central concept of the rational choice perspective, namely the choice-structuring properties of a crime.

THE RATIONAL CHOICE PERSPECTIVE IN CRIMINOLOGY

The rational choice perspective addresses decision making carried out by an offender in the course of a specific crime (Clarke & Felson, 1993; Cornish & Clarke, 1986; Piquero & Tibbetts, 2002). The basic assumption of this perspective is that criminals are rational individuals who weigh the costs and benefits of criminal opportunities in order to decide whether or not to act. Cost-benefit analysis may be sophisticated in well-planned crimes and minimal in violent, impulsive crimes. According to Cohen and Felson (1979), when a criminal is highly motivated to commit a crime, he analyses the value of the target and the magnitude of the interferences with his criminal project. For example, if a highly motivated sexual aggressor of women finds a woman sexually attractive, and judges that the probability that somebody (e.g., husband, father, friend, or passer-by) interfering with his plan to offend is low, he will choose to commit a sexual assault. During the assault, however, he may reassess the probability of interference and interrupt his crime. Consequently, decisional processes and choices are involved in the planning and enactment of violent crimes, even those that seem impulsive and irrational.

Criminals' rationality is bounded by several factors (Cornish & Clarke, 1987; Johnson & Payne, 1986). In fact, an offender's cost-benefit analysis may not take into account every possibility, both because such an analysis is time-consuming and because the relevant information is only partially available to him. In addition, an offender's cognitive deficits may restrict his information processing concerning the crime. Consequently, criminals usually rely on heuristics based on the success and failure of previous criminal activities, rather than on a fully rational cost-benefit analysis. The course of action selected by an offender is usually the first minimally satisfactory one identified, rather than the optimal one.

Each type of crime involves specific information processing that leads to a sequence of choices and actions, known variously as the crime-commission process or the *crime script* (Cornish, 1994). For example, the offender's motivations, the targets, and the guardians (any person who may interfere with a criminal project, such as a parent, police officer, or security guard) are not the same for a bank robbery as they are for a sexual assault of a woman. First, a sexual aggressor must be motivated to commit a sexual assault (e.g., as a result of sadistic sexual fantasies and urges, anger, sexual arousal), and may also be in a state of alcohol- or drug-induced, disinhibition that favours actions compatible with his motivations. Second, he has to select a 'hunting field', a place where he can find victims (e.g., red-light district, private home) (Beauregard, Proulx, Rossmo *et al.*, 2007). Third, he has to identify the time he is most likely to have access to victims in his hunting field. Fourth, he must select a victim according to her desirability, vulnerability and accessibility. Fifth, he has to choose a victim-contact strategy. Finally, he must adjust his behaviours to overcome the victim's resistance during their transportation to the crime site and during the sexual aggression. This offender-victim interaction plays an important role in the crime script, since it is closely related to the level of victim injury and, sometimes, to murder. In addition to these decisions, the aggressor may, at each step of the script, evaluate the risk of a variety of negative outcomes for him. Such outcomes include somebody helping the victim, and the victim having enough information about the offender to identify him to the police and secure conviction and incarceration.

In each step of the crime script, information processing may be sophisticated, minimal, or absent. Some offenders carefully plan their offences, watching their victims for weeks, and gathering information on their life styles. These offenders often have a rape kit, and their modus operandi is usually closely linked to their deviant sexual fantasies. Some others are in a state of anger and sexual arousal during the hours preceding the crime. They have no precise plan, but are prepared to take advantage of any opportunity to commit a brutal sexual assault. This is the minimal level of rationality in sexual offending, since decision making about the crime begins with victim access. Finally, for some aggressors, information processing related to hunting field and victim selection is unnecessary, since the motivation to commit a sexual offence arises after initial contact with the victim. This would be the case, for example, for a burglar who decides, on the basis of a minimal and opportunistic cost-benefit analysis, to sexually assault a woman who is sleeping in the bedroom he breaks into.

In the analysis of the choices and actions related to a specific type of crime, knowledge about scripts identified for other types of crime is of limited usefulness. For each type of crime, choices and actions are shaped by a constellation of specific external constraints, i.e., the *choice-structuring properties of a crime* (Cornish & Clarke, 1987). For example, to commit a bank robbery, a criminal must overcome the security measures (e.g., alarm system, bullet-proof glass, armed security guard), persuade the staff to give him a significant amount of money and leave the crime site rapidly and in a safe manner. All of this must be done as fast as possible, in a public place where there is a high probability of finding guardians (e.g., policemen) who may interfere with the crime. The interaction of these external constraints is not random but rather driven by an internal logic that permits only a limited number of ways to commit a bank robbery.

THE RATIONAL CHOICE PERSPECTIVE APPLIED TO SEXUAL OFFENDING

Turning now to the sexual assault of an adult woman, we can see that there are also specific external constraints that shape the decisions and actions of offenders. For example, the crime site must be an isolated place where nobody can stop the assault. Also, this crime site must remain isolated long enough to permit the offender to gratify himself sexually. Finally, the offender must prevent the victim from escaping, and obtain compliance with his demands. Just as in bank robbery, the sexual assault of a woman is subject to specific external constraints, i.e., choice-structuring properties that determine the limited number of ways this type of crime can be committed.

In addition to external constraints, there are also internal constraints that influence the crime script. According to Tibbetts and Gibson (2002), criminal propensity, which is not equally distributed in the population, has an impact on decision making related to a crime. For example, psychopaths are impulsive and remorseless, and lack empathy for their victims (Hare, 2003; Herve & Yulle, 2007). Accordingly, their crime scripts are usually unsophisticated and the assaults they commit may involve a high level of coercion, to overcome their victims' resistance (Trassler, 1993). Furthermore, as pointed out by Yochelson and Samenow (1976), during the preparation phase of a crime, psychopaths have a tendency to underestimate the risk of being hurt or apprehended, and exaggerate the benefits of a crime. They named this process *corrosion*. Thus, sexual aggressors who have psychopathic personality traits (internal constraints) commit their crimes in an impulsive way and use instrumental violence (the minimal violence necessary to attain their ends). When these offenders are highly motivated to obtain without delay sexual gratification (internal constraints) and in a state of disinhibition following drug, or alcohol, consumption (internal constraints), their cost-benefit analysis is minimal. In addition, empathy for the victim – something which might otherwise stop their criminal projects – is absent. On the other hand, sexual aggressors overwhelmed by sadistic sexual fantasies (internal constraints) carefully plan their offences and may wait for the optimal conditions (a suitable victim without any guardians) for a long time. When the assault does occur, it involves high levels of physical and/or psychological violence (e.g., humiliation) uncorrelated to the level of victim resistance. These coercive acts are largely a function of their sadistic sexual fantasies. In sexual aggressors, internal constraints may be stable factors such as psychopathy and sadistic sexual preferences, or they may be state-situational factors such as sexual arousal, anger and disinhibition following drug or alcohol consumption.

According to Piquero and Tibbetts (1996), identifying crime scripts requires taking into account the interaction between external and internal constraints. Based on structural equation models, they concluded "a significant portion of the effects of individual propensities were indirect via more situational rational choice variables" (p. 8). They also stated that "rational choice variables appear to be essential in models of criminal offending. However, not only are individual trait measures equally important for inclusion, but these disposition measures tend to condition or interact with the effects of rational choice variables" (p. 10). Psychopathy and deviant sexual preferences are two dispositional traits which may influence decision processes in sexual aggressors.

The crime script is a function of the interaction between internal and external constraints, but also of the bounded rationality of criminals. As a result, there are a limited number of crime scripts for each type of crime (Tibbetts & Gibson, 2002). In sexual aggressors of women, taxometric studies have identified four main types of offenders: sadistic, angry, opportunistic, and compensatory. Since these types are prototypical, aggressors may exhibit only some of the characteristics associated with each of them. Overall, the literature suggests that there are four main types of sexual aggressors of women: we will now outline these in some detail.

The Sadistic Type

Sadistic sexual aggressors of women (rapists or sexual murderers) have been described in several studies (Beauregard & Proulx, 2002; Brittain, 1970; Gratzer & Bradford, 1995; Groth & Birnbaum, 1979; Knight & Prentky, 1990; Marshall *et al.*, 2002; Marshall & Kennedy, 2003; Proulx *et al.*, 1999; Proulx, Blais & Beauregard, 2006; Warren, Hazelwood & Dietz, 1996). This type of sexual aggressor had received other labels, such as assaultive offender (Gebhard *et al.*, 1965), organised sexual murderer (Ressler, Burgess & Douglas, 1988), compulsive sexual murderer (Revitch & Schlesinger, 1981, 1989), murderer motivated to carry out fantasies (Beech *et al.*, 2005), calculated pain infliction (Beech, Ward & Fisher, 2006), and sexually motivated sex murderer (Clarke & Carter, 2000). These studies highlighted the fact that during the hours before their crime, sadistic sexual aggressors are overwhelmed by sadistic sexual fantasies and by negative emotions such as anger and anxiety. In addition, prior to the offence, a large proportion of perpetrators are intoxicated by psychoactive substances (alcohol, drugs).

The sadistic sexual aggressor carefully plans the way his offence will be executed. The location of the offence is selected. Also, he prepares a rape kit, which may include tape, handcuffs, rope, knife and a gun. Finally, he selects an unknown victim according to specific criteria related to his deviant sexual fantasies. Some sadistic sexual aggressors choose a prostitute, while some others select a vulnerable victim, such as a young small woman who looks insecure.

At the beginning of the crime phase, the victim is abducted and sequestered; she may be bound and gagged. When the victim is under the sadistic sexual aggressor's control, he forces her to commit a variety of sexual acts, such as fellatio, sexual intercourse, and anal sex. Furthermore, in some cases, he may torture (burning, biting, flagellating) his victim and mutilate her sexual body areas. Also, the sadistic sexual aggressor humiliates his victim verbally (insults) and physically (urinating or ejaculating in her face). Some of them perform bizarre actions such as washing and shaving their victim's body. The level of injury is high, and murder may ensue. In the latter case, the body is hidden. The expressive violence used in the commission of this type of sexual aggression is far more than that necessary to overpower the victim and perform sexual acts. Surprisingly, a small proportion of victims physically defend themselves. This type of sexual aggression is of a long duration.

The Angry Type

The angry type is part of a number of typologies of sexual aggressors of women (Beauregard & Proulx, 2002; Beech *et al.*, 2006; Groth & Birnbaum, 1979; Knight & Prentky, 1990; Proulx *et al.*, 1999). This type of sexual aggressor is also named explosive offender (Gebhard *et al.*, 1965), disorganised sexual murderer (Ressler *et al.*, 1988), catathymic sexual murderer (Revitch & Schlesinger, 1981, 1989), grievance-motivated (Beech *et al.*, 2005), and aggressive dyscontrol murderer (Clarke & Carter, 2000). Sexual aggressors of this type report feeling intense anger and a desire for revenge against women (misogynistic anger) in the hours preceding their crimes. In addition, they consume excessive amounts of alcohol and drugs. They rarely, however, indicate having deviant sexual fantasies. These aggressors do not premeditate their sexual offences and do not seek out specific victims. They choose a woman who is immediately available – and may not even be familiar to the aggressor – as a target for their anger.

An angry-type sexual aggressor of women uses a blitz attack to initiate an offence. He rarely takes the time to bind his victim. His aim is to hurt her physically and psychologically. To do so, he humiliates his victim and may beat and stab her. In the initial stages of the assault, this gratuitous, expressive violence occurs in the absence of victim resistance. But in the course of the offence, which is usually of a short duration, a majority of victims physically resist their aggressor. Such a resistance may exacerbate the aggressor's anger and increase the brutality of his crime. Such extreme violence usually causes serious physical injury to the victims, and a significant proportion of them die. In the cases that do involve the death of the victim, the body is left at the crime scene.

Opportunistic Type

The opportunistic type is described in some typologies of rapists and of sexual murderers of women (Knight & Prentky, 1990; Proulx *et al.*, 1999). The amoral delinquent in the typology of Gebhard *et al.* (1965), and the sexually motivated type in the classification of Beech *et al.* (2005) are opportunistic types of sexual aggressors. In the hours preceding their sexual assaults, opportunistic offenders are not angry and do not have deviant sexual fantasies. However, they are usually in a state of disinhibition due to drugs and alcohol consumption. Opportunistic aggressors are psychopaths who focus on their immediate needs, with neither empathy nor respect for others' wishes. Their sexual assaults are part of a polymorphic antisocial lifestyle.

The opportunistic sexual aggressor does not plan his offence and does not select a victim according to specific criteria. In fact, his assault is an impulsive predatory act provoked by situational factors. For example, during the commission of a burglary, he decides to assault a woman he finds attractive. Also, he may assault a woman encountered in a bar; if she refuses to have sex with him, this type of offender may act on distorted male cognitions such as 'male sexual drive is uncontrollable', which means that the offender considers women to be the cause of uncontrollable male sexual arousal (Beech *et al.*, 2006).

Opportunistic sexual aggressors of women use instrumental violence during the commission of their offence. There is no evidence of gratuitous violence. Victims are rarely injured or humiliated. This type of aggressor may say to his victim, *Do what I want and I will not hurt you.* If the victim resists, however, he may use sufficient force to obtain her compliance, but will rarely bind her. Finally, it is seldom that he uses a weapon during an assault. If he kills his victim, it is to eliminate a witness.

Compensatory Type

The power rapist (Groth & Birnbaum, 1979), and the sexual non-sadistic rapist (Knight & Prentky, 1990) are considered to commit rape to compensate for an underlying feeling of inadequacy. These aggressors are described as insecure and as having low self-esteem. For them, the aims of their assaults are to control women and to be considered a good lover by them. Also, these aggressors have overwhelming rape fantasies during the hours preceding their crimes. Finally, they have cognitive distortions which favour the sexual domination of women.

Compensatory sexual aggressors carefully plan their offences, and select their victims according to specific criteria. The victims may be abducted and sequestered, but are rarely bound. During the commission of the crime, the aggressor uses instrumental violence to overpower his victim. He may use a weapon to intimidate the victim, but will not use it to hurt her. Victims are not injured or humiliated. These offences are usually of long duration.

AIM OF THE STUDY

Several typologies of sexual aggressors of women have been proposed, with four types being recurrent. Unfortunately, some of the typologies outlined above are based on clinical judgement only, which precludes verification of the validity of the clustering procedure employed (Groth & Birnbaum, 1979). Some other typologies were developed with data originating from small samples (Revitch & Schlesinger, 1981). In addition, Knight and Prentky's typology is based on modus operandi variables, as well as psychological and developmental factors. Finally, these typologies did not investigate every component of the crime scripts of sexual aggressors of women or the way these components are linked together in the crime script. Consequently, the aim of the study discussed in this chapter was to develop a typology of sexual aggressors of women (rapists, sexual murderers) on the basis of crime-script variables only. Such an approach, we would argue, is necessary to the investigation of choice-structuring properties (internal and external constraints) in crime scripts of sexual aggressors of women.

METHODS

Subjects

A total of 180 adult males who were convicted of at least one sexual offence against an extrafamilial female at least 16 years old were included in this study. A victim was considered as extrafamilial if her relationship with the offender was one of the following: stranger, acquaintance, neighbour, or friend. Our sample included a total of 63 sexual murderers of women and 117 non-homicidal sexual aggressors against women. The majority of the subjects were Caucasian (87%) and the average age at the time of the intake assessment was 33.7 years (SD = 9.2). Only a third (32.3%) of these offenders were married or in a relationship when they committed their sexual crimes. None of the subjects had an intellectual disability, or had major mental disorders such as psychosis or mood disorders.

All the non-homicidal sexual aggressors and 14 of the sexual murderers were imprisoned at the Regional Reception Center (RRC) in Ste-Anne-des-Plaines, Quebec, a maximum security institution of Correctional Service Canada. These men stayed in this institution for approximately eight weeks each, while their correctional risk level and treatment needs were assessed prior to their transfer to other institutions. The remaining 49 sexual murderers were incarcerated in other institutions of Correctional Service Canada (Quebec region). Subjects had an average of 9.9 previous charges (SD = 17.0) for non-sexual non-violent crimes, 2.5 (SD = 4.2) for non-sexual violent crimes, 0.5 (SD = 1.1) for hands-on sexual crimes and 0.09 (SD = 0.7) for hands-off sexual crimes. The participation rate was 93%. We used the data related to the first sexual offence that matched our inclusion criteria, because a majority of our subjects had only one victim.

Procedure

Before participation in this study, subjects signed a consent form indicating that the information to be gathered would be used for research purposes only. Each subject was interviewed by a criminologist and a psychologist about his crime. In addition, information from official sources such as police records and victim statements was also gathered. For the sexual murderers, we consulted the autopsy reports and the crime scene photographs. In case of discrepancies between self-reported and official information, the latter was considered more valid and was used in the current study.

Modus Operandi Variables

Our study included 13 variables related to the modus operandi. Of these, eight were coded as absent/present: selection of victim, kidnapping of victim, use of a weapon, use of physical restraints, mutilation of victim, victim forced to perform sexual acts, humiliation of victim, search for victim-specific characteristics. The remaining variables were: level of force (minimal/more than necessary), time spent with victim (less than 30 minutes/more than 30 minutes), reaction to victim resistance (without physical coercion/with physical coercion), premeditation of the crime (no/non-structured premeditation/structured premeditation) and the type of injury inflicted on the victim (none/injury/death).

Victimology Variables

Four victimology variables were included in our study: victim is a prostitute (absent/present), victim comes from a dysfunctional environment (absent/present), relationship of victim to offender (stranger/acquaintance/friend), and age of victim (16–29/30–39/$\geq$40).

Situational Variables

Six situational variables were included in the study: offender use of alcohol prior to the crime (absent/present), offender use of drugs prior to the crime (absent/present), deviant fantasies prior to crime (absent/present), victim resistance (passive/active), pre-crime affect (anger/depression/excitation/unknown), and time of crime (day/night/both night and day).

Data Analysis

The data were first submitted to multiple correspondence analysis (MCA) using multi-way tables. MCA is a geometric technique that provides a powerful representation of the associations between multi-level categorical variables, in the form of a low-dimensional graphical representation of the association between rows and columns of a table (Clausen, 1998). MCA provides a visualisation of the association, along with some descriptive statistics that indicate the number of dimensions. MCA may be seen as similar to principal component analysis, since it allows researchers to reduce a complex data matrix into a simpler one without loss of meaningful information. In this study, MCA was used in order to: (a) explore the relationship between the modus operandi, victimology, and situational variables related to crime scripts; and (b) reduce the number of variables used in the identification of crime scripts.

Although MCA provides a good representation of the data, a more comprehensive approach is needed to identify crime scripts. One such approach involves the use of complementary clustering techniques. As the starting points and outputs of MCA and clustering techniques are different, the use of both types of techniques is recommended when dealing with complex data sets (Lebart, 1994). It is more efficient to perform clustering techniques with a limited number of dimensions obtained from MCA than with a large set of variables. Thus, the clustering technique provides a hierarchical classification of the set of cases characterised by the first set of coordinates created by the MCA procedure. Ward's aggregation criterion was applied, as it has been shown that it results in a minimal loss of inertia at each step and ensures good compatibility between MCA and classification (Greenacre, 1988). The concept of inertia is analogous to that of variance and indicates how much of the 'variance' each dimension explains (Clausen, 1998). MCA and hierarchical clustering were performed using SPAD (Decisia, version MN 5.6.0), a specialised software package (Lebart, Morineau & Lambert, 2003).

In order to determine the number of dimensions to retain in the MCA solution, the 'Elbow criterion' is applied. This scree test has been proposed by Cattell (1966) for use within the context of factor analysis. The output of MCA provides eigenvalues plotted by increasing dimensionality, resulting in a falling curve. The point at which this curve flattens out (the 'elbow' of the curve), after a relatively steep downward trend, indicates the right dimensionality (Clausen, 1998). The same procedure has been applied to the study of the hunting process scripts of serial sex offenders (Beauregard *et al.*, 2007).

RESULTS

The Multiple Correspondence Analysis extracted a four-dimensional solution from the offence process variables. These four dimensions explained a total of 33.49% of the inertia (Dimension 1: 10.90%; Dimension 2: 9.68%; Dimension 3: 6.82%; Dimension 4: 6.10%). *Dimension 1* discriminates between offenders who display a high level of physical coercion in their crimes (react to victim resistance by using physical violence, physically injure the victim, kill the victim, use a level of force more than necessary), and those who display a low level (encounter no or passive victim resistance, do not injure their victim, use minimal force). *Dimension 2* contrasts sexual aggressors of women who exhibit a high investment in their crime with those with low investment. Highly invested sexual aggressors premeditate their crimes, have deviant sexual fantasies, and search for specific victim characteristics. *Dimension 3* describes the lethality of the sexual assault, (the level of physical coercion, with the highest level corresponding to the death of the victim). Offenders displaying high lethality kill and mutilate their victims, but do not humiliate or force them to perform sexual acts, as opposed to low-lethality offenders, who are more inclined to injure and humiliate their victims, and force them to perform sexual acts. Finally, *Dimension 4* describes the degree of planning of the sexual assault. Compared to those who score low on this dimension, offenders who score high plan their assault, specifically select their victims (most commonly a prostitute), search for specific victim characteristics, and commit their crimes at night. These latter crimes are premeditated and preceded by sexual arousal and deviant sexual fantasies.

Table 11.1 shows the distribution of sexual assaults in the three clusters resulting from the Hierarchical Cluster Analysis carried out with our four dimensions of offending process.

The first cluster, *Sadistic*, represents 27% (N = 49) of the sexual assaults. These offenders have deviant sexual fantasies and carefully premeditate their assaults, which occur in either the day or the night. They select, kidnap, restrain, humiliate and mutilate their victims, and use more force than necessary during their sexual assaults. Offenders following such crime scripts search for distinctive characteristics in the victim and are most likely to spend more than 30 minutes with the victim during the crime. In cases where the victim resists, offenders use physical violence. The attack often results in the death of the victim.

The second cluster, *Angry*, accounts for 41% (N = 74) of the sexual assaults. Sexual aggressors of women following this crime script are characterised by the emotion of anger prior to the crime. Typically, the victim is a prostitute aged between 30 and 39 years old, although these offenders do not look for distinctive victim characteristics.

Table 11.1 Percentages of events and test-values for the three clusters of offence pathways

	Sadistic N = 49 (27.22%)			Angry N = 74 (41.11%)			Opportunistic N = 57 (31.67%)		
		%	Test-Values		%	Test-Values		%	Test-Values
Pre-crime affect	–	–	–	Anger	37.84	2.65	–	–	–
Offender use of alcohol prior to crime	–	–	–	–	–	–	No	50.88	3.43
Offender use of drugs prior to crime	–	–	–	–	–	–	–	–	–
Deviant fantasies prior to crime	Yes	59.18	5.40	No	91.89	5.01	–	–	–
Premeditation	Structured	61.22	4.81	No	60.81	7.31	–	–	–
Time of crime	Both	18.37	2.33	Night	82.43	2.68	–	–	–
Victim selection	Yes	69.39	4.94	No	85.14	5.55	None	87.72	10.62
Type of injury	Death	59.18	4.35	Injury	47.30	3.01	–	–	–
Age of victim	–	–	–	30 to 39	29.73	2.89	–	–	–
Relationship	–	–	–	–	–	–	Friend	24.56	2.51
Kidnapping	Yes	22.45	2.76	No	97.30	2.77	No	68.42	2.72
Weapon	–	–	–	–	–	–	–	–	–
Restraints	Yes	34.69	4.43	No	94.59	2.63	–	–	–
Level of force	More than necessary	97.96	5.63	More than necessary	93.24	6.10	Minimal	87.72	11.30
Mutilation	Yes	38.78	6.65	No	98.65	3.54	No	100.00	3.44
Specific victim characteristics	Yes	40.82	3.75	No	94.59	4.26	–	–	–
Victim is a prostitute	–	–	–	Yes	20.27	2.75	–	–	–
Victim from dysfunctional environment	–	–	–	–	–	–	–	–	–
Humiliation of the victim	Yes	48.98	2.41	–	–	–	No	80.70	2.71
Victim forced to commit sexual acts	–	–	–	–	–	–	–	–	–
Victim resistance	Physical violence	87.76	4.11	Active	82.43	3.91	Passive	64.91	5.64
Reaction to victim resistance	–	–	–	Physical violence	86.49	5.30	Without physical violence	85.96	9.50
Time spent with victim	More 30 minutes	77.55	3.99	–	–	–	–	–	–

Contrary to the sadistic crime script, offenders do not present deviant sexual fantasies, the crime is committed at night, and there is no premeditation, victim selection, kidnapping or use of restraints. Offenders use more force than necessary to commit their sexual assaults but do not mutilate the victim. In this script, the victim is likely to resist actively, which triggers a reaction of physical violence in the offender and ultimately results in injuries to the victim.

The third crime script, *Opportunistic*, accounts for 32% (N = 57) of sexual assaults. In these cases, a minimal level of violence is used on a victim who is a friend of the offender. The offender does not consume alcohol prior to the crime or kidnap the victim. There is no humiliation or mutilation of the victim. Usually, the victim offers passive resistance to the offender, which results in the absence of injury.

DISCUSSION OF FINDINGS FROM THE STUDY

Typologies of Sexual Aggressors of Women

Sadistic sexual aggressors reported having deviant sexual fantasies during the hours before their sexual offence, which was carefully planned. During the offence, the victim was humiliated, mutilated and seriously injured (and sometimes even killed). This sadistic crime script is similar to the one described in previous typological studies (Beauregard & Proulx, 2002; Beech *et al.*, 2005; Knight & Prentky, 1990; Proulx *et al.*, 1999), except for two pre-crime variables – anger and alcohol consumption. Since these variables are self-reported, more inter-study variation is to be expected. Also, in our study, we did not infer that anger was present if the modus operandi involved expressive violence. In fact, anger was only considered present when it was explicitly self-reported.

Angry sexual aggressors reported having been angry and intoxicated (alcohol, drugs) in the hours before their offence, which was not planned. Also, they did not indicate having had deviant sexual fantasies during these hours. In the course of the sexual offence, the victim was humiliated and seriously injured. In addition, the victim actively resisted, provoking a physically violent response from the aggressor. This angry crime script perfectly matches those in previous typological studies, with the exception of alcohol consumption.

Opportunistic sexual aggressors of women did drink alcohol during the hours preceding their sexual crime. They used instrumental violence, but did not humiliate, mutilate or injure their victim. The victim passively resisted and this resistance was not met with physical violence from the offender. As with the other crime scripts, our results agree with those from previous typological studies.

Our results did not include a compensatory sexual aggressor type. This type of offender is also absent from several other typologies (Beauregard & Proulx, 2002; Beech *et al.*, 2005; Polaschek *et al.*, 2001; Proulx *et al.*, 1999; Ressler *et al.*, 1988; Revitch & Schlesinger, 1981). What can explain this discrepancy among typologies? Firstly, since the compensatory sexual aggressor used instrumental violence only and never killed his victim, his absence from sexual murderer typologies is obvious. Secondly, because his criminal activities focus on sexual offences of relatively low gravity, the compensatory sexual aggressor has incarceration sentences of short duration. Consequently, in our study, which was carried out with subjects serving long sentences in maximum security institutions, the compensatory type of sexual aggressors of women is under-represented. Finally, since this offender type is largely defined on the basis of personality characteristics (e.g., insecurity, low self-esteem), his identification was highly improbable in a typology developed with crime-script variables only.

Sexual Aggression Crime Scripts

Our results, as well as those from previous typological studies, indicate that there is a small number of prototypes of sexual aggressors of women, even though a diversity of clinical, theoretical and statistical methods have been used to investigate this issue. In the introduction to this chapter, we suggested that this situation is due to the choice-structuring properties of sexual crimes, i.e., the internal and external constraints that shape crime scripts. In fact, combinations of these constraints allow only a limited number of crime scripts of sexual aggressors of women. We will now examine the interaction between internal and external constraints in each of the three types of sexual aggressors of women (sadistic, angry and opportunistic) present in our sample.

In *sadistic sexual aggressors*, deviant sexual fantasies are strong internal constraints that not only constitute a motivation to offend, but also shape the nature of the modus operandi of their crimes. Also, in order that his crime matches his sadistic sexual fantasies, this type of offender must carefully plan his offence. For example, he must determine the means of overpowering the victim he selects on the basis of distinctive characteristics. His strategy for overcoming the victim typically will involve a variety of physical restraints (e.g., handcuffs, rope, tape) and the transporting of the victim to a pre-selected location (kidnapping). Because the victim's resistance is minimal during the offence and involves a high level of coercion, typical of the sadistic offender (i.e., humiliation, mutilation, physical injuries and sometimes death) his strategy is usually successful. Finally, because these offences are so well planned, they can be enacted without any interference during the day or the night. Sadistic sexual aggressors also typically have sophisticated strategies to deal with both their internal constraints (deviant sexual fantasies, distinctive characteristics of victims) and external constraints (victim resistance, interference by guardians).

The major internal constraint of the *angry* sexual aggressor is intense anger – no sexual fantasies shape his modus operandi. This aggressor uses the sexual aggression of women as a means to cope with his anger. Tension reduction catharsis is the aim of his aggression. He does not plan his offence and he does not select a victim with distinctive characteristics. Therefore, a prostitute is a readily accessible victim, particularly at night. Furthermore, the angry offender uses more force than necessary to obtain the compliance of his victim, who typically sustains extensive physical injuries. Also, he does not use physical restraints and kidnapping to overpower his victim. In such a context, active resistance from the victim is expected, as is a brutal reaction on the part of the offender. This escalation of coercion in the face of resistance has been demonstrated by Ullman and Knight (1995). Unlike in sadistic offenders, however, such resistance does not provoke an increase in the level of coercion, which is already at the extreme end of the continuum (i.e., mutilation, death).

The *opportunistic* sexual aggressor has no anger or deviant sexual fantasies as internal constraints that shape the modus operandi of his sexual aggression. In addition, since his offence is not planned, he has no weapon and physical constraints to overpower his victim. However, since his goal is to achieve sexual gratification, he does not humiliate or mutilate his victim; in fact, he uses a minimal amount of force to achieve victim compliance. In this case, victim resistance is minimal.

CONCLUSIONS

Sexual aggression, like other types of crime, has specific choice-structuring properties. Important external constraints include victim resistance and victim refusal to actively participate in sexual activities. In addition, the offender must ensure that he has enough time alone with the victim to achieve his goals. Internal constraints, in sexual aggressions of women, differ as a function of the crime script. Thus, for some offenders the constraint is a sadistic sexual fantasy, for others it is intense anger, and for yet others it is unbounded sexual gratification. Our results suggest, consistent with the model of Tibbetts and Gibson (2002), that external and internal constraints interact with each other to produce a limited number of crime scripts. This is as valid for sexual aggressions as for any other types of crime.

Although the cognitive-emotional *states* of the offender before, during and after the sexual aggression (the internal constraints of crime scripts) are situational factors, they are not independent of *traits* (stable internal constraints such as personality disorders). In sadistic sexual aggressors, sadistic sexual fantasies are related to a sexual preference for sadistic rape (Proulx *et al.*, 1994; Proulx *et al.*, 2006) and a proclivity to use deviant sexual activities to cope with stressful situations (Proulx, McKibben & Lusignan, 1996). Anger and impulsivity in angry sexual aggressors are related to a borderline personality disorder which is characterised by emotional and behavioural instability, and by intense negative emotions (Proulx *et al.*, 1999). Finally, in opportunistic aggressors, unbounded sexual gratification is associated with psychopathy – a tendency to assert one's sexual and non-sexual needs with no consideration for others' will (Knight & Prentky, 1990; Proulx *et al.*, 1999). These stable internal constraints have also been conceptualised as implicit theories (views of the world), which induce the motivation to offend in both sexual aggressors (Polaschek & Ward, 2002) and sexual murderers (Beech *et al.*, 2005).

This study of crime scripts in sexual aggressors of women has emphasised the role of internal and external constraints in shaping modus operandi. The interactions between these constraints are also crucial elements of crime scripts. Apart from these constraints, which include the enduring characteristics of the offender (traits), situational factors also play an indirect role in shaping the characteristics of the modus operandi (Piquero & Tibbetts, 1996). In future studies, situational factors (internal and external constraints) as well as time-stable individual characteristics (e.g., sexual preferences, personality disorders, implicit theories and intellectual capabilities) must be analysed with structural-equation modelling to elucidate the processes involved in the commission of a sexual assault of an adult woman.

REFERENCES

Beauregard, E. & Proulx. J. (2002). Profiles in the offending process of non-serial sexual murderers. *International Journal of Offender Therapy and Comparative Criminology, 46*, 386–399.

Beauregard, E., Proulx, J., Rossmo, K., *et al.* (2007). Script analysis of hunting process of serial sex offenders. *Criminal Justice and Behavior, 34*, 1069–1084.

Beauregard, E., Proulx, J. & St-Yves, M (2007). Angry or sadistic? Two types of sexual murderers. In J. Proulx, E. Beauregard, M. Cusson& A. Nicole (Eds), *Sexual Murders: A Comparative Analysis and New Perspectives* (pp. 123–141). Chichester, UK: John Wiley & Sons, Ltd.

Beech, A.D., Fisher, D. & Ward, T. (2005). Sexual murderers' implicit theories. *Journal of Interpersonal Violence, 20*, 1366–1389.

Beech, A.D., Ward, T. & Fischer, D. (2006). The identification of sexual and violent motivations in men who assault women: Implications for treatment. *Journal of Interpersonal Violence, 21*, 635–643.

Brittain R.P. (1970). The sadistic murderer. *Medicine, Science and the Law, 10*, 198–207.

Cattell, R.B. (1966). The scree test for the number of factors. *Multivariate Behavioral Research, 1*, 245–276.

Clarke, J. & Carter, A. (1999). Sexual murderers: Their assessment and treatment. *Paper presented at the 18th Annual ATSA research and treatment conference*, Orlando, Florida, September.

Clarke, J. & Carter, A. (2000). Relapse prevention with sexual murderers. In D.R. Laws, S.M. Hudson & T. Ward (Eds), *Remaking relapse prevention with sex offenders: A sourcebook* (pp. 389–401). Thousand Oaks, CA: Sage.

Clarke, R.V. & Felson, M. (1993). *Routine activity and rational choice*. New Brunswick, NJ: Transaction Publishers.

Clausen, S.-E. (1998). *Applied correspondence analysis: An introduction*. Sage university paper series on quantitative applications in the social sciences, 121. Beverly Hills, CA: Sage.

Cohen, L. & Felson, M. (1979). Social change and crime rate trends: A routine activity approach. *American Sociological Review, 44*, 588–608.

Cornish, D.B. (1994). Crime as scripts. In D. Zahm& P. Cromwell (Eds), *Proceedings of the international seminar on environmental criminology and crime analysis*, University of Miami, Coral Gables, Florida, 1993. Tallahassee, FL: Florida Statistical Analysis Center, Florida Criminal Justice Executive Institute, Florida Department of Law Enforcement.

Cornish, D.B. & Clarke, R.V. (1986). Introduction. In D.B. Cornish& R.V. Clarke (Eds), *The reasoning criminal: Rational choice perspectives on offending* (pp. 1–16). New York: Springer-Verlag.

Cornish, D.B. & Clarke, R.V. (1987). Understanding crime displacement: An application of rational choice theory. *Criminology, 25*, 901–916.

Gebhard, P., Gagnon, J., Pomeroy, W. & Christensen, C. (1965). *Sex offenders: An analysis of types*. New York: Harper and Row.

Gratzer, T. & Bradford, M.W. (1995). Offender and offense characteristics of sexual sadists: A comparative study. *Journal of Forensic Sciences, 40*, 450–455.

Greenacre, M. (1988). Clustering the rows and columns of a contingency table. *Journal of Classification, 5*, 39–51.

Greenacre, M. & Blasius, J. (1994). *Correspondence analysis in the social sciences.* San Diego, CA: Academic Press.

Groth, A.N. & Birnbaum H.J. (1979). *Men who rape.* New York: Plenum.

Hare, R.D. (2003). *The Hare Psychopathy Checklist-Revised.* Toronto, Ontario, Canada: Multi-Health Systems.

Herve, H. & Yulle, J.C. (2007). *The psychopath: Theory, research, and practice.* Mahwah, NJ: Lawrence Erlbaum Associates.

Johnson, E. & Payne, J. (1986). The decision to commit a crime: An information processing analysis. In D.B. Cornish& R.V. Clarke (Eds), *The Reasoning criminal: Rational choice perspectives on offending* (pp. 170–185). New York: Springer-Verlag.

Knight, R.A. (1999). Validation of a typology for rapists. *Journal of Interpersonal Violence, 14,* 303–330.

Knight, R.A. & Prentky, R.A. (1990). Classifying sexual offenders: The development and corroboration of taxonomic models. In W.L. Marshall, D.R. Laws& H.E. Barbaree (Eds), *Handbook of sexual assault: Issues, theories, and treatment of the offender* (pp. 23–52). New York: Plenum Press.

Lebart, L. (1994). Complementary use of correspondence analysis and cluster analysis. In M. Greenacre& J. Blasius (Eds.), *Correspondence analysis in the social sciences* (pp. 163–178). San Diego, CA: Academic Press.

Lebart, L., Morineau, A. & Lambert, T. (2003). *SPAD. Version MN 5.6.0,* Système portable pour l'analyse des données. Paris: Decisia.

Marshall, W.L. & Kennedy, P. (2003). Sexual sadism in sexual offenders: an elusive diagnosis. *Aggression and Violent Behavior, 8,* 1–22.

Marshall, W.L., Kennedy, P., Yates, P. & Serran, G. (2002). Diagnosing sexual sadism in sexual offenders: Reliability across diagnosticians. *International Journal of Offender Therapy and Comparative Criminology, 46,* 668–676.

Piquero, A.R. & Tibbetts, S.G. (1996). Specifying the direct and indirect effects of low self-control and situational factors on offenders' decision making: Toward a more complete model of rational offending. *Justice Quarterly, 13,* 481–510.

Piquero, A.R. & Tibbetts, S.G. (2002). *Rational Choice and Criminal Behavior: Recent Research and Future Challenges.* New York: Routledge.

Polaschek, D.L.L., Hudson, S.M., Ward, T. & Siegert, R.J. (2001). Rapists' offense processes: A preliminary descriptive model. *Journal of Interpersonal Violence, 16,* 523–544.

Polaschek, D.L.L. & Ward, T. (2002). The implicit theories of potential rapists: What our questionnaires tell us. *Aggression and Violent Behavior, 7,* 385–406.

Proulx, J., Aubut, J., McKibben, A. & Côté, M. (1994). Penile responses of rapists and non-rapists to rape stimuli involving physical violence or humiliation. *Archives of Sexual Behavior, 23,* 295–310.

Proulx, J., Blais, E. & Beauregard, E. (2006). Sadistic sexual aggressors. In W.L. Marshall, Y.M. Fernandez, L.E. Marshall & G.A. Serran (Eds), *Sexual offender treatment: Controversial issues* (pp. 61–77). Chichester, UK: John Wiley & Sons, Ltd.

Proulx, J., McKibben, A. & Lusignan, R. (1996). Relationship between affective components and sexual behaviors in sexual aggressors. *Sexual Abuse: A Journal of Research and Treatment, 8,* 279–289.

Proulx, J., St-Yves, M., Guay, J.-P. & Ouimet, M. (1999). Les agresseurs sexuels de femmes: Scènarios délictuels et troubles de la personnalitè. In J. Proulx, M. Cusson & M. Ouimet (Eds), *Les violences criminelles* (pp. 157–185). Saint-Nicholas, QC: Les Presses de l'Université Laval.

Ressler, R.K., Burgess, A.W. & Douglas, J.E. (1988). *Sexual homicide: Patterns and motives.* New York: Lexington Books.

Revitch, E. & Schlesinger, L.B. (1981). *Psychopathology of homicide.* Springfield, IL: Charles C. Thomas.

Revitch, E. & Schlesinger, L.B. (1989). *Sex murder and sex aggression: Phenomenology, psychopathology, psychodynamics and prognosis.* Springfield, IL: Charles C. Thomas.

Tibbetts, S.G. & Gibson, C.L. (2002). Individual propensities and rational decision making: recent findings and promising approaches. In A.R. Piquero & S.G. Tibbetts (Eds), *Rational choice and criminal behavior: Recent research and future challenges* (pp. 3–24). New York: Routledge.

Trassler, G. (1993). Conscience, opportunity, rational choice and crime. In R.V. Clarke & M.S. Felson (Eds), *Routine activity and rational choice*. New Brunswick, NJ: Transaction Publishers.

Ullman, S.E. & Knight, R.A. (1995). Women's resistance strategies to different rapist types. *Criminal Justice and Behavior*, *22*, 263–283.

Warren, J., Hazelwood, R. & Dietz, P. (1996). The sexually sadistic serial killer. *Journal of Forensic Sciences*, *41*, 970–974.

Yochelson, S. & Samenow, S.E. (1976). *The Criminal personality: A profile for change*. New York: Jason Aronson.

12

Internet Sex Offenders

DAVID MIDDLETON

INTRODUCTION

Practitioners working in the field of assessment and treatment of sexual offenders will be aware that there has been a phenomenal increase in the volume of convictions for offences related to possession of, making and distributing indecent images of children. For England and Wales, in the five years between 1999 and 2004 there was an almost 500% increase in convictions from 238 to 1162 (Middleton, 2007). This trend appears to have been reflected in North America (Taylor & Quayle, 2006). The estimates of the volume of Internet traffic associated with viewing indecent images of children suggests an increasing scale of activity which outstrips current law enforcement activity.

In June 2004 the leading UK telecommunications company, BT launched an operation to block customer access to sites containing indecent images of children listed by the Internet Watch Foundation. At the time BT announced it had blocked 10,000 hits a day. By February 2006, some 18 months later, the number of attempted hits to these sites had risen to 35,000 per day (BBC News Online, 2006). Since BT is estimated to have approximately one-third of the UK domestic market as an Internet Service Provider (ISP), (and there is no reason to suppose that BT customers have a disproportionate interest in viewing these images than other ISPs), it is possible that the total volume of activity would be in the region of 100,000 attempts per day to log on to sites hosting indecent images of children.

The assessment of sexual offenders has focused increasingly on combining an actuarial approach to risk assessment by considering *static* risk factors, with *dynamic stable and acute* risk factors. Therefore, it will be important to discover if these assessments are appropriate for those convicted of Internet-related sexual offence (ISO) behaviour. In addition the common theme which assessors will be required to address is whether the person looking at indecent images of children is also likely to engage in contact offences against children. Equally it is important to examine current models of sexual

Assessment and Treatment of Sex Offenders: A Handbook. Edited by Anthony Beech, Leam Craig and Kevin Browne. © John Wiley & Sons Ltd, 2009.

offending against the emerging characteristics of Internet sexual offenders to ascertain whether as suggested by Quayle *et al.* (2000) individuals who access child pornography via the Internet are a new type of offender or whether those with a pre-disposition to child sexual abuse are responding to new opportunities provided by the 'affordability, accessibility and anonymity' (Cooper, 1998, p. 24) provided by the Internet.

This chapter will attempt to provide an overview of contemporary research into the characteristics, and assessment, of those who have been convicted of such offences in England and Wales. It remains the case that while the growth of problematic Internet use has been meteoric, the collection of research data and evaluation of assessment and treatment outcomes has trailed far behind in both volume and pace (Middleton, 2004). Many of the findings reported in this chapter can only be described as indicative since samples are too small in most cases to form definitive conclusions and it is not known whether the characteristics of those who are convicted differ from those, and it must be assumed they are the majority, who are never brought within the criminal justice system.

DO MODELS OF CONTACT CHILD SEXUAL ABUSE FIT WITH INTERNET OFFENDING?

It is common practice to group together Internet offenders with contact child sexual abusers for the purposes of psychological assessment and treatment. Furthermore, theories of child sexual abuse are assumed to be effective in explaining the behaviour of individuals who access, distribute and create child pornography. However, this link appears to be based on assumption rather than the application of comprehensive theories and models of aetiology that contact sex offender treatment and assessment is based on.

Middleton *et al.* (2006) sought to test one such model in an analysis of Internet sexual offenders. One of the most recent theories of the development of child sexual abuse is Ward and Siegert's (2002) Pathways Model. In this model the authors use a 'theory-knitting' approach, identifying and integrating the most salient features of the previous theories of child sexual abuse, while simultaneously addressing the limitations, to build one comprehensive and multi-factorial aetiological framework. By incorporating Marshall and Barbaree's (1990) description of the effects of developmental adversities in the offence process, Hall and Hirschman's (1992) comprehensive discussions of typology, and the psychological vulnerabilities involved in child sexual abuse described by Finkelhor (1984), Ward and Siegert developed the multi-factorial model that suggests that there are multiple aetiological pathways leading to child sexual abuse.

Each of the pathways is associated with a set of core primary psychological mechanisms that act as vulnerabilities which, when interacting with each other, can lead to the individual sexually abusing a child. It is postulated that these dysfunctional psychological mechanisms are initially caused and then influenced by learning events, and biological and cultural factors, each of which can exert both a proximal and distal influence on behaviour. The model proposes four core mechanisms, corresponding to those suggested in previous theories: (1) intimacy and social skill deficits; (2) distorted sexual scripts; (3) emotional dysregulation; and (4) antisocial cognitions, each of which have a distinct aetiology. However, the nature of the interactions between the psychological mechanisms in the Pathways Model, as with Hall and Hirschman's (1992) model, denote that all sexual offences involve intimacy, sexual, cognitive and arousal components, but each pathway has a unique core set of primary mechanisms that impact on the others (Ward & Sorbello, 2003).

The first aetiological pathway, *intimacy deficits*, contains offenders who are hypothesised to possess normal sexual scripts and only offend at specific times, for example, at times of prolonged loneliness, at times of rejection, or if their adult relationships are compromised or unsatisfactory.

The second aetiological pathway, *deviant sexual scripts*, contains individuals who have subtle distortions of sexual scripts and dysfunctional attachment styles (Ward, Hudson & Marshall, 1996), where interpersonal closeness is only achieved via sexual contact.

The third aetiological pathway, *emotional dysregulation*, contains individuals who possess normal sexual scripts but have difficulties in the self-regulation of emotions (Thompson, 1994).

The fourth aetiological pathway, *antisocial cognitions*, contains individuals who do not have distortions in their sexual scripts but possess general pro-criminal attitudes and beliefs and whose offending reflects this antisocial tendency.

Finally, there is a fifth pathway, *multiple dysfunctional mechanisms*, that contains individuals who have developed distorted sexual scripts coinciding with dysfunctions in all of the other primary psychological mechanisms. They will display major flaws in their implicit theories of the appropriateness of sexual contact with children and the sexual sophistication of the child. This group is likely to exhibit a multitude of offending behaviours.

In considering the implication for individuals who engage in sexualised behaviour associated with Internet use, Middleton *et al.* (2006) used a sample collected from the caseloads of 15 Probation Service regions of the National Probation Service of England and Wales, and comprised 72 male sexual offenders who had been convicted of an index offence involving possessing and/or distributing images of child pornography, or the production, possession and/or distribution of pseudo-sexual images involving child pornography. Of the participants 48% were married or co-habiting, 48% were single or divorced and 4% were widowed. Of the 75% (N = 54) of the sample for whom information on the gender of the victim (based on the images collected in the index offence) was available, 76% viewed images depicting female victims, 6% viewed images depicting male victims, and 18% viewed images depicting both male and female victims. No information was available regarding whether or not the offenders collected child pornography exclusively or collected both adult and child pornography.

Each offender in the sample had completed the standardised battery of psychometric tests used by the National Probation Service as an assessment tool for nationally accredited treatment programmes, including those used with Internet offenders (Beech, Fisher & Beckett, 1999; Mandeville-Norden, Beech & Middleton, 2005).

The psychometric data for each offender was analysed to assign the offenders to one of the five pathways outlined by Ward and Siegert (2002). This was carried out on the basis of their scores on the primary psychometric indicators for the dysfunctional psychological mechanisms involved in each pathway. An elevated score in the primary indicator psychometric (at least one standard deviation above the mean score for sexual offenders reported by Beech *et al.*, 1999) for one pathway and average or below average scores in the other measures would consequently lead to that offender being assigned to the pathway indicated by the elevated score. An elevated score in all primary indicator psychometrics (at least one standard deviation above the mean score for sexual offenders reported by Beech *et al.*, 1999) would consequently lead to that offender being assigned to the multiple dysfunctional mechanisms pathway.

Of the sample 60% (N = 43) offenders reported elevated scores in one or more of the psychometric indicators. The rest of the sample (N = 29) did not report elevated scores in any of the measures. Of those who reported elevated psychometric scores 33 could be relatively easily assigned to one of the five pathways, as follows:

Pathway 1 – intimacy deficits (35%, N = 15). All of the members of this group evidenced high levels of emotional loneliness. None reported high levels of difficulty controlling negative emotions and none reported high levels of cognitive distortions about children and sex, most of this group also reported low levels of self-esteem.

Pathway 2 – distorted sexual scripts (5%, N = 2). All of the members of this group had high measurable levels of emotional congruence (with children). None reported being emotional, lonely, difficulty controlling negative emotions, or any evidence of cognitive distortions about children and sex. None of the offenders assigned to this pathway demonstrated any problems in level of self-esteem.

Pathway 3 – emotional dysregulation (33%, N = 14). All of the members of this group reported difficulty dealing with negative emotions. None reported high levels of emotional loneliness, high levels of cognitive distortions about children and sex, or high levels of emotional congruence with children, although most (N = 10) reported high scores indicating low levels of empathetic concern for victims of sexual abuse.

Pathway 4 – antisocial cognitions (2%, N = 1). The offender assigned to this pathway demonstrated high levels of cognitive distortions regarding the appropriateness of sexual contact with children, but no other problems.

Pathway 5 – multiple dysfunctional mechanisms (2%, N = 1). The offender assigned to this pathway demonstrated elevated scores on all four primary pathway indicators.

Multiple pathway individuals. It was found that 10 men (23%) showed elevated scores in two or three of the main indicators pf pathway identification.

The fact that such a proportion of this Internet offender sample could be separated into the five distinct pathways by their primary deficits suggests that the Internet offender population is not a homogenous group and is as diverse within itself as other sex offender groups such as rapists, or child abusers, and also that the Internet offender sample here shares similar psychological deficits as other sex offender groups.

To test this model further data were collected on a larger sample of Internet offenders ($N = 213$) and compared with a sample of contact sexual offenders against children ($N = 191$). The sample was again drawn from offenders under supervision of the National Probation Service. Comparisons between contact offenders and Internet offenders are shown in Table 12.1.

It can be seen from Table 12.1 that there are a number of similarities between both groups, in particular the largest clusters for both Internet and contact offenders are the *intimacy deficits* and *emotional dysregulation* groups. However, it is also interesting that the Internet offender sample has a larger range of offenders than the contact offenders. For example, on this sample more Internet offenders were scored dysfunctional in all four psychological domains, recording high scores for measures of *intimacy deficits*, *emotional dysregulation*, *distorted sexual scripts*, and *antisocial cognitions* than contact offenders. It is possible that this reflects the reality that the term 'Internet offender' is used as a label for a large range of behaviours and offender types. Quite simply Internet offenders are a heterogeneous subgroup of sexual offenders.

As for the prevalence of particular pathways in the Internet sample, the most common pathway was again the *intimacy deficits* pathway. The primary mechanism hypothesised by Ward and Siegert (2002) for this group is the formation of insecure attachments leading to low levels of social skills and self-esteem. Low self-esteem was certainly common in this group, who recorded a high level of co-morbidity with low self-esteem compared to the other pathways. According to Ward and Siegert, the primary cause of sexually abusive behaviour within this group is the need to engage in a sexual relationship with another person to alleviate loneliness and to compensate for a lack of intimacy. The Internet offender may display a fearful-dismissive attachment style (Ward, Hudson & Marshall, 1996), and consequently may be attracted to use the Internet for sexual purposes at times of loneliness and dissatisfaction to create a pseudo-intimacy, due to low estimations of efficacy in initiating and maintaining intimacy in more appropriate adult relationships. For such individuals, images depicting children are less fearful and the child a more accepting partner, and they may use

Table 12.1 Comparisons between contact sexual offenders and Internet sexual offenders

	Contact sexual offenders (N = 191)	Internet sexual offenders (N = 213)
High on all measures	28 (15%)	38 (28%)
High on most measures	2 (2%)	22 (16%)
Intimacy deficits	31 (25%)	27 (20%)
Distorted sexual scripts	9 (7%)	7 (5%)
Emotional dysregulation	26 (21%)	23 (17%)
Antisocial cognitions	10 (8%)	4 (3%)
Intimacy and emotional dysregulation	18 (15%)	14 (10%)
Total of sub-sample	124	135
Low scores on all measures	67	78

the Internet as a maladaptive strategy to avoid their perceived likelihood of failure in adult relationships.

The second largest group in the Internet sample belonged to the *emotional dys-regulation* pathway. It is suggested that for individuals in this group strong negative mood states result in a lack of control and, in conjunction with sexual desire, can lead to the individual seeking contact with children to meet their sexual needs. In situations where the individual cannot effectively manage their negative emotions they can become disinhibited and/or use sex as a soothing strategy. Self-esteem was found to be high or low in this group, depending on the psychological makeup of the individual. This group may use the Internet to access both adult and, under certain circumstances, child pornography during times of emotional dysphoria, and to alleviate the strong negative emotions connected with this and increase feelings of well-being. The related disinhibition found in this group, it is hypothesised, would allow the user to justify their behaviour by externalising it as a loss of control rather than an intentionally chosen strategy to alleviate their mood state. As regards impulsivity, 86% of offenders in this pathway scored above average on a scale to measure impulsivity (the Barratt Impulsivity Scale; Barratt, 1994) suggesting that these offenders may act without thinking or demonstrate little regard for the consequences of their behaviour, which may add to the perception that their choices are not responsible for their offending.

It should also be noted that almost half of the coded sample could not be assigned to any of the five aetiological pathways outlined by Ward & Siegert (2002). These individuals recorded no problems with intimacy or dealing with negative emotions, no distortions in their sexual scripts, and no antisocial cognitions, regarding the appropriateness of sexual contact with children, and yet have been prosecuted for using the Internet to access abusive images of children. This appears to suggest that there is a population of Internet offenders who do not share the psychological vulnerabilities typically displayed by sex offenders.

One explanation of this could be that these individuals have completed the self-report psychometrics in a way that underestimates and/or masks their deficits. A further explanation is that these individuals have a preference for adult pornography, but accessed child pornography when given the opportunity for its immediate sexually gratifying effects without regard for the consequences of their actions (as most scored quite highly on some of the impulsivity measures used in the study). Therefore, it may be a case that these individuals display deficits more attributable to problematic Internet use than a primary goal of satisfying deviant sexual preference. If this were the case then the elevated Internet use is explained not only by the material accessed, but also as a process by which other emotional needs are met (Quayle & Taylor, 2003). Evidence for this would be the associated rituals employed by certain users in each Internet session and total absorption in the session in which users become oblivious not only to prior anxieties or mood states, but also the passage of time.

Support for findings that Internet offenders report higher levels of intimacy deficits or emotional dysregulation comes in a number of small studies. Laulik, Allam and Sheridan (2006) assessed a sample of 30 Internet offenders under community supervision using the Personality Assessment Inventory (PAI; Morey, 1991). They found that there were significant differences between Internet offenders and a normative population in both interpersonal functioning and affective difficulties. The combination of *Low Dominance* and *Low Warmth* scale scores on the PAI for the sample is indicative, the authors to suggest, of a rejecting and submissive interpersonal style, which is thought to preclude effective interaction with others. The study also found higher than usual levels of depression amongst the sample and in particular that this corresponded with increased usage of the Internet for accessing indecent images. This correlation supports Morahan-Martin and Schumacher's (2000) assertions, that viewing indecent images of children may be used as a mechanism to escape from negative mood states and provide individuals with, albeit temporary, psychological and physical relief from unpleasant feelings.

In another study, Webb, Craissati and Keen (2007) used psychometric analysis to examine a sample of 90 Internet offenders. They suggest a tentative typology stemming from four clusters of Internet offenders in their study: *Type One* offenders have been in long-term intimate relationships and have reasonably good psychological functioning, and it would appear that their offending behaviour appears to be triggered by relatively recent life events; *Type Two* offenders have sustained intimate relationships but have more evident psychological difficulties throughout their adult life. Life events appear to trigger deterioration in psychological health that often takes the form of increased sexual preoccupation; *Type Three* offenders were found not to be in any measurable long-term intimate relationships, and had clear personality difficulties, including difficulties with sexual self- regulation; *Type Four* offenders similarly had not been in a long-term intimate relationship but appeared to be more stable than *Type Three* offenders, in that they had fewer psychological difficulties. These may have experienced life events and or sexual self-regulation difficulties prior to the onset of offending.

In summary, in assessing Internet sexual offenders it may useful to examine for any evidence of intimacy deficits, particularly difficulty in entering age-appropriate relationships, perhaps coupled with a more socially isolated pre-disposition. Alternatively the individual may appear able to make and sustain intimate relationships, but is not able to gain support within the relationship for dealing with emotional stressors, and there may also be a decline in the sexual activity within the relationship. Finally, any evidence of high emotional identification with children may indicate sex as a coping strategy and that they seek to use the Internet, and sites depicting children, either to relieve stress or to seek pseudo-intimacy.

EVIDENCE FOR 'CROSSOVER' FROM VIEWING IMAGES TO THE COMMISSION OF CONTACT SEXUAL OFFENCES

Frequently assessors will be faced with an individual who has been convicted of possession of large quantities of indecent images of children, but who professes not to have been sexually aroused to children. Theoretically, Check and Guloien (1989) note that "men who are predisposed to aggression are particularly vulnerable to negative influences from pornography" (p. 171). While Marshall (2000) states that it is possible to "infer from the available literature that pornography exposure may influence . . . the development of sexual offending in some men" (p. 74). Such individuals would be those who have experienced childhood development of vulnerability that in turn leads to a variety of problems including "a greater focus on sex, and the need to control events during sex" (Marshall (2000, p. 73). Therefore, viewing indecent images of children on the Internet can be used as an aid in generating inappropriate sexual fantasy which in turn is reinforced through masturbation. The escalation model, described by Sullivan and Beech (2004) suggests that users of these images report that they normalise the fantasy and this 'disinhibits' the user, i.e., as the viewer becomes familiar and bored with the pornography viewed, they seek out more 'intense' content. The combination of disinhibition, increased risk taking, and the need to seek more intense experiences, suggests the possibility of escalating behaviour into seeking opportunities for 'real-life experiences' and potential contact sexual abuse. It is of course the case that the production of any indecent image viewed must inherently involve exploitation and abuse of the child; however, for many Internet offenders this fact has either been blocked or misattributed into offence-supporting cognitions such as the children were willing or enjoyed the activity.

However, Marshall cautions against ascribing a direct causal link between viewing pornography and contact sexual offending, suggesting that viewing pornography may accelerate a process already underway or may further justify an established set of antisocial beliefs.

As for empirical evidence of the link between the possession of child pornography and contact sexual offending, Seto, Cantor and Blanchard (2006) found, in a sample of 100 individuals convicted of the possession of child pornography, that this group as a whole showed greater sexual arousal to children (measured by phallometric assessment), and higher levels of arousal than a sample of known contact child sexual abusers. While, Marshall (1988) indicates that more than one-third of child abusers had at least occasionally been incited to commit an offence by exposure to pornographic material. However, such studies often rely on self-report by sex offenders. More objective data has been reported in a study in the West Midlands Probation Area by Wilcox *et al.* (2005), who found 86% of contact sexual offenders admitted using pornography as a precursor to offending when asked during a polygraph examination.

However, other evidence is less supportive of the view that crossover offending is present in the majority of cases, or that escalation is inevitable. Wolak *et al.* (2005) reported that 40% of cases in their USA sample had convictions for both possession and contact offences, labelled *dual offenders*. A further 15% both possessed indecent images and attempted to sexually victimise children by soliciting undercover investigators posing online as minors. However, most of these *dual offenders* were detected in investigations. In that the law enforcement agencies who were investigating child contact offence allegations, also found collections of pornography in these cases. This may indicate that many contact offenders use pornography (some or all of which may be downloaded via the Internet) but this does not provide evidence that offenders who possess downloaded images inevitably become contact child sexual offenders.

Wolak *et al.* note that, in cases which originated as investigations of allegations of possession of indecent images, only 14% of cases both possessed child pornography and had evidence of contact sexual abuse of children, 2% possessed material and attempted to solicit undercover investigators posing as children, and 84% possessed indecent images (but investigators found no evidence of contact child sexual abuse or attempts at victimisation). Wolak *et al.* therefore suggest that only 17% cases of possession in their sample resulted in contact offences. Also, it is not clear from the study whether this is an indication of escalation in offence behaviour. Again, one explanation could be that many of those detected in the sample were established sexual offenders, already engaged in contact offences and the possession of indecent images was just another facet of their abusive behaviour.

In summary, viewing indecent images of children can be used to stimulate, develop and fuel sexual fantasy. Frequent use may be linked to sexual pre-occupation and attitudes that normalise deviant behaviour with potential victims. Undoubtedly some sexual offenders appear to use pornography to increase arousal pre-offence. Again it appears from the evidence available to date, that there is not a substantial generic risk of escalation but clearly there are subgroups of Internet offenders who expand their online activities from viewing to engaging in communication with children, a group who progress to arranging meetings with children for sexual abuse and a proportion who move to contact sexual abuse with children known to them or whom they have targeted for abuse. However, many men may use pornography but do not appear to sexually assault others, therefore assessment needs to focus on the context and meaning of pornography for each individual, along with an assessment of evidence of other dynamic factors associated with sexual offence behaviours.

IS THE VOLUME OR TYPE OF IMAGE RELATED TO RISK?

The Sentencing Guidelines Council (SGC) (2006) recommends that Courts in England and Wales assess the level of seriousness for sentencing for offences involving porno-graphic images of children by the use of a five-point scale. *Level One* images are classed as depicting erotic posing with no sexual activity; *Level Two* images depict non-penetrative sexual activity between children, or solo masturbation by a child; *Level Three* images depict non-penetrative sexual activity between adults and chil-dren; *Level Four* images depict penetrative sexual activity involving a child or children, or both children and adults; *Level Five* images depict sadism, or penetration of or by an animal.

The Guidelines set out a range of starting points for sentences ranging from six years' imprisonment for the offender who is involved in the production of *Level Four* or *Five* images; two years' imprisonment for production of *Level One* to *Level Three* images. For possession of *Level Four/Five* images the Guidelines recommend a starting point of 12 months' imprisonment and lesser sentences for possession of levels below this. However, the Guidelines also allow for the sentences to be influenced by the volume of images. For example, possession of a large quantity of *Level Three* images attracts a starting point of 26 weeks' imprisonment while a small amount of *Level Three* images attracts a starting point of 12 weeks' imprisonment. Unfortunately neither 'large' nor 'small' is defined in the Guidelines. Adjustments to the starting point for sentence can be made by applying aggravating or mitigating factors. For example, an aggravating factor is if the collection is 'systematically stored or organised, indicating a sophisticated approach to trading or a high level of personal interest' (p. 99).

In an attempt to relate the level of image viewed with risk Osborn (2006) assessed 74 Internet offenders, under community supervision using Risk Matrix 2000 (Thornton *et al.*, 2003) (an actuarial measure of risk, see below), and correlated risk level with the possession of the SGC Levels. The results showed that the offenders categorised as most high risk viewed images of lower severity on the SGC scale than lower risk offenders. Offenders also categorised in the highest category had not viewed images with the highest severity (*Level Five*). Even if a larger sample was able to demonstrate a stronger link, one must wonder whether type of image is a particularly strong indicator of deviant sexual interest. For example, if an individual is able to obtain strong arousal to images of children, clothed, or partially clothed which may not even fall in to *Level One* this may suggest a greater problem of deviant arousal, and therefore risk to children, than an individual who requires images depicting sexual penetration.

In practice therefore, there is only limited support for the approach of basing sentencing on these factors in terms of risk assessment and one must conclude that these elements of sentencing reflect the need for the Courts to reflect public abhorrence of the increasingly graphic levels of activity depicted rather than the risk posed by the offender. Unfortunately the unintended consequence may be that the length of sentence passed by a Court could be interpreted as reflecting the level of risk and monitoring or treatment of the offender required to protect the public. Clearly there is a need for further research on the implications of type of image viewed and size of collection.

ASSESSING INTERNET SEXUAL OFFENDERS

Assessing Level of Risk

The most common actuarial risk assessment tool used in the National Probation Service, HM Prison Service, and by the police forces in England and Wales is Risk Matrix 2000 (Thornton *et al.*, 2003). This instrument combines static (historical) factors such as *age, previous criminal history, previous sexual history* with four aggravating factors: *male victims, previous non-contact offences, stranger victims, inability to sustain a long-term relationship.* By giving a weighting to the identified risk factors RM2000 provides a probability of reconviction from Low, Medium, High and Very High, and it has demonstrated to have high predictive accuracy (see Chapter 4 of this volume) in predicting future offending. However, as regards assessing risk in Internet offenders, these were not included in the validation studies for RM2000 (as there were no offenders convicted of such offences when these studies had taken place). The question arises therefore whether RM2000 has validity for assessment of Internet sexual offenders. Clearly to answer this question a further validation study based on assessment and follow-up of this offender group is required.

However, since this process could take several years, the National Probation Service, HM Prison Service and Association of Chief Police Officers (ACPO) have agreed with the primary author of RM2000 (David Thornton) to use RM2000 with some modifications. These include omitting the aggravating factor relating to non-contact offending, and to score the *stranger* factor only if there was an attempt to meet the victim within 24 hours of viewing the image (in practice most unlikely to be found in case histories).

However, it should be noted that there is some evidence that the use of *previous criminal convictions* as a risk factor can be helpful. Seto and Eke (2005) looked at the criminal records of 201 adult males who had been convicted of possession, distribution or production of child pornography, on the Ontario Sex Offender Registry in Canada, in order to identify potential predictors of later offences. The results of the Seto and Eke study suggested that offenders with prior criminal records were significantly more likely to offend again generally; that is both sexual and non-sexual offending. The study also found that those with contact sexual offences reconvicted at a higher rate both for sexual and non-sexual offences. In total, over a 2.5 year period, 17% of the sample re-offended; however, only 6% committed new child pornography offences and 4% commit contact sexual offences.

In a later paper Seto and Eke (2006) extended the follow-up period to 3.6 years on 198 offenders from the original sample. It was found that 6.6% had committed a new contact sexual offence, during the extended follow-up period, while 7.1% had committed a new child pornography offence. The overall rate for any new offence was 22%. Interestingly Seto and Eke found that the most consistently significant predictor of new offences was violent offence history. Men with more extensive violent offence histories (non-sexual or sexual) were more likely to offend again, sexually or non-sexually. Prior non-contact offences, including prior child pornography convictions were not a significant predictor of new offences.

However, the sample in the Seto and Eke (2006) study appears to have a high proportion of prior offenders. They found that 57% of their sample had one or more prior convictions, 24% had prior contact sexual offences, 17% had prior non-contact sexual offences, and 15% had prior child pornography offences. This, together with the relatively small sample size, may have led to a bias in the reported results. Wolak, Finkelhor and Mitchell (2005) examined a sample of 1,713 arrests in the USA for possession of child pornography in the 12 months beginning July 2000. They found that only 22% had prior convictions for previous non-sexual offences; 11% had prior violence convictions, and 11% had prior sexual offence convictions against children.

Other studies suggest a lower level of risk. In the UK, for example, Webb *et al.* (2007) reported that only 8% of their sample of 90 Internet offenders in the UK had any previous convictions. While O'Brien and Webster (2007), in a study of 123 incarcerated and community-based Internet offenders, found that the mean number of any previous convictions for the sample was .40 (S.D. 1.3; Range 0–10) and the mean for previous sexual convictions against children was .10 (S.D. .57; Range 0–5) leading to the conclusion that "the total number of previous convictions for sexual offences against children in the sample was considered to be low" (p. 20).

Assessing Level of Need for Treatment (Dynamic Risk)

Dynamic (changeable) risk factors can be identified as two types: *stable* and *acute dynamic* risk factors (Hanson & Harris, 2000).

Stable dynamic risk factors are those factors that are relatively constant personality characteristics of the offender but can also be subject to change; hence they form the targets for sex offender treatment (Beech, Fisher & Thornton, 2003). Examples of *stable dynamic* risk factors include: offence-specific problems known to be associated with sexual offending such as: [deviant] sexual interests, pro-offending attitudes, social and emotional problems, and self-management difficulties (Allam, 2000; Beech *et al.*, 1999; Hanson & Bussière, 1998; Marshall & Serran, 2000; Rice *et al.*, 1994; Thornton, 2002). Such problems may be in the area of poor problem recognition, poor problem solving, lack of consequential thinking, issues around self-management, especially impulsivity and anger control (Fisher & Beech, 1998; Fisher & Howells, 1993; Hanson & Scott, 1995). Further problem areas may be associated with low self-esteem, lack of assertiveness and an inability to achieve or sustain intimacy in relationships (Bumby & Hansen 1997; Garlick, Marshall & Thornton, 1996; Hudson & Ward, 1997; Marshall, Anderson & Fernandez, 1999; Smallbone & Dadds, 1998). It should be noted that all kinds of offenders exhibit characteristics of poor self-management and poor social adequacy, however it is the combination of these characteristics together with the offence-specific problems, that distinguish sexual offenders.

The most clearly articulated attempt to formulate these dynamic risk factors into a structured assessment tool has been suggested by Thornton's (2002) Structured Risk Assessment (SRA) model and in particular the subsection which is the Initial Deviance Assessment (IDA). Each of the IDA domains (Sexual Interests, Distorted Attitudes, Social and Emotional Functioning, and Self-Management) has a list of more specific psychological functions, impairment of which, as noted above, is associated with repetitive sexual offending (Thornton, 2002). The SRA has been adapted by the National Probation Service, and HM Prison Service, into the Structured Assessment of Risk and Need (SARN; Webster *et al.*, 2006) as the preferred static and dynamic risk assessment tool for sex offenders in treatment. The evidence from the analysis of psychometric profiles in the studies, cited in this chapter (Laulik *et al.*, 2006; Middleton *et al.*, 2006; Webb *et al.*, 2007), suggests that these risk domains are equally relevant for the assessment of Internet sex offenders.

Acute dynamic factors are capable of changing more rapidly than stable factors, and are seen by Beech and Ward (2004) as triggering factors. The factors include: *substance misuse*, *collapse of social supports*, *victim acquisition behaviours*, and *negative emotional states*, the presence of which increase risk (Hanson & Harris,

2000). In addition factors such as *conflict in intimate relationships* and *hostility* have also been associated with sexual recidivism (Hanson & Morton-Bourgon, 2005). In assessing evidence for these factors it is important to distinguish between the general presence of these factors and changes in the level of presentation in each case (Hanson, personal communication, 8th December 2006).

Hanson and Harris (2004) have developed the STABLE-2000 and ACUTE-2000 tools as a way of monitoring stable and acute dynamic risk factors for sexual offenders under supervision in the community. A full description and complete version of these tools is available in Hanson *et al.* (2007).

Assessing Level of Sexual Preoccupation

In addition assessors need to examine the degree, extent and frequency of use of the Internet for sexual purposes. There has been some debate in the literature (e.g., Cooper *et al.*, 1999; Pratarelli & Browne, 2002; Young, 1998) that Internet offenders develop the characteristics of addiction (see Chapter 11). Others (e.g., Beard & Wolfe, 2001; Caplan, 2002; Quayle & Taylor, 2003) suggest that while there is undoubtedly evidence of escalation in terms of hours spent online, particularly for those who are also into collecting volumes of indecent images, the case for addiction is not clear.

Therefore, assessors need to consider whether there is evidence of sexual preoccupation or sexually compulsive behaviour in the individual case. This approach was endorsed by the Correctional Services Accreditation Panel (personal communication, 14th December 2005, Professor D. Grubin) in relation to the Internet Sex Offender Treatment Programme (i-SOTP), developed by Middleton and Hayes (2006) for the National Offender Management Service (NOMS).

An attempt at quantifying sexual preoccupation was made by Kafka (1997) in a study of a group of outpatient males with paraphilias. It was found that a persistent *total sexual outlet* (TSO) of seven, or more, orgasms per week for six months could be considered as the lower boundary for hypersexual desire in males. This was two to three times greater than the most commonly observed one to three TSO per week in a sample of adult males (Seidman & Reider, 1994). In Kafka's study, masturbation was found to be the most predominant sexual behaviour, with offenders reporting spending 1–2 hours per day engaging in sexual fantasies, urges and sexual outlet behaviours related exclusively to their unconventional sexual proclivities. This finding is seen as important diagnostically, especially when linked to other studies, which have demonstrated that increased sex drive is correlated with aspects of sexual aggression in sex offenders (e.g., Malamuth, 1986). While Knight, Prentky & Cerce (1994) found that in sex offenders, high TSO is robustly associated with the total number of paraphilias, use of pornography, expressed aggression and sadism.

Collecting behaviour is a feature of Internet pornography use, new images, or missing parts of sets, are often sought. Those who trade, organise their collections systematically often spending a great deal of time on and offline obsessively cataloguing and indexing their photographs (Quayle & Taylor, 2003). Status is attached to the volume of collections, having parts of missing series and distributing new images. The phenomenon of collecting linked to compulsivity in Internet usage is noted frequently. Accessing Internet child pornography is used as a way of creating a private and intensely arousing world where it is possible to go beyond normal limits. Initially usage can be associated with feelings of regaining control in users but this quickly changes for some to feelings of loss of control (Kennedy-Souza, 1998). Therefore, assessors may wish to assess for Obsessive Compulsive Disorder (DSM-IV-TR, 2000, American Psychiatric Association, 2000).

CONCLUSIONS

The increasing level of prosecutions for offences relating to Internet sexual offending has led to a rapid increase in requests for assessment of these offenders. The level of Internet sex offender research remains limited and typically uses small samples, which are open to bias in the reported results. In the vacuum of reliable offence-specific research practitioners have relied on the findings from both the general sex offender assessment literature, and more particularly on that relating to sex abusers who have committed contact offences against children. For the most part this practice appears valid. The predisposing factors relating to child sexual abuse (dynamic risk factors) appear frequently enough in both offender groups to suggest that for the moment, assessments based on similar tools can distinguish between differing levels of risk and deviance. However, more research is clearly needed to develop offence-specific assessment tools and in analysing the particular factors that can lead an individual from seeking to view indecent images of children to moving into the commission of contact offences.

REFERENCES

Allam, J. (2000). *Community-based treatment for child sex offenders*. Unpublished doctoral thesis. University of Birmingham.

American Psychiatric Association (2000). *Diagnostic and Statistical Manual of Mental Disorders, Fourth Edition, Text Revision*. Washington, DC: American Psychiatric Association.

Barratt, E.S. (1994). Impulsiveness and aggression. In J. Monahan & H.J. Steadman (Eds), *Violence and mental disorder: Developments in risk assessment* (pp. 21–79). Chicago, IL: University of Chicago.

BBC News Online (2006, February 7). BT sounds child web porn warning. http://news.bbc.co.uk/1/hi/uk/4687904.stm

Beard, K.W. & Wolfe, E.M. (2001). Modification in the proposed diagnostic criteria for Internet addiction. *CyberPsychology and Behavior, 4*, 377–383.

Beech, A.R., Fisher, D. & Beckett, R.C. (1999). STEP 3: An Evaluation of the Prison Sex Offender Treatment Programme. Available from: Home Office Publications Unit, 50, Queen Anne's Gate, London, SW1 9AT, England. Available electronically from: www.homeoffice.gov.uk/rds/pdfs/occ-step3.pdf

Beech, A.R., Fisher, D. & Thornton, D. (2003). Risk assessment of sex offenders. *Professional Psychology: Research and Practice, 34*, 339–352.

Beech, A.R. & Ward, T. (2004). The integration of etiology and risk in sex offenders: A theoretical model. *Aggression and Violent Behavior, 10*, 31–63.

Bumby, K.M. & Hansen, D.J. (1997). Intimacy deficits, fear of intimacy, and loneliness among sexual offenders. *Criminal Justice and Behavior, 24*, 315–331.

Caplan, S.E. (2002). Problematic Internet use and psychosocial well-being: Development of a theory-based cognitive-behavioral measurement instrument. *Computers in Human Behavior, 18*, 5553–5575.

Check, J.V.P. & Guloien, T.H. (1989). Reported proclivity for coercive sex following repeated exposure to sexually violent pornography, non-violent pornography and erotica. In D. Zillmann & J. Bryant (Eds), *Pornography: Research advances and policy considerations* (pp. 159–184). Hillsdale, NJ: Erlbaum.

Cooper, A. (1998). Sexuality and the Internet: Surfing into the new millennium. *CyberPsychology and Behavior, 1*, 187–193.

Cooper, A., Putnam, D.E., Planchon, L.A. & Boies, S.C. (1999). Online sexual compulsivity: Getting tangled in the net. *Sexual Addiction and Compulsivity: The Journal of Treatment and Prevention, 6*, 79–104.

Finkelhor, D. (1984). *Child sexual abuse: New theory and research.* New York: Free Press.

Fisher, D. & Beech, A.R. (1998). Reconstituting families after sexual abuse: The offender's perspective. *Child Abuse Review, 7*, 420–434.

Fisher, D. & Howells, K. (1993). Social relationships in sexual offenders. *Sexual and Marital Therapy, 8*, 123–135.

Garlick, Y., Marshall, W.L. & Thornton, D. (1996). Intimacy deficits and attribution of blame among sexual offenders. *Legal and Criminological Psychology, 1*, 251–258.

Hall, G.C.N. & Hirschman, R. (1992). Sexual aggression against children: A conceptual perspective of etiology. *Criminal Justice and Behavior, 19*, 8–23.

Hanson, R.K. & Bussière, M.T. (1998). Predicting Relapse: A meta-analysis of sexual offending recidivism studies. *Journal of Consultancy and Clinical Psychology, 66*, 348–362.

Hanson, R.K. & Harris, A.J.R. (2000). Where should we intervene? Dynamic predictors of sexual offense recidivism. *Criminal Justice and Behavior, 27*, 6–35.

Hanson, R.K. & Harris, A.J.R. (2004). *The Dynamic Supervision Project: Project overview.* Available from: Department of the Solicitor General of Canada, 340 Laurier Ave West, Ottawa, Ontario, Canada.

Hanson, R.K., Harris, A.J.R., Scott, T.-L. & Helmas, L. (2007). Assessing risk of sexual offenders on community supervision: The Dynamic Supervision Project 2007-05). Available at: www.ps-sp.gc.ca/res/cor/rep/_fl/crp2007–05-en.pdf

Hanson, R.K. & Morton-Bourgon, K. (2004). Predictors of sexual recidivism. Available electronically from: www.psepcsppcc.gc.ca/publications/corrections/pdf/200402_e.pdf

Hanson, R.K. & Scott, H. (1995). Assessing perspective-taking among sexual offenders and non-sexual criminals: Risk predictors and long-term recidivism. *Sexual Abuse: A Journal of Research and Treatment, 7*, 259–277.

Hudson, S.M. & Ward, T. (1997). Intimacy, loneliness, and attachment style in sex offenders. *Journal of Interpersonal Violence, 12*, 325–339.

Itzin, C. (1992) Pornography and civil liberties: Freedom, harm and human rights in C. Itzin, *Pornography: Women, violence and civil liberties.* Oxford: Oxford University Press.

Kafka, M.P. (1997). Hypersexual desire in males: An operational definition and clinical implications for males with paraphilias and paraphilia-related disorders. *Archives of Sexual Behavior, 26*, 505–526.

Kennedy-Souza, B.L. (1998). Internet addiction disorder. *Interpersonal Computing and Technology: An Electronic Journal for the 21st Century, 6*, 1–2.

Knight, R.A., Prentky, R.A. & Cerce, D.D. (1994). The development, reliability and validity of an inventory for the multidimensional assessment of sex and aggression. *Criminal Justice and Behavior, 21*(1), 72–94.

Laulik, S., Allam, J. & Sheridan, L. (2006). Psychopathology in Internet child sex offenders. Presented at NOTA Annual Conference, York, September 2006.

Malamuth, N.M. (1986). Predictors of naturalistic sexual aggression. *Journal of Personality and Social Psychology, 50*, 953–962.

Mandeville-Norden, R., Beech, A. & Middleton, D. (2006). The development of the Sex Offender Psychometric Scoring System (SOPSSys) for use in the Probation Service. *Probation Journal, 53*, 89–94.

Marshall, W.L. (1988). The use of sexually explicit stimuli by rapists, child molesters and non-offenders. *The Journal of Sex Research, 25*, 267–288.

Marshall, W.L. (2000). Revisiting the use of pornography by sexual offenders: Implications for theory and practice. *The Journal of Sexual Aggression, 6*, 67–77.

Marshall, W.L., Anderson, D. & Fernandez, Y. (1999). *Cognitive behavioural treatment of sexual offenders*. Chichester: John Wiley & Sons, Ltd.

Marshall, W.L. & Barbaree, H.E. (1990). An integrated theory of the etiology of sexual offending. In W.L. Marshall, D.R. Laws & H.E. Barbaree (Eds), *Handbook of sexual assault: Issues, theories and treatment of the offender* (pp. 257–275). New York: Plenum.

Marshall, W.L. & Serran, G.A. (2000). Improving the effectiveness of sexual offender treatment. *Trauma, Violence & Abuse, 1*, 203–222.

Middleton, D. (2004). Current treatment approaches. In M.C. Calder (Ed.), *Child Sexual abuse and the Internet: Tackling the new frontier* (pp. 99–112). Trowbridge: Cromwell Press.

Middleton, D. (2007). *Internet Offenders – the Challenge of Assessment*. Paper by invitation to Royal College of Psychiatrists, Forensic Division, Annual Residential Conference, 7–9 February 2007, Prague.

Middleton, D., Elliott, I.A., Mandeville-Norden, R. & Beech, A.R. (2006). An investigation into the application of the Ward and Siegert pathways model of child sexual abuse with Internet offenders. *Psychology, Crime and Law, 12*, 589–603.

Middleton, D. & Hayes, E. (2006). *The Internet Sex Offender Treatment Programme (I-SOTP): Theory Manual*. London: National Offender Management Service, Home Office. Available from: Interventions Unit, 1st Floor, Abell House, John Islip St., London SW1P 4LH, UK.

Morahan-Martin, J. & Schumacher, P. (2000). Incidents and correlates of pathological Internet use among college students. *Computers in Human Behavior, 13*, 13–29.

Morey, L.C. (1991). *The Personality Assessment Inventory: Professional Manual*. Odessa, FL: Psychological Assessment Resources.

O'Brien, M.D. & Webster, S.D. (2007). The Construction and Preliminary validation of the Internet Behaviours and Attitudes Questionnaire (IBAQ). *Sexual Abuse: A Journal of Research and Treatment, 19*, 237–256.

Osborn, J. (2006). The Suitability of Risk Matrix 2000 for use with Internet Offenders. Unpublished MSc Thesis. University of Birmingham.

Pratarelli, M.E. & Browne, B.L. (2002). Confirmatory factor analysis of Internet use and addiction. *CyberPsychology and Behavior, 5*, 53–64.

Quayle, E., Holland, G., Linehan, C. & Taylor, M. (2000). The Internet and offending behaviour: A case study. *The Journal of Sexual Aggression, 6*, 78–96.

Quayle, E. & Taylor, M. (2003). Model of problematic Internet use in people with a sexual interest in children. *CyberPsychology and Behavior, 6*, 93–106.

Rice, M.E., Chaplin, T.C., Harris, G.T. & Coutts, J. (1994). Empathy for the victim and sexual arousal among rapists and non-rapists. *Journal of Interpersonal Violence, 9*, 435–449.

Sentencing Guidelines Council (SGC) (2006). Draft Guidelines on the Sexual Offences Act 2003 available at: http://www.sentencing-guidelines.gov.uk/docs/draft-guidelines-sexual-offences.pdf

Seto, M.C., Cantor, J.M. & Blanchard, R. (2006). Child pornography offences are a valid diagnostic indicator of pedophilia. *Journal of Abnormal Psychology, 115*, 610–615.

Seto, M.C. & Eke, A.W. (2005). The criminal histories and later offending of child pornography offenders. *Sexual Abuse: A Journal of Research and Treatment, 17*, 201–210.

Seto, M.C. & Eke, A.W. (2006). Extending the Follow-up of Child Pornography Offenders Reported by Seto and Eke (2005). Poster presented at the 25th Annual Conference of the Association for the Treatment of Sexual Abusers (ATSA), Chicago, September 2006.

Smallbone, S.W. & Dadds, M.R. (1998). Childhood attachment and adult attachment in incarcerated adult male sex offenders. *Journal of Interpersonal Violence, 13*, 555–573.

Sullivan, J. & Beech, A. R. (2004). Assessing Internet sex offenders. In M.C. Calder (Ed.), *Child sexual abuse and the Internet: Tackling the new frontier* (pp. 69–84). Trowbridge: Cromwell Press.

Swets, J.A., Dawes, R.M., & Monahan, J. (2000). Psychological science can improve diagnostic decisions. *Psychological Science in the Public Interest, 1*, 1–26.

Taylor, M. & Quayle, E. (2006). The Internet and abuse images of children: Search, precriminal situations and opportunity. In R. Wortley & S. Smallbone (Eds), *Situational prevention of child sexual abuse.* New York: Criminal Justice Press/Willan Publishing.

Thornton, D. (2002). Constructing and testing a framework for dynamic risk assessment. *Sexual Abuse: A Journal of Research and Treatment, 14*, 139–153.

Thornton, D., Mann, R., Webster, S. *et al.* (2003). Distinguishing and Combining Risks for Sexual and Violent Recidivism. In R. Prentky, E. Janus, M. Seto & A.W. Burgess (Eds), *Understanding and managing sexually coercive behavior. Annals of the New York Academy of Sciences, 989*, 225–235.

Thompson, R.A. (1994). Emotional regulation: A theme in search of definition. *Monographs of the Society for Research in Child Development, 59*, 25–52.

Ward, T., Hudson, S.M. & Marshall, W.L. (1996). Attachment style in sexual offenders: A preliminary study. *Journal of Sex Research, 33*, 17–26.

Ward, T. & Siegert, R.J. (2002). Toward a comprehensive theory of child sexual abuse: A theory-knitting perspective. *Psychology, Crime and Law, 8*, 319–351.

Ward, T.S. & Sorbello, L. (2003). Explaining child sexual abuse: Integration and elaboration. In T. Ward, D.R. Laws & S.M. Hudson (Eds), *Sexual Deviance: Issues and controversies* (pp. 3–20). London: Sage.

Webb, L., Craissati, J. & Keen, S. (2007). Characteristics of child Internet pornography offenders: A comparison with child molesters. *Sexual Abuse: A Journal of Research and Treatment, 19*, 449–465.

Webster, S.D, Mann, R.E., Carter, A.J., Long, J., Milner, R., O'Brien, M.D., Wakeling, H., and Ray, N. (2006). Inter-rater reliability of dynamic risk assessment with sexual offenders. *Psychology, Crime and Law, 12*, 439–452.

Wilcox, D., Sosnoski, D., Warberg, B. & Beech, A. (2005). Sexual history disclosure using the polygraph in a sample of British sex offenders in treatment. *Polygraph, 34*, 171–183.

Wolak, J., Finkelhor, D. & Mitchell, K.J. (2005). Child pornography possessors arrested in Internet-related crimes: Findings from the National Juvenile Online Victimization Study. Virginia: The National Center for Missing and Exploited Children.

Young, K. (1998). Internet addiction: The emergence of a new clinical disorder. *CyberPsychology and Behavior, 1*, 237–244.

13

The Assessment of Treatment-Related Issues and Risk in Sex Offenders and Abusers with Intellectual Disability

WILLIAM R. LINDSAY

JOHN L. TAYLOR

INTRODUCTION

Although lagging behind the significant developments which have been seen in work on mainstream offenders, there have been considerable developments over the last 15 years in work with offenders with intellectual disability (ID) in general, and specifically sex offenders. At the outset, we must recognise the problem of definition in the population. Within the field, it is reasonably well established (e.g., Holland, 2004) that a number of factors influence the way clients are defined within the population of offenders with ID. The way in which these factors come to bear may influence local referral rates (prevalence rates) significantly.

The first issue relates to the definition of the population itself. Both Holland (2004) and Lindsay (2002) have noted that some men with ID who engage in an incident or incidents of inappropriate sexual behaviour are not brought to the attention of the Criminal Justice System. It may be felt by carers and those around the individual that it is not appropriate to involve the police following the perpetration of the incident. Reasons might include the fact that individuals involved consider that the perpetrator does not have *mens rea* and as a result cannot be held responsible since he cannot understand the laws and regulations of society. There may be a number of other reasons why such incidents are not brought to the attention of the authorities such as the fact that those around the individual may agree that it is not in the interests of the victim or the establishment to make such an incident public and a decision is

Assessment and Treatment of Sex Offenders: A Handbook. Edited by Anthony Beech, Leam Craig and Kevin Browne. © John Wiley & Sons Ltd, 2009.

made to deal with it internally. Therefore, this chapter is entitled 'Sexual Offenders and Abusers' to include this class of men.

A second, more technical issue with definition is that of the means of measuring IQ and inclusion criteria. As for the latter, most forensic services (and therefore studies which target these services in their research questions) would not include individuals who lack *mens rea*. Therefore, generally those individuals with a moderate intellectual disability, IQ < around 50, would not be included. However, Noble and Conley (1992), in their review of people with ID in the penal system in the USA, reported some surveys finding individuals with an IQ as low as 25. There are no recent detailed studies of this nature but it does seem astonishing to include anyone in the forensic services who is likely to have such a poor understanding of the illegal nature of an incident that they have perpetrated. At the other end of the range of ID, some services will have a very strict cut-off of IQ 70, while others will include one or two standard errors (up to IQ 75). This makes a considerable difference in terms of numbers included in the study since these four extra IQ points constitute around 3% of the population.

A second issue in relation to inclusion is the type of assessment used by the study or by the service being studied. The essential point of note is whether or not full intellectual assessment is used, such as the Wechsler Adult Intelligence Scale – Third Edition [UK](WAIS- III[UK]), or an IQ screening. A Quick Test has been mentioned in previous reports and is the assessment most frequently mentioned by Noble and Conley (1992) in their review of people with ID and the penal system. They note that the Quick Test is a screening method that consistently over-estimates the number of individuals in the lower IQ categories and, as a result, they do not recommend it for use. However, the police are increasingly obliged to provide special assistance to vulnerable suspects during interview and initial detention. Therefore Hayes (2002) has argued that ID should be identified as early as possible in the criminal justice process and has developed the Hayes Ability Screening Index (HASI; Hayes, 2000) in an attempt to address the issue of early identification of the presence of ID. However, the HASI includes around one in five participants as a false positive with no false negatives and is therefore likely to over-include individuals without ID at a rate of about 20%. The author herself stresses that the HASI should always be followed by detailed diagnostic assessment using appropriate IQ and adaptive behaviour tests. The previous paragraphs illustrate the extent to which one must take care with assessment in this field, even prior to assessing offence-related issues, and the importance of ensuring that assessments employed are sensitive to the comprehension levels of the individual being assessed.

RISK ASSESSMENT IN SEXUAL OFFENDERS WITH ID

Static Risk Assessment

There have been considerable developments in the identification of risk factors for future offending with the corresponding development of risk assessments of increasing accuracy (see Chapters 3 and 4 of this volume). Until recently, these developments had not spread to the field of ID. Lindsay, Elliot and Astell (2004) conducted a study to review the predictive potential of a range of previously identified variables and assess their relationship with recidivism. They employed 52 male sex offenders who had an average IQ of 64.3 (range: 56/75 IQ points); at least one year had elapsed since conviction for the index offence; the mean period of discharge was 3.3 years. It included 15 static/historical variables and 35 proximal/dynamic variables, all of which had either been identified in previous research or added on the basis of clinical experience. The significant variables to emerge from the regression models included antisocial attitude, poor relationship with mother, low self-esteem, lack of assertiveness, poor response to treatment, offences involving physical violence, staff complacency, an attitude tolerant of sexual crimes, low treatment motivation, erratic attendance and unexplained breaks from routine, deterioration of family attitudes, unplanned discharge and poor response to treatment. While most readers of this chapter will be unsurprised by these emerging variables, what was most notable in the study were the variables not associated with recidivism. Although employment history, criminal lifestyle, criminal companions (antisocial influences), diverse sexual crimes and deviant victim choice have been highly associated with recidivism in studies on mainstream offenders, they did not emerge from this study. Perhaps this points to the way in which those of us working in this field should adjust our perceptions. For example, very few individuals with ID have an employment history reflected in the fact that this does not emerge as a significant variable. However, individuals often have alternative regimes of special educational placements, occupational placements and the like which serve to make up the weekly regime. Non-compliance with this regime did emerge as a significant variable suggesting that individuals with ID should be judged in relation to their peers. This in turn suggests that the individual working with that offender should have a basic grasp of the general cultural context of people with ID. For example, we have known of probation officers, used to mainstream offenders and their employment histories, who have excused non-attendance of an ID offender at their occupational placement saying "it sounds really boring – I wouldn't enjoy it either". Alternatively, they may make allowances for the ID offender on the basis of their disability with statements like "you can't really expect too much of him given his handicap". On the basis of the research, and our experience, this is precisely the wrong thing to do. Lindsay (2005) has written of the theoretical and practical importance of engaging offenders with ID with society in the form of interpersonal contacts, occupational placements and so on. This emerges as a clear risk factor which has important ramifications for management of the offender.

In a specific test of clinical and actuarial prediction, McMillan, Hastings and Coldwell (2004) compared actuarial assessment and clinical judgement for the prediction of physical violence in a forensic ID sample. They studied 124 individuals over a one-year follow-up period and found that static/actuarial methods resulted in medium to high effect sizes for prediction (ROC AUC 0.77). They also found predictive values significantly above chance for structured clinical risk assessments. Therefore these authors found that it was possible to make reasonable predictions of who was at risk for violence in forensic populations with ID. Although this study was on violence rather than sexual offences, it serves as a specific illustration of the predictive value of static variables.

The first evaluation of a standard risk assessment when it is applied to individuals with ID was conducted by Quinsey, Book and Skilling (2004) with the Violence Risk Appraisal Guide (VRAG). They carried out a 16-month follow-up of 58 clients of whom 67% exhibited antisocial behaviour and 47% exhibited a violent or sexual misbehaviour. They found that the VRAG showed significant predictive value with a medium effect size. They also showed that monthly staff ratings of client behaviour were significantly related to antisocial incidents. One of the interesting developments in this study was that they substituted the Psychopathy Checklist-Revised (Hare, 1991), a very technical item on the VRAG, with the Child and Adolescent Taxon (CAT) which is a much simpler measure of antisociality. Quinsey *et al.* (2005), in their revision of the VRAG, have found that the CAT can substitute the PCL-R with no significant reduction in accuracy. They concluded that the VRAG was a reasonably accurate estimate of long-term risk in this client group.

There is one previous report in which actuarial risk assessment is used with sex offenders with ID. However, although Harris and Tough (2004) report that they have found the measures to predict reasonably well in their population, they do not present the data. Rather, they employ the RRASOR (Hanson, 1997) as a means of allocating 81 sex offenders with ID into their services. By accepting referrals of only low or medium risk, as judged by the RRASOR, they argue that they can target limited resources at an appropriate group.

Over the last 10 years, several groups of researchers have compared the predictive accuracy of different risk assessment instruments on a range of databases containing actuarial information on mainstream offenders (Barbaree *et al.*, 2001; Bartosh *et al.*, 2003; Sjöstedt & Långström, 2002). For example, Harris *et al.* (2003) compared the VRAG, its companion assessment for sex offenders, the Sex Offender Risk Appraisal Guide (SORAG) (Quinsey *et al.*, 2005), the RRASOR and the Static-99 (Hanson & Thornton 1999) in the prediction of recidivism for 396 sex offenders in Canada. All four instruments predicted recidivism with significantly greater accuracy than chance. Prediction of violent recidivism was considerably higher for the VRAG and SORAG with effect sizes large for violent recidivism and moderate for sexual recidivism.

Lindsay *et al.* (2008) have recently made the first such comparison of actuarial risk assessments with a mixed group of 212 violent and sexual offenders with ID. Seventy-three participants in their sample were drawn from high secure services, 70 from medium/low secure services and 69 from a community forensic service. They employed the VRAG, which assesses risk for violent incidents, the Static-99, which assesses risk for sexual incidents, and the RM2000 (Thornton *et al.*, 2003) which has sections for assessing risk of violence (RM2000/V) and risk for sexual incidents (RM2000/S). Following up participants for one year, they found that the VRAG was a reasonable predictor for future violent incidents with a medium effect size (AUC = 0.72), Static-99 was a reasonable predictor for future sexual incidents with a medium effect size (AUC = 0.71) and the RM2000/V (AUC = 0.61) and the RM2000/S (AUC = 0.62) predicted somewhat less well with small effect sizes. The authors wrote that the findings on the RM2000 should not discourage future research since because it is relatively simple to use, it has the potential for considerable utility if it can be found to have similar predictive ability to other risk assessments. However, this study does give further validation to both the VRAG and Static-99 which have had endorsement from the results of several studies and researchers across cultures and countries. Lindsay *et al.* (2008) compared the three separate cohorts using these risk assessments and found that the VRAG and combined RM2000 scores (RM2000/C) showed an orderly pattern among the groups with the high secure participants having higher scores than the medium secure participants who in turn had higher scores than the low secure participants. The trend was more notable on the VRAG than the RM2000/C. Interestingly, there were similar numbers of sex offenders across all three groups and this was reflected in the lack of difference between the groups on the Static-99.

Although there are not many studies on which to base a conclusion about Static/Actuarial Risk Assessment, these studies do provide some encouragement on the applicability of these assessments to offenders with ID. There are now two independent evaluations of the VRAG and the one which was not conducted by the authors of the assessment found a marginally higher predictive value. One study has found medium effect sizes for the predictive value of the Static-99 while another report has used its predecessor, the RRASOR. Although the effect sizes on prediction were smaller, the RM2000/C did discriminate between groups of high secure, medium/low secure and community offenders. Because of its ease of use and potential utility, it warrants further study.

Assessment of Personality Disorder

Assessment of personality disorder (PD) will be discussed in this chapter because aspects of PD have been linked strongly with offending and recidivism in mainstream populations. The crucial finding is that certain PDs and especially antisocial PD is a reasonable predictor of future aggression and is significantly more prevalent among inmates of correctional settings (Fazel & Danesh, 2002). In addition, psychopathy as measured by the Psychopathy Checklist-Revised (PCL-R; Hare 1991) is related to certain PDs, including antisocial PD, and also successfully predicts future aggression in a range of populations of criminals (Grettan *et al.*, 2001; Hill, Neumann & Rogers, 2004). A final important finding is that antisocial PD and the PCL-R make significant contributions to the prediction of recidivism in a range of offences (Harris *et al.*, 2003). Therefore, from a number of points of view, research on PD has been shown to produce extremely important findings in relation to the planning and development of services and treatment.

There has been a slow but steady flow of research on ID and PD from early idiosyncratic writings to recent more systematic investigations (see Lindsay, 2006, for a review). Alexander and Cooray (2003), in their review of the field, comment on the lack of diagnostic instruments, the difference between classificatory systems (ICD-10 and DSM-IV), confusion of definition and personality theory and the difficulties of distinguishing personality disorder from other problems integral to ID, for example, communication problems, sensory disorders and developmental delay. They conclude "the variation of the co-occurrence of personality disorder in (*intellectual disability*) with prevalence rates ranging from 1% to 91% ... is too large to be explained by real differences" (p. 28). They recommend tighter diagnostic criteria, greater use of behavioural observation and increased use of informant information. Naik, Gangada-jran and Alexander (2002) held these cautions in mind when they conducted a study of 230 outpatients with ID in which they found a prevalence rate of PD of 7%. Of those individuals diagnosed with PD, 59% were classified with dissocial/antisocial PD, 28% emotionally unstable PD and 10% with both diagnoses. They found a high percentage of co-morbidity with AXIS I disorders and 59% had had one or more admissions to hospital.

Lindsay *et al.* (2006a) in a study on the same population reported above (70 offenders with ID from a high secure setting, 73 from a medium/low secure setting and 69 from a community forensic setting) took some care to address previous criticisms of PD research in that extensive training of research assistants and clinical informants was conducted, care was taken to ensure inter-rater reliability, and multiple information sources were employed including file reviews, clinical informants, carers and nursing staff. They reported an overall rate of 39% of participants diagnosed as having a PD and given that the three cohorts were administratively selected for having been referred to offender services for people with ID, they argued that the relatively high rate of diagnosis seemed reasonable. By the far the most common diagnosis in these samples was antisocial PD with participants in the high security setting having a significantly greater rate of diagnosis. Those diagnosed with PD were found to have a significantly higher level of risk for violence, as measured by actuarial measures of risk, from those with no diagnosis of PD. However, those with a PD diagnosis did not differ from those without on actuarial measures of risk of sexual recidivism. Those authors went on to combine PD classifications with PCL-R data to construct a simple dimensional system of increasing indications of PD. They found strong relationships between increasing indications of PD and actuarial measures of risk for future violence. Relationships with actuarial measures of sexual risk were significant but less strong. In a further analysis of their data, Lindsay *et al.* (2007b) found that similar factor structures emerged from personality disorder data in this client group as those found in mainstream studies. In an analysis of PD data from 168 participants from high secure hospitals, Blackburn *et al.* (2005) found that two super-ordinate factors emerged representing 'acting out' and 'anxious-introverted' underlying personality difficulties. These reflected similar super-ordinate factors to emerge from a previous study by Morey (1988) in a study of 291 university students. In a similar confirmatory factor analysis, Lindsay *et al.* (2007b) found that two super-ordinate factors emerged representing 'acting out' and 'anxious/avoidant/inhibited'. These two factors accounted for a similar amount of variance as the Blackburn *et al.* study (38%) and were essentially orthogonal. These findings add weight to the emerging picture that a classification of PD, if used with caution and based on appropriate information, may have similar utility in offenders with ID as it does with mainstream offenders. However, it should be remembered, particularly with reference to this volume on sex offenders, that the relationship between PD and risk for sexual offending was not as strong as the relationship between PD and risk for violent offending.

Assessment of Dynamic Risk and Offence-Related Issues

Thornton (2002) has developed a frame work for the consideration of dynamic risk factors in sex offenders which clearly includes issues that would be considered for offence-related interventions. Dynamic risk factors are more amenable to change through therapeutic intervention and we shall include all of these various factors in this section of the chapter. Thornton (2002) set out four domains: *Domain 3* is socio-affective functioning. This refers to the way in which the individual being assessed relates to other people and includes aspects of negative affect such as anger, anxiety, depression and low self-esteem. In relation to sexual incidents, low self-esteem and loneliness have been found to feature prior to incidents of inappropriate or violent sexual behaviour (Beech *et al.*, 2002). *Domain 2* relates to distorted attitudes and beliefs and there has been considerable interest in relation to cognitive distortions for sex offenders (Ward & Hudson, 2000; Ward, Johnston & Marshall, 1998). *Domain 4*, self-management, referred to the individual's current ability to engage in appropriate problem solving, impulse control and a general ability to regulate their own behaviour. Clearly transient deficits in such self-regulation would be relevant to the assessment of increased immediate risk. Self-regulation has also been employed as the fundamental principle grading recent developments in the assessment and treatment for sex offenders (Ward & Hudson, 2000; Ward, Hudson & McCormack, 1999; Ward *et al.*, Chapter 16 this volume). *Domain 1* mentioned in the frame work was offence-related sexual preference, split into sexual preference and sexual drive.

Lindsay, Elliot and Astell (2004) reviewed a number of dynamic variables in relation to sex offence recidivism and found that antisocial attitude, low self-esteem, attitudes tolerant of sexual crimes, low treatment motivation, deteriorating treatment compliance and staff complacency all contributed to the predictive model. The most significant dynamic predictors were antisocial attitude, denial of crime, allowances made by staff and deteriorating compliance. Quinsey, Book and Skilling (2004) conducted a field trial of dynamic indicators with 58 participants. They found that a rating of inappropriate and antisocial behaviour was the best predictor of subsequent inappropriate violent or sexual behaviour. In addition, there were differences between clients who precipitated and those who did not precipitate incidents on the dynamic variables of compliance, dynamic antisociality and inappropriate/antisocial behaviour. These two studies attest to the predictive utility of dynamic risk variables and we will now go on to consider variables within each of Thornton's four categories in more detail.

Socio-affective functioning

The personal attribute which emerges most frequently from studies reviewing dynamic variables is that of antisocial and hostile attitude. Hostility and anger in individuals with ID are areas which have attracted a reasonable amount of research when compared with other dynamic risk variables. Novaco and Taylor (2004) sought to evaluate the reliability and validity of anger assessment procedures with 129 male inpatients with ID, most of whom had forensic histories. In this study, specially modified self-report measures of *anger disposition* (Novaco Anger Scale (NAS); Novaco, 2003; Spielberger State-Trait Anger Expression Inventory (STAXI); Spielberger, 1996), *anger reactivity* (provocation inventory (PI); Novaco, 2003), and informant rated *anger attributes* (Ward Anger Rating Scale (WARS); Novaco, 1994) were investigated with regard to their internal consistency, stability and concurrent and predictive validity. The STAXI and NAS showed substantial intercorrelations, providing evidence for concurrent validity for these instruments. WARS staff ratings for patient anger based on ward observations were found to have high internal consistency and to correlate significantly with patient anger self-reports. Anger, self-reported by the participants, was significant related to their record of assaultive behaviour in hospital. Predictive validity was assessed retrospectively, examining patient assault behaviour in the hospital as predicated by patient rated anger in a hierarchical regression analysis. Controlling for age, length of stay, IQ, violent offence and personality measures, the NAS total score was found to be significantly predictive of whether the patient had physically assaulted others in the hospital and the total number of physical assaults.

In a further development, Taylor *et al.* (2004) developed the Imaginal Provocation Test (IPT) as an additional idiographic anger assessment procedure with people with ID that taps key elements of the experience and expression of anger, is sensitive to change associated with anger treatment and is easily modifiable for idiographic uses. The IPT produces four indices relevant to the individual client's experience of anger: anger reaction, behavioural reaction, a composite of anger and behavioural reaction and anger regulation. They administered the IPT to 48 patients prior to beginning an anger treatment and showed that the indices had respectable internal reliabilities. The assessment had reasonable concurrent validity when correlated with the STAXI and NAS. Therefore it would appear that there are rapid, flexible and sensitive idiographic assessments of anger among people with ID and that these assessments have reasonable psychometric properties. Alder and Lindsay (2007) also produced a provocation inventory which is easily accessible and easy to use. A factor analytic study revealed five factors, the first of which was threat to self-esteem. These factors can be considered as basic self-schema and poor self-esteem considered a major dynamic risk factor in sex offenders by several authors (Beech *et al.*, 2002; Boer, Tough & Haaven, 2004). Therefore the assessment developed by Alder and Lindsay (2007) may provide a quick assessment of threat to self-esteem in this client group.

Although hostile attitude and anger emerge persistently from studies assessing risk for future violent and sexual incidents, it has to be acknowledged that sex offenders with ID tend to show lower levels of anger than other offenders with ID. Lindsay *et al.* (2006) in a study of 247 offenders with ID found that sex offenders showed significantly lower levels of anger and aggression than other male offenders or female offenders. However, where anger is present, it may be a particularly potent dynamic risk factor.

Lindsay *et al.* (2006b) also found that sex offenders were recorded as showing lower levels of anxiety than other male offenders or female offenders. A similar finding was also reported by Lindsay and Skene (2007) in a study of a mixed group of 105 people with ID. They found that the subgroup of men who had committed inappropriate sexual behaviour reported lower levels of anxiety and depression on the Beck Anxiety Inventory and the Beck Depression Inventory. Therefore although anxiety and depression may be salient features prior to incidents, they may feature less often in some subgroups of sex offenders with ID.

Finally, in relation to the all-encompassing domain of socio-affective functioning, loneliness has been found to be a feature prior to incidents of inappropriate or violent sexual behaviour for mainstream offenders (Garlic, Marshall & Thornton, 1996). In a recent study, Steptoe *et al.* (2006) reported some interesting findings when they compared a group of 28 sex offenders with ID with 28 members of a control group. Although the sex offender group participants reported the same opportunities as other participants, they seemed to choose to take advantage of these opportunities less often than control participants. In addition, they appeared to have more impoverished relationships than control participants but reported being quite happy with a more restricted range of relationships. This led to the conclusion that while sex offenders might appear lonelier than other groups of individuals with ID, this may reflect a more self-contained way of life. Lindsay (2005) has stressed the importance of promoting social contact and community identification in sex offenders with ID both from a practical and theoretical standpoint. Such increased social inclusion allows others to monitor the individual sex offender and also ensures that their views and attitudes are constantly being reviewed and even challenged by ordinary social contact. Steptoe *et al.* (2006) used the Significant Other Scale (Power, Champion & Aris, 1988) and the life experience checklist (Ager, 1990) both of which were useful in eliciting such information from this client group.

A range of assessments have been developed and adapted to gather reliable and valid information from this client group. These assessments include the NAS, the IPT, the Beck Anxiety Inventory, the Beck Depression Inventory, the Significant Other Scale and the Life Experience Checklist. All of these tests represent a significant beginning in assessing a range of dynamic risk variables relating to the socio-affective functioning of sex offenders with ID.

Distorted cognitions and beliefs

Some work has been completed on knowledge and beliefs in relation to sexual interaction with sex offenders with ID. With this client group it is important not only to review cognitive distortions but also to consider the level of sexual knowledge an individual may have. Indeed, one of the first hypotheses put forward to account for inappropriate sexual behaviour in this group was that lack of sexual knowledge may lead the individual to attempt inappropriate sexual contact precisely because they are unaware of the means to establish appropriate interpersonal and sexual relationships.

This hypothesis of 'counterfeit deviance' was first mentioned by Hingsburger, Griffiths and Quinsey (1991) and was noted by Luiselli (2000) to be the most influential basis for the development of treatment services for this client group. The term refers to behaviour which is undoubtedly deviant but may be precipitated by factors such as lack of sexual knowledge, poor social and heterosexual skills, limited opportunities to establish sexual relationships and sexual naivety rather than a preference or sexual drive towards inappropriate objects. Therefore mediation should focus on educational issues and developmental maturation rather than inappropriate sexuality. Griffiths, Quinsey and Hingsburger (1989) gave a number of examples illustrating the concept of counterfeit deviance and developed a treatment programme, part of which was based significantly on sexual and social education.

In a review of variables associated with the perpetration of sexual offences in men with ID, Lindsay (2005) noted that, surprisingly, there are no controlled tests of this hypothesis. This is despite the fact that the notion is relatively easy to test under controlled conditions. Counterfeit deviance would suggest that some men with ID commit sexual offences because they have poorer social-sexual knowledge, do not understand the rules and mores of society and are unaware of taboos relating to sexuality. Therefore, men with ID who have committed sexual offences should have poorer social-sexual knowledge than those who do not. Two sets of authors have thrown some doubt on this as an explanation. Lambrick and Glaser (2004) note that features of poor sexual knowledge and social skills are also found in sex offenders without disability and that this may merely indicate a propensity to be detected rather than to commit offences. They also report experience in their service of a number of such individuals who have excellent social skills and understanding of issues to do with sexuality. A second source of relevant information comes from Lunsky et al. (2007) in a study using their revision of the Social-Sexual Knowledge & Attitudes Assessment Tool (SSKAAT-R). They report reference group scores for sex offenders and controls on each of the subscales on the SSKAAT. There are no significant differences between the two groups on any subscale which clearly does not support a hypothesis which suggests that lack of sexual knowledge is a primary reason for committing inappropriate sexual behaviour.

Sexual knowledge, sexual attitudes and sex education have been the focus of several studies and assessments over the last 25 years. The first assessment of sexual knowledge and attitudes designed for people with ID, and the most widely employed over that period, has been the Socio-Sexual Knowledge and Attitudes Test (SSKAT), originally developed by Wish, McCombs and Edmondson (1979) and recently updated by Griffiths and Lunsky (2003). Michie et al. (2006) completed a test of counterfeit deviance by comparing the sexual knowledge of groups of sex offenders with ID and control participants using the SSKAT. In the first study comparing 17 male sex offenders with 20 controls, they found that of 13 subscales in the SSKAT, 3 comparisons, birth control, masturbation and sexually transmitted diseases, showed significant differences between the groups and in each case the sex offenders had higher levels of sexual knowledge. There were no differences between the groups on age or IQ. In a second comparison, 16 sex offenders were compared with 15 controls. There were significant differences between the groups on seven scales and in each case the sex offenders showed a higher level of sexual knowledge. Michie *et al.* (2006) then pooled the data for all 33 sex offenders and 35 control participants. They found a significant positive correlation between IQ and SSKAT total score for the control group (r = 0.71) but no significant relationship between IQ and SSKAT total score for the sex offender cohort (r = 0.17). They presented two possible reasons for this finding. The first was that, by definition, all of the sex offender cohort have some experience of sexual interaction. It is unlikely that these experiences of sexual interaction are random and one might therefore conclude that these sex offenders have given some thought and attention to sexuality at least in the period prior to the perpetration of the inappropriate sexual behaviour or sexual abuse. Therefore we can be sure that they have at least some experience of sexual activity which is not the case for the control participants. The second possible explanation was that these individuals have a developmental history of increased sexual arousal. This in turn may have led to selective attention and interest in sexual information gained from informal sources. Such persistence of attention would lead to greater retention of information through rehearsal and perhaps to a higher level of associated appropriate sexual activity such as masturbation. These behavioural and informal educational experiences would lead to a higher level of sexual knowledge. In this latter hypothesis, sexual arousal and sexual preference is hypothesised to have an interactive effect with knowledge acquisition and, perhaps, attitudes and beliefs. From this information it is clear that it is important to assess sexual knowledge in offenders with ID.

Although a number of assessments have been developed to assess cognitive distortions in sex offenders, it is generally recognised that the language should be simplified considerably in order to be understood by individuals with ID. Kolton, Boer and Boer (2001) employed the Abel and Becker Cognition Scale with 89 sex offenders with ID (although their degree of cognitive ability was not mentioned). They found that the response options of the test needed to be changed from a 4-choice system (1 = agree, 4 = strongly disagree) to a dichotomous system (agree/disagree) to reduce extremity bias of the sample. The revised assessment provided 'adequate' total score to item correlations and test-retest reliability, and internal consistency was 'acceptable' (values not reported), and preserved the psychometric and integrity of the assessment. Other tests, such as the Bumby Rape and Molest Scales (1996) have not been used with this client group but have the drawbacks of having contained in their syntax complex concepts, difficult words and complex response choices.

Lindsay, Whitefield and Carson (2007a) reported on the development of the Questionnaire on Attitudes Consistent with Sexual Offences (QACSO) which is designed to be suitable for offenders with ID. The QACSO contains a series of scales which evaluates attitudes across a range of different types of offence including rape and attitudes to women, voyeurism, exhibitionism, dating abuse, homosexual assault, offences against children and stalking. They compared 41 sex offenders with ID, 34 non-sexual offenders with ID, 30 non-offenders with ID and 31 non-ID controls who had not committed sexual offences. The Questionnaire has a Flesch reading ease score of 88.21 although all items require to be read to participants with ID because few have literacy skills. The assessment was revised following tests of reliability, discriminant validity and internal consistency in order to ensure that all three psychometric properties were robust. It is found that six of the seven scales on the QACSO were valid and reliable measures of cognitive distortions held by sex offenders with ID (the exception was homosexual assault). Lindsay *et al.* (2006c) also found that the rape and offences against children scales in particular discriminated between offenders against adults and offenders against children in the hypothesised direction with offenders against adults having higher scores on the rape scale and lower scores on the offences against children scale than the child molesters. Therefore, it would appear that the cognitive distortions in sex offenders with ID can be assessed with some reliability and validity. However, these authors were cautious when considering the relationship of cognitive distortions to risk. They wrote that changes in attitudes may reflect a number of processes such as suppression, influence by social desirability and even lying. They recommended that the results from the QACSO should be considered in relation to the range of risk assessment variables within the contexts suggested by Thornton (2002).

Self-management and self-regulation

Self-regulation has become germane to the assessment and treatment of sex offenders since the publication of Hudson and Ward (2000), and Hudson, Ward and McCormack (1999) self-regulation pathways in the perpetration of sexual offences and recidivism. The model has had some validation from independent experiments (e.g., Bickley & Beech, 2002) in mainstream offenders and has recently extended to the field of ID. The model itself is clearly explained elsewhere in this volume (Chapter 16) and will not be outlined here. Langdon, Maxted and Murphy (2007) in a study of 34 men with a history of inappropriate sexual behaviour, found that the population could be reliably classified using the self-regulation pathways model. There was partial support for the hypothesis that approach offenders with ID would have higher levels of cognitive distortions, less victim empathy and a history of engaging in more prolific offending behaviour. Passive offenders were found to have lower levels of general intellectual functioning and poorer sexual knowledge. In their study, 82% of the sample were classified as having approach goals with only 18% avoidant goals.

While there is some developing evidence that the self-regulation model may be applicable to sex offenders with ID, the Thornton (2002) domain refers predominantly to deficits in self-regulation and ability to engage in appropriate problem-solving strategies and impulse control. The developing field of social problem solving (McMurran *et al.*, 2001) has not spread to the field of offenders with ID. The work that does exist is generally related to problem-solving skills with respect to self-regulation of anger. The NAS has sections on the cognitive, behavioural and physiological self-regulation of the emotion of anger and the results from the work of Novaco and Taylor (2003) have already been discussed above.

Impulsivity is an interesting personal characteristic which is often cited in relation to sex offenders in general and also sex offenders with ID. Ward and Hudson (1998) in their elucidation of the offence pathways of mainstream sex offenders have clarified some issues on impulsivity. In their hypothetical account, which as noted above has been subsequently validated through independent research studies, not all pathways rely on impulsive reactions from the sex offender. Indeed, one of the main pathways, approach/explicit, does not invoke impulsivity at all and the extent to which it is incorporated into other pathways is variable. For example, if an offender employs an approach automatic pathway in which they engage in routine high-risk behaviours without the explicit intention to offend, one could argue that they are arranging their routines in order to maximise the probability of offending opportunities. In this way, the impulsivity would not appear to play a significant part in the offence cycle. Indeed, several authors (Cohen *et al.*, 2002; Nussbaum *et al.*, 2002) have conducted studies in which it appeared that sex offenders were less impulsive than other types of offenders when the personality traits were measured systematically.

Having said that, Glaser and Deane (1999) hypothesised that impulsivity was involved in a range of offending in men with ID. They compared 19 sex offenders with 23 other types of offenders and found very few differences between the two cohorts. As a result, they felt that impulsivity may be involved in both types of offending rather than feature in one or the other. Parry and Lindsay (2003) compared 22 sex offenders with 6 non-offenders and 13 other types of offenders using the Barratt Impulsiveness Scale adapted to suit the client group. They found that the sex offenders reported lower levels of impulsiveness than other types of offenders. However, they felt that there may be subgroups of clients with ID who do indeed have higher levels of disinhibition and impulsivity and that this should be incorporated into assessment and treatment considerations.

There is very little work on social problem solving and offenders with ID. One of the main social problem-solving inventories, the Social Problem-Solving Inventory-Revised (D'Zurilla, Nezu & Maydeu-Olivares, 2000) although used widely in mainstream offenders (McMurran *et al.*, 2001) has seldom been used in offenders with ID. Hamilton *et al.* (2006) have piloted the use of the SPSI with this client group and have found that if it is suitably modified, it can be used reliably. In addition, they conducted a preliminary factor analysis on the 25 items and found a fairly logical and reasonably simple factor structure which incorporated the original development of the test. The SPSI consists of 25 items which provide five problem-solving styles: positive orientation, negative orientation, impulsive problem-solving style, rational problem-solving style and avoidant problem-solving style. In their pilot study, Hamilton *et al.* (2006) found that three factors emerged accounting for 63% of the variance: negative/avoidant style, positive/rational style and impulsive problem-solving style. Therefore there are some preliminary indications that it may be possible to assess problem-solving style of sexual offenders using a suitably adapted established assessment.

Sexual preference and sexual drive

The hypothesis of counterfeit deviance has already been discussed above and has been the most prevalent theoretical model in the development of sex offender treatment in the field of ID. However, in mainstream sex offender work, inappropriate sexual preference and sexual drive have been suggested as primary motivation by several authors (Blanchard *et al.*, 1999; Harris *et al.*, 2003). Although some of this work is beginning to extend to men with lower intellectual functioning, perhaps the main instances can be drawn from studies which have noted previous sexual offending and patterns of offending in cohorts of referred clients. Day (1994) reported in a study of 31 sexual offenders referred to his clinic, that all of them had previous recorded incidents of inappropriate sexual behaviour or sexual offences. On the other hand, Glaser and Deane (1999) found no differences between the number of previous sex offences in their cohorts of sex offenders and non-sex offenders with ID. Lindsay *et al.* (2002) found that for 62% of referrals there was either a previous conviction for a sexual offence or clear documented evidence of sexual abuse having been perpetrated by the individual. When one considers that any incident of sexual abuse is typically met with a great deal of criticism towards the offending individual on the part of his victim's family or his caregivers, which would be a considerable disincentive to the further commission of additional sexual offences, then one must conclude that sexual drive and sexual preference are likely to be significant factors.

Two important studies, although not directly relevant, can inform on this issue. Blanchard *et al.* (1999) investigated patterns of sexual offending in 950 participants. They found that sex offenders with intellectual disabilities were more likely to commit offences against younger children and male children. Although the proportion of variance is not high, this information, coming as it does from a well-conducted series of studies, constitutes evidence that inappropriate sexual preference plays at least some role in this client group. They also reported that their results suggest that choices of male or female victims by offenders with intellectual disability were not primarily determined by accessibility (or other circumstantial factors) but, rather, by their relative sexual interest in male and female children. Cantor *et al.* (2005) have recently published a detailed meta-analytic study of previous reports which have included reliable data on IQ and sexual offending. In a re-analysis of data on 25,146 sex offenders and controls, they found a robust relationship between lower IQ and sexual offending but specifically, lower IQ and paedophilia. They had hypothesised that "a third variable – a perturbation of prenatal or childhood brain development – produces both paedophilia and low IQ" (p. 565). They go on to accept that psychosocial influences are likely to be important but incomplete in explaining paedophilia emphasising the importance of investigating the range of hypotheses presented for the genesis of sexual offending. However, this information on the relationship between intellectual ability and sexual preference, coming as it does from a highly reliable research group, presents more persuasive evidence than the essentially anecdotal accounts of previous authors (e.g., Day, 1994; Lindsay *et al.*, 2004). Therefore sexual drive and sexual preference are likely to be important components within any treatment programme and Lindsay (2005) has argued that self-regulation and self-control of any inappropriate sexual drive or preference is an essential aspect of any treatment programme. Treatment issues directed at these aspects of personal sexual preference are outlined in Chapter 20.

CONCLUSION

In this chapter we have reviewed the current state of literature on assessment of risk in sex offenders with ID. Our knowledge on static risk factors has begun to develop considerably and there have now been two studies on the applicability of existing risk assessments to this client group. Both studies (Quinsey, Book & Skilling, 2004; Lindsay *et al.*, 2008) have found predictive results that are broadly consistent with the literature on mainstream offending for the VRAG and Static-99. Results on the RM2000 were somewhat poorer but the authors urged further research work since this particular assessment has wide applicability and accessibility. The Static-99 in particular appeared relevant for use with sex offenders with ID since Harris and Tough (2004) reported that its predecessor the RRASOR was used effectively in treatment services for this client group in the Toronto area. Therefore there are some positive results regarding assessment of static/actuarial risk.

We have considered dynamic risk variables in accordance with the Thornton (2002) classification of social/affective, cognitive and attitudinal, self-regulation and sexual preference/drive. These are the issues which would be targeted for treatment in relevant services and because of this, there is a reasonably rich literature upon which to draw. A few studies have been conducted which confirm the relevance of these dynamic risk variables in the prediction of incidents for this client group. A number of studies have demonstrated the reliability and validity of assessments for use with these clients on these relevant variables. Notably they include assessments of hostility, emotional instability, personal relationships, cognitive distortions that might be considered supportive of sexual offences, and self-regulation. Two important studies (Blanchard *et al.*, 1999; Cantor *et al.*, 2005) also attest to the importance of considering self-regulation of sexual preference drive during treatment. The field of sex offenders with intellectual disability has been making some reasonable progress over the last 15 years and we are now at the point where treatment services are becoming more effective and we can have more confidence in the reliability and validity of assessments to monitor the progress of treatment. It is to be hoped that the next 15 years will witness researchers continuing to develop the field.

REFERENCES

Ager, A. (1990). *The Life Experience Checklist*. Kidderminster, UK: British Institute of Learning Disabilities.

Alder, L. & Lindsay, W.R. (2007). Exploratory factor analysis and convergent validity of the Dundee Provocation Inventory. *Journal of Intellectual and Developmental Disabilities, 32*, 179–188.

Alexander, R. & Cooray, S. (2003). Diagnosis of personality disorders in learning disability. *British Journal of Psychiatry, 182* (Suppl. 44) S28–S31.

Barbaree, H.E., Seto, M.C., Langton, C.M. & Peacock, E.J. (2001). Evaluating the predictive accuracy of six risk assessment instruments for adult sex offenders. *Criminal Justice and Behavior, 28*, 490–521.

Bartosh, D.L., Garby, T., Lewis, D. & Gray, S. (2003). Differences in the predictive validity of actuarial risk assessments in relation to sex offender type. *International Journal of Offender Therapy and Comparative Criminology, 47,* 422–438.

Beech, A., Friendship, C., Erikson, M. & Hanson, R.K. (2002). The relationship between static and dynamic risk factors and reconviction in a sample of UK child abusers. *Sexual Abuse: A Journal of Research and Treatment, 14,* 155–167.

Bickley, J.A. & Beech, A.R. (2002). An investigation of the Ward and Hudson pathways model of the sexual offence process with child abusers. *Journal of Interpersonal Violence, 17,* 371–393.

Blackburn, R., Logan, C., Renwick, S.J.D. & Donnelly, J.P. (2005). Higher order dimensions of personality disorder: Hierarchical and relationships with the five factor model, the interpersonal circle and psychopathy. *Journal of Personality Disorders, 19,* 597–623.

Blanchard, R., Watson, M., Choy, A. *et al.* (1999). Paedophiles: Mental retardation, mental age and sexual orientation. *Archives of Sexual Behavior, 28,* 111–127.

Boer, D.P., Tough, S. & Haaven, J. (2004). Assessment of risk manageability of developmentally disabled sex offenders. *Journal of Applied Research in Intellectual Disabilities, 17,* 275–284.

Bumby, K.M. (1996). Assessing the cognitive distortions of child molesters and rapists: Development and validation of the MOLEST and RAPE scales. *Sexual Abuse: A Journal of Research and Treatment, 8,* 37–54.

Cantor, J.M., Blanchard, R., Robichaud, L.K. & Christensen, B.K. (2005). Quantitative reanalysis of aggregate data on IQ in sexual offenders. *Psychological Bulletin, 131,* 555–568.

Cohen, L.J., Gans, S.W., McGeoch, P.G., *et al.* (2002). Impulsive personality traits in male paedophiles versus healthy controls: Is paedophilia an impulsive-aggressive disorder? *Comprehensive Psychology, 43,* 127–134.

Day, K. (1994). Male mentally handicapped sex offenders. *British Journal of Psychiatry, 165,* 630–639.

D'Zurilla, T.J., Nezu, A.M. & Maydeu-Olivares, A. (2000). *Manual for the Social Problem-Solving Inventory-Revised.* North Tonawanda, NY: Multi-Health Systems.

Fazel, S. & Danesh, J. (2002). Serious mental disorder among 23,000 prisoners: Systematic review of 62 surveys. *Lancet, 16,* 545–550.

Garlic, Y., Marshall, W.L. & Thornton, D. (1996). Intimacy deficits and attribution of blame among sex offenders. *Legal and Criminological Psychology, 1,* 251–258.

Glaser, W. & Deane, K. (1999). Normalisation in an abnormal world: A study of prisoners with intellectual disability. *International Journal of Offender Therapy and Comparative Criminology, 43,* 338–350.

Grettan, H.M., McBride, M., Hare, R.D. *et al.* (2001). Psychopathy and recidivism in adolescent sex offenders. *Criminal Justice and Behavior, 28,* 427–449.

Griffiths, D. & Lunsky, Y. (2003). *Socio-Sexual Knowledge and Attitudes Assessment Tool (SSKAAT-R).* Wood Dale, Illinois: Stoelting Company.

Griffiths, D.M., Quinsey, V.L. & Hingsburger, D. (1989). *Changing inappropriate sexual behaviour: A community-based approach for persons with developmental disabilities.* Baltimore: Paul Brooks Publishing.

Hamilton, C., Doyle, M.C., Lindsay, W.R. & Goodall, J. (2006). Adaptation and psychometric evaluation of the Social Problem-Solving Inventory-Revised (SPSI-R). *Journal of Applied Research in Intellectual Disabilities, 19,* 258.

Hanson, R.K. (1997). *The development of a brief actuarial risk scale for sexual offence recidivism.* (User report 1997-04.) Ottawa: Department of the Solicitor General of Canada.

Hanson, R.K. & Thornton, D. (1999). *Static-99: Improving actuarial risk assessments for sex offenders.* (User report 1999-02.) Ottawa: Department of the Solicitor General of Canada.

Hare, R.D. (1991). *The Hare Psychopathy Checklist-Revised.* Toronto, Ontario: Multi-Health Systems.

Harris, G.T., Rice, M.E., Quinsey, V.L. *et al.* (2003). A multi-site comparison of actuarial risk instruments for sex offenders. *Psychological Assessment, 15,* 413–425.

Harris, A.J.R. & Tough, S. (2004). Should actuarial risk assessments be used with sex offenders who are intellectually disabled? *Journal of Applied Research in Intellectual Disabilities, 17,* 235–242.

Hayes, S.C. (2000). *Hayes Ability Screening Index (HASI) Manual.* University of Sydney, Sydney: Behavioural Sciences in Medicine.

Hayes, S.C. (2002). Early intervention or early incarceration? Using a screening test for intellectual disability in the criminal justice system. *Journal of Applied Research in Intellectual Disability, 15,* 120–128.

Hill, C.D., Neumann, C.S. & Rogers, R. (2004). Confirmatory factor analysis of the Psychopathy Checklist: Screening version in offenders with Axis-I disorders. *Psychological Assessment, 16,* 90–95.

Hingsburger, D., Griffiths, D. & Quinsey, V. (1991). Detecting counterfeit deviance: Differentiating sexual deviance from sexual inappropriateness. *Habilitation Mental Health Care Newsletter, 10,* 51–54.

Holland, A.J. (2004). Criminal behaviour and developmental disability: An epidemiological perspective. In W.R. Lindsay, J.L. Taylor & P. Sturmey (Eds), *Offenders with developmental disabilities* (pp. 23–34). Chichester: John Wiley & Sons, Ltd.

Hudson, S.M., Ward, T. & McCormack, J.C. (1999). Offence pathways in sexual offenders. *Journal of Interpersonal Violence, 14,* 779–798.

Kolton, D.J.C., Boer, A. & Boer, D.P. (2001). A revision of the Abel and Becker Cognition Scale for intellectually disabled sexual offenders. *Sexual Abuse: A Journal of Research & Treatment, 13,* 217–219.

Lambrick, F. & Glaser, W. (2004). Sex offenders with an intellectual disability. *Sexual Abuse: A Journal of Research and Treatment, 16,* 381–392.

Langdon, P.E., Maxted, H. & Murphy, G.H. (2007). An exploratory evaluation of the Ward and Hudson Offending Pathways Model with sex offenders who have intellectual disabilities. *Journal of Intellectual and Developmental Disabilities, 32,* 94–105.

Lindsay, W.R. (2002). Research and literature on sex offenders with intellectual and developmental disabilities. *Journal of Intellectual Disability Research, 46* (Suppl. 1) 74–85.

Lindsay, W.R. (2005). Model underpinning treatment for sex offenders with mild intellectual disability: Current theories of sex offending. *Mental Retardation, 43,* 428–441.

Lindsay, W.R. (2006). Personality Disorder. In N. Bouras & G. Holt (Eds), *Psychiatric and behavioural disorders in developmental disabilities and mental retardation* (pp. 336–359). Cambridge: Cambridge University Press.

Lindsay, W.R., Elliot, S.F. & Astell, A. (2004). Predictors of sexual offence recidivism in offenders with intellectual disabilities. *Journal of Applied Research in Intellectual Disabilities, 17,* 299–305.

Lindsay, W.R., Hogue, T., Taylor, J.L., *et al.* (2006a). Two studies on the prevalence and validity of personality disorder in three forensic intellectual disability samples. *Journal of Forensic Psychiatry and Psychology, 17,* 485–506.

Lindsay, W.R., Hogue, T., Taylor, J.L., *et al.* (2008). Risk assessment in offenders with intellectual disabilities: A comparison across three levels of security. *International Journal of Offender Therapy and Comparative Criminology, 52,* 90–111.

Lindsay, W.R., Michie, A.M., Whitefield, E., *et al.* (2006c). Response patterns on the Questionnaire on Attitudes Consistent with Sexual Offending in groups of sex offenders with intellectual disability. *Journal of Applied Research in Intellectual Disabilities, 19,* 47–54.

Lindsay, W.R. & Skene, D.D. (2007). The Beck Depression Inventory II and the Beck Anxiety Inventory in people with intellectual disabilities: Factor analyses and group data. *Journal of Applied Research in Intellectual Disability, 20,* 401–408.

Lindsay, W.R., Smith, A.H.W., Law, J., *et al.* (2004). Sexual and non-sexual offenders with intellectual and learning disabilities: A comparison of characteristics, referral patterns and outcome. *Journal of Interpersonal Violence, 19,* 875–890.

Lindsay, W.R., Smith, A.H.W., Law, J., *et al.* (2002). A treatment service for sex offenders and abusers with intellectual disability: Characteristics of referrals and evaluation. *Journal of Applied Research in Intellectual Disability, 15,* 166–174.

Lindsay, W.R., Steele, L., Smith, A.H.W., *et al.* (2006b). A community forensic intellectual disability service: Twelve-year follow-up of referrals, analysis of referral patterns and assessment of harm reduction. *Legal & Criminological Psychology, 11,* 113–130.

Lindsay, W.R., Steptoe, L., Hogue, T.E., *et al.* (2007b). Internal consistency and factor structure of personality disorders in a forensic intellectual disability sample. *Journal of Intellectual & Developmental Disabilities*, *32*, 134–142.

Lindsay, W.R., Whitefield, E. & Carson, D. (2007a). An assessment for attitudes consistent with sexual offending for use with offenders with intellectual disability. *Legal & Criminological Psychology*, *12*, 55–68.

Luiselli, J.K. (2000). Presentation of paraphilias and paraphilia-related disorders in young adults with mental retardation: Two case profiles. *Mental Health Aspects of Developmental Disabilities*, *3*, 42–46.

Lunsky, Y., Frijters, J., Griffiths, D.M., *et al.* (2007). Sexual knowledge and attitudes of men with intellectual disabilities who sexually offend. *Journal of Intellectual and Developmental Disability*, *32*, 74–81.

McMillan, D., Hastings, R. & Coldwell, J. (2004). Clinical and actuarial prediction of physical violence in a forensic intellectual disability hospital: A longitudinal study. *Journal of Applied Research in Intellectual Disabilities*, *17*, 255–266.

McMurran, M., Fyffe, S., McCarthy, L. *et al.* (2001). Stop and think!: Social problem-solving therapy with personality disordered offenders. *Criminal Behaviour and Mental Health*, *11*, 273–285.

Michie, A.M., Lindsay, W.R., Martin, V. & Grieve, A. (2006). A test of counterfeit deviance: A comparison of sexual knowledge in groups of sex offenders with intellectual disability and controls. *Sexual Abuse: A Journal of Research and Treatment*, *18*, 271–279.

Morey, L.C. (1988). The categorical representation of personality disorder: A cluster analysis of DSM III-R personality features. *Journal of Abnormal Psychology*, *97*, 314–321.

Naik, B.I., Gangadharan, S.K. & Alexander, R.T. (2002). Personality disorders in learning disability – the clinical experience. *British Journal of Developmental Disabilities*, *48*, 95–100.

Noble, J.H. & Conley, R.W. (1992). Toward an epidemiology of relevant attributes. In R.W. Conley, R. Luckasson & G. Bouthilet (Eds), *The criminal justice system and mental retardation* (pp. 17–54). Baltimore, MD: Paul Brookes Publishing.

Novaco, R.W. (1994). Anger as a risk factor for violence among the mentally disordered. In J. Monahan & H.J. Steadman (Eds), *Violence in mental disorder: Developments in risk assessment*. Chicago: University of Chicago Press.

Novaco, R.W. (2003). *The Novaco Anger Scale and Provocation Inventory Manual (NAS-PI)*. Los Angeles: Western Psychological Services.

Novaco, R.W. & Taylor, J.L. (2004). Assessment of anger and aggression in offenders with developmental disabilities. *Psychological Assessment*, *16*, 42–50.

Nussbaum, D., Collins, M., Cutler, J., *et al.* (2002). Crime type and specific personality indices: Cloninger's TCI impulsivity, empathy and attachment subscales in non-violent, violent and sexual offenders. *American Journal of Forensic Psychology*, *20*, 23–56.

Parry, C. & Lindsay, W.R. (2003). Impulsiveness as a factor in sexual offending by people with mild intellectual disability. *Journal of Intellectual Disability Research*, *47*, 483–487.

Power, M., Champion, L. & Aris, S.J. (1988). The development of a measure of social support: The Significant Others Scale (SOS). *British Journal of Clinical Psychology*, *27*, 349–358.

Quinsey, V.L., Book, A. & Skilling, T.A. (2004). A follow-up of deinstitutionalised men with intellectual disabilities and histories of antisocial behaviour. *Journal of Applied Research in Intellectual Disabilities*, *17*, 243–254.

Quinsey, V.L., Harris, G.T., Rice, M.E. & Cormier, C.A. (2005). *Violent offenders, appraising and managing risk* (2nd edn). Washington DC: American Psychological Association.

Sjöstedt, G. & Långström, N. (2002). Assessment of risk for criminal recidivism among rapists: A comparison of four different measures. *Psychology, Crime and Law*, *8*, 25–40.

Spielberger, C.D. (1996). *State-Trait Anger Expression Inventory Professional Manual*. Florida: Psychological Assessment Resources Inc.

Steptoe, L., Lindsay, W.R., Forrest, D. & Power, M. (2006). Quality of life and relationships in sex offenders with intellectual disability. *Journal of Intellectual and Developmental Disabilities*, *31*, 13–19.

Taylor, J.L., Novaco, R.W., Guinan, C. & Street, N. (2004). Development of an imaginal provocation test to evaluate treatment for anger problems in people with intellectual disabilities. *Clinical Psychology and Psychotherapy*, *11*, 233–246.

Thornton, D. (2002). Constructing and testing a framework for dynamic risk assessment. *Sexual Abuse: A Journal of Research and Treatment*, *14*, 139–153.

Thornton, D., Mann, R., Webster, S. *et al.* (2003). Distinguishing and combining risks for sexual and violent recidivism. *Annals of the New York Academy of Sciences*, *989*, 225–235.

Ward, T. & Hudson, S.M. (1998). A model of the relapse process in sexual offenders. *Journal of Interpersonal Violence*, *13*, 700–725.

Ward, T. & Hudson, S.M. (2000). A self-regulation model of the relapse prevention process. In D.R. Laws, S.M. Hudson & T. Ward (Eds), *Remaking relapse prevention with sex offenders: A source book* (pp. 79–101). Thousand Oaks: Sage.

Ward, T., Johnston, I. & Marshall, W.L. (1998). Cognitive distortions in sex offenders: An integrative review. *Clinical Psychology Review*, *17*, 479–507.

Wish, J.R., McCombs, K.F. & Edmonson, B. (1979). *The socio-sexual knowledge and attitudes test*. Wood Dale, IL: Stoelting Company.

14

The Peaks: Assessing Sex Offenders in a Dangerous and Severe Personality Disorders Unit

TODD E. HOGUE

INTRODUCTION

The aim of this chapter is to detail the strategy being used for the assessment of sexual offenders within the Peaks, a specialist unit for the treatment of personality disordered individuals within a high security hospital setting. As such it is important to have an understanding of the type of population that is likely to be treated within the unit; a conceptual understanding of how factors related to personality disorder and risk are addressed within the unit and then how the strategy for assessing the needs of sexual offenders fits within that context.

Within England and Wales the provision of forensic mental health services for individuals who have a personality disorder has been very limited. Historically, classification as 'psychopathically disordered' under the Mental Health Act (1983), often with a corresponding label of 'untreatable', has led to an exclusion from services rather than a route to provision. It is only during the past five years that there has been the political impetus to develop specific services for those with a personality disorder. The guidance *Personality disorder: No longer a diagnosis of exclusion* published by the National Institute for Mental Health in England (2003) has acted as the basis for the development of non-forensic services for people with personality disorders. At the same time, the Dangerous and Severe Personality Disorder (DSPD) Programme had been the focus of recent Home Office developments relating to personality disordered individuals within forensic settings.

Assessment and Treatment of Sex Offenders: A Handbook. Edited by Anthony Beech, Leam Craig and Kevin Browne. © John Wiley & Sons Ltd, 2009.

The DSPD Programme (www.dspdprogramme.gov.uk) has guided the piloting of new services for individuals thought to be of a high risk (dangerous) and with severe personality disorder which is linked to their risk. Bell *et al.* (2003) and Sizmar and Noutch (2006) provide an overview of the initiative while the DSPD Planning and Delivery Guide (DSPD Programme, 2005) provides factual information about the delivery of DSPD services in high security settings. There was considerable initial controversy regarding establishing these kinds of services and concerns over the types of individuals who might be treated within them (e.g., Pilgrim, 2002; Royal, 2002). Although concerns over the possibility that DSPD services will be over-inclusive in detaining individuals there is little known about the types of individuals who will be detained in such services.

The DSPD Planning and Delivery Guide (DSPD Programme, 2005) states the general criteria for inclusion in a DSPD unit as:

- He is more likely than not to commit an offence that might be expected to lead to serious physical or psychological harm from which the victim would find it difficult or impossible to recover; and,
- He has a severe disorder of personality; and,
- There is a link between the disorder and the risk of offending.

Decisions about suitability are informed by a structured assessment process where the general criteria have been operationalised through the use of a number of structured assessment tools to guide decisions regarding the level of risk and severity of personality disorder. For risk, the processes used include the Historical Clinical Risk Management-20 (HCR-20; Webster *et al.*, 1997), Violence Risk Scale (VRS; Wong & Gordon, 2000), Static-99 (Hanson & Thornton, 2000) and Risk Matrix-2000 (RM2000; Thornton *et al.*, 2003). The working definition of severe personality disorder used by the DSPD Programme suggests an individual has severe personality disorder if they have any of the following: (1) a PCL-R score of 30 or more, (2) a PCL-R score of 25–29 inclusive and one DSM-IV personality disorder diagnosis, other than antisocial personality disorder, or (3) two or more DSM-IV diagnoses.

THE POPULATION WITHIN THE PEAKS

The Peaks is located within the Rampton Hospital, one of three high security forensic hospitals in England. Although it was expected that the DSPD criteria would select a fairly heterogeneous population with a wide range of different clinical and risk-related needs, there was little objective evidence of what the population would consist of prior to its initial opening. The Peaks has now been open for over two years and an increasingly clear picture is developing of the extent of the heterogeneity of the population.

Many individuals have a history of both sexual and violent offending so that the priority of treatment is not always clear. For the first 46 individuals admitted to the

Peaks, over half (51%) have sexually motivated index offence and in most of these cases the index offence included acts of violence. Almost all have a previous conviction for violence (92%) with approximately a third having previous convictions for sexual offences (32%) or arson (32%).

The group has a high average Hare PCL-R (Hare, 2003) score with 78% of the population having a score of 25 or more and 24% having a score of 30 or greater, which reflects at least in part the personality disorder admission criteria. All admissions satisfied the 'definite' or 'probable' criteria for antisocial personality disorder with a large proportion satisfying the 'definite' or 'probable' criteria for borderline personality disorder (64%). There are also a significant number of patients meeting the criteria for paranoid (49%) and narcissistic (27%) personality disorder.

What was unexpected was the extent to which the population presented with problems in specific areas of neuropsychological functioning. Just over a third of the population had assessed Intelligence Quotients (IQs) in the extremely low or borderline range (35.5%) (IQ < 79). Neuropsychological testing highlighted a range of problems with large proportions of the population presenting problems with memory (38%), attention (27%), executive functioning (33%) and language (16%). In fact over half of the population (61%) present with one area of functioning in the bottom fifth percentile of the distribution. In addition the population presents with a wide range of other clinical needs including affective, behavioural and cognitive disorders.

A large proportion (81%) of those admitted have a history of suicide attempts or episodes of self-harm. Similarly a high proportion of new admissions have self-harmed since being admitted to the Peaks. While there is an active risk of suicide or self-harm, clinical interventions are targeted at managing self-destructive behaviour over interventions for other types of clinical problems.

The overall picture of the initial population within the Peaks is that of a heterogeneous population with a diversity of different clinical and criminological needs. Most of the individuals admitted to the unit have been deemed as failing in previous treatment attempts, rejected from participating, or found to be unwilling to engage in the process. Often in other services, these individuals would have been considered to be 'untreatable'.

THE PEAKS APPROACH TO TREATMENT

By definition, all the patients within the Peaks have a personality disorder or psychopathy. Given the complex and heterogeneous nature of the population's needs, a range of different interventions are likely to be needed to address the needs of the patient group (Livesley, 2001, 2003). Livesley (2001) suggests that a meta-theoretical model is necessary to systematically incorporate the range of different models and theoretical inputs that are necessary with such a personality disordered patient group. The philosophical and theoretical underpinnings of the Peaks have been described elsewhere (Hogue *et al.*, 2007). The general ethos of the unit has a considerable impact on the approach taken to the assessment and treatment of sexual offenders within the unit. In particular, the unit takes a motivational perspective where motivating and engaging the individual in their treatment is central, and it is recognised that due to the diverse needs of the patient group, an individually tailored approach to assessment and treatment is the most appropriate (Blackburn, 2004).

Within the unit, the treatment of personality disorder is seen from a biopsychosocial perspective (Livesley, 2001; Sperry, 2003) with assessments and treatment interventions reflecting this. It is recognised that the treatment provided involves multiple domains of pathology (Livesley, 2001) and that the lower the level of 'treatability,' the greater the need to combine and integrate treatment modalities and approaches (Sperry, 2003). It is important that individuals are assessed regarding their amenability to treatment (Sperry, 2003) and that a central focus of the assessment and treatment process is focused on developing and maintaining a positive level of motivation and a collaborative relationship as part of the therapeutic process (Jones, 2002; Livesley, 2003; Sainsbury, Krishnan & Evans, 2004). Developing such a therapeutic alliance with personality disordered individuals may be one of the most difficult parts of the therapeutic process (Benjamin, 1993). As such there is a focus on engaging and motivating the individual to engage in the collaborative process from the start of the initial assessment through until the completion of therapeutic interventions. Although our approach comes from a personality disorder perspective, the underlying principles are the same in relation to sex offender assessment and treatment (see Shingler & Mann, 2006).

Sperry (2003) points out that effective treatment with personality disordered individuals is likely to be tailored to their specific needs and that the more it is tailored, the more likely treatment is to respond to specific client factors. This individualised approach is consistent with the integrated approach to treatment proposed by Livesley (2001, 2003), which strongly influences the approach within the unit. Although there is recognition that there may be core difficulties resulting from the manifestation of the personality disorder, the specific needs will vary on an individual basis. To accommodate these differences the model of working within the unit is to focus on the individualised needs of each patient and to identify a treatment pathway that is likely to address their specific treatment needs, taking into consideration clinical presentation, motivation and responsivity factors and criminogenic needs. As such, an individualised approach based on a functional analysis of need is used to inform treatment planning (Hogue et al., 2007; Howells, Day & Thomas-Peters, 2004). Consistent with this individualised approach a single case model is promoted in the first instance as the most viable way to assess and monitor clinical change with the population, at least in this early stage of implementation (Davies, Howells & Jones, 2007).

CLINICAL STRATEGY

As previously indicated the Peaks utilises an individualised model of assessing and treating patients within the unit. Hogue et al. (2007) provides a general overview to the functioning of the Peaks and the processes which are used to underpin ongoing clinical work. Although the approach to treatment within the Peaks had always been strongly influenced by the work of Livesley (2001, 2003) there has not been an explicit attempt to match the treatment pathway utilised within the unit to a particular treatment model. Following a recent review of the provision of assessment and treatment within the unit, it was decided to develop the service more explicitly in line with a phased model, which integrates the types of clinical needs presented by the individual with the stage and focus of their care within the unit. This has a potentially significant impact on the assessment and treatment of sexual offenders within the unit as they should all, at the point of referral to the sex offender programme, be at a similar stage in their treatment pathway. Jones (2007) describes in detail specific modifications used to accommodate responsivity issues when undertaking sex offender treatment with such a personality disordered population.

A brief description of the clinical strategy that is used (see Table 14.1) will help the reader understand where sex offender treatment fits within the treatment pathway, and also the impact that this structure has on the assessment process within the unit. Livesley (2003) argues that a five-phase strategy can be used to structure intervention strategies with personality disordered individuals. Within the Peaks, this structure is being used to focus the treatment planning that is undertaken and to allow for a clear understanding of what the needs of the patient and focus of interventions are at different stages of treatment.

Stage One: Assessment – Know What You Need

Most patients will start at the assessment stage when admitted to the Peaks. The focus at this initial stage is on containing affective and behavioural instability and undertaking a comprehensive assessment of the individual's needs. The main goals at this stage are similar to Livesley's *containment* phase in treatment, with the focus being to better understand the patient's needs. During this stage, the core DSPD assessments and a comprehensive assessment of clinical needs and risk is undertaken, as described later. This stage would be consistent with the identification of an individual's needs from within the risk, needs, responsivity model (Andrews & Bonta, 2003).

Stage Two: Personality – Manage Yourself

Following the assessment stage, patients move into stage two where the focus is on personality issues. At this stage, the core clinical targets are related to a reduction in symptom behaviour and improved self-control. This matches Livesley's (2003) control and regulation phase in treatment. Although treatment for each person is individualised, some general assumptions are made about the typical model of progress. At this stage treatment interventions include Dialectical Behaviour Therapy (DBT) (Linehan, 1993) and Cognitive Analytic Therapy (CAT) (Ryle, 1995; Ryle & Kerr, 2002) as well as participation in community meetings (Dolan, Warren & Norton. 1997; Lees, Manning & Rawlings, 1999) and undertaking problem solving and other

Table 14.1 The Peaks: Therapeutic strategy

Time	Therapeutic Stage	Targets	Therapeutic Intervention	Planned Environment
Needs based	**Pre-therapy: SAFETY:** [Be safe] Focus on the management of extreme manifestations of behaviour which pose a threat to self or others	• **Ensure safety of patients and staff** • **Manage inappropriate high risk behaviour** • **Goals to move to stage 1 assessment or reintegrate at appropriate point in treatment pathway**	• **Contingency Management** • **Individual interventions (e.g., CBT, CAT etc.)** • **Motivational Interviewing** • **Psychologically-Informed Relationship Management**	**HDU** • Highest levels security & observation • Externalised behaviour control/management • Room-based • Strict boundary management • Ethos: Psychological support of staff
0–6 months	**Stage 1: ASSESSMENT:** [Know what you need] Focus on assessment of need and the containment of affective and behavioural instability while engaging the patient in the therapeutic process	• **Contain affective and behavioural instability** • **Assessment of current and future need** • **Initiate therapeutic participation** • **Form therapeutic alliance** • **Motivation-engagement**	• **Orientation Group** • **Men Talking** • **Coping Skills** • **Therapeutic Assessment Process** • **Motivation/engagement** • **Formulation (e.g., CBT, CAT etc.)**	**Assessment Ward** • High levels security & observation • Mainly externalised behaviour control • Ward-based • Strong boundary management • Psychological assessment of need • Ethos: Engagement/motivation – initial therapeutic alliance
6 months – 2 years	**Stage 2: PERSONALITY:** [Manage yourself] Focus on control and regulation related to the reduction of symptoms and improved self-regulation of affect and impulses to ensure ability to partake in therapy	• **Control and regulation to reduce symptoms** • **Develop cognitive and interpersonal skills** • **Improve self-regulation, interpersonal interactions and impulse control**	• **DBT: Stabilise/skill deficits** • **CAT: Emotional, cognitive, relationship and self problems** • **Thinking skills/problem solving etc.** • **Social learning therapy meetings** • **Individual therapy: e.g., CBT, CAT Schema etc.**	**Treatment Ward (Main)** • Group and individual therapy • Ward- and CRB-based • Focus on current coping and interpersonal behaviour • Limited patient autonomy • Ethos: Managing current affect and behaviour & develop therapeutic alliance
2–4 years	**Stage 3: OFFENDING:** [Manage your future] Focus to change the cognitive, affective and situational factors contributing to problem behaviour with an emphasis on future offending and risk behaviour	• **Exploration and change of cognitive, affective and situational factors contributing to long-term problem behaviour** • **Focus: offending and long-term problematic behaviours**	• **Violence programme** • **Sex offence programme** • **Substance misuse** • **Trauma work** • **Address long-term problems through CBT/Schema/CAT, Psychodynamic, Music therapy etc.**	**Treatment Ward (Continuing)** • Group and individual therapy • Focus on future offence/problem behaviour • Higher patient autonomy • Ethos: Addressing long-term needs maintaining therapeutic alliance
4 years +	**Stage 4: TRANSITION:** [Move on] Focus on developing and implementing a new, more integrated, adaptive sense of self in preparation of movement forward	• **Integration and synthesis** • **Promote adaptive functioning** • **Develop, practice and display long-terms skills for managing offending/behaviour** • **Planning transition from the Peaks**	• **Relapse prevention** • **Therapeutic community principles?** • **Rehabilitation work** • **Good lives** • **Transitional visits**	**Transition Ward** • Practical focus on transition planning • Increased patient autonomy • Ethos: Addressing issues relating to moving forwards, endings and transition

Staff supervision, training, and support

Formulation informed application of therapeutic interventions Cross unit approaches: e.g., Neuropsychology, MDT working, unit ethos skills-building interventions focused at improving the individual's ability to manage themselves.

At this stage, treatment is focused on improving self-management skills, and addressing difficulties related to affect and impulse control. Such difficulties often result in having a negative effect on the individual's ability to interact effectively with others and to successfully engage in treatment (Hogue & Jones, 1999). Treatment at this stage can be seen as focusing on responsivity issues within the risk, needs and responsivity model (Andrews & Bonta, 2003). Although it can be argued some of the targets addressed at this stage are non-criminogenic needs, the level of affective-regulation and impulse control problems within a severely personality disordered population are such that without addressing them the individual, "cannot, does not, or will not focus on treatment to reduce criminogenic needs" (Ogloff & Davis, 2004, p. 233).

Many of the clinical needs addressed at this stage within the context of the treatment pathway for individuals with a personality disorder are consistent with vulnerability factors in an aetiological model of risk (Beech & Ward, 2004), dysfunctional mechanisms within Ward and Siegert's (2002) pathways model or more recent mapping of traits as vulnerability factors within the context of understanding risk in sexual offenders (Ward, Polaschek & Beech, 2006). The point is that when working with a group of severely personality disordered individuals most of the trait/stable dynamic factors are likely to be present and the assessment and treatment of these factors is part of a general model of addressing the needs of individuals with personality disorders (Livesley, 2001, 2003, 2007; Sperry, 2003) rather than specific to the treatment of sexual offenders as such.

Stage Three: Offending – Manage Your Future

Consistent with Livesley's (2003) exploration and change phase, the third stage of treatment within the Peaks relates to focusing on changing the cognitive, affective and situational factors related to problem behaviours. Within the context of a high-risk personality disordered population, this phase focuses on changing the long-term problem behaviours and offending behaviour which led to them being in DSPD as a high-risk individual. High-risk offence-related behaviour is managed throughout the individual's treatment within the Peaks. However, at an earlier stage in the programme the focus of interventions is primarily on managing any violent, sexual or offence paralleling behaviour (Jones, 2004). The development of sufficient intra- and interpersonal support assists the individual in coping with the potential distress and related difficulties of engaging in offence-specific work.

Within the risk-needs responsivity model this stage concentrates on the long-term risk that the individual presents through addressing the criminogenic risk factors related to both their offence history and the psychological deficits related to dynamic risk factors. Individuals are likely at this stage to undertake work to modify maladaptive repetitive patterns of thinking through schema work (Young, Klosko &

Weishar, 2003) or further CAT therapy (Ryle, 1995; Ryle & Kerr, 2002). Although schema-based work was initially seen as specific to the treatment of personality disorder, this is increasingly seen as important within the context of sex offender treatment (Mann & Shingler, 2006).

It is at this stage where individuals undergo the sex offender specific assessments and the pre-treatment assessment process. The individual would then undertake the Sex Offender Group and related therapy as part of their treatment pathway. Jones (2007) presents the types of modifications to traditional sexual offender programmes used within the Peaks. Following the treatment process they are reassessed with respect to clinical change. The critical point is that by the time an individual gets to this stage in their treatment pathway they will have undertaken a range of therapeutic interventions aimed at addressing some of the core interpersonal deficits and vulnerabilities related to their personality disorder. Such clinical interventions should already have addressed, or at least partially addressed, a number of dynamic factors seen to be related to sex offence risk (Beech & Ward, 2004; Hanson, 2006; Ward, Polaschek & Beech, 2006) (e.g., impulsivity, intimacy deficits, etc).

Stage Four: Transition – Move On

The final stage in the clinical strategy focuses on the *integration and synthesis* stage of treatment (Livesley, 2003). The focus is on maintaining and integrating and the skills and changes made with the view to putting them into practice in the future. The Good Lives Model (Ward & Brown, 2004; Ward & Stewart, 2003) and related principles are embedded throughout the treatment pathway. At this stage the focus is on the development of an adapted relapse plan (Laws & Ward, 2006) and a positive approach to adaptive functioning when the individual moves from the Peaks.

PD/RISK RELATIONSHIP

Although the therapeutic orientation of the Peaks is focused from a personality disorder perspective, this is not to say that criminogenic needs and the risks that the patient presents are not explicitly addressed as part of their treatment. Increasingly both stable (e.g., intimacy deficits, sexual self-regulation, etc.) and acute (e.g., substance use, negative mood, etc.) dynamic risk factors (Hanson, 2006; Hanson & Harris, 2000) have been recognised as important factors in predicting risk. Recently developed risk assessments such as the SARN (Mann et al., unpublished; Webster *et al.*, 2006) incorporate judgements about dynamic factors which essentially represent the interpersonal functioning of the individual. Such psychological dispositions or 'trait' factors are argued as having an important mediating role in understanding the influence of triggering and contextual events on the level of risk (Beech & Ward, 2004) while others argue that the measurement of such personality traits are central to developing an individually tailored risk assessment (Craig *et al.*, 2004). The argument has been made that most of the stable and acute dynamic risk factors map onto the areas of personality dysfunction represented in having a personality disorder and that intervening to address the personality disorder/dysfunction acts to change the level of dynamic risk presented by the individual (Hogue, 2005, 2006). This underlying principle that working to intervene with the personality disorder of the individual also acts to address the level of risk that the individual presents is central to the treatment model within the Peaks. The overall ethos of treatment within the Peaks is aimed at addressing general personality and risk factors with the offence-specific treatments aimed at addressing those additional specific personality and risk factors that apply for that individual.

ASSESSMENT WITHIN THE PEAKS

To understand the assessment process for sexual offenders within the Peaks, it is important to understand the range of other assessment processes which are generally undertaken and the extent to which this is used to inform the assessment process with sexual offenders.

It is important to stress the context of this initial assessment process and the extent to which it is intended to be a positive therapeutic experience for the patient. The aim throughout is to facilitate as collaborative assessment process as possible. Most of the patients sent to the Peaks have a history of treatment failure or rejection which makes them reluctant to engage in a new assessment process. Added to this, many of the patients arrive near to the time when otherwise they might be moving into the community and it is natural for them to be concerned about the consequence of obtaining a DSPD label and the potential indeterminate nature of their detention. Great efforts are made to ensure that the process is motivating to the patient with a focus on developing a good therapeutic relationship to maximise the quality of the assessment information (Jones, 2002). This approach also has the equally important potential of creating a positive experience for the patient of success in coping with a difficult process. A motivational, Good Lives Model (Ward & Stewart, 2003) approach is a central part of the ethos of the unit where the need to provide a motivational milieu for the start of the initial assessment process through to completion of an individual's treatment programme is seen as critical (Hogue et al., 2007).

THE CORE ASSESSMENT PROCESS

A comprehensive initial assessment is completed with all patients following admission to the Peaks (see Table 14.2). The assessment process is carried out by a multidisciplinary team. A central requirement of this initial assessment is to determine if the individual meets the DSPD criteria for admission to a DSPD unit. The Planning and Delivery Guide (DSPD Programme, 2005) outlines a number of different measures used to assess both risk and personality disorder which need to be undertaken as part of the initial assessment process. The intention is to ensure that a consistent approach is taken to making decisions regarding the risk, personality disorder and functional link decisions, which are critical for placement within the DSPD programme.

These initial assessments, along with a standardised set of background information, are collected on all patients within the Peaks. This *common data set* is intended to act as a set of standardised information to facilitate cross-site programme evaluation (DSPD Programme, 2005). The common data set consists of information relating to demographic factors, criminal history, risk factors in the form of standardised risk assessment measures, assessments of mental disorder including both Axis I and Axis II diagnosis and an assessment of PCL-R psychopathy. While the core DSPD assessment is sufficient to comment on risk and prevalence of personality disorder it does not provide sufficient information on the full range of clinical needs presented by the population. A set of additional assessment measures and processes are therefore undertaken as part of ongoing clinical work to identify the relevant treatment needs for the individual and to assist in making decisions regarding a suitable treatment pathway.

Responses to these measures provide a baseline level of psychological functioning and individual need. This information is used to assist in the overall formulation of their personality, offending and the links between the two. It identifies treatment needs and assists in identifying referrals for particular therapeutic interventions and the appropriate sequencing of interventions into an appropriate treatment pathway. These assessments are also used to monitor clinical change over time and evaluate the overall effectiveness of treatment within the Peaks. As such, a number of measures are repeated on an annual basis and information regarding treatment participation is recorded.

All of this clinical information and the accompanying formulation of treatment needs are available to those professionals providing the sex offender treatment programme within the unit. Given the treatment model that we are using where treatment needs are related to your stage in the clinical pathway, it would be expected that most individuals starting to engage in sex offence specific treatment would be some way along their treatment pathway where issues of affective control and self-regulation have already been identified and addressed as treatment targets.

SEX OFFENDER TREATMENT SUITABILITY

Sex offender treatment within the Peaks is undertaken as a multidisciplinary clinical activity with joint working throughout the process. As a result, both the agreed assessment process and the content of the therapeutic programme is a result of multidisciplinary planning. Facilitators are responsible for the collection and interpretation of the psychometric measures outlined and should liaise with ward staff regarding observational assessment of clinical progress throughout the programme. The psychophysiological and cognitive assessments of sexual interests are to be carried out by the phallometric technician within the Peaks unit.

Table 14.2 General assessment measures used within the Peaks

	DSPD Common Dataset Measures	Annual Re-administration
Risk	VRS – Violence Risk Scale	✓
	HCR-20	✓
	RM2000 – Risk Matrix 2000	
	Static-99	
	SARN – Structured Assessment of Risk and Need	
	PCL-R/PSL:SV	
Personality	IPDE – International Personality Disorder Examination	
	SCID I – Structured Clinical Interview DSM Axis I	
	WAI – Working Alliance Inventory	✓
	Combined TNA Measures	
General	PAI – Psychological Assessment Inventory	✓
Self-regulation	SPSI-R:S - Social Problem-Solving Inventory-Revised	
	Emotional Self-Regulation Scale & UPPS Impulsive Behaviour Scales	
	Trauma Symptom Index	
	STAXI – State Trait Anger Inventory	
Biological/Physical	NEO FFI – NEO Five Factor Inventory	
	TCI – Temperament and Character Inventory	✓
Interpersonal	Relationship Style Questionnaire	
	Circle – Chart of Interpersonal Reactions in Closed Living Environments	✓
	Working Alliance Inventory	✓
	Behavioural Rating of PD	✓
Core Beliefs	PICTS – Psychological Inventory of Criminal Thinking Scales	
	Schedule of imagined violence	
	Young Schema Questionnaire	
	BAS – Blame attribution inventory	
	TRRS – Treatment Readiness and Responsivity Scale	
Maladaptive Behaviour	DAST – Drug Abuse Screening Test	
	SADD – Short Alcohol Dependence Data	
	SUST – Substance Use Screening Tool	
	SCJ Risk – Structured Clinical Judgment: Risk (including HCR-20)	✓

(Continued)

Table 14.2 Continued

	DSPD Common Dataset Measures	Annual Re-administration
	Neuropsychology	
Intelligence	WAIS-III – Wechsler Adult Intelligence Test WTAR – Wechsler Test of Adult Reading	
Memory	AMIPB – Adult Memory and Information Processing Battery, Story Recall AMIPB – Adult Memory and Information Processing Battery, Figure Recall	
Attention	Trail making test (A and B) TEA – Test of Everyday Attention	
Executive	Stroop FAS – Verbal Fluency Test WCST – Wisconsin Card Sorting Test	
Speech and Language	SCOLP – Speed and Capacity of Language Processing Test (Vocabulary and Speed)	
Dissimulation	Rey 15 – Rey 15 Item Memory Test TOMMS	
Mood	HADS – Hospital Anxiety and Depression Scale	

As indicated earlier, it is assumed that patients being referred for sex offender treatment will be at the appropriate stage in their treatment pathway. By the time they are referred for assessment they should have completed the core DSPD assessments as well as the more comprehensive treatment needs analysis described earlier. These earlier assessments will have informed previous decisions regarding treatment planning and the patient is likely to be at the offence or manage your future stage of treatment input. It is envisaged that all patients requiring the SOG (Sex Offender Group) will have first engaged in therapeutic work related to the necessary skills and abilities to manage their affective stability. This is likely to include having participated in DBT or CAT with the expectation that they will have participated in and developed appropriate skills for affect regulation and problem solving such that they are able to apply these where necessary during participation in the sex offender group.

All of the previously undertaken assessments, formulations of treatment need based on these assessments and the reports of the individual's response to earlier interventions are used to inform the assessment for sex offender treatment. In addition, sex offender specific measures are collected in order to better understand the needs of the patient and to monitor treatment efficacy in terms of pre- and post-intervention measures.

The formal minimum criteria for inclusion on the Sex Offender Group are as follows:

- Has completed DBT group or similar group, focused on building skills;
- Has completed a treatment needs analysis incorporating a preliminary functional analysis of the index offence and any other significant sexual offending;
- Has completed an analysis of characteristic behaviour associated with personality disorder;
- Consider level of stability, e.g., level and type of self-harm, evidence of emotional regulation skills, seclusions and the ability to make use of group work settings.

A patient's overall suitability for the SOG is assessed using the following broad criteria, although this list is not exhaustive:

- Iatrogenic Effects: possible negative effects of participation like self-injury or increased suicide risk;
- Neuropsychological Deficits: to the extent that any deficits will limit the individual's ability to participate and or benefit from the intervention;
- Motivation: excessively low motivation may require additional motivational work to encourage the individual to participate;
- Paranoia: excessively paranoid individuals may find it particularly difficult to participate in group aspects of the programme, it may be necessary to consider medication or other interventions;
- Total denial of offence, to the extent that this impacts on their willingness and ability to participate;
- Other: there may in some cases be idiographic factors that impact on an individual's suitability for treatment.

THE ASSESSMENT MODEL

The assessment strategy for the Sex Offender Treatment Groups will take a four-tiered approach, designed to provide a comprehensive assessment and evaluation system. This is based on four key areas:

- Self-report, as identified by psychometric instruments;
- Observational, as identified by ward reports and other assessment instruments;
- Psychophysiological, as identified by phallometric assessment;
- Cognitive, as identified by cognitive and neuropsychological tests.

Assessments from all four areas are administered prior to group work, and repeated afterwards to evaluate clinical change. The use of multiple information sources has been utilised in the assessment of treatment need for psychopathic offenders (Chromis, 2005) and an accurate assessment of personality disorder (Spitzer, 1983). It is believed that by adopting a multi-domain approach, a more comprehensive and accurate assessment is achieved.

THE STRUCTURED ASSESSMENT OF RISK AND NEED (SARN)

The Structured Assessment of Risk and Need (SARN; see Webster *et al.*, 2006) is a standardised needs assessment process used within the HM Prison Service. The SARN covers four domains: sexual interest, distorted attitudes, social and emotional functioning, and self-management. The structure of the SARN is useful in assisting a formulation of the needs of the individual and has been used as part of the evaluation of treatment programmes which provides useful information on the treatment of comparable populations (Beech *et al.*, 2005). Although the overall assessment process within the Peaks contains additional assessment information than within the Prison Service (e.g., neuropsychological testing, different observational information, etc.) the overall structure of utilising the four domain model is maintained. Briefly the four domains include the following: Domain One relates to *sexual interests* and includes assessment of sexual preoccupation, sexual preference for children, sexual preference for violence and other offence-related socially deviant sexual interests. Domain Two relates to distorted attitudes and beliefs regarding sexual offending and includes assessments of adversarial sexual attitudes, sexual entitlement, child abuse supportive beliefs, rape supportive beliefs, and beliefs that women are deceitful. Domain Three covers social and emotional functioning and includes assessments of inadequacy, grievance thinking and lack of emotional intimacy. Domain Four relates to general problems in self-management and includes assessments of life-style impulsivity, poor cognitive problem solving, and poor emotional control.

Use of the SARN is part of the common DSPD dataset (DSPD Programme, 2005) and is used within the Peaks as part of the standardised assessment process for those individuals with a history of sexual offending. As such, the SARN, and the related four problem domains model, help to structure the way in which sex offence assessments are undertaken in the Peaks, including the pre- and post-assessment of change following completion of treatment. The following description of the assessment pathway and the information collected within the assessment process should be read with the use of the SARN assessment structure in mind.

THE ASSESSMENT PATHWAY

A critical aspect of the assessment process is to determine the suitability of the individual to the type of treatment offered and the extent to which individual factors may interfere with or limit their ability to engage effectively in therapy. This is particularly important with this client group given the severity of their personality disorder and the prevalence of neuropsychological problems. The basis assessment pathway for assessing sexual offenders within the unit is shown in Figure 14.1.

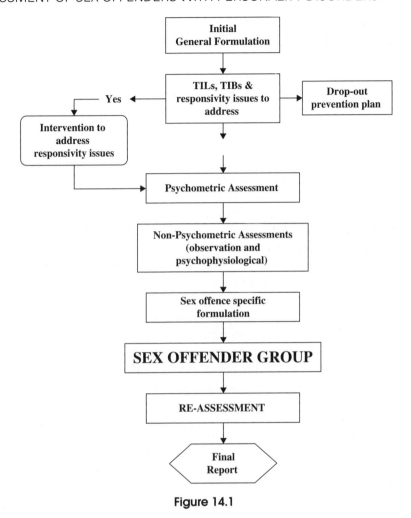

Figure 14.1

INITIAL GENERAL FORMULATION

For all patients, a functional analysis of their sexual offending behaviour should have been undertaken as part of their ongoing clinical work prior to referral for the SOG. Prior to undertaking any sex offence-specific assessment, facilitators are advised to review existing formulations carried out during the earlier assessment and treatment process. Particular attention should be paid to formulations relating to offence-related behaviours and responsivity issues. The intention is to develop as comprehensive a picture as possible related to the responsivity needs of the individual. To the extent that clear information and a related formulation are not available on these issues then it is the responsibility of the facilitator to develop them prior to formal assessment.

RESPONSIVITY ISSUES: ASSESSMENT OF THERAPY INTERFERING BEHAVIOURS (TIBs) AND LIMITATIONS (TILs)

The first step of the assessment process is to consider the responsivity issues applicable for each individual case. As indicated earlier this is a complex population with a wide range of clinical needs. Jones (Chapter 22, this volume) highlights the importance of considering responsivity issues and modifying treatment interventions to accommodate the responsivity issues of a personality disordered population. This is important in terms of ensuring continued participation in treatment and limiting the likelihood to which interventions may have iatrogenic effects (Jones, 2007).

Therapy interfering behaviours (TIBs) have been coined as those behaviours that an individual presents which limits their ability to suitably engage in the treatment process. The most common TIBs may involve a lack of motivation, denial or minimisation of offending, or particular traits of personality disorder (such as paranoia). Such therapy interfering behaviours must be identified prior to group treatment. The information from the completed treatment needs analysis and information from the ward psychologist regarding current functioning should be sought to provide an overview of possible therapy interfering behaviours. Such difficulties may include the potential for 'borrowing' offence patterns from other patients, or the adoption of others' fantasies. Other examples of TIBs include: dropping out; fabricated engagement; inability to emotionally engage; therapy contingent change (adapting to the therapeutic context but failing to generalise); active and passive deception; denial; and problematic behaviour with peers in group-based interventions.

It is important that those factors regarded as therapy interfering limitations (TILs) are also identified for each individual patient. TILs include difficulties with memory; problem solving; attention and concentration; speech and language; and intellectual functioning. The assessment is primarily neuropsychological in nature, and many test results are audited from files from the first stage assessment process. Cognitive profiles may be generated for individual patients to identify cognitive support needs. In addition, some patients may have been assessed regarding other key neuropsychological factors, such as emotional regulation and processing, and these are also woven into any formulation and treatment plan where available. Assessment of learning and memory for session content will be conducted with each patient through the use of a free-recall model, and it is planned that this work will be carried out by either facilitators at the beginning of each individual session, or by nursing staff on the ward.

DROP-OUT PREVENTION PLAN

This plan should take the form of a contract devised between facilitator and patient identifying all possible TILs and TIBs that may influence motivation and responsivity during group treatment. Identified within this plan are the steps that the facilitators and individual patients will take should TIBs or TILs be interfering with the patient's ability to engage in, or stay in, the therapeutic process. By clearly identifying possible future difficulties and the corresponding steps that need to be taken should difficulties arise, a sense of therapeutic collaboration is reinforced between patient and facilitator. Most importantly there is an a priori plan available as to what steps should be taken to maximise the likelihood that the individual patient will be maintained in therapy.

THE SELF-REPORT DOMAIN

Psychometric Tests

A series of self-report measures are used as part of the standardised assessment process. The standard battery of psychometric assessments used within the Prison Service has been adopted as the core of the self-report assessment battery. A detailed description of these measures is outlined in HMPS Revised Psychometric Assessment Battery Manual: Version 3 (Offending Behaviour Programmes Unit, 2004) and a list of the specific sex offender assessments used can be seen in Table 14.3. These measures are intended

Table 14.3 Self-report measures used for sex offender specific assessment

Measure	Source
Self-Esteem	Thornton (1995)
Impulsivity	Eysenck & Eysenck (1978)
Ruminations	Capara (1986)
Interpersonal Reactivity Index	Davis (1980)
Locus of Control	Levenson (1974)
Emotional Control	Roger & Najarian (1989)
Relationship Style Questionnaire	Dutton et al. (1994)
Paulhus Deception Scales: The Balanced Inventory of Desirable Responding	Paulhus (1984)
Social Problem-Solving Inventory-Revised	D'Zurilla, Nezu & Maydeu-Olivares (2002)
Sex Offence Attitudes Questionnaire	Items from OBPU and Hogue, T.E. (1994)
Sex with Children is Justifiable Questionnaire	Marshall (1995)
Women are deceitful	OBPU, unpublished
Rape myths	Burt (1980)
Entitlement to sex	Hanson, Grizzarelli & Scott (1994)
Openness to women	OBPU, unpublished
Openness to men	OBPU, unpublished
Children and Sex Questionnaire	Beckett (1987)
Hypermasculinity Inventory	Mosher & Sirken (1984)
Relapse Prevention Interview	Beckett et al. (1997)
UCLA Emotional Loneliness Scale	Russell, Peplan & Cutrona (1980).
WHO Quality of Life Measure	The World Health Organization
Groups Environment Scale	Moos (2002)
Multiphasic Sex Inventory	Nichols & Molinder (1984)
Sex Offence Information Questionnaire	Hogue (1998)
Sexual Interest Card Sort	Abel & Becker, 1985

to cover the four problem domains identified within the SARN as well as providing additional information specific to individual case formulation and management.

While most of the self-report assessment measures will be administered just prior to the individual engaging in the Sex Offender Group. However, some measures will have been previously collected as part of the initial DSPD assessment and sex offender screening process and will not be re-administered if a limited amount of time (under six months) has passed and the clinical view is that the measure would still represent the functioning of the individual.

Other Assessments

A number of other self-report-based measures are also used within the assessment process. In keeping with a single case design methodology, repertory grid, diary keeping and the monitoring of ideographically factors are also included in the assessment process.

Repertory grids (Fransella & Bannister, 1977; Horley, 2003; Houston, 1998) are useful ways in which to assess a patient's relationships and offence behaviour. Some patients will have completed a 'relationship' grid during Treatment Needs Analysis or as part of an earlier stage of therapy. This earlier relationship grid may be used or it may be decided that it is necessary to carry out another 'relationship' grid prior to sex offender treatment. In addition, an offence-focused grid should be conducted looking specifically at factors relevant to the individual's index offence and their history or pattern of sexual offending.

Diary keeping will be used where deemed appropriate and related to the specific needs of the patient. This is most often used in the case of patients being required to keep a log of their moods, masturbatory fantasies or other sexual behaviour or offence-related thoughts and behaviours. The general model of use is for the assessor to work with the patient in a collaborative manner to identify the relevant factors to monitor and to design the diary in conjunction with the patient which can then be reviewed routinely during individual sessions.

OBSERVATIONAL DOMAIN

Ward Behaviour

It is important that in addition to the observations made within the group programme individuals are observed within the ward context and their ongoing daily behaviour. Some of this is done within the context of weekly ongoing individual sessions that are undertaken by one of the group facilitators to support and extend the work being undertaken within the group-based programme. The model being used here is similar to that of Dialectical Behaviour Therapy (Linehan, 1993) with group-based training and individual support aimed at maintaining the individual in treatment and strengthening individual learning points. This also allows for individual observation of how the individual is functioning outside the group and the extent to which any clinical changes appear to be generalising to their ward-based behaviour. To assist in this process there will be a training programme for ward staff to increase their understanding of the relevant ongoing behaviours and attitudes that should be fed back to group facilitators as part of an ongoing assessment.

A structured recording of ongoing ward behaviour in the form of the Daily Behaviour Rating Scale (DBRS) is also used (Beeley & Hogue, 2006; Hogue & Samuda, 1999). This is a formalised system of structuring the nursing observations of the patient's ongoing behaviour which is undertaken twice daily. Although this system allows for the recording of violent and other behaviour, the most relevant item within this context is the recording of any observed sexualised behaviour. Nursing staff rate the presence of sexualised behaviour, possible presence of less serious sexualised behaviour, or no evidence of sexualised behaviour twice daily. This observational information of sexual behaviour is integrated into the assessment process and monitored over time as one measure of clinical change. In addition, formal systems of recording incidents (e.g., violence), security information and concerns, or periods of seclusion from other patients are also monitored.

Goal Attainment Scaling (GAS)

Although not strictly an observational measure, the Goal Attainment Scaling (GAS) system developed for use with sexual offenders (Hogue, 1994; Stirpe, Wilson & Long, 2001) is designed to structure facilitator's judgements about the ongoing behaviour and clinical presentation of individuals undertaking sexual offence treatment. Originally the GAS was focused on measuring nine clinical targets (e.g., acceptance of guilt, recognise cognitive distortions, etc.) and three engagements targets (disclose personal information, motivation to change behaviour, etc.). Each of the dimensions was rated on an anchored five-point scale rated from *very risky* (-2) to *very appropriate* ($+2$) with the minimum *acceptable* attitude or behaviour being rated zero. The GAS has been shown to be a useful system for monitoring treatment needs and change (Hogue, 1994; Stirpe, Wilson & Long, 2001). Four additional ratings have been added to the GAS to cover treatment areas thought specifically relevant for use with a personality disordered population and to match with the specific treatment targets of the programme (see Table 14.4). Using all available information to inform their ratings, programme facilitators rate the patient's functioning and presentation prior to, during and after treatment participation.

PSYCHOPHYSIOLOGICAL DOMAIN

The use of phallometric assessment, or penile plethysmography (PPG), has a long history of use in the assessment of sexual offenders. Essentially, phallometry allows

Table 14.4 Extended goal attainment scaling system for use in the Peaks

THE PEAKS UNIT: INDIVIDUAL CLINICAL RATING FORM – REVISED VERSION

NAME: _____ NUMBER: _____ DATE: _____

RATER: _____ GROUP & SESSION NUMBER: _____

Use the guideline below to rate the behaviour and attitudes of the offender during interview and/or therapy. Remember that a middle score of '0' represents the minimum acceptable behaviour/attitudes. Less than acceptable behaviour should be rated −2 or −1; better than acceptable performance should be rated +1 or +2.

	− 2 'VERY RISKY' ATTITUDE OR BEHAVIOUR	− 1 'RISKY' ATTITUDE OR BEHAVIOUR	0 MINIMUM 'ACCEPTABLE' ATTITUDE OR BEHAVIOUR	+1 'APPROPRIATE' ATTITUDE OR BEHAVIOUR	+2 VERY 'APPROPRIATE' ATTITUDE OR BEHAVIOUR	Enter a rating for each of the clinical scales
1) ACCEPTANCE OF GUILT FOR THE OFFENCE	Insists on his innocence, denies any participation in the offence	Minimises his role, attributes blame to victim, situation & others	Admits guilt and his role as charged	Fully admits guilt, exonerates victim of any blame or responsibility	Admits guilt, recognises deviant motivation for the offence	
2) SHOW INSIGHT INTO VICTIM ISSUES	No understanding of victim issues, sees little/no physical or mental stress/impact	Some understanding but does not fully understand extent of physical/mental harm	Shows good understanding of victim issues relating to sexual abuse	Understands full extent of mental and physical harm and related impact on life	Full understanding including long-term effects on victim's family, spouse etc.	
3) SHOW EMPATHY FOR THEIR VICTIMS	No understanding of the harm to victims, seen as unharmed or enjoying the abuse	Little understanding, rationalising victims coped OK, and are no worse for experience	Shows genuine empathy for the victims of his offence	Shows full empathy/understanding of the mental/physical harm to their victims	Shows full empathy/understanding, wishes to undo the long-term harm caused	
4) ACCEPT PERSONAL RESPONSIBILITY	Accepts little or no responsibility, blames victim, situation and others; does not see actions as deviant	Accepts partial responsibility claiming victim/situation also to blame, or claims 'one-off' situation	Accepts full responsibility for the offence and his behaviour	Accepts complete responsibility, sees need to seek help and change behaviour	Full responsibility, places no blame on victim, fully sees need to change to avoid offences	
5) RECOGNISE COGNITIVE DISTORTIONS	Totally fails to understand the role cognitive distortions play in his offending	Partially recognises cognitive distortions but only sees them as partially applicable	Recognises role of cognitive distortions relating to sexual offending behaviour	Recognises personal use of cognitive distortions, avoids/challenges CDs	Fully understands CDs, active change of current/past distortions, reoffence	
6) MINIMISE CONSEQUENCE	Fully minimises his role and any negative consequences	Recognises some effect but minimises his role or the effect of his offending	Does not minimise the effects of his offending	Does not minimise, thinks about the wide range of impact without minimisation	Does not minimise, actively accepts all the consequences of his offending	
7) UNDERSTAND LIFE-STYLE DYNAMICS	Sees no relationship between his life-style and his sexual offending	Has partial understanding of life-style and offence, but little/no need to change	Understands how his life-style relates to his offending	Recognises life-style dynamics, realises need to change in future	Recognises life-style dynamics, actively seeks realistic ways to change, as a must	
8) UNDERSTAND OFFENCE CYCLE	Denies the crime was anything more than a spontaneous act, no precursors/cycle	Unable to identify cycle, may claim lack of memory or only partially applicable	Recognises offence/deviant cycle and the relationship to his offending	Identifies cycle as related to his offence, begins thinking how to change cycle	Identifies cycle, actively seeks ways of interrupting cycle to avoid future offences	
9) IDENTIFY RELAPSE PREVENTION CONCEPTS	No understanding of relapse prevention concepts, unwilling to accept avoidance of HRTs and HRSs	Shows only partial or superficial understanding, cannot easily identify HRTs and HRSs	Shows a clear understanding of relapse prevention concepts as applied to sexual offending	Shows good understanding, able to actively relate concepts to his offence/release	Fully understands, able to understand proactive avoidance of HRTs & HRSs in the future	

10) DISCLOSE PERSONAL INFORMATION	Refuses to disclose personal information even if trivial, even when pressured	Reluctantly discloses personal information, which is usually trivial or superficial	Willing to disclose personal information as necessary	Willing to share most personal information and details	Openly shares and discusses intimate information in an open and receptive manner
11) PARTICIPATE IN TREATMENT	Does not participate in the group even when encouraged or cajoled to do so	Participates in group only when encouraged or cajoled to do so	Participates in group as required	Fully participates in the group, encourages other to do likewise	Actively participates, encourages others, seeks understanding beyond limit of group
12) MOTIVATION TO CHANGE BEHAVIOUR	Not motivated to change, no perceived genuine interest in changing behaviour	Motivation to change; inconsistent, transient or inappropriate reason to change	Motivated to change his behaviour	Well motivated to change in consistent and enduring manner for safety of others	Consistently well motivated to change, actively encourages others
13) UNDERSTAND OFFENCE-RELATED SCHEMA	No understanding of offence-related schema	Shows only partial or superficial understanding	Understands the schema related to his offending	Shows good understanding	Fully understands. Is able to demonstrate ability to manage his behaviour and identify triggers for core schemas
14) EMOTIONAL REGULATION	Completely unable to regulate emotional responses even with encouragement	Displays some ability to control emotional responses	Able to control emotional responses to acceptable degree	Able to control emotional responses to all circumstances	Consistently able to control emotional responses and understands antecedents to these responses
15) IDENTIFIES ANTECEDENTS	No understanding of offence antecedents	Shows only partial or superficial understanding of offence antecedents	Recognises the antecedents to his offending behaviour	Shows good understanding of offence antecedents	Fully understands; able to plan ahead to avoid or counter antecedents in future
16) STRATEGY FOR POSITIVE LIFESTYLE	Refuses/not motivated to consider positive lifestyle and prefers criminal lifestyle	Inconsistent motivation to adhere to or plan for positive lifestyle	Has discussed and understood strategy for positive lifestyle	Has discussed, understood and planned for positive lifestyle	Has planned for, and is attempting to adhere to, positive lifestyle

PLEASE NOTE: This form is used to assess the overall level of risk that a sexual offender presents in terms of the attitudes and behaviours that he has expressed. It is important that this form is completed by a trained member of the therapy team who knows the assessed individual well. For pre-treatment, rating should be done on the basis of assessment interview(s)/personal officer knowledge. Post treatment ratings should be completed by a member of the therapy teams who facilitated the individual's treatment group.

an individual's pattern of sexual arousal to be measured. Within the forensic context this is most often used to assess the extent to which an individual shows evidence of displaying inappropriate sexual interest, for example, sexual interest in children or preferential interest in coercive or forceful sex. Although there is a long history of the use of phallometric assessment this is not without concerns over the use and application of the process (see Kalmus & Beech, 2005; Marshall & Fernandez, 2003).

However, the physiological assessment of deviant sexual interest has been shown to be one of the best single predictors of future sexual recidivism (Hanson & Bussière, 1998; Hanson & Morton-Bourgon, 2005). Deviant arousal is included as a relevant factor in a number of different risk assessment tools including the SARN. In addition to the prediction of future risk it may be that the modification of an individual's pattern of sexual interests is one of the identified treatment goals. If this is the case then the use of phallometric assessment is one way to evaluate the effectiveness of the treatment intervention. As such, it is intended that all individuals participating in the Sex Offender Group will be screened and assessed for patterns of inappropriate arousal.

Individuals referred to the SOG will be assessed prior to attending and after attending the SOG. Where additional clinical work is undertaken specifically to target the patterns of sexual arousal, then the individual will be reassessed at the end of this piece of work specifically to evaluate the efficacy of the clinical intervention. All of the assessment processes will use visual and/or audio assessment stimuli where the assessments are tailored specifically to the offence type and clinical needs of the individual, in line with recent guidance about assessments needing to be targeted and proportionate (National PPG Users Forum, 2006).

COGNITIVE DOMAIN

The aim of the cognitive domain is to utilise cognitive process-based assessments to examine the extent to which individuals process information relevant to their sexual offending differently from non-offenders. The main task that will be initially utilised is that of the Implicit Association Test (IAT). The IAT is a task initially developed by Greenwald, McGhee and Schwartz (1998) to measure the extent to which two concepts are associated. The IAT has been used to measure beliefs about violence in psychopathic murders (Gray et al., 2003) and child sexual offenders (Gray et al., 2005; Mihailides, Devilly & Ward, 2004). Although the use of the IAT with sexual offenders is a fairly new process, one of the advantages is that it is non-transparent and difficult to fake (Banse, Seise & Zerbes, 2001). It has been agreed that the IAT will be used as part of the ongoing clinical evaluation of patients participating in sex offender treatment but that the use of the IAT would be reviewed as part of the ongoing evaluation process. Should this initial evaluation prove positive then the IAT will be formally included in the assessment process. However, if the evaluation is negative then the process will either be modified or the IAT removed from the assessment protocol.

ASSESSMENT REPORTING

Initial Report

All of the information collected as part of the assessment process should be integrated into a comprehensive report outlining the treatment needs of the individual. The assessment measures and processes outlined are intended to be used with all those individuals within the Peaks where it is necessary to undertake treatment for their sexually inappropriate behaviour. Given the treatment model used within the Peaks and the range of other assessment processes that are used, the sex offender specific assessment needs to be seen as integrated into the overall assessment and treatment process. As such the initial sex offence assessment report should be completed at the end of the introductory module to the Sex Offender Group. This allows for group administration of some of the measures as well as time to undertake the observational and judgement bases of the assessment process. Central to this initial report will be the formulation of responsivity issues, the drop-out prevention plan and any recommendations relating to specialist assessment and or treatment that needs to occur with each particular individual. For example, this might include individual support about abuse issues or assistance with therapy tasks/homework due to neuropsychological deficits. This initial report also provides a summary of the psychological testing scores which is used as a baseline from which to measure future change.

Post-Treatment Report

Following completion of the treatment programme an end of treatment report is undertaken. This report focuses on the extent to which identified treatment needs have been addressed by the treatment interventions provided as part of the sex offender treatment process. The post-treatment report is based on: retesting of the psychometric assessment battery, observation of behaviour change over time, retesting of phallometric assessments, the GAS observations of group facilitators regarding the achievement of treatment goals all of which contribute to the rescoring of the SARN and the overall judgement of treatment progress/success. The focus at this stage is the extent to which treatment goals have been addressed and the existing level of risk that the individual presents. To the extent that the individual stays within the Peaks then their ongoing behaviour is monitored and contributed to future assessments of risk and needs with the SARN structure being used annually to monitor change and need.

CONCLUSIONS

This chapter overviews how sex offender specific treatment fits within the clinical strategy used within the Peaks and describes in some detail the assessments and related assessment processes that are used. It is important that the specific assessment and treatment of sexual offenders, as described above, are seen within the context of an overall clinical strategy developed to address the treatment needs of a personality disordered population. As such, the types of assessments used and the timing of treatment participation are interdependent with the general treatments and assessments used within the Peaks and need to be read with this in mind. It is also equally important that the reader understands that the aim of such a comprehensive assessment process is to inform and direct the clinical treatment of each individual.

REFERENCES

Andrews, D.A. & Bonta, J. (2003). *The psychology of criminal conduct* (3rd edn). Cincinnati, OH: Anderson Publishing.

Abel, G. & Becker, J. (1985). Sexual interest card sort. In A.C. Salter (1988), *Treating child sex offenders and victims: A practical guide* (pp. 301–309). Newbury Park, CA: Sage.

Banse, R., Seise, J. & Zerbes, N. (2001). Implicit attitudes towards homosexuality: Reliability, validity and controllability of the IAT. *Zeitschrift fur Experimentelle Psychologie, 48*, 145–160.

Beckett, R.C. (1987). The Children and Sex Questionnaire. (Available from: Richard Beckett, Room FF39, The Oxford Clinic, Littlemore Health Centre, Sandford Rd, Littlemore, Oxford, OX44XN, England.)

Beckett, R.C., Fisher, D., Mann, R. & Thornton, D. (1997). The Relapse Prevention Questionnaire and Interview. In H. Eldridge (Ed.), *Therapists' Guide for Maintaining Change: Relapse Prevention Manual for Adult Male Perpetrators of Child Sexual Abuse.* California, USA: Sage Publications.

Beech, A.R., Oliver, C. Fisher, D. & Beckett, R.C. (2005). *STEP 4: The Sex Offender Treatment Programme in prison: Addressing the offending behaviour of rapists and sexual murderers.* Birmingham, UK: The Centre for Forensic and Family Psychology. http://www.hmprisonservice.gov.uk/assets/documents/100013DBStep_4_SOTP_report_2005.pdf

Beech, A.R. & Ward, T. (2004). The integration of etiology and risk in sexual offenders: A theoretical framework. *Aggression and Violent Behavior, 10*, 31–63.

Beeley, C. & Hogue, T.E. (2006). Daily Behaviour Rating Scale: Monitoring risk and clinical need. Paper presented at DSPD Research Conference, 5–6 December 2006, Leeds, UK.

Bell, J., Campbell, S., Erikson, M. *et al.* (2003). An overview: DSPD programme concepts and progress. *Issues in Forensic Psychology, 4*, 11–23.

Benjamin, L.S. (1993). *International diagnosis and treatment of personality disorders.* New York: Guilford Press.

Blackburn, R. (2004). What works with mentally disordered offenders? *Psychology Crime and Law, 10*, 297–308.

Burt, M. (1980). Cultural myths and support for rape. *Journal of Personality and Social Psychology, 39*, 217–230.

Capara, G.V. (1986). Indications of aggression: The Dissipation-Rumination Scale. *Personality and Individual Differences, 7*, 763–769.

Chromis (2005). *Chromis programme for violent offenders.* Offending Behaviour Programmes Unit, HM Prison Service. Available from: OBPU, Abel House, John Islip St., London SW1P 4LH, UK.

Craig, L.A., Browne, K.D., Hogue, T.E. & Stringer, I. (2004). New directions for assessing risk for sexual offenders. In G. Macpherson & L. Jones (Eds), *Issues is Forensic Psychology: Risk Assessment and Management.* Leicester: British Psychological Society.

Davies, J., Howells, K. & Jones, L. (2007). Using single case approaches in personality disorder and forensic services. *British Journal of Forensic Psychiatry and Psychology, 18*(3), 353–367.

Davis, M.H. (1980). A multi-dimensional approach to individual differences in empathy. *JSAS Catalogue of Selected Documents in Psychology, 10*, 85–100.

Dolan, B., Warren, F. & Norton. K. (1997). Changes in borderline symptoms one year after therapeutic community treatment for severe personality disorder. *British Journal of Psychiatry, 171*, 274–279.

DSPD Programme. (2005). *Dangerous and severe personality disorder (DSPD) high secure services for men: Planning and delivery guide*. London: Home Office. http://www.dspdprogramme.gov.uk/media/pdfs/High_Secure_Services_for_Men.pdf

Dutton, D.G., Saunders, K., Starzomski, A. & Bartholomew, K. (1994). Intimacy-anger and insecure attachment as precursors of abuse in intimate relationships. *Journal of Applied Social Psychology, 24*, 1367–1387.

D'Zurilla, T.J., Nezu, A.M. & Maydeu-Olivares, A. (2002). *Social Problem-Solving Inventory-Revised. Technical Manual*. Toronto: Multi-Health Systems.

Eysenck, S.B.G. & Eysenck, H.J. (1978). Impulsivity and venturesomeness: Their place in a dimensional system of personality description. *Psychological Reports, 43*, 1247–1255.

Fransella, F. & Bannister, D. (1977). *A Manual for Repertory Grid Technique*. London: Academic Press.

Greenwald, A.G., McGhee, J.L. & Schwartz, J.L. (1998). Measuring individual differences in implicit cognition: The Implicit Association test. *Journal of Personality and Social Psychology, 74*, 1464–1480.

Gray, N.S., Brown, T., MacCulloch, M.J. *et al.* (2005). An implicit test of the associations between children and sex in pedophiles. *Journal of Abnormal Psychology, 114*, 304–308.

Gray, N.S., MacCulloch, M.J., Smith, J. *et al.* (2003). Violence viewed by psychopathic murderers. *Nature, 423*, 497–498.

Hanson, R.K. (2006). Stability and change: Dynamic risk factors for sexual offenders. In W.L. Marshall, Y.M. Fernandez, L.E. Marshall & D.A. Serran (Eds), *Sexual offender treatment: Controversial issues* (pp. 17–31). Chichester: John Wiley & Sons, Ltd.

Hanson, R.K. & Bussière, M.T. (1998). Predicting relapse: A meta-analysis of sexual offender recidivism studies. *Journal of Consulting and Clinical Psychology, 66*, 348–362.

Hanson, R.K., Gizzarelli, R. & Scott, H. (1994). The attitudes of incest offenders: Sexual entitlement and acceptance with children. *Criminal Justice and Behavior, 21*(2), 187–202.

Hanson, R.K. & Harris, A.J. (2000). Where should we intervene? Dynamic predictors of sexual offence recidivism. *Criminal Justice and Behavior, 27*, 6–35.

Hanson, R.K. & Morton-Bourgon, K. (2005). The characteristics of persistent sexual offenders: A meta-analysis of recidivism studies. *Journal of Consulting and Clinical Psychology, 73*, 1154–1163.

Hanson, R.K. & Thornton, D. (2000) Improving risk assessment for sex offenders: A comparison of three actuarial scales. *Law and Human Behavior, 24*, 119–136.

Hare, R.D. (2003). *The Psychopathy Checklist-Revised* (2nd edn). Toronto: Multi-Health Systems.

Hogue, T.E. (1994). Goal attainment scaling: A measure of clinical impact and risk assessment with sexual offenders. In N.C. Clark & G. Stephenson (Eds), *Rights and risks: The application of forensic psychology*. Leicester: British Psychological Society.

Hogue, T.E. (1998). *The Sex Offence Information Questionnaire: The development of a self-report measure of offence-related denial in sex offenders*. Unpublished PhD thesis, University of Wales, Cardiff.

Hogue, T.E. (2005). The link between risk and PD. Presented at International Conference on the Management and Treatment of Dangerous Offenders, September 28–30, York, UK.

Hogue, T.E. (2006). Personality Disorder treatment and risk reduction. Paper presented at The BPS Northern Ireland Branch Conference: The Assessment and Management of Personality Disordered Offenders, Belfast, NI, December 2006.

Hogue, T.E. & Jones, L. (1999). PD attrition rates: Comparisons and suggestions. Poster presented at the 5th Anglo-Dutch Conference on Personality Disorder and Forensic Psychiatry, Amsterdam, February 1999.

Hogue, T.E., Jones, L., Talkes, K. & Tennant, A. (2007). The Peaks: A Clinical Service for those with Dangerous and Severe Personality Disorder. *Psychology Crime and Law, 13*, 57–68.

Hogue. T.E. & Samuda, S. (1999). Measuring change: Developing a daily measure of risk behaviour. Paper presented at the 9th Annual Conference of the British Psychological Society, Division of Criminal and Legal Psychology, Cambridge, September 1999.

Horley, J. (2003). *Personal construct perspectives on forensic psychology*. Hove: Brunner-Routledge.

Houston, J. (1998). *Making sense with offenders. Personal constructs, therapy and change*. Chichester: John Wiley & Sons, Ltd.

Howells, K., Day, A. & Thomas-Peters, B. (2004). Changing violent behaviour: Forensic mental health and criminological models compared. *The Journal of Forensic Psychiatry and Psychology, 15*(3), 391–406.

Jones, L.F. (2002). An individual case formulation approach to the assessment of motivation. In M. McMurran (Ed.), *Motivating offenders to change: A guide to enhancing engagement in therapy* (pp. 31–54). Chichester: John Wiley & Sons, Ltd.

Jones, L.F. (2004). Offence paralleling behaviour as a framework for assessment and interventions with offenders. In A. Needs & G. Towl (Eds), *Applying psychology to forensic practice* (pp. 34–63). Oxford: BPS Blackwell.

Jones, L.F. (2007). Iatrogenic interventions with personality disordered individuals. *Psychology Crime and Law, 13*, 69–79.

Kalmus, E. & Beech, A.R. (2005). Forensic assessment of sexual interest: A review. *Aggression and Violent Behavior, 10*, 193–217.

Laws, R.D. & Ward, T. (2006). When one size doesn't fit all: The reformulation of relapse prevention. In W L. Marshall, Y.M. Fernandez, L.E. Marshall & D.A. Serran (Eds), *Sexual offender treatment: Controversial issues* (pp. 241–254). Chichester: John Wiley & Sons, Ltd.

Lees, J., Manning, N. & Rawlings, B. (1999). Therapeutic community effectiveness: A systematic international review of therapeutic community treatment for people with personality disorders and mentally disorder offenders. York: NHS Centre for Reviews and Dissemination, University of York.

Levenson, H. (1974). Multidimensional locus of control in prison inmates. *Personality and Social Psychology Bulletin, 1*, 354–356.

Linehan, M.M. (1993). *Cognitive-behavioral treatment of borderline personality disorder*. New York: Guilford Press.

Livesley, W.J. (2001). A framework for an integrated approach to treatment. In W.J. Livesley (Ed.), *Handbook of personality disorder: Theory, research and treatment* (pp. 570–600). New York: Guilford Press.

Livesley, W.J. (2003). *Practical management of personality disorder*. New York: Guilford Press.

Livesley, W.J. (2007). The relevance of an integrated approach to the treatment of personality disordered individuals. *Psychology Crime and Law, 13*, 27–46.

Mann, R.M., O'Brien, M., Rallings, M. *et al.* (unpublished). *Manual for the Structured Assessment of Risk and Need for Sex Offenders (SARN-SO)*. Available from: Sex Offender Treatment Programme Team, Offending Behaviour Programmes Unit, HM Prison Service, Room 725 Abel House, John Islip St., London SW1 4LH, UK.

Mann, R.E. & Shingler, J. (2006). Schema-driven cognition in sexual offenders: theory, assessment and treatment. In W.L. Marshall, Y.M. Fernandez, L.E. Marshall & D.A. Serran (Eds), *Sexual offender treatment: Controversial issues* (pp. 174–185). Chichester: John Wiley & Sons, Ltd.

Marshall, W.L. (1995). Sex with Children is Justifiable Questionnaire. Available from: OBPU, Abel House, John Islip St, London SW1P 4LH, UK.

Marshall, W.L. & Fernandez, Y.M. (2003). *Phallometric testing with sexual offenders: Theory, research and practice*. Brandon, VT: Safer Society Press.

Mihailides, S., Devilly, G.J. & Ward, T. (2004). Implicit cognitive distortions and sexual offending. *Sexual Abuse: A Journal of Research and Treatment, 16*, 333–350.

Moos, R.H. (2002). *A Social Climate Scale. Group Environment Scale Manual. Developments, Applications, Research* (3rd edn). Redwood City, CA: Mind Garden Inc.

Mosher, D.L. & Sirken, M. (1984). Measuring a macho personality constellation. *Journal of Research in Personality, 18*, 150–163.

National Institute for Mental Health in England (2003). *Personality disorder: No longer a diagnosis of exclusion. Policy implementation guidance for the development of services for people with personality disorder.* Gateway Reference 1055. London: NIMHE.

National PPG Users Forum (2006). *Penile plethysmography (PPG) assessments guidance.* Information available from the British Psychological Society, Leicester, England.

Nichols, H.R. & Molinder, I. (1984). *Multiphasic Sex Inventory. A Test to assess the Characteristics of the Sexual Offender.* Available from the authors: 437 Bowes Drive, Tacoma, WA 98466, USA.

Offending Behaviour Programmes Unit (OBPU) (2004). *Sex Offender Treatment Programme Revised Psychometric Assessment Battery Manual: Version 3: Scales, items and descriptions.* London: HM Prison Service. Available from: OBPU, Abel House, John Islip St., London SW1P 4LH, UK.

Offending Behaviour Programme Unit (OBPU) (2007). *Sex Offender Treatment Programme Revised Psychometric Assessment Manual: Version 4, Scales, Items and Descriptions.* London: HM Prison Service.

OBPU (Date unknown). Openness to Men Questionnaire. Available from: OBPU, Abel House, John Islip St., London SW1P 4LH, UK. For further details, see OBPU (2007) above.

OBPU (Date unknown). Openness to Women Questionnaire. Available from: OBPU, Abel House, John Islip St., London SW1P 4LH, UK. For further details, see OBPU (2007) above.

Ogloff, J.R.P. & Davis, M.R. (2004). Advances in offender assessment and rehabilitation: Contributions of the risk-needs-responsivity approach. *Psychology Crime and Law, 10*, 229–242.

Paulhus, D.L. (1984). Two Component Models of Socially Desirable Responding. *Journal of Personality and Social Psychology, 46*, 598–609.

Pilgrim, D. (2002). DSPD: From futility to utility. *Clinical Psychology, 20*, 5–8.

Roger, D. & Najarian, B. (1989). The Construction and Validation of a New Scale for Measuring Emotion Control. *Personal Individual Differences, 10*(8), 845–853.

Royal, S. (2002). Double jeopardy. *Mental Health Today, August*, 12–13.

Russell, D., Peplan, C.A. & Cutrona, C.A. (1980). The revised UCLA Loneliness Scale: Concurrent and discriminant validity evidence. *Journal of Personality and Social Psychology, 39*, 472–480.

Ryle, A. (1995). *Cognitive Analytic Therapy; Developments in Theory and Practice.* Chichester: John Wiley & Sons, Ltd.

Ryle, A. & Kerr, I.B. (2002). *Introducing Cognitive Analytic Therapy: Principles and Practice.* Chichester: John Wiley & Sons, Ltd.

Sainsbury, L., Krishnan, G. & Evans, C. (2004). Motivating factors for male forensic patients with personality disorder. *Criminal Behaviour and Mental Health, 14*, 29–38.

Shingler, J. & Mann, R. (2006). Collaboration in clinical work with sexual offenders: Treatment and risk assessment. In W.L. Marshall, Y.M. Fernandez, L.E. Marshall & D.A. Serran (Eds), *Sexual offender treatment: Controversial issues* (pp. 225–239). Chichester: John Wiley & Sons, Ltd.

Sizmar, S. & Noutch, T. (2006). Dangerous and severe personality disorder services. *The British Journal of Forensic Practice, 7*, 33–38.

Sperry, L. (2003). *Handbook of diagnosis and treatment of DSM-IV-TR personality disorders* (2nd edn). New York: Brunner-Routledge.

Spitzer, R.L. (1983). Psychiatric diagnosis: Are clinicians still necessary? *Comprehensive Psychiatry, 24*, 399–411.

Stirpe, T.S., Wilson, R.J. & Long, C. (2001). Goal attainment scaling with sexual offenders: A measure of clinical impact at post-treatment and community follow-up. *Sexual Abuse: A Journal of Research and Treatment, 13*, 65–77.

Thornton, D. (1995). Self-esteem Questionnaire. (Unpublished). Available from: Dr. David Thornton, Sand Ridge, Sand Ridge Secure Treatment Center, 1111 North Road, PO Box 700 Mauston, WI 53948–0700, USA.

Thornton, D., Mann, R., Webster, S. *et al.* (2003). Distinguishing and combining risks for sexual and violent recidivism. In R. Prentky, E. Janus, M. Seto & A.W. Burgess (Eds), Understanding and Managing Sexually Coercive Behavior. *Annals of the New York Academy of Sciences, 989*, 225–235.

Ward, T. & Brown, M. (2004). The Good Lives Model and conceptual issues in offender rehabilitation. *Psychology Crime and Law*, *10*, 243–257.

Ward, T., Polaschek, D.L.L. & Beech, A.R. (2006). *Theories of sexual offending*, Chichester: John Wiley & Sons, Ltd.

Ward, T. & Siegert, R. J. (2002). Toward a comprehensive theory of child sexual abuse: A theory-knitting perspective. *Psychology Crime and Law*, *9*, 319–351.

Ward, T. & Stewart, C.A. (2003). The treatment of sex offenders: risk management and good lives. *Professional Psychology: Research and Practice*, *34*, 453–460.

Webster, C.D., Douglas, K.S., Eaves, D. & Hart, S.D. (1997). *HCR-20 Assessing risk for violence* (Version 2). Vancouver: Mental Health and Law Policy Group, Simon Fraser University.

Webster, S.D., Mann, R.E., Carter, A.J. *et al.* (2006). Inter-rater reliability of dynamic risk assessment with sexual offenders. *Psychology, Crime and Law*, *12*, 439–452.

Wong, S. & Gordon, A. (2000). *The Violence Risk Scale*. (Unpublished.) Available from the authors: Saskatoon Regional Psychiatric Centre, Saskatoon, Canada.

The World Health Organization (WHO). The WHOQOL Group, Department of Mental Health, WHO, CH-1211, Geneva 27, Switzerland.

Young, J.E., Klosko, J.S. & Weishar, M.E. (2003). *Schema therapy*. New York: Guilford.

15

Predicting Risk of Sexual Recidivism in Juveniles: Predictive Validity of the J-SOAP-II

ROBERT A. PRENTKY

ANN PIMENTAL

DEBORAH J. CAVANAUGH

SUE RIGHTHAND

INTRODUCTION

Over the past decade, there has been a quantum change in attitudes to juvenile sexual offenders, moving from one extreme in which frank instances of sexual battery were attributed to adolescent sexual experimentation to the opposite extreme in which juveniles were labeled as 'sexually violent predators', subject, in some jurisdictions in the United States, to indeterminate civil commitment (Trivits & Reppucci, 2002). Barbaree, Hudson and Seto (1993) observed that, "Prior to the 1980s, the predominant view of the sexual offenses committed by juveniles was that they constituted a nuisance value only reflecting a 'boys-will-be-boys' attitude . . . these acts were seen as examples of experimentation and therefore as innocent" (p. 10). Barbaree *et al.* (1993) went on to note, however, that by the early 1990s "the tendency to minimize the sexual crimes of juveniles has been reduced substantially" (p. 10). Indeed, this attitudinal shift in the direction of exceptionally harsh sanctions was eloquently captured by Chaffin and Bonner (1998) in their editorial entitled: "Don't shoot, we're your children: Have we gone too far in our response to adolescent sexual abusers and children with sexual

Assessment and Treatment of Sex Offenders: A Handbook. Edited by Anthony Beech, Leam Craig and Kevin Browne. © John Wiley & Sons Ltd, 2009.

behavior problems?" Perhaps unwittingly, this increased attention to juvenile sexual offenders seems to have also served as a catalyst for what has been characterized, at least in the United States, as a state of 'moral panic' (Selvog, 2001).

These polarized reactions can be explained, at least in part, by two separate realities. According to the extant empirical literature, the sexual recidivism rates of juvenile sexual offenders are indeed quite low (e.g., Kahn & Chambers, 1991; Lab, Shields & Schondel, 1993; Prentky *et al.*, 2000; Rasmussen, 1999; Schram, Milloy & Rowe, 1991; Sipe, Jensen & Everett, 1998; Smith & Monastersky, 1986). On the other hand, data from multiple sources suggest that a small group of juveniles who repeat crimes of sexual assault are indeed notable for their dangerousness (Alexander, 1999; Association for the Treatment of Sexual Abusers, 2001; Becker 1990; Center for Sex Offender Management, 2002; Hunter, 2000; Långström & Grann, 2000; Worling & Curwen, 2001; Worling & Långström, 2003). Fueled by profound misconceptions about the prevalence and magnitude of risk posed by these youth, harsh, punitive laws have been adopted in the United States (e.g., registration and community notification laws, and, most recently, civil [indeterminate] commitment laws), (Caldwell, 2002; Letourneau, 2006; Letourneau & Miner, 2005; Trivits & Reppucci, 2002; Zimring, 2004). Such statutory management of juvenile sexual offenders *demands* reliable, valid methods for assessing the risk posed by these youth. Judgments about degree of risk clearly are central to all management decisions, including those having to do with civil commitment and need for (or level of) registration.

The increased legal attention to the problems posed by sexually coercive/aggressive adolescent boys and girls has increased the urgency for progress in research on risk assessment with juveniles. Despite noble efforts by a small cohort of researchers, the absence of any risk assessment scale with clearly demonstrated predictive validity severely undermines the efficacy of these legal management strategies. It is reasonable to conclude that research efforts devoted to untangling problems associated with assessment of risk among juvenile sexual offenders fail to match even remotely the *presumed* gravity of the behavior, as reflected by the more extreme laws alluded to.

The empirical literature on risk assessment has focused largely on the identification of individual risk predictors. This is a logical, indeed essential, *first* step in the development of a valid risk assessment scale; it is not the end goal. Individual risk predictors are typically weak when used in isolation. As Hanson and Bussière (1998) warned, no risk predictors, even the more robust variables identified by their meta-analysis, were strong enough to be relied on as separate predictors of risk. The critical next step involving the design and testing of scales combining multiple risk predictors has come only very recently. We begin by reviewing briefly the extant literature on risk predictors and proceed to a discussion of a test of the predictive validity of one of the existing scales designed to assess risk in adolescent sexual offenders, the Juvenile Sex Offender Assessment Protocol-II (J-SOAP-II; Prentky & Righthand, 2003). Although we may pose many questions of a risk assessment scale (e.g., Can we discriminate between the youth detained in residential facilities and the youth treated in the community? Are different levels of risk associated with different adverse life experiences?), the question universally posed is whether the scale can *predict* with some degree of accuracy those youth who reoffend sexually. Thus, the question of *predictive validity*, as opposed to other types of validity, assumes center stage in empirical research on juvenile risk assessment.

REVIEW OF RISK PREDICTORS

The literature on presumptive risk predictors for juvenile sexual offenders is quite substantial. Rich (2003), for example, listed 136 different risk predictors that he gleaned from the clinical and empirical literature. As we indicated earlier, however, the vast majority of these risk predictors are only weakly related, if related at all, to sexual reoffense. Indeed, most of these risk predictors have never been examined empirically with respect to reoffense. Of those predictors listed by Rich, no more than two dozen have ever been scrutinized empirically, and those are the ones that we will briefly discuss. Several recent comprehensive reviews of this literature are available (Rich, 2003; Worling & Långström, 2003).

Discerning which predictors have adequate cross-study empirical support is complicated for a variety of reasons: (1) some studies examined only adolescents while others included varying numbers of pre-adolescents; (2) although most studies included only males, some included females; (3) although most studies were drawn from the juvenile justice system, some came from the child welfare system; and (4) while some studies focused on residential samples, others used community-based samples. Overall, however, there appears to be some reasonable consensus regarding those risk predictors that are empirically defensible and those that are not.

Worling and Långström (2003) reviewed a wide range of risk predictors, separating them broadly into four categories based on the judged amount of empirical support. To be classified as 'Supported' the predictors had to be validated by a recent meta-analysis, have at least two independent follow-up studies, and not have any contradictory evidence. According to Worling and Långström (2003), predictors in the *supported* category *included:* (1) deviant sexual interest, (2) prior criminal sanctions for sexual offending, (3) sexual offending against multiple victims, (4) sexual offending against a stranger, (5) social isolation, and (6) failure to participate in specialized treatment for sexual offending.

One of the interesting areas of ambiguity is antisociality. According to Worling and Långström (2003), antisociality would be considered *possible* as a risk predictor. Antisociality (e.g., having a 'socially deviant lifestyle'), however, is one of the two robust dimensions for predicting risk among *adult* sex offenders (Hanson & Bussière, 1998; Hanson & Morton-Bourgon, 2005), as well as among generic samples of delinquent youth (e.g., Hawkins *et al.*, 1998). Juvenile sexual offenders have also been characterized as high in delinquency and impulsive, antisocial behavior (Ageton, 1983; Awad & Saunders, 1991; Awad, Saunders & Levene, 1984; Becker, Cunningham-Rathner & Kaplan, 1986; Caldwell, 2002; Fehrenbach *et al.*, 1986; Hagan *et al.*, 2001; Knight & Prentky, 1993; Prentky & Knight, 1993; Shoor, Speed

& Bartelt, 1966; Spaccarelli *et al.*, 1997; Van Ness, 1984). Ageton's (1983) integrated delinquency model, borrowing from social-control, strain and social-learning theories, pointed to juvenile sexual offenders as primarily delinquent and hence difficult to distinguish from other delinquents with no known history of sexual assault. A study of chronic delinquents by Spaccarelli *et al.* (1997) found essentially no differences between juveniles arrested for sexual assault and juveniles arrested for non-sexual, violent assault, supporting the earlier study by Ageton (1983).

Delinquency essentially represents a continuum of impulsive, antisocial behaviors, ranging from running away and truancy to serious crimes involving interpersonal violence. From the standpoint of assessing risk, delinquency is a behaviorally complex dimension that may include *static* risk predictors (e.g., *number of prior offenses, having been arrested before age 16, having committed multiple types of offenses*), *stable dynamic* risk predictors (e.g., *impulsivity* and *anger management problems*) and perhaps even *acute dynamic* risk predictors, such as *alcohol* and *drug abuse*. This complexity lends ambiguity to its role as a risk predictor among adolescents who are generally known for their developmentally-normative impulsive and risk-taking behavior. Depending on how delinquency is assessed and the composition of the study sampled, delinquency may, or may not, discriminate between *persisters* and *desisters*.

Although a number of studies (Kahn & Chambers, 1991; Lab, Shields & Schondel, 1993; Långström, 2002; Rasmussen, 1999; Sipe, Jensen & Everett, 1998; Worling & Curwen, 2001) have shown that a history of non-sexual offending is *not* associated with committing a subsequent sexual offense, Nisbet, Wilson and Smallbone (2004) found a significant correlation between a history of non-sexual offenses and sexual reoffense. Indeed, youth with such a history were three times more likely to commit a subsequent sexual offense as an adult. Clearly, a sample with a higher base rate of non-sexual criminal behavior would be more likely to yield a positive association between such behavior and sexual recidivism.

Worling and Curwen (2001) found sexual interest in children (as assessed by self-reported sexual fantasies of children, child-victim grooming behaviors, and intrusive sexual assault activities) was associated with sexual recidivism. Similarly, Schram, Milloy and Rowe (1991) found a trend between therapist-assessed *deviant arousal* and sexual reoffending. Kenney, Keogh and Seidler (2001) also found that juveniles with a *prior charge* for sexual offending were more likely to report deviant sexual fantasies involving young children or the use of force. By contrast, however, Gretton *et al.* (2001) found that penile plethysmograph (PPG) assessment findings were *not* related to sexual reoffending. Using the same data set as Schram *et al.*, 1991, Kahn and Chambers (1991) found only a small, non-significant difference in deviant arousal between juveniles who reoffended sexually and those who did not. In general, documenting compelling evidence to support the risk-relevance of sexual deviance, particularly when it has been defined in terms of PPG-assessed deviant arousal, has been elusive.

A reasonable explanation for these inconclusive findings was offered by Hunter and Becker, who cautioned that juveniles may not yet have developed a fixed pattern of sexual arousal and interest (Hunter, Goodwin & Becker, 1994). Another possible explanation is that adolescents are so universally responsive to sexually explicit materials that it is difficult to differentiate normal from deviant arousal. Finally, even if 'sexual preference' could be assessed reliably in adolescence, it may only be those youngsters with sexual attraction to much younger children that are identified using deviant sexual interest as a risk predictor.

Another predictor with support from several studies is *prior sanctions* for sexual offending (Långström, 2002; Långström & Grann, 2000; Ross & Loss, 1991; Schram, Milloy & Rowe, 1992). This predictor is, of course, entirely consistent with the adult sex offender risk assessment literature. Individuals who are apprehended and punished but nevertheless persist in their sexual offending are considered to be at higher risk (Långström, 2002; Långström & Grann, 2000; Schram *et al.*, 1991). Again, consistent with the literature on risk among adult sex offenders, an *offense committed against a stranger* or *more than one victim* has also been found to be correlated with reoffense (Långström, 2002; Smith & Monastersky, 1986; Worling, 2002). Having *multiple victims* and reoffending after a previously charged sexual offense may reflect persistent deviant sexual interests and behavior (Långström, 2002; Långström & Grann, 2000; Ross & Loss, 1991; Schram *et al.*, 1991).

Juveniles who hold *attitudes supportive of sexual deviancy* (Kahn & Chambers, 1991), along with those individuals who *failed to complete a sexual offense-specific treatment program* (Borduin *et al.*, 1990; Seabloom *et al.*, 2003; Worling & Curwen, 2001), are also reportedly at increased risk. *Denial*, however, has been shown to have an *inverse* relationship to recidivism (Kahn & Chambers, 1991; Långström & Grann, 2000; Worling, 2002). As Worling (2005) speculated, "Perhaps some mechanisms that result in denial of the sexual offense (e.g., extreme shame, embarrassment, or fear of sanctions) also act to reduce the odds of a future sex offense" (pp. 18–19).

As with adult sexual offenders, failure to express *empathy* for one's victim is *not* predictive of reoffense (Långström & Grann, 2000; Smith & Monastersky, 1986). This is most likely due to the considerable difficulty in measuring empathy reliably. Although problems assessing *empathy* and *remorse* are clearly evident with adults as well, these problems are especially vexing with children and adolescents, because the emergence of the capacity for empathy is age-related (Bee, 1997; Berk, 2001; Hoffman, 1982, 1988, 1991). Research clearly supports the general conclusion that adults possess a greater capacity for empathy than children, and that older children are more empathetic and prosocial than younger children (Hoffman, 1991). Older children are better able to recognize emotional states in others, are more capable of relating to and sharing others people's feelings, are better able to feel empathy for different kinds of people, and are better able to express their empathy by being generous toward others (Harris, Olthof & Terwogt, 1981). Younger children, by contrast, have greater self-involvement, frequently objectify others, and are more likely to express empathy only toward people that are like themselves in age, ethnicity and gender (Bee, 1997). In general, the mechanism that seems to be most frequently identified to explain differences, including age-related differences, in capacity for empathy is perspective taking (i.e., the ability to take someone else's point of view) (Selman, 1976).

A *history of sexual victimization* (i.e., the youth's history of having been a victim of sexual assault) has generally *not* been predictive of reoffense (Hagan & Cho, 1996;

Långström, 2002; Rasmussen, 1999; Worling & Curwen, 2001). Although a large proportion of juvenile sexual offenders have been sexually abused prior to committing their first offense, the research is quite inconclusive with respect to the predictive efficacy of this adverse life experience (Worling & Långström, 2006). Childhood sexual abuse, like other forms of abuse, becomes critical in the presence of a variety of other factors (Kaufman & Zigler, 1987), such as the *age of onset*, the *duration* of the abuse, the child's *relationship* to the perpetrator, the *invasiveness* and/or *violence* in the abuse, the co-occurrence of other types of abuse, the availability of *supportive caregivers*, the *ego strength* of the child at the time of the abuse, and treatment (Prentky, 1999). Thus, sexual abuse may only differentiate between those who are at lower or higher risk of reoffense when it is examined in a more refined way by focusing on one of more of the morbidity factors mentioned above, such as age of onset, duration or intrusiveness (Burton, 2000, 2003). When studies examine the more serious expressions of sexual abuse, such as restricting cases to those involving *early onset* or *penetration*, the results clearly favor predictive efficacy. In general, the role of a history of sexual abuse as a moderator of sexually aggressive outcome appears to be highly complex and interactive with other life experiences (cf. Prentky *et al.*, 1989).

Committing a sexual offense against a *male victim* has also been inconclusive as a risk predictor among juveniles (Långström & Grann, 2000; Rasmussen, 1999; Smith & Monastersky, 1986; Worling, 1995; Worling & Curwen, 2001), as well as adults (Prentky, Knight & Lee, 1997). Some studies have found higher rates of sexual recidivism among juveniles who have victimized males (Smith & Monastersky, 1986), whereas others have not (e.g. Rasmussen, 1999). Rasmussen (1999) found higher rates of sexual recidivism among juveniles who had multiple female victims. Worling (1995) found, however, that 75% of juvenile offenders who assaulted one male child reported a history of sexual abuse, compared with 25% of those juveniles who assaulted a female child. Varied results were also reported for past sexual assaults against *a child victim* (Hagan & Cho, 1996; Kahn & Chambers, 1991; Långström, 2002; Rasmussen, 1999; Sipe, Jensen & Everett, 1998; Smith & Monastersky, 1986; Worling & Curwen, 2001). Mixed results have also been reported for *use of threats*, *violence or weapons* in a previous sexual assault (Kahn & Chambers, 1991; Långström, 2002).

Although there are indeed some risk predictors that appear to have comparable utility for adult and juvenile offenders, there are many more predictors that either have very limited utility or must be tailored for use with adolescents. The major risk-relevant difference between adults and juveniles is *age* itself. Even under 'normal' conditions, adolescence is a time of extraordinary maturational change in virtually all domains of development, from physical and biological to cognitive, social, sexual and emotional (cf. Hann, 2001; Keating, 1990; Reyna & Farley, 2006; Steinberg & Scott, 2003; US Department of Health and Human Services, 1999, 2001). Numerous studies document the pervasive developmental 'flux' of adolescents. Even the central nervous system in adolescents is immature (cf. Reyna & Farley, 2006). The frontal lobe, for example, a brain region associated with impulsivity, continues to mature into the mid-twenties (Reyna & Farley, 2006). A recent conference hosted by the

New York Academy of Sciences was devoted entirely to the topic of adolescent brain development (Dahl & Spear, 2004).

In addition to physical growth, there are marked changes in both reproductive and stress hormones that are associated with maturational changes in sexual arousal, emotional intensity and lability, changes in sleep and appetite, and risk-taking behaviors. Risk-adversity, in particular, increases with age, and in adolescence, the hedonic motive overshadows rational recognition of adverse outcomes. As Steinberg (2004) noted, "increased risk taking in adolescence is normative, biologically driven, and inevitable" (p. 57). As Reyna and Farley (2006) observed, "The scientific literature confirms the commonsense belief that adolescence is a period of inordinate risk taking" (p. 7). Laboratory studies underscore the inverse relation between age and risk taking: risk taking decreases from childhood to adolescence and again from adolescence to adulthood (e.g., Levin & Hart, 2003; Reyna, 1996; Rice, 1995). These experimental studies, however, belie the undeniable reality of risk taking as a cardinal feature of adolescents. The explanation is most likely another critical feature of adolescence – substantially increased *opportunity* to engage in risk behavior (Moffitt, 1993; Spear, 2000).

To further complicate matters, a substantial proportion of the youth that are assessed for risk have been subjected to varying degrees of maltreatment, and indeed, in some cases, the abuse is *real time* (i.e., occurring within roughly the same time frame as the risk assessment). Childhood abuse and maltreatment is a robust, and many would say universal, risk predictor in antisocial behavior (Brown & Bzostek, 2003; Meyers *et al.*, 1995; Rivera & Widom, 1990; Stewart, Dennison, & Waterson, 2002), and in fact, the same holds true for juvenile sexual offenders (Burton, 2003; Burton & Smith-Darden, 2001; Ford & Linney, 1995; Knight & Prentky, 1993). In addition to the obvious emotional and psychological impact of maltreatment, there is a substantial literature documenting permanent brain damage that may be associated with early and protracted maltreatment (e.g., DeBellis, 2005; DeBellis *et al.*, 1999a; DeBellis *et al.*, 1999b; Teicher, 2000, 2002). Such abuse produces a cascade of stress-related hormones (principally cortisol and adrenalin) in the young, developing brain, permanently altering the development of certain structures (e.g., hippocampus, corpus callosum and prefrontal cortex) (Teicher, 2000, 2002; Teicher *et al.*, 2003). Thus, we must take into account not only the developmentally normative biological changes that occur in adolescence but whatever developmentally aberrant, abuse-induced, biological changes that occur as well.

All-in-all, the task of assessing risk in this population of pervasively developmentally immature and often abuse-reactive youth is highly complex and not to be equated with the task of assessing risk in adults. Adolescence is characterized, even under the best of conditions, by poor decision making, as rational decisions give way to intense emotions. In addition, there is, of course, a complex social chemistry in which peers become powerful influences on behavior. In sum, adolescence is a developmental twilight zone between childhood and adulthood that is characterized by radical emotional changes in response to hormonal shifts, high-intensity feelings, emotionally-charged, impulsive, risky behaviors, and poor decision making. Most of all, it is a time of *change*. Change cannot be captured by static or fixed risk predictors. Optimal risk prediction in this population *must* take into account the pervasive developmental flux that defines this transitional period in our lives. In addition, the life circumstances of adolescents may change rapidly, often within a very short time frame. Thus, the risk 'temperature' of an adolescent is arguably much more in flux and unstable than that of an adult, increasing the importance of stable and acute dynamic risk related predictors. Refining dynamic risk predictors for juveniles is a consummate challenge and the ultimate quest in improving risk and needs management decisions for this population.

Despite the ample concern about the risk posed by juvenile sexual offenders, not to mention the copious literature, both clinical and empirical, on risk predictors that may be associated with recidivism among juvenile sexual offenders, there are, to the best of our knowledge, only three empirically-driven programs aimed at developing and validating a risk assessment instrument for sexually abusive youth. These efforts include those of Worling and his colleagues and others (Bourgon, Morton-Bourgon & Madrigrano, 2005; Bremer & Dellacecca, 2006; McCoy & Murrie, 2006; Skowron, 2004; Worling, 2004; Worling & Curwen, 2001), Epperson and his colleagues (Epperson *et al.*, 2006), and Prentky, Righthand and their colleagues (Fanniff & Becker, 2006; Hecker *et al.*2002; Martinez, Rosenfeld & Flores, 2004; McCoy & Murrie, 2006; Parks & Bard, 2006; Prentky *et al.*, 2000; Prentky, 2006; Righthand, Carpenter & Prentky, 2001; Righthand *et al.*, 2000; Righthand *et al.*, 2005; Waite *et al.*, 2005).

The fruits of these preliminary efforts are reported in Table 15.1. As may be observed, although some progress has been made, this domain of research is very much in its infancy. To the best of our knowledge, there have only been six peer-reviewed reports published. Perhaps more to the point, there are only four follow-up studies that have reported predictive accuracy using Receiver Operating Characteristics analysis (ROC values), and only *one* (Worling, 2004) has appeared in a peer-reviewed journal.

In the balance of this chapter, we report on and discuss a validity study conducted on one such scale, the *Juvenile Sex Offender Assessment Protocol-II* (J-SOAP-II; Prentky & Righthand, 2003). To the best of our knowledge, this is the first use of the J-SOAP with a child welfare sample and the first application of the J-SOAP to pre-adolescents. Whether it is the J-SOAP-II or some other promising alternative, conducting the minimal research necessary to develop a reliable and accurate method of assessing risk of sexual aggression in adolescents must be a high priority given the laws that have been implemented to curb such behavior (Adam Walsh Act, 2006).

METHOD

In 1998, the Commonwealth of Massachusetts established a program to screen out and evaluate children and adolescents who were deemed at risk to engage in dangerous behaviors, including sexually inappropriate and coercive behaviors, thereby endangering other children. This program, Assessment for Safe and Appropriate Placement

Table 15.1 Validity studies

Risk Assessment Tool	Sample Size	Validity Studies	Reported ROC Values[†]
ERASOR			
Bremer & Dellacecca (2006)	397 NR age range	Discriminant	–
Bourgon et al. (2005)**	137 males 12–19 age range	Discriminant	–
Skowron (2004)	110 males 12–19 age range	Predictive	.71
Worling (2004)**	136 males 12–18 age range	Predictive	.72
J-SORRAT			
Epperson et al. (2006)*	636 males 12–17 age range	Predictive	.91
J-SOAP			
Prentky (2006)	551 males: 331 pre-adol. (<12 years old) 220 adol. (>12 years old)	Predictive	.82 .80
Parks & Bard (2006)**	156 males 12–17 age range	Predictive	–
Righthand et al. (2005)**	153 males 7–20 age range	Concurrent & Discriminant	–
Waite et al. (2005)**	261 males 8–18 age range	Discriminant	– (Scale 2 only)
Martinez et al. (2004)	61 males 12–19	Predictive	–
Hecker et al. (2002)	54 males NR	Predictive	.79 (Scale 1 only)
Prentky et al. (2000)**	96 males 9–20 age range	Concurrent	–

NR = Not Reported
† = Sexual Reoffense
* = Published
** = Peer-reviewed

(ASAP), had the principal mandate of evaluating youth in the custody of the Department of Social Services (DSS) who had been removed from abusive homes and placed elsewhere, often in foster care, because of their dysfunctional and frequently abusive backgrounds, in order to improve the management and care of those youth and to reduce the likelihood of those youth sexually abusing (further victimizing) other children or peers.

With the support of DSS, we began a research project in 2001 aimed at developing a protocol for improving discretionary and management decisions for those youth that had been flagged for an ASAP evaluation. With additional support from the National Institute of Justice (2002-IJ-CX-0029), we initiated and completed a seven-year follow-up study (1998–2005) of these DSS children to test the predictive efficacy of the J-SOAP-II within this population. Many of the youth who were first ASAP evaluated in 1998 and 1999 were 14–17 years old at the time, and therefore had reached adulthood by the end of our study in 2005.

TERMINOLOGY

We typically refer to the participants in our study as *youth* rather than as 'juvenile sexual offenders'. The majority of our child welfare sample were never arrested or adjudicated for a sexual offense and were not in any 'legal' sense juvenile sexual offenders. Moreover, when we do use the word 'juvenile', it is *not* synonymous with adolescent. Many of the youth in our sample committed their first hands-on sexual offense *prior* to the age of 12. Although, in our analyses, we separate adolescents and pre-adolescents, we use the term 'juveniles' to refer to all of the youth in our sample.

Sexual 'reoffense' was defined as any new inappropriate or coercive 'hands-on' sexual behavior. 'New' referred to any behavior that came *after* the ASAP evaluation. Since most of the youth in our sample were not adjudicated, we could not use conventional criminal justice system dispositional markers (e.g., charge, arrest, conviction, or incarceration) to determine 'reoffense'.

PARTICIPANTS

Participants were 192 boys on whom we had total J-SOAP-II scores. These 192 youth were part of a larger ASAP dataset. We divided our sample into pre-adolescents ($n = 123$) and adolescents ($n = 69$). This distinction was made using the *age of first hands-on sexual offense* variable. The preadolescent – adolescent split was <12 and 12–17. Average age at the time of the ASAP evaluation was 11.62 ($SD = 2.52$) for the pre-adolescents and 13.93 ($SD = 1.59$) for the adolescents $F(1, 190) = 49.25$, $p < .001$ (see Table 15.2) for a description of these samples. Notably, the age at *first hands-on* sex offense occurred, on average, three and a half years prior to the ASAP evaluation for the pre-adolescents ($M = 8.06$). By contrast, age at first hands-on sex offense among the adolescents was, on average, only 6 months prior to the ASAP evaluation. Overall, among the pre-adolescents, age at first inappropriate sexual behavior ($M = 7.71$) was very shortly before the age at first hands-on sexual offense ($M = 8.06$) but three and a half years before the ASAP evaluation ($M = 11.62$). Among the adolescents, age at first inappropriate sexual behavior ($M = 11.48$) was close to two years before the first hands-on sexual offense ($M = 13.30$), which was close in time to the ASAP evaluation ($M = 13.93$).

Although the majority of the sample were Caucasian (58% of the pre-adolescents and 72% of the adolescents, the pre-adolescents were more ethnically mixed, with almost 19% being Hispanic and 14% being coded as 'other' (Cape Verdean, Portuguese, Mixed). Roughly 10% of both groups were African-American. IQ was coded

Table 15.2 Demographic characteristics

Total $N = 192$	Pre-Adolescent Boys $n = 123$	Adolescent Boys $n = 69$	χ^2
Race[a]:			7.46
Caucasian	58.1%	72.4%	
African-American	9.0%	10.1%	
Hispanic	18.8%	14.4%	
Other	13.9%	2.8%	
			F
IQ:			
M/SD	92.22/15.80	90.24/14.40	0.61
Range	55–134	57–121	
Age at Time of ASAP Evaluation:			
M/SD	11.62/2.52	13.93/1.59	49.25****
Age at First Hands-On Sexual Offense:			
M/SD	8.06/2.20	13.30/1.30	328.86****
Age at First Inappropriate Sexual Behavior:			
M/SD	7.71/2.29	11.48/3.02	92.17****

NOTE: *p<.05, ****p<.001

as the highest Full Scale (FS) score reported in the youth's DSS record. The mean FS IQ was 92.22 ($SD = 15.80$) for the pre-adolescents and 90.24 ($SD = 14.40$) for the adolescents.

PROCEDURE FOR DATA COLLECTION

In conjunction with retrieving post-ASAP information from DSS records and DSS social workers, we worked closely with the Criminal History Systems Board (CHSB) and the Sex Offender Registry Board (SORB). Both agencies allowed us access to their criminal records. We confirmed a youth's criminal justice involvement from their Criminal Offender Record Information (CORI). The CORIs included information regarding charges, arraignment dates and dispositions, including juvenile adjudications. The follow-up time *began* on the date of the ASAP evaluation and *ended* on the date of the last documented information that we had on a particular individual.

The first task of this project was to create a coding dictionary. The focus of this outcome project was twofold: (1) to examine *outcome* defined in terms of reoffense, or re-commission of sexually inappropriate behavior, and (2) to examine outcome defined in terms of static, stable and dynamic risk factors. The coding dictionary consisted of 89 items. The final version of the coding dictionary covered demographic data, stable dynamic risk factors, response to treatment, the continuation of sexually inappropriate behaviors, penal history and acute dynamic risk factors at the time of a reoffense, as well as information regarding activities that resulted in criminal sanctions. In addition, the items on the J-SOAP-II were coded.

THE J-SOAP-II SCALE

The J-SOAP-II is an empirically-informed assessment guide developed to assist clinicians in identifying factors that may increase or decrease the risk of sexual and criminal
non-sexual recidivism by youth with histories of sexually coercive behavior (Prentky
& Righthand, 2003). The J-SOAP-II was designed to be used with boys in the age
range of 12 to 18 who have adjudications for contact sexual offenses or have histories of contact sexually coercive behavior that have not resulted in adjudication. The
present study is the first application of the J-SOAP to a sample of pre-adolescents. By
assisting users in identifying relevant areas of risk and patterns among risk factors,
the J-SOAP-II can facilitate the identification of risk-related needs that, if effectively
addressed, may reduce the risk of repeat offending and, help these youth to develop
prosocial, non-abusive relationships and lifestyles.

J-SOAP-II consists of four scales:

1. Sexual Drive/Sexual Preoccupation;
2. Impulsive, Antisocial Behavior;
3. Intervention; and
4. Community Stability.

Scale 1 (e.g., *Prior legally charged sex offenses, Number of sexual abuse victims,
Male child victim*, and *Sexual victimization history*) and Scale 2 (e.g., *Ever arrested
before age 16, Multiple types of offenses*, and *History of physical assault and/or exposure to family violence*) assess risk factors that may be primarily considered fixed
or static in nature, though some of the items on these two scales clearly are more
dynamic in nature (e.g., *Sexualized aggression* and *Sexual drive and preoccupation*
on Scale 1, and *Caregiver consistency* and *Pervasive anger* on Scale 2). Scales 3 and
4 assess stable and acute dynamic risk factors. Scale 3, in particular, may function
at two levels, tapping both acute dynamic risk (i.e., change in risk status as a function of treatment intervention), as well as stable dynamic risk (e.g., relative absence
of *Empathy* or *Remorse* capturing the affective deficits in the four-factor, structural
models of psychopathy [Forth, Kosson & Hare, 2003] and poor *Quality of peer relationships* reflecting social skills deficits). Scale 4 assesses adequacy of adjustment in
the community with both acute dynamic risk factors (e.g., *Stability of current living
situation, School stability* and *Positive support systems*) and more stable dynamic risk
factors (e.g., *Management of anger* and *Management of sexual urges*).

Overall, we were able to code reliably 26 out of the 28 items included in the
J-SOAP-II. The two items that we could not assess reliably were *Prior legally charged
sex offenses* and *Degree of planning*, both on Scale 1. Prior legally charged sex offenses
could not be coded, since very few of the youth in our DSS sample were legally
charged or adjudicated for any sexual offense prior to their ASAP evaluation. Degree
of planning is coded on the J-SOAP-II according to the 'modus operandi' of the
youth's sex offenses. We were unable to code this facet of offense history with adequate
reliability. Thus, the total J-SOAP score used in this study is based on 26, not 28, items.

Results

Reliability

Inter-rater reliability was calculated as the percent of agreement between two independent, 'blind coders' using a random selection of 15% of all cases. Overall, 65 variables (98%) had good to excellent agreement ($\geq .80$). Of those 65 items, the percent of agreement for 54 fell between 1.00–.91, while the percent of agreement for the other 11 fell between .80–.89. We were able to achieve a high degree of reliability in our codings due to a wealth of data in the DSS files and a coding dictionary that included precise definitions and concrete examples. Only one variable (Quality of peer relationships) had moderate agreement of (.79).

Reoffense rates

The average follow-up time for the pre-adolescents ($M = 46.95$ months; $SD = 19.03$) was significantly longer than the average follow-up time for the adolescents ($M = 40.62$; $SD = 19.42$) $F (1, 190) = 4.82$, $p < .03$.

Among the pre-adolescents, 37 reoffended sexually (30.6% of the pre-adolescent sample), extending over a period of 67 months. Over three-quarters of the pre-adolescent reoffenses (78.5%) occurred within the first 24 months. Among the adolescent boys, 16 reoffended sexually (23% of the adolescent sample), extending over a period of 63 months. Over 85% of the adolescent failures (86.2%) occurred within the first 24 months.

Two noteworthy observations are that: (1) most youth who persisted did so within the first 24 months, and (2) the highest failure rate was observed among the pre-adolescent boys.

Outcome prediction using J-SOAP-II

Binomial logistic regression was used to predict the dichotomous dependent outcome variable (sexual reoffense) (Table 15.3). The independent variable was the J-SOAP-II total scale score. We tested the null hypothesis of no significant difference in J-SOAP-II scores between those who reoffended sexually and those who apparently did not, using the Likelihood Ratio (LR) goodness-of-fit test and the Wald test. The Wald statistic is a test of whether an effect exists (the effect, in this case, is the ability of the J-SOAP to discriminate between sexual reoffenders and non-reoffenders). Simply stated, the Wald statistic tests the significance of a particular explanatory variable, in this case J-SOAP-II. If the Wald test is significant, we would conclude that the parameters associated with the variable are not zero, and that the variable should be retained in the model. When there is a single variable (as in the present case with J-SOAP-II), a t-test can be used to check whether the parameter is significant (Altman, 1991). For a single parameter, the Wald test is simply the square of the t-statistic.

Table 15.3 Logistic regression

Parameter	Estimate	S.E.	X^2 (Wald)	χ^2 (LR)[a]
Pre-Adolescent Boys				
J-SOAP Total Score	0.176	.04	19.82[****]	31.20[****]
Intercept	−6.482	1.34		
Adolescent Boys				
J-SOAP Total Score	0.133	.05	8.25[***]	11.39[****]
Intercept	−5.595	1.62		

[a]$H_0: \beta = 0$
[***]$p < .005$
[****]$p < .001$

Among both the pre-adolescent and the adolescent boys, there are large, highly significant LR and Wald chi-square values, revealing a statistically strong association between the J-SOAP-II predicted outcomes and the actual outcomes. The Wald values suggest a strong *effect* of J-SOAP-II in identifying reoffenders and non-reoffenders.

Predictive Accuracy as Assessed by ROC Analysis

The Receiver Operating Characteristics (ROC) curve estimates predictive accuracy by plotting sensitivity by 1-specificity. Sensitivity is the true positive rate of prediction (i.e., how likely the prediction will be positive when the person is truly dangerous). Specificity is the true negative rate of prediction (i.e., how likely the prediction will be negative when the person is truly not dangerous). Thus, the ROC curve captures both types of potential error (false negatives and false positives). Although there is no uniformly accepted index of accuracy for predictive models using dichotomous dependent variables (Ash & Schwartz, 1994), the C statistic, derived from ROC analysis, is generally regarded as an index that should be reported (Harrell *et al.*, 1984). The C statistic reflects the area under the curve (AUC) derived by plotting sensitivity by 1-specificity. AUC corresponds to the probability of accurately predicting that a randomly selected, truly dangerous individual is more likely to be dangerous than a randomly selected, truly non-dangerous individual. As a basis for comparison, Mossman (1994) examined 58 studies of violence prediction, finding that the median AUC for all 58 studies was .73, and the weighted average was .78. Chance prediction would yield an AUC of .50. To be sure, of course, the studies reviewed by Mossman involved prediction of violence in *adult* populations. To the best of our knowledge, there are no equivalent AUC guidelines for predicting violence among children. One might surmise, however, given the daunting problems associated with accurate estimation of risk of violence in children, that the AUC values would be lower in studies of risk prediction with children.

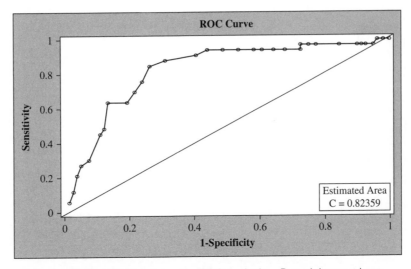

Figure 15.1 J-SOAP total score ROC analysis – Pre-adolescent boys

Figure 15.1 presents the results of the Receiver Operating Characteristics (ROC) analysis for the pre-adolescent boys only. Remarkably, when the J-SOAP-II full-scale score was used to predict sexual recidivism the *C* value was .824, with a concordance of 81.2% (i.e., there was agreement between the prediction using the J-SOAP-II score and the actual outcome 81% of the time) (see Table 15.4). The optimal *probability* level for the pre-adolescents was .30, yielding a sensitivity of 75.8% and a corresponding specificity of 76.2%. Greater sensitivity (84.8%) could be achieved at a slightly lower probability (.28).

Figure 15.2 presents the results of the Receiver Operating Characteristics (ROC) analysis for the adolescent boys only. When the J-SOAP-II full-scale score was used to predict sexual recidivism for the adolescent boys the *C* value was .803, with a

Table 15.4 Association of predicted probabilities with observed outcomes

Parameter	Concordant (%)	C^a	Optimum Probability Level for Classification[b]		
			p level	Sensitivity	Specificity
Pre-Adolescent Boys					
J-SOAP Total	81.2	.824	.28	84.8	73.8
Score			.30	75.8	76.2
			.32	75.8	76.2
Adolescent Boys					
J-SOAP Total	79.4	.803	.22	78.6	70.4
Score			.24	78.6	77.8
			.26	71.4	77.8

[a]Estimated area under curve from ROC analyses
[b]$\geq$.70 for sensitivity <u>and</u> specificity

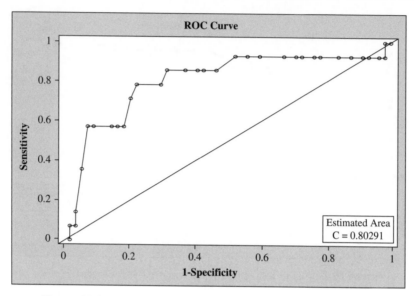

Figure 15.2 J-SOAP total score ROC analysis – Adolescent boys

concordance of 79.4%. The optimal *probability* level for the adolescents was .24, yielding a sensitivity of 78.6% and a corresponding specificity of 77.8%.

As noted above, based on the summary findings of Mossman (1994), these *C* values for J-SOAP-II, when used with these two groups of pre-adolescents and adolescents examined separately, are remarkably high (*C*: .824, .803, respectively). These *C* values correspond to Cohen's *d* (1988) values of roughly 1.24 to 1.30, and point-biserial correlations (r_{pb}) of .528 to .545 (Rice & Harris, 2005). A large effect size, as defined by Cohen (1988), would be a *d* of .80 or higher and the corresponding r_{pb}, assuming a base rate of 25%, would be .327 (Rice & Harris, 2005). We regard these results as remarkable, given the extraordinary methodological problems associated with assessment of risk in children and adolescents who have committed sexual offenses. These results are comparable to the best results reported on the Violence Risk Appraisal Guide (VRAG), a seasoned, much researched instrument for assessing risk of violence among adults (Rice & Harris, 2005).

Comparative efficacy of static and dynamic scales for predicting reoffense

We compared the predictive efficacy of the static and the dynamic scales by running a simple regression analysis, using sexual reoffense as the dependent variable and two predictors (the total static score [Scales 1 + 2] and the total dynamic score [Scales 3 + 4]). Among the pre-adolescent boys, the correlation between reoffense and the static scales (S1+2) and the dynamic scales (D3+4) was .30 and .49, respectively. The standardized regression coefficients (beta) were: S1 + 2 = .08 ($t = 0.925$, $p < .357$)

and D3 + 4 = .45 (t = 5.10, p < .001). Among the adolescent boys, the correlation between reoffense and the static scales (S1+2) and the dynamic scales (D3+4) was .34 and .37, respectively. The standardized regression coefficients (beta) were: S1 + 2 = .23 (t = 1.95, p < .06) and D3 + 4 = .27 (t = 2.30, p < .02).

DISCUSSION

The extraordinarily difficult task of assessing accurately the risk posed by adolescent sexual offenders is made all the more urgent by the recent imposition of harsh legal sanctions targeting these youngsters. These sanctions, primarily community notification and civil commitment, are management strategies that assume the ability to discriminate among youth with regard to degree of risk for reoffending sexually. Although progress has been made, we are still in the rudimentary stages of testing promising risk assessment scales developed for juvenile sex offenders.

Like any scale that is developed to assess risk, J-SOAP-II requires ongoing validation on diverse samples. Further revision and adaptation will undoubtedly occur as we learn more about how J-SOAP-II works with different groups (by gender, by age/developmental stage, perhaps by typological status [e.g., rapist or child molester], perhaps by placement [e.g., community-based, child welfare system, juvenile justice system]). Despite significant methodological challenges, we have made notable progress and the returns on predictive validity studies thus far, including the present one, have been encouraging.

The study briefly reported in this chapter represents the first examination of the predictive validity of the J-SOAP-II using a sample of boys drawn from the child welfare system and the first attempt to apply the J-SOAP to pre-adolescents. The failure rate for new hands-on sexual offenses for the pre-adolescents (30.6%) was notably higher than the equivalent failure rate for the adolescents (23%). Over three-quarters of all new offenses for both pre-adolescents and adolescents were committed within 24 months after the ASAP evaluation. The J-SOAP-II performed comparably for the pre-adolescents and adolescents in predicting sexual reoffense, with AUC values of .82, and .80, respectively. For both the pre-adolescents and the adolescents, the score derived from the combined dynamic scales (3 + 4) outperformed the score derived from the combined static scales (1 + 2). This was especially true for the pre-adolescents, wherein the combined static score was weak (β = .08) compared with the combined dynamic score (β = .45). Among adolescents, although the two combined scores were comparable (β = .23 & .27), only the combined dynamic score was significant. These results would certainly seem to support the general conclusion that acute and stable dynamic risk predictors are critically important, indeed indispensable, for the younger youth.

The higher failure rate of the pre-adolescents compared with adolescents may lend some support for heightened risk associated with earlier onset. In general, younger adolescents are more likely to engage in risky sexual behavior than older adolescents (Reyna & Farley, 2006). In the delinquency literature, moreover, there is a robust finding that persistence into adulthood and/or degree of violence are associated with an earlier age of onset of antisocial behavior (e.g., Lipsey & Derzon, 1998; Loeber et al., 1998; Sullivan, Veysey & Dorangrichia, 2003). Further evidence from the present study that early onset of sexually inappropriate and coercive behaviors may be associated with greater persistence of *sexual* offending is suggested by the significantly greater number of sexual abuse victims among the pre-adolescents ($M = 4.41$ compared to 3.14 for the adolescents; $F = 4.97$, $p < .05$) and the significantly greater number of total separate incidents of sexually coercive and inappropriate behaviors ($M = 15.47$ compared with 10.57 for the adolescents; $F = 4.40$, $p < .05$). The pre-adolescents, moreover, had a significantly higher score on Scale I (*Sexual drive and preoccupation*) of the J-SOAP-II, $F(1, 190) = 4.25$, $p < .05$.

Adolescents are on an evolving developmental trajectory, and, as Cicchetti and Rogosch (2002) pointed out, "changes in the balance of risk and protective processes have the potential to alter the direction" of the trajectory (p. 10). The changing blend of normative developmental transitions during adolescence and risk-relevant adverse life events speaks to the fluid nature of "the dynamic interplay of risk and protective processes operating during adolescence" (Cicchetti & Rogosch, 2002, p. 10). Advances in understanding these complex, interactive events in the lives of juvenile sex offenders, a prerequisite for developing empirically informed treatment and risk assessment models, has been compromised by the absence of a sound theoretical framework (Kirsch & Becker, 2006). We concur with Kirsch and Becker. Although we clearly have made progress in developing experimental scales for assessing risk in adolescents, the absence of a well-grounded theory has undermined the refinement, if not the sophistication, of these scales.

With juveniles, one useful approach may be to draw upon the concept of equifinality from system's theory (von Bertalanffy, 1968), in which diverse starting points lead to a similar outcome. One illustration of equifinality with potential relevance is the development and expression of antisocial personality disorder, APD (Cicchetti & Rogosch, 2002). With APD, correlations between externalizing, delinquent and antisocial behaviors in childhood, adolescence and adulthood tend to be, at best, moderate, suggesting a variety of different paths leading to a common outcome. Clearly, in the case of juvenile sex offenders, there are a multitude of paths that lead to a similar outcome of sexually abusive and coercive behavior.

The only notable divergence with respect to outcome appears to be the intended age range of the targeted victims. As mentioned earlier, youth that offend against similar-age peers and/or adults tend to share characteristics in common with general delinquents and adult rapists. By contrast, youth who target much younger victims (i.e., 4–5 years younger than themselves), tend to share characteristics in common with adult child molesters. This may prove to be a salient difference with respect to risk prediction, requiring, at the very least, that the testing of risk assessment models for juvenile sex offenders disaggregate these two victim-age preference outcomes. It should be noted, of course, that not all juveniles who offend against younger victims fall into this latter category of individuals that 'look like' adult child molesters. Some juveniles target younger victims simply because they are readily available and more easily controlled.

As we noted earlier, however, taxonomic differentiation along the lines of what Hunter *et al.* (2003) proposed is essential for sorting out these risk-relevant dimensions.

A theoretical approach to risk assessment with juvenile sex offenders that is highly relevant, albeit admittedly unrealistic as a short-term goal for basic research in this area, emerges from the original writings of Thom (1975) on catastrophe theory. Catastrophe theory essentially seeks to explain, and indeed predict, non-linear changes in behavior. Such a model would propose that a minor change in one variable can prompt a 'catastrophic' (large) change in another variable. One type of catastrophe model ('cusp') has been used to predict alcohol use in adolescents (Clair, 1998), and the relapse process in addictive disorders in adults (Hufford *et al.*, 2003). The overarching theoretical model that embraces catastrophe theory is non-linear dynamic systems theory, which seeks to explain the behavior of complex, inherently non-linear systems. The risky behavior of adolescents, including indiscriminate sexual behavior, would certainly appear, given everything we know about such behavior, to be captured better by non-linear models.

CONCLUSION

Recent laws having the intended purpose of managing juvenile sexual offenders are characteristically punitive and carry exceptionally harsh sanctions (Chaffin & Bonner, 1998; Hunter & Lexier, 1998; Trivits & Reppucci, 2002). These laws take for granted our ability to assess risk reliably among juveniles. These laws make other unwarranted assumptions as well, including the stability of risk status once assessed. Although progress on the development of risk models is evident, the pace has been hampered by the paucity of resources and support necessary to conduct large scale validity studies of promising scales. Meanwhile, the widespread practice of classifying juvenile sex offenders according to their presumptive level of risk and rendering management decisions based on those classifications continues. It is imperative, at the least, that we keep in mind the serious unintended consequence of mislabeling youth as 'dangerous' when they are not. We may inadvertently produce the very outcome that we are trying to avoid. Not only do we stigmatize youth, with all of the predictable debilitating consequences of such stigma, but we may expose low risk youth to high risk environments and high risk peers, thereby creating 'dangerousness' where there was not before. In summary, inappropriate use of restrictive management strategies through uninformed and inaccurate risk decisions will inevitably result in a larger proportion of mistakes that translate into a significant and unnecessary human and monetary cost to society. The goal of avoiding these 'false positive mistakes' requires a sophisticated, empirically informed understanding of how to assess risk in adolescents.

Eighteen years ago Wald and Woolverton (1990) wrote an influential article on "Risk assessment: The emperor's new clothes", in which they cataloged numerous problems that threatened the integrity of the then newly designed risk assessment scales for the child welfare system. Rycus and Hughes (2003) concluded, 13 years later, that although "formal risk assessment has become tightly woven into the fabric of child welfare practice ... there is still little research to support the reliability and validity of many models, and the literature continues to raise provocative and disturbing questions about all aspects of risk assessment" (p. 6). We are once again confronted by "provocative and disturbing questions" about the premature and inappropriate use of risk assessment for managing adolescent's problematic behaviors.

Risk assessment with adolescents must be accomplished with utmost care and only with procedures that have been subjected to rigorous empirical scrutiny. We should emphasize, however, that, in our view, risk assessment per se, is not the desired end goal. A risk *and* needs assessment that focuses on risk reduction and risk management is the *most* desirable outcome for fostering a healthier, prosocial lifestyle. The ultimate worth of a scale such as the J-SOAP-II is the direction it provides its user in identifying protective factors and remediable needs.

REFERENCES

Adam Walsh Child Protection & Safety Act (2006). *Sex Offender Registration and Notification Act (SORNA)*, Public Law 248–109.

Ageton, S.S. (1983). *Sexual assault among adolescents*. Lexington, MA: Lexington Books.

Alexander, M. (1999). Sex offender treatment efficacy revisited. *Journal of Sexual Abuse: A Journal of Research and Treatment, 111*, 101–116.

Altman, D.G. (1991). *Practical statistics for medical research*. London: Chapman & Hall.

Ash, A.S. & Schwartz, M. (1994). Evaluating the performance of risk-adjustment methods: Dichotomous measures. In L.I. Lezzoni (Ed.), *Risk adjustment for measuring health care outcomes* (pp. 313–346). Ann Arbor, NI: Health Administration Press.

Association for the Treatment of Sexual Abusers (2001, June). Brief for the Association for the Treatment of Sexual Abusers: As amicus curiae in support of petitioner. *Kansas v. Crane.* 2001, WL 670067 (U.S.) (pp. 1–12). Brief is available at: http://web2.westlaw.com

Awad, G.A. & Saunders, E. (1991). Male adolescent sexual assaulters, clinical observations. *Journal of Interpersonal Violence, 6*, 446–460.

Awad, G.A., Saunders, E. & Levene, J. (1984). A clinical study of male adolescent sex offenders. *International Journal of Offender Therapy and Comparative Criminology, 20*, 105–116.

Barbaree, H.E., Hudson, S.M. & Seto, M.C. (1993). Sexual assault in society: The role of the juvenile sexual offender. In H.E. Barbaree, W.L. Marshall & S.M. Hudson (Eds), *The juvenile sex offender* (pp. 1–24). New York: Guilford Press.

Becker, J.V. (1990). Treating adolescent sexual offenders. *Professional Psychology: Research and Practice, 21*, 362–365.

Becker, J.V., Cunningham-Rathner, J. & Kaplan, M. (1986). Adolescent sexual offenders: Demographics, criminal, and sexual histories and recommendations for reducing future offenses. *Journal of Interpersonal Violence, 1*, 431–443.

Bee, H. (1997). *The developing child* (8th edn) (pp. 341–343). New York: Addison-Wesley Educational Publishers, Inc.

Berk, L. (2001). *Development through the lifespan* (2nd edn) (pp. 252–253). Boston, MA: Allyn & Bacon.

Borduin, C.M., Henggeler, S.W., Blaske, D.M. & Stein, R.J. (1990). Multisystemic treatment of adolescent sexual offenders. *International Journal of Offender Therapy and Comparative Criminology, 34*, 105–113.

Bourgon, G., Morton-Bourgon, K.E. & Madrigrano, G. (2005). Multisite investigation of treatment for sexually abusive juveniles. In B.K. Schwartz (Ed.), *The sex offender: Issues in assessment, treatment, and supervision of adult and juvenile populations* (Vol. 5) (pp. 15–1 to 15–17). Kingston, NJ: Civic Research Institute.

Bremer, J.F. & Dellacecca, K. (2006, April). *Evidence for a continuum of care: Sex offense risks for juveniles in residential and outpatient populations based on the use of the ERASOR.* Poster presented at the 21st National Adolescent Perpetrator Network Conference, Atlanta, GA.

Brown, B.V. & Bzostek, S. (2003, August). Violence in the lives of children. *Child Trends Databank*, retrieved online at: www.childtrendsdatabank.org.

Burton, D.L. (2000). Were adolescent sexual offenders children with sexual behaviour problems? *Sexual Abuse: A Journal of Research and Treatment, 12,* 37–48.

Burton, D.L. (2003). Male adolescents: Sexual victimization and subsequent sexual abuse. *Child and Adolescent Social Work Journal, 29,* 277–296.

Burton, D.L. & Smith-Darden, J. (2001). *The 2000 Safer Society Survey Report.* Rutland, VT: Safer Society Press.

Caldwell, M.F. (2002). What we do not know about juvenile sexual reoffense risk. *Child Maltreatment, 7,* 291–302.

Center for Sex Offender Management (2002, June). *An overview of sex offender management.* Silver Springs, MD: Author.

Chaffin, M. & Bonner, B. (1998). Don't shoot, we're your children: Have we gone too far in our response to adolescent sexual abusers and children with sexual behavior problems? *Child Maltreatment, 3,* 314–316.

Cicchetti, D. & Rogosch, F.A. (2002). A developmental psychopathology perspective on adolescence. *Journal of Consulting and Clinical Psychology, 70,* 6–20.

Clair, S. (1998). A cusp catastrophe model for adolescent alcohol use: An empirical test. *Nonlinear Dynamics, Psychology, and Life Sciences, 2,* 217–241.

Cohen, J. (1988). *Statistical power analysis for the behavioral sciences* (2nd edn). Hillsdale, NJ: Lawrence Erlbaum.

Dahl, R.E. & Spear, L.P. (Eds) (2004). *Adolescent brain development: vulnerabilities and opportunities.* Annals Vol. 1021. New York: The New York Academy of Sciences.

DeBellis, M.D. (2005). The psychobiology of neglect. *Child Maltreatment, 10,* 150–172.

DeBellis, M.D., Baum, A.S., Birmaher, B. *et al.* (1999a). Developmental traumatology. Part I: Biological stress systems. *Biological Psychiatry, 45,* 1259–1270.

DeBellis, M.D., Keshavan, M.S., Clark, D.B. *et al.* (1999b). Developmental traumatology. Part II: Brain development. *Biological Psychiatry, 45,* 1272–1284.

Epperson, D.L., Ralston, C.A., Fowers, D. *et al.* (2006). Actuarial risk assessment with juveniles who offend sexually: Development of the Juvenile Sexual Offense Recidivism Risk Assessment Tool-II (JSORRAT-II). In D. Prescott (Ed.), *Risk assessment: Theory, controversy, and emerging strategies of youth who have sexually abused* (pp. 118–169). Oklahoma City, OK: Wood & Barnes Publishing.

Fanniff, A.M. & Becker, J.V. (2006). Specialized assessment and treatment of adolescent sex offenders. *Aggression and Violent Behavior, 11,* 265–282.

Fehrenbach, P.A., Smith, W. Monastersky, C. & Deisher, R.W. (1986). Adolescent sex offenders: Offender and offense characteristics. *American Journal of Orthopsychiatry, 56,* 225–233.

Ford, M.E. & Linney, J.A. (1995). Comparative analysis of adolescent sexual offenders, violent non-sexual offenders, and status offenders. *Journal of Interpersonal Violence, 10,* 56–70.

Forth, A.E., Kosson, D.S. & Hare, R.D. (2003). *The Psychopathy Checklist: Youth Version.* Toronto, Canada: Multi-Health Systems.

Gretton, H.M., McBride, M., Hare, R.D. *et al.* (2001). Psychopathy and recidivism in adolescent sex offenders. *Criminal Justice and Behavior, 28,* 427–449.

Hagan, M.P. & Cho, M.E. (1996). A comparison of treatment outcomes between adolescent rapists and child sexual offenders. *International Journal of Offender Therapy and Comparative Criminology, 40,* 113–122.

Hagan, M.P., Gust-Brey, K.L., Cho, M.E. & Dow, E. (2001). Eight-year comparative analyses of adolescent rapists, adolescent child molesters, other adolescent delinquents, and the general population. *International Journal of Offender Therapy and Comparative Criminology, 45*, 314–324.

Hann, D.M. (Ed.) (2001). *Taking stock of risk factors for child/youth externalizing behavior problems.* Washington, DC: National Institute of Mental Health.

Hanson, R.K. & Bussière, M.T. (1998). Predicting relapse: A meta-analysis of sexual offender recidivism studies. *Journal of Consulting and Clinical Psychology, 66*, 348–362.

Hanson, R.K. & Morton-Bourgon, K. (2005). The characteristics of persistent sexual offenders: A meta-analysis of recidivism studies. *Journal of Consulting and Clinical Psychology, 73*, 1154–1163.

Harrell, F.E., Lee, K.L., Califf, R. *et al.* (1984). Regression modeling strategies for improved prognostic prediction. *Statistics in Medicine, 3*, 143–152.

Harris, P.L., Olthof, T. & Terwogt, M.M. (1981). Children's knowledge of emotion. *Journal of Child Psychology and Psychiatry, 22*, 247–261.

Hawkins, J.D., Herrenkohl, T.L., Farrington, D.P. *et al.* (1998). A review of predictors of youth violence. In R. Loeber & D.P. Farrington (Eds), *Serious and violent juvenile offenders: Risk factors and successful interventions* (pp. 106–146). Thousand Oaks, CA: Sage Publications.

Hecker, J., Scoular, Righthand, S. & Nangle, D. (2002, Oct.). *Predictive validity of the J-SOAP over 10-plus years: Implications for risk assessment.* Paper presented at the Annual Meeting of the Association of Treatment of Sexual Abusers, Montreal, Quebec, Canada.

Hoffman, M.L. (1982). Development of prosocial motivation: Empathy and guilt. In N. Eisenberg (Ed.), *The development of prosocial behavior* (pp. 281–314). New York: Academic Press.

Hoffman, M.L. (1988). Moral development. In M.H. Bornstein & M.E. Lamb (Eds), *Developmental Psychology: An advanced textbook* (2nd edn) (pp. 497–548). Hillsdale, NJ: Erlbaum.

Hoffman, M.L. (1991). Empathy, cognition, and social action. In W.M. Kurtines & J.L. Gewirtz (Eds), *Handbook of moral behavior and development, Volume 1* (pp. 275–303). Hillsdale, NJ: Erlbaum.

Hufford, M.H., Witkiewitz, K., Shields, A.L. *et al.* (2003). Relapse as a non-linear dynamic system: Application to patients with alcohol use disorders. *Journal of Abnormal Psychology, 112*, 219–227.

Hunter, J.A. (2000). Understanding juvenile sexual offenders: Research findings and guidelines for effective management and treatment. *Juvenile Justice Fact Sheet.* Charlottesville, VA: Institute of Law, Psychiatry, and Public Policy, University of Virginia.

Hunter, J.A. (2006). Understanding diversity in juvenile sexual offenders: Implications for assessment, treatment and legal management. In R.E. Longo & D.S. Prescott (Eds), *Current perspectives: Working with sexually aggressive youth and youth with sexual behavior problems* (pp. 63–78). Holyoke, MA: NEARI Press.

Hunter, J.A., Figueredo, A.J., Malamuth, N.M. & Becker, J.V. (2003). Juvenile sex offenders: Toward the development of a typology. *Sexual Abuse: A Journal of Research and Treatment, 15*, 27–48.

Hunter, J.A., Goodwin, D.W. & Becker, J.V. (1994). The relationship between phallometrically measured deviant sexual arousal and clinical characteristics in juvenile sexual offenders. *Behavior, Research and Therapy, 32*, 533–538.

Hunter, J.A., Hazelwood, R.R. & Slesinger, D. (2000). Juvenile perpetrated sexual crimes: Patterns of offending and predictors of violence. *Journal of Family Violence, 15*, 81–93.

Hunter, J.A. & Lexier, L.J. (2003). Ethical and legal issues in the assessment and treatment of juvenile sex offenders. *Child Maltreatment: Journal of the American Professional Society on the Abuse of Children, 3*, 339–348.

Kahn, T.J. & Chambers, H.J. (1991). Assessing reoffense risk with juvenile sexual offenders. *Child Welfare, 70*, 333–345.

Kaufman, J. & Zigler, E. (1987). Do abused children become abused parents? *American Journal of Orthopsychiatry, 57*, 186–192.

Keating, D. (1990). Adolescent thinking. In S.S. Feldman & G.R. Elliot (Eds), *At the threshold: The developing adolescent* (pp. 54–89). Cambridge, MA: Harvard University Press.

Kenney, D.T., Keogh, T. & Seidler, K. (2001). Predictors of recidivism in Australian juvenile sex offenders: Implications for treatment. *Sexual Abuse: A Journal of Research and Treatment, 13*, 131–148.

Kirsch, L.G. & Becker, J.V. (2006). Sexual offending: Theory of problem, theory of change, and implications for treatment effectiveness. *Aggression and Violent Behavior, 11*, 208–224.

Knight, R.A. & Prentky, R.A. (1993). Exploring characteristics for classifying juvenile sex offenders. In H.E. Barbaree, W.L. Marshall & S.M. Hudson (Eds), *The juvenile sex offender* (pp. 45–79). New York: Guilford Press.

Lab, S.P., Shields, G. & Schondel, C. (1993). Research note: An evaluation of juvenile sex offenders. In H.E. Barbaree, W.L. Marshall & S. Hudson (Eds), *The juvenile sex offender* (pp. 45–83). New York: Guilford Press.

Långström, N. (2002). Long-term follow-up of criminal recidivism in young sex offenders: Temporal patterns and risk factors. *Psychology, Crime and Law, 8*, 41–58.

Långström, N. & Grann, M. (2000). Risk for criminal recidivism among young offenders. *Journal of Interpersonal Violence, 15*, 855–871.

Letourneau, E.J. (2006). Legal consequences of juvenile sex offending in the United States. In H.E. Barbaree & W.L. Marshall (Eds), *The juvenile sex offender* (2nd edn) (pp. 275–290). New York: Guilford Press.

Letourneau, E.J. & Miner, M.H. (2005). Juvenile sex offenders: A case against the legal and clinical status quo. *Sexual Abuse: A Journal of Research and Treatment, 17*, 293–312.

Levin, I. & Hart, S. (2003). Risk preferences in young children: Early evidence of individual differences in reaction to potential gains and losses. *Journal of Behavioral Decision Making, 16*, 397–413.

Lipsey, M.W. & Derzon, J.H. (1998). Predictors of violence and serious delinquency in adolescence and early adulthood: A synthesis of longitudinal research. In R. Loeber & D.P. Farrington (Eds), *Serious and violent juvenile offenders: Risk factors and successful interventions* (pp. 86–105). Thousand Oaks, CA: Sage.

Loeber, R., Farrington, D.P., Stouthamer-Loeber, M. & Van Kammen, W.B. (1998). *Antisocial behavior and mental health problems: Explanatory factors in childhood and adolescence.* Mahawah, NJ: Lawrence Erlbaum Associates.

Martinez, R., Rosenfield, B. & Flores, J. (2004, March). *Predictive validity of the J-SOAP-II for sexual offending minority youth.* Paper presented at the Annual Meeting of American Psychology-Law Society, Scottsdale, AZ.

McCoy, W.K. & Murrie, D. (2006, March). *Use of JSOAP and ERASOR in community sample.* Paper presented at the Annual Meeting of American Psychology-Law Society, St Petersburg, FLA.

Meyers, W.C., Scott, K.S., Burgess, A.W. & Burgess, A.G. (1995). Psychopathology, biopsychosocial factors, crime characteristics, and classification of 25 homicidal youths. *Journal of American Academy of Child and Adolescent Psychiatry, 34*, 1483–1489.

Moffitt, T.E. (1993). Adolescence-limited and life-course persistent antisocial behavior: A developmental taxonomy. *Psychological Review, 100*, 674–701.

Mossman, D. (1994). Assessing predictions of violence: Being accurate about accuracy. *Journal of Consulting and Clinical Psychology, 62*, 783–792.

Nisbet, I.A., Wilson, P.H. & Smallbone, S.W. (2004). A prospective longitudinal study of sexual recidivism among adolescent sex offenders. *Sexual Abuse: A Journal of Research and Treatment, 16*, 223–234.

Parks, G.A. & Bard, D.E. (2006). Risk factors for adolescent sex offender recidivism: Evaluation of predictive factors and comparison of three groups based upon victim type. *Sexual Abuse: A Journal of Research and Treatment, 28*(4), 319–342.

Prentky, R.A. (1999). Child sexual molestation. In V.B. Hasselt & M. Hersen (Eds), *Handbook of psychological approaches with violent offenders* (pp. 267–300). New York: Kluwer Academic/Plenum Publishers.

Prentky, R.A. (2006). *Risk management of sexually abusive youth: A follow-up study.* Final Technical Report submitted to National Institute of Justice, (2002-IJ-CX 0029). Available at: www.ncjrs.gov/pdffiles/nij/grants/214261/pdf

Prentky, R.A., Harris, B., Frizzell, L. & Righthand, S. (2000). An actuarial procedure for assessing risk in juvenile sex offenders. *Sexual Abuse: A Journal of Research and Treatment, 12*, 71–93.

Prentky, R.A. & Knight, R.A. (1993). Age of onset of sexual assault: Criminal and life history correlates. In G.C.N. Hall, R. Hirschman, J.R. Graham & M.S. Zaragoza (Eds), *Sexual aggression: Issues in etiology, assessment, and treatment* (pp. 43–62). London: Taylor & Francis.

Prentky, R.A., Knight, R.A. & Lee, A.F.S. (1997). Risk factors associated with recidivism among extrafamilial child molesters. *Journal of Consulting and Clinical Psychology, 65*, 141–149.

Prentky, R.A., Knight, R.A., Sims-Knight, J.E. *et al.* (1989). Developmental antecedents of sexual aggression. *Development and Psychopathology, 1*, 153–169.

Prentky, R.A. & Righthand, S. (2003). *Juvenile Sex Offender Assessment Protocol-II (J-SOAP-II) Manual.* Washington, DC: Office of Juvenile Justice and Delinquency Prevention's Juvenile Justice Clearinghouse (NCJ 202316).

Rasmussen, L.A. (1999). Factors related to recidivism among juvenile sexual offenders. *Sexual Abuse: A Journal of Research and Treatment, 11*, 69–86.

Reyna, V.F. (1996). Conceptions of memory development with implications for reasoning and decision making. *Annals of Child Development, 12*, 87–118.

Reyna, V.F. & Farley, F. (2006). Risk and rationality in adolescent decision making: Implications for theory, practice, and public policy. *Psychological Science in the Public Interest, 7*, 1–44.

Rice, C.L. (1995). *The effects of outcome attractiveness and framing on children's risky decision making.* Unpublished master's thesis, University of Arizona, Tucson.

Rice, M.E. & Harris, G.T. (2005). Comparing effect sizes in follow-up studies: ROC area, Cohen's *d* and *r*. *Law and Human Behavior, 29*, 615–620.

Rich, P. (2003). *Juvenile sexual offenders: Understanding, assessing, and rehabilitating.* Hoboken, NJ: John Wiley & Sons, Inc.

Righthand, S., Carpenter, E.M. & Prentky, R.A. (2001, November). *Risk assessment with juveniles who sexually offended: A comparative analysis of community and residential youths.* Poster session presented at the Annual Meeting of the Association for the Treatment of Sexual Abusers, Treatment Conference, San Antonio, TX.

Righthand, S., Prentky, R.A., Hecker, J.E. *et al.* (2000). *JJPI-Maine Juvenile Sex Offender Risk Assessment Schedule (J-SOAP).* Poster session presented at the Annual Meeting of the Association for the Treatment of Sexual Abusers, 19th Annual Research and Treatment Conference, San Diego, CA.

Righthand, S., Prentky, R.A., Knight, R.A. *et al.* (2005). Factor structure and validation of the *Juvenile Sex Offender Assessment Protocol* (J-SOAP). *Sexual Abuse: A Journal of Research and Treatment, 17*, 13–30.

Rivera, B. & Widom, C.S. (1990). Childhood victimization and violent offending. *Violence and Victims, 5*, 19–35.

Ross, J. & Loss, P. (1991). Assessment of the juvenile sex offender. In G.D. Ryan & S.L. Lane (Eds), *Juvenile sexual offending: Causes, consequences, and correction* (pp. 199–251). Lexington, MA: Lexington Books.

Rycus, J.S. & Hughes, R.C. (2003). *Issues in risk assessment in child protective services: Policy white paper.* Retrieved online October 2, 2006 from the North American Resource Centre for Child Welfare website at: www.narccw.com

Schram, D.D., Milloy, C.D. & Rowe, W.E. (1991, Sept.). *Juvenile sex offenders: A follow-up study of reoffense behavior.* Olympia, WA: Washington State Institute for Public Policy.

Seabloom, W., Seabloom, M.E., Seabloom, E. *et al.* (2003). A 14-to-24 year longitudinal study of a comprehensive sexual health model treatment program for adolescent sex offenders: Predictors of successful completion and subsequent criminal recidivism. *International Journal of Offender Therapy and Criminology, 47*, 113–122.

Selman, R.L. (1976). Social-cognitive understanding: A guide to educational and clinical practice. In T. Lickona (Ed.), *Moral development and behavior: Theory, research, and social issues* (pp. 299–316). New York: Holt, Rinehart & Winston.

Selvog, H.H. (2001). Social state to penal state, moral panic and sex offenders: Megan's Law as a result of moral panic. *Justice Policy Journal, 1*, 72–93.

Shoor, M., Speed, M.H. & Bartelt, C. (1966). Syndrome of the adolescent child molester. *American Journal of Psychiatry, 122*, 783–789.

Sipe, R., Jensen, E.L. & Everett, R.S. (1998). Adolescent sexual offenders grown up: Recidivism in young adulthood. *Criminal Justice and Behavior, 25*, 109–124.

Skowron, C. (2004). *Differentiation and predictive factors in adolescent sexual offending.* Unpublished doctoral dissertation. Carelton University, Ottawa, Ontario, Canada.

Smith, W.R. & Monastersky, C. (1986). Assessing juvenile sexual offenders' risk for reoffending. *Criminal Justice and Behavior, 13*, 115–140.

Spaccarelli, S., Bowden, B., Coatsworth, J.D. & Kim, S. (1997). Psychosocial correlates of male sexual aggression in a chronic delinquent sample. *Criminal Justice and Behavior, 24*, 71–95.

Spear, L.P. (2000). The adolescent brain and age-related behavioral manifestations. *Neuroscience and Biobehavioral Reviews, 24*, 417–463.

Steinberg, L. (2004). Risk taking in adolescence: What changes and why? *Annals of the New York Academy of Sciences, 1021*, 51–58.

Steinberg, L. & Scott, E.S. (2003). Less guilty by reason of adolescence: Developmental immaturity, diminished responsibility, and the juvenile death penalty. *American Psychologist, 58*, 1009–1018.

Stewart, A., Dennison, S. & Waterson, R. (2002). Pathways from maltreatment to juvenile offending. *Trends and Issues in Crime and Criminal Justice, 241*, 1–6.

Sullivan, C.J., Veysey, B.M. & Dorangrichia, L. (2003). Examining the relationship between problem history and violent offending in high-risk youth. *Journal of Offender Rehabilitation, 38*, 17–39.

Teicher, M.H. (2000). Wounds that time won't heal: The neurobiology of child abuse. *Cerebrum: The Dana Farber Forum on Brain Science, 2*, 50–67.

Teicher, M.H. (2002). Scars that won't heal: The neurobiology of child abuse. *Scientific American, 283*, 68–75.

Teicher, M.H., Andersen, S.L., Polcari, A. *et al.* (2003). The neurobiological consequences of early stress and childhood maltreatment. *Neuroscience and Biobehavioral Reviews, 27*, 33–44.

Thom, R. (1975). Catastrophe theory: Its present state and future perspectives. In A. Manning (Ed.), *Dynamical systems-Warwick1974: Lecture notes in mathematics No. 468* (pp. 366–389). Berlin: Springer-Verlag.

Trivits, L.C. & Reppucci, N.D. (2002). Application of Megan's Law to juveniles. *American Psychologist, 57*, 690–704.

US Department of Health and Human Services (1999). *Mental health: A report of the Surgeon General.* Rockville, MD: Author.

US Department of Health and Human Services (2001). *Youth violence: A report of the Surgeon General.* Rockville, MD: Author.

Van Ness, S.R. (1984). Rape as instrumental violence: A study of youth offenders. *Journal of Offender Counseling Services and Rehabilitation, 9*, 161–170.

von Bertalanffy, L. (1968). *General systems theory.* New York: Braziller.

Waite, D., Keller, A., McGarvery, E.L. *et al.* (2005). Juvenile sex offender re-arrest rates for sexual, violent non-sexual and property crimes: A ten-year follow-up. *Sexual Abuse: A Journal of Research and Treatment, 17*, 313–331.

Wald, M.S. & Woolverton, M. (1990). Risk assessment: The emperor's new clothes. *Child Welfare, 69*, 483–511.

Worling, J.R. (1995). Sexual abuse histories of adolescent male sex offenders: Differences on the basis of the age and gender of their victims. *Journal of Abnormal Psychology, 104*, 610–613.

Worling, J.R. (2002). Assessing risk of sexual assault recidivism with adolescent sexual offenders. In M.C. Calder (Ed.), *Young people who sexually abuse: Building the evidence base for your practice* (pp. 365–375). Lyme Regis, UK: Russell House.

Worling, J.R. (2004). The estimate of risk of adolescent sexual offense recidivism (ERASOR): Preliminary psychometric data. *Sexual Abuse: A Journal of Research and Treatment, 16*, 235–254.

Worling, J.R. (2005). Assessing sexual offense risk for adolescents who have offended sexually. In B.K. Schwartz (Ed.), *The sex offender: Issues in assessment, treatment, and supervision of adult and juvenile populations*, Vol. 5 (pp. 18–1 to 18–17). Kingston, NJ: Civic Research Institute.

Worling, J.R. & Curwen, T. (2001). *The "ERASOR": Estimate of Risk of Adolescent Sexual Recidivism* (Version 2.0). Toronto, Ontario, Canada: Safe-T Program, Thistletown Regional Centre.

Worling, J.R. & Långström, N. (2003). Assessment of criminal recidivism risk with adolescents who have offended sexually: A review. *Trauma, Violence, & Abuse, 4*, 341–362.

Worling, J.R. & Långström N. (2006). Risk of sexual recidivism in adolescents who offend sexually: Correlates and assessment. In H.E. Barbaree & W.L. Marshall (Eds), *The juvenile sex offender* (2nd edn) (pp. 219–247). New York: Guilford Press.

Zimring, R.E. (2004). *An American travesty: Legal responses to adolescent sexual offending*. Chicago, IL: The University of Chicago Press.

PART FOUR
Interventions

16

Models of Offender Rehabilitation: The Good Lives Model and The Risk-Need-Responsivity Model

TONY WARD

RACHAEL M. COLLIE

PATRICE BOURKE

INTRODUCTION

The effective treatment of sex offenders depends on the availability of valid assessment measures and procedures, and powerful interventions. Assessment and treatment modules in turn are underpinned by rehabilitation theories, essentially maps of the intervention process. The primary aim of theories of rehabilitation is to provide therapists with guidance on issues such as the values and aims of intervention, aetiological commitments and treatment targets, and how to integrate the technical and process aspects of treatment (e.g., therapist factors).

It is fair to say that the issue of offender rehabilitation is a controversial and contested one. The flashpoints include debate over the effectiveness of rehabilitation and claims that even if treatment does reduce reoffending sex offenders do not deserve the opportunity to learn new skills and ultimately a chance at better lives. Instead, the argument goes, they should be humanely contained and the focus of sentencing on retribution rather than treatment. However, what is increasingly clear is that it is possible to reduce reoffending rates by treating or rehabilitating sex offenders as opposed to simply incarcerating them (Andrews & Bonta, 2003; Hollin, 1999). Furthermore, treatment can be cost-effective as well as harm reducing. Despite some dissenting views (e.g., Whitehead & Lab, 1990), most recent comprehensive reviews of what

Assessment and Treatment of Sex Offenders: A Handbook. Edited by Anthony Beech, Leam Craig and Kevin Browne. © John Wiley & Sons Ltd, 2009.

works in the correctional domain agree that some types of rehabilitation programmes are extremely effective in reducing reoffending rates (e.g., Andrews & Dowden, 2005, 2006). For example, Lipsey's (1992) examination of almost 400 studies of juvenile delinquency treatment programmes led to the conclusion that cognitive behavioural interventions that were delivered in a rigorous and appropriate manner resulted in considerable reductions in reoffending (i.e., by at least 10%). Thus active attempts to change the characteristics of offenders associated with crime can reduce future risk.

On the other hand, deterrence-based approaches and diversion do not appear to provide any kind of significant treatment effect. The evidence suggests that deterrent type approaches which include intensive supervision programming, boot camps, scared straight, drug testing, electronic monitoring and increased prison sentences are ineffective in reducing recidivism (e.g., Gendreau *et al.*, 2000; MacKenzie, Wilson & Kider, 2001). In fact, a recent review of randomly assigned evaluations of scared straight programmes, Petrosino, Turpin-Petrosino and Fincknaeuer (2000) concluded that most actually increased recidivism (by up to 30%).

The empirical evidence seems to be quite straightforward and persuasive – treat the offender rather than simply punish and do not focus all correctional resources on deterrence. The push for utilising empirically supported interventions in sex offender programmes is underpinned by two types of reasons. First, there is the proposal that because public resources are scarce it is important not to squander them and therefore to only adopt intervention strategies that have been empirically evaluated as effective. The resources referred to comprise financial, material and human capital, and thus include correctional personal (e.g., psychologists, social workers, prison officers, teachers, trainers and so on), materials (e.g., buildings, handouts, books, etc.), and specialised agencies (e.g., institutions that promote change such as specialised drug and alcohol services). The second type of reasons is more abstract and in effect constitutes a set of claims based on the contrasting ethical claims of community and offenders. On the one hand it is claimed that the safety needs of the community can best be served by reducing recidivism rates and hence minimising the degree of harm and setback to the interests of individuals; the focus is squarely on the interests of the community and harm reduction. On the other hand, a second focus is on offenders' welfare and the argument is that their interests are more likely to be facilitated by the adoption of effective interventions by correctional treatment agencies. There is thus tension between the push for offender rights and the rights of the community to be safe from future threats (Ward, Gannon & Birgden, 2007). In other words, the contemporary debate in correctional, social and political arenas is not really about the utilisation of 'What Works' but rather concerns how best to employ effective interventions and whose interests are paramount. Fundamentally, it is a matter of human interests, rights and goods.

In this chapter we discuss the frequently neglected question of what actually constitutes a correctional *rehabilitation theory* as opposed to aetiological or treatment theories. We then briefly examine an example of a risk management rehabilitation theory, the Risk-Need-Responsivity model (RNR), and an example of a strength-based approach, the Good Lives Model (GLM). Finally, we conclude the chapter with some reflections on the future of sexual offender rehabilitation. The two theories of rehabilitation examined in this chapter apply to both general and sex offenders and it is assumed that any comment relating to one of these groups also applies to the other unless otherwise noted.

THE NATURE OF REHABILITATION THEORY

Attempts to help individuals reform their ways and lead productive and satisfying lives have been evident for thousands of years through religious and philosophical writings. True, in less enlightened times the contingencies were often particularly harsh and the threat of extreme punishment a primary means of modifying deviant behaviour, such as physical violence. The fact that the roots of offender rehabilitation are ancient means that today it is possible to identify conflicting and diverse discourses underlying correctional policies concerning offender treatment. The presence of contested ideas and values has created a wealth of different terminologies associated with the reintegration of criminals. Criminal justice workers and professionals speak of 'treating', 'rehabilitating', 'reintegrating', encouraging 'desistence from crime', offender 'rehabilitation', or 'redirecting' offenders (Andrews & Bonta, 2003; Ward & Stewart, 2003). Each of these terms has slightly different connotations derived from networks of core values and assumptions about the nature of crime and offenders. For example, 'treatment' has its roots in the medicalisation of crime and viewing offenders as suffering from some form of disorder of the body or mind (Ward & Maruna, 2007). While, the notion of 'reintegration' suggests that individuals who have committed criminal offences are somewhat estranged from the moral community and need to acknowledge responsibility for their offences and the process of change in order to be accepted back (Ward & Maruna, 2007).

Our major aim in this chapter is to briefly critically examine two broad approaches to sex offender rehabilitation or reintegration. While fully aware of the subtle differences in meaning of different terms for the process of reintegration we use the terms above as synonyms. In our view there is a common thread of meaning that runs through all the various labels used to refer to the process of modifying offenders' criminal tendencies and dispositions in order to reduce the harm to society and result in better lives for the individuals themselves. Thus in this chapter, we will primarily use the term 'rehabilitation' to denote this process.

FEATURES OF A GOOD REHABILITATION THEORY

We would argue that a good theory of sex offender rehabilitation should specify the aims of therapy, provide a justification of these aims in terms of its core assumptions about aetiology and the values underpinning the approach, identify clinical targets and outline how treatment should proceed in the light of these assumptions and goals (Ward & Marshall, 2004). In order to be able to adequately describe and evaluate the

RNR (Risk-Need-Responsivity Model) and GLM (Good Lives Model) models it is first necessary to identify the features of a rehabilitation theory. Somewhat surprisingly we have found that the nature of rehabilitation tends to be taken for granted in the correctional and sexual offending fields and very little has been said about what actually constitutes a *rehabilitation theory* as opposed to a treatment or aetiological theory. Typically, the terms 'treatment', 'therapy' and 'rehabilitation' are used interchangeably as if they refer to the same thing. In our opinion using these terms interchangeably runs the risk of confusing distinct types of theories and their associated referents: normative theories concerning the legitimate aims of treatment as found in policy debates; aetiological theories explaining why crimes occur and how to prevent them; treatment theories concerning how to implement certain strategies and why targeting specific factors is likely to be effective; and finally, overarching theories of rehabilitation.

This is unfortunate and can only lead at best to confusion about how to proceed when working therapeutically with sex offenders and at worse to a failure to provide correctional workers with a comprehensive framework for dealing with the complexities of correctional practice. Typically, there is little attention to policy or aetiological theories and most often what is presented to individuals working with sex offenders are manual-based programmes that prescribe in great detail techniques for modifying criminal behaviour. In our view all the different types of theories have something to offer but only if elements of each are integrated into a coherent rehabilitation theory.

The terms theories of 'treatment' or 'therapy' refer to theories that incorporate psychological principles and concrete strategies and are applied in clinical settings to change the behaviour of sex offenders. They are in effect local theories of change and specify how to effect reductions in offence-related problems using certain types of techniques. In our view, the term 'rehabilitation theory' is broader in nature and refers to the overarching aims, values, principles and aetiological assumptions that are used to guide interventions with sex offenders and instruct therapists how to translate these rather abstract principles into work with different people.

A rehabilitation theory is essentially a *hybrid* theory comprised of values, core principles, aetiological assumptions and practice guidelines. In effect, it contains elements of normative, aetiological, practice/treatment theories within it while being somewhat broader in scope. It contains multiple levels and enables therapists to intervene with offenders in diverse and rational ways. Without a rehabilitation theory, therapists will be unaware of the broad aims (i.e., reduce risk, enhance functioning) of treatment and their relationship to the causes of sexual offending.

We propose that there are *three* levels, or components, to rehabilitation theories: (1) a set of general principles and assumptions that specify the values that underlie rehabilitation practice and the kind of overall aims for which clinicians should be striving; (2) aetiological assumptions that serve to explain sexual offending and identify its functions, at least in a general sense; and (3) the intervention implications of both the set of values, aims and principles, and the aetiological assumptions. We will now describe each of these components in more detail.

General Principles and Assumptions

Every rehabilitation theory has a number of general metaphysical, epistemological (knowledge-based) and ethical assumptions concerning the purpose and nature of the key actors associated with rehabilitation that underlie its practical suggestions. In our experience, these are often tacit and require teasing out. *Metaphysical* assumptions concern the nature of the entities involved in the rehabilitation process and outline their core features and processes. This could include specifying the nature of risk (e.g., is it discrete or dynamic), whether or not sex offenders have value as persons (e.g., are they moral strangers or simply estranged from the rest of the community), are sex offenders redeemable, what constitutes human nature more generally, and sex offenders in particular, are people best viewed as part of nature, or are they cultural products or a mixture, and so on.

The basic *epistemological* assumptions really spell out what constitutes knowledge and how research that informs practice should be undergone, and hence will include recommendations about research designs, analytic strategies and what kind of evidence is admissible when deciding on best practice with offenders. In addition, the core epistemological assumptions contained in a rehabilitation theory should inform researchers and practitioners about what knowledge consists of and what threshold is required when making decisions about offenders (e.g., risk assessment, probation reports, etc.). A good example of the broad epistemological assumptions concerns the merits of qualitative versus quantitatively derived data and the location of such methods in epistemological theories. For example, constructive approaches to knowledge tend to privilege personal or lived experience while positivist, empiricist research and theories favour more objective methods.

Values are a particularly important set of resources as they represent foundational or core standards used to construct ways of living and hence identities. They bestow a sense of meaning, significance and purpose on human lives and are at the heart of the rehabilitation process. A value judgement asserts that specific types of qualities, which are evaluated as positive or negative, characterise aspects of the world or people (Kekes, 1993; Rescher, 1993). Values play a significant role in rehabilitation theories as they serve to identify therapeutic goals (e.g., to promote a good life or to reduce community risk) and to constrain rehabilitative attempts (e.g., we should not subject offenders to empirically unsupported interventions or expose them to unnecessarily stressful situations). In addition, the weightings of offenders' interests relative to those of the community will be stated and function to constrain therapeutic and bureaucratic decision making. Although we must reiterate our earlier point that often these assumptions are implicit and not fully expressed.

Aetiological Assumptions

Aetiological or causal assumptions (component 2) help therapists and probation officers to understand *how* to target specific variables as well as indicating *what* to target. The aetiological component of a rehabilitation theory is clearly linked to the level above (i.e., basic assumptions) and will incorporate the entities and processes that exist in any causal claims. The aetiological component bridges the gap between the core assumptions (component 1) and practice guidelines (component 3). In order for therapists to effectively target the most appropriate characteristics of sex offenders they need to know which of the bewildering array of variables evident are causally related to offending and which if modified will result in reduced reoffending rates. However, in order to identify and eliminate the most relevant problems presented by sex offenders they need to have certain values in mind, for example, to reduce risk to the community, allow victims to achieve resolution, enhance offenders' well-being, and/or engage in ethical practice (e.g., respect offenders' rights, ensure all offenders receive equal resources, ensure victims' rights are considered alongside those of offenders and so on). This is essentially the point we made earlier that scientific explanations track interests and values: researchers with different interests are likely to pursue quite different research projects and therefore intervention strategies. In other words, if there is no theory or research on sex offenders' needs, it is unlikely to figure in practice guidelines and therapeutic programmes.

Rehabilitation theories should not be confused with aetiological theories of a general type (e.g., general theories of crime) or of particular types of offences (e.g., sexual offences). The major function of rehabilitation theories is to provide a comprehensive guide to clinicians when working with offenders. The aetiological component of such theories is quite general in scope. It only serves to sketch out the causal factors that culminate in general criminal actions or sexual offending and to depict their relationships with each other. In a sense it provides an *overview* of the kinds of factors that are likely to cause sexual crimes and on its own does not constitute a complete explanation. In effect because rehabilitation theories are hybrid theories containing elements of different types of theories, they cannot be expected to provide the same kind of value that the more specific theories do in their own particular domains. In a sense, they hover above the more specific theories and draw from them core assumptions and factors. Ultimately the content-rich or domain-specific theories (e.g., theories of crime) feed into or provide the more abstract rehabilitation with theory content. This should be an ongoing process but an explicit and critical one. That is, policy makers, researchers and practitioners should deliberately evaluate their best rehabilitation theories in light of new research and either adjust the theory or reject it for a better alternative.

Intervention Implications

A good rehabilitation theory should also specify the most suitable style of treatment (e.g., skills-based, structured, etc.), inform therapists about the appropriate attitudes to take toward sex offenders, address the issue of motivation and clarify the role and importance of the therapeutic alliance. The kind of guidance given to therapists will vary according to the core assumptions and aetiological elements described earlier. The three components are conceptually linked in that the overriding aims of rehabilitation should be consistent with the demonstrated causes of crime and the types of treatment interventions ought to follow from both aetiological assumptions and core value commitments.

Although theories of therapy assume the relevance and truthfulness of some aetiological theories, they do not aim to explain why individuals commit sexual offences but instead concentrate on informing clinicians how to effect behavioural changes in offenders. In other words, there are various types of theories associated with sex offenders: rehabilitation theories, aetiological theories, policy/normative theories and treatment theories.

One more issue remains: how should rehabilitation theories be evaluated? Because they are hybrid theories we suggest a two-fold evaluation strategy. First, each of the three components of the theory should be critically examined to ascertain whether of not there are problems of coherence, scope, etc. This is possible because sometimes important values are missing (i.e., ones accepted by the community) or rather dubious assumptions made about offenders. Furthermore, the evidential base of the various aetiological claims can be examined and the various methods used to collect data critically appraised. Second, an overall judgement can be made of the rehabilitation theory's value, taking into account its strengths and weaknesses relative to its rivals and also itself.

If a rehabilitation theory is coherent and a strong or 'good' theory, it is able to account for the agreed upon facts of sexual offending (by virtue of its aetiological assumptions), has sufficient unifying power to incorporate important facets of rehabilitation (such as motivation, therapeutic alliance, skills acquisition, etc.), is relatively simple, has sufficient explanatory depth to clarify whether certain causal factors should be targeted in treatment, is both internally and externally consistent, and results in innovative and effective therapy.

THE RISK-NEED MODEL OF OFFENDER REHABILITATION

The most prominent rehabilitation approach for offenders is associated with risk detection and management, the focus being squarely on estimating the degree to which individuals constitute a menace to the community and then setting out to reduce or minimise their risk factors in the most cost-efficient manner. Individuals are viewed as bearers of risk, potential agents of harm or hazards. The rehabilitation approach most closely aligned to the risk management perspective is the RNR (Andrews & Bonta, 2003). Indeed, empirical research supports the utility of the RNR of offender treatment, a perspective that focuses primarily on the management of risk (Ward, Melser & Yates, 2007).

The assumptions underlying the RNR model are well established in criminal justice agencies and non-government agencies throughout the western world to the point where it can be regarded as the received or orthodox position concerning rehabilitation. In essence, the RNR proposes that correctional interventions should be structured according to three core rehabilitation principles: risk, need and responsivity (Andrews & Bonta, 1998; Hollin, 1999). Perhaps the most well-known rehabilitation assumption is that the most effective and ethical approach to the treatment of offenders is to target *dynamic risk factors* (i.e., criminogenic needs) that are causally related to criminal behaviour (Andrews & Bonta, 2003; Gendreau & Andrews, 1990; McGuire, 2000). This is termed the *need* principle. A second important guiding assumption is the *risk* principle, which specifies that the treatment of offenders ought to be organised according to the level of risk they pose to society. The third major assumption is the *responsivity* principle, which is primarily concerned with the problem of matching the delivery of correctional interventions to certain characteristics of offenders, for example, motivation, learning style and ethnic identity, and making the changes necessary in their lives to desist from further offending. A fourth relatively minor principle, the principle of *professional discretion*, states that clinical judgement should override the above principles if circumstances warrant. This principle allows for treatment flexibility and innovation under certain circumstances.

In terms of the three components of rehabilitation theory the RNR has the following commitments (for a fuller description and evaluation of the RNR, see Ward & Maruna, 2007; Ward, Melser & Yates, 2007).

Principles, Aims and Values

First, the major aim of offender rehabilitation is to reduce harm to the community. Considerations of the offender's welfare are secondary to this, with the caveat that any interventions must not unnecessarily intentionally harm him or violate commonly accepted professional ethical standards. Second, individuals are likely to vary with respect to their predisposition to commit crimes. The features that are associated with offending come from a range of variables including biological, psychological, social, cultural, personal, interpersonal and situational factors. Third, the most important treatment targets are those offender characteristics that research associates with potentially reduced recidivism rates. Everything else is at best of marginal relevance and at worst, potentially obstructive and harmful.

Fourth, the severity of risk (i.e., whether low, medium, or high) is assumed to co-vary with the number of criminogenic needs, and additionally, the severity or strength of each need. That is, lower risk sex offenders will have few, if any, criminogenic needs while higher risk offenders will display a significant range of such needs. Risk factors are viewed as discrete, quantifiable characteristics of offenders and their environments that can be identified and measured (from the Psychology of Criminal Conduct Perspective (PCC) and inferred from the General Personality and Social Psychology Perspective on Criminal Conduct (GPSPP)). Thus the conceptualisation of risk is from an individualist perspective.

Aetiological Assumptions of the RNR

According to the RNR, there are a number of major risk factors (known as the 'big eight') for general offending and these are causally linked to criminal conduct or function as markers for causes: antisocial attitudes, antisocial associates, a history of antisocial behaviour, antisocial personality pattern, problematic circumstances at home, difficulties at work or school, problems with leisure activities, and substance abuse. An empirically informed aetiological theory of crime should be based on these risk factors and outline their relationships to each other (where known) and actual incidents of crime. Thus, theory construction is a *bottom-up* process in the sense that theoretical constructs are constrained by the detection of empirical regularities. Specific sexual dynamic risk factors include deviant sexual interests, cognitive distortions, intimacy deficits, emotional regulation and general regulation difficulties (Beech & Ward, 2004).

The proximal cause of offending is the framing of an immediate (high-risk) situation in such a way that the rewards of criminal activity are evaluated as outweighing the costs. It is not clear what psychological mechanisms actually mediate the process of reward/cost appraisal. According to the RNR model the possible mechanisms include self-efficacy expectations, intentions, or perception of the density of rewards inherent in a situation. More distal causes of an individual's predisposition to experience the problems outlined above include developmental adversity (e.g., sexual or physical abuse, neglect) and growing up in environment where antisocial norms have been modelled, or where the opportunities to lead a crime-free life are significantly low. Once a crime has been committed its effects are likely to reinforce further offending and the individual concerned will be responsive to environmental and internal cues that signal the presence of offending opportunities.

Practice Implications

It is apparent that the principles of risk, need and responsivity are consistent with the RNR model's overall aims and aetiological assumptions. First, the *risk* principle is concerned with the match between individuals' level of risk for reoffending and the amount of treatment/interventions they should receive. The assumption is that risk is a rough indicator of clinical need and therefore according to this principle, high-risk sex offenders should receive the most treatment, typically at least 200 hours of cognitive behavioural interventions (Beech & Mann, 2002; Hollin, 1999).

Second, according to the *need* principle, treatment programmes for sexual and non-sexual offenders should primarily focus on changing criminogenic needs – that is, dynamic offender characteristics that, when changed, are associated with reduced recidivism rates. These include pro-offending attitudes, aspects of antisocial personality (e.g., impulsiveness), poor problem-solving abilities, substance abuse, deviant sexual interests, high hostility and anger, and criminal associates (Andrews & Bonta, 2003).

Third, the *responsivity* principle is used to refer to the use of a style and mode of intervention that engages the interest of the client group and takes into account their relevant characteristics such as cognitive ability, learning style and values (Andrews & Bonta, 2003). In other words, responsivity is concerned with how the individual interacts with the treatment environment and covers a range of factors and situations.

In conjunction with empirical validation, Andrews and Bonta (2003) stress that there are six main principles needed for effective rehabilitation. They argue that treatment programmes should be: (1) cognitive behavioural in orientation; (2) highly structured, specifying the aims and tasks to be covered in each session; (3) implemented by trained, qualified and appropriately supervised staff; (4) delivered in the correct manner and as intended by programme developers to ensure treatment integrity; (5) manual-based; and (6) housed within institutions with personnel committed to the ideals of rehabilitation and a management structure that supports rehabilitation.

Comments on the RNR

A major strength is the fact that a strong empirical base underpins the theory and therefore assessment and treatment strategies are carefully evaluated and tested to ensure their validity and reliability (McGuire, 2000). There is now mounting research evidence for the three principles underlying treatment indicating that lowered recidivism rates are a direct result of treating higher risk general and sex offenders more intensively, targeting criminogenic needs and matching treatment to the particular features of offenders such as learning style and motivation, etc. (e.g., Andrews & Bonta, 2003; Andrews and Dowden, 2006; Beech & Ward, 2004; Dowden & Andrews, 2003, 2004; Lipsey, 1992; Lösel, 1995; Lowenkamp, Latessa & Holsinger, 2006). This particular strength underlines the empirical adequacy and practical utility of the RNR model. Although, not all the empirical evidence is supportive (see Antonowicz, 2005).

In recent years, clinicians and researchers have challenged certain aspects of the RNR model and argued that concentrating on reducing dynamic risk factors (criminogenic needs) is a *necessary* but *not sufficient* condition for effective correctional interventions (Maruna, 2001; Ward & Stewart, 2003). One of the major concerns is the perceived narrowness of the RNR model and its failure to adopt a more constructive or positive approach to treatment. It has been argued that it is necessary to broaden the scope of correctional interventions to take into account the promotion of human goods (i.e., approach goals). That is, experiences, activities, or states of affairs which are strongly associated with well-being and higher levels of personal satisfaction and social functioning.

Researchers, clinicians and correctional workers who are critical of the RNR model point to its rather impoverished nature and inability to provide those involved with rehabilitation with sufficient tools to engage and work with offenders in the process of behaviour change. What they mean by this claim is that a set of principles that are essentially oriented toward risk management and the allocation of scare rehabilitation resources are unlikely to help deal with the complexities and demands of forensic practice.

In brief, those critical of the RNR model assert that:

1. Motivating offenders by concentrating on eliminating or modifying their various dynamic risk factors is extremely difficult. One thing individuals want to know is how can they live better lives, what are the positive rewards in desisting from crime;

2. The RNR model tends to neglect or underemphasise the role of narrative identity and agency (i.e., self-directed, intentional actions designed to achieve valued goals) in the change process. Thus an important component of living an offence-free life appears to be viewing oneself as a different person with the capabilities and opportunities to achieve personally endorsed goals;

3. The RNR model appears to be associated with a rather restricted and scientifically obsolete view of human nature. It seems to ignore the established fact that human beings are biologically embodied organisms who quite naturally seek and require certain kinds of experiences and activities (i.e., human goods) in order to live balanced and personally fulfilling lives;

4. The RNR model does not appreciate the relevance and crucial role of treatment alliance in the therapeutic process. Any type of enduring change depends on the capacity of the offender to trust his or her therapist enough to absorb the skills and 'lessons' imparted in therapy. This means that despite the claims of proponents of the RNR model, so-called non-criminogenic needs such as personal distress and low self-esteem are essential clinical targets; failure to address them is likely to result in a weak therapeutic alliance. Researchers have demonstrated that the creation of a sound therapeutic alliance requires an array of interventions that are not directly concerned with targeting risk and it has been established that a good therapeutic alliance is a necessary feature of effective therapy with offenders (Marshall, Fernandez, Serran *et al.*, 2003);

5. The RNR model is fundamentally a psychometric model (i.e., derived from and in part based on data from reliable and valid measures of criminal behaviour) and tends to be preoccupied with offenders' risk profiles (or traits) and downplays the relevance of contextual or ecological factors in offender rehabilitation. This is a serious problem and ignores the fact that offenders, like all human beings are embedded in various social and cultural systems that facilitate and constrain their behaviour;

6. The RNR model is often implemented in practice in a 'one-size-fits-all' manner and fails to adequately consider the specific needs, values and issues of individual offenders. Indeed, the typical way in which the RNR model is operationalised is at variance with its own principle of responsivity. At the very least, the fact that the RNR model is implemented in a large scale, heavily manualised and prescriptive manner makes it hard to accommodate the unique characteristics of offenders.

THE GOOD LIVES MODEL OF OFFENDER REHABILITATION

The second approach to correctional rehabilitation takes a more humanistic stance towards the reintegration of both sexual and non-sexual offenders. According to this perspective in the course of their daily lives offenders, like all other people, attempt to secure beneficial outcomes such as good relationships, a sense of mastery and recognition from others that they matter (Ward & Stewart, 2003). One of the core assumptions of more positive approaches to offender rehabilitation is that all people by virtue of their shared human nature and aspirations seek primary goods. The search for primary goods is hypothesised to result in a sense of personal or narrative identities (Gillet, 1999; Singer, 2001; Woolfolk, 1998). Thus all humans seek certain goods and construct their identities through the realisation of these goods in certain types of activities and lifestyles (Emmons, 1999, 2003; Nussbaum, 2001). Of course, local circumstances and access to varying resources in the form of learning opportunities and social capital is likely to result in diverse ways of living and values. Just how successful individuals are in the construction of adaptive identities is crucially dependent on whether or not they possess the necessary capabilities, resources and opportunities (internal and external conditions) to secure personally valued goals in certain circumstances. One of the advantages of looking at sexual and general offending in a richer and more constructive manner is that it is able to reconcile risk- and goods-orientated discourses. For example, criminogenic needs (dynamic risk factors) can be viewed as representing distortions or omissions in these necessary conditions; risk assessment points to obstacles in the quest for a good and satisfying life (Ward & Stewart, 2003). Because individuals are naturally predisposed to desire, and require, certain types of human goods for a fulfilling and satisfactory life, they will still attempt to secure them despite the presence of such obstacles. This can result in dysfunctional or antisocial behaviour.

The array of attitudes and assumptions comprising more constructive views of rehabilitation is evident in theories of rehabilitation such as the Good Lives Model (GLM; Ward & Gannon, 2006; Ward & Stewart, 2003). The GLM is a theory of rehabilitation that endorses the viewpoint that offenders are essentially human beings with similar needs and aspirations to non-offending members of the community. The GLM is based around two core therapeutic goals: to promote human goods and to reduce risk. According to Ward and his colleagues, a focus on the promotion of specific goods or goals in the treatment of sex offenders is likely to automatically eliminate (or reduce) commonly targeted dynamic risk factors (i.e., criminogenic needs). By contrast, Ward argues that focusing *only* on the reduction of risk factors is unlikely to promote the full range of specific goods and goals necessary for longer term desistence from offending.

In terms of the three-component structure of rehabilitation theories the GLM has the following commitments.

Principles, Aims and Values

First, according to the GLM, both sexual and non-sexual offenders are naturally disposed to seek a range of primary human goods that if secured will result in greater self-fulfilment and sense of purpose. In essence, a primary human good is defined as an experience, activity or situation that is sought for its own sake and is intrinsically beneficial. The possession of primary goods enhances people's lives and increases their level of functioning and personal satisfaction. Examples of primary human goods are: relatedness, mastery, autonomy, creativity, physical health and play (Emmons, 1999; Murphy, 2001; Nussbaum, 2000; Ward & Stewart, 2003). Primary goods are rather abstract and generally people do not specify them as goals when talking about the things that are most important to them. In fact what they most often refer to when asked about their reasons for acting in certain ways or engaging in personal projects are the *means* utilised in the attempt to achieve certain outcomes. Thus, instrumental goods are means for achieving primary human goods and only have value because of their association with the former. For example, the primary good of relatedness could be sought through different types of personal relationships such as friendships or romantic relationships. The available research indicates that all primary goods need to be present in individuals' lives to some extent if they are to achieve high levels of well-being (e.g., Emmons, 1999). However, there is also room for individual prefer- ences with respect to the weighting of the various goods. It is typically the case that individuals vary in the importance they accord to the various goods with some placing greater importance on mastery at work and others on feeling connected to the commu- nity. This is an important issue because the differential weighting of a good tends to reveal peoples' core commitments and therefore is indicative of their narrative identity.

Second, individuals' overarching or more heavily weighted goods reveal the kind of person they wish to be, and the kind of lives they want. This claim is dependent on the assumption that to some degree people are *self-constituting*, that is, they create themselves by the way they lead their lives and the meanings they attach to their experiences. A good example of the relationship between identity and goods empha- sis is those individuals who weigh the primary good of mastery at work highly. Such individuals tend to cultivate the development of work-related expertise and look for opportunities to tackle difficult problems and to impress others with their commit- ment and achievements. Therefore, it is to be expected that he or she would prize attributes and experiences that are closely associated with this good. These would include spending time at work, being engaged in further training and skill enhance- ment opportunities, being a good communicator (depending on the job), developing a strong sense of fidelity at work, wanting to be viewed as reliable and competent and so on. These activities and experiences, in turn, serve to constitute the person's narrative identity; by pursuing experiences and activities that realise the good of mastery at work, the person *becomes* a certain type of individual with specific interests, lifestyle and goals.

Third, the GLM is based around two core therapeutic goals: to promote human goods and to reduce risk. According to Ward and his colleagues, a focus on the promotion of specific goods or goals in the treatment of sex offenders is likely to automatically eliminate (or reduce) commonly targeted dynamic risk factors (i.e., criminogenic needs). By contrast, Ward argues that focusing *only* on the reduction of risk factors is unlikely to promote the full range of specific goods and goals necessary for longer term desistence from offending.

Fourth, because people are conceptualised to be constituted from, and to be embed- ded within, complex systems, risk is viewed as multifaceted rather than purely individualistic (Denny, 2005). In addition, risk is seen as contextualised and it is to be expected that an adequate risk management plan would need to take into account offenders' particular lifestyles and environments.

Etiological Assumptions of the GLM

First, approaching the aetiological factors from a GLM perspective enables us to appreciate the role of human goods in offending behaviour, and also, to understand the relationship between psychological deficits (e.g., impulsivity) and offenders' offence-related goals. The GLM guided analysis goes beyond deficit aetiological theories by encouraging clinicians to think clearly about just what it is that the person is *seeking* when committing the offence.

Second, from the perspective of the GLM, there are two routes to the onset of sexual and non-sexual offending, direct and indirect (Purvis, 2005; Ward & Gannon, 2006). The *direct* pathway is implicated when offending is a primary focus of the (typically implicit) cluster of goods and strategies associated with an offender's life plan. What this means is that the individual concerned seeks certain types of goods directly through criminal activity. The *indirect* route occurs when the pursuit of a good or set of goods creates a ripple effect in the person's personal circumstances and these unanticipated effects increase the chances of sexual offending occurring.

Third, criminogenic needs are *internal* or *external obstacles* that frustrate and block the acquisition of primary human goods. What this means is that the individual concerned lacks the ability to obtain important outcomes (i.e., goods) in his life, and in addition, frequently is unable to think about his life in a reflective manner. We suggest that there are four major types of difficulties often evident in offenders' life plans: problems of scope, inappropriate means, conflict and lack of capabilities.

Practice Implications

First, an important therapeutic task involves managing the balance between the approach goal of promoting offender goods and the avoidance goal of reducing risk.

Second, a related consideration concerns the attitude of the therapist to the offender and the importance from the perspective of the GLM of adapting a constructive, humanistic approach. That is, individuals who commit offences act from a common set of goals stemming from their underlying human nature. They warrant our respect for their capacity to change and the fact that their offending is directly or indirectly associated with the pursuit of the ingredients of a good life.

Third, the GLM recommends that there should be some degree of tailoring of therapy to match individual offenders' particular good lives plan and their associated risk factors (i.e., problems with the internal and external conditions). What we have in mind here is that the offender's particular strengths, interests, values (weightings of goods), social and personal circumstances, and environments are taken into account when constructing a reintegration plan. In other words, a more 'holistic' treatment perspective is taken, based on the core idea that the best way to reduce risk is by helping offenders live more fulfilling lives. In addition, therapy is tailored to each offender's good lives plan while still being administered in a systematic and structured way.

Fourth, a systematic assessment of an offender's social, psychological and sexual functioning, should result in good lives-oriented case formulation and an associated treatment plan. The therapist then constructs a good lives reintegration plan for the offender based on the above considerations and information. Thus taking into account the kind of life that would be fulfilling and meaningful to the individual (i.e., primary goods, secondary goods, and their relationship to ways of living and possible environments); the clinician notes the capabilities or competencies he requires to have a reasonable chance of putting the plan into action. A treatment plan is then developed.

Finally, the GLM functions as a regulatory ideal and is therefore deeply pragmatic. It asks therapists to develop an intervention plan that seeks to capitalise on offenders' interests and preferences and to equip them with the capabilities they need to realise their plan in the environment into which they are likely to be released. Constraints relating to offenders' abilities, the provision of resources, and the degree of support in their environments moderate the nature of such plans. The aim is to promote whichever goals are possible taking into account each offender's unique set of circumstances.

Comments on the GLM

The GLM is a very new theory of offender rehabilitation and therefore is still at the point of being theoretically elaborated, debated and critiqued. It has been presented as an advance over the RNR because of its ability to include both goods promotion and risk management aims within its policy and practice guidelines. This enables correctional workers to employ empirically supported interventions in a way that capitalises on offenders' desires to live worthwhile lives and in the process of helping them to achieve this goal reduces their risk of harming others.

In our view, there are two key issues to consider when evaluating the GLM. First, does it incorporate elements of practice that are essential if individuals are to significantly alter their antisocial tendencies? For example, are programmes consistent with the principles and assumptions of the GLM able to motivate offenders to enter into therapy? Do they address issues of narrative dignity and meaning? Will they reduce the likelihood of offenders committing additional crimes and therefore ensure that the risk to the community is reduced? Can they account for the importance of criminogenic and non-criminogenic needs and do they provide an account of how risk factors develop and why they are important intervention targets? The second evaluation issue concerns the theoretical and empirical robustness of the GLM. The key questions here revolve around the GLM's capacity to provide a comprehensive account of the rehabilitation process, one that is empirically supported and conceptually coherent.

In brief, our assessment is that the GLM does a good job in integrating aspects of practice already established as important and is particularly useful in addressing motivational issues. In terms of its advantages over the RNR, it manages to integrate aspects of practice that are viewed as important by correctional workers but which the RNR does not deal with particularly well. These include, the importance of identity formation, motivating offenders to participate in, and to persist with, correctional programmes, accounting for the importance of the therapeutic alliance (non-criminogenic needs), working in a more holistic, constructive way, indicating the necessity of tailored, more flexible intervention approaches, and clarifying the role of values in the change process.

However, whether the GLM can add value to specific programmes directly based on it is still unclear. Our argument is that it is possible to reduce risk if primary goods are promoted in a systematic way, tapping into an offender's particular priorities and also taking into account his ecology and personal characteristics. This aspect of the GLM showcases its theoretical coherence (internal consistency) and external consistency. The GLM is starting to be utilised in sex offender and general offender programmes in a number of countries throughout the world. These include: Ireland (Granada Treatment Programme – sex offenders), England (adult HMP sex offender programmes and adolescent sex offenders [GMAP, general forensic patients]), Canada (Corrections Canada – adult sexual offenders), Australia (Victoria – adult and adolescent sex offenders, general offenders), New Zealand (adult sexual and non-sexual offenders, intellectually disabled offenders, adolescent offenders), and the United States (sexual and non-sexual offenders, forensic mental health patients).

CONCLUSIONS

In this chapter we have explored two different rehabilitation theories, the Risk-Need-Responsivity Model and the Good Lives Model. Each of these theories is illustrative of a particular approach to the question of how best to reduce crime and to reintegrate sexual and non-sexual offenders into the community. The RNR is associated with a risk management approach and as such tends to regard offender welfare as of secondary interest and at best simply a means to an end of increased community safety. By way of contrast, the GLM proposes that advancing offenders' needs in the right way will also reduce risk.

Where do we go from here? There appear to be quite conflicting tendencies at play within the current correctional scene. On the one hand there is an impressive body of evidence indicating that sexual and non-sexual offenders can be effectively reintegrated into the community provided they participate in specific types of programmes. On the other, it appears that western societies are becoming risk aversive and more conservative in their attitude toward offenders (Denny, 2005). Thus we have the odd situation where more sophisticated and powerful interventions are being hampered by severe sentencing regimes and overly restrictive monitoring of offenders. We certainly appreciate the need to reduce the harm offenders can inflict on a vulnerable community but in our determination to ensure personal safety it is imperative that we do not lose our perspective and humanity.

REFERENCES

Andrews, D.A. & Bonta, J. (1998). *The psychology of criminal conduct* (2nd edn). Cincinnati, OH: Anderson.

Andrews, D.A. & Bonta, J. (2003). *The psychology of criminal conduct* (3rd edn). Cincinnati, OH: Anderson.

Andrews, D.A. & Dowden, C. (2005). Managing correctional treatment for reduced recidivism: A meta-analytic review of programme integrity. *Legal and Criminological Psychology, 10*, 173–187.

Andrews, D.A. & Dowden, C. (2006). Risk principle of case classification in correctional treatment. *International Journal of Offender Therapy and Comparative Criminology, 50*, 88–100.

Antonowicz, D.H. (2005). The Reasoning and Rehabilitation program: Outcome evaluations with offenders. In M. McMurran & J. McGuire (Eds), *Social problem solving and offending: Evidence, evaluation, and evolution* (pp. 163–181). New York, John Wiley & Sons, Inc.

Beech, A.R. & Mann, R.E. (2002). Recent developments in the treatment of sexual offenders. In J. McGuire (Ed.), *Offender rehabilitation: effective programmes and policies to reduce reoffending* (pp. 259–288). Chichester: John Wiley & Sons, Ltd.

Beech, A. & Ward, T. (2004). The integration of etiology and risk in sexual offenders: A theoretical framework. *Aggression and Violent Behavior, 10*, 31–63.

Denny, D. (2005). *Risk and society*. London, UK: Sage.

Dowden, C. & Andrews, D.A. (2003). Does family intervention work for delinquents? Results of a meta-analysis. *Canadian Journal of Criminology and Criminal Justice, 45*, 327–342.

Dowden, C. & Andrews, D.A. (2004). The importance of staff practice in delivering effective correctional treatment: A meta-analytic review of core correctional practice. *International Journal of Offender Therapy and Comparative Criminology, 48*, 203–214.

Emmons, R.A. (1999). *The psychology of ultimate concerns*. New York: Guilford.

Emmons, R.A. (2003). Personal goals, life meaning, and virtue: wellsprings of a positive life. In C.L.M. Keyes & J. Haidt (Eds), *Flourishing: Positive psychology and the life well-lived*. Washington, DC: American Psychological Association.

Gendreau, P. & Andrews, D.A. (1990). Tertiary prevention: What a meta-analysis of the offender treatment literature tells us about 'what works'. *Canadian Journal of Criminology, 32*, 173–184.

Gendreau, P., Goggin, C., Cullen, F.T. & Andrews, D.A. (2000). The effects of community sanctions and incarceration on recidivism. In L.L. Motiuk & R.C. Serin (Eds), *Compendium 2000 on effective correctional programming* (pp. 18–21). Ottawa: Correctional Services Canada.

Gillet, G. (1999). *The mind and its discontents: An essay in discursive psychiatry*. Oxford, UK: Oxford University Press.

Hollin, C.R. (1999). Treatment programs for offenders: Meta-analysis, 'what works' and beyond. *International Journal of Law and Psychiatry, 22*, 361–372.

Kekes, J. (1989). *Moral tradition and individuality*. Princeton, NJ: Princeton University Press.

Lipsey, M. (1992). Juvenile delinquency treatment: A meta-analytic inquiry into the variability of effects. In T. Cook (Ed.), *Meta-analysis for explanation: A casebook*. New York: Russell Sage Foundation.

Lösel, F. (1995). What recent meta-evaluations tell us about the effectiveness of correctional treatment. In G. Davies, S. Loyd-Bostock, M. McMurran & C. Wilson (Eds), *Psychology, law and criminal justice: International developments in research and practice* (pp. 537–554). New York: Walter de Gruyter.

Lowenkamp, C., Latessa, E. & Holsinger, A. (2006). The risk principle in action: What have we learned from 13,676 offenders and 97 correctional programs? *Crime and Delinquency, 52*, 77–93.

MacKenzie, D., Wilson, D. & Kider, S. (2001). Effects of correctional boot camps on offending. *Annals of the American Academy of Political and Social Science, 578*, 126–143.

Marshall, W.L., Fernandez, Y.M., Serran, G.A., *et al.* (2003). Process variables in the treatment of sexual offenders. *Aggression and Violent Behaviour, 8*, 205–234.

Maruna, S. (2001). *Making good: How ex-convicts reform and rebuild their lives*. Washington, DC: American Psychological Association.

McGuire, J. (2000). Explanations of criminal behaviour. In J. McGuire, T. Mason & A. O'Kane (Eds), *Behaviour, crime and legal processes: A guide for legal practitioners* (pp. 135–159). Chichester: John Wiley & Sons, Ltd.

Murphy, M.C. (2001). *Natural law and practical rationality.* New York, NY: Cambridge University Press.

Nussbaum, M.C. (2000). *Women and human development: The capabilities approach.* Cambridge: Cambridge University Press.

Petrosino, A., Turpin-Petrosino, C. & Fincknaeuer, J. (2000). Well-meaning programs can have harmful effects! Lessons from experiments of programs such as scared straight. *Crime and Delinquency, 46,* 354–379.

Purvis, M. (2005). *Good Lives plans and sexual offending: A preliminary study.* Unpublished doctoral dissertation, University of Melbourne, Australia.

Rescher, N. (1993). *A system of pragmatic idealism. Vol. II: The validity of values.* Princeton, NJ: Princeton University Press.

Singer, J.A. (2005). *Personality and psychotherapy: Treating the whole person.* New York: Guilford Press.

Ward, T. & Gannon, T. (2006). Rehabilitation, etiology, and self-regulation: The Good Lives Model of sexual offender treatment. *Aggression and Violent Behavior, 11,* 77–94.

Ward, T., Gannon, T. & Birgden, A. (2007). Human rights and the treatment of sex offenders. *Sexual Abuse: A Journal of Research and Treatment, 19,* 195–216.

Ward, T. & Marshall, W.L. (2004). Good lives, aetiology and the rehabilitiation of sex offenders: A bridging theory. *Journal of Sexual Aggression, 10,* 153–169.

Ward, T. & Maruna, S. (2007). *Rehabilitation: Beyond the risk paradigm.* London, UK: Routledge.

Ward, T., Melser, J. & Yates, P.M. (2007). Reconstructing the Risk-Need-Responsivity Model of offender rehabilitation. *Aggression and Violent Behavior, 12,* 208–228.

Ward, T. & Stewart, C.A. (2003). The treatment of sex offenders: Risk management and good lives. *Professional Psychology: Research and Practice, 34,* 353–360.

Whitehead, J. & Lab, S. (1989). A meta-analysis of juvenile correctional treatment. *Journal of Research in Crime and Delinquency, 26,* 276–295.

Woolfolk, R.L. (1998). *The cure of souls: Science, values, and psychotherapy.* San Francisco: Jossey-Bass.

17

Modifying Sexual Preferences

WILLIAM L. MARSHALL

MATT D. O'BRIEN

LIAM E. MARSHALL

INTRODUCTION

In the early applications of a behavioural (and subsequently a cognitive behavioural) approach to the treatment of sexual offenders, the key issue was thought to be a sexual interest in the specific deviant acts involved in the offence (Laws & Marshall, 2003). This notion derived from McGuire, Carlisle and Young's (1965) influential conditioning theory of the acquisition of deviant sexual interests, and later entrenched in Abel and Blanchard's (1974) account of the role of fantasy in sexual deviations. This issue was so central to early treatment approaches that Bond and Evans (1967) stated that once deviant sexual preferences were changed to normal preferences, treatment was essentially complete. This over-simplified view, however, was soon overturned as treatment providers began to expand the issues addressed in treatment (Marshall & Laws, 2003). However, concern remains for the role of deviant sexual interests and strategies are typically provided to modify such interests.

The first step in the process of treating deviant interests is to establish their presence or not. Contrary to the assumptions of the early behaviour therapists, not all men convicted of sexual offences display deviant sexual interests (Marshall & Fernandez 2003). The usual, and most objective, way of assessing sexual preferences is to employ phallometry (Launay, 1999) (see Chapter 8 for a comprehensive review of this assessment procedure). Phallometry (sometimes called 'plethysmography' or 'PPG') assesses the magnitude of penile erectile responses to various sexual stimuli including both deviant and appropriate sexual scenes. In a review by Marshall and Fernandez (2003) it was found that among non-familial child molesters some 50% displayed arousal at phallometric testing that indicated deviance. For incest offenders deviance

Assessment and Treatment of Sex Offenders: A Handbook. Edited by Anthony Beech, Leam Craig and Kevin Browne. © John Wiley & Sons Ltd, 2009.

Table 17.1 Criteria for the identification of deviant sexual interests

1. Sexual history reveals high rates of deviant acts that are persistent over an extended period of time.
2. Phallometric evaluations reveal either: (a) equal or greater arousal to deviant than to normative sexual acts, or (b) arousal to deviant acts is equal or greater than 30% full erection (i.e., approximately 9–10 mm of increase in penile circumference).
3. The offender reports persistent deviant sexual fantasies that he cannot resist.
4. The offender reports, or staff report, that he displays sexualised behaviour toward them.
5. Staff report that he is collecting inappropriate images from magazines and newspapers, or that he is persistently watching television shows depicting his preferred class of victims.
6. Client's institutional records show he has previously attempted to sexually assault staff or other inmates.

Adapted from Marshall, Marshall, Serran & Fernandez (2006).

is far less frequently identified at phallometric testing. While there is disagreement about how many rapists show deviant arousal, in large-scale studies some 30% appear deviant. Thus, if we are to rely on phallometric test results, then not all sexual offenders are deviant.

As a result of these issues, we have formulated a set of criteria to determine when, and if, a specific sexual offender requires interventions designed to modify sexual interests. Table 17.1 describes these criteria.

As can be seen, it is not just deviant arousal displayed at phallometric assessment that indicates a need to intervene. Interestingly, the evidence suggests that criteria 1 and 2 in our set are typically redundant; that is, if an offender has a history of numerous sexual offences over many years then he is very likely to show deviant arousal at phallometric evaluations. Note that institutional behaviour can provide a basis for inferring sexual problems beyond what might be revealed by the client's history or his arousal at assessment. This somewhat neglected source of information might also reveal sexual preoccupation that is not necessarily deviant. In such cases medications such as the selective serotonin reuptake inhibitors can be very useful (Kafka, 1994). Sexual preoccupation, as we (Marshall & Marshall, 2001) have shown, occurs at a far higher frequency among sexual offenders than is apparent in a comparison group of community-based non-offenders, suggesting that overcoming sexual preoccupation should be a treatment target with sexual offenders. Unfortunately very few sexual offender programmes address this issue.

CONTEXT OF INTERVENTIONS

It is important, when employing procedures (whether behavioural or medical) for modifying sexual interests, to ensure that these procedures are embedded within the context of all other relevant issues addressed in the treatment programme. The client needs to recognise the relevance for effective and appropriate sexual functioning of each other issue addressed in treatment. For example, the skills and attitudes (both toward others and toward himself) he is acquiring regarding relationships, empathy, self-esteem, and coping styles are directly relevant to the sexual aspects of relationships and this needs to be made clear to the client. His formulation of future life plans, particularly those based on a Good Lives Model (see Chapter 16), must reflect his changed sexual interests and his changed sexual interests must be integrated into these plans. An offender who has sought children for sexual solace during stressful periods will need to not only have plans to avoid situations where opportunities to molest children are present, he will also need to identify ways in which he can meet potential partners based on his changed sexual interests.

Perhaps most important of all, the modification of sexual interests should occur in the context of an appropriate course of sex education. Healthy sexual functioning requires a reasonable knowledge of the range of normative or acceptable sexual activities. Our approach is to consider as acceptable all sexual behaviours that are either solitary or that involve a consenting partner. Since sexual offenders appear to be rather more prudish than others about sexual activities, it is necessary, by open discussion, to diminish this prudishness particularly for behaviours that are known to facilitate sexual satisfaction. Discussions of these behaviours in an open and accepting style are helpful.

Some unusual sexual behaviours, such as fetishisms, are thought by many people (including, unfortunately, some treatment providers) to reflect deviance such that when they are present in sexual offenders it is thought to be necessary to eliminate them. However, unless a functional relationship between the eccentric sexual behaviour and sexual offending can be demonstrated, any attempt to eliminate the fetish (or whatever other non-offending sexual behaviour is present) will simply reflect the therapist's own prejudices.

CHANGING SEXUAL INTERESTS

The assumption underlining attempts to modify sexual interests has been that these interests were acquired rather than inborn and that therefore the client can learn new ways of expressing his sexual appetite. Whether this is perfectly true or not it does appear that sexual interests are modifiable, although it must be said that a significant body of evidence has not yet been published concerning the effectiveness of procedures used to change these interests. In the context of these remarks it is important to note that behaviour does not have to be acquired in order for it to be modifiable. We are all born with a self-interested disposition, otherwise we would not have survived as a species, but most of us learn to temper this self-interest in order to function effectively within a social context.

Proceeding on the assumption that sexual interests can be changed we will frame our account of the procedures in terms derived from the extensive body of knowledge on human and animal learning. Without becoming too complex we will briefly outline some basic notions.

First, it is important to note that any persistent behaviour must have effects for the person enacting the behaviour that are seen as pleasurable or beneficial to the person. Behaviours, on the other hand, that produce unpleasant experiences or result in unpleasant consequences, are unlikely to be maintained. These are the basic principles of Skinner's (1938) operant conditioning account of behaviour. Second, it is important to understand the notion of extinction. Extinction refers to a reduction in the frequency of a behaviour that was previously enacted at a higher rate. This occurs when either the rewards elicited by the behaviour are removed or an alternative behaviour is acquired that produces even greater rewards. In fact, extinction is never simply the passive loss of a behaviour but always the replacement by another behaviour (Falls, 1998).

BEHAVIOURAL PROCEDURES

Although the procedures that have been developed to increase prosocial sexual interests and to decrease deviant interests are described as 'behavioural', in fact each procedure has a significant cognitive component and clear strong emotional qualities. However, in the sexual offender treatment literature they are still described as either behaviour therapy or behaviour modification procedures, so we will use those terms.

Broadly speaking there are two main types of behaviour modification techniques. Aversion techniques involve the pairing of deviant images with an aversive experience where the aim is to reduce interest in the deviant activities. In some, or perhaps all, of these techniques it is not always clear that the putative aversive stimuli function as such. Certainly there is no clear evidence that the changes induced by these procedures are the result of conditioned aversion (Marshall & Eccles, 1993; McConaghy, 1993). The other set of techniques involve associating appropriate sexual images with an experience that is presumed to be rewarding (usually masturbation).

The evidence base for these behaviour modification procedures is, unfortunately, not strong (Hunter & Lexier, 1998; Laws & Marshall, 1991). In particular, there is a dearth of recent studies on the efficacy of these techniques with sexual offenders and the studies that are available all have limitations. There are no large-scale controlled studies that unequivocally support the efficacy of any one of these procedures. Most of the reports in the literature are simply case descriptions (e.g., Maletzky, 1985; Marquis, 1970). However, some reports are either reasonably well-controlled single-case designs that permit inferences about the efficacy of the procedures (e.g., Kremsdorf, Holman & Laws, 1980; Marshall, 1979, 2006a, 2006b, 2007) or they are designed in such a way as to encourage confidence in the idea that it was the specific intervention that produced the observed changes (Laws, Meyer & Holman, 1978; Marshall, 1974). In addition, there are reports of group studies that permit reasonably confident inferences about effectiveness (Alford et al., 1987; Hunter & Goodwin, 1992; Johnston, Hudson & Marshall, 1992).

Deviant sexual preference, as measured phallometrically, is a significant predictor of sexual recidivism (Hanson & Bussière, 1998). Therefore, despite the lack of convincing evidence in support of particular techniques, it would be remiss not to address deviant arousal in treatment programmes for sexual offenders. McGrath, Cumming and Burchard (2003) indicate that approximately 60% of treatment programmes for adult sexual offenders that responded to a large scale North American survey reported using techniques to modify sexual interests. Over 50% of programmes treating adolescent sexual offenders reported using these procedures, while 35% of residential programmes for children (under age 12 years) also employed arousal control techniques. We admit to being shocked and dismayed that such intrusive procedures are being used with such young children whose sexual expressions are still being formed. With children we would have thought a more positively focused approach would have produced changes in sexual interests without direct intervention.

Aversion Techniques

Aversion techniques involve the pairing of the offence-related sexual thoughts/images with an aversive experience, the expectation being that this association will reduce sexual responses to the offence-related imagery. These procedures rely on theoretical notions that have extensive supporting evidence. These notions stem from Skinner's (1938) idea that behaviours that are followed by unpleasant events will show a future decline in frequency and intensity. The human and animal literature is replete with demonstrations that this is so (Ayres, 1998; Barker, 2001; Domjan, 1998). McGrath *et al.* (2003) note that between 18% and 49% of surveyed programmes for adults reported using one or another aversive technique to reduce deviant interests, while between 5% and 39% used these procedures with adolescents. In McGrath *et al.*'s surveys they asked about the use of four aversive procedures: aversive behavioural rehearsal, covert sensitisation, odour aversion, and minimal arousal conditioning. Unfortunately McGrath *et al.* appear to have identified ammonia aversion with odour aversion so it is not clear what respondents meant when they indicated their use of odour aversion. Ammonia aversion is mediated by the pain centres of the brain and not by the olfactory bulb. In addition, McGrath *et al.* did not ask about the use of faradic aversion (i.e., the use of an unpleasant, but tolerable, electric shock as the aversive stimulus). This procedure was by far the most popular in the early days of the use of behaviour therapy to modify sexual interests (Bancroft, 1971, 1974; Marshall, 1973), but its use rapidly declined. Quinsey and Earls (1990) noted that reports of the use of faradic aversion had all but disappeared by the time of their review, but they pointed out that its disappearance did not seem to be based on evidence showing that it was ineffective. Indeed, one of the best experimental studies evaluating procedures to modify deviant interests involved faradic aversion. Quinsey, Chaplin and Carrigan (1980) found that a signalled punishment procedure very effectively reduced the phallometric responses of child molesters to sexual stimuli depicting children. However, since it is no longer in use, we will not review in any more detail the research regarding faradic aversion.

Shame Aversion

Shame aversion was first described by Serber (1970). He applied the procedure to a variety of clients with various sexual behaviours that they identified as problematic;

at least four of these behaviours (i.e., voyeurism, paedophilia, exhibitionism and frot-teurism) were sexual offences. Serber stumbled upon this procedure by accident. He was photographing a client in the process of cross-dressing in order to produce images to present in faradic aversion sessions. The client expressed extreme distress and shame at being watched and was unable to become sexually aroused. Serber imme-diately recognised the potential therapeutic value of this procedure. Subsequently, Serber applied shame aversion to eight clients. Two or more staff were recruited to be the observers. They openly watched each client enact a simulation of his deviant behaviour, offering no comments but simply staring at the client.

This procedure seems obviously fraught with ethical and practical problems. For example, for a frotteur, Serber asked 'an attractive girl' to allow the client to rub himself against her while being watched by several other people. For a paedophile a young woman was recruited as a substitute for the child molester's usual victim. During the cross-dresser's treatment the client broke down repeatedly, cried, and asked for the session to stop. Apparently this request was not granted. Between sessions the cross-dresser reported nightmares and anxiety. These obviously troublesome features and consequences are hardly justified by what Serber saw as the reductions in the problematic behaviours. In fact Serber's (1970; Serber & Wolpe, 1972) reports of the benefits were simply anecdotal.

What is really surprising is that this ethically dubious procedure is still practiced under the title 'aversive behaviour rehearsal'. McGrath *et al.* (2003) report that this procedure is employed in 22.8% of the North American community programmes for adults they surveyed and in 18.3% of the adult institutional programmes. Even more dismaying, it is used in 18.2% of residentially-based programmes for adolescents and in 15% of programmes for children (aged 11 years and under). What dreadful effects such an explicitly shaming procedure might have on such young people can only be imagined.

Ammonia Aversion

Ammonia aversion has been a popular aversion strategy used in the treatment of sexual offenders, particularly exhibitionists (Abel & Rouleau, 1990; Ball & Seghorn, 1999; Colson, 1972; Maletzky, 1991; Marshall & Fernandez, 1998; Wolpe, 1969). This simple and portable procedure is best implemented when clients report a high frequency of deviant thoughts throughout each day that are experienced as intrusive to the extent that they interfere with everyday tasks. Ammonia aversion requires the client to carry, at all times, a small vial of smelling salts (ammonium carbonate mixed with ammonium water and various aromatic substances). The client is instructed to take a rapid inhalation from the opened bottle, whenever an unwanted sexual thought or urge occurs. The effects of inhaling this aversive agent are mediated by the pain system (as opposed to the olfactory system as in foul odour aversion) and so it has an instant effect of removing the inappropriate thoughts. This gives the client the opportunity to replace these thoughts with some non-sexual thoughts and actions. The procedure is seen as a combination of punishment (the inhalation of the ammonia) and aversion relief (i.e., associating prosocial thoughts with the termination of the aversive experience).

Marshall, Anderson and Fernandez (1999) note that although this procedure makes good sense, there are no satisfactorily controlled studies that demonstrate its efficacy. Earls and Castonguay (1989) produced changes in a child molester's sexual responses to children by using ammonia aversion, however, despite these effects being largely maintained at one-year follow-up the client still experienced slightly elevated arousal to 'passive' scenes involving male and female children. In a reasonably well-controlled single case study, Marshall (2006a) demonstrated that the introduction of ammonia aversion in the treatment of an exhibitionist markedly reduced both urges to expose and actual incidents of exposure. These results were maintained at 12 months follow-up. Furthermore, Marshall found that these reductions in exhibitionistic behaviours markedly improved the client's mood and strengthened his self-confidence, thereby allowing him to expand his social life, begin a relationship and plan educational upgrading to obtain a secure job.

Marshall's (2006a) case report demonstrates the potential value of ammonia aversion used as a continuously available self-management technique for controlling exhibiting urges and behaviours. Although the use of ammonia aversion has been reported almost exclusively with exhibitionists, we have employed it with other problematic high frequency compulsive sexual behaviours. For example, we have used it in prison and community settings with child molesters who report high frequency deviant fantasies or intrusive sexual thoughts about children. In our experience one of the key factors in the success of this procedure is to ensure that clients keep daily records of the relevant problematic behaviours. It has been frequently found that after the euphoria produced by the initial reduction in deviant thoughts or acts, clients fail to perceive subsequent less dramatic gains and lose enthusiasm. As a result they typically become inconsistent in their use of the smelling salts and the problem behaviours return. Daily monitoring of their deviant thoughts, urges, or acts, keeps the client alert to the gradual, if at times marginal, improvements and this maintains their devoted use of the procedure.

In summary, these is some (albeit limited) evidence to support the value of ammonia aversion. It appears to be most usefully employed with clients who have high frequency deviant fantasies, urges or behaviours. In particular, ammonia aversion can provide sexual offenders who are in the community, with an immediate strategy to control the expression of deviant urges until a full treatment programme can produce sufficient benefits.

Olfactory Aversion

This procedure involves associating relevant deviant images/thoughts with the inhalation of a foul odour. There have been a number of descriptions of procedures utilising noxious odours in the literature (e.g., Colson, 1972; Dougher, 1995; Kennedy & Foreyt,

1968; Morganstern, 1974) none of which have provided objective outcome data. The foul odours that have been employed have included valeric acid, mercapto-ethanol, and rancid meat. However, any malodorous substance, that is known to be safe to inhale, can be used.

One problem that the use of foul odours presents is the typically rapid sensory adaptation of the olfactory receptors (Rolls & Rolls, 1997). This rapid loss of the sense of repugnance of any particular odour means that strategies have to be adopted to ensure that the odour continues to be experienced as unpleasant. There are two ways to achieve this goal. First, it is wise to employ more than one foul odour and to switch the odours to be presented on successive pairings of the odours and the deviant stimuli.

Marshall, Keltner and Griffiths (1974) showed that olfactory aversion was effective in eliminating a range of problematic appetitive behaviours including sexual deviations. The best study to date, as applied to the treatment of sexual offenders, was described by Laws, Meyer and Holman (1978). This study involved a sexual sadist inhaling gaseous valeric acid while viewing slides of sadistic content. The sadist's sexual responses, as measured phallometrically, showed significant changes with treatment. However Laws *et al.* provided only anecdotal suggestions of a change in actual sadistic behaviour at post-treatment follow-up.

Marshall (2006b) described a case study of a child molester whose deviant preferences were modified using a combination of olfactory aversion and masturbatory reconditioning. This client was asked to generate a list of sexual fantasies involving children. Once ten 60-second fantasies had been identified they were recorded onto audiotape. The client then chose from a collection of coloured pictures of female children aged 6–10 years (his preferred age range), those he considered to be sexually exciting. A similar set of appropriate fantasies and slides were generated. During treatment the audiotapes were presented via headphones and the slides were presented on a screen directly in front of the client. The apparatus used to deliver foul odours included a small nasal mask that allowed for the delivery of one of several bad odours as well as mentholated air to clear nasal mucosa between foul odour inhalations.

Each trial consisted of the client holding the mask over his nose while listening to one of the deviant fantasies and watching an associated slide. The bad odour was delivered at this point. This was followed by a concurrent termination of the fantasy, image and odour, and a blast of mentholated air. To create the conditions necessary to produce 'aversion relief' (Thorpe *et al.*, 1964), one of the appropriate fantasies and slides was then presented. The intention was to enhance the attractiveness of the appropriate stimuli by associating it with relief from the aversive experience (i.e., negative reinforcement). There were five trials per session with two sessions each week for four weeks, resulting in a total of 40 pairings of the deviant images and the foul odours. In addition to these procedures, the client was given a vial of a foul odour of his choice to carry with him and inhale from whenever he experienced sexual feelings towards children. This was designed to facilitate generalisation outside the office-based sessions.

The foul odour procedure was employed as the initial intervention, and was found to produce significant reductions in arousal responses to sexual stimuli depicting young girls. Olfactory aversion resulted in no changes in arousal or fantasies involving adult females, which suggested that it was not simply attention to the client's problems that produced the benefits. Subsequent application of directed masturbation (see later section for a description) had the effect of increasing sexual interests in adult females to a level that was approximately normal.

The use of olfactory aversion should be considered with clients who have a high frequency of intense offence-related thoughts, and a high level of sexual preoccupation. However, since the office-based use of aversive procedures may have a negative effect on the therapist/client relationship, aversion procedures should not be the first choice but used only when less intrusive procedures prove ineffective.

Minimal Arousal Conditioning

This procedure was originally described by Steve Jensen (see McGrath, 2001) but he has not published anything on it as yet. Minimal arousal conditioning (MAC), in its basic form, has the client listen to a prepared, individualised, deviant script until he begins to become sexually aroused. At this point the client self-administers repetitive inhalations of ammonia (as many as 20). The client then repeats this process until he can listen to the deviant script to the end without becoming aroused. This is an innovative procedure that makes good sense in terms of what is known about aversive processes but unfortunately it has not received much attention in the literature.

Gray (1995) compared his modified version of MAC with verbal satiation (see later description) and reported benefits with MAC but not with satiation. However, closer examination of Gray's data suggests that both procedures were effective with possibly a small advantage for MAC. Using phallometric assessments as his indicator of treatment-induced changes, Gray reports responses that, when converted to deviant indices (DI), indicate normative responding after treatment for both groups. Both MAC and satiation groups were clearly deviant prior to the interventions but both interventions produced responding that was within the normal range (DIs less that 0.8) at post-treatment evaluations. Clearly MAC is worth pursuing in larger-scale controlled studies but until these are completed we cannot recommend its use.

Covert Sensitisation/Covert Association

Cautela (1967) described an aversion-based procedure that was conducted entirely in imagination for use with a variety of problematic appetitive behaviours. Covert sensitisation, as this procedure was called, required the client to imagine enacting the problematic behaviour and then immediately to imagine an undesirable consequence. The consequences Cautela employed were meant to be something of a match with the problem behaviour. For example, a client with an excessive fondness for chocolate cake would imagine eating the cake and then switch to imagining being sick and throwing-up; a homosexual man was told to imagine he was fellating another man when he suddenly noticed puss oozing from the man's penis. Whether sexual offenders would see such consequences as meaningful and likely to occur is open to question. However, in this form covert sensitisation has been used with sexual offenders by numerous clinicians (Dougher *et al.*, 1987; Hayes, Brownell & Barlow, 1978; Hughes, 1977; Moergen, Merkel & Brown, 1990; Rangaswamy, 1987; Stava, Levin & Schwanz, 1993).

Maletzky (1973, 1980; Maletzky & George, 1973) reported the use of what he called "assisted covert sensitisation". He suggested that the aversiveness of covert consequences was not strong enough on its own to produce reliable changes in the target behaviour so he added the presentation of unpleasant odours to coincide with the client imagining the consequences. Maletzky (1980) reported 100% success with 100 sexual offenders (paedophiles and exhibitionists). A success rate this high is surprising and definitely requires replication which to date has not happened.

A variation on covert sensitisation that appears to have promise was described by Weinrott, Riggan and Frothingham (1997). They outlined a vicarious sensitisation procedure that involved audiotaped descriptions of individualised crime scenarios followed by videotaped depictions of individually relevant aversive scenes that included "legal, social, physical, and emotional consequences" (p. 708). Clients were exposed to 300 such trials over 25 treatment sessions. A well-controlled study demonstrated that both phallometric evaluations and self-reports showed significant reductions in deviant interests as a result of this treatment (Weinrott *et al.*, 1997). Although vicarious sensitisation has elements consistent with covert sensitisation it also has features of shame aversion. As we noted with shame aversion, the induction of shame in sexual offenders appears to be counter-therapeutic so we do not recommend the use of vicarious sensitisation. In addition, it is rather expensive and time-consuming to produce the individually tailored videotapes.

Covert association is derived from covert sensitisation. It was renamed by Marshall (Marshall, 2007; Marshall *et al.*, 2006) for two reasons. First to distinguish it from the original way it was implemented by Cautela (1967) and typically applied in the sexual offender field (Dougher, 1995; Maletzky, 1991). Second, Marshall's view is that the effective element of the procedure is not the aversiveness of the consequences but simply the association between imagining the deviant sequence and imagining the possible consequences.

In Cautela's procedure, the imagined consequences (e.g., nausea) were not always realistically related to the targeted problem behaviour and this might be expected to reduce the salience, and therefore the effectiveness of the procedure. In addition, the rationale underlying covert sensitisation depended upon the maintenance of the aversive properties of the imagined consequences. Clinicians employing covert sensitisation have repeatedly told us (and this matches our experience) that clients say that after repeating the consequences several times, they lose their aversive properties. This would be expected of covertly imagined consequences since they are likely to be attenuated versions of real life stimuli, and low intensity stimuli rapidly lose their effects (Peeke & Petrinovich, 1984). Another potential problem with Cautela's (1967) description of covert sensitisation is that it involved imagined evocation of only the terminal aspects of the targeted behaviour. Given that all problematic acts involve a chain of behaviours and associated thoughts and feelings, and because evidence indicates that such behavioural chains are most effectively suppressed when early steps are punished (Axelrod & Apsche, 1983), it would seem better to use such behavioural chains in treatment rather than just the terminal act.

It was in response to these considerations that Marshall (2007) designed a modified version of covert sensitisation which he referred to as "covert association". Some aspects of Marshall's procedure are consistent with the way others have employed covert sensitisation (Barnard *et al.*, 1989; Travin & Protter, 1993).

Covert association requires clients to construct several offence sequences, some of which replicate the behavioural/emotional/thought chains of their offences while others are reconstructions of their typical deviant fantasies. The start-point for these sequences is at a somewhat distal point from the actual abusive behaviours; in fact, at the point where an intention to abuse is at least vaguely formed. Five or more sequences are formed, each of which is broken up into six to eight steps. Each offence sequence is written on a pocket-sized card. The client, with assistance from the therapist, constructs personally relevant and realistic, if unlikely, meaningful negative consequences to offending. Examples of these have included: being caught in the act by the child's father; being denigrated by the client's own family; being identified in the press as a sexual offender; losing his job and friends; and being sent to prison. Different variations of these consequences are written on the reverse of each card.

The client is instructed to carry these cards with him at all times, and to read each sequence and its consequences on at least three occasions every day. In the early stages of this procedure the client is told to read each sequence through to the terminal behaviour before reading the consequences. Over the weeks of practice he is to move the interruption of the sequence, and the reading of the consequences, to progressively earlier steps in the sequence until by 4–6 weeks he is reading the consequences at the point when he is contemplating initiating the offence or fantasy sequence.

In their survey of North American treatment programmes for sexual offenders, McGrath *et al.* (2003) found that covert sensitisation was the most consistently employed procedure for modifying deviant sexual interests. Forty-eight percent of adult programmes and over 35% of juvenile programmes used covert sensitisation whereas the next most commonly used procedure was olfactory aversion at 25.3%. Despite this popularity, there is little in the way of supportive evidence for the covert sensitisation (Quinsey & Earls, 1990).

To date there is only one case report of the use of covert association. Marshall (2007) designed a reasonably well-controlled implementation of covert association with a child molester who reported having abused at least 10 boys over a 12-year period. Marshall employed repeated phallometric assessments of the client's arousal to boys of his preferred age and also to adult males and adult females. In addition, the client kept daily records of his sexual urges and fantasies concerning these same three groups of people. Final results, which were enduring at two-year follow-up, revealed reductions in arousal and in urges and fantasies concerning boys, associated with strong sexual interests in adult males. At two years follow-up the client had initiated a sexual relationship with an adult male. This was a first for him since it involved romantic and affectionate elements whereas his prior sexual contacts with adult males had all been brief and strictly sexual.

Masturbatory-Based Techniques

These procedures all employ masturbation, either in attempts to enhance appropriate sexual interests or as a strategy to generate a state that is unresponsive to sexual stimuli. This latter state (called the 'refractory period' – see Masters, Johnson & Kolodny, 1985) provides the basis for deconditioning arousal to deviant images and acts.

Enhancing Appropriate Interests

Various procedures have been described that pair masturbatory-induced sexual arousal with the presentation of images or thoughts that depict appropriate sexual behaviours. Thorpe, Schmidt and Castell (1963) employed what later became known as the 'thematic shift' approach, Marquis (1970) described 'orgasmic reconditioning' and Maletzky (1980) utilised what he called 'directed masturbation'. Each of these procedures requires the client to either watch images of appropriate sex, or imagine such scenes, while masturbating to orgasm, although each procedure employs a slightly different way of doing this. There is no evidence showing that any one of these procedures is better than the others but it must be said that there is not strong evidence to support any of them (see Laws & Marshall, 1991). Whichever specific strategy is chosen (we prefer the 'thematic shift' technique), the crucial feature is to ensure that sexually appropriate thoughts are associated with significant sexual arousal induced by masturbating. This is best achieved by having the client associate the thoughts with what Masters *et al.* (1985) called the "plateau stage" of sexual arousal.

Clients are instructed to employ the procedure each time they masturbate. Persistent application of the procedure should inevitably result in the enhancement of the sexual attractiveness of the appropriate sexual stimuli, although as we have noted, the published evidence is not strong. In a quasi-controlled single case study of a problematic fetish-related behaviour in a young adult male, Marshall (1974) demonstrated positive effects for the use of the thematic shift technique. Repeated phallometric assessments revealed that after an aversion-based procedure had reduced the fetishistic interests, thematic shift gradually produced increased sexual arousal to peer-aged adult females.

In the study mentioned earlier concerning the use of olfactory aversion, Marshall (2006) also employed directed masturbation to enhance responses to adult females once the aversive procedure had produced its effects. In this procedure the client was simply instructed to use images of appropriately aged women while masturbating. Three weeks of persistent practice led to markedly enhanced sexual arousal to women and a corresponding increase in the frequency of sexual urges and fantasies concerning women. In an earlier well-controlled single case study, Marshall (1979) demonstrated similar benefits for directed masturbation.

Oddly enough in McGrath *et al.*'s (2003) survey, only 19% of programmes reported using one or another form of this masturbatory-based approach despite the fact that almost 40% employed one or another form of satiation, which depends for its efficacy on the creation of a masturbatory-induced refractory state. At present, masturbation associated with appropriate fantasies or images appears to be the only approach that has been systematically employed to enhance appropriate sexual interests despite the poverty of evidence in support of these procedures.

Decreasing Deviant Interests

We have already discussed aversive-based procedures for reducing deviant interests. Here we will describe satiation procedures. These procedures, when properly employed, associate deviant thoughts/fantasies with a state where the client is unresponsive to sexual stimuli. Shortly after orgasm (within two minutes of orgasm) men enter what is called a 'refractory state'; that is, a state where otherwise sexually provocative stimuli elicit little or no sexual responses. The refractory state rarely lasts less than 20 minutes. Having clients rehearse every variation on their deviant sexual themes during this refractory period should reduce the sexual valence of the deviant acts since the refractory state is, by definition, a period of non-reward. Associating high frequency behaviours with the absence of a rewarding consequence leads to the rapid extinction of the behaviours (Falls, 1998).

Satiation therapy, as this approach is called, was first described for use with sexual offenders by Marshall and Lippens (1977) and later demonstrated to be effective in two experimentally-controlled single case studies (Marshall, 1979). In these early applications of satiation, Marshall had the clients continue to masturbate after ejaculation. His hope was that this would not only extinguish arousal to deviant images, it would also discourage masturbating to such images. Unfortunately this requirement to continue to masturbate post-orgasm made the procedure unattractive to many clients leading to high refusal rates. Laws *et al.* (1987) dropped the requirement to continue masturbating and called their version "verbal satiation". We adopted these changes by having our clients simply verbalise aloud every variant they can create on their deviant images for no more than 10 minutes after 2 minutes post-orgasm. It remains crucial, however, to induce a refractory state immediately prior to verbalising the deviant fantasies. Indeed, we always combine directed masturbation (or thematic shift) with satiation.

Evidence on the efficacy of satiation procedures is more substantial than is the case with any of the other techniques described in this chapter. Several group studies have provided support for the utility of satiation therapy with sexual offenders (Alford *et al.*, 1987; Hunter & Goodwin, 1992; Hunter & Santos, 1990). Johnston, Hudson and Marshall (1992) evaluated the combination of directed masturbation followed by satiation. Pre- to post-treatment phallometric assessments revealed marked reductions in deviant arousal and a post-treatment index (deviant responses divided by appropriate responses) that reflected normative responding.

CONCLUSIONS

We believe that the combination used by Johnston *et al.* (i.e., directed masturbation to both enhance appropriate interests and to induce a refractory state, followed by satiation) represents the best currently available approach to changing sexual interests, and is to be preferred over any aversion-based technique. Aversion procedures are most usefully employed when other behavioural procedures fail, although pharmacological interventions are also useful in these cases (Bradford, 2000) and may be the better choice for high-risk sexual offenders who are in a community setting.

What is most clear from this review of behavioural procedures is that far more research is needed to generate confidence in their utility. This is particularly pressing given that so many programmes employ these techniques (McGrath *et al.*2003). It is time that clinicians made the effort to collect data on their use of behavioural procedures aimed at enhancing appropriate sexual interests and decreasing deviant interests.

REFERENCES

Abel, G.G. & Blanchard, E.B. (1974). The role of fantasy in the treatment of sexual deviation. *Archives of General Psychiatry, 30*, 467–475.

Abel, G.G. & Rouleau, J.L. (1990). The nature and extent of sexual assault. In W.L. Marshall, D.R. Laws & H.E. Barbaree (Eds), *Handbook of sexual assault: Issues, theory and treatment of the offender* (pp. 9–21). New York: Plenum Press.

Alford, G.S., Morin, C., Atkins, M. & Schoen, L. (1987). Masturbatory extinction of deviant sexual arousal. *Journal of Behaviour Therapy and Experimental Psychiatry, 18*, 59–66.

Axelrod, S. & Apsche, J.(Eds) (1983). *The effects of punishment on human behaviour.* New York: Academic Press.

Ayres, J.J.B. (1998). Fear conditioning and avoidance. In W. O'Donohue (Ed.), *Learning and behaviour therapy* (pp. 122–145). Boston: Allyn & Bacon.

Ball, C.J. & Seghorn, T.K. (1999). Diagnosis and treatment of exhibitionism and other sexual compulsive disorders. In B.K. Schwartz (Ed.), *The sex offender: Theoretical advances, treating special populations and legal developments*, Vol. *III* (pp. 28.1–28.16). Kingston, NJ: Civic Research Institute.

Bancroft, J. (1974). *Deviant sexual behaviour.* Oxford, UK: Clarendon Press.

Bancroft, J.H.J. (1971). The application of psychophysiological measures to the assessment and modification of sexual behaviour. *Behaviour Research and Therapy, 9*, 119–130.

Barker, L.M. (2001). *Learning and behaviour: Biological, psychological, and sociocultural perspectives* (3rd edn). Upper Saddle River, NJ: Prentice Hall.

Barnard, G.W., Fuller, A.K., Robbins, L. & Shaw, T. (1989). *The child molester: An integrated approach to evaluation and treatment.* New York: Brunner/Mazel.

Bond, I.K. & Evans, D.R. (1967). Avoidance therapy: Its use in two cases of underwear fetishism. *Canadian Medical Association Journal, 96*, 1160–1162.

Bradford, J.M.W. (2000). The treatment of sexual deviation using a pharmacological approach. *Journal of Sex Research, 37*(3), 248–257.

Cautela, J.R. (1967). Covert sensitization. *Psychological Reports, 20*, 459–468.

Colson, C.E. (1972). Olfactory aversion therapy for homosexual behaviour. *Journal of Behaviour Therapy and Experimental Psychiatry, 3*, 185–187.

Domjan, M. (1998). *The principles of learning and behaviour* (4th edn). Pacific Grove, CA: Brooks/Cole Publishing.

Dougher, M.J. (1995). Behavioural techniques to alter sexual arousal. In B.K. Schwartz & H.R. Cellini (Eds), *The sex offender: Corrections, treatment and legal practice*, Vol. *I* (pp. 15.1–15.8). Kingston, NJ: Civic Research Institute.

Dougher, M.J., Crossen, J.R., Ferraro, D.P. & Garland, R.J. (1987). Covert sensitization and sexual preference: A preliminary analogue experiment. *Journal of Behaviour Therapy and Experimental Psychiatry*, *18*, 231–242.

Earls, C.M. & Castonguay, L.G. (1989). The evaluation of olfactory aversion for a bisexual pedophile with a single case study multiple baseline design. *Behaviour Therapy*, *20*, 137–146.

Falls, W.A. (1998). Extinction: A review of theory and evidence suggesting that memories are not erased with nonreinforcement. In W. O'Donohue (Ed.), *Learning and behaviour therapy* (pp. 205–229). Boston: Allyn & Bacon.

Gray, S.R. (1995). A comparison of verbal satiation and minimal arousal conditioning to reduce deviant arousal in the laboratory. *Sexual Abuse: A Journal of Research and Treatment*, *7*, 143–153.

Hanson, R.K. & Bussière, M.T. (1998). Predicting relapse: A meta-analysis of sexual offender recidivism studies. *Journal of Consulting and Clinical Psychology*, *66*, 123–142.

Hayes, S.C., Brownell, K.D. & Barlow, D.H. (1978). The use of self-administered covert sensitisation in the treatment of exhibitionism and sadism. *Behaviour Therapy*, *9*, 283–289.

Hughes, R.C. (1977). Covert sensitization treatment of exhibitionism. *Journal of Behaviour Therapy and Experimental Psychiatry*, *8*, 177–179.

Hunter, J.A. & Goodwin, D.W. (1992). The clinical utility of satiation therapy with juvenile sex offenders: Variations and efficacy. *Annals of Sex Research*, *5*, 71–80.

Hunter, J.A. & Lexier, L.J. (1998). Ethical and legal issues in the assessment and treatment of juvenile sex offenders. *Child Maltreatment*, *3*, 339–348.

Hunter, J.A. & Santos, D. (1990). The use of specialized cognitive-behavioural therapies in the treatment of juvenile sexual offenders. *International Journal of Offender Therapy and Comparative Criminology*, *34*, 239–248.

Johnston, P., Hudson, S.M. & Marshall, W.L. (1992). The effects of masturbatory reconditioning with non-familial child molesters. *Behaviour Research and Therapy*, *5*, 559–561.

Kafka, M.P. (1994). Sertraline pharmacotherapy for paraphilias and paraphilia-related disorders: An open trial. *Annals of Clinical Psychiatry*, *6*, 189–195.

Kennedy, W.A. & Forety, J. (1968). Control of eating behaviour in obese patients by avoidance conditioning. *Psychological Reports*, *23*, 571–573.

Kremsdorf, R., Holmen, M. & Laws, D. (1980). Orgasmic reconditioning without deviant imagery: A case report with a pedophile. *Behaviour Research and Therapy*, *18*, 203–207.

Launay, G. (1999). The phallometric measurement of offenders. *Criminal Behaviour and Mental Health*, *9*, 254–274.

Laws, D.R. & Marshall, W.L. (1991). Masturbatory reconditioning with sexual deviates: An evaluative review. *Advances in Behaviour Research and Therapy*, *13*, 13–25.

Laws, D.R. & Marshall, W.L. (2003). A brief history of behavioural and cognitive behavioural approaches to sexual offenders. Part 1. Early developments. *Sexual Abuse: A Journal of Research and Treatment*, *15*, 75–92.

Laws, D.R., Meyer, J. & Holmen, M.L. (1978). Reduction of sadistic sexual arousal by olfactory aversion: A case study. *Behaviour Research and Therapy*, *16*, 281–285.

Laws, D.R., Osborn, C.A., Avery-Clark, C. *et al.* (1987). *Masturbatory satiation with sexual deviates*. Unpublished manuscript. University of South Florida, Florida Mental Health Institute, Tampa.

Maletzky, B.M. (1973). Assisted covert sensitization: A preliminary report. *Behaviour Therapy*, *7*, 139–140.

Maletzky, B.M. (1980). Assisted covert sensitization. In D.J. Cox & R.J. Daitzman (Eds), *Exhibition: Description, assessment, and treatment* (pp. 187–251). New York: Garland STPM Press.

Maletzky, B.M. (1985). Orgasmic reconditioning. In A.S. Bellack & M. Hersen (Eds), *Dictionary of behaviour therapy techniques* (pp. 157–158). New York: Pergamon Press.

Maletzky, B.M. (1991). *Treating the sexual offender*. Newbury Park, CA: Sage Publications.

Maletzky, B.M. & George, F.S. (1973). The treatment of homosexuality by 'assisted' covert sensitization. *Behaviour Research and Therapy, 11*, 655–657.

Marquis, J.N. (1970). Orgasmic reconditioning: Changing sexual object choice through controlling masturbation fantasies. *Journal of Behaviour Therapy and Experimental Psychiatry, 1*, 263–271.

Marshall, W.L. (1973). The modification of sexual fantasies: A combined treatment approach to the reduction of deviant sexual behavior. *Behaviour Research and Therapy, 11*, 557–564.

Marshall, W.L. (1974). A combined treatment approach to the reduction of multiple fetish-related behaviours. *Journal of Consulting and Clinical Psychology, 42*, 613–616.

Marshall, W.L. (1979). Satiation therapy: A procedure for reducing deviant sexual arousal. *Journal of Applied Behavioural Analysis, 12*, 377–389.

Marshall, W.L. (2006a). Ammonia aversion with an exhibitionist: A case study. *Clinical Case Studies, 5*, 15–24.

Marshall, W.L. (2006b). Olfactory aversion and directed masturbation in the modification of deviant preferences: A case study of a child molester. *Clinical Case Studies, 5*, 3–14.

Marshall, W.L. (2007). Covert association: A case demonstration with a child molester. *Clinical Case Studies, 6*, 218–231.

Marshall, W.L., Anderson, D. & Fernandez, Y.M. (1999). *Cognitive behavioural treatment of sexual offenders*. Chichester, UK: John Wiley & Sons, Ltd.

Marshall, W.L. & Eccles, A. (1993). Pavlovian conditioning processes in adolescent sex offenders. In H.E. Barbaree, W.L. Marshall & S.M. Hudson (Eds), *The juvenile sex offender* (pp. 118–142). New York: Guilford Press.

Marshall, W.L. & Fernandez, Y.M. (1998). Cognitive-behavioural approaches to the treatment of the paraphilias: Sexual offenders. In V.E. Caballo (Ed.), *International handbook of cognitive and behavioural treatment for psychological disorders* (pp. 281–312). Oxford, UK: Elsevier Science.

Marshall, W.L. & Fernandez, Y.M. (2003). *Phallometric testing with sexual offenders: Theory, research, and practice*. Brandon, VT: Safer Society Press.

Marshall, W.L., Keltner, A. & Griffiths, E. (1974). *An apparatus for the delivery of foul odours: Clinical applications*. Unpublished manuscript. Queen's University, Kingston, Ontario, Canada.

Marshall, W.L. & Laws, D.R. (2003). A brief history of behavioural and cognitive behavioural approaches to sexual offender treatment: Part 2. The modern era. *Sexual Abuse: A Journal of Research and Treatment, 15*, 93–120.

Marshall, W.L. & Lippens, K. (1977). The clinical value of boredom: A procedure for reducing inappropriate sexual interests. *Journal of Nervous and Mental Disorders, 165*, 283–287.

Marshall, L.E. & Marshall, W.L. (2001). *Sexual compulsivity as part of sexual offending behaviour*. Workshop presented at the National Conference of the National Council on Sexual Addiction and Compulsivity, San Diego, CA, May 2001.

Marshall, W.L., Marshall, L.E., Serran, G.A. & Fernandez, Y.M. (2006). *Treating sexual offenders: An integrated approach*. New York: Routledge.

Masters, W.H., Johnson, V.E. & Kolodny, R.C. (1985). *Human sexuality* (2nd edn). Boston: Little, Brown.

McConaghy, N. (1993). *Sexual behaviour: Problems and management*. New York: Plenum Press.

McGrath, R.J. (2001). Using behavioural techniques to control sexual arousal. In M.S. Carich & S.E. Mussack (Eds), *Handbook for sexual abuser assessment and treatment* (pp. 105–116). Brandon, VT: Safer Society Press.

McGrath, R.J., Cumming, G.F. & Burchard, B.L. (2003). *Current practices and trends in sexual abuser management: The Safer Society 2002 Nationwide Survey*. Brandon, VT: Safer Society Press.

McGuire R.J., Carlisle J.M. & Young B.G. (1965). Sexual deviations as a conditioned behaviour: A hypothesis. *Behaviour Research and Therapy, 2*, 185–190.

Moergen, S.A., Merkel, W.T. & Brown, S. (1990). The use of covert sensitization and social skills training in the treatment of an obscene telephone caller. *Journal of Behaviour Therapy and Experimental Psychiatry, 21*, 269–275.

Morgenstern, K. (1974). Cigarette smoking as a noxious and self-managed aversion therapy for compulsive eating. *Behaviour Therapy, 2*, 255–260.

Peeke, H.V.S. & Petrinovich, L.(Eds) (1984). *Habituation, sensitization, and behaviour*. New York: Academic Press.

Quinsey, V.L., Chaplin, T.C. & Carrigan, W.F. (1980). Biofeedback and signaled punishment in the modification of inappropriate sexual age preferences. *Behaviour Therapy*, *11*, 567–576.

Quinsey, V.L. & Earls, C.M. (1990). The modification of sexual preferences. In W.L. Marshall, D.R. Laws& H.E. Barbaree (Eds), *The handbook of sexual assault: Issues, theories and treatment of the offender* (pp. 279–295). New York: Plenum Press.

Rangaswamy, K. (1987). Treatment of voyeurism by behaviour therapy. *Child Psychiatry Quarterly*, *20*, 73–76.

Rolls, E.T. & Rolls, J.H. (1997). Olfactory sensory-specific satiety in humans. *Physiology & Behaviour*, *61*, 461–473.

Serber, M. (1970). Shame aversion therapy. *Journal of Behaviour Therapy and Experimental Psychiatry*, *1*, 213–215.

Serber, M. & Wolpe, J. (1972). Behaviour therapy techniques. In H.L.P. Resnick & M.E. Wolfgang (Eds), *Sexual Behaviours* (pp. 239–254). Boston: Little Brown.

Skinner, B.F. (1938). *The behaviour of organisms: An experimental analysis*. New York: Appleton-Century.

Stava, L., Levin, S.M. & Schwanz, C. (1993). The role of aversion in covert sensitization treatment of pedophilia: A case report. *Journal of Child Sexual Abuse*, *2*, 1–13.

Thorpe, J.G., Schmidt, E., Brown, P. & Castell, D. (1964). Aversion-relief therapy: A new method for general application. *Behaviour Research and Therapy*, *2*, 71–82.

Thorpe, J.G., Schmidt, E. & Castell, D.A. (1963). A comparison of positive and negative (aversive) conditioning in the treatment of homosexuality. *Behaviour Research and Therapy*, *1*, 357–362.

Travin, S. & Protter, B. (1993). *Sexual perversion: Integrated treatment approaches for the clinician*. New York: Plenum Press.

Weinrott, M., Riggan, M. & Frothingham, S. (1997). Reducing deviant arousal in juvenile sex offenders using vicarious sensitization. *Journal of Interpersonal Violence*, *12*, 704–728.

Wolpe, J. (1969). *The practice of behaviour therapy*. New York: Pergamon Press.

18

Advances in the Treatment of Adult Incarcerated Sex Offenders

RUTH E. MANN

WILLIAM L. MARSHALL

INTRODUCTION

The purpose of this chapter is to explore how treatment procedures for adult sexual offenders have advanced in the last two decades. In particular, this chapter will examine some popular treatment targets for sexual offenders such as cognitive distortions, victim empathy and relapse prevention. Have these approaches stood the test of time, or do adjustments need to be made to long-standing treatment models to incorporate the latest research and clinical developments? We will summarise the evidence base for modern treatment procedures and draw conclusions about the current state of the art in terms of content, style and implementation of treatment.

One thing has not changed in the last two decades and looks unlikely to change. Sexual offending remains a pressing societal problem which attracts massive media coverage and public concern. Legislators and policy makers are under constant pressure to reassure the public that plenty is being done about the problem of sexual offending. Treatment providers work within this climate to provide therapy, with the aim of reducing recidivism by known offenders. We are in an era where the general public wants sexual offenders to be as socially excluded as possible, but social exclusion is likely to raise rather than reduce risk. Those who provide treatment to sexual offenders have to rise above the stigma attached to their client group in order to see them as men who can change, and to communicate this sense of hope to their clients, colleagues and the general public.

In the late 1980s and early 1990s, most sexual offender treatment involved three major activities: identifying and challenging cognitive distortions (Murphy, 1990), enhancing victim empathy (Pithers, 1994) and relapse prevention (Laws, 1989).

Assessment and Treatment of Sex Offenders: A Handbook. Edited by Anthony Beech, Leam Craig and Kevin Browne. © John Wiley & Sons Ltd, 2009.

Treatment providers were cautioned not to trust their clients (Salter, 1988) who, it was expected, would generally minimise the nature and extent of their abusive behaviour. It was assumed that sexual offenders planned and fantasised about offending beforehand. If they denied this, therapists were to challenge them robustly (Salter, 1988). These assumptions and practices will now be considered in more detail, and critiqued in terms of subsequent research and theory.

COGNITIVE DISTORTIONS

In the 1980s, two main texts (Salter, 1988; Finkelhor, 1984) influenced the practice of sexual offender treatment. Both texts emphasised the importance of the role of 'cognitive distortions' in causing and maintaining sexual offending. In Finkelhor's 'Four Preconditions' descriptive theory of child sexual abuse, he proposed that one stage through which offenders must pass in order to offend was 'overcoming internal inhibitions'. In this stage, offenders needed to adjust their thinking so that any reservations about offending were overcome. Programmes based on Finkelhor's model took the line that internal inhibitions were overcome by employing 'cognitive distortions'. While this term has been over-used (Maruna & Mann, 2006), the definition of cognitive distortion is usually accepted to mean the process of deliberately generating excuses and justifications to oneself for what is known to be a deviant act (e.g., Murphy, 1990). The term cognitive distortions therefore encompassed denial, minimisation, excuses and justifications. Salter (1988) guided therapists to respond robustly to cognitive distortions. She advised therapists that some offenders admit their offending but justify it, perhaps by blaming the victim or by stating that the offence caused no harm. Others may admit the behaviour but explain it with reference to external causes such as alcohol, work stress, or their wife's behaviour. According to Salter, the primary purpose of a sexual offender treatment group was to "identify and confront cognitive distortions, rationalizations and excuses for offending" (p. 114). Salter was not alone in her emphasis on cognitive distortion as a major cause of offending. The vast criminological literature into neutralisation theory rested on the same assumption (for a review, see Maruna & Copes, 2005). This theory posited that all criminals minimise the seriousness of criminal acts; hence, this mental process of minimisation or justification could be characterised as 'criminal thinking'.

Consequently, sexual offender treatment in the 1980s dedicated considerable time to hearing offenders describe their offending, and then challenging any instances of denial, minimisation, justification or excusing that were found to be part of their accounts. Therapists saw cognitive distortions as deliberate strategies generated by the offender to give himself permission to offend. Therapists assumed that if the treatment process could stop offenders from justifying their previous offending, they would be less likely to offend again.

These assumptions have now been challenged. Maruna and Copes (2005) published a comprehensive critique of neutralisation theory, concluding that after 50 years of research, there was insufficient evidence to support the theory. With specific reference to sexual offender treatment, Maruna and Mann (2006) suggested that the idea that cognitive distortions cause offending could be a fundamental attribution error; that is, an error based on over-dispositional explanations for behaviour. Furthermore, they argued, the assumption that because most offenders offer excuses and justification, such phenomena must have played a causal role in offending, is a logical fallacy. The co-existence of two phenomena cannot lead to an assumption of direction of cause. Maruna and Mann reviewed a large body of literature to show that excuse making following (non-criminal) transgressions is widely regarded as normal, healthy and socially desirable. They found barely any evidence in either the psychological or criminological literature that lack of excuse making (popularly known as 'taking responsibility for offending') reduces risk of recidivism.

Maruna and Mann (2006), and Mann and Beech (2003), pointed out that researchers (and clinicians) define cognitive distortions in different ways, so that the term can refer to any or all of the following: denial, minimisation, justifications, excuses, attitudes, beliefs and schemas. Clearly there are too many different cognitive phenomena absorbed into one term and the concept is dangerously imprecise as a result. Clinicians who subscribe to the broad and insufficiently defined goal of 'reducing cognitive distortions' could end up conveying to offenders that *any* account of why they offended is unacceptable.

On the other hand, we do not mean to suggest that offenders' cognitions are irrelevant to their offending or their treatment. The important issue is to be able to distinguish between those cognitions that are important (i.e., related to risk) and those that are not. Minimisation, justifications and excuses all tend to occur after the offence has taken place (and hence are also sometimes referred to as 'post-hoc rationalisations'). However, cognitions that take place prior to and during the offence are likely to be representations of underlying attitudes and schemas which play a direct role in the commission of the offence (Mann & Beech, 2003).

There are several implications for evidence-based practice. First, as denial and minimisation do not raise risk for recidivism (Hanson & Morton-Bourgon, 2004), these phenomena should not be a primary goal for treatment. Generally, denial and minimisation should be regarded as problems only insomuch as they prevent an offender from identifying and addressing his criminogenic needs. So, it does not matter if an offender denies that his victim was aged six, insisting that she was aged eight. Either way, he acknowledges that he abused a pre-pubescent child. It does matter if he denies that she was six, insisting that she was sixteen, because this denial would preclude him from discussing sexual arousal to younger children. It does not matter if an acquaintance rapist claims that he misread signals and thought he was getting the go-ahead, because he still essentially acknowledges that he failed to properly consider if his victim was consenting and will be able to consider possibilities such as his judgement being impaired by sexual preoccupation or sexual entitlement beliefs. It does matter if he insists that the sex was consenting and she only 'cried rape' when she later regretted the encounter, because this scenario does not encourage him to consider his own offence-relevant schemas.

Second, therapists should consider being more tolerant of post-hoc neutralisations that involve unstable, external attributions for offending. In fact, such attributions can be therapeutically helpful, as they can act as indicators of specific problems that may require targeting in treatment (Dean *et al.*, 2007; Maruna & Mann, 2006). For example, a man who claims that his offending was caused by stress is indicating that he has trouble managing life problems. A man who states that his offences would not have happened if he had not been drunk is revealing that he has certain sexual interests that he cannot always inhibit.

The primary targets when working with offenders' cognitions should be offence-supportive attitudes (e.g., a child abuser's belief that sex does not harm children) and schema-related beliefs (e.g., a rapist's suspicious, hostile, vengeful orientation towards others). Schema-related beliefs do not necessarily occur immediately prior to offending, but they are often seen in the earlier stages of an offence chain. Such beliefs seem to play a role in offending by causing emotional distress, which can in turn increase vulnerability to impulses to offend (Mann, 2005). Offence-supportive attitudes produce situation-specific misinterpretations of victim behaviour so that an offender can ignore the possibility that his offending is harmful in that given situation (Mann *et al.*, 2007). For example, an offender who believes that children are sexual beings may interpret innocent child-like displays of affection as sexual signals. He therefore will continue with an offence, believing that his behaviour is in line with the child's intentions, and failing to process the child's signals that suggest otherwise. It is a well-documented consequence of cognitive schemas that they focus attention on schema-relevant behaviour, and filter out schema-disconfirming information. In essence, certain schemas enable us to only see what we want to see.

VICTIM EMPATHY

In the 1980s, victim empathy was a core component of sexual offender programmes. The Safer Society survey of North American treatment provision for sexual offenders (Knopp, Freeman-Longo & Stevenson, 1992) reported that 94% of programmes contained a significant victim empathy component. Salter (1988) noted that [in treatment] "sex offenders must show progress in developing empathy for their victims" (p. 177). The basis for this belief was that development of empathy would inhibit future sexual abuse, and increase motivation to engage in cessation-oriented treatment (Hildebran & Pithers, 1989). An underlying assumption was that once offenders realised how truly damaging sexual abuse was, they would not want to do it again.

Marshall, Anderson and Fernandez (1999) pointed out that these assumptions were unfortunately not supported by research. They emphasised "the poverty of evidence that sexual offenders actually lack empathy, or that these treatments are effective" (p. 86). Subsequently, a large-scale meta-analytic study of risk predictors for sexual recidivism failed to find any relationship between empathy deficits and recidivism risk (Hanson & Morton-Bourgon, 2005).

One problem might be measurement. Empathy has a number of components (Marshall *et al.*, 1995) including cognitive elements (perspective taking), an emotional element (compassion) and a behavioural element (acting to comfort or reduce suffering). Self-report questionnaires, a generally well-validated approach for assessing sexual offenders (Beech, 1998), may well be able to measure the cognitive element but are less useful in assessing compassion or action taken to alleviate suffering. Another problem is that if offenders do lack empathy, this is likely to apply only to their own sexual offence victims (Beckett *et al.*, 1994; Fernandez & Marshall, 2003; Fernandez *et al.*, 1999). It is particularly problematic to measure the different elements of empathy in relation only to an offender's specific victim.

Does this mean that victim empathy work has no place in an evidence-based treatment programme? Despite the above argument, we do not advocate removing victim empathy entirely. Clinicians frequently report that empathy sessions appear to be something of a turning point for offenders, in the way originally conceptualised by Hildebran and Pithers (1989). Furthermore, offenders themselves report that empathy interventions are a very meaningful component of treatment (Beech, Fisher & Beckett, 1999; Wakeling, Webster & Mann, 2005).

We suggest that what was previously thought of as a victim empathy deficit could usefully be reconceptualised with reference to cognitive deconstruction theory (Baumeister, 1991) as applied to sexual offending by Ward, Hudson and Marshall (1995). Cognitive deconstruction theory proposed that offences are committed in the context of powerful emotional states for the offender. Strongly negative emotional states can lead a person to enter a state of 'cognitive deconstruction', where information processing becomes concrete and self-serving. In the presence of a potential victim, and with the accompanying complication of sexual arousal, cognitive deconstruction may lead an offender to focus only on information that is congruent with offending being a desirable course of action. Information such as victim resistance is filtered out; literally, not even noticed.

A re-conceptualisation of victim empathy work could see it as an activity which assists each offender in re-evaluating the way in which he processed information at the time of the offence. Empathy work should therefore be a very specific, targeted, activity for each offender, focusing on his recall of the experiences and reactions of the victim at the time, and encouraging re-processing of previously unrecognised visual or behavioural cues of distress. Techniques to assist this process include in particular role play based on psychodrama principles (Mann, Daniels & Marshall, 2002). Offenders often describe an apparently paradoxical effect of such role plays: as the offender achieves a greater realisation of the harm he caused, he experiences a subjective sense of relief. It seems likely that this phenomenon can be explained by cognitive dissonance: the demands of maintaining an increasingly untenable set of beliefs becomes more and more uncomfortable as disconfirming evidence mounts, so that the shift to a new belief is eventually experienced as relieving.

It should be noted that victim empathy work places particular demands on the therapist. Therapists who easily identify with the victim's perspective can become overpowered with empathic compassion for the victim during victim empathy work. If unrecognised, unchecked or unmanaged, such feelings can translate into punitive rather than therapeutic goals on the part of the therapist (Pithers, 1997).

Recent texts on sexual offender treatment have de-emphasised victim empathy (e.g., Marshall *et al.*, 2006). But, in our view, abandoning this area of work would be premature. Offenders' views about what works for them should not be lightly dismissed, especially if they are not self-serving.

RELAPSE PREVENTION

Laws (1989) edited a textbook on how the relapse prevention approach (RP), originally developed for substance misusers, could be adapted for sexual offender treatment. This highly influential text was adopted with alacrity by sexual offender treatment providers, probably because of its clear exposition of how to translate theory into practice (Laws & Ward, 2003). The Californian Sex Offender Treatment Evaluation Project (SOTEP; Marques *et al.*, 1989) became the blueprint for relapse prevention work with sexual offenders. In fact, this project evolved the idea of relapse prevention from its original conceptualisation as an adjunctive, maintenance-focused programme that would follow change-oriented treatment, to a model of treatment in its own right.

The SOTEP model of RP was a highly structured programme, which involved three main activities. First, offenders in the programme were assisted in constructing an offence chain (Nelson & Jackson, 1989), involving a detailed description of the sequence of events (with associated thoughts, moods and behaviours) that led up to the offence. SOTEP participants then examined their chain in detail in order to identify the elements that constituted their individual high-risk situations. The use of the term 'situation' in this context encompassed internal situations such as thoughts, actions and feelings as well as external situations such as places (e.g., parks) and incidents (e.g., seeing a lost child). Third, each participant then worked out escape, avoidance and coping strategies that could be used to manage each high-risk situation so that offending would not re-occur.

Unfortunately, the randomised allocation experiment that tested SOTEP's effectiveness concluded that the offenders who received this treatment programme recidivated at the same rate as those who received no treatment at all (Marques *et al.*, 2005). While some would take this as the ultimate evidence that sexual offenders cannot be treated, this conclusion would be overly hasty. The SOTEP evaluation simply showed that a *highly-structured RP approach* did not reduce recidivism. By the end of its life-span, the SOTEP directors had already articulated the limitations of the programme that they were evaluating (Marques *et al.*, 2000). First, they realised that without preparatory motivational work, offenders may reject the avoidance nature of traditional RP. That is, RP is focused by definition on situations which must be managed, controlled or avoided. It is not an intervention that would naturally lead to offenders feeling that they are growing or developing in psychological maturity or getting closer to their full potential. In order for an offender to benefit from a traditional RP intervention, he would have to be very committed already to avoiding future offending. In fact, the SOTEP staff felt that the men who failed (reoffended) after treatment had not been persuaded during their time in SOTEP that they wanted to give up offending. Second, SOTEP focused on the identification of risk factors as its main activity. Consequently, with hindsight, it was realised that there was insufficient focus on behavioural practice of coping skills. Third, the SOTEP directors commented that they consider the programme to have been too highly structured. The structure allowed offenders to apparently succeed in meeting programme goals (such as constructing a comprehensive cognitive behavioural offence chain) without them necessarily having addressed their 'difficult issues'.

The SOTEP has been incomparably important in advancing our knowledge about what works with sexual offenders. It is now acknowledged that offenders cannot be assumed to be intrinsically motivated to change when they enter a treatment programme. They may well be entering treatment for extrinsic reasons only, particularly if the programme is located in a penal institution, or if attendance is mandated as part of parole. Therefore the first lesson to be learned from SOTEP is that sexual offender treatment must begin with a focus on developing intrinsic motivation to avoid offending in the future. This motivation must be continually revisited throughout the duration of treatment. Intrinsic motivation can be built through explicit work, such as exercises to consider personal goals for a more fulfilling life; and through therapist behaviours, particularly reward and reinforcement (Fernandez, Shingler & Marshall, 2006). Programmes will also be more motivational if they focus on what the offender can achieve, rather than what he must give up (Mann et al., 2004). Such an 'approach goal focus' should be communicated through individual exercises (see Mann et al., 2004) and through the broader programme ethos. Programmes based explicitly on Ward's Good Lives Model of offender rehabilitation (Ward, Mann & Gannon, 2007), or containing elements of this model (Marshall et al., 2006) tend to be approach goal focused (Ward & Mann, 2004). It is our view that the Good Lives Model (see Chapter 16) should be adopted, imparted and evaluated as the framework for self-management work.

The SOTEP evaluation also indicated that interventions for sexual offenders should have a strong skills-building focus. More time and energy should be devoted to developing skills than to simply raising awareness of risk factors. The acquisition of new skills can be generalised to situations outside the therapy room through activities such as behavioural experiments and diary-keeping (Fernandez et al., 2006). For programmes located in secure institutions this poses a challenge. It is important that the practice of new skills is reinforced, not punished; and this therefore requires the cooperation and support of residential staff as well as treatment staff. Often the culture in penal establishments is such that this cooperation cannot be assumed, so it rests on treatment providers to work collaboratively and motivationally with prison staff in order to ensure their support.

TREATMENT STYLE AND THERAPY PROCESS

Salter (1988) recommended that sexual offenders should continually be challenged and confronted with their denial and justification: "The process of treating child sex offenders is heavily weighted in the direction of confrontation. Treatment requires continual confrontation" (p. 93). Although she cautioned that confrontation should not involve hostility, her examples included telling the offender that the therapist does not trust him, does not believe him, and does not see his issues as a problem. These sorts of statements, encouraging a confrontational style towards sexual offenders, continued to appear in the treatment literature into the 1990s (Mark, 1992; Prendergast, 1991) and have led to treatment practices that offenders can perceive as authoritarian if not downright aggressive.

By the mid-1990s, the influence of movements such as motivational interviewing (MI; Miller & Rollnick, 1991) started to reach the world of sex offender treatment. MI was a pioneering approach to people with addictive problems, also traditionally a group that were deemed to require confrontational treatment. MI suggested that confrontational approaches will backfire, pushing the client into a defensive corner. Instead, MI involved helping a client create his own self-motivational statements, using gentle techniques such as creating cognitive dissonance, rolling with resistance and expressing empathy.

When Marshall and his colleagues began a series of studies to define a successful treatment style with sexual offenders, it was therefore of little surprise that his findings closely matched the recommended style of MI. Marshall's studies (summarised in Marshall, 2005) involved the study of videotapes from HM Prison Service's Sex Offender Treatment Programme (SOTP). First, Marshall created a checklist of therapist behaviours and established that this scale could be reliably applied by trained observers. Next he used the scale to rate therapist behaviours in groups that had been successful or unsuccessful in achieving the aims of the programme. The rater was blind to the success category of the group they were rating. Four therapist characteristics emerged as the most important predictors of group success: expression of empathy, a warm manner, use of verbal reward, and directiveness (Marshall *et al.*, 2003). These four features combined accounted for between 40% and 60% of the variance on indices of change. Furthermore, a confrontational style was negatively related to the achievement of goals. Marshall (2005) concluded that the message to therapists working with sexual offenders is, "Do not challenge harshly" (p. 112).

Most treatment for sexual offenders is delivered as group therapy (see Mann & Fernandez, 2006, for a discussion of why this is so). Therefore, there is a need for therapists to understand the role of group process in helping a group achieve its aims. The processes of any group may be a forceful agent of change, but this issue has been under-researched in sexual offender treatment. Beech and his colleagues (Beech & Fordham, 1997; Beech & Hamilton-Giachritsis, 2005) have conducted the most useful studies of this topic to date. For example, Beech and Fordham (1997) analysed scores on the Group Environment Scale (GES; Moos, 1986) for a number of probation programmes. Using a similar methodology to the Marshall studies, they compared the GES profiles of successful groups to those of unsuccessful groups. The most successful group was characterised by high scores on scales measuring group cohesion, perceived leader support, emotional expressiveness, independence, task orientation and innovation. That is, successful group leaders encouraged a friendly atmosphere, and were practical, well-organised, and comfortable with displays of emotion. Beech and Fordham also reported that some group leaders were insufficiently aware of the power of group process and failed to recognise their own role in setting the group norms. They noted that group leaders and group members tended to have different perceptions of the group environment. In comparison with group members, leaders tended to have a more positive view of the group's success; over-estimating the help they provided, the control that they had, and the level of change that was taking place.

These findings have clear implications for the facilitation and management of sexual offender groups. It is apparent that training, monitoring and supervision of therapists should focus on style as much as content. It is also apparent that treatment providers should seek feedback from their clients about how their treatment style is perceived, rather than relying on their own judgement.

In summary, there have been considerable developments in the way in which sexual offender treatment is delivered. Confrontation is no longer seen as an appropriate tactic to adopt with sexual offenders. There has been clear identification of the personal and group management skills required to deliver treatment successfully. Sexual offender treatment providers and managers who incorporate these findings into practice are more likely to effect changes in their clients and reductions in recidivism.

RISK AND NEED ASSESSMENT AND TREATMENT PLANNING

As recently as 15 years ago, actuarial procedures to determine risk of recidivism for sexual offenders were not available. Generally, all sexual offenders were assumed to be high risk by the nature of their offences. There have been major advances over the last 15 years in our understanding of static and dynamic risk factors, and our ability to assess these risk factors via structured procedures.

The reconviction rates for sexual offending are much lower than the general public believe them to be. Harris and Hanson (2004) concluded the report of their large-scale study into reconviction rates by stating that:

> *Most sexual offenders do not reoffend sexually over time. This may be the most important finding of this study, as this finding is contrary to some strongly held beliefs. After 15 years, 73% of sexual offenders had not been charged with, or convicted of, another sexual offence. The sample was sufficiently large that very strong contradictory evidence is needed to substantially change these recidivism estimates (p. 17).*

In particular, sexual reconviction rates for sexual offenders who are judged to be low risk are very low indeed (e.g., less than 5% over a 5-year follow-up, in comparison with a 50% rate for the very high risk group; Thornton *et al.*, 2004), begging the question whether such offenders actually require treatment at all. On the other hand, high-risk offenders may require more than the standard components of sexual offender treatment (Friendship, Mann & Beech, 2003). It is now the case that reliable static risk scales (Hanson & Thornton, 2000) and dynamic risk assessment frameworks (Thornton, 2002) exist, and psychometric measures have proven their value by differentiating risk and need levels (Beech, 1998; Craig *et al.*, 2007). There is, therefore, little excuse for providing treatment that is not preceded by careful risk and need assessment, so that the treatment activities chosen can be tailored to the exact needs of each programme. Such individualisation is achievable even within manualised treatment programmes (McMurran & Duggan, 2005).

In terms of treatment 'dose', the risk principle of the Risk-Need-Responsivity Model of offender rehabilitation (Andrews & Bonta, 2003) states that treatment dose should be related to risk, with higher risk offenders receiving more treatment. Friendship *et al.* (2003) found that high-risk sexual offenders did not respond to a 160-hour treatment programme, but that the same programme was very effective in reducing reconvictions for medium-risk offenders. Rapists and sexual murderers also seemed to require longer treatment than the 160-hour programme, with continuing needs relating to dysfunctional thinking patterns (such as grievance thinking) and socio-affective difficulties (Beech *et al.*, 2005). Beech, Fisher and Beckett (1999) found that lower-risk offenders responded as well to an 80-hour programme as they did to a 160-hour programme. These studies suggest that an increase in treatment dose is necessary as risk increases, with high-risk offenders probably needing around 300 hours of treatment for an impact on recidivism to be observed.

RECOMMENDED CONTENT FOR A COMPREHENSIVE PROGRAMME FOR SEXUAL OFFENDERS

The treatment targets for a comprehensive treatment programme for sexual offenders should reflect those issues that have been found to raise risk of recidivism (Hanson & Bussière, 1998; Hanson & Morton-Bourgon, 2005). Such criminogenic targets should be expressed in a way that is congruent with the Good Lives Model of offender rehabilitation (Ward & Mann, 2004; Ward *et al.*, 2007) (see Chapter 16). Established treatment targets for sexual offenders are grouped below into four areas or domains, and suggested treatment approaches are described for each domain.

Sexual Interests

Details of the behavioural procedures and medications to modify sexual interests are provided in another chapter in this book (see Chapter 17 by Marshall, O'Brien & Marshall) so we will not describe them here except for the changes we have introduced to the standard approaches.

In the early days of behavioural, and subsequently cognitive behavioural, programmes for sexual offenders, it was believed that conditioned deviant sexual interests were the primary, if not the only, source that drove deviant sexual behaviours (see, e.g., Abel & Blanchard, 1974; Bond & Evans, 1967; McGuire, Carlisle & Young, 1965). Phallometric (or PPG) assessments were seen as the crucial method of assessing these problematic sexual interests as well evaluating the effects of treatment. While the perceived centrality of deviant sexual interests in both theory and treatment has diminished over the years, these interests and their assessment live on as part of most programmes for sexual offenders. Recent critical appraisals of phallometry (Barbaree & Peacock, 1995; Marshall & Fernandez, 2000, 2001, 2003; O'Donohue & Letourneau, 1992; Simon & Schouten, 1992, and Chapter 8 of this book), have revealed the limitations of the procedure to detect deviance and it is far from clear that all sexual offenders have such deviant interests. Among non-familial child molesters, if we eliminate those who refuse to do the assessment, as well as those who fail to respond to any stimulus, less than 40% display arousal to children. Furthermore, the majority of non-familial child molesters who have only one known victim respond normally at phallometric assessment. Among rapists, only 30% respond significantly to non-consenting or forceful sex; less than 20% of incest offenders and even fewer exhibitionists appear deviant at phallometric testing. Thus while for some sexual offenders it may be necessary for treatment to address deviant sexual interests, this is not an issue for most such clients. Even for those who display deviant arousal it may be unnecessary to specifically target these interests. For example, Marshall (1997) demonstrated among a small group (N = 12) of child molesters, specifically chosen because both their phallometric results (high deviant arousal) and their offence histories (numerous victims each, violence in the offences, and very intrusive sexual behaviours) revealed strong deviance, that treatment aimed at the usual broad set of targets, *except deviant interests*, had the effect of eliminating deviant responses at post-treatment phallometric assessments. Marshall suggested that because treatment provided these men with the attitudes, skills and sense of self-worth necessary to function effectively in adult, prosocial sexual relationships, deviant interests no longer served the purpose of compensating for these pre-treatment deficiencies and so the deviant responses simply extinguished. Of course this was a small study so we should be cautious about over-interpreting the meaning of these findings. However, Marshall's findings do suggest that all the elements in today's comprehensive treatment programmes may be importantly interrelated such that enhancing positive lifestyle changes may have the effect of diminishing prior deviant sexual interests.

If treatment providers take the more cautious view that reducing deviant interests should be a target of treatment, then the procedures outlined by Marshall *et al.* in Chapter 17 of this book should be implemented. Insofar as behaviour modification procedures (as these behavioural interventions are usually described) are employed we suggest that the least aversive procedures be tried first so as to both emphasise the positive approach we have been advocating here and to ensure that as little damage as possible is done to the client-therapist relationship.

Perhaps one effective way to do this, while still directly attempting to diminish deviant interest, is to explicitly place the procedures in the context of the rest of the programme and to more specifically indicate how the diminution of deviant interests unlocks the potential to develop the skills necessary to lead a more satisfying and fulfilling life (i.e., the good life). All too often procedures aimed at addressing deviant interests are done quite separately from the rest of the programme without making the connection clear. Those behaviour modification procedures that require special equipment (e.g., most aversive procedures) of necessity must be done on an individual basis rather than described within the context of group treatment sessions. This makes it hard for clients to see the connection between the use of these procedures and what goes on in the rest of the programme. Even if the therapist attempts to make these connections (which in our experience seems to happen rarely) most clients will likely have difficulty recognising the relationship. Procedures that involve modifying the fantasy content of masturbation (i.e., thematic shift, orgasmic reconditioning, or directed masturbation techniques), and the post-orgasmic deliberate evocation of deviant fantasies (i.e., satiation) can readily be presented in group sessions and their implementation reported at these sessions. Even if just one or two of the group members have identified deviant interests (either by self-report or by phallometric results), the presentation of these masturbatory-based procedures can usefully be outlined in the group context since some of the other group members will likely have at least transitory deviant fantasies. These latter group members, although not the focus of the introduction of these procedures, will then have the information about how to implement the procedures and can, therefore, utilise them whenever they feel it is useful.

In Chapter 17 of this book by Marshall *et al.*, modifications are described to the traditional way some of the behavioural techniques have been implemented. If readers decide to employ one or another of the behavioural techniques to modify sexual interests, we recommend they follow the procedural descriptions outlined in Marshall *et al.*'s chapter as their recommendations fit rather better with basic psychological research than does the way these techniques have traditionally been employed. We also wish to refer readers to the concerns Marshall *et al.* raise in their chapter about the use of behavioural techniques to modify presumed deviant interests in young males who have engaged in troublesome sexual behaviours. Young males, perhaps particularly those who have sexual behaviour problems, are still in the process of forming their sexual interests and their sense of identity, so that employing some of these procedures may convey all kinds of unintentional messages to such vulnerable individuals. The well-documented negative impact of labelling (see Marshall, 1999; Rosenhan, 1973) is perhaps most pronounced in this group so we need to avoid taking such risks with young people. Identifying a young male as a *sexual offender* and placing him in a sexual offender programme, is likely by itself to cause him to see himself as nothing more than a sexual offender without the additional implementation of procedures to modify deviant arousal.

Finally, if medications (e.g., SSRIs or anti-androgens) are to be used to facilitate control over expressions of sexual behaviour, then certain precautions are necessary.

There seems to be little doubt that such medications can be useful (Bradford, 2000) particularly for sexual offenders who meet criteria for sexual compulsivity or sexual addiction or who represent a serious danger to reoffend in a significantly harmful way (e.g., sexual sadists). However, when medications are employed they should most usefully be seen as adjuncts to psychological interventions rather than effective treatments on their own. Our view is that such medications can reduce sexual preoccupation to levels that eliminate the distracting effects of these preoccupations such that the client is then able to focus on the relevant issues in cognitive behavioural programmes. Once this state is attained, the medications can be gradually reduced while the offender continues in psychological treatment. This should allow the client, with encouragement from the therapist, to shift his attribution of control over his sexual thoughts from the medication to himself, which is an essential step to the long-term maintenance of an offence-free disposition.

Offence-Supportive Cognitions

Sexual offender treatment should focus on addressing offence-supportive attitudes such as the belief that children enjoy sex and are unharmed by it (Ward & Keenan, 1999; Mann et al., 2007). Other important forms of offence-supportive cognition include entitlement thinking (Hanson, Gizzarelli & Scott, 1994), hostile grievance thinking (Mann, 2005), and suspiciousness of women (Malamuth & Brown, 1994). It is more important to target these issues than to 'challenge' minimisations and excuses for offending (Maruna & Mann, 2006), as noted earlier. We strongly suggest the use of more sophisticated cognitive therapy and schema-focused therapy techniques (Mann & Shingler, 2005). Any belief that offending is not harmful can be effectively addressed through perspective-taking role plays such as those described by Mann, Daniels and Marshall (2003) and Daniels (2005).

Relationships

In the 1980s, social skills training was an important component of sexual offender treatment, but this activity became less valued as emphasis increased on cognitive distortion, victim empathy and relapse prevention. In the mid-1990s and beyond, a number of studies into attachment styles of sexual offenders were reported, suggesting that intimacy and attachment are important issues for sex offenders (Smallbone & Dadds, 1998, 2000; Stirpe et al., 2006; Ward et al., 1995). It appears we have traversed something of a circle, arriving back at a place where work on relationship skills is again recognised as important in terms of reducing recidivism risk. Ward, McCormack and Hudson (1997) identified a useful list of relationship skills where sexual offenders believe themselves to be deficient. These include, among others, self-disclosure, trust, expression of affection, the giving and receiving of support, and conflict resolution. The breadth of this list suggests that a comprehensive approach to relationship training is necessary with sexual offenders.

Stirpe *et al.* (2006) further recommended that attachment work should be carefully tailored, based on an understanding of each individual's attachment style and associated maladaptive beliefs. Relevant beliefs that preclude a rewarding experience of intimacy can involve negative views of self or other or both. For instance, men who hold hostile interpersonal schemas, such as those who over-value dominance and vengeance in their relationships with others (Mann, 2005), are unlikely to achieve more successful intimacy unless these schemas are modified.

Low self-esteem is a core issue in insecure attachment. While the Hanson meta-analyses of sexual offender risk factors (Hanson & Bussière, 1995; Hanson & Morton-Bourgon, 2005) found no relationship between low self-esteem and recidivism risk, some recent individual studies have suggested otherwise (Thornton, Beech & Marshall, 2004; Webster *et al.*, 2007). Marshall and colleagues (e.g., Marshall *et al.*, 1997) have made arguments for the importance of raising sexual offenders' self-esteem, and more recent implicit technologies for measuring low self-esteem (e.g. Greenwald & Farnham, 2000) provide a promising new direction for understanding the nature of any dysfunctional self-view in offenders.

Furthermore, it seems likely that problematic low self-esteem in sexual offenders will be accompanied by low other-esteem. Hence, in our view a comprehensive treatment programme should address these issues side-by-side. To raise self-esteem while other-esteem remains low may not be sufficient to reduce the likelihood of further offending.

Self-Management

Dynamic risk factor studies of sexual offenders (e.g., Hanson & Morton-Bourgon, 2005) confirm that sexual offenders share many risk factors with non-sexual offenders, including lifestyle impulsivity, poor problem solving and poor emotional control. Hence, a comprehensive treatment programme for sexual offenders should incorporate the standard rehabilitation approaches used more widely with non-sexual offenders, such as cognitive skills training (particularly focused on problem solving and management of impulsivity), emotional management training and aggression replacement training. As these treatments are comprehensively described elsewhere (e.g., Bernfeld, Farrington & Leschied, 2001; Goldstein *et al.*, 2004; Hollin & Palmer, 2006; McGuire, 2002), we will not describe these in further detail here.

FUTURE DIRECTIONS?

As research and clinical practice with sexual offenders continues to evolve at some speed, it is vital that treatment providers are committed to developing their programmes in response to emerging findings. It is usually inadvisable to introduce new procedures on the basis of untested theory, or unreplicated research, but it is also irresponsible to continue with outdated practices that are focused on irrelevant goals or involve counter-productive approaches. There are important arguments for manualising and standardising treatment procedures so that treatment is delivered with sufficient integrity that it can be evaluated. However, a manualised programme must recognise the influence of the therapist-client relationship, and must provide the capacity to flexibly respond to each individual. Changing treatment from one day to the next is not recommended for a variety of reasons, not the least of which is that it would effectively eliminate any meaning that might be attached to an outcome evaluation. Instead, considered reviews of treatment content and style from time to time are encouraged, provided that changes in procedures are documented in terms of their rationale and implementation date. This sort of documentation process allows future evaluators to identify where changes were made and makes it possible to compare different procedures. For instance, a study of procedures developed to enhance victim empathy (Webster et al., 2005) was able to compare two alternative approaches to determine which procedures were more effective.

We also advise that treatment providers engage in research themselves. A divide between clinicians and researchers limits the work of both. Clinicians often make the best researchers, because they know what questions to ask and what questions need answering. Research threads that have proved, or would prove, particularly productive in moving forward our understanding of the detail of effective treatment, include the examination of treatment failures and successes, the investigation of sexual offenders' own experiences during treatment (e.g., Garrett et al., 2003; Wakeling et al., 2005), and designs based on the realistic evaluation model (Pawson & Tilley, 1997).

Debate continues about the overall impact of sexual offender treatment on recidivism rates. One problem is that evaluations, given the requirement for sample size and reasonable follow-up periods, necessarily lag behind treatment developments. That is, by definition, a treatment programme that has run for 5 years and been followed up for 5 years will have been designed 10 years previously by the time the evaluation concludes. A comprehensive programme such as that we have outlined above, drawing its goals and techniques from the most recent research and theory into sexual offending, has yet to be evaluated and as such, its effectiveness in terms of the ultimate test – significant reductions in serious recidivism – is untested. However, we hope that we have made the case for the relevance of each component, and the overall approach, based on patterns observed across an enormous and fast-growing research literature into the pressing social phenomenon of sexual offending.

REFERENCES

Abel, G.G. & Blanchard, E.B. (1974). The role of fantasy in the treatment of sexual deviation. *Archives of General Psychiatry, 30,* 467–475.

Andrews, D.A. & Bonta, J. (2003). *The psychology of criminal conduct* (3rd edn). Cincinnati, OH: Anderson Publishing.

Barbaree, H.E. & Peacock, E.J. (1995). Assessment of sexual preferences in cases of alleged child sexual abuse. In T. Ney (Ed.), *True and false allegations of child sexual abuse: Assessment and case management* (pp. 242–259). New York: Brunner/Mazel.

Baumeister, R.F. (1991). *Escaping the self*. New York: Basic Books.

Beckett, R.C., Beech, A.R., Fisher, D. & Fordham, A.S. (1994). Community-based treatment for sex offenders: An evaluation of seven treatment programmes. *Home Office Occasional Report*, 1–216. Available from: Home Office Publications Unit, 50, Queen Anne's Gate, London, SW1 9AT, England.

Beech, A.R. (1998). A psychometric typology of child abusers. *International Journal of Offender Therapy and Comparative Criminology*, *42*, 319–339.

Beech, A.R., Fisher, D. & Beckett, R.C. (1999). An Evaluation of the Prison Sex Offender Treatment Programme. UK Home Office Occasional Report. Available from: Home Office Publications Unit, 50, Queen Anne's Gate, London, SW1 9AT, England. Available electronically from: www.homeoffice.gov.uk/rds/pdfs/occ-step3.pdf

Beech, A.R. & Fordham, A.S. (1997). Therapeutic climate of sexual offender treatment programmes. *Sexual Abuse: A Journal of Research and Treatment*, *9*, 219–237.

Beech, A.R. & Hamilton-Giachritsis, C.E. (2005). Relationship between therapeutic climate and treatment outcome in group-based sexual offender treatment programs. *Sexual Abuse: A Journal of Research and Treatment*, *17*, 127–140.

Beech, A.R., Oliver, C., Fisher, D. & Beckett, R. (2005). STEP 4: The Sex Offender Treatment Programme in prison: Addressing the offending behaviour of rapists and sexual murderers. Birmingham, UK: University of Birmingham Centre for Forensic and Family Psychology.

Bernfeld, G.A., Farrington, D.P. & Leschied, A.W.(Eds) (2001). *Offender rehabilitation in practice: Implementing and evaluating effective programmes*. Chichester, UK: John Wiley & Sons, Ltd.

Bond, I.K. & Evans, D.R. (1967). Avoidance therapy: Its use in two cases of underwear fetishism. *Canadian Medical Association*, *96*, 1160–1162.

Bradford, J.M.W. (2000). The treatment of sexual deviation using a pharmacological approach. *Journal of Sex Research*, *37*, 248–257.

Craig, L.A., Thornton, D., Beech, A.R. & Browne, K.D. (2007). The relationship of statistical and psychological risk markers to sexual reconviction. *Criminal Justice and Behavior*, *34*, 314–329.

Daniels, M. (2005). The use of role play to develop victim empathy and relapse prevention. In B.K. Schwartz (Ed.), *The sex offenders: Issues in assessment, treatment, and supervision of adult and juvenile populations*, Volume 5 (8.2–8.17). Kingston, NJ: Civic Research Institute.

Dean, C., Mann, R., Milner, R. & Maruna, S. (2007). Changing Child Sexual Abusers Cognitions. In T.A. Gannon, T. Ward, A.R. Beech & D. Fisher (Eds), *Aggressive offenders' cognition: Theory, research and practice* (pp. 116–134). Chichester, UK: John Wiley & Sons, Ltd.

Fernandez, Y.M. & Marshall, W.L. (2003) Victim empathy, social self-esteem and psychopathy in rapists. *Sexual Abuse: A Journal of Research and Treatment*, *15*, 11–26.

Fernandez, Y.M., Marshall, W.L., Lightbody, S. & O'Sullivan, C. (1999). The Child Molester Empathy Measure: Description and examination of its reliability and validity. *Sexual Abuse: A Journal of Research and Treatment*, *11*, 17–31.

Fernandez, Y.M., Shingler, J. & Marshall, W.L. (2006). Putting 'behaviour' back into cognitive behavioural treatment of sexual offenders. In W.L. Marshall, Y.M. Fernandez, LE. Marshall & G.A. Serran (Eds), *Sexual offender treatment: Issues and controversies* (pp. 211–224). Chichester, UK: John Wiley & Sons, Ltd.

Finkelhor, D. (1984). *Child sexual abuse: New theory and research*. New York: The Free Press.

Friendship, C., Mann, R.E. & Beech, A.R. (2003). Evaluation of a national prison-based treatment programme for sexual offenders in England and Wales. *Journal of Interpersonal Violence*, *18*, 744–759.

Garrett, T., Oliver, C., Wilcox, D.T. & Middleton, D. (2003). Who cares? The views of sexual offenders about the treatment they receive. *Sexual Abuse: A Journal of Research and Treatment*, *15*, 323–338.

Goldstein, A.P., Nensen, R., Daleflod, B. & Kalt, M. (2004). *New perspectives on aggression replacement training*. Chichester, UK: John Wiley & Sons, Ltd.

Greenwald, A.G. & Farnham, S.D. (2000). Using the Implicit Association Test to measure self-esteem and self-concept. *Journal of Personality and Social Psychology*, *79*, 1022–1038.

Hanson, R.K. & Bussière, M.T. (1998). Predicting relapse: A meta-analysis of sexual offender recidivism studies. *Journal of Consulting and Clinical Psychology, 66*, 348–362.

Hanson, R.K., Gizzarelli, R. & Scott, H. (1994). The attitudes of incest offenders: Sexual entitlement and acceptance of sex with children. *Criminal Justice and Behavior, 21*, 187–202.

Hanson, R.K. & Morton-Bourgon, K. (2005). The characteristics of persistent sex offenders: A meta-analysis of recidivism studies. *Journal of Consulting and Clinical Psychology, 73*, 1154–1163.

Hanson, R.K. & Thornton, D. (2000). Improving risk assessments for sex offenders: A comparison of three actuarial scales. *Law and Human Behaviour, 24*, 119–136.

Harris, A.J.R. & Hanson, R.K. (2004). *Sex offender recidivism: A simple question.* (Report No. 2004-03.) Ottawa: Public Safety and Emergency Preparedness Canada.

Hildebran, D. & Pithers, W.D. (1989). Enhancing offender empathy for sexual abuse victims. In D.R. Laws (Ed.), *Relapse prevention with sex offenders* (pp. 236–243). New York: Guilford Press.

Hollin, C.R. & Palmer, E.J. (2006). *Offending behaviour programmes: Development, application and controversies.* Chichester, UK: John Wiley & Sons, Ltd.

Knopp, F.H., Freeman-Longo, R.E. & Stevenson, W. (1992). *Nationwide survey of juvenile and adult sex offender treatment programmes.* Orwell, VT: Safer Society Press.

Laws, D.R. (1989). *Relapse prevention with sex offenders.* New York: Guilford Press.

Laws, D.R. & Ward, T. (2003). When one size doesn't fit all: The reformulation of relapse prevention. In W.L. Marshall, Y.M. Fernandez, L.E. Marshall & G.A. Serran (Eds), *Sexual offender treatment: Controversial issues* (pp. 241–254). Chichester, UK: John Wiley & Sons, Ltd.

Malamuth, N.M. & Brown, L.M. (1994). Sexually aggressive men's perceptions of women's communications: Testing three explanations. *Journal of Personality and Social Psychology, 67*, 699–712.

Mann, R.E. (2005). *An investigation of the nature, content and influence of schemas in sexual offending.* Unpublished PhD thesis, University of Leicester, England.

Mann, R.E. & Beech, A.R. (2003). Cognitive distortions, schemas and implicit theories. In T. Ward, D.R. Laws & S.M. Hudson (Eds), *Sexual deviance: Issues and controversies* (pp. 135–153). Thousand Oaks, CA: Sage.

Mann, R.E., Daniels, M. & Marshall, W.L. (2003). The use of role plays in developing empathy. In Y.M. Fernandez (Ed.), *In their shoes: Examining the issue of empathy and its place in the treatment of offenders* (pp. 132–148). Oklahoma City, Oklahoma: Wood 'n' Barnes.

Mann, R.E. & Fernandez, Y.M. (2006). Sex offender programmes: Concept, theory and practice. In C.R. Hollin & E. Palmer (Eds), *Offending behaviour programmes: Development, application and controversies* (pp. 155–177). Chichester, UK: John Wiley & Sons, Ltd.

Mann, R.E. & Shingler, J. (2005). Schema-driven cognition in sexual offenders: theory, assessment and treatment. In W.L. Marshall, Y.M. Fernandez, L.E. Marshall & G.A. Serran (Eds), *Sexual offender treatment: Controversial issues* (pp. 173–186). Chichester, UK: John Wiley & Sons, Ltd.

Mann, R.E., Webster, S.D., Schofield, C. & Marshall, W.L. (2004). Approach versus avoidance goals in relapse prevention with sexual offenders. *Sexual Abuse: A Journal of Research and Treatment, 16*, 65–75.

Mann, R.E., Webster, S.D., Wakeling, H.C. & Marshall, W.L. (2007). The measurement and influence of child abuse supportive beliefs. *Psychology, Crime and Law, 13*, 443–458.

Mark, P. (1992). Training staff to work with sex offenders. *Probation Journal, 39*, 1–13.

Marques, J.K., Day, D.M., Nelson, C. & Miner, M. (1989). The Sex Offender Treatment and Evaluation Project: California's relapse prevention program. In D.R. Laws (Ed.), *Relapse prevention with sex offenders* (pp. 247–267). New York: Guilford Press.

Marques, J.K., Nelson, C., Alarcon, J-M. & Day, D.M. (2000). Preventing relapse in sexual offenders: what we learned from SOTEP's experimental program. In D.R. Laws, S.M. Hudson & T. Ward (Eds), *Remaking relapse prevention with sex offenders* (pp. 321–340). Thousand Oaks, CA: Sage.

Marques, J.K., Wideranders, M., Day, D.M. *et al.* (2005). Effects of a relapse prevention program on sexual recidivism: Final results from California's Sex Offender Treatment Evaluation Project (SOTEP). *Sexual Abuse: A Journal of Research and Treatment, 17*, 79–107.

Marshall, W.L. (1997). The relationship between self-esteem and deviant sexual arousal in non-familial child molesters. *Behavior Modification, 21,* 86–96.

Marshall, W.L. (1999). Theoretical perspectives of abnormal behavior. In W.L. Marshall & P. Firestone (Eds), *Abnormal psychology: Perspectives* (pp. 23–48) Toronto: Prentice Hall.

Marshall, W.L. (2005). Therapist style in sex offender treatment: Influence on indices of change. *Sexual Abuse: A Journal of Research and Treatment, 17,* 109–116.

Marshall, W.L., Anderson, D. & Fernandez, Y.M. (1999). *Cognitive behavioural treatment of sexual offenders.* Chichester, UK: John Wiley & Sons, Ltd.

Marshall, W.L., Champagne, F., Sturgeon, C. & Bryce, P. (1997). Increasing the self-esteem of child molesters. *Sexual Abuse: A Journal of Research and Treatment, 9,* 321–333.

Marshall, W.L. & Fernandez, Y.M. (2000) Phallometric testing with sexual offenders: Limits to its value. *Clinical Psychology Review, 20,* 807–822.

Marshall, W.L. & Fernandez, Y.M. (2001). Los delincuentes sexuales en la actualidad. In W.L. Marshall (Ed.), *Agresores sexuales* (pp. 84–119) Barcelona, Spain: Ariel Publishing.

Marshall, W.L. & Fernandez, Y.M. (2003). *Phallometric testing with sexual offenders: Theory, research, and practice.* Brandon, VT: Safer Society Press.

Marshall, W.L., Hudson, S.M., Jones, R. & Fernandez, Y.M. (1995). Empathy in sex offenders. *Clinical Psychology Review, 15,* 99–113.

Marshall, W.L., Marshall, L.E., Serran, G.A. & Fernandez, Y.M. (2006). *Treating sexual offenders: An integrated approach.* New York: Routledge.

Marshall, W.L., Serran, G.A., Fernandez, Y.M. *et al.* (2003). Therapist characteristics in the treatment of sexual offenders: Tentative data on their relationship with indices of behaviour change. *Journal of Sexual Aggression, 9,* 25–30.

Maruna, S. & Copes, H. (2005). What have we learned in five decades of neutralization research? *Crime and Justice: A Review of Research, 32,* 221–320.

Maruna, S. & Mann, R.E. (2006). A fundamental attribution error? Rethinking cognitive distortions. *Legal and Criminological Psychology, 11,* 155–177.

McGuire, J. (Ed.) (2002). *Offender rehabilitation and treatment: Effective programmes and policies to reduce reoffending.* Chichester, UK: John Wiley & Sons, Ltd.

McGuire, R.J., Carlisle, J.M. & Young, B.G. (1965). Sexual deviations as conditioned behaviour: A hypothesis. *Behaviour Research and Therapy, 3,* 185–190.

McMurran, M. & Duggan, C. (2005). The manualization of a treatment programme for personality disorder. *Criminal Behaviour and Mental Health, 15,* 17–27.

Miller, W.R. & Rollnick, S. (1991). *Motivational interviewing: Preparing people to change addictive behaviour.* New York: Guilford.

Moos, R.H. (1986). *Group environment scale manual* (2nd edn). Palo Alto, CA: Consulting Psychologists Press Inc.

Murphy, W.D. (1990). Assessment and modification of cognitive distortions in sex offenders. In W.L. Marshall, D.R. Laws & H.E. Barbaree (Eds), *Handbook of sexual assault: Issues, theories, and treatment of the offender* (pp. 331–342). New York: Plenum.

Nelson, C. & Jackson, P. (1989). High-risk recognition: The cognitive-behavioural chain. In D.R. Laws (Ed.), *Relapse prevention with sex offenders* (pp. 247–267). New York: Guilford Press.

O'Donohue, W. & Letourneau, E. (1992). The psychometric properties of the penile tumescence assessment of child molesters. *Journal of Psychopathology and Behavioral Assessment, 14,* 123–174.

Pawson, R. & Tilley, N. (1997). *Realistic evaluation.* London: Sage Publications.

Pithers, W.D. (1994). Process evaluation of a group therapy component designed to enhance sex offenders' empathy for sexual abuse survivors. *Behaviour Research and Therapy, 32,* 565–570.

Pithers, W.D. (1997). Maintaining treatment integrity with sexual abusers. *Criminal Justice and Behavior, 24,* 34–51.

Prendergast, W.E. (1991). *Treating sex offenders in correctional institutions and outpatient clinics: A guide to clinical practice.* New York: Haworth Press.

Rosenhan, D.L. (1973). On being sane in insane places. *Science, 179*, 250–258.

Salter, A.C. (1988). *Treating child sex offenders and victims: A practical guide*. Newbury Park, CA: Sage.

Simon, W.T. & Schouten, P.G. (1992). Problems in sexual preference testing in child sexual abuse cases: A legal and community perspective. *Journal of Interpersonal Violence, 7*, 503–516.

Smallbone, S.W. & Dadds, M.R. (1998). Childhood attachment and adult attachment in incarcerated adult male sex offenders. *Journal of Interpersonal Violence, 13*, 555–573.

Smallbone, S.W. & Dadds, M.R. (2000). Attachment and coercive sexual behaviour. *Sexual Abuse: A Journal of Research and Treatment, 12*, 3–15.

Stirpe, T., Abracen, J., Stermac, L. & Wilson, R. (2006). Sexual offenders' state of mind regarding childhood attachment: A controlled investigation. *Sexual Abuse: A Journal of Research and Treatment, 18*, 289–302.

Thornton, D. (2002). Constructing and Testing a Framework for Dynamic Risk Assessment. *Sexual Abuse: A Journal of Research and Treatment, 14*, 139–154.

Thornton, D., Beech, A. & Marshall, W.L. (2004). Pre-treatment self-esteem and post-treatment sexual recidivism. *International Journal of Offender Therapy and Comparative Criminology, 48*, 587–599.

Wakeling, H.C., Webster, S.D. & Mann, R.E. (2005). Sexual offenders' treatment experience: A qualitative and quantitative investigation. *Journal of Sexual Aggression, 11*, 171–186.

Ward, T., Hudson, S.M. & Marshall, W.L. (1995). Cognitive distortions and affective deficits in sex offenders: A cognitive deconstructionist interpretation. *Sexual Abuse: A Journal of Research and Treatment, 7*, 67–83.

Ward, T., Hudson, S.M., Marshall, W.L. & Siegert, R. (1995). Attachment style and intimacy deficits in sexual offenders: A theoretical framework. *Sexual Abuse: A Journal of Research and Treatment, 7*, 317–335.

Ward, T. & Keenan, T. (1999). Child Molesters' Implicit Theories. *Journal of Interpersonal Violence, 14*(8), 821–838.

Ward, T., McCormack, J. & Hudson, S.M. (1997). Sexual offenders' perceptions of their intimate relationships. *Sexual Abuse: A Journal of Research and Treatment, 9*, 57–74.

Ward, T. & Mann, R.E. (2004). Good lives and the rehabilitation of sex offenders: A positive approach to treatment. In A.L. Linley & S. Joseph (Eds), *Positive psychology in practice* (pp. 598–616). Hoboken, NJ: John Wiley & Sons, Inc.

Ward, T., Mann, R.E. & Gannon, T.A. (2007). The Good Lives Model of offender rehabilitation: Clinical implications. *Aggression and Violent Behaviour, 12*, 87–107.

Webster, S.D., Bowers, L.E., Mann, R.E. & Marshall, W.L. (2005). Developing empathy in sex offenders: The value of offence re-enactments. *Sexual Abuse: A Journal of Research and Treatment, 17*, 63–77.

Webster, S.D., Mann, R.E., Wakeling, H.C. & Thornton, D. (2007). Further validation of the Short Self-Esteem Scale with sexual offenders. *Legal and Criminological Psychology, 12*, 207–216.

19

A Community Residential Treatment Approach for Sexual Abusers: A Description of the Lucy Faithfull Foundation's Wolvercote Clinic and Related Projects

HILARY ELDRIDGE

DONALD FINDLATER

INTRODUCTION

Named after its founder, Baroness Faithfull of Wolvercote, the Lucy Faithfull Foundation is a child protection charity operating UK wide and specialising in safeguarding children from sexual abuse. To this end, it assesses and treats people perpetrating, and affected by, child sexual abuse and has contributed to research into developing effective interventions. Its policy is to collaborate with individuals and agencies internationally to develop a more child sensitive and offender aware culture in our society. One of its aims is, and has been, to provide high-quality sex offender treatment.

The aim of this chapter is to describe one aspect of this approach: the community residential programme for child sexual abusers, at the Wolvercote residential clinic. It was set up in 1995 in the grounds of a Surrey Hospital and closed in 2002, when the lease from the Department of Health ended. In 2004 the Home Office announced that further residential facilities would be established and Lucy Faithfull Foundation has been working with them to this end. In this chapter we describe how we would further enhance a new residential programme's effectiveness by the addition of new

Assessment and Treatment of Sex Offenders: A Handbook. Edited by Anthony Beech, Leam Craig and Kevin Browne. © John Wiley & Sons Ltd, 2009.

therapies and approaches, based on feedback from ex-residents and informed by new research about treatment.

PROGRAMME DESCRIPTION

The Wolvercote programme was developed from its predecessor, Gracewell, which closed in 1993. Gracewell was successful in treating sexual offenders, particularly high-risk offenders (Beckett *et al.*, 1994). A combination of political support and research showing positive treatment outcome (Beckett *et al.*, 1994) led to the opening of the new clinic in 1995 (described by Eldridge & Wyre, 1998). While open, Wolvercote Clinic assessed and treated 112 offenders and assessed 193 more. In 1999, it received accreditation status from the Prison Service's Accreditation Panel. This status continued when the Panel was superseded by the Joint Prison/Probation Services Accreditation panel of international sex offender treatment experts (Rex *et al.*, 2003).

The residents' experience at the Wolvercote Clinic was strongly skills based. This included skills in recognising and dealing with emotional and physical risk factors, managing painful feelings, developing social and life skills, developing positive thinking skills, developing assertive behaviours, intimacy skills, sexual fantasy management, and enhanced thinking skills. Many residents had engaged in previous treatment programmes, which had some impact on offence minimisation and attitudes towards children and victims, but they needed additional work in affective, interpersonal areas as well.

Most residents fell into the category defined as *high deviance* (Beech, 1998; Thornton & Beech, 2002) (see Chapter 4) in that they deviated strongly from non-offenders on a battery of psychometric tests, and hence were seen as being at high level of dynamic risk (Thornton, 2002). The Clinic also accepted men who were harder to categorise accurately on initial assessment, such as previously undetected, often intelligent, repeat offenders. Such men were characterised by high levels of denial, apparent respectability and manipulation of communities and families. Despite a social veneer they were often emotionally lonely and lacked intimacy skills. Highly deviant men are hard to treat in ordinary group-work programmes because their deficits in the affective/interpersonal area are more pervasive, often anchored in their own traumatic childhood experiences. Studies show that even where sex offenders were not directly sexually victimised as children, their backgrounds are frequently physically or emotionally abusive (Bentovim, 1996; Cox & Daitzman 1980; Dhawan & Marshall 1996; Finkelhor, 1984; Langevin, Paitich & Russon 1984; Marshall, 1993; Rada, 1978; Tingle *et al.*, 1986). In some cases, these experiences needed to be addressed in individual therapy, which the Clinic provided. For others the experience of living in a positive environment was more important to the development of a less fearful view of the world. In order to be treated effectively, these men not only needed more extensive work, but also interventions and a context for them that attempted to counter early learning. Hence, the emphasis was on focused groups and individual therapy operating within a learning environment, which took account of the men's general functioning deficits.

Wherever possible, the Clinic tried to maintain or develop positive external support networks throughout the resident's stay as these were seen as a vital part of an offence-free future. However, some residents had families, which included vulnerable children whose protection was always of paramount importance. Consequently, some relationships had to end or to change significantly. In such cases, the resident was supported through this loss and help was at hand to find safe new social networks. Funding permitting, therapists worked directly with residents' family members or provided consultancy to other agencies doing such work.

The environment fostered a collaborative approach between staff and residents. For many of the residents the Clinic provided one of their first experiences of non-abusive relationships, of giving and receiving empathic responses. Many came from backgrounds which fostered negative schema of the world and negative or abusive beliefs, attitudes and behaviours. Fundamental human needs had not been met positively. They learned, via their experiences, to meet these needs through abusive sexual and non-sexual behaviours. In fact, many had developed a perception that the commission of abusive sexual acts was in itself a fundamental need. In the programme this was recognised and explicitly discussed, and the environment was designed to provide safety in which the men could question core beliefs, attitudes and behaviours, which they previously viewed as essential to their well-being. The men learned to question the means by which they had tried to meet their needs and learned non-abusive ways of meeting them. Where residents had particular difficulty in self-management of intrusive, offence-related sexual fantasies, we used fantasy modification techniques including thought stopping, urge surfing, verbal satiation and covert sensitisation. The primary aim was to help them develop 'healthy' sexual fantasies, which would not support abusive behaviour.

The main methods of treatment used were cognitive behavioural with a clear focus on relapse prevention and the development of a positive offence-free life. There was extensive use of group-work including role play, and art- and drama-based techniques to create opportunities to identify skill deficits and to learn and practice new skills. Hence, the Clinic also provided an environment in which cognitive behavioural techniques were used to develop new thinking and new skills could be learned and practised. This environment was particularly important in facilitating the change process, as a critical feature of the high deviancy offenders was their affective deficits. The interplay between thoughts, feelings and behaviours was more easily addressed in a holistic way within the 'total environment' of the Clinic.

The need for new learning was identified on an on-going basis: objectives were set, practice took place and was evaluated by self, group and therapists. Evaluation included behavioural observation both in and outside the Clinic by all types of staff, by referrers, other residents, relevant others and self-report. The resident review system provided routine evaluation of progress. The lack of certain skills and their relationship to a resident's past offending as well as its relevance to an offence-free future was explored in each of his quarterly reviews. The reviews also determined the means whereby the resident could demonstrate and document skill acquisition and development through his residential key-worker and other residential staff. Skills development

Table 19.1 Residential programme in outline

4 week Assessment - psychometric tests - group exercises - individual exercises - observation in formal and informal settings **2–4 week Pre-intervention phase** - overcoming the blocks to effective intervention - in-depth identification of offending pattern/s - beginning to identify a relapse prevention/new life plan **6–12 month Treatment programme: intervention/relapse prevention** - 'rolling' group-work programme - enhanced thinking skills and supplementary groups - learning from the past: strategies for the future group (focused on learning from personal childhood/adolescent experiences) - individual therapy - skills practice within a positive living environment **Monitoring and evaluation** - videotaped recording system - repeat psychometric tests and reviews at regular intervals - observation in formal and informal settings - monitoring the relapse prevention/new life plan in action

was a regular item within the key-worker sessions, alongside a Behavioural Assessment Checklist which was undertaken quarterly and also used within the quarterly review.

We will now describe the programme in detail, as shown schematically in Table 19.1.

Assessment

On arrival each new resident met with a senior member of the Clinic team. He was welcomed and started his induction. This began with reading and signing up to the Clinic Rules and the Resident's Charter, the reasons for which were explained. These documents introduced him to the Wolvercote ethos, the key theme of which was a collaborative approach to assessment and treatment: a therapeutic alliance, but in the context of Lucy Faithfull Foundation's guiding principle of protecting children.

All men entering the Clinic completed psychometric tests (Fisher, Beech & Browne, 1999) to identify the presence of offending related problems. Over three-quarters of treatment entrants had significant problems in the area of social adequacy often related to their own childhood experiences of abuse and/or neglect. Approximately, one-third had problems in directly offence-related thinking such as offence minimisation and distorted perceptions of children and of victims. Risk, both absolute and contextual, was assessed, together with treatment need. The four-week assessment period provided time for disclosure of further offences, space for families and communities away from the offender, and opportunity for motivational work as well as for assessment of ability and willingness to engage in treatment. Pre- and post-assessment psychometric tests were used as well as individual and group-work based on a manualised programme.

The new resident was also asked to make a recording, in which he answered the questions: What were my offences? What were the effects? Who is to blame? This was kept as a benchmark indicating his thinking on arrival, and was revisited at the end of assessment, so that he and those working with him, both in and outside the clinic, could assess changes. The new resident was then inducted into the residential environment by one of the team of residential workers, who also searched his personal belongings to ensure no prohibited items came into the Clinic, to make appropriate arrangements regarding medication and items that the resident could not retain during residence, for example, mobile phone, camera.

A designated resident who was making good progress and had demonstrated his ability to be a positive 'culture carrier', then provided a guided tour of the premises, introducing the man to the other residents, acquainting him with the Clinic routine and, finally, showing him his bed-space. All but a few of the rooms at the Clinic were shared, so the new resident would share with others. These men were also in the assessment programme and provided important practical and emotional support over the four weeks of assessment work ahead. Before the end of his first day, the new resident would begin work on the psychometric tests for completion over the following 24–36 hours. Over the next two days, the new resident met his allocated therapist who would be involved in two-thirds of his daily group-work sessions and who would undertake individual sessions based on the Assessment Workbooks. He met with his residential key-worker, who would provide practical support in adjusting to the residential environment as well as in dealing with issues in the external world.

Throughout this four-week assessment period, the resident worked through his personal Assessment Workbooks and wrote a 'life story'. His participation in group-work gave him the opportunity to demonstrate his improving understanding of his own offending through session contributions, where offence accounts were explored. Many residents talked about 'the light bulbs going on in my head' when they found that in questioning others, they were in fact questioning themselves.

Some men were referred to the Clinic for assessment only. Such assessments were intended for use in decisions by Family Courts or social workers about contact with children, or in decision making by Bishops about continued suitability, or not, for ministry, or in decisions by criminal courts about sentence for an offence. Other men were referred for assessment with a view to intervention. Of the 305 men who were assessed, 112 progressed into the intervention programme, the bulk of these being criminal justice or church referrals.

Pre-Intervention

After completion of the assessment phase, offenders who were recommended and funded for treatment, entered a two- to four-week pre-intervention phase in which tasks relating to preparation for the main programme and work on overcoming blocks to programme receptivity were started. These included problematic beliefs related to personal experiences of childhood abuse, fear of change, fear of feelings and fear of the reaction of family members to admission of the scale of offending. Realistic positive thinking was taught from the pre-intervention stage. Identification of personal risk factors and pattern/s of offending also began at that point. Skills training took place in accordance with individual need identified with the therapist.

At this stage work began to develop networks of people who would help monitor and support the resident during the programme and post-discharge. Where family members were involved the safeguarding of children was the first consideration, so with this in mind, personal relationships often needed to be re-evaluated and re-negotiated.

Intervention

The resident's stay in the intervention programme lasted for up to 12 months, and in some cases up to 15 months. This followed a similar weekly structure to that set in assessment. Formal programme work was seen as his 'employment', requiring attention and commitment for 40–50 hours per week including personal written work. Group-work sessions would occupy three hours of each weekday, with homework, (either personal, in pairs or group based), requiring three or more hours per day. Each man was expected to contribute to the life of the resident community by assisting in domestic chores, attending weekly 'Residents' Meetings', potentially holding one or more of the 'positions' identified to ensure the good organisation of the community. Membership of the resident body and the holding of positions of responsibility were part of the programme and were essential to the maintenance of the Clinic ethos, to the 'Positive living and learning environment'. For most residents this environment provided the opportunity for developing and practising new skills that would be an important component of their Relapse Prevention and New Life Plan.

Staff employed a range of methods in teaching skills and facilitating practice. They modelled assertiveness and social skills; reviewed with the resident the outcome of a confrontation or negative event, and helped residents work out and rehearse different approaches for a more positive outcome. They showed how problem-solving skills learned on the 'Enhanced thinking skills' course run at the Clinic could be applied in practice. They explained that dilemmas are part of everyone's life and that seeking a resolution (compromise) is more beneficial than holding out for a specific solution at all costs. Books, musical instruments, art materials, exercise and games equipment were commonly used in the teaching of social competence skills.

The discussions in the 'Learning from the past – strategies for the future' group, helped residents better understand their early personal histories and plan ways of dealing with these experiences in an abuse-free new life. This was particularly important for residents who had experienced abuse in childhood. Staff encouraged the development of a new, more positive lifestyle in which residents could feel and demonstrate concern and respect for each other, feel better about themselves and begin to relate more confidently to other adults.

The programme manuals included the rationale for each formal core element, its aims and objectives, exercises and matching worksheets for the participants, and

Eldridge's 1998 'Maintaining Change' workbook (Eldridge, 1998). The treatment manuals provided explicit instruction about how the men should be encouraged to identify skill deficits, identify new skills and plan how to learn and practise them. Residents were encouraged to develop skills relevant to their personal needs and to identify skill deficits and learn new skills related to the content of the group-work modules. Detailed relapse prevention/new life planning was an ongoing process throughout the programme.

Beech and Fordham (1997) reported that treatment groups rated as cohesive by group members were significantly more effective in producing measurable progress. At Wolvercote, the treatment group was essentially the entire resident population of approximately 24 men at any given time. They were divided into smaller groups for different kinds of group-work. Hence, we were concerned not just with the cohesiveness of the smaller groups but also of the whole community.

The programme 'rolled' in that it had four formal core elements, each containing four modules, which were different from but not more advanced than each other. This meant that a new person could join the programme at the beginning of any new two-week module. Where a particularly advanced piece of work was required, for example, re-enactments in the Victim awareness/empathy modules (see below), there was an explicit strategy which enabled the two treatment groups to be divided into those who were ready to do this work and those who were not. To complete the programme a resident had to participate in all the modules. If he left early the work he had missed was noted in the final report and recommendations were made about how these omissions could be rectified.

Each two-week module included two days in which learning was related to individual offence patterns and relapse prevention/new life planning. Great emphasis was placed on the need to individualise this work. Each block of four modules was followed by an offending pattern review in which all learning within formal group and informal settings was brought together and applied to individual offending patterns and offence-free life development. This targeted all relevant criminogenic factors and helped the men to apply and internalise learning.

The core elements of the programme were selected because of their known relationship to sex offending, especially for high deviancy child abusers. These were as follows:

Victim awareness/empathy

There is extensive evidence available indicating that empathy inhibits aggression (e.g., Clarke, 1980; Feshback, 1982, 1987; Mehrabian & Epstein, 1972; Parke & Slaby, 1983). Studies by Pithers (1994) and Marshall et al. (1995), for example, have shown that empathy training packages can be effective in reducing empathy deficits. Whilst some of the residents had victim-specific empathy deficits, others had more generalised deficits. Many described this core element as crucial in helping them change the way they felt about and behaved towards others.

Fantasy in offending

The relationship between deviant sexual fantasy/arousal and offending is described by a number of researchers (Beckett, 1994; Deu & Edelmann, 1997; Hanson & Bussière, 1998; Prentky *et al.*, 1989; Ressler *et al.*, 1986; Wolf, 1984). Consequently, the aim was to raise awareness of this problem and to assist residents to learn skills to manage any deviant fantasies as well as to develop healthy and appropriate sexual fantasies. The group-work on the role of fantasy in offending was supplemented by individual fantasy management work tailored to personal need.

Sexuality and relationships

A deficit common to sex offenders is the failure to develop the capacity for intimacy in relations with adults. This may have its roots in poor intimacy relations with adults (Marshall, 1989) producing emotional loneliness, leading to the hope of finding intimacy through sexuality and through less threatening partners. Child abusers have typically been found to have a preoccupied, or fearful, attachment style (Hudson & Ward, 1997) neither of which are conducive to the development of positive relationships (Beech & Mitchell, 2005). Consequently, the aim was to promote thinking patterns in which relationships are seen in a realistic way, not in extremes of good or bad; to encourage the learning of skills and gaining of knowledge to help develop non-abusive adult social, and if appropriate, sexual relationships; and to encourage and motivate participants to develop non-abusive, responsible and consenting approaches to sexuality and relationships.

Assertiveness and self-efficacy

Under-assertiveness, and associated social and relationship problems are particularly common among child molesters (Fisher & Howells 1993). Beckett *et al.* (1994) recommended the inclusion of this element in treatment programmes, commenting that assertive behaviour is dependent on perceived self-efficacy and that lack of skills in this area can lead to social and emotional isolation. The emphasis of this core element was on the development of positive realistic thinking and responsible assertive behaviour. Skills practice in everyday life situations was vital and the residential environment provided opportunity to practice seven days a week.

Weekends were less structured than weekdays, with the opportunity for greater periods of relaxation. But, as with weekdays, residents were not free to come and go but could participate in approved supervised outings. Residents were required to work together to produce an 'Outings Charter' including a comprehensive code of conduct with the protection of children at its heart. The staff members supervising and escorting the outings met with all the participants in advance to agree a plan and ensure that everyone was properly briefed. Whilst, newer residents were most closely supervised by staff, residents who had progressed in treatment were expected to contribute to the oversight process. They were organised into twos and threes to hold each other to account. The whole group met for a de-brief session on their return, where residents were expected to raise any issues for themselves and each other. Any such matters were referred to formal group sessions where links with offence- related thoughts, feelings and behaviour were explored. Outings typically involved sightseeing, shopping days in major towns or cities away from the immediate vicinity, visits to museums, art galleries, stately homes, trips to the theatre or cinema to see productions approved by the Clinic Manager.

Living an Offence-Free Life after Discharge from the Clinic

Planning for discharge began during Pre-intervention. Progress reviews took place quarterly throughout the programme. These involved the resident himself, his key therapist and a member of the residential and psychology team, his referrer (e.g., Probation Officer, Social Worker, Bishop) and one or two members of his close family or a personal friend/supporter. Meetings focused around his progress (or lack of it) in all aspects of the Programme, including group and individual work, life skills development, contributions to the resident body and Clinic ethos, maintenance of external relationships, and involvement and performance on trips out of the Clinic. The resident himself was required to complete a revised version of his personal relapse prevention plan, which addressed all aspects relevant to his future resettlement and goals for an offence-free life. These included accommodation, leisure, employment, contact with adults and children, dealing with sexual fantasy, anticipating, avoiding and managing risky situations and managing offence-related problems such as alcohol and anger.

Developing and maintaining new thinking and new behaviours to attain a personally satisfying, abuse-free life, takes place over a lifetime. Consequently, the identification of a support network of appropriate, informed adults was a critical part of each resident's Personal Relapse Prevention Plan. Many men had one or more family members or close friends who were prepared to be involved in the Review meetings and who had additional contact with the resident and with his key therapist. Such contact ensured that those involved with the resident during his stay at the Clinic and crucially after discharge, had a sufficient understanding of his past offending behaviour and Relapse Prevention/New Life Plan to enable them to support him effectively. However, a number of men had no personal friends or family, or those identified were unsuitable to fulfil the necessary role. For those people, Circles of Support and Accountability provided a vital way forward.

In 2000 the Public Protection Unit of the Home Office supported a Conference, organised by the Society of Friends, the subject of which was 'Circles of Support and Accountability'. The concept of 'Circles' was developed in Canada with the support of the Mennonite Church and the Corrections Service. High-risk sex offenders, on being discharged into the community and into potential (and risky) isolation, were 'surrounded' by a group of volunteers, operating under a 'covenant' agreed with them.

The volunteers engaged with the offender or 'core member' on a daily basis and met with him as a group on a weekly basis. The aim of the Circle was to provide both practical and emotional support to the offender as he aimed to maintain an offence-free life *and* to hold him accountable for his future behaviour.

The Home Office provided a grant to allow the Clinic to develop one of three Circles projects in the UK, specifically for residents leaving Wolvercote without adequate personal support in the community to which they were discharged. Working collaboratively with the other two projects, specifically in Thames Valley and Hampshire, a volunteer training programme and battery of essential documentation was constructed to ensure the appropriate and responsible development of Circles in the UK. The project engages volunteers with high-risk offenders and thus had to be designed and managed in such a way as to reassure statutory agencies, volunteers and offenders themselves that this new and ground-breaking scheme was credible and responsible.

By 2001 Circles of Support and Accountability had been established for two residents of Wolvercote, commencing immediately prior to their discharge. In addition to undertaking the recruitment, selection and training of the four volunteer members of each Circle, the Clinic Manager himself became a volunteer in these 'pilots'. Each Circle anticipates an initial 12 months commitment from both the core member and the volunteers. The volunteers offer support according to need on a regular and practical basis and challenge unhelpful or concerning attitudes or behaviour. They notify the public protection agencies should the core member show signs of increased risk of offending.

One of the first Circles for an ex-resident supported him in employment and career development, in friendship and partnership choices, in enjoying recreational pursuits and in celebrating achievements and anniversaries. Critically, it assisted in his social interaction and four years on some Circle volunteers still have sporadic contact with him. His life is now progressing satisfactorily, and to date successfully, without their daily involvement.

Having subsequently developed Circles for a number of other ex-residents, the closure of the Clinic in 2002 prompted the extension of the project to other known or convicted offenders, including members of the clergy with or without convictions, female offenders and other high-risk offenders subject to Multi-Agency Public Protection Arrangements. The involvement of a small number of community volunteers in the support and management of sex offenders living in their locality appears, to the authors, to be a more productive and protective involvement than that anticipated by 'Sarah's/Megan's Law'.

THE EFFECTIVENESS OF THE PROGRAMME

The programme was positively evaluated by ongoing post-treatment analysis of individual progress and by a reconviction study. Prior to leaving the programme, residents repeated the psychometric tests they had undertaken on arrival. A method of analysis

Table 19.2 Analysis of % improving in specific risk factors

Risk Factors	% Improving
Offence-related thinking	
Minimising own offending	82%
Distorted images of children	78%
Distorted images of victims	87%
Affective/interpersonal factors	
Submissiveness	72%
Self-rejection	72%
Emotional loneliness	70%

was devised by Dr David Thornton, Head of HM Prison Service Offending Behaviour Programmes Unit, who monitored the effectiveness of the programme for the Home Office. This made it possible to track significant improvements made by individual residents. The following analysis (as shown in Table 19.2) was completed shortly prior to closure in 2002 and shows the percentage of 91 treatment completers starting the programme with a specific risk factor who demonstrated major improvement, i.e. more than one standard deviation, in that area by the time they left Wolvercote.

Most of the residents fell into the 'high deviance' category on arrival, so they had to change hugely to reach a score within the range of Beckett *et al.*'s (1994) non-offending sample. However, generally, over three-quarters of the men who entered treatment with specific risk factors showed a major improvement post-treatment, indicating positive learning.

A Home Office-commissioned study (Ford & Beech, 2004), examined the reconviction rates of a sample of 51 ex-Wolvercote residents who had completed at least six months treatment and had been (at risk) in the community for at least two years. A five-year follow-up study was also conducted, but as offenders left the programme at different times, only 19 men had been in the community for sufficient time to be included in this part of the study (Beech & Ford, 2006).

Risk of reconviction was calculated in the sample using Thornton's Risk Matrix 2000 (RM2000), which focuses on static (historical) and aggravating factors (Thornton *et al.*, 2003). The men in the sample were also classified as high or low deviance based on their pre-treatment scores on a battery of offence-related and socio-affective psychometric measures as described earlier. Fifty-two percent of the sample were classified as high deviance and 45% were high risk, 28% were both high deviance and presented high or very high risk. Treatment effects were also examined. To be deemed 'treated' the individual's scores on both sets of measures (offence specific and socio-affective) had to fall within the 'normal' range after change (i.e., scores were indistinguishable from non-offenders on the measures used).

Ford and Beech found a reconviction rate of 10% (N = 5) in their sample of 51 programme completers. However, only men predicted to be at very high (N = 2) or high risk (N = 3) on RM2000 were reconvicted. Four of these men were classified as high deviance. All five of the reconvicted men had failed to reach the study's criteria for a fully treated profile.

The study suggests a relationship between treatment outcome, as measured psychometrically, and sexual reconviction rates, in that none of the men in the sample who achieved the 'treated' profile were reconvicted of a sexual offence, including four high deviance men. Ford and Beech commented that the Wolvercote programme was able to effect change (i.e., reach the study's definition of a 'treated' profile) in 20% of high deviance offenders – twice as effective as alternative programmes available at the time.

However, men who made significant progress at Wolvercote but did not achieve the score for the 'treated profile' also did well. Eighty-six percent of the sample who left the programme without a fully treated profile remained unconvicted at the five-year follow-up. This included 22 men categorised as high deviance. We hypothesise that the combination of factors targeted and methods used within the positive living, learning environment, together with the length of stay, encouraged the development of thought, feeling and behaviour change as well as the maintenance of positive living skills.

LESSONS LEARNED FROM THE CLINIC

During our work with offenders in assessment and intervention we explored whether and in what ways they had felt guilty about their thoughts or behaviour; whether they had attempted to manage these, or had sought help or support in doing so. The vast majority identified times when they had attempted to desist, when they had experienced feelings of guilt and remorse, and when they lacked any awareness of where to go for help or support to avoid committing an offence. For many, offending-linked behaviours commenced during adolescence.

In our contact with family and friends of residents we explored attitudes or behaviours that they had witnessed in the offender that might have alerted them to the fact of his risk and prompted them to intervene to prevent the subsequent abuse. Almost always, these individuals recollected concerns, but either had no idea where to get advice about what to do, did not know how to interpret what they witnessed, or could not accept their loved one was a 'paedophile'. The media representation of sex offenders was identified as a significant obstacle to recognition and response. In our work with family and friends of offenders we shared knowledge about patterns of offending. We provided them with 'alert lists' of what to look for in the behaviour and attitudes of the person they were supporting and provided contact details of individuals or agencies the family or friend could contact at times of concern. Often, we were told, 'If only I had known this before.'

These experiences, combined with ongoing contact with the inspirational Fran Henry of Stop it Now! US, prompted us to create Stop it Now! UK and Ireland supported by government departments, other leading children's charities, statutory and voluntary sector agencies.

STOP IT NOW!

Based on the US model, Stop it Now! is a public education campaign aimed at preventing the sexual abuse of children by giving adults the sound information (via leaflets, posters and media exposure) they need to recognise worrying thoughts, attitudes and behaviour in themselves or others and enabling them to take steps that will protect a child. Stop it Now! has three principal target groups:

- Offenders and potential offenders
- Friends and family of offenders and potential offenders
- Parents and carers of young people with sexually worrying behaviour.

The knowledge and experience gained at the Wolvercote Clinic was key to the information that was provided to the public and the confidence to develop this work. In addition, staff experience in work with offenders, families and victims provides the backbone of a freephone Helpline that supports the Stop it Now! campaign by providing a confidential resource to adults. Remarkably, in the first three years of helpline operation, some 35% of callers (45% of calls) to the Helpline were adults – mostly, but not exclusively men – concerned about their own sexual thoughts or behaviour towards children (Eldridge *et al.*, 2006). Concerns about Internet-related behaviours, including the viewing and possession of child pornography and online grooming, have increased in volume since the Helpline's inception in 2001. The Public Protection Unit of the Home Office, the DfES and grant-making trusts such as the Henry Smith Charity, have to date provided most of the funding for Stop it Now!

ENHANCING THE PROGRAMME IN THE LIGHT OF NEW RESEARCH AND FEEDBACK FROM EX-RESIDENTS

During the four years since the Clinic closed, there have been developments in the field of sex offender treatment that we would incorporate into the relocated Clinic programme and regime. In addition, we have been able to follow up ex-residents and have learned about what helps them maintain an offence-free life. Ex-residents have commented on what they carried with them as important messages from the Clinic. They highlighted the clear message of child protection which involved 'coming to terms with themselves, what they had done and that they have a problem'. Some talked of feeling protected and safe enough within the environment to change their lives. The men also felt that a really valuable aspect of Wolvercote was being with other offenders who had an understanding of their thoughts and behaviour and therefore they were able to challenge each other effectively.

Research supports methods used at Wolvercote Clinic. However, in future work with offenders who presented similar problems to Wolvercote residents, we would increase our emphasis on the areas described below.

Individualising the Interventions

Ex-residents commented that they would have preferred more individualised treatment with their therapists. This view is supported by research on pathways to reoffending (Ward *et al.*, 2004). Ward has shown the importance of tailoring interventions to suit individual needs. Wolvercote Clinic staff and residents contributed to this work in the UK by assisting researchers to identify their pathways (Bickley & Beech, 2002). For example, men who plan their offending and have few inhibitions about it need a different approach to those who believe it is wrong and try to avoid offending. Those for whom sexually abusive behaviour is meeting, or perceived to be meeting, fundamental human needs for affiliation and attachment need different approaches from those who can already meet these needs in appropriate ways.

At the Wolvercote Clinic, residents' relapse prevention work incorporated plans for leading a new life in which human needs were met in non-abusive ways. The 'Good Lives' model developed by Ward and Stewart (2003) confirms our view that this work is vital to the prevention of reoffending. The Good Lives Model (see Chapter 16) is a strength-based approach concerned with promoting offenders' goals alongside managing their risk, as a rehabilitation approach. Consequently, it can work with innovations that are designed to evaluate progress, such as polygraphy and visual screening.

The Good Lives Model assumes that like all human beings, offenders seek feelings, activities and experiences that are likely to increase psychological well-being. These include healthy living and functioning, knowledge, success in play and work, autonomy and self-directedness, freedom from emotional turmoil and stress, friendship, community, a sense of finding meaning and purpose to life, happiness and creativity. Human beings seek ways of securing such goods. They develop a sense of who they are and what really matters from what they do: a sense of personal identity and meaning and fulfilment in their lives (Ward, Mann & Gannon, 2007).

Each person's 'new life plan' needs to take account of all the above and to relate to the individual's past and present life experiences and to the environment in which he is likely to be discharged. He also needs to have a key role in making decisions about it and building it himself, thereby increasing a sense of self-efficacy. The concept of a positive and realistic offence-free lifestyle (Eldridge, 1998) was built into the Wolvercote programme. Each resident was encouraged to develop a personally satisfying non-abusive lifestyle throughout his period in residence. However, in future we would emphasise and individualise this work more strongly and incorporate it more fully into all the programme elements. We would spend more time focusing on personal identity and values and on practical manifestations such as hobbies and lifestyle. New approaches to sex offender management by the criminal justice agencies would help to formalise links into the home area from the earliest stage. In addition, Circles of Support and Accountability would be developed earlier in the programme in preparation for successful rehabilitation on discharge.

Engaging with the Effects of Childhood Abuse and Neglect

Many of the Clinic's residents had been sexually, physically and emotionally abused in childhood. Consequently, the life experiences they brought to the work reduced their receptivity to change. Although we worked with this, in future we would want to understand it more fully in each case. In assessment we would use the Trauma Symptom Inventory to ascertain the presence of post-traumatic stress disorder and the Attachment Style Interview and use the findings to inform clinical interventions and risk management.

The growing knowledge of brain development has increased our understanding of how early abuse and neglect may have a profound effect on an individual's later adjustment. The effects on behaviour, emotional well-being, interpersonal relationships and cognitive functioning are known to have their counterparts in brain structure, chemistry and function. A further aspect of child abuse is the significant neurobiological stress which a young, maltreated child experiences. Secure attachment protects the developing brain from the worst effects of the stress response (Glaser, 2006) but such attachment did not typify our residents. The neural mechanisms that emerge in infancy continue to affect affiliative behaviours throughout life. Therefore dysfunction of the attachment system can result in problems in both early development and adulthood (Nelson & Panksepp, 1998).

Beech and Mitchell (2005) argue that negative experiences in childhood can have an effect on oxytocin function, vasopressin function and raised corticosteroid release resulting in hippocampal and striatal damage. Serotonin (5HT) is one of the main neurotransmitter substances in the central nervous system and is involved in the regulation of arousal, attention and mood. Oxytocin and vasopressin have been found to be dependent upon the level of serotonin. Levels of corticosteroids have been found to be inversely correlated with serotonin. Beech and Mitchell argue that drugs that modulate the level of serotonin may be useful in the treatment of attachment-related problems. Selective serotonin reuptake inhibitors (SSRIs) are antidepressant drugs which can block the reuptake of serotonin allowing concentrations of it to increase in particular areas of the brain.

The adjunctive use of such drug therapy with sex offenders is still in its early stages, but Beech and Mitchell cite evidence of improvements in relation to decreases in deviant fantasies, in abnormal sexual behaviours and in obsessions and compulsions regarding abusive sexual behaviour. They add that SSRIs mediate neurochemicals that underlie social behaviours, so the real benefits of their use is to increase affiliative feelings and behaviours which lead to a decrease in the motivation or compulsion to engage in deviant thoughts and behaviours. In residential treatment such interventions may have particular value for highly fixated individuals who feel trapped by their own obsessions and need extra help in self-management.

In treating the effects of childhood abuse, we would also explore the application of compassionate mind training. This is a therapeutic approach that attempts to compensate for the effects of early abuse by stimulating new brain pathways. Gilbert (2005) suggests that compassion is an emergent property of our minds that is dependent on the interaction of complex processes that include genes, psychological systems, early life experiences and social ecologies. Early attachment relationships create the contexts for developing compassion for others as well as for the self. Compassionate mind training was developed for people who have histories of abuse and attachment problems, are highly externally and internally threat focused, cannot self-soothe, have difficulties regulating emotions, have rigid and inflexible thinking patterns and experience difficulties in interpersonal and self-to-self relating (Gilbert, 2006). This description applies to many of the Wolvercote high deviance residents.

Ongoing Therapy and Follow-Up

Anticipation of the closure of the Clinic, with a number of residents part-way through the programme, prompted the development of non-residential support and intervention services to ensure that interventions were completed and to help create an environment where treatment gains could be nurtured and supported. The Home Office funded work with those ex-residents who needed it, alongside an out-of-office-hours Helpline that all ex-residents and Circles volunteers could telephone for advice and support. Feedback from ex-residents and public protection professionals has confirmed that these services have provided effective preventive support that reduced the risk of reconviction.

CONCLUSIONS

Through its assessment work, the Clinic assisted public protection, child protection and other agencies and individuals to understand the risk of those assessed, enabling them to better protect children as a consequence. Through its intervention work, the Clinic significantly reduced the risk of those men who completed the programme. It also assisted public and child protection agencies, the clients, themselves, and their support networks, to manage risk into the future. The staff involved in this intensive work have subsequently made an invaluable contribution to the training of professionals, including police, probation and social workers, both within the UK and abroad, enabling them to better discharge their duties.

In addition knowledge gained through the work of the Clinic has been used to contribute to reviews of the criminal law, and to enquiries conducted by government agencies, charitable organisations and faith communities to enhance their child protection policies and arrangements. Through projects including Circles of Support and Accountability and Stop it Now! UK and Ireland, the Lucy Faithfull Foundation is ensuring that the public is better informed and supported in its essential role in the prevention of child sexual abuse.

REFERENCES

Beckett, RC. (1994). Cognitive-behavioural treatment of sex offenders. In T. Morrison, M. Erooga & R.C. Beckett (Eds.), *Sexual offending against children: Assessment and treatment of male abusers* (pp. 80–101). London: Routledge.

Beckett, R., Beech, A., Fisher, D. & Fordham, A.S. (1994). *Community-based treatment for sex offenders: An evaluation of seven treatment programmes*. Available from: Home Office Publications Unit, 50, Queen Anne's Gate, London, SW1 9AT, UK.

Beech, A.R. (1998). Towards a psychometric typology for assessing pretreatment level of problems in child abusers. *Journal of Sexual Aggression, 3*, 24–38.

Beech, A. & Ford, H. (2006). The relationship between risk, deviance, treatment outcome and sexual reconviction in a sample of child sexual abusers completing residential treatment for their offending. *Psychology, Crime and Law, 12*, 685–701.

Beech, A.R. & Fordham, A.S. (1997). Therapeutic climate of sexual offender treatment programs. *Sexual Abuse: A Journal of Research and Treatment, 9*, 219–237.

Beech, A.R. & Mitchell, I.J. (2005). A neurobiological perspective on attachment problems in sexual offenders and the role of selective serotonin reuptake inhibitors in the treatment of such problems. *Clinical Psychology Review, 25*, 153–182.

Bentovim, A. (1996). Trauma-organised systems in practice: implications for work with abused and abusing children and young people. *Clinical Child Psychology and Psychiatry, 1*, 513–524.

Bickley, J. & Beech, A.R. (2002). An empirical investigation of the Ward and Hudson self-regulation model of the sexual offence process with child abusers. *Journal of Interpersonal Violence, 17*, 371–393.

Clarke, K.B. (1980). Empathy: A neglected topic in psychological research. *American Psychologist, 35*, 187–190.

Cox, D.J. & Daitzman, R.J. (1980). *Exhibitionism: Description, assessment and treatment*. New York: Garland.

Deu, N. & Edelmann, R.J. (1997). The role of criminal fantasy in predatory and opportunist sex offending. *Journal of Interpersonal Violence, 12*, 18–29.

Dhawan, S. & Marshall, W.L. (1996). Sexual abuse histories of sexual offenders. *Sexual Abuse: A Journal of Research and Treatment, 8*, 7–15.

Eldridge, H.J. (1998). *Maintaining change: A personal relapse prevention manual*. Thousand Oaks, CA: Sage.

Eldridge, H.J. (1998a). *Therapist guide for maintaining change: Relapse prevention for adult male perpetrators of child sexual abuse*. Thousand Oaks, CA: Sage.

Eldridge, H.J., Fuller, S., Findlater, D. & Palmer, T. (2006). *Stop it Now! UK and Ireland Helpline Report 2002–2005*. Birmingham, UK: The Lucy Faithfull Foundation.

Eldridge, H.J. & Wyre, R. (1998). The Lucy Faithfull Foundation's residential programme for sexual offenders. In W.L. Marshall, S.M. Hudson, T. Ward & Y.M. Fernandez (Eds), *Sourcebook of treatment programs for sexual offenders* (pp. 79–92). New York: Plenum.

Feshback, N.D. (1982). Empathy training and the regulation of aggression: Potentialities and limitations. *Academic Psychology Bulletin, 4*, 399–413.

Feshback, N.D. (1987). Parental empathy and child adjustment/maladjustment. In N. Eisenberg & J. Strayer (Eds.), *Empathy and its development* (pp. 271–291). New York: Cambridge University Press.

Finkelhor, D. (1984). *Child sexual abuse: New theory and research*. New York: Viking Press.

Fisher, D. & Beech, A. (1998). Reconstituting families after sexual abuse: The offender's perspective. *Child Abuse Review, 7*, 420–434.

Fisher, D. Beech, A.R. & Browne, K.D. (1999). Comparison of sex offenders to non-offenders on selected psychological measures. *International Journal of Offender Therapy and Comparative Criminology, 43*, 473–491.

Fisher, D. & Howells, K. (1993). Social relationships in sexual offenders. *Sexual and Marital Therapy, 8*, 123–136.

Ford, H. & Beech, A. (2004). The effectiveness of the Wolvercote Clinic residential treatment programme in producing short-term treatment changes and reducing sexual reconvictions. Available electronically from: http://www.probation.homeoffice.gov.uk/output/Page32.asp

Gilbert, P. (Ed.) (2005). *Compassion: conceptualisations, research and use in psychotherapy*. Hove, East Sussex: Routledge.

Gilbert, P. (2006). Working with shame, self-attacking and the compassionate mind. Paper presented at the 4th Tools to Take Home Conference, Birmingham, 26 April 2006.

Glaser, D. (2006). Neurobiological effects of child maltreatment. Paper presented at Child and Family Training Conference, Institute of Child Health, London, 14 July 2006.

Hanson, R.K. & Bussière, M.T. (1998). Predicting Relapse: A meta-analysis of sexual offender recidivism studies. *Journal of Consulting and Clinical Psychology, 66,* 348–362.

Hudson, S.M. & Ward, T. (1997). Intimacy, loneliness and attachment style in sexual offenders. *Journal of Interpersonal Violence, 12,* 323–339.

Langevin, R., Paitich, D. & Russon, A. (1984). Are rapists sexually anomalous, aggressive, or both? In R. Langevin (Ed.), *Erotic preference, gender identity, and aggression in men: New research studies* (pp. 13–38). Hillsdale, NJ: Lawrence Erlbaum.

Marshall, W.L. (1989). Invited essay: Intimacy, loneliness and sexual offenders. *Behavior Research and Therapy, 27,* 491–503.

Marshall, W.L. (1993). The role of attachment, intimacy, and loneliness in the etiology and maintenance of sexual offending. *Sexual and Marital Therapy, 8,* 109–121.

Marshall W.L., Hudson S.M., Jones R. & Fernandez Y.M. (1995). Empathy in sex offenders. *Clinical Psychology Review, 15,* 99–113.

Mehrabin, A. & Epstein, N. (1972). A measure of emotional empathy. *Journal of Personality, 40,* 525–543.

Nelson, E.E. & Panksepp, J. (1998). Brain substrates of infant—mother attachment, contributions of opioids, oxytocin, and norepinephrine. *Neuroscience & Biobehavioral Reviews, 22,* 437–452.

Parke, R.D. & Slaby, R.G. (1983). The development of aggression. In E.M. Hetherington (Ed.), *Manual of child psychology, Vol. 4: Socialization, personality and social development* (pp. 549–641). New York: John Wiley & Sons, Inc.

Pithers, W.D. (1994). Process evaluation of a group therapy component designed to enhance sex offenders' empathy for sexual abuse survivors. *Behavior Research and Therapy, 32,* 565–570.

Prentky, R.A., Burgess, A.W., Rokous, F. *et al.* (1989). The presumptive role of fantasy in serial sexual homicide. *American Journal of Psychiatry, 146,* 887–891.

Rada, R.T. (1978). *Clinical aspects of the rapist.* New York: Grune & Stratton.

Ressler, R.K., Burgess, A.W., Douglas, J.E. *et al.* (1986). Sexual killers and their victims: Identifying patterns through crime scene analysis. *Journal of Interpersonal Violence, 1,* 288–308.

Rex, S., Lieb, R., Bottoms, A. & Wilson, L. (2003). Accrediting Offender Programmes: A process-based evaluation of the Joint Prison/Probation Services Accreditation Panel. Home Office Research Study, 273. Available from: www.homeoffice.gov.uk/rds/pdfs2/hors273.pdf.

Thornton, D. (2002). Constructing and testing a framework for dynamic risk asessment. *Sexual Abuse: A Journal of Research and Treatment, 14,* 139–154.

Thornton, D. & Beech, A.R. (2002). Integrating statistical and psychological factors through the structured risk assessment model. *Poster presented at the 21st Association for the Treatment of Sexual Abusers Conference.* Montreal, Canada, October 2002.

Thornton, D., Mann, R., Webster, S. *et al.* (2003). Distinguishing and combining risks for sexual and violent recidivism. In R.A. Prentky, E.S. Janus & M.C. Seto (Eds), *Sexually coercive behaviour: Understanding and management. Annals of the New York Academy of Sciences, 989,* 225–235.

Tingle, D., Barnard, G.W., Robbins, L. *et al.* (1986). Childhood and adolescent characteristics of pae-dophiles and rapists. *International Journal of Law and Psychiatry, 9,* 103–116.

Ward, T., Bickley, J., Webster, S.D. *et al.* (2004). *The self-regulation model of the offense and relapse process: A manual. Vol. 1: Assessment.* Victoria, BC. Canada: Pacific Psychological Assessment Corporation.

Ward, T., Mann, R.E. & Gannon, T. (2007). The Good Lives Model of offender rehabilitation: clinical implications. *Aggression and Violent Behavior, 12,* 87–107.

Ward, T. & Stewart, C.A. (2003). The treatment of sex offenders: Risk management and good lives. *Professional Psychology: Research and Practice, 34,* 353–360.

Wolf, S.C. (1984). A multifactor model of deviant sexuality. Paper presented at *Third International Conference on Victimology,* Lisbon, November 1984.

Issues/Interventions for Specific Populations

PART FIVE

Issues: Interventions for
Specific Populations

20

Treatment for Men with Intellectual Disabilities and Sexually Abusive Behaviour

GLYNIS MURPHY

NEIL SINCLAIR

INTRODUCTION

Historically, the sexuality of people with intellectual disabilities appears to have been a challenging issue. During the eugenics era, in the early 1900s, people with intellectual disabilities were sometimes considered to be asexual and 'eternal children' (Kempton & Kahn, 1991; McCarthy, 1999) and yet sometimes considered to be excessively sexual, likely to reproduce to excess, thereby "... damaging the national gene pool ..." (Craft, 1996, p. 97). These two beliefs, that "society needed protection from the sexuality of people with intellectual disability and that people with intellectual disability needed protection from sex in society" (McCarthy, 1999, p. 53) were of course contradictory, and are reminiscent of Wolfensberger's description of the historical stereotypes of people with intellectual disabilities as a "menace to society" and as the "eternal child" (Wolfensberger & Thomas, 1983, pp. 36 & 25 respectively). The contradictory nature of these two beliefs and their translation into practices within services for people with intellectual disabilities is described in the following quote from Ann Craft:

> There is the mythology that such individuals have extra high levels of sex drives and rampant sexual appetites, but have none of the internal mechanisms which ... keep our own expressions of sexuality under ... control. There is also the myth that people with learning disabilities are not really sexual at all. Their bodies may grow and develop but in essence they are Peter Pans, eternal asexual children, whatever their chronological

---

Assessment and Treatment of Sex Offenders: A Handbook. Edited by Anthony Beech, Leam Craig and Kevin Browne. © John Wiley & Sons Ltd, 2009.

age. These two myths inter-twine so that ... services ... both exercised strict control over sexual opportunities, and worked simultaneously on the principle that if we did not mention 'sex' they would not feel sexual, be sexual, or engage in sexual activity (1996, p. 97).

Attitudes have changed since the eugenics period, however, and people with intellectual disabilities are increasingly recognised as having full citizenship rights, as asserted in the United Nations Declaration on the Rights of Mentally Retarded Persons in 1971 (United Nations, 1971) and the United Nations Convention on the Rights of Persons with Disabilities in 2006 (United Nations, 2006). This declaration and convention specifically address the right to choose a lifestyle, the right to vote (and see Beckman, 2007), to marry and to have a family life. They also both specifically address, through Article 6 in the 1971 Declaration and Articles 12 and 16 in the 2006 Convention, the right to equal treatment before the law and protection from abuse.

Nevertheless, it has transpired in a variety of studies that people with intellectual disabilities are particularly vulnerable to being victims of abuse, especially sexual abuse (Brown, Stein & Turk, 1995; Buchanen & Wilkins, 1991; Furey, 1994; Hard & Plumb, 1987; McCarthy & Thompson, 1997; Sobsey, 1994; Turk & Brown, 1993), more so than other vulnerable groups (Brown & Stein, 1998). Many of the perpetrators of that abuse are themselves people with intellectual disabilities (42% of perpetrators, according to Furey, 1994; 53% according to Brown *et al.*, 1995) and they are predominantly men (88% men according to Furey, 1994; 96% men according to Brown *et al.*, 1995).

PREVALENCE

Very often, sexually abusive behaviour by men with intellectual disabilities goes unreported (Murphy, 2007). This is especially likely if the victim is also someone with intellectual disabilities (Brown & Thompson, 1997b; Green, Gray & Willner, 2002; Thompson, 1997) and it seems to be less likely if the victim is a non-disabled child (see Lindsay *et al.*, 2006). Thompson (1997), for example, found over 70% of offences against children, but only 11% of offences against another person with intellectual disabilities, were reported to the police.

Even when sexually abusive behaviour by men with intellectual disabilities *is* reported, the police frequently do not proceed with the case, especially when the alleged victim has intellectual disabilities (Brown & Thompson, 1997a; Brown *et al.*, 1995; McCarthy & Thompson, 1997; Thompson, 1997). While some men do go to court and receive prison sentences (Lund, 1990; Hayes, 1991) or are diverted out of custody (e.g., in England, are detained under the Mental Health Act, see Day, 1994; Walker & McCabe, 1973) or given Probation or Community Rehabilitation Orders (Lindsay & Smith, 1998; Thompson, 1997), many men simply continue to live in community settings without any formal legal sanction (Lindsay *et al.*, 2006).

At times, there have been assertions that men with intellectual disabilities are more likely to commit sexual crimes, in comparison to non-disabled men (Cullen, 1993;

Hawk, Rosenfeld & Warren, 1993; Nezu, Nezu & Dudek, 1998) but it is actually impossible to verify such an assertion. One of the early influential studies was that of Walker and McCabe (1973) who investigated a 90% sample of all the men with mental disorders detained in hospital, following conviction for offences, under the mental health legislation in England. Of the 960 men so detained, about one-third had intellectual disabilities and two-thirds had mental health needs and/or personality disorder. It transpired that of the total number of sexual crimes committed by the cohort, two-thirds of them were committed by the one-third of the cohort that had intellectual disabilities. This has sometimes been interpreted as meaning that men with intellectual disabilities are particularly likely to commit sexual offences. In fact, of course, it means nothing of the kind. For example, it is known that very few sexual crimes are reported to the police (Darke, 1990; Murphy, 2007), and even fewer end in convictions, so that very little is known about the perpetrators of the 'invisible' sexual crimes, whether these are men with or without disabilities. Moreover, numerous selective filters operate between a crime being notified to the police and the offender being convicted and sent to hospital under mental health legislation (see Table 20.1). It has to be concluded that Walker and McCabe's data cannot be interpreted to mean that men with intellectual disabilities are particularly prone to commit sexual crimes.

Other data on the relative prevalence of sexually abusive behaviour in men with intellectual disabilities and in men without disabilities can be subject to similar criticisms. For example, Hayes (1991) showed men with intellectual disabilities in prison in Australia were as likely to be there due to conviction following a sexual offence as were men without disabilities (4% of both groups had committed sexual offences). However, this cannot be interpreted to mean that men with and without disabilities are equally likely to commit sexual offences because of the many filters which operate differentially for people with and without an intellectual disability as described in Table 20.1. In the absence of good total population studies it has to be concluded that the prevalence of sexual offending in men with intellectual disabilities is unknown, and that while there is strong evidence that it is especially prevalent in men (that is, most sexual offenders are men), it cannot be said to be especially prevalent in men with intellectual disabilities (Murphy & Mason, 2007; Murphy, 2007).

CHARACTERISTICS

There has been relatively little research into the characteristics of men with intellectual disabilities and sexually abusive behaviour, but it appears that they tend to come from chaotic, violent and neglectful families where parents often have criminal histories themselves (Day, 1994; Fortune & Lambie, 2004; Gilby, Wolf & Goldberg, 1989). They frequently show other challenging behaviours, such as aggression, and may have other non-sexual convictions (Day, 1994; Fortune & Lambie, 2004; Gilby *et al.*, 1989; Lindsay *et al.*, 2002; Lindsay *et al.*, 2006; Lund, 1990), with a history of mental health problems being common (Day, 1994; Lindsay, Elliot & Astell, 2004; Lindsay *et al.*, 2006; Lund, 1990). They have an increased likelihood of a history of

Table 20.1 Filters in the Criminal Justice System

Factors that will decrease likelihood of prosecution and/or conviction	Criminal Justice System process	Factors that will increase likelihood of prosecution and/or conviction
Staff may not report. Victim may not report (especially if victim has ID &/or not able to tell anyone)	Victim with/without intellectual disabilities (or staff) reports to police	Men with ID very closely supervised (compared to non-disabled men)
	↓	
Police may not bother to arrest suspect, especially if victim has severe ID	Police apprehend suspected man	Men with ID less able to evade police than non-disabled men
	↓	
Police may decide not to interview suspect if he has ID	Police interview the suspect	Suspect may not say he has ID, may not understand his rights, may be suggestible & easily led on interview
	↓	
AA &/or lawyer, if called, may help protect against e.g., false confession	AA &/or lawyer can be called by police	AA may not be called & issues above may be problematic. Lawyer may not be called &/or may not know how to communicate with men with ID
	↓	
Suspect may simply be sent home if police decide not to proceed	Suspect charged or released without charge	Suspect may be thought more dangerous & 'out of control' if he has ID
	↓	
Suspect may be sent to hospital as unfit to plead or under MHA e.g., for assessment	Suspect appears in court ↓	When suspect appears in court he may not understand his rights or the process, may appear unreliable to judge/jury
	Suspect convicted	

sexual abuse as victims themselves (Gilby *et al.*, 1989; Lindsay *et al.*, 2001; Lindsay *et al.*, 2006; Mitchie *et al.*, 2006) and they commit the full range of sexual offences (Day, 1994; Fortune & Lambie, 2004; Lindsay *et al.*, 2002; Thompson, 1997), and frequently reoffend (Day, 1994; Gilby *et al.*, 1989; Klimecki, Jenkinson & Wilson, 1994; Lindsay *et al.*, 2006). Like non-disabled sex offenders, men with intellectual disabilities who engage in sexually abusive behaviour often show cognitive distortions (Lindsay *et al.*, 1998a, b, c; Lindsay, Carson & Whitefield, 2000). Where they differ from non-disabled sex offenders is that the men with intellectual disabilities seem to have more male victims (Blanchard, Watson & Choy, 1999; Fortune & Lambie, 2004; Gilby *et al.*, 1989; Murrey, Briggs & Davis, 1992) and are possibly more opportunistic and less focused on particular types of victims (Blanchard *et al.*, 1999; Gilby *et al.*, 1989). There is some suggestion that they may be less likely to be violent during their sexual offences than non-disabled men and less likely to commit penetrative offences (Murrey *et al.*, 1992) but this may be a result of other factors, such as being more closely supervised in general than other men and therefore perhaps more easily detected at earlier stages of offending.

TREATMENT

For community-based intellectual disability services, the presence of men with sexually abusive behaviour and intellectual disabilities poses a dilemma: clearly these men need treatment but often none seems to be available. The leading treatment for non-disabled sex offenders seems to be cognitive behaviour therapy (Aos, Miller & Drake, 2006; Brooks-Gordon, Bilby & Wells, 2006; Hanson *et al.*, 2002; Kenworthy *et al.*, 2003; Marshall, 1996) and currently, in the UK, the probation service runs an accredited treatment programme of this kind for non-disabled men (Beckett *et al.*, 1994). However, probation-run programmes do not normally accept men with intellectual disabilities (indeed their cut-off is usually at IQ 80). In UK prison settings, which also run an effective CBT programme called SOTP (Sex Offender Treatment Programme) for non-disabled men (Beech, Fisher & Beckett, 1999; Friendship, Mann & Beech, 2003; Grubin & Thornton, 1994), an adapted sex offender treatment programme (ASOTP) is sometimes offered for men with limited cognitive skills, i.e. with IQ below 80 (e.g. Hill & Hordell, 1999; Rogers & Fairbanks, 2003; Williams, Wakeling & Webster, 2007). A few areas of the country also have specific sex offender treatment programmes for men with intellectual disabilities, usually based in clinics or hospitals. Nevertheless, most studies have evaluated very small samples of men either in the UK (Charman & Clare, 1992; Craig, Stringer & Moss, 2006; Garrett, 2006; Lindsay *et al.*, 1998a, b, c; Rose *et al.*, 2002) or elsewhere (Griffiths, Quinsey & Hingsburger, 1989; Haaven, Little & Petre-Miller, 1990; Nezu *et al.*, 1998; O'Connor, 1996; Swanson & Garwick, 1990). Only a few studies had relatively larger samples:

- Lindsay and Smith (1998) compared reoffending rates for 14 men, half of whom had one year of CBT treatment and half of whom had two years of CBT treatment (all were living in the community on probation orders). They found that two years of treatment was more effective.

- In a separate study, Lindsay *et al.* (2006) showed a 70% reduction in harm amongst a group of 29 sexual offenders with intellectual disabilities who had a history of repeated offending, following community-based cognitive behavioural treatment.
- Williams *et al.* (2007) showed significant pre-/post-treatment change in a group of over 150 men with cognitive deficits (not all of whom had intellectual disabilities), treated in prison using the ASOTP programme.

THE SOTSEC-ID MODEL: PURPOSE

The lack of real treatment options for men with intellectual disabilities in many parts of the country in the UK led to the setting up of a group called the Sex Offender Treatment Services Collaborative in Intellectual Disabilities (SOTSEC-ID) in 2000. SOTSEC-ID is a group of clinical and forensic therapists (mainly psychologists but also some nurses and psychiatrists) who collaborate in the provision of group CBT for men with intellectual disabilities and sexually abusive behaviour (see www.kent.ac.uk/tizard/sotsec). The group includes therapists working in the community and in low/medium secure hospitals, and all therapists in the group run the SOTSEC-ID treatment model, using the same assessment measures and being guided by a common treatment manual (Sinclair, Booth & Murphy, 2002). The group has three aims:

- To be a forum within which clinicians who are engaged in treating this client group may meet to discuss treatment issues and ethical issues which this type of work raises;
- To provide appropriate training and dissemination of the SOTSEC-ID cognitive behavioural treatment (CBT) approach for this client group;
- To collect a data set of sufficient size to allow a proper test of the effectiveness of group CBT for this client group.

The first aim is achieved through meetings, every 6–8 weeks, of interested professionals. Most of these are therapists running SOTSEC-ID groups and the majority are experienced in working with people with intellectual disabilities in a variety of service settings. They are sometimes less experienced in working with sexually abusive men using group cognitive behavioural treatment. The SOTSEC-ID meetings thus provide a vital setting for peer support and for peer supervision and advice in a new area of treatment endeavour (Gabbay, Kiemle & Maguire, 1999).

The SOTSEC-ID group also arranges, once yearly, a two-day SOTSEC-ID training event (for therapists who are already professionally qualified), to teach therapists the elements of the SOTSEC-ID assessment and treatment model before they begin to run a group themselves. Other training events are run periodically, on topics relevant to SOTSEC-ID, at the request of members, with recent topics including such issues as risk assessment, the role of pornography in maintaining offending, involvement of carers, and other types of treatment for men with an intellectual disability.

SOTSEC-ID members also collaborate in providing data for the research project that is evaluating treatment effectiveness. Men who receive assessment and treatment through SOTSEC-ID are asked if they would consent to be part of the research project. If they consent, their pre- and post-group assessment and follow-up data are entered in the collaborative dataset; if they decline, they can still continue with the treatment but their assessment data are not collected onto the database. All SOTSEC-ID groups use a common assessment and treatment framework within which treatment can be provided in a standard way, so that there is some assurance of standardisation and model fidelity for comparative research purposes.[1] The group also collects data on waiting list controls, provided these men consent, in order to be more certain about treatment effectiveness.

THE SOTSEC-ID MODEL: DEFINITIONS AND ASSESSMENT

Defining Sexually Abusive Behaviour

By no means all men with intellectual disabilities and sexually abusive behaviour have been convicted of an offence (see discussion above) and consequently the definition of sexually abusive behaviour has been an important issue for the project. SOTSEC-ID defines sexually abusive behaviour as any sexually related behaviour for which:

- the other person was not consenting (or was unable to consent), and
- the behaviour would be defined as illegal within the jurisdiction in which it occurred.

This definition excludes sexual behaviours that may be considered unusual but which are not illegal (for example, cross-dressing).

Normally the proof for whether a sexual offence has occurred is provided through the criminal justice process. However, if the alleged perpetrator was diverted out of the criminal justice system due to having an intellectual disability or other mental disorder, or the sexually abusive behaviour was not reported to the usual authorities (e.g., the police), then eye-witness accounts of the sexually abusive behaviour (e.g., by the victims or other witnesses), would suffice to establish the probability that sexually abusive behaviour occurred. (Sinclair et al., 2002, p.4, parenthesis added).

This definition is deliberately broad and acknowledges that a large number of incidents of sexually abusive behaviour are often not reported to the authorities. Nevertheless it does exclude some of the kinds of sexual behaviours that sometimes cause men to be referred to the groups, even though they have done nothing illegal (such as cross-dressing; developing 'crushes' on staff).

---

[1] The research has been funded by the Department of Health, the Bailey Thomas Fund and Care Principles.

Assessment Measures

Assessment measures for men with intellectual disabilities and sexually abusive behaviour are not well researched, in comparison to measures for non-disabled men (Keeling, Beech & Rose, 2007). Frequently, men with intellectual disabilities struggle to understand the wording and scales of measures designed for mainstream offenders, so all measures used on the SOTSEC-ID project have either been developed specifically for men with intellectual disabilities or have been adapted particularly for this group.

There are three sets of assessment measures used in the project:

- Initial or screening variables and measures (Table 20.2)
- Dependent variables and measures: Process (Table 20.3)
- Dependent variables and measures: Outcome (Table 20.4)

The initial or screening measures describe important characteristics of the clients such as degree of intellectual disability, adaptive behaviour and receptive language, as well as the presence of a co-morbid mental health diagnosis, and whether the client falls within the continuum of autistic spectrum disorders. These measures also allow clinicians to determine whether an individual client referred to the group meets the inclusion criteria for the research.

Facilitators also record initial family, educational, forensic and sexual history for each man, using the Men's Group Background Information and Database Schedule – Phase One, which provides a systematic way of collecting such information.

The aim of the treatment is to reduce sexually abusive behaviour and it is hypothesised that this will be achieved through positive change in men's sexual attitudes and

Table 20.2 Initial or screening variables and measures

Variable	Measure
Intelligence	Wechsler Adult Intelligence Scale – Third Edition (WAIS-III; Wechsler, 1997)
Adaptive Behaviour	Vineland Scales of Adaptive Behavior (Sparrow *et al.*, 1984)
Receptive Language	British Picture Vocabulary Scale-II (BPVS-II; Dunn *et al.*, 1997)
Mental Health	Psychiatric Assessment for Adults with a Developmental Disability (mini PAS-ADD; Prosser *et al.*, 1997)
Autism	The Diagnostic Criteria Checklist (operationalises DSM-IV criteria for autism) (Howlin, 1997)
History & background (including all sexually abusive behaviour)	Men's Group Background Information and Database Schedule – Phase One

Table 20.3 Dependent variables and measures: Process

Variable	Measures	ID Specific Yes/No
Sexual Knowledge	Sexual Attitudes and Knowledge (SAK; Heighway & Webster, 2007)	Yes
Distorted Cognitions	(a) Questionnaire on Attitudes Consistent with Sex Offences (QACSO; Lindsay, Carson & Whitefield, 2000	Yes
	(b) Sexual Offenders Self-Appraisal Scale (SOSAS; Bray & Forshaw, 1996)	Yes
Victim Empathy	Victim Empathy Scale (Beckett & Fisher, 1994) – Adapted	No – but adapted

knowledge, reductions in the degree of minimisation, denial for the offence(s) and blame for the victim, and improvements in the degree of victim empathy (these are process variables, i.e., those dependent variables that are believed to mediate between the treatment and the outcome of reoffending). Measures of these characteristics are administered before the start and at the end of the treatment programme, and at six-month follow-up (see Murphy *et al.*, 2007 for details). In addition, one of them, the Questionnaire on Attitudes Consistent with Sex Offending (QACSO) is administered mid-way through the treatment programme.

Finally, Table 20.4 describes the dependent variables of most importance: the number of alleged sexually abusive behaviours and/or the number of convictions for sexual offences. These are assessed during treatment and for up to six months following the treatment programme. They are recorded on the Men's Group Background Information and Database Schedules – Phase Two and Three.

Table 20.4 Dependent variables and measures: Outcome

Variable	Measures
Recidivism: during treatment (Men's Group Background Information and Database Schedule – Phase Two)	• Sexually abusive behaviour not reported to the police • Allegations of sexual offending behaviour reported to the police • Convictions for sexual offending behaviour
Recidivism: post-treatment (Men's Group Background Information and Database Schedule – Phase Three)	• Sexually abusive behaviour not reported to the police • Allegations of sexual offending behaviour reported to the police • Convictions for sexual offending behaviour

THE SOTSEC-ID MODEL: TREATMENT

A treatment manual has been developed to provide a common framework for treatment with this group of clients, partly to guide therapists but also to provide some assurance of standardisation and model fidelity for comparative research purposes. Treatment manuals are made available to those running groups at a low cost and therapists are asked to adhere to the manual and, for the moment, only to share the manual with others running the SOTSEC-ID model (in order to prevent contamination of the model).

The predominant model in intellectual disability services has for some time included a constructional and positive approach to antisocial behaviours (Cullen, 1993), which has some similarity to the positive therapeutic approach to sexual offender treatment outlined by Marshall, Anderson and Fernandez (1999). This therapeutic approach has been adopted in the SOTSEC-ID model and is a feature of the treatment manual and training, and thus focuses on building a positive and respectful relationship with the client by focusing on their strengths and positive options for the future. This approach seeks a positive therapeutic relationship with each perpetrator without supporting offence-related thinking or attitudes, and in some small ways the approach anticipated recent developments which are critical of an overemphasis on risk management and a deficit-behaviour approach in the non-disabled sex offender literature (Ayland & West, 2006; Ward & Marshall, 2004). The components of the treatment reflect the hypothesis that reductions in sexually abusive behaviour will result from positive change in men's sexual attitudes and knowledge, increases in self-esteem, an increase in victim empathy, and a reduction in cognitive distortions in relation to sexual offending. These issues form the main focus of the treatment programme, the components of which are described below.

Social and Therapeutic Framework

The first part of the treatment seeks to establish the social and therapeutic framework within which the group treatment will proceed. This includes the positive therapeutic engagement described above, as well as establishing group rules, addressing initial denial, and developing group social skills. In the first group meeting, following introductions and ice-breakers, the men discuss the rules of the group themselves. They often need relatively little guidance here, except for some assistance in framing the confidentiality rule (see Table 20.5 for an example of one group's rules). This collaborative exercise helps the men feel that, as well as being present to learn, they can also have some control over what happens in the group, although this is necessarily limited. Following rule setting, the men then discuss why they have come to the group and what they expect from the group. This is an important first step in admitting that they engage in sexually abusive behaviour. Many men will only be able to say, at this stage, that they are present because they have a problem with sex, although some men may be more open. Experience has shown that if men are pushed too hard at this point to admit to their sexually abusive behaviour, many will not return to the group and,

Table 20.5 Typical group rules

1. Take turns to talk
2. Listen to each other
3. No swearing in anger
4. What we say is private except to protect others
5. No bad touching
6. Take some time out if angry
7. No shouting
8. Disagree gently
9. Support and help each other
10. Come each week and be on time
11. Coffee break at 3pm

given that about half of the men are there voluntarily (because they have not been convicted of an offence), the pace at which they come to admit the extent of their sexually abusive behaviour has to be handled very carefully.

Human Relations and Sex Education

Several studies have shown that men with intellectual disabilities and sexually abusive behaviour are not less knowledgeable than other men with intellectual disabilities about sexual matters (Mitchie *et al.*, 2006; Talbot & Langdon, 2006). Nevertheless, men (and women) with intellectual disabilities are less knowledgeable about sexual matters than non-disabled people (Murphy & O'Callaghan, 2004; Talbot & Langdon, 2006), so they clearly lack sexual knowledge of various kinds.

The purpose of the sex education module for the men with intellectual disabilities and sexually abusive behaviour in SOTSEC-ID treatment is to provide:

- A common knowledge base and understanding for human sexuality and relationships, including consent and legal issues;
- 'Permission' to talk about sexuality and sexually abusive behaviour;
- Opportunities to challenge any myths/beliefs/attitudes/cognitive distortions regarding relationships, behaviour or gender roles, which may contribute to sexually abusive behaviour.

The content is broadly based around two main components: general sex education aimed at those who have gaps in their basic sexual knowledge, and specific education/discussion on areas that are hypothesised to be less understood or known by men with an intellectual disability who engage in sexually abusive behaviours, such as legal vs. illegal behaviours, the consequences of such behaviours and issues of consent. There are considerable numbers of helpful sex education resources available that are generally relied on for this part of the programme, including slide packages (such as Kempton, 1988), pictorial packs (such as Cambridge, 1997; McCarthy &

Thompson, 1992) and videos (e.g., South East London Health Promotion Services, 1992; Family Planning Association of New South Wales, 1993).

The Cognitive Model

There is evidence that men with intellectual disabilities and sexually abusive behaviour show very similar cognitive distortions to men without disabilities who commit sexual offences (Lindsay, 1998a,b,c; Lindsay *et al.*, 2007), and so the SOTSEC-ID model includes a cognitive approach to changing sexually abusive behaviour, through changing the men's cognitive distortions.

This phase of the treatment introduces men to the cognitive model of human behaviour, i.e., to the idea that changing the way people think about their experiences will change how people respond emotionally and thus how they respond behaviourally (Beck, 1976; Ellis & Greiger, 1977). This component of treatment seeks to identify, challenge and change cognitive distortions in the men's thinking that are supportive of sexual offending, replacing them with more adaptive cognitions. A simple 'Thoughts, Feelings, Actions' framework is used to introduce the men to the cognitive model of behaviour change, beginning with everyday examples, moving on to challenging behaviour/offending, and finally to sexual offending examples. This process is illustrated with some actual (anonymised) examples in Tables 20.6 and 20.7. The cognitive

Table 20.6 Cognitive model applied to challenging behaviour/offending

Situation: Another resident accused me of stealing his stuff

Thoughts	**Feelings**	**Actions**
What I thought	**And felt**	**And did**
He's an animal.	Very annoyed	Dirty look
He's rubbish.	Explosive	Called him a liar
Should be in prison.	Aggressive	Pushed him into the wall
Take around the corner and give a good kicking.	Stressed	
	Self-righteousness	
What I will think next time	**I would feel this**	**I would do this**
He's a human being.	Still annoyed, but calmer	Walk off without saying or doing anything
If I hurt him it makes it worse for him and me.		
He's jealous – behaving silly.		

Table 20.7 Cognitive model applied to sexual offending

Situation: Young girl sits on my knee on a family visit

Thoughts	**Feelings**	**Actions**
What I thought	**And felt**	**And did**
I want to touch her.	Sexy	Sat her on knee
I'll touch her when my family is not looking.	Attracted to her	Cuddled her
I'm in control.	Powerful	Put my arms right around her
I want her on my knee so that I can do something to her.	Aroused	Nuzzled her neck
	Excited	
	Happy	
	Glad	
What I will think next time	**I would feel this**	**I would do this**
Will someone catch me?	She will hate me	Put her down
I'll be seen.	I should stay away from children	Stand up so she can't sit on my lap
I'll get into trouble.	Risky situation	Don't touch her physically
She might not like it.		
People around help keep her safe.		
Touching her will damage her.		

restructuring from cognitive distortions to more adaptive thoughts, and the effect on feelings and actions, can be seen in the top and bottom half respectively of each of table.

Sexual Offending Model

Finkelhor (1984) developed a model that included four preconditions that he argued needed to be met in order for sexual offending to occur. This four-step framework was modified for the Adapted Sex Offender Treatment Programme (ASOTP), developed jointly by HM Prison Service and Janet Shaw Clinic (1999), and then further adapted for the present programme in the Treatment Manual. The model provides a framework within which facilitators and participants can discuss and understand the men's sexually abusive behaviour, especially the various stages or steps involved in the offending process. This part of the programme is intended to help the men understand that their previous behaviour did not occur in a random or unexplained fashion, but that they planned to offend (and therefore that they can plan not to offend). The

Table 20.8 Table to show the Finkelhor (1984), ASOTP (1999) and SOTSEC-ID (2002) sex offending models

Finkelhor (1984)	ASOTP (1999)	SOTSEC-ID (2002)
Motivation to abuse	Thinking/having sexy thoughts	Thinking not OK sexy thoughts. (Thinking about sexually abusive behaviour, having a 'not OK' sexual fantasy, or internal 'film')
Overcoming internal inhibitors	Making it OK to offend	Making it OK or Making Excuses (Making excuses about why offending, is 'OK' – lying to self)
Overcoming external inhibitors	Setting up a situation in which you can offend	Planning to offend (Planning access to a victim)
Overcoming victim resistance	Making the victim do what you want	Offending (Engaging in sexually abusive behaviour)

model provides a relatively simple framework for understanding sexual offending and forms a basis for the later development of relapse prevention. Finkelhor's (1984) four preconditions, the ASOTP adaptation and our own modification are shown in Table 20.8.

Each man is required to consider these steps in relation to his own past behaviour, and to apply the model to his own previous sexual offending. This means that each man is helped to identify the specific 'Not OK sexy thoughts' he has, the specific 'Making it OK' or 'Excuses' distortions he tells himself, and the specific 'Planning to offend' strategies he uses, as well as details about the type and nature of his offences. There are usually significant cognitive distortions underlying all stages, especially the 'Making it OK' stage, so the cognitive model integrates effectively with the sexual offending model. With the help of other men in the group, these cognitive distortions are restructured and offence prevention strategies developed for each of the four stages. As can be seen in the examples given (Tables 20.9 and 20.10) this produces an offending and a non-offending pathway, with Table 20.9 showing the model being applied to a general sex offending example taken from a television programme, and Table 20.10 showing an application to one of the men's past offences.

Victim Empathy

Empathy has long been considered important for regulating and/or mediating prosocial behaviour, motivating altruism and inhibiting aggression. In general, most research has suggested that empathy consists of a number of components, particularly cognitive and emotional components, and many measures of empathy reflect this division (Davis, 1983; Marshall *et al.*, 1999, pp.73–92).

Table 20.9 Applying the 4-stage model to a general sex offending example:
A storyline in a recent TV programme

Stage	Offending examples	Non-offending examples
Thinking not OK sexy thoughts	Thinking about drugging women to have sex with them	Imagine doing some gardening Being a radio DJ or sports reporter Woman sees me and exposes me
Making it OK	Thinking: I won't get caught I won't go to prison It's just a bit of fun They enjoy it They are asking for it	Thinking: I will get caught I could go to prison It's not fun, they don't enjoy it They are being assaulted They are not asking to be drugged or raped
Planning	Go to pub/club Buy some drugs Go out at night Go somewhere quiet . . . looking for an opportunity	Avoid clubs Don't buy drugs Watch DVD Have pizza Keep busy
Offending	Sexually assault someone	Stay away from sexual assaults

Nevertheless, whilst it might be expected that non-disabled men who commit sexual offences would have low levels of general empathy, this does not appear to be the case (Joliffe & Farrington, 2004; Marshall *et al.*, 1999). Such men do seem to have low levels of empathy for *victims of sexual offences*, however, especially their own victims (Beckett & Fisher, 1994), and it appears that low victim empathy may be related to some of the cognitive distortions that sex offenders hold, in that both minimisation of harm and victim blaming may be the result of low victim empathy.

With respect to men with intellectual disabilities and sexually abusive behaviour, there is also some evidence that they too show poor empathy with their victims, which improves with treatment (Murphy *et al.*, 2007). In the SOTSEC-ID model, various methods are used in the treatment to try to increase victim empathy. Initially the men are supported to talk about times when they were victims of harassment, bullying or abuse. This is often a key session in the SOTSEC-ID treatment as many men have been abused themselves, including having been victims of sexual abuse and they usually find it helpful to discuss how they felt (see example in Table 20.11). The group then works towards getting the men to think about how victims of sexual abuse, generally, might feel (this often includes role playing victims). Finally they are helped to face up to how their own victims felt, something which most men find very hard.

Table 20.10 The 4-stage model applied to a man's specific sex offending history

Stage	Offending example	Non-offending example
Thinking not OK sexy thoughts	Thinking of touching vulnerable people in between their legs Thinking of having sex with them (raping them)	Distract myself with thinking of Liverpool winning the cup Legal fantasy of consensual sex with woman over 16 Turn off: victim's family shouting at me
Making it OK	Thinking: I'm just going to do it anyway Nobody will find out I don't care what the victim thinks or feels I'm going to hurt them really bad, I'll be fine They can't report me I'm going to get a kick out of it I'm in control I will never get caught	Thinking: I did it and got caught People found out and they shouted at me I damaged them and they might never get over it If I hurt them, I'll get caught and put under section But there might be cameras I didn't in the end I'm not in control now I did get caught
Planning	Plan to do it when no-one around Wait until everyone has gone home I didn't tell anyone else about plans Choose vulnerable people	Let people know the risk I pose Stay in own room and sleep Talk to staff about plans and illegal fantasies and get help Avoid being around vulnerable people Watch DVDs/Listen to music at night
Offending	Sexual offending	Remember I could get sent to prison: stay away from sexual offending

Relapse Prevention

Relapse prevention is designed to address the difficulty encountered in most sex offender treatment programmes, that of recidivism or failure of maintenance (George & Marlatt, 1989). The purpose of relapse prevention strategies is to provide the client with a range of strategies and tactics that will reduce the probability of encountering situations in which a lapse is likely, and reduce the likelihood of lapses becoming relapses.

Such strategies are needed because regardless of how powerful the initial treatment effect is, maintenance relies on self-administration of strategies and tactics to avoid relapse, and if such strategies are not explicitly addressed in treatment, the client is less likely to have the appropriate skills and knowledge to apply them (Pithers *et al.*, 1983).

Table 20.11 How victims feel (the men as victims)

They Said or Did	I Felt
When called names 'imbecile', 'spastic', 'wanker', 'pillock'	• Feel punished for something you didn't do
	• Feel hurt and want to talk to someone
Picked on in playground	• Feel scared
	• Feel like running away
	• Feeling embarrassed
Being hit on the head by strangers	• Terrible
	• Angry
In the market, being called a 'nutter'	• Annoyed
'There's the nutter again'	• Wound up
	• Felt scared
'Do you want to fight?'	• Felt like running away
Being called at from cars ('I like your shorts')	• Angry
People chanting song tunes at you	• Terrible
	• Angry
People ringing up and leaving horrible messages	• Feel like hitting them
Being pulled into a garage and attacked by a stranger when I was a child	• I can still remember his clothes, shoes, how he looks, the smell in there
	• I was scared to go out
	• I couldn't forget it
When my dad started on me (sexual abuse)	• I thought it was my fault
	• It affected my schoolwork. I started playing up
	• I felt I couldn't tell anyone
	• I won't ever forget it. I tried to.

Towards the end of the treatment, a number of sessions are spent developing detailed relapse prevention plans for each client. These serve as a distillation of the group treatment programme and 'therapeutic work' undertaken, and are designed to be shared with relevant parties such as the man's key-worker, Care Manager, Probation Officer and similar. They can be carried around in abbreviated forms on portable cards, as well as being included in longer forms in care plans, risk management plans and the like.

Post-Treatment

The serious consequences of the men's offending behaviour on their victims means that steps have to be taken following the treatment to help reduce the chance of recidivism. Several different strategies have been used to help the men from committing further offences. At the lowest level of response, the relapse prevention plan developed for each man is used as a basis for risk management with services responsible for monitoring the individual. Services are encouraged to re-refer to psychology or the treatment group if circumstances arise that potentially increase the risk of reoffending.

On many of the treatment sites, maintenance groups are held on a regular basis (e.g., every two, four or six weeks) to monitor the relapse prevention plan, and assist the client to deal with other issues and problems which may otherwise increase the risk of offending. Occasionally, men are included in a further year-long treatment group (see Murphy *et al.*, 2007). Which strategy, or combination of strategies, is adopted depends, as always, on the individual being treated, his treatment response, and local circumstances and resources.

Involvement of Carers

Groups have differed in the extent to which it has been possible to involve carers, but most have run several sessions for carers, usually one session near the start of the year-long treatment, one in the middle of the year and one at the end (often in parallel with the Men's Group sessions). This is much less than some probation programmes for non-disabled offenders have been able to do, probably as a result of the very restricted resources available in most CLDTs for these kinds of programmes. Given the limited resources, the main aims are to demystify the treatment and provide carers with a guide to how to support the men when they are not in the group.

DISCUSSION

The characteristics of the men who are enrolled in the SOTSEC-ID group treatment (Murphy *et al.*, 2006; Murphy *et al.*, 2007) are very much as described in previous literature (Day, 1994; Gilby *et al.*, 1989; Lindsay *et al.*, 2001, 2002): they have mild or borderline intellectual disabilities, often have dual diagnoses and had difficult childhood circumstances, frequently having been abused themselves when young. They often had long histories of sexually abusive behaviour and tended only to be convicted if the victim was a child, as others have also reported (Green *et al.*, 2002; Thompson, 1997).

By no means all of the men who came for treatment agreed to participate in the research, but those who did agree mostly stayed to the end of the treatment group, making significant progress in terms of their sexual knowledge, victim empathy and cognitive distortions (Murphy *et al.*, 2006; Murphy *et al.*, 2007). In a previous study, Rose *et al.* (2002) demonstrated that a closed group intervention lasting 16 weeks (for 2 hours per week) for a group of 5 men which focused on sex education, identifying feelings and enhancing empathy, sexual fantasies, offending cycles and planning how not to reoffend, had some effect in improving empathy and cognitive distortions, in some men. However, the numbers were very small and no statistically significant effects were detected. Craig *et al.* (2006), on the other hand, in a 7-month CBT treatment group found no changes in cognitive distortions for 6 men, although none reoffended in the following 12 months. Lindsay and colleagues, in contrast, in a series of studies, have shown that group CBT, involving some victim empathy work, challenging of cognitive distortions about responsibility, intent, harm done to the victim and relapse prevention did reduce cognitive distortions in treated men (Lindsay *et al.*, 1998a, b, c) and those receiving two years of treatment did better in terms of reoffending rates than those with one year of treatment (Lindsay & Smith, 1998). It seems possible therefore that men with intellectual disabilities can gain sexual knowledge quite quickly but need lengthy treatment before they show significant changes to their victim empathy or cognitive distortions.

Most of the men in SOTSEC-ID groups manage not to engage in sexually abusive behaviour during the period when the group is running. However, occasionally men continued to engage in sexually abusive behaviour, mainly non-contact offences, either during and/or after the end of the group. Surprisingly, the police often seemed very reluctant to arrest such men and we would argue that this is not helpful to the men, as it means they are receiving two different messages: in the group, they are told this kind of behaviour is illegal and if the police know about it they will be arrested and may go to court, whereas in actuality it may seem to them that they can reoffend with impunity if the police fail to take action. There was some evidence in SOTSEC-ID groups that men on the autistic spectrum found it particularly difficult to prevent themselves reoffending (Murphy *et al.*, 2006; Murphy *et al.*, 2007), perhaps partly because of their difficulties in understanding other people's perspectives and feelings, and partly because, for some men, their non-contact offences had become part of their rigid daily routine.

Clearly, the SOTSEC-ID study has a number of strengths and a number of limitations. One of the strengths is that the cognitive behavioural treatment approach has been simplified so that it is suitable for men with intellectual disabilities. The treatment length is longer than periods shown to be too short, such as those of Rose *et al.* (2002) and Craig *et al.* (2006), and can be increased with successive treatments to build up to two-year lengths, as found effective by Lindsay and Smith (1998) for intellectually disabled sex offenders. Another strength is that the measures used were designed or adapted for men with intellectual disabilities (cf. Craig *et al.*, 2006) and covered sexual knowledge and victim empathy as well as cognitive distortions (cf. Lindsay *et al.*, 1998a, b, c). Moreover, all sexually abusive behaviour was logged before, during and after the group, rather than just convictions (cf. Craig *et al.*, 2006; Lindsay & Smith, 1998).

However, there were also a number of limitations to the study. These included the difficulty of obtaining full sets of assessment data from busy clinicians so that the data for some men is not complete for some measures. In addition, the fact that by no means all of the men enrolled in treatment consented to be part of the research, has meant that it is possible the data will overestimate the effectiveness of treatment (assuming that the more challenging men refuse to be part of the research). Some researchers have not sought men's consent, arguing that their behaviour means they have no right to refuse to take part in research (Brown & Thompson, 1997a) but we would disagree. Finally, another limitation is that there were few men in the waiting list control group. Other trials of group treatment for men with intellectual disabilities and sexually abusive behaviour (e.g., Craig *et al.*, 2006; Lindsay & Smith, 1998; O'Connor, 1996; Rose *et al.*, 2002; Swanson & Garwick, 1990) have also lacked a no-treatment comparison group. Nevertheless, the lack of control groups makes it very difficult to conclude whether or not the men did better (in terms of sexual knowledge, empathy, cognitive distortions and reoffending) than they would have done without treatment.

Despite these limitations, the SOTSEC-ID model does appear to be a promising model of treatment for men with intellectual disabilities and sexually abusive behaviour. Over the next few years it is hoped that further data will accrue allowing us to evaluate the effectiveness of the treatment over a longer period of time and against a larger group of comparison men.

REFERENCES

Aos, S., Miller, M. & Drake, E. (2006). *Evidence-based adult corrections programs: What works and what does not*. Olympia, WA: Washington State Institute for Public Policy.

Ayland, L. & West, B. (2006). The good way model: A strengths-base approach for working with young people, especially those with intellectual disabilities, who have sexually abusive behaviour. *Journal of Sexual Aggression, 12*, 189–201.

Beck, A.T. (1976). *Cognitive therapy and the emotional disorders*. New York: International Universities Press.

Beckett, R. & Fisher, D. (1994). Victim empathy measure. In R.C. Beckett, A. Beech, D. Fisher & A.S. Fordham (Eds), *Community-based treatment for sex offenders: An evaluation of seven treatment programmes*. London: Home Office.

Beckett, R., Beech, A., Fisher, D. & Fordham, A.S. (1994). *Community-based treatment for sex offenders: An evaluation of seven treatment programmes*. London: Home Office.

Beckman, L. (2007). Political equality and the disenfranchisement of people with intellectual impairments. *Social Policy and Society, 6*, 13–23.

Beech, A.R., Fisher, D. & Beckett, R.C. (1999). An Evaluation of the Prison Sex Offender Treatment Programme. UK Home Office Occasional Report. Available from: Home Office Publications Unit, 50, Queen Anne's Gate, London, SW1 9AT, England. Available electronically from: www.homeoffice.gov.uk/rds/pdfs/occ-step3.pdf

Blanchard, R., Watson, M. & Choy, A. (1999). Pedophiles: Mental retardation, maternal age and sexual orientation. *Archives of Sexual Behavior, 28*, 111–127.

Bray, D. & Forshaw, N. (1996). *Sex Offender's Self-Appraisal Scale. Version 1.1*. Lancashire Care NHS Trust.

Brooks-Gordon, B., Bilby, C. & Wells H. (2006). A systematic review of psychological interventions for sexual offenders. I: Randomised control trials. *Journal of Forensic Psychiatry and Psychology, 17*, 442–466.

Brown, H. & Stein, J. (1998). Implementing Adult Protection policies in Kent and East Sussex. *Journal of Social Policy, 27*, 371–396.

Brown, H., Stein, J. & Turk, V. (1995). The sexual abuse of adults with learning disabilities: a second incidence study. *Mental Handicap Research, 8*, 3–24.

Brown, H. & Thompson, D. (1997a). The ethics of research with men who have learning disabilities and abusive sexual behaviours: A minefield in a vacuum. *Disability & Society, 12*, 5.

Brown, H. & Thompson, D. (1997b). Service responses to men with intellectual disabilities who have unacceptable or abusive sexual behaviours: The case against inaction. *Journal of Applied Research in Intellectual Disabilities, 10*, 176–197.

Buchanen, A.H. & Wilkins, R. (1991). Sexual abuse of the mentally handicapped: difficulties in establishing prevalence. *Psychiatric Bulletin, 15*, 601–605.

Cambridge, P. (1997). *HIV, sex and learning disability*. Brighton: Pavilion Publishing.

Charman, T. & Clare, I.C.H. (1992). Education about the laws and social rules relating to sexual behaviour. *Mental Handicap, 20,* 74–80.

Craft, A. (1996). The moral map – overview and context. In J. Churchill, A. Craft, A. Holding & C. Horrocks (Eds), *It Could Never Happen Here: The Prevention and Treatment of Sexual Abuse of Adults with Learning Disabilities in Residential Settings* (Revised edition). Chesterfield: ARC/NAPSAC.

Craig, L., Stringer, I. & Moss, T. (2006). Treating sexual offenders with learning disabilities in the community. *International Journal of Offender Therapy and Comparative Criminology, 50,* 369–390.

Cullen, C. (1993). The treatment of people with learning disabilities who offend. In K. Howells & C.R. Hollin (Eds), *Clinical approaches to the mentally disordered offender.* Chichester: John Wiley & Sons, Ltd.

Darke, J.L. (1990). Sexual aggression: Achieving power through humiliation. In W.L. Marshall, D.R. Laws & H.E. Barbaree (Eds), *Handbook of sexual assault: Issues, theories and treatment of the offender* (pp. 55–72). New York, Plenum Press.

Davis, M.H. (1983). Measuring individual differences in empathy. *Journal of Personality and Social Psychology, 44,* 113–126.

Day, K. (1994). Male mentally handicapped sex offenders. *British Journal of Psychiatry, 165,* 630–639.

Dunn, L.M., Dunn, L.M., Whetton, C. & Burley, J. (1997). *The British Picture Vocabulary Scale* (2nd edn). National Foundation for Educational Research. Windsor, England: NFER-NELSON.

Ellis, A. & Grieger, R. (1977). *Handbook of rational-emotive therapy.* New York: Springer.

Family Planning Association of New South Wales (1993). *Feeling sexy, feeling safe.* A sex education video for people with intellectual disabilities. New South Wales, Australia: Family Planning Association.

Finkelhor, D. (Ed.) (1984). *Child Sexual Abuse: New Theory and Research.* New York: Free Press.

Fortune, C.A. & Lambie, I. (2004). Demographic and abuse characteristics in adolescent male sexual offenders with 'special needs'. *Journal of Sexual Aggression, 10,* 63–84.

Friendship, C., Mann R. & Beech, A. (2003). Evaluation of a national prison-based treatment program for sexual offenders in England and Wales. *Journal of Interpersonal Violence, 18,* 744–759.

Furey, E.M. (1994). Sexual abuse of adults with mental retardation: Who and where? *Mental Retardation, 32,* 173–180.

Gabbay, M.B., Kiemle, G. & Maguire, C. (1999). Clinical supervision for clinical psychologists: Existing provision and unmet needs. *Clinical Psychology and Psychotherapy, 6,* 404–412.

Garrett, H. (2006). Development of a community-based sex offender treatment programme for adult male clients with a learning disability. *Journal of Sexual Aggression, 12,* 63–70.

George, W.H. & Marlatt, G.A. (1989). Introduction. In D.R. Laws (Ed.), *Relapse prevention with sex offenders.* New York: Guilford Press.

Gilby, R., Wolf, L. & Goldberg, B. (1989). Mentally retarded adolescent sex offenders: A survey and pilot study. *Canadian Journal of Psychiatry, 34,* 542–548.

Green, G., Gray, N.S. & Willner, P. (2002). Factors associated with criminal convictions for sexually inappropriate behaviour in men with learning disabilities. *Journal of Forensic Psychiatry, 13,* 578–607.

Griffiths, S.D.M., Quinsey, V.L. & Hingsburger, D. (1989). *Changing inappropriate sexual behaviour: a community-based approach for persons with developmental disabilities.* Baltimore, MD: Paul H. Brookes.

Grubin, D. & Thornton, D. (1994). A national programme for the assessment and treatment of sex offenders in the English prison system. *Criminal Justice and Behavior, 21,* 55–71.

HM Prison Service & Janet Shaw Clinic (1999). *Sex Offender Treatment Programme: Adapted Programme.* London, Programme Development Section, HM Prison Service.

Haaven, J., Little, R. & Petre-Miller, D. (1990). *Treating intellectually disabled sex offenders: A model residential program.* Orwell, VT: Safer Society Press.

Hanson, R.K., Gordon, A., Harris, A.J.R. *et al.* (2002). First report of the collaborative outcome data project on the effectiveness of psychological treatment for sex offenders. *Sexual Abuse: A Journal of Research and Treatment, 14,* 169–194.

Hard, S. & Plumb, W. (1987). Sexual abuse of persons with developmental disabilities. A case study. Unpublished manuscript.

Hawk, G.L., Rosenfeld, B.D. & Warren, J.I. (1993). Prevalence of sexual offences among mentally retarded criminal defendants. *Hospital and Community Psychiatry, 44*, 784–786.

Hayes, S. (1991). Sex offenders. *Australia and New Zealand Journal of Developmental Disabilities, 17*, 220–227.

Heighway, S. M. & Webster, S. K. (2007). *STARS: Skills training for assertiveness, relationships building and sexual awareness*. Arlington, Texas: Future Horizons Inc.

Hill, J. & Hordell, A. (1999). The Brooklands sex offender treatment programme. *Learning Disability Practice, 1*, 16–21.

Howlin, P. (1997). The Diagnostic Criteria Checklist. Unpublished manuscript. St George's Medical School.

Joliffe, D. & Farrington, D.P. (2004). Empathy and offending: A systematic review and meta-analysis. *Aggression and Violent Behaviour, 9*, 441–476.

Keeling, J., Beech, A.R. & Rose, J.L. (2007). Assessment of intellectually disabled sexual offenders: the current position. *Aggression and Violent Behavior, 12*, 229–241.

Kempton, W. (1988). *Life Horizons I & II*. Santa Monica: James Stanfield and Co.

Kempton, W. & Kahn, E. (1991). Sexuality and people with intellectual disabilities: A historical perspective. *Sexuality & Disability, 9*, 93–111.

Kenworthy, T., Adams, C.E., Bilby, C. *et al.* (2003). Psychological interventions for those who have sexually offended or are at risk of offending. *Cochrane Database of Systematic Reviews, Art. No: CD004858. DOI: 10.1002/14651858*.

Klimecki, M.R., Jenkinson, J. & Wilson, L. (1994). A study of recidivism among offenders with intellectual disability. *Australia and New Zealand Journal of Developmental Disabilities, 19*, 209–219.

Lindsay, W.R., Carson, D. & Whitefield, E. (2000). Development of a questionnaire on attitudes consistent with sex offending for men with intellectual disabilities. *Journal of Intellectual Disability Research, 44*, 368.

Lindsay, W.R., Elliot, S.F. & Astell, A. (2004). Predictors of sexual offence recidivism in offenders with intellectual disabilities. *Journal of Applied Research in Intellectual Disabilities, 17*, 299–305.

Lindsay, W.R., Law, J., Quinn, K. Smart, N., & Smith, A.H.W. (2001). A comparison of physical and sexual abuse histories: sexual and non-sexual offenders with intellectual disability. *Child Abuse and Neglect, 25*, 989–995.

Lindsay, W.R., Marshall, L., Neilson, C., Quinn, K., & Smith, A.H.W. (1998b). The treatment of men with a learning disability convicted of exhibitionism. *Research in Developmental Disabilities, 19*, 295–316.

Lindsay, W.R., Neilson, C., Morrison, F. & Smith, A.H.W. (1998a). The treatment of six men with a learning disability convicted of sex offences with children. *British Journal of Clinical Psychology, 37*, 83–98.

Lindsay, W.R., Olley, S., Jack, C., Morrison, F., & Smith, A.H.W. (1998c). The treatment of two stalkers with intellectual disabilities using a cognitive approach. *Journal of Applied Research in Intellectual Disabilities, 11*, 333–344.

Lindsay, W.R. & Smith, A.H.W. (1998). Responses to treatment for sex offenders with intellectual disability: a comparison of men with one and two year probation sentences. *Journal of Intellectual Disability Research, 42*, 346–353.

Lindsay, W.R., Smith, A.H.W., Law, J., Quinn, K., Anderson, A., Smith, A., Overend, T., & Allan, R. (2002). A treatment service for sex offenders and abusers with intellectual disability: characteristics of referrals and evaluation. *Journal of Applied Research in Intellectual Disabilities, 15*, 166–174.

Lindsay, W.R., Steele, L., Smith, A.H.W., Quinn, K., & Allan, R. (2006). A community forensic intellectual disability service: Twelve-year follow-up of referrals, analysis of referral patterns and assessment of harm reduction. *Legal and Criminological Psychology, 11*, 113–130.

Lindsay, W.R., Whitefield, E. & Carson, D. (2007). An assessment for attitudes consistent with sexual offending for use with offenders with intellectual disabilities. *Legal and Criminological Psychology, 12*, 55–68.

Lund, J. (1990). Mentally retarded criminal offenders in Denmark. *British Journal of Psychiatry, 156,* 726–731.

Marshall, W.L. (1996). Assessment, treatment and theorising about sex offenders: developments during the past twenty years and future directions. *Criminal Justice and Behavior, 23,* 162–199.

Marshall, W.L., Anderson, D. & Fernandez, Y. (1999). *Cognitive behavioural treatment of sexual offenders.* Chichester: John Wiley & Sons, Ltd.

McCarthy, M. (1999). *Sexuality and women with learning disabilities.* London: Jessica Kingsley.

McCarthy, M. & Thompson, D. (1992). *Sex and the 3Rs: Rights, Responsibilities and Risks.* Brighton: Pavilion Publishing.

McCarthy, M. & Thompson, D. (1997). A prevalence study of sexual abuse of adults with intellectual disabilities referred for sex education. *Journal of Applied Research in Intellectual Disabilities, 10,* 105–124.

Mitchie, A.M., Lindsay, W.R., Martin, V. & Grieve, A. (2006). A test of counterfeit deviance: a comparison of sexual knowledge in groups of sex offenders with intellectual disability and controls. *Sexual Abuse: A Journal of Research and Treatment, 18,* 271–278.

Murphy, G.H. (2007). Intellectual disabilities, sexual abuse and sexual offending. In A. Carr, G. O'Reilly, P. Noonan Walsh & J. McEvoy (Eds), *Handbook of intellectual disability and clinical psychology practice* (pp. 831–866). London: Routledge.

Murphy, G. & Mason, J. (2007). People with intellectual disabilities who are at risk of offending. In N. Bouras (Ed.), *Psychiatric and behavioural disorders in intellectual and developmental disabilities* (2nd edn) (pp. 173–201). Cambridge: Cambridge University Press.

Murphy, G. & O'Callaghan, A.C. (2004). Capacity to consent to sexual relationships by adults with intellectual disabilities. *Psychological Medicine, 34,* 1347–1357.

Murphy, G.H., Powell, S., Guzman, A-M. & Hays, S.J. (2007). Cognitive behavioural treatment for men with intellectual disabilities and sexually abusive behaviour: A pilot study. *Journal of Intellectual Disabilities Research, 51,* 902–912.

Murphy, G.H., Sinclair, N., Hays, S.J. *et al.* (2006). *Effectiveness of group cognitive-behavioural treatment for men with learning disabilities at risk of sexual offending.* Final report to the Department of Health.

Murrey, G.H., Briggs, D. & Davis, C. (1992). Psychopathically disordered, mentally ill and mentally handicapped sex offenders: A comparative study. *Medicine, Science and the Law, 32,* 331–336.

Nezu, C.M., Nezu A.M. & Dudek, J.A. (1998). A cognitive behavioural model of assessment and treatment for intellectually disabled sex offenders. *Cognitive and Behavioural Practice, 5,* 25–64.

O'Connor, H. (1996). A problem-solving intervention for sex offenders with an intellectual disability. *Journal of Intellectual and Developmental Disability, 21,* 219–235.

Pithers, W.D., Marques, J.K., Gibat, C.C. & Marlatt, G.A. (1983). Relapse prevention with sexual aggressives. In J.G.S. Greer & I.R. Stuart (Eds), *The sexual aggressor.* New York: Van Nostrand/Reinhold.

Prosser, H., Moss, S., Costello, H., Simpson, N. & Patel, P. (1997). The Mini-PAS-ADD (Psychiatric Assessment Schedule for Adults with Developmental Disability). Brighton: Pavilion Publishing.

Rogers, J. & Fairbanks, A. (2003). ASOTP. Applying the adapted sex offender treatment programme for patients with cognitive deficits. *Forensic Update, 74,* 6–11.

Rose, J., Jenkins, R., O'Connor, C. *et al.* (2002). A group treatment for men with intellectual disabilities who sexually offend or abuse. *Journal of Applied Research in Intellectual Disabilities, 15,* 138–150.

Sinclair, N., Booth, S.J. & Murphy, G.H. (2002). *Cognitive Behavioural Treatment for Men with Intellectual Disabilities who are at Risk of Sexual Offending: A Treatment Manual.* Unpublished manuscript.

Sobsey, D. (1994). *Violence and abuse in the lives of people with disabilities: The end of silent acceptance?* Baltimore, MD: Paul H. Brookes.

South East London Health Promotion Services (1992). *My choice, my own choice.* A sex education video for people with learning disabilities.

Sparrow, S.S., Balla, D.A. & Cicchetti, D.V. (1984). *Vineland Adaptive Behavior Scales.* Circle Pines, MN: American Guidance Service.

Swanson, C.K. & Garwick, G.B. (1990). Treatment for low functioning sex offenders: group therapy and interagency coordination. *Mental Retardation, 28,* 155–161.

Talbot, T.J. & Langdon, P. (2006). A revised sexual knowledge assessment tool for people with intellectual disabilities: Is sexual knowledge related to sexual offending behaviour? *Journal of Intellectual Disability Research, 50,* 523–531.

Thompson, D. (1997). Profiling the sexually abusive behaviour of men with intellectual disabilities. *Journal of Applied Research in Intellectual Disabilities, 10,* 125–139.

Turk, V. & Brown, H. (1993). The sexual abuse of adults with learning disabilities: results of a two-year incidence survey. *Mental Handicap Research, 6,* 193–216.

United Nations (1971). Declaration on the Rights of Mentally Retarded Persons (Resolution adopted by the General Assembly during its 26th session, 20 December 1971). New York: Author. *General Assembly Official Records Suppl. No. 29 (A/8429), 93.*

United Nations (2006). Convention on the Rights of Persons with Disabilities, adopted 13 December 2006. New York: Author. *General Assembly Official Records. A/RES/61/106.*

Walker, N. & McCabe, S. (1973). *Crime and insanity in England.* Edinburgh: Edinburgh University.

Ward, T.W. & Marshall, W.L. (2004). Good lives, aetiology and the rehabilitation of sex offenders: A bridging theory. *Journal of Sexual Aggression, 10,* 153–169.

Wechsler, D. (1997). *Wechsler Adult Intelligence Scale* (3rd edn). (WAIS-III). London: Psychological Corporation.

Williams, F., Wakeling, H. & Webster, S. (2007). A psychometric study of six self-report measures for use with sexual offenders with cognitive and social functioning deficits. *Psychology, Crime and Law, 13,* 505–522.

Wolfensberger, W. & Thomas, S. (1983). *PASSING: Program Analysis of Service Systems Implementation of Normalization Goals.* Toronto: National Institute on Mental Retardation.

21

Interventions with Sex Offenders with Mental Illness

TANYA GARRETT

BRIAN THOMAS-PETER

INTRODUCTION

In this chapter, we will discuss the psychological treatment of those sexual offenders with mental illness (MI). Although MI is often associated with other disorders we are not seeking to address sexual offenders with learning disabilities (Murphy & Sinclair, Chapter 20 of this volume) or those with personality disorder (Jones, Chapter 22 of this volume). There will be areas of overlap with these populations as there are likely to be different issues in such cases. Instead, we intend to concentrate on those with severe and enduring mental health difficulties. In considering psychological treatment for this population, a sound psychological formulation (Gardner, 2005) is important in order to establish the connection, if any, between the mental illness and the offending behaviour (Sahota & Chesterman, 1988), and hence to assist in determining appropriate treatment options. We refer to mentally ill sexual offenders in this chapter as being 'vulnerable' because of their capacity to relapse in terms of their mental health needs and because of the consequent need to tailor treatment accordingly, the treatment seeks to minimise the risk of undermining their mental health.

It could be argued that while treating sexual offenders who suffer from a form of mental illness is not new to forensic mental health specialists, the implications of a mental illness on treating sexual offending has not been systematically considered. This may be the result of the tendency of forensic mental health services in the United Kingdom to focus on mental health issues rather than the Risk-Need paradigm (Howells, Day & Thomas-Peter, 2004) that has dominated offender management. Mental health services in England and Wales have neglected offending behaviour to the extent that the Government introduced and passed the Mental Health Act 2007, which purports to have at its foundation a balance of meeting need and managing risk to

Assessment and Treatment of Sex Offenders: A Handbook. Edited by Anthony Beech, Leam Craig and Kevin Browne. © John Wiley & Sons Ltd, 2009.

the public. There is no longer doubt about the obligation that health services have in addressing offending behaviour. However, there has been insufficient examination of the motivation for offending in those with mental illness. Hodge and Renwick (2002) make this point when they argue:

> [T]here has been a remarkable lack of consideration given to the factors underpinning mentally disordered offenders' motivation for engagement and participation in the treatment process ... this disregard of motivational matters occurs despite the fact that ... these factors often bear heavily on clinical decision making regarding critical issues such as continuing detention and perceived dangerousness ... examination of motivational issues in this population is long overdue (p. 221).

Consequently, relatively little attention has, thus far, been afforded to the question of what adaptations may need to be made within mental health settings to the traditional interventions that have been offered to sexual offenders in prison or probation settings. We will attempt to address these issues here.

PREVALENCE

It could be argued that accommodating mental health issues within these traditional settings has long been neglected, despite the occurrence of mental health problems among prisoners (Singleton *et al.*, 1998). On behalf of the Department of Health, Singleton *et al.* (1998) sought to establish a baseline of the prevalence of psychiatric problems among prisoners in England and Wales. Prisoners were randomly selected from a list of all inmates. Selected prisoners were asked to take part in an initial interview (88% complied) and a random subsample of 20% was followed up for more detailed examination (75% complied). This resulted in a total of 3,142 full interviews at the initial stage and 505 follow-up interviews. Singleton *et al.* found that 10% of men on remand and 7% of sentenced men in a random subsample who took part in a follow-up clinical interview were assessed as having a functional psychosis (such as schizophrenia or manic depression) in the year prior to interview. A more general review of the criminogenic, psychiatric and psychological needs of offenders can be found in Thomas-Peter (2006).

Of the population, individuals with mental illness constitute only a small minority of sexual offenders (Sahota & Chesterman, 1988). The mental illnesses which such individuals might have include those with reactive depression with suicidal features, acute psychotic reactions with schizophrenic features, bipolar disorder and paranoid psychosis.

Information regarding the number of sexual offenders with mental illness is limited, though there are Home Office statistics available for restricted patients (a subgroup of patients detained compulsorily under the Mental Health Act, 1983) with a history of sexual offending. The proportion of restricted patients with mental illness with a history of sexual offending increased from 8.9% of all restricted patients admitted to National Health Service secure mental health facilities in 1983, to 9.5% in 1994 (Sahota & Chesterman, 1988). However, the percentage has subsequently decreased, with the figure for 2002 being 7.8% (Home Office, 2003). When the figures for unrestricted hospital inpatients are considered, it can be seen that the proportion of sexual offenders with mental illness has not changed significantly over the period 1992–2002; the figures are 5.9% in 1992, compared with 5.3% in 2002. There are no figures available for individuals with mental illness and a history of sexual offending who are currently managed as outpatients by mental health professionals. Neither are there data in relation to the proportion of imprisoned sexual offenders with mental illness, though it is well documented that a significant number of prisoners have mental health difficulties (Gunn, 1977; Singleton *et al.*, 1998), with levels of psychosis similar to that found in the general population; and a subgroup of these individuals will be sexual offenders.

Sahota and Chesterman (1998) suggest that less than 8% of men charged with sexual offences have an underlying mental illness, and that there are "few individuals for whom mental illness is said to be the cause of sexual offending" (p. 271). Craissati and Hodes (1992) suggest that police records show that only 0.3% of men charged with rape have a mental illness, but that sexual offences committed by psychotic men are likely to be "bizarre, violent and terrifying experiences for the victim". Hence, this group of individuals is perhaps of disproportionate concern to the general public, particularly in the current climate of public vigilance in relation to sexual offenders generally.

There are reports of patients who experience command hallucinations in the context of a schizophrenic illness, having sexually offended, or attempted to do so, as a direct response to auditory hallucinations (Jones, Huckele & Tanaghow, 1992). Other studies suggest that violence in general perpetrated by mentally ill individuals (including presumably sexual violence) may be attributable to delusions, jealousy or revenge (Taylor, 1985), but that half of psychotic men in one study claimed "ordinary, non-psychotic motives" for their offending behaviour (Taylor, 1985).

Much of the research and statistical information available in this field concerns male patients; however, Sahota and Chesterman (1998) note that in one available study of female sexual offenders, it appeared to be indecency offences which were connected to mental illness.

The only available study describing a population of mentally disordered sexual offenders is that of Craissati and Hodes (1992) who considered an inpatient sample of 11 patients admitted to a regional secure unit over a period of 4 years. Of their sample 10 had diagnoses of schizophrenia, one had a diagnosis of affective psychosis and the mean age was 25.7 years (range 19–30). Nine of the sample were Afro-Caribbean, although seven of these were born in the UK. One subject was white and one was a British born Asian. The offences reported within the sample were rape, indecent assault, buggery and attempted rape. Sometimes these sexual offences occurred in conjunction with physical violence such as grievous bodily harm. Generally the sexual offences were not overtly violent, though over half of the subjects had discontinued their psychotropic medication and had been deteriorating in mental state for some weeks prior to the offence. A minority were experiencing hallucinations at the time of the offence, and all but one were psychotic or developing psychosis prior to the offence, that is, their "normal inhibitory controls were breaking down" (p. 848). Hence, Craissati and Hodes suggest that mentally ill sex offenders are "not akin to the sociopathic type cited in the literature" (p. 848), but rather, tend to execute their offences impulsively.

TREATMENT ISSUES

There are aspects of traditional cognitive behavioural sexual offender treatment which are likely to be applicable both to mentally ill and non-mentally ill sex offenders. These might include work to address offence-related attitudes, cognitive distortions, cycles of offending and relapse prevention. There is no reason to believe that the same crimonogenic factors that influence non-mentally ill offenders will not also influence mentally ill offenders (see Howells, Day & Thomas-Peter, 2004). For some time, it has been acknowledged that among psychotic patients who offend sexually, the motives for offending are unlikely to be directly attributable to the illness (Taylor, 1985). However, it has also been suggested (Sahota & Chesterman, 1988) that mental illness may enable the offender to overcome inhibition and may increase motivation for offending, either through direct experience of psychosis, phenomena such as command hallucinations, or disinhibition and social disengagement. Whatever the causal mechanism is for these offences committed by people with mental illness, the important question for this chapter is the extent to which the presence of mental illness should influence treatment for sexual offending.

Traditionally, psychological treatment of sexual offenders has concentrated on the provision of group-based intervention, often undertaken on an outpatient basis (e.g., Hollin *et al.*, 2004), such as sexual offenders on Community Rehabilitation Orders with a condition of attendance at a group programme for sexual offenders run by the Probation Service. Treatment for detained sexual offenders, again, is generally undertaken on a group basis, usually within the prison service (e.g., Beech, Fisher & Beckett, 1998). However, we propose that such a 'groups for all' strategy might be counterproductive if applied to sexual offenders with mental health problems. While there are similar concerns about the safety of inmates of any kind institution who are labelled as 'sexual offenders', there are additional concerns about those who live among the mentally ill. First, in a mental health setting, there are patients who experience paranoid and delusional beliefs regarding sexual offenders. Secondly, if it can be argued that sexual offences arise through the disinhibiting effect of mental illness, so might violent behaviour occur by the same mechanism of disinhibition. In this way the content of belief, nature of associated emotion and behavioural expression of those with mental illness towards those who offend sexually, provide cause for concern. This illustrates one of the difficulties of setting up a group treatment programme for mentally ill sexual offenders in an inpatient setting. To identify a patient as a sexual offender by requiring them to attend a group programme which is clearly identified as 'the sex offenders' group', may place them at risk of harm from other service users.

There are similar problems with dealing with sexual offenders in any closed institution, but there may be additional implications of living in fear, for the mental well-being of those with mental illness.

Furthermore, in this population there are often difficulties in relation to patients' willingness to engage in treatment, which may be related to their current mental status. For example, those individuals who are currently experiencing significant psychotic symptoms may be unable to participate in any psychological endeavour until their symptoms have abated. These issues may, of course, be somewhat different in a long-term facility, where patients' mental states will often be more settled. To put this in another way, sexual offenders with mental illness are not always ready when the programme is ready. This requires special consideration, timing, preparation and flexibility.

There are two related issues that need to be considered in the question of dealing with sexual offending among the mentally ill. The first is the impact of stress, associated with treatment, on the probability of relapse in mental illness and risk of reoffending. The second is the extent to which we can moderate our interventions to minimise these risks. These issues are in part a matter of acknowledging a substantial body of knowledge (Malla *et al.*, 1990), although the mechanism by which stress causes relapse is unclear (Gispen-de Wied, 2000). In any case, the association between stress and relapse has been available to psychology for some time, but it has failed to influence conventional forensic interventions.

CONFRONTING OFFENDERS AS A MECHANISM OF CHANGING THEM

It is far from certain whether the use of challenging techniques that have been commonly used in forensic interventions will positively change attitudes, risk-related behaviours or the motivation of individuals in treatment, and may even make things worse, especially for vulnerable subjects. Latterly this is starting to be acknowledged, through the recognition that working positively with offenders is likely to yield more favourable results and that an excessive focus on risk may lead to unhelpful confrontational strategies (Marshall *et al.*, 2005).

While Boster and Mongeau (1984) conclude that threat and fear can add positively to attitude change, several factors work against this. Considerable evidence supports the finding that where individuals believe that they do not have the skills to cope with threat or fearful circumstances, a 'threat appeal' to attitudes has an opposite or 'boomerang' effect on attitudes (Petty & Wegener, 1998). The foundation work supporting this derives from the protective motivation theory offered by Rogers (1983). As this applies to the mentally ill, it may be argued that the cognitive depletion that often accompanies recurring bouts of schizophrenia or the cognitive debilitation arising from medication, reduces the real and perceived capacity of the mentally ill to cope with challenge, and hence they may be more resistant to change; worse, more likely to harden their attitudes against those who seek to change them.

A better known framework within which to consider confrontation is Cognitive Dissonance Theory (Festinger, 1957), which is one of several theories postulating a general motive to maintain cognitive consistency. In brief, where a belief and attitudes or an attitude and behaviour are not congruent, they are described as 'dissonant'. The mental state associated with this is argued to be aversive, and individuals will be motivated to redress this by making them congruent and this implies changing an attitude. Within the treatment for sexual offenders, we might consider that confronting someone with the inconsistencies of their beliefs, actions and representation of events amounts to a deliberate creation of dissonance, in the hope that it will be resolved with a change of attitude. However, it is naive to be confident that change will occur in the direction hoped for. Resolution can occur equally well with the rejection of the therapist's perspective. Conventionally, individuals may bolster their pro-offending beliefs and commitment to denial by finding independent means of making apparently disparate beliefs seem congruent. Alternatively, they may minimise the significance of one of the dissonant beliefs (Simon, Greenberg & Brehm, 1995).

There is some evidence to suggest that where an attitude and behaviour are dissonant, it is the attitude that is more likely to change in order to become congruent with the behaviour, than vice versa (Festinger & Carlsmith, 1959, cited in Gilbert, Fiske & Lindsay, 1998). This means that among vulnerable offenders where the fragile belief, "I am a good person" is juxtaposed, through a confrontational process, with "harming children is bad", the dissonance may be resolved by the reduction of self-esteem rather than a change of behaviour. If low self-worth is associated with offending or self-harm, the therapeutic process has put this offender and the public at risk.

Convincing evidence is also available to indicate that the aversive experience created by dissonance can be indirectly alleviated, not by a reconfiguration of cognitions or related behaviour, but by any other means that would make someone feel less unpleasant. This would include the use of substances (Steele, Southwick & Critchlow, 1981), watching movies (Cooper, Fazio & Rhodewaldt, 1978) or whatever means of discomfort reduction occurs first (Aronson, Blanton & Cooper, 1995), which would include, for sex offenders, masturbation to deviant images and perhaps offending behaviour. In other words, we are at risk of generating offence-related behaviour through the process of confrontation.

THE IMPACT OF GROUP INTERVENTIONS

There is evidence that for some people intensive group interactions such as those found in a Therapeutic Community will have harmful effects[1] (Rice, Harris & Cormier,

---

[1] All Therapeutic Communities share the primary characteristic of using the influence of the social group to contain and change behaviour. It is the social exchange between members of the community that is the therapeutic process.

1992). This has recently influenced the Prison Service in the UK to develop special programmes for those with high Psychopathy Checklist-Revised (PCL-R; Hare, 1991) scores. The Prison Service Sex Offender Treatment Programme (SOTP) has explicitly acknowledged the importance of treatment style (SOTP Theory Manual, 2000) in managing all sex offenders. The initiative for this has come from empirical research (Beech & Fordham, 1997) about the therapeutic climate of treatment programmes and the relationship of this to outcome. However, there has been evidence for almost half a century from social psychology that there are risks associated with poorly conducted group work, in respect of attitude change, that have not been addressed by recent changes to programmes.

In general, the process of asking offenders to reveal their stories in front of others has a range of undesirable consequences for vulnerable offenders, and perhaps others. This process of exposing a group of people to the persuasive message of the therapist, one by one, emulates a well researched area known as the effects of 'forewarning' on attitude change. In summary, the evidence suggests that as an audience becomes aware that their individual attitudes will be challenged and as they hear the 'attack arguments' being made, they prepare themselves with counter-arguments, providing they have the time (Brehm, 1966; Freedman & Sears, 1965; Petty & Cacioppo, 1977). In fact, even before the arguments are known, simply knowing that someone is going to try and persuade you that they are right and you are wrong about something is enough to prepare individuals to resist the persuasive impact of the message (Petty & Cacioppo, 1979). There are methods to counter this effect associated with 'distraction', but they are generally not to be found in conventional sex offender programmes.

The group process in treating sex offenders has additional likely effects that may be undesirable. If someone thinks they are accountable to others in respect of an unimportant topic, but is unsure of how their opinion will be received, their inclination is to adopt a moderate position on the topic to start with. As the group's view becomes known, the attitude of the presenter will move in the direction of the group (Caikin, 1980). However, this is not the situation in treating sex offenders who usually have a good idea of what is coming. In these circumstances, individuals are likely to choose the most defensible position in anticipation of the interaction with the audience (Chen, Shechter & Chaiken, 1996). Of course, this means that they are encouraged by the process of treatment to minimise, deny and obscure the truth of what they have done, as they have learned that this is the most defendable way to represent themselves.

Other evidence argues strongly that where an individual has already expressed a view on a matter of real importance to them, the process of being subsequently accountable to an audience leads them to justify their initial position and polarise their attitudes against the audience (Cialdini, Petty & Cacioppo, 1981; Lambert *et al.*, 1996; Tetlock, 1992; Tetlock, Skitka & Boettger, 1989). In other words, it may be highly undesirable to ask sex offenders to tell their story to a group, knowing that it is a distortion, and then have them defend themselves against opposing views, in a public forum. This is because we know before asking them to do this that it may make that story more difficult to change subsequently.

The risks associated with a conventional approach of treating offenders in groups involving the expectation of disclosure and the systematic confronting of issues includes:

- Undermining the credibility of workers,
- Hardening of offence-supportive attitudes,
- Encouraging defensive or helpless reactions,
- Creating dissonance with unpredictable resolutions,
- Increasing offending potential,
- Promoting superficial adaptation to treatment circumstances.

The process of treatment is also at risk of being elongated by virtue of the increased difficulty associated with overcoming better-defended attitudes.

Some Possible Solutions

Attending to individual needs and capacities of those we seek to change is not new to psychological therapy, but it may be underdeveloped when addressing sexual offending among the mentally ill. The link between the forensic 'need' and helping individuals change has two modern sources of guidance that might be useful starting points. The first is the new literature on 'readiness' for psychological treatment (see Hodge & Renwick, 2002; Howells & Day, 2003; Ward *et al.*, 2004), and the second is an older theme developed by Hubble, Duncan and Miller (1999) in their edited volume of what works in psychological therapy. The former focuses on the characteristics of the offender and the context in which therapy may occur. The latter offers accumulated wisdom about the psychology of change. Both need to be understood to make best use of treatment opportunities with the mentally ill.

The concept of readiness has been recently applied to those with personality disorder (Howells, Day & Bryan, 2005) and is broadly defined as the presence of characteristics (states or dispositions) within either the client or the therapeutic situation that promotes engagement in therapy and enhances therapeutic change. Described as a more inclusive concept than 'responsivity', readiness considers cognitive, affective, behavioural, volitional and personal identity factors within the individual. The concept also accounts for external readiness conditions in which the conditions of treatment, its timing and availability of supportive factors is seen as increasing readiness for therapy.

An important aspect of this contribution to psychological therapy in corrections is the implication that the effectiveness of psychological therapy programmes cannot be evaluated properly unless considered in the context of external readiness factors. It is also evident that we cannot assume groups of offenders being subjected to, for example, CBT programmes, will be homogenous with respect to internal readiness. Several problems arise from this. It is probable that therapy will have a more positive outcome on those with relatively high treatment readiness. A programme designed for high readiness offenders will be seen as less effective when the group is comprised of both low and high readiness participants, as the treatment effect is likely to be diluted. The second problem is the effect on those who would otherwise benefit (high readiness individuals) of having low readiness individuals in the programme. It is probable that this effect is not likely to be positive and as a consequence, CBT psychological treatment may be appraised as having had a poor impact on those it should have done really well with, causing the programme to display poor general outcome.

As yet, there are no guidelines about what 'readiness' conditions should prevail to ensure the best outcome from psychological therapies addressing offending behaviour with those with mental health problems. However, some guidance may be available. Hubble *et al.* (1999, p. 6) have argued that outside of a small number of examples where particular kinds of patients can be shown to improve in response to a particular intervention no significant differences among approaches to therapy can be demonstrated. However, models/techniques of therapy do make a contribution to positive client change. They constitute one of four factors that reliably account for most of the variance in positive change among clients. These are:

- *Extra-therapeutic factors* (accounting for 40% of client change) outside of the therapy process but which aid recovery. They might include social support, spiritual faith, membership in the community, and the support of family.
- *Relationship factors* (accounting for 30% of client change) include common therapeutic relationship-mediated variables such as caring, empathy, warmth, acceptance, affirmation and encouraging risk taking.
- *Hope/expectancy factors* (accounting for 15% of client change) (or placebo factors) are associated with the faith of both therapist and client that a positive outcome is possible and likely from the therapy undertaken.
- *Model/technique factors* (accounting for 15% of client change). Hubble *et al.* argue that all successful interventions, in one way or another, facilitate change by preparing people to be different in their understanding, experience of emotion and behaviour.

In a medium-secure mental health facility in the UK, we have developed a 'modular' programme for psychiatric patients who have a history of sexual offending, which seeks to exploit the last three of these factors. There are insufficient numbers of subjects to report on outcome, but the strategy has been useful to us in demonstrating that this group can be engaged in therapeutic work without apparent deterioration in mental health, providing it is done in a way that they can tolerate.

A programme was developed including a number of modules, a curriculum of issues to be covered, and a set of homework tasks to use with individual clients. Key to the success of this was the use of clinicians who were familiar to each patient. This meant the quality of relationship between clinician and patient was maximised and the learning style and capacity of each patient could be considered in respect of each module and the pace of therapy.

The treatment programme is provided and evaluated (psychometrically, clinically and via client feedback) by the Psychology Department, with the involvement of other disciplines such as medical and social work personnel.

The attitude of the therapists is seen as central to the treatment process, particularly in the light of research which shows that confrontational style on the part of therapists is negatively related to achievement of treatment goals, and empathy, warmth, rewardingness, flexibility and directiveness are all positively related to indices of beneficial change (Marshall, 2005). Lea, Auburn and Kibblewhite (1999) suggest that in order to maintain appropriate attitudes and values, and hence to effect therapeutic change in sexual offenders, professionals require ongoing training and support. This would seem particularly necessary when professionals are working with a group doubly disadvantaged in terms of others' perceptions, by their mental illness and their status as sexual offenders. Hence, robust training and supervision processes are in place for therapists providing treatment, which include explicit discussion of therapists' attitudes and feelings towards the clients and their offending behaviour. Flexibility includes providing time at the beginning of each session for the individual to discuss any current issues or concerns, such that matters relating to their mental state can be addressed in sessions. This may, at times, necessitate a delay in offending-focused work in order to deal with current difficulties which often relate to mental health issues.

THE DENIAL TRAINING PHASE

An important aspect of the treatment programme is what we refer to as 'denial training'. Initially the client is discouraged from disclosing their offending or why they offended. The principle here, which is shared with those in treatment, is that we must do everything to ensure they get the story 'right at the first attempt'. This is difficult because often they have already committed themselves to a story with relatives or other agencies, but it is important that we do not compound these falsifications and make them even more difficult to change. The first few sessions are spent understanding the concept of denial. They learn that denial is expected, normal, and adaptive in many circumstances, but it also has serious consequences which can put themselves and others at risk, and obstruct their own opportunities to establish a conventional life. For each individual we develop a general denial profile, which identifies the kinds of issues that are denied in everyday life, their motives for denial and the various methods that they may employ to deny things to themselves and others.

It is helpful to remove from vulnerable offenders the threat of being 'damned if they do' say why they have offended and 'damned if they don't'. Often offenders complain that they are reluctant to explain themselves because, when they do, they are accused of making excuses or shifting the blame to others. If they do not explain themselves, they are accused of being in denial, without insight or of obstructing treatment. To deal with this offenders are encouraged to distinguish between an 'explanation' and an 'excuse' and recognise the importance of this distinction.

THE DISCLOSURE PHASE

From early in the sessions it is made clear that a full understanding of each individual and complete disclosure is an iterative process. Disclosure is acknowledged to be a difficult process in which mistakes and omissions are likely to be made. Several features of how this is done may be of interest. They are reminded of how important it is to get it right first time and they are advised that they are likely to need help to do this. They are also warned that they are likely to make mistakes, but they must be vigilant if what they say sounds like the subject's denial profile. At any time, individuals have the right to add to their previous statements or employ what is described as the 'elastic clock'. This metaphorical device allows patients to go back to when they made any statement or disclosure and change it, without penalty or castigation. Why should there be castigation? These changes invariably represent reflections that are associated with accepting more responsibility or culpability.

The programme takes the view that 'incomplete' disclosure is tolerable in some circumstances. There are times when that last morsel of information adds significantly to our understanding of an offender's behaviour and risk. However, the marginal utility of pursuing that information is often small or even negative. While there is a world of difference between being the tenth victim and being not victimised at all, there is often hardly any useful clinical difference between an offender accepting responsibility for nine or ten very similar offences. The conflict of dealing with differences of this kind serve only to distort the function of therapy and in these circumstances we do the public and the victims a disservice by a preoccupation with marginal information rather than risk reduction.

Participants are invited to provide their story and then we reflect on how that representation works for them, as an excuse or explanation. Confrontation on these matters is not necessary and neither would it be helpful.

The disclosure phase includes formulation work relating to the individual's sexual offending, and we discuss the contributory factors from individuals' histories. We include in this process matters relating to the individual's mental health problems, and their influence on the offending behaviour. For example, the role of delusions and impulse control issues are considered. The formulation is represented diagrammatically (Ryle, 1991), initially on a flipchart sheet, and a typed copy is then given to the offender for future reference. We reduce counter-argument formation by staying as close to what was done and how it was done rather than why it was done. We do get to the question of 'why', but in the first instance the facts are important to get right. Subsequently many aspects of the programme are very similar to those contained within traditional approaches.

THE CYCLE OF OFFENDING PHASE

As their initial disclosure is completed, we have found it helpful to assist offenders to order their thoughts by explicitly employing Finkelhor's (1984) stages of offending model. These stages allow us to focus on the motivation to offend, how a person overcomes internal inhibitions to offending, how they create the opportunity to offend and overcome the resistance of the victim. This is a process of inquiry and exploration rather than assumptions and expectations. This teaches offenders much about themselves as individuals, and the speed and quality of the work done in this phase is directly linked to how well we have completed the denial and disclosure phases. Wolf's (1984) original cycle of offending provides a useful framework to assist offenders seeing the repeated pattern of behaviour but it has limited value in any particular case.

The experience of this small programme is that it is more helpful to distinguish between a 'foundation cycle' of pathology and an 'offence cycle'. The foundation cycle of pathology depicts the development of needs that may subsequently be met by offending behaviour, but which may then exist independently of the original pathology.

Case Example

One patient experienced powerlessness, helplessness and isolation as a child and these feelings continued into adulthood, when he became capable of depression and self-harm. His social inhibition and poor confidence resulted in him being unable to express himself adequately with the result that he developed passive-aggressive strategies to recoup self-esteem within an unsatisfactory relationship. He was left with a high need for affiliation, acceptance and intimacy, made worse by his capacity to ruminate about unfairness and his sense of being deserving. Nothing of this history would necessarily result in him becoming a sex offender, but it does help us understand his helplessness and self-harm. The offence cycle in this case began when he started bathing his children, resentful that his partner had abandoned him to these tasks to go out with friends. It transpired that it was good fun, the children enjoyed it and seemed to welcome his attention and responded affectionately. He began to fantasise and eventually created the opportunity to offend by encouraging his partner to go out. He found ways of justifying his behaviour and thereby he removed any brake on his conduct. The offence cycle continued for a matter of months, during which time his needs were met while his children were damaged. When it all came to light, the foundation cycle of pathology re-emerged with depression and self-harm.

In this case there was a real risk of precipitating significant mental health problems and self-harm. He demonstrated this summarily when he attended a traditional group programme that resulted in a hospital admission following an overdose. Despite this, his risk had to be addressed. He was very reluctant to attend our programme, but was persuaded to simply turn up, without obligation to say anything in the first few sessions. He found himself able to participate fully after several sessions and once he came to understand his own denial and how obvious it was to others, he disclosed the full extent of his abusive behaviour.

Our experience is that once the offence cycle has been established, it has a life of its own and has the potential to continue, regardless of any resolution of the foundation cycle of pathology. However, this does not mean that it is only the offence cycle issues that must be addressed. Without dealing with some of the foundation cycle issues, the offence cycle is always at risk of being started again, in the right circumstances.

VICTIM EMPATHY MODULE

The victim empathy module would be recognised by anyone familiar with the process and includes: Victim apology letters; Developing empathic knowledge through teaching of the effects of child sexual abuse; Evocation of childhood feelings; Reading and viewing video accounts of adult survivors of child sexual abuse; Perspective-taking exercises; Review of cognitive distortions.

THE RELAPSE PREVENTION PHASE

The relapse prevention plan for each individual takes a common form (see Laws, 1989) although it is simplified to suit the abilities of the clients. It has been helpful to construct a relapse prevention 'checklist' for each person, drawing on each of the previous phases. This checklist, and a list of appropriate responses where a concern is raised, is transferred to a pocket-size laminated card that is to be referred to at daily or weekly intervals, or at times of emergency. During this phase we refer explicitly to techniques for controlling impulses, as the research shows poor impulse control to be an important factor in sexual offending (Marlatt, 1989). Patients are encouraged to identify specific techniques for coping when their mental state is deteriorating, and to include in their relapse prevention plan a list of reasons why they do not wish to reoffend, to use as an aide-memoire at such times.

From a psychological perspective, relapse prevention is also thought to be the intervention of choice with individuals who have bipolar disorder (e.g., George, 1998). Hence, where appropriate, a relapse prevention plan directly focusing on the interplay between the individual's sexual offending and their mental health issues, can be prepared, and should cover, for example, issues of disinhibition, eye contact and personal space which are likely to be important in individuals with mental health difficulties who have sexually offended.

It is essential that concurrent with treatment focusing on offending behaviour, there is ongoing intervention relating to the mental illness issues, including medication-based treatment and psychological intervention such as mental health awareness and symptom-focused work. There needs to be regular communication between members of the team providing treatment so that intervention can be tailored to the individual's current situation and mental state. This highlights the importance of ensuring that, although a treatment 'manual' is useful to guide therapists, therapists are aware that they should regard it as a guide and not as something to be applied rigidly.

CONCLUSIONS AND RECOMMENDATIONS

This chapter has described issues to be taken into account when considering the provision of offence-focused treatment to sexual offenders with mental health difficulties, an under-developed and under-researched topic. This clientele constitutes a small, but publicly visible subgroup of sexual offenders. An example of a treatment programme developed in a medium-secure mental health facility is described. This emphasises the importance of adapting traditional group-based approaches, offering individually-tailored treatment focusing on therapist attitudes, including flexibility, and formulation, taking into account issues relating to the offenders' mental health difficulties. Denial training, disclosure, cycle of offending, victim empathy and relapse prevention phases are central to this process as well as ensuring that mental health issues are concurrently addressed. It is suggested that such treatment will offer the best possible protection to offenders themselves and to the public, by seeking to avoid some of the potential pitfalls within traditional treatment approaches.

REFERENCES

Aronson, J., Blanton, H. & Cooper, J. (1995). From dissonance to disidentification: Selectivity in the self-affirmation process. *Journal of Personality and Social Psychology, 68*, 986–996.

Beech, A., Fisher, D. & Beckett, R. (1998). *Step 3: An evaluation of the prison sex offender treatment programme.* London: HMSO. UK Home Office Occasional Report. Home Office Publications Unit, 50, Queen Anne's Gate, London, SW1 9AT, England. Available electronically from: www.homeoffice .gov.uk/rds/pdfs/occ-step3.pdf

Beech, A.R. & Fordham, A. (1997). Therapeutic climate of sex offender treatment programs. *Sexual Abuse: A Journal of Research and Treatment, 9*, 219–237.

Boster, F.J. & Mongeau, P. (1984). Fear arousing persuasive messages. In R.N. Bostrom (Ed.), *Communication Yearbook*, Volume 8 (pp. 330–375). Beverley Hills, CA: Sage.

Brehm, J.W. (1966). *A theory of psychological reactance.* San Diego, CA: Academic Press.

Chaikin, S. (1980). Heuristic versus systemic information processing in the use of source versus message cues in persuasion. *Journal of Personality and Social Psychology, 39*, 752–766.

Chen, S., Shechter, D. & Chaikin, S. (1996). Getting at the truth or getting along: Accuracy versus impression motivated heuristic and systemic processing. *Journal of Personality and Social Psychology, 71*, 262–275.

Cialdini, R.B., Petty, R.E. & Cacioppo, J.T. (1981). Attitude and attitude change. *Annual Review of Psychology, 32*, 357–404.

Cooper, J., Fazio, R.H. & Rhodewalt, F. (1978). Dissonance and humour: Evidence for the undifferentiated nature of dissonance arousal. *Journal of Personality and Social Psychology, 36*, 280–285.

Craissati, J. & Hodes, P. (1992). Mentally ill sex offenders: the experience of a regional service unit. *British Journal of Psychiatry, 161*, 846–849.

Festinger, L. (1957). *A theory of cognitive dissonance.* Palo Alto, CA: Stanford University Press.

Finkelhor, D. (1984). *Child sexual abuse: New theory and research*. New York: The Free Press.

Freedman, J.L. & Sears, S.O. (1965). Warning distraction and resistance to influence. *Journal of Personality and Social Psychology, 95*, 262–266.

Gardner, D. (2005). Getting it together: Integrative approaches to formulation. *Clinical Psychology Forum, 15*, 10–15.

George, S. (1998). Towards an integrated treatment approach for manic depression. *Journal of Mental Health, 7*(2), 145–156.

Gilbert, D., Fiske, S. & Lindsay, G. (1998). *The handbook of social psychology* (4th edn, Volume 1). Boston, MA: McGraw Hill.

Gispen-de Wied, C.C. (2000). Stress in schizophrenia: an integrative view. *European Journal of Pharmacology, 405*(1–3), 375–384.

Gunn, J. (1977). Criminal behaviour and mental disorder. *British Journal of Psychiatry, 130*, 317–329.

Hare, R.D. (1991). *Manual for the Hare Psychopathy Checklist-Revised*. Toronto, Canada: Multi-Health Systems.

Hodge, J. & Renwick, S.J. (2002). Motivating mentally abnormal offenders. In M. McMurran (Ed.), *Motivating offenders to change: A guide to engagement in therapy* (pp. 221–234). Chichester: John Wiley & Sons, Ltd.

Hollin, C., Palmer, E., McGuire, J. *et al.* (2004). *Pathfinder programmes in the Probation Service: A retrospective analysis*. Home Office Publications Unit, 50, Queen Anne's Gate, London, SW1 9AT, England.

Home Office. (2003). *Statistics of mentally disordered offenders 2002 (England and Wales)*. Home Office Publications Unit, 50, Queen Anne's Gate, London, SW1 9AT, England.

Howells, K. & Day, A. (2003). Readiness for anger management: Clinical and theoretical issues. *Clinical Psychology Review, 23*, 319–337.

Howells, K., Day, A. & Bryan, J. (2005). Readiness for Treatment in High Risk Offenders with Personality Disorders. International Association of Forensic Mental Health Services, 5th Annual Conference, Melbourne, Australia, April 18–21, 2005.

Howells, K., Day, A. & Thomas-Peter, B.A. (2004). Changing violent behaviour: Criminological and Psychiatric Models Compared. *Journal of Forensic Psychiatry and Psychology, 15*, 391–406.

Hubble, M.A., Duncan, B.L. & Miller, S.D. (Eds), (1999). *The heart and soul of change: What works in therapy*. Washington, DC: American Psychological Association.

Jones, G., Huckele, P. & Tanaghow, A. (1992). Command hallucinations, schizophrenia and sexual assault. *Irish Journal of Psychological Medicine, 9*, 47–49.

Lambert, J.A., Cronin, S., Chasten, A.L. & Lickel, B. (1996). Private versus public expressions of racial prejudice. *Journal of Experimental Social Psychology, 32*, 437–459.

Laws, D.R. (Ed.) (1989). *Relapse prevention with sex offenders*. New York: Guilford.

Lea, S., Auburn, T. & Kibblewhite, K. (1999). Working with sex offenders: the perceptions and experiences of professionals and paraprofessionals. *International Journal of Offender Therapy and Comparative Criminology, 43*, 103–119.

Malla A.K., Cortese, L., Shaw T.S. & Ginsberg, B. (1990). Life events and relapse in schizophrenia. A one-year prospective study. *Social Psychiatry and Psychiatric Epidemiology, 25*, 221–224.

Marlatt, G.A. (1989). How to handle the PIG. In R. Laws (Ed.), *Relapse prevention with sex offenders* (pp. 227–235). New York: Guilford Press.

Marshall, W.L. (2005). Therapist style in sexual offender treatment: Influences on indices of change. *Sexual Abuse: A Journal of Research and Treatment, 17*, 109–116.

Marshall, W.L., Ward, T., Mann, R. *et al.* (2005). Working positively with sexual offenders. *Journal of Interpersonal Violence, 20*, 1096–1114.

Petty, R.E. & Cacioppo, J.T. (1977). Forewarning, cognitive responding and resistance to persuasion. *Journal of Personality and Social Psychology, 35*, 645–655.

Petty, R.E. & Cacioppo, J.T. (1979). Effects of forewarning of persuasive intent and involvement on cognitive responses. *Personality and Social Psychology Bulletin, 5*, 173–176.

Petty, R.E. & Wegener, D.T. (1998). Attitude change, multiple roles for persuasion variables. In D.T. Gilbert, S.T. Fiske. & G. Lindsay (Eds), *The handbook of social psychology* (4th edn, Volume 1) (pp. 323–390). Boston, MA: McGraw Hill.

Rice, M.E., Harris, G.T. & Cormier, C.A. (1992). An evaluation of a maximum security therapeutic community for psychopaths and other mentally disordered offenders. *Law and Human Behavior, 16,* 399–412.

Rogers, R.W. (1983). Cognitive and physiological processes in fear appeals and attitude change: A revised theory of protection motivation. In J.T. Cacioppo & R.E. Petty (Eds), *Social psychophysiology: A sourcebook* (pp. 153–176). New York: Guilford.

Ryle, A. (1991). *Cognitive-analytic therapy: Active participation in change.* Chichester: John Wiley & Sons, Ltd.

Sahota, K. & Chesterman, P. (1988). Sexual offending in the context of mental illness. *The Journal of Forensic Psychiatry, 9,* 267–280.

Sex Offender Treatment Programme (SOTP) (2000). *Theory Manual.* Offending Behaviour Treatment Team. HM Prison Service, Offending Behaviour Programmes Unit. London: Home Office.

Simon, L., Greenberg, J. & Brehm, J. (1995). Trivialisation: The forgotten mode of disonance reduction. *Journal of Personality and Social Psychology, 68,* 247–260.

Singleton, N., Meltzer, H., Gatward, R.*et al.* (1998). *Psychiatric morbidity among prisoners in England and Wales; Summary Report.* Office of National Statistics on behalf of the Department of Health, London. Available from The Stationery Office at: http://www.tsoshop.co.uk/bookstore.asp?FO=1159966&Action=Book&ProductID=0116210451.

Steel, C.M., Southwick, L. & Critchlow, B. (1981). Dissonance and alcohol: Drinking your troubles away. *Journal of Personality and Social Psychology, 41,* 831–846.

Taylor, P. (1985). Motives for offending among violent and psychotic men. *British Journal of Psychiatry, 147,* 491–498.

Tetlock, P.E. (1992). The impact of accountability on judgment and choice: Towards a social contingency model. *Advances in Experimental Social Psychology, 25,* 361–376.

Tetlock, P.E., Skitka, L. & Boettger, R. (1989). Social and cognitive strategies of coping with accountability: Conformity, complexity and bolstering. *Journal of Personality and Social Psychology, 57,* 632–641.

Thomas-Peter B.A. (2006). The needs of offenders and the process of changing them. In G. Towl (Ed.), *Psychology Research in Prisons* (pp. 40–53). Oxford: Blackwell.

Ward, T., Day, A., Howells, K. & Birgden, A. (2004). The multifactor offender readiness model. *Aggression and Violent Behavior, 9,* 645–673.

Wolf, S.C. (1984). *A multifactor model of deviant sexuality.* Paper presented at the Third International Conference on Victimology, Lisbon, Portugal.

22

Working with Sex Offenders with Personality Disorder Diagnoses

LAWRENCE JONES

INTRODUCTION

In this chapter interventions addressing risk of sexual reoffending with people with personality disorder diagnoses will be explored. As there is very little evidence of any particular approach working with this group it is important to recognise that we are in the course of a developmental process, as opposed to presenting the 'definitive model' of treatment. Because of the heterogeneity and complexity in this population formulation-based interventions need to be informed by a wide range of theoretical perspectives and are inevitably complex. The field is too young to arrive at a definitive model, and to do so, even if it were evidence based, would potentially represent premature closure. Practice needs to be an evolving process building on emerging evidence, clinical experience and critical reflection.

PERSONALITY DISORDER AMONG SEX OFFENDERS

While, the construct of personality disorder is problematic (e.g., Livesley, 2001) the literature on personality disorder and sexual offending suggests some utility for the construct of personality. In this section this literature is reviewed. Langevin *et al.* (1988) found that 90% of sexual offenders had at least one personality disorder and that sexual offenders as a group were more avoidant, dependent, passive aggressive, schizoid, and less narcissistic and obsessional, when compared with non-sex offenders. Ahlmeyer *et al.* (2003) found that sex offenders generally were more schizoid, avoidant, depressive, dependent, self-defeating and schizotypal. General population offenders were, by contrast, more antisocial, narcissistic and sadistic. Jones (2007) in

Assessment and Treatment of Sex Offenders: A Handbook. Edited by Anthony Beech, Leam Craig and Kevin Browne. © John Wiley & Sons Ltd, 2009.

a review of the literature suggested that whilst there was no consistent link between specific personality disorders and particular offences, there was a tendency for mixed offenders and offenders against adults to have personality disorders identified by Blackburn (1998) as being in the dominant section of the interpersonal circle (narcissistic, antisocial, histrionic), and offenders against children in the submissive section (schizoid, dependent, avoidant). This pattern is suggested by Jones's (1997) proposal that people tend to offend against others that they consider to be equal or lower than they are in perceived dominance. The presence of personality disorder in differing types of sexual abuse will now be briefly examined.

Rape

Proulx *et al.* (1994) note that models of sexual offending do not give much role to personality, other than antisocial and narcissistic personality. They highlighted the heterogeneity of rapists and the tendency for theorists to develop 'one-size-fits-all' models. In their own study, they found that 'more physically violent' rapists were more antisocial, and less violent rapists had a higher incidence of avoidant, dependent, passive-aggressive and schizoid personality disorders. Bogaerts, Vanheule and Declercq (2005) present a case for personality disorders facilitating 'sexually abusive acts' and review evidence that rapists are more antisocial and narcissistic. Proulx *et al.* (1994) proposed that the interpersonal and intra-personal processes associated with sex offenders' personality disorder are likely to be manifested during the offence process. The offence is conceptualised as a replication in the sexual domain of the habitual mode of relating associated with an individual's personality disorder. They give the example of an individual with antisocial personality disorder who characteristically perceives himself as a victim of injustice and then, uses this sense of injustice to justify violent behaviour. In relationships, they suggest, this individual is likely to see himself as a victim of injustice, become angered and then potentially offend sexually. Moreover Proulx *et al.* propose that sexual offending can be analysed in terms of affective processes, driven by personality; the personality disorder underpinning a characteristic way of interacting and feeling, is played out in the offence process. Fantasies are also seen to replay this characteristic interactive style.

Sexual Homicide

Porter *et al.* (2003) found a higher incidence of high Psychopathic Checklist-Revised (PCL-R; Hare 1991) scorers amongst sexual homicides. Briken, Nika and Berner (1999) found narcissism, chronic isolation and 'tendency to perversity' to be higher amongst people who had committed repeat sexual homicides when compared with those that had committed a single sexual homicide. Hill *et al.* (2004) found the following prevalence of personality disorders in a sample of sexual murderers: antisocial (27.1%), borderline (18.7%), sadistic (17.5%), NOS (13.9%), schizoid (16.3%), avoidant (12.7%), and narcissistic (9.6%). Beech *et al.* (2006) identified three types of serious sexual offenders:

1. *Grievance motivated offenders* with more borderline and paranoid traits, an anger motive, external locus of control, high impulsivity, low self-restraint, a high level of justification for rape, a high level of reported hostility to women; were likely to be in a relationship break-up before the offence; and their offences were likely to include repeated uncontrolled beatings and stabbings.
2. *Sexually motivated offenders* were more narcissistic, predominantly sexually motivated, more likely to have sexual previous convictions than violent ones, more socially integrated, have fewer substance abuse problems, are not impulsive, hold less negative views about relationships, have fewer rape-supporting beliefs and attitudes, have lower levels of anger and interpersonal aggression, are more likely to attack a stranger, are more likely to have one main partner prior to offence, to acknowledge going through 'stages of rape' (Multiphasic Sex Inventory Rape Scale; Nichols & Molinder 1984), and to be motivated to work on their problems.
3. *Sadistic offenders* (see section below on sadistic offenders).

Child Abuse

The evidence for personality disorder among child abusers is mixed. Marshall (1996) and Shea (1996) both found that personality disorder did not distinguish 'paedophiles' from normal controls. However, Raymond *et al.* (1999) found 60% of a sample of child sex offenders met *Diagnostic and Statistical Manual of Mental Disorders, Fourth Edition* (DSM-IV; APA, 2000) criteria for at least one personality disorder. Bogaerts *et al.* (2005) found that 'paedophiles' showed more dependent, avoidant and schizoid personality disorders than rapists and more schizoid and antisocial traits than non-sexual offenders. The diagnostic confusion around Asperger's syndrome, autistic spectrum disorders or pervasive developmental disorders, and schizoid personality disorder (e.g., case 'IJ' in Murrie *et al.*, 2002) needs to be borne in mind. The observations in the literature about 'theory of mind' difficulties amongst sex offenders (e.g., Keenan & Ward 2004) is also suggestive of some commonality between autistic spectrum disorders and some kinds of sexual offending. Bogaerts, Vervaeke and Goethals (2004) concluded that narcissistic, schizoid and avoidant personality disorders were more typical of intra-familial offenders and antisocial, narcissistic and passive-aggressive personality disorders were more typical of extra-familial child offenders. Ahlmeyer *et al.* (2003), comparing child sex offenders with rapists, found child sex offenders to be more dependent.

Bogaerts, Vanheule and Desmet (2006) argue that schizoid personality disorder is particularly associated with insecurely attached child sexual offending. They hypothesise that this is due to being blocked from engaging in adult relationships by bad experiences with age-appropriate adults, sexual dysfunction or limited relational and social skills. They also argue that they find children to be emotionally congruent and feel comfortable in their presence. They highlight the importance of using a positive therapeutic relationship to develop an understanding of their attachment and abusive histories, possibly using Cognitive Analytic Therapy (e.g. Pollock, Stowell-Smith and Göpfert, 2006).

Psychopathic Sexual Offending

Psychopathy is associated more with the nature and severity of sexual violence than with its likelihood (e.g. Hart *et al.*, 2003). Porter *et al.* (2000), for example, found that most offenders who offended against both adults and children were high PCL-R scorers and rapists were generally higher in their scores on the PCL-R than child 'molesters'. They identify psychopathy as being associated with sadistic sexual arousal (see also Rice, Harris & Quinsey, 1990; Serin, 1994) and higher levels of violence in the commission of sexual offences. Porter *et al.* (2003) found that there were high levels of psychopathy amongst sexual homicides and that offences of high PCL-R scorers had higher levels of sadistic and gratuitous violence in them. Hare *et al.* (2000) conclude that the offences of sexual offenders with high PCL-R psychopathy tend to be more violent or sadistic in comparison to non-psychopathic sexual offenders. Jackson and Richards (2007), and Vess, Murphy and Arkowitz (2004) also identify offence types associated with different levels of psychopathy; rapists and mixed offenders having the highest scores and 'child molesters' having the lowest scores. Knight and Guay (2006) propose three types of sexual 'psychopathic' offending: opportunistic, pervasively angry and overtly sadistic. These are similar to the clusters identified by Beech *et al.* (2006).

Sadistic Offending

Whilst sadistic personality is no longer described in DSM, it is consistently used as a construct in the forensic literature (Hare, Cooke & Hart, 1999). Gratzer and Bradford (1995) found that sadistic sexual offenders more often experienced emotional detachment (82%) during the offence and often experienced sexual dysfunction (50%); they also found that 86% met the criteria for antisocial personality disorder. Marshall, Kennedy and Yates (2002) found no difference in the incidence of antisocial personality between sadistic and non-sadistic offenders. They also found that sadistic sexual offenders had a higher incidence of 'murderous fantasies'. Proulx and Beauregard (2005) and Proulx, Blais & Beauregard (2006) found that sadistic offenders had a higher incidence of schizoid personality disorder, scored higher on schizoid, avoidant and schizotypal scales of the Millon Clinical Multiaxial Inventory (MCMI; Millon, 1994) and lower on the Histrionic scale when compared with non-sadistic offenders. Proulx and Beauregard (2005) reviewed the literature on sadistic offenders and suggested that the long-term developmental antecedents typically were: social isolation, low self-esteem, deviant sexual fantasies, 'sexual incompetence', paraphilias (voyeurism, exhibitionism, fetishism) and they were often physically abused as children. Immediate antecedents to the offence were: low self-esteem, deviant sexual fantasies and careful planning. Proulx *et al.* (2006) found specific and generalised conflicts with women, anger, sexual excitement and deviant sexual fantasies as antecedents in the 48 hours before the offence and offences more often involved: planning, victim selection, kidnapping or unlawful confinement, victim being tied up, bondage, weapon use, expressive violence, humiliation, mutilations (including mutilation of erogenous zones) and insertion of objects in the vagina. Crimes more often involved strangulation, the body being found completely naked, post-mortem intercourse, and post-mortem mutilation.

Berner, Berger and Hill (2003) highlight the distinction between sadism as a paraphilia and sadistic personality disorder. They found, in a forensic psychiatric sample, that only half of those with a sexually sadistic paraphilia also met criteria for sadistic personality disorder; but two-thirds of those with a diagnosis of sadistic personality disorder also had a diagnosis of sexual sadism. Prognosis was seemingly unaffected by sadistic personality or by sexual sadism as a paraphilia. They also found that of those who met criteria for sadistic personality disorder 31.6% met criteria for borderline personality disorder and 42.1% for antisocial personality disorder.

Eher *et al.* (2004) found DSM-IV Axis I sexual sadists exhibited a higher prevalence of clusters A and B personality disorders, were higher on measures of risk and evidenced a higher prevalence of anal manipulation, inserting objects into the victim's genitals, violent acts against the victim's neck like choking and weapons use.

Beech *et al.* (2006) in their typology of sexual homicides identified a sadistic offenders' subgroup who were characterised by: a high incidence of strangulation or stabbing as the method of killing, mutilation of victims, post-mortem sexual interference, absence of relationship prior to the offence, a prior interest in guns and torture (e.g., may have a history of torturing animals), sadistic fantasies and planning offences.

INTERVENING WITH PERSONALITY DISORDERED SEX OFFENDERS

Jones (1997) suggested the clinical utility of a treatment hierarchy for prioritising interventions with personality disordered offenders including sex offenders. Adapting the model suggested by Linehan (1993) for DBT he suggested that any form of therapy interfering behaviour was a critical target for intervention. This was suggested for three reasons: (1) because it would aim to prevent the often predictable attrition process associated with people with personality disorder diagnoses; (2) the drop-out process itself was hypothesised to be a reflection of similar processes evident in offending and relapse processes – where commitment not to offend has in some way been compromised (when it is there); (3) the therapy interfering behaviour was also likely to reflect key interpersonal themes that run through that person's life-history reflecting core schema and patterns of behaving being activated and played out.

A model of change involving an initial increase in distressing emotions and loss of self-esteem, during the process of experiencing therapy-induced change (Jones, 1997), highlighted a critical point in interventions where the distress associated with change could be resolved by either changing beliefs or using old means of managing distress linked with offending, or simply dropping out of therapy. Whilst these processes are there for all offenders it is hypothesised that they are more significant for personality disordered offenders with issues around trust, emotional disregulation, emotion evasion strategies or limited capacity for experiencing distress.

Livesley (2003) argues for a similar principle when he indicates the following sequence of 'phases' for intervention:

1. *Safety:* Interventions should ensure safety of patient and others;
2. *Containment:* Interventions targeting affective and behavioural instability;
3. *Control and regulation:* Targeting reduction of symptoms and self-regulation of affects and impulses;
4. *Exploration and change:* Targeting cognitive, behavioural and situational factors associated with problems;
5. *Integration and synthesis:* Targeting developing a new integrated sense of self.

The treatment pathway for a person who has a personality disorder diagnosis and who has committed a sexual offence needs to follow this kind of sequence. It would be unethical to intervene prematurely addressing offending or trauma-related issues if the problems around emotional regulation and coping skills haven't already been addressed.

This section will now examine particular approaches to treatment.

Attrition Prevention Planning

Linehan's (1993) Dialectical Behaviour Therapy (DBT) emphasises the importance of targeting Therapy Interfering Behaviour (TIBs) and Jones (1997) suggests a model for using DBT with offenders that targeted TIBs including offending behaviour or offence-related behaviour. Individual's patterns of TIBs are collaboratively identified at the start of the intervention and then predictions about future possible TIBs are used to develop an attrition prevention plan. This uses the same framework as is eventually used for the relapse prevention component of the intervention. As such it serves as an introduction to the model of relapse prevention – socialisation to the model. Another advantage of this strategy is that when the relapse prevention plan is eventually developed many of the high-risk situations that are identified are the same as those identified as HRSs for dropping out of an intervention.

Jones (1997, 2003) highlighted the importance of focusing on therapy interfering behaviour (from Linehan's DBT approach) and Safran and Muran's (2000) concept of therapeutic ruptures as a focus for intervention addressing problems with relationships. This concept has been developed in the behavioural and the cognitive behavioural literatures, via the work of Kohlenberg and Tsai (1995) and Koerner, Kohlenberg and

Parker (1996) (the behavioural theorists who most informed Linehan's 1993 model), who highlight the importance of focusing on 'clinically relevant behaviour' in the session. Jones (1997) identified the problem with psychoeducational interventions not addressing the here and now manifestation of clinically relevant material and suggested that in-treatment offence-related material emerging in daily life and in the session was a key target for offence-focused interventions. Relapse prevention themes overlap significantly with themes around attrition prevention.

Offence Disclosure Work

Jones (2002a) in exploring the kinds of factors leading to drop-out amongst referrals to a sex offender group found a common theme of people leaving the group at the point when they heard others' disclosures. This was for a variety of reasons, see section on adverse responses to treatment below. In order to prevent this from happening in future groups a process whereby the detailed offence disclosure work was taken out of the group and done individually with more than one clinician was introduced. Besides preventing adverse reactions to peer accounts this also enabled patients who had committed bizarre or atypical offences to explore their offences without having to manage the group reaction. The two clinicians took different roles in the session, one taking an active exploratory, questioning and collaborative role, the other taking an observational role watching the process issues in the session. Their task was to try and monitor for collusive avoidance or overbearing challenging in the session. Particularly monitoring the interpersonal dynamics of who was in 'control' and who was taking a passive role and what levels of overt and covert hostility were around in the room.

The aim of offence disclosure work is to obtain an account of the offence where the individual recognises the kinds of choices that they made and the way this built up to an offence. The model of interaction is not so much Socratic as motivational interviewing (Miller & Rollnick, 2002) and solution focused (see below) where a focus on self-regulation strategies that had been previously effective was required.

Working on offences that had not been explored previously in a range of different adversarial and therapeutic contexts was used in order to deconstruct the individuals' over-rehearsed narratives and to allow fresh thinking about the underpinning reasons for the offence. Behavioural try-outs that had not resulted in offending are a good source of information, as are patterns of interacting in a range of contexts including developmental contexts, which parallel the offence (e.g., chasing games in the playground or teenage discovery and enactment of sexual maturation). Detailed charting of the different aspects of the offence is made. Minimisation and denial are analysed with a view to establishing what function they serve for the individual. They are construed as adaptations to a range of experiences as opposed to simply as deliberate obstruction.

Solution-Focused Offence Work

There has been little emphasis in models of intervention on identifying ways in which offenders have successfully managed their offending behaviour, both in their current settings and in the past. The reason an individual might choose to try and regulate their own behaviour can vary; however, the likelihood is that even with the most impulsive individuals there is evidence that they have been able to successfully manage their offending behaviour at times. The solution-focused approach (e.g., De Shazar, 1988), suggested by Jones (2002a) as an approach to intervention and other related narrative approaches (e.g., White, 2007) are fundamentally client centred and are aimed at developing a way of thinking about problems that empowers the client and instils hope in the possibility of change. Using this strategy highlights the possibility that as clinicians we can fail to assess and work with an individual's own change beliefs (Jones, 2002b) and repertoire of existing self-regulation strategies. The Ward and Hudson (1998) pathways model identifies the avoidance explicit pathway which involves misguided attempts to self-regulate. It does not, however, specify effective previous attempts at self-regulation. Solution-focused approaches involve a number of basic strategies: looking for exceptions when an individual has effectively managed their behaviour (before or after the offence); and developing a 'what works' agenda for the individual case based on previous interventions, self-regulation episodes and responses to these. The starting point is that the individual is not offending most of the time and therefore is doing something that is effective. This strategy can also be used to identify coping strategies with people who show an approach explicit pathway. For them the self-management may have been a part of their detection and conviction evasion strategy. Every offender is likely to have some skills in managing their offending behaviour; getting these out into the open is a useful first step and can validate the individual's sense of themselves as being able to manage themselves. When strategies have been used and have failed it is important to analyse what went wrong with them. Rather than 'installing' a new repertoire of skills and implicitly dismissing existing strengths, this approach starts by assuming some degree of skill and competence, validates that and offers to elaborate and build on existing structures of coping.

Solution-focused interventions are part of a broader family of interventions called 'narrative therapies' (e.g., White, 2007) which focus on working within an individual's own framework for making sense of the world (as opposed to imposing one upon them). Even offenders taking the approach explicit pathway (Ward & Hudson, 1998) are usually able to describe ways in which they manage their urges to offend even if it is simply to avoid detection.

Empathy Formulation

Having an analysis of the reasons for a particular individual not being able to empathise at the time of the offence is a critical task. In a recent review of the theoretical literature on empathy deficits amongst sex offenders Ward, Polaschek and Beech (2006) highlight the range of different ways in which empathy deficits could be a contributory factor for offending behaviour. For each individual case there is a need to develop an empathy formulation identifying how extensive the deficit is, what kinds of empathy strengths the individual has and proposing hypotheses about the possible causal factors leading to the current presentation.

Empathy formulations can draw on a range of literatures for suggestions. Gilbert's (2005) recent development of the construct of compassion, to self and others, has much in common with the construct of empathy. Gilbert highlights the notion that an individual who is un-empathic and uncompassionate towards others may also relate to themselves in this way. Useful models of empathy, such as the perception-action model (Preston & DeWaal, 2002) and Decety and Jackson's (2004) functional model can provide a framework for thinking about how empathy can be de-railed or disrupted. It is also important to conceptualise different ways in which empathy can take the form of sadistic enjoyment (e.g., Singer *et al.*'s (2006) work on enjoyment of perceived distress in others when they are perceived to be 'cheats' and behaving unfairly).

Baumeister (2003) identifies decision making and active responding as resources of the self that can be adversely affected by stressors such as lack of sleep; as a limited resource it can be depleted leaving the individual vulnerable to impulsive and insensitive behaviour. The concept of a limited resource has also been explored by DeWall *et al.* (2007). Understanding ways in which state variables can impact on this limited resource and impact on the ability to empathise in a particular context is a key role for an empathy formulation.

Recent work by DeWall and Baumeister (2006) suggests that social exclusion can have profound effects on interpersonal functioning. It can heighten emotional numbness and insensitivity to pain and emotion in self and others; under this formulation, empathy deficits may be partly a result of being members of an 'out-group' and experiencing the self as excluded.

Blair *et al.*'s (1997) work identifying deficits in identifying distress in others' facial expressions as a characteristic of psychopaths as identified by the PCL-R suggests one potentially critical dynamic factor in empathy deficits. Blair *et al.*'s work did not control for state variables and this may have confounded his findings. Assessing and developing an understanding of capacity to recognise and respond to facial expressions of distress may be an important strategy (particularly if this is, as Blair contends, a critical trigger for the violence inhibition mechanism [VIM]). Venn *et al.* (2005) argue that capacity to recognise facial expressions is very much state dependent and indeed can be impacted by pharmacological agents. Pollak *et al.* (2000) identify different kinds of deficit in emotional face recognition amongst children who had experienced different kinds of abuse; neglect being associated with a general deficit in discriminating emotional expressions, physically abused children with a response bias for angry faces. Philippot, Kornreich and Blairy (2003) also describe significant deficits in recognition of emotion in faces (including not recognising distress in others) associated with alcohol consumption. There are thus numbers of pathways leading to deficits in responding to distress in others.

Schema Work

Bernstein, Arntz and de Vos (2007) have evidenced the utility of schema therapy approaches with personality disordered offenders. Ward's (2000) concept of an 'implicit theory' is an example of schema that are held outside conscious awareness. Ward *et al.* (2006) point out that implicit theories are also a feature of personality disorder, they illustrate this by linking implicit theories found in both rapists and child sex offenders of *Entitlement* and *Dangerous world* with Baumeister, Bushman and Campbell's (2000) account of narcissism. Taking this idea further we find that the *Dangerous world* implicit theory, one version of which is summarised by Ward *et al.* (2006) by the phrase 'it's just a dog-eat-dog world', is identical to Beck, Freeman and Davis' (2007) account of the core beliefs of people with antisocial personality disorder where he uses the phrase 'it's a dog-eat-dog world and in a dog-eat-dog world the safest place to be is top dog' to capture them. The 'uncontrollability' implicit theory is an account of an individual's relationship with themselves where one part of them, their urges and emotions, overwhelms another part of them – possibly the observing or the agentic part of them. Framed in these terms it can be seen as an example of Gilbert's (2000) account of individuals having relationships with themselves involving rank status where one part of them is allowed to dominate another. It is also part of a possible 'condemnation narrative' (Maruna, 2001) as a way of thinking that prevents the possibility of change.

One might expect those child sex offenders identified as schizoid or dependent to hold the *adults are dangerous* version of the dangerous world implicit theory because these personality disorders are associated with a submissive interpersonal stance. Jones (1997) found some evidence for child sex offenders being more submissive in group contexts, and hypothesised that individuals tend to offend against those whom they see as less dominant than themselves. Identifying and working with an individual's schema relating to self, and others, is a critical task for interventions with this group. It is not possible to bring about change without some kind of revision at this level. Identifying and working with schema at a content level is useful for an individual to get a sense of the kinds of schema that they make use of regularly. However, schema usually operate at a number of levels and are difficult therefore to change simply through dissonance induction or Socratic questioning. Ward (2000) advocates the approach of instructing sex offenders in how to be better scientists by making their own assumptions more explicit.

Lee (2005) highlights the need for other strategies, usually experiential – such as behavioural experiments and the use of gestalt and imagery work suggested by Young (e.g., Bernstein *et al.*, 2007; Young, Klosko & Weishaar, 2003), in order to overcome what she terms the 'heart – head lag'. Changing schema requires that they be activated in some way. Working with offence paralleling behaviour (OPB) in the clinical setting is a critical strategy for working with schemas that are in the process of being activated and therefore are potentially most open to revision. Clinicians cannot activate some kinds of schema without running into ethical problems; offence paralleling behaviour (OPB) work (Jones, 2004, 2007) relies on natural occurrences of schema activation in order to bring about change. Instead of responding to acting-out and crises in the institutional setting by managing them and moving on, they are used as a critical opportunity to learn. The way in which they are managed inevitably either reinforces the problem or begins to change it.

Individual Intervention

For some individuals group-based interventions are not suitable. Individual interventions need to be developed as an alternative. This is particularly true for those who have unusual needs or who typically respond poorly to groups. Individuals with strong traits of suspiciousness and difficulty trusting others (possibly with a paranoid personality disorder diagnosis) can really struggle in a group context where their tendency towards misattribution of hostile intent can be amplified. Overly anxious individuals also struggle in this kind of context. Individuals with an impulsive extravert personality who struggle to stop talking can sabotage the group for others and can sometimes be better managed in an individual intervention.

Formulation Driven Interventions

Perkins *et al.* (1998) describe a 'tension' between 'individually tailored' idiographic interventions delivered individually and group-based programmes 'designed around general criminogenic factors'. They conclude that 'the decision as to whether a group-based environment is the best treatment for a particular offender is a matter of clinical judgement'. Ward (2000) and Drake and Ward (2003) (see also Chapter 5) suggest that formulation-based interventions are appropriate if any one of the following conditions is met:

1. Complex cases;
2. Unusual cases where there is confusion as to how to categorise a particular patient;
3. When standardised treatment has failed;
4. When there are significant threats to the therapeutic relationship.

People with sex offending histories and personality disorder diagnoses generally meet all of these criteria.

While it is not within the scope of this chapter to present a theoretical account of personality disordered offending, a number of theoretical models are useful for the practitioner developing formulations with this population, examples include: the model of personality offered by Blackburn *et al.* (2005) highlighting interpersonal theory; Buschman and van Beek's (2003) model of personality disordered sex offenders; Jones's (2004) account of potentially criminogenic states associated with interpersonal hostile dominance; Ward and Beech's (2006) Integrated Theory of Sexual Offending; Gannon, Polaschek and Ward's (2005) account of social cognition; and Dowset and Craissati's (2007) account of working with personality disordered offenders in the community.

Avoidance of negative mood state is often hypothesised as an antecedent in the offending and personality disorder CBT literatures. Formulations around hypomanic and related dysphoric processes can also be useful ('approach active' offending in Ward and Hudson's relapse model). Addressing positive affective states (associated with Behavioural Activating System activation, see Gray, 1994, and Watson, 2000) and positive cognitive distortions (self-world and future) can be important. For example, the opposite distortions to depression: jumping to positive conclusions, under-estimate risk, minimisation of problems and overvaluing immediate gratification, exaggeration of current and future resources, high utility for gains, low demands for information to assess risk, discounting of losses and regret, and over-estimation of the ability to replicate behaviour can be worked with (Leahy, 2005). Palmer and Gilbert (1997) have developed a CBT framework for working with some of these issues that are useful with offenders exhibiting this kind of process in their offending.

Targeting Offence Paralleling Behaviour

McDougall, Clarke and Fisher (1994) highlight the utility of looking at in-treatment behaviour as a measure of risk. Jones (1997, 2004) identified offence paralleling behaviour (OPB) as a critical target for intervention. An understanding of OPB can be developed through serial analysis of an individual's offences. In addition near offences and patterns of behaviour that paralleled the offence (e.g., same antecedents but ending in episode of self-harm) are identified and analysed. Current OPB past offending and childhood antecedents are combined into a formulation of the individual's offence processes. This formulation can then be used to link together a range of interventions in different settings (i.e., individual work, crisis behaviour on the ward, group-based intervention).

Working on Issues around the Client's Own Abusive Developmental Experiences

Johnson *et al.* (1999) found that early childhood trauma victims are considerably more likely than those who were not abused or neglected to have Personality Disorders (PD) and elevated PD symptoms, particularly those PD within the Cluster B spectrum as outlined within DSM-IV-TR (APA, 2000). Craissati, McClurg and Browne (2002a, b) also highlight the role of sexual abuse in the development of sexual offending. Spitzer *et al.* (2006) found that patients in a high secure hospital had a high incidence of 'complex PTSD' associated with a range of traumatic experiences.

Vivian-Byrne (2002) highlights the value of working with abuse issues when working with sex offenders and argues for developing a methodology for doing this based on systemic therapy. Saradjian (1996), working with female sex offenders, is perhaps one of the few clinicians who gives an account of using CBT case formulations which include the impact of abuse, as a framework for intervention.

However, it is probably a mistake to see traumatic experiences as being the only or the most important aetiological factor in the development of sexual offending. Raine (2002), for example, has argued that the critical factor in the development of some violent offending was the combination of a neurological deficit and abusive or poor parenting; it is likely that sexual offending amongst personality disordered offenders is driven by a similar interaction between developmental and neurological factors. One model for the way in which abuse impacts on offending highlights emotional avoidance, of own or others' distress, or attentional avoidance (transdiagnostic processes; Harvey *et al.*, 2004); if these processes are systematically targeted then for some individuals abuse-focused intervention could be useful. The clearest role for addressing abuse is with individuals who describe 'enjoying' the experience and therefore what they have done is not harming their victims. Helping them to recognise the impact of abuse on them could help them to recognise the impact on their victims. Allam, Middleton and Browne (1997) argue, for instance, that sex offenders who have been abused need to address their own abuse before they can experience empathy towards their victims. Whilst it is not necessary or sufficient to address abuse to develop empathy, for individuals where there appears to be a clear link between aspects of their offending and aspects of their experience of abuse this can be a useful approach. Indeed Gilbert's (2005) approach to developing compassion for others is predicated on developing compassion for the self also, whatever process is played out towards others in the offence is likely to also be played out with the self in the relationship with the self.

THREATS TO EFFECTIVE INTERVENTION

Responsivity Issues

One way of conceptualising personality disorder is to see it as a feature of an individual's presentation that impacts on their capacity to respond to an intervention. The importance of addressing responsivity was highlighted by Andrews and Bonta (2003) who argued that interventions are more effective if they are delivered in a way that is made more accessible to the individual involved in the intervention. This entails identifying what kinds of intervention are most likely to be effective for an individual. One approach to this is to look at what has previously been effective for an individual; it is also important, however, to identify what has been ineffective or iatrogenic in previous interventions.

Treatment Drop-Out

There is some evidence that dropping out of treatment or having treatment terminated is associated with an adverse outcome for offenders undertaking some kinds of sex offender intervention. The direction of the causality is not clear, however. Does treatment drop-out cause increased reconviction, or does a prior propensity to offending lead both to treatment drop-out and to higher rates of eventual offending? There is evidence that personality disorder is associated with higher risk of dropping out of treatment. Langevin (2006) identified antisocial personality disorder as a predictor of starting treatment but not finishing it (suggesting some form of instrumental engagement). Anecdotal evidence from practitioners working in high secure settings suggests that the majority of those referred for sex offender interventions have experienced at least one previous similar intervention and often more. It is consequently essential that any intervention addresses treatment retention issues as a priority. This problem is highlighted by the work of Seager, Jellicoe and Dhaliwal (2004) who argue that treatment effects are often spurious and that interventions for sex offenders act as 'a prolonged screening instrument for sex offenders whose failure to comply with treatment attendance predicted higher rates of recidivism'. They found that non-completers were six times more likely to incur a new sexual or violent conviction. Also, in a review of factors that lead to treatment drop-out one frequent factor reported by patients as an antecedent to their dropping out of the group was listening to (or anticipating listening to) accounts of sexual offending by others in the group. This was particularly the case with patients who have experienced sexual abuse themselves. This is corroborated by Craissati and Beech (2001) who found that those who drop out of sex offender groups are more likely to have experienced childhood trauma and psychological difficulties.

Adverse Outcome from Treatment

Various authors have argued that interventions with people who have high PCL-R is counterproductive (Seto & Barbaree, 1999). However, reanalysis of this data using more complete recidivism data and an improved research methodology (Langton, 2000) failed to find this effect. The high PCL-R scorers recidivated at the rate predicted by an actuarial measure. This debate, however, continues. Harris and Rice (2006) argue that the evidence from therapeutic communities (Ogloff, Wong & Greenwood, 1990; Rice, Harris & Cormier, 1992) and prison-based programmes evaluated by Hare *et al.* (2000) indicate that interventions with people with high PCL-R scores are likely to result in increased rates of recidivism.

A recent study by Looman and Abracen (2005) found that sexual offenders with high PCL-R scores whose risk was rated as having changed during an intervention recidivated at the same rate as 'non-psychopaths' and conclude that it is possible to intervene effectively with this group. They did, however, find that this was only true for those who, whilst high on the PCL-R overall rating, were not high on glibness/ grandiosity and poor behavioural controls/impulsivity items. Whilst we should always be mindful of the possibility of interventions having an adverse effect, the evidence is simply not strong enough to support the contention that they are made worse (see D'Silva, Duggan & McCarthy, 2004, for recent review).

Jones (2002a) indicated that a critical factor in delivering interventions with personality disordered offenders in high secure settings was the fact that most of them had previously been involved in unsuccessful interventions and that many of these previous interventions had been iatrogenic in some ways. A critical issue is to identify, on a group and on a case-by-case basis, what leads to people dropping out and addressing this as a priority. Jones (2002a, 2007b) argues any intervention is potentially harmful and proposed the following as possible adverse reactions leading to drop-out or non-responsiveness (based on the accounts of individuals referred to a sex offender group):

Learned non-responsiveness due to repeated failure of interventions. Jones (2002a, 2007b) identified a model for possible inoculation in the social psychological literature (Pfau *et al.*, 1990). Essentially inoculation theory holds that it is possible to prevent belief change by exposure to 'weak attacks' that are unsuccessful.

Fragility particularly in the face of confrontational interventions. A theme in the literature on working with patients with narcissistic (and other Cluster 'B' personality disorders) traits is their limited capacity to tolerate feelings associated with challenging or exposure to dissonance.

Paranoid personality disorder and suspiciousness in group contexts. Patients with paranoid traits often find group contexts difficult to manage. The group can trigger feelings of suspiciousness and amplify their sense of persecution.

Learning about detection evasion skills. Another way in which interventions can be potentially harmful with this group is that they can give patients the opportunity to reflect on detection evasion skills that they might want to emulate.

Increasing repertoire of offending skills. There is some evidence that interventions addressing offending behaviour can increase offending repertoires. For example, Buschman and van Beek (2003) report a personality disordered sex offender who borrowed an offence pattern from one of the other patients in his therapy group.

OUTCOME STUDIES

There is little evidence in the literature about the efficacy of interventions with personality disordered sexual offenders. There can be a number of different outcomes from an intervention with sex offenders, these include: (a) becoming worse; (b) changing current sexually impulsive behaviour that impacts on life in a custodial setting, and results in victims; (c) reducing risk of reoffending; and (d) increasing manageability in the community. With the exception of the first, all of these outcomes are valid targets for interventions. Most of the literature, however, looks at reconviction as an outcome.

HM Prison Grendon Therapeutic Community

Thornton *et al.* (2000) reported significant attitudinal change amongst personality disordered sex offenders in the Grendon Therapeutic Community, and that changes were more significant amongst those attending a CBT group within the therapeutic community, and for those with more than one previous sexual conviction. They suggest that, in line with Beckett *et al.* (1994), specialist supportive provision, providing a high number of hours of intervention is more likely to impact on reconviction for more deviant sex offenders, such as the personality disordered population at Grendon. Whilst they question the outcome in terms of the possibility that it could be accounted for by a process of differential attrition, this is the only outcome study looking at the impact of an intervention with this population on reconviction.

Forensic Psychiatric Centre (FPC) Veldzicht

Buschman and van Beek (2003) report a study at the FPC looking at sex offender treatment that found a 'poor outcome'. It is likely that a significant proportion of this group would have met criteria for personality disorder diagnosis. They speculated that the following factors would have contributed to the lack of efficacy:

1. Focusing on 'general problems' like drugs, alcoholism and employment problems and failing to target 'sexual deviancy, sexual fantasies, cognitive distortions associated with these fantasies, stress-related problems like lack of self-efficacy and inadequate self-regulation';
2. Using mostly individual work that 'holds the risk of the client grooming the therapist';
3. A significant proportion of the intervention time being used to reduce behaviour problems resulting from hospitalisation.

They report clinical observations about a revised intervention, designed for working with personality disordered sex offenders and based on the pathways model. Of 32 cases treated, those that had been released indicated that they have a 'more structured way of looking at themselves' and that 'in the short term it helped them to use their relapse prevention plans more effectively'. Two cases reported psychotic episodes in their offences and received individualised interventions using the adapted pathways model. Two cases evidenced sexually sadistic offence paralleling behaviour and were put on a 'long-stay programme'. Three were identified as meeting criteria for pervasive developmental disorder and were treated using 'chemical castration'. Two patients with an approach explicit pathway associated with a 'well-regulated positive emotional state' were taken into treatment 'to collect more information' on them and were put on intensive supervision by probation officers who used the adapted pathways model as a framework. Out of the remaining 25 one reoffended during 'resocialisation'; one almost reoffended but was stopped when it was recognised that the way in which he was violating his conditions of parole showed a similar pattern as his offence pattern'. Most of this 25 violated alcohol/drugs issues in their relapse prevention plans, but it was considered that these violations were not 'severe' and that they were 'able to control themselves more effectively than before treatment'.

CONCLUSIONS

Sex offenders with personality disorder diagnoses present clinicians with a significant challenge and the development of models for intervening with this population is still in its infancy. Hopefully clinicians will find this chapter useful for conceptualising and developing interventions both on a group and individual basis for working with this population. There are many questions that need to be examined more carefully in order to facilitate progress in this field. How many hours of intervention time are likely to be most effective and is there a point where length of intervention becomes iatrogenic? Does personality integration enhance the generalisation of change processes? To what extent are change processes specific to 'being in a therapeutic relationship'; with consequent loss of gains following the ending of the relationships? (see Twenge *et al.*, 2007). How do we best measure change in this population?

REFERENCES

Ahlmeyer, S., Kleinsasser, D., Stoner, J. & Retzlaff, P. (2003). Psychopathology of incarcerated sex offenders. *Journal of Personality Disorders, 17*, 306–318.

Allam, J., Middleton, D. & Browne, K.D. (1997). Different clients, different needs? Practice issues in community-based treatment for sex offenders. *Criminal Behaviour and Mental Health, 7*, 69–84.

American Psychiatric Association (APA) (2000). *Diagnostic and statistical manual of mental disorders DSM-IV-TR* (4th edn). Washington DC: American Psychiatric Association.

Andrews, D.A. & Bonta, J. (2003). *The psychology of criminal conduct* (3rd edn). Cincinnati, OH: Anderson.

Baumeister, R.F. (2003). Ego depletion and self-regulation failure: A resource model of self-control. *Alcoholism: Clinical and Experimental Research, 27*, 1–4.

Baumeister, R.F., Bushman, B.J. & Campbell, W.K. (2000). Self-esteem, narcissism, and aggression: Does violence result from low self-esteem or from threatened egotism? *Current Directions in Psychological Science, 9*, 26–29.

Beck, A.T., Freeman, A. & Davis, D.D. (2007). *Cognitive therapy of personality disorders*. New York: Guilford Press.

Beckett, R.C., Beech, A.R., Fisher, D. & Fordham, A.S. (1994). *Community-based treatment of sex offenders: An evaluation of seven treatment programmes*. Home Office Occasional Paper. London: Home Office.

Beech, A.R., Oliver, C., Fisher, D. & Beckett, R.C. (2006). *STEP 4: The Sex Offender Treatment Programme in prison: Addressing the offending behaviour of rapists and sexual murderers*. Home Office Occasional Paper. London: Home Office. Available electronically from www.hmprisonservice.gov.uk/assets/documents/100013DBStep_4_SOTP_report_2005.pdf

Berner, W., Berger, P. & Hill, A. (2003). Sexual Sadism. *International Journal of Offender Therapy and Comparative Criminology, 47*, 383–395.

Bernstein, D.P., Arntz, A. & de Vos, M. (2007). Schema-focused therapy in forensic settings: A theoretical model and recommendations for best clinical practice. *International Journal of Forensic Mental Health, 6*(2), 169–183.

Blackburn, R. (1998). Psychopathy and personality disorder: implications of interpersonal theory. In D.J. Cooke, A.E. Forth & R.D. Hare (Eds), *Psychopathy: Theory, research and implications for society* (pp. 269–301). Amsterdam: Kluwer.

Blackburn, R., Logan, C., Renwick, S.J.D. & Donnelly, J.P. (2005). Higher order dimensions of personality disorder: Hierarchical structure and relationship with the five-factor model, the interpersonal circle and psychopathy. *Journal of Personality Disorders, 19*, 597–623.

Blair, R.J., Jones, L., Clark, F. & Smith, M. (1997). The psychopathic individual: A lack of responsiveness to distress cues? *Psychophysiology, 34*, 192–198.

Bogaerts, S., Vanheule, S. & Declercq, F. (2005). Recalled parental bonding, adult attachment style and personality disorders in child molesters: A comparative study. *The Journal of Forensic Psychiatry and Psychology, 16*, 445–458.

Bogaerts, S., Vanheule, S. & Desmet, M. (2006). Personality disorders and romantic adult attachment a comparison of secure and insecure attached child molesters. *International Journal of Offender Therapy and Comparative Criminology, 50*, 139–147.

Bogaerts, S., Vervaeke, G. & Goethals, J. (2004). A comparison of relational attitude and personality disorders in the explanation of child molestation. *Sexual Abuse: A Journal of Research and Treatment*, *16*, 37–47.

Briken, P., Nika, E. & Berner, W. (1999). Abteilung fur sexualforschung, universitatsklinik fur psychiatrie und psychotherapie, Hamburg-Eppendorf. [Sexual homicide: a data collection from psychiatric records] *Fortschritte der Neurologie-Psychiatrie*, *67*, 189–199.

Buschman, J. & van Beek, D.J. (2003). A clinical model for the treatment of personality disordered sexual offenders: an example of theory-knitting. *Sexual Abuse: A Journal of Treatment and Research*, *15*, 183–199.

Craissati, J. & Beech, A. (2001). Attrition in a Community Treatment Program for Child Sexual Abusers. *Journal of Interpersonal Violence*, *16*, 205–221.

Craissati, J., McClurg, G. & Browne, K. (2002a). Characteristics of perpetrators of child sexual abuse who have been sexually victimized as children. *Sexual Abuse: A Journal of Research and Treatment*, *14*, 225–238.

Craissati, J., McClurg, G. & Browne, K. (2002b). The parental bonding experiences of sex offenders: A comparison between child molesters and rapists. *Child Abuse and Neglect*, *26*, 909–921.

Decety, J. & Jackson, P.L. (2004). The functional architecture of empathy. *Behavioral and Cognitive Neuroscience Reviews*, *3*, 71–100.

De Shazar, S. (1988). *Clues: Investigating solutions in brief therapy*. New York: Norton.

DeWall, C.N. & Baumeister, R.F. (2006). Alone but feeling no pain: Effects of social exclusion on physical pain tolerance and pain threshold, affective forecasting, and interpersonal empathy. *Journal of Personality and Social Psychology*, *91*, 1–15.

DeWall, C.N., Baumeister, R.F., Stillman, T.F. & Gailliot, M.T. (2007). Violence restrained: Effects of self-regulation and its depletion on aggression. *Journal of Experimental Social Psychology*, *43*, 62–76.

Dowsett, J. & Craissati, J. (2007). *Managing personality disordered offenders in the community: A psychological approach*. London: Routledge.

Drake, D.R. & Ward, T. (2003). Practical and theoretical roles for the formulation-based treatment of sexual offenders. *International Journal of Forensic Psychology*, *1*, 71–84.

D'Silva, K., Duggan, C. & McCarthy, L. (2004). Does treatment really make psychopaths worse? A review of the evidence. *Journal of Personality Disorders*, *18*, 163–177.

Eher, R., Schilling, F., Fruehwald, F. & Frottier, P. (2004). *Violent sexual offenses in relation to paraphilias and personality disorders*. International Academy of Sex Research Conference. June16–19, Helsinki, Finland.

Gannon, T.A., Polaschek, D.L.L. & Ward, A. (2005). Social Cognition and Sex Offenders. In M. McMurran & J. McGuire (Eds), *Social problem solving and offenders* (pp. 223–247). Chichester, UK: John Wiley & Sons, Ltd.

Gilbert, P. (2000). Social mentalities: Internal 'social' conflicts and the role of inner warmth and compassion in cognitive therapy. In P. Gilbert & K.G. Bailey (Eds), *Genes on the couch: Explorations in evolutionary psychotherapy* (pp. 118–150). Hove: Brenner-Routledge.

Gilbert, P. (2005). Compassion and cruelty: A biopsychosocial approach. In P. Gilbert (Ed.), *Compassion: Conceptualisations, research and use in psychotherapy*. London: Brunner-Routledge.

Gratzer, T. & Bradford, M.W. (1995). Offender and offence characteristics of sexual sadists: a comparative study. *Journal of Forensic Sciences*, *40*, 450–455.

Gray, J.A. (1994). Personality dimensions and emotion systems. In P. Ekman & R.J. Davidson (Eds), The nature of emotion: fundamental questions (pp. 329–331). New York: Oxford University Press.

Hare, R.D. (1991). *The Hare Psychopathy Checklist-Revised*. Toronto: Multi-Health Systems.

Hare, R.D., Cooke, D.J. & Hart, S.D. (1999). Psychopathy and Sadistic Personality Disorder. In T. Millon, P. Blaney & R. Davis (Eds), *Oxford textbook of psychopathology* (pp. 555–584). Oxford: Oxford University Press.

Hare, R.D., Clark, D., Grann, M. & Thornton, D. (2000). Psychopathy and the predictive validity of the PCL-R: An international perspective. *Behavioral Sciences and the Law*, *18*, 623–625.

Hart, S.D., Kropp, P.R., Laws, D.R. *et al.* (2003). *The Risk for Sexual Violence Protocol (RSVP): Structured professional guidelines for assessing risk of sexual violence.* Vancouver: Simon Fraser University.

Harvey, A., Watkins, E., Mansell, W. & Shafran, R. (2004). *Cognitive behavioural processes across psychological disorders: A transdiagnostic approach to research and treatment.* Oxford: Oxford University Press.

Hill, A., Briken, P., Habermann, N. & Berner, W. (2004). The relevance of sadism for recidivism in sexual murderers. Paper presented at International Academy of Sex Research (IASR) conference, Helsinki, Finland, June 2004.

Jackson, R.L. & Richards, H.J. (2007). Diagnostic and Risk Profiles Among Civilly Committed Sex Offenders in Washington State. *International Journal of Offender Therapy and Comparative Criminology, 51*, 313–323.

Johnson, G.J., Cohen, P., Brown, J. *et al.* (1999). Childhood maltreatment increases risk for personality disorders during early adulthood. *Archives of General Psychiatry, 56*, 600–606.

Jones, L. (1997). Developing models for managing treatment integrity and efficacy in a prison-based TC: The Max Glatt Centre. In E. Cullen, L. Jones & R. Woodward (Eds), *Therapeutic communities for offenders* (pp. 121–157). Chichester: John Wiley & Sons, Ltd.

Jones, L. (2002a). *Iatrogenic interventions with 'personality disordered' offenders.* Division of Forensic Psychology conference. Manchester, November 2002.

Jones, L. (2002b). An individual case formulation approach to the assessment of motivation. In M. McMurran (Ed.), *Motivating offenders to change: A guide to enhancing engagement in therapy.* Chichester: John Wiley & Sons, Ltd.

Jones, L.F. (2003). Therapy interfering behaviour, iatrogenic intervention histories and offence paralleling behaviour: some responsivity issues in working with sex offenders with 'personality disorder'. Paper presented at British and Irish Group for the Study of Personality Disorder, Dublin, February 2003.

Jones, L. (2004). Offence paralleling behaviour (OPB) as a framework for assessment and interventions with offenders. In A. Needs & G. Towl (Eds), *Applying psychology to forensic practice* (pp. 34–63). Oxford: Blackwell.

Jones, L. (2007a). What does the literature say about personality disordered sex offenders ? NOTA Conference, Edinburgh, September 2007.

Jones, L. (2007b). Iatrogenic interventions with personality disordered offenders. *Behaviour, Crime and Law, 13*, 69–79.

Keenan, T. & Ward, T. (2004). A theory of mind perspective on cognitive, affective, and intimacy deficits in child sexual offenders. *Sexual Abuse: A Journal of Research and Treatment, 12*, 49–60.

Knight, R.A. & Guay, J.P. (2006). The role of psychopathy in sexual coercion against women. In C.J. Patrick (Ed.), *Handbook of psychopathy* (pp. 512–532). New York: Guilford Press.

Koerner, K., Kohlenberg, R.J. & Parker, R. (1996). Diagnosis of personality disorder: A radical behavioral alternative. *Journal of Consulting and Clinical Psychology, 64*, 1169–1176.

Kohlenberg, R.J. & Tsai, M. (1995). Functional analytic psychotherapy: A behavioral approach to intensive treatment. In W. O'Donohue & L. Krasner (Eds), *Theories of behavior therapy: Exploring behavior change* (pp. 637–658). Washington, DC: American Psychological Association.

Langevin, R. (2006). Acceptance and completion of treatment among sex offenders. *International Journal of Offender Therapy and Comparative Criminology, 50*, 402–417.

Langevin, R., Lang, R., Reynolds, R. *et al.* (1988). Personality and sexual anomalies: an examination of the Millon Clinical Multiaxial Inventory. *Annals of Sex Research, 1*, 13–32.

Langton, C.M. (2000). Contrasting approaches to risk assessment with adult male sex offenders: an evaluation of recidivism prediction schemes and the utility of supplementary clinical information for enhancing predictive accuracy. Unpublished doctoral dissertation. University of Toronto, Canada.

Leahy, R.L. (2005). Clinical implications in the treatment of mania: Reducing risk behavior in manic patients. *Cognitive and Behavioral Practice, 12*, 89–98.

Lee, D.A. (2005). The perfect nurturer: A model to develop a compassionate mind within the context of cognitive therapy. In P. Gilbert (Ed.), *Compassion: Conceptualisations, research and use in psychotherapy* (pp. 326–351). London: Routledge.

Linehan, M. (1993). *Cognitive behavioral treatment of borderline personality disorder*. New York: Guilford.

Livesley, W.J. (2001). Conceptual and taxonomic issues. In W.J. Livesley (Ed.), *Handbook of personality disorders: Theory, research, and treatment* (pp. 3–38). New York: Guilford.

Livesley, W.J. (2003). *Practical management of personality disorder*. New York: Guilford.

Looman, J. & Abracen, J. (2006). *Psychopathy subtypes, treatment performance and recidivism*. Paper presented at the 25th Annual Conference of the Association for the Treatment of Sexual Abusers, Chicago, September 2006.

Marshall, W.L. (1996). Assessment, treatment and theorizing about sex offenders. Development in the past twenty years and future directions. *Criminal Justice and Behavior*, *23*, 162–199.

Marshall, W.L., Kennedy, P. & Yates, P. (2002). Issues concerning the reliability and validity of the diagnosis of sexual sadism applied in prison settings. *Sexual Abuse: A Journal of Research and Treatment*, *14*, 301–311.

Maruna, S. (2001). *Making good: How ex-convicts reform and rebuild their lives*. Washington, DC: American Psychological Association.

McDougall, C., Clarke, D.A. & Fisher, M.J. (1994). Assessment of violent offenders. In M. McMurran & J. Hodge (Eds), *The assessment of criminal behaviours of clients in secure settings* (pp. 68–93). London: Jessica Kingsley Publishers.

Miller, W.R. & Rollnick, S. (2002). *Motivational interviewing: Preparing people for change* (2nd edn). New York: Guilford Press.

Millon, T. (1994). Millon Clinical Multiaxial Inventory III Manual. Minneapolis, MN: National Computer Systems.

Murrie, D.C., Warren, J.I., Kristiansson, M. & Dietz, P.E. (2002). Asperger's syndrome in forensic settings. *International Journal of Forensic Mental Health*, *1*, 59–70.

Nichols, H.R. & Molinder, I. (1984). *Multiphasic Sex Inventory*. Available from Nichols and Molinder, 437 Bowes Drive, Tacoma, WA, 98466, USA.

Ogloff, J., Wong, S. & Greenwood, A. (1990). Treating criminal psychopaths in a therapeutic community program. *Behavioral Sciences and the Law*, *8*, 81–90.

Palmer, A. & Gilbert, P. (1997). What psychologists can do to help. In V.P. Varma (Ed.), *Managing manic depressive disorder* (pp. 42–61). London: Jessica Kingsley.

Perkins, D., Hammond, S., Coles, D. & Bishopp, D. (1998). *Review of sex offender treatment programmes*. Department of Psychology Broadmoor Hospital: Document Prepared for the High Security Psychiatric Services Commissioning Board (HSPSCB). Retrieved 17 November 2007 from: http://www.ramas.co.uk/report4.pdf

Pfau, M., Kenski, H., Nitz, M. & Sorenson, J. (1990). Efficacy of inoculation strategies in promoting resistance to political attack messages: Application to direct mail. *Communication Monographs*, *57*, 25–43.

Philippot, P., Korenreich, C. & Blairy, S. (2003). Nonverbal deficits and interpersonal regulation in alcoholics. In P. Philippot, E.J. Coats & R.S. Feldman (Eds), *Nonverbal behavior in clinical context* (pp. 209–231). New York: Oxford University Press.

Pollak, S.D., Ciccheti, D., Hornung, K. & Reed, A. (2000). Recognizing emotion in faces: Developmental Effects of Child Abuse and Neglect. *Developmental Psychology*, *36*, 679–688.

Pollock, P. H., Stowell-Smith M. & Göpfert M. (2006). *Cognitive analytic therapy for offenders: A new approach to forensic psychotherapy*. London: Routledge.

Porter, S., Fairweather, D., Drugge, J. *et al.* (2000). Profiles of psychopathy in incarcerated sexual offenders. *Criminal Justice and Behavior*, *27*, 216–233.

Porter, S., Woodworth, M., Earle, J. *et al.* (2003). Characteristics of sexual homicides committed by psychopathic and non-psychopathic offenders. *Law and Human Behavior*, *27*, 459–470.

Preston, S.D. & DeWaal, F.B.M. (2002). Empathy: Its ultimate and proximate bases. *Behavioral and Brain Sciences*, 25, 1–72.

Proulx, J., Aubut, J., Perron, L. & McKibben, A. (1994). Troubles de la personnalitéet viol implications théoriques et cliniques. *Criminologie*, 27, 33–53.

Proulx, J. & Beauregard, E. (2005). *Sadistic sexual aggressors and sexual murderers: Empirical and theoretical issues*. Paper presented at the 8th International Investigative Psychology conference. Retrieved from: www.i-psy.co.uk/conferences/8/presentations/jean_proulx.ppt

Proulx, J., Blais, E. & Beauregard, E. (2006). Sadistic sexual aggressors. In W.L. Marshall, Y.M. Fernandez, L.E. Marshall & G.A. Serran (Eds), *Sexual offender treatment: Controversial issues* (pp. 61–77). Chichester: John Wiley & Sons, Ltd.

Raine, A. (2002). Biosocial studies of antisocial and violent behavior in children and adults: A review. *Journal of Abnormal Child Psychology*, 30, 311–326.

Raymond, N.C., Coleman, E., Ohlerking, F. *et al.* (1999). Psychiatric comorbidity in pedophilic sex offenders. *American Journal of Psychiatry*, 156, 786–788.

Rice, M., Harris, G. & Cormier, C. (1992). An evaluation of maximum-security therapeutic community for psychopaths and other mentally disordered offenders. *Law and Human Behavior*, 16, 399–412.

Rice, M.E., Harris, G.T. & Quinsey, V.L. (1990). A follow-up of rapists assessed in a maximum security psychiatric facility. *Journal of Interpersonal Violence*, 5, 435–448.

Safran, J.D. & Muran, J.C. (2000). *Negotiating the therapeutic alliance: A relational treatment guide*. New York: Guilford.

Saradjian, J. (1996). *Women who sexually abuse children: From research to clinical practice*. New York: John Wiley & Sons, Inc.

Seager, J.A., Jellicoe, D. & Dhaliwal, G.K. (2004). Refusers, drop-outs and completers: Measuring sex offender treatment efficacy. *International Journal of Offender Therapy and Comparative Criminology*, 48, 600–612.

Serin, R.C. (1994). Psychopathy and violence in criminals. *Journal of Interpersonal Violence*, 6, 423–431.

Seto, M.C. & Barbaree, H. (1999). Psychopathy, treatment behavior, and sex offender recidivism. *Journal of Interpersonal Violence*, 14, 1235–1248.

Shea, W.M. (1996). Personality characteristics of child molesters, non-sex offending criminal child abuse controls, and normals as differentiated by the Millon Clinical Multiaxial Inventory II. *Dissertation Abstracts International, Section B: The Sciences and Engineering*, 56, 5184 B.

Singer, T., Seymour, B., O'Doherty, J.P. *et al.* (2006). Empathic neural responses are modulated by the perceived fairness of others. *Nature*, 439, 1–4.

Spitzer, C., Chevalier, C., Gillner, M. *et al.* (2006). Complex post-traumatic stress disorder and child maltreatment in forensic patients. *The Journal of Forensic Psychiatry and Psychology*, 17, 204–216.

Thornton, D., Mann, R., Bowers, L. *et al.* (2000). Sex offenders in a therapeutic community. In J. Shine (Ed.), *A compilation of Grendon research* (pp. 30–35). Available from HM Prison Grendon, Grendon Underwood, Aylesbury, Bucks.

Twenge, J.M., Baumeister, R.F., DeWall, C.N. *et al.* (2007). Social exclusion decreases prosocial behavior. *Journal of Personality and Social Psychology*, 92, 56–66.

Venn, H.R., Watson, S., Gallagher, P. & Young, A. (2005). Facial expression perception: an objective outcome for treatment studies in mood disorder? *International Journal of Neuropsychopharmacology*, 9, 229–245.

Vess, J., Murphy, C. & Arkowitz, S. (2004). Clinical and demographic differences between sexually violent predators and other commitment types in a state forensic hospital. *Journal of Forensic Psychiatry and Psychology*, 15, 669–681.

Vivian-Byrne, S.E. (2002). Using context and difference in sex offender treatment: An integrated systemic approach. *The Journal of Sexual Aggression*, 8, 59–73.

Ward, T. (2000). The role of formulation-based treatment for sexual offenders. *Behavior Change*, 17, 251–264.

Ward, T. & Beech, A.R. (2006). An integrated theory of sexual offending. *Aggression and Violent Behavior, 11*, 44–63.

Ward, T. & Hudson, S.M. (1998). A self-regulation model of the offense process. *Sexual Abuse: A Journal of Research and Treatment, 10*, 141–157.

Ward, T., Polaschek, D.L.L. & Beech, A.R. (2006). *Theories of sexual offending*. Chichester: John Wiley & Sons, Ltd.

Watson, D. (2000). *Mood and temperament*. New York: Guilford Press.

White, M. (2007). *Maps of narrative practice*. New York: Norton.

Young, J., Klosko, J. & Weishaar, M. (2003). *Schema therapy: A practitioner's guide*. New York: Guilford Press.

23

Understanding the Complexities and Needs of Adolescent Sex Offenders

PHIL RICH

INTRODUCTION

Working with adolescent sexual offenders and sexually reactive children is a substantially different proposition from work with adult offenders. This is primarily because sexually abusive behaviour, in both children and adolescents, appears far more tied to developmental issues than sexual deviance, in terms of the emergence of personality, psychological development, response to the social environment and social messages, and the myriad of forces that shape and define the emotions, cognitions, relationships and behaviour of children and adolescents.

More specifically, it is both how we *understand* sexually reactive children and sexually abusive adolescents, compared to adult sexual offenders, that is different; as well as the way that we actually define and provide treatment for these different populations. Here, it is important to highlight that we are discussing, not two, but three populations, because although we tend to group children and adolescents who engage in sexually abusive behaviour under the label of 'juvenile sexual offenders', these are two distinct populations in their own right, with acute differences between them. Although this chapter focuses on how we understand and treat adolescent sexual offenders, just as we conceptualise differences between adolescent and adult sexual offenders, we similarly conceptualise differences between sexually abusive post-pubescent adolescents and sexually abusive pre-pubescent children. Expanding this idea further, we also note other discrete populations included under the rubric of 'juvenile sexual offender', including teenage (and younger) girls, cognitively challenged children and adolescents, and other subpopulations that include adolescents

Assessment and Treatment of Sex Offenders: A Handbook. Edited by Anthony Beech, Leam Craig and Kevin Browne. © John Wiley & Sons Ltd, 2009.

from distinctly different cultures, for instance. If we fail to recognise and acknowledge these differences, we risk building a 'one-size-fits-all' mentality which is not only unlikely to provide depth in understanding our clients and the roots of their behaviour, but also limits specialisation in treatment for different treatment groups. Further, as it has become a near tenet of current treatment that sexual offenders are not a homogeneous group, we risk failing to live up to our own stated beliefs that great heterogeneity exists, not simply *within* the larger group of 'sexual offenders' but *across* different groups, by age, gender, cognitive and intellectual capacity, level of psychological/psychiatric functioning, and ethnic and cultural background.

This is a useful place, then, to open this chapter, by noting that as we consider sex offender specific treatment, it is important to bear in mind that there are many subpopulations within the larger category of 'sexual offender'. Although this chapter focuses on male adolescent offenders, we recognise that we can apply some of the same ideas to other groups of young persons, including girls and young women, children, and cognitively (intellectually) impaired juveniles, but also that there significant differences among these subpopulations.

DISTINGUISHING BETWEEN ADOLESCENT AND ADULT SEXUAL OFFENDERS

In many substantial ways, work with juvenile sexual offenders is much like mental health and developmental work with any troubled child, involving relationship building, the exploration and development of attitudes, beliefs, and interests, the emergence of empathy and social connectedness, and the influence and context of the family. Compared to adult sexual offenders, sexually abusive youth are far less fixed, if fixed at all, in their social, emotional, attitudinal, behavioural and, in this case, sexual preferences and interests. Accordingly, they are far more amenable to treatment, which, therefore, has the clear capacity to eliminate the problem of sexually abusive behaviour by the time the child, or adolescent reaches young adulthood.

Regardless of their behaviour, adolescents are still very much in the developmental process, have few fixed ideas or beliefs, are easily influenced and shaped by their social environment, and are still very experimental in their behaviours and attitudes as they try out and develop life scripts and personal identities. Rather than having the fixed ideas, interests, and motivations that characterise adults, adolescents are far more fluid in every aspect of their lives[1], and this is a normative aspect of the human developmental cycle. This is as true for juvenile sexual offenders as it is of any adolescent. In addition, adolescents are more open and more used to the educational and learning process as it permeates their lives in a way not true for most adults,

---

[1]This is not so true in the case of cognitively impaired adolescents, who do form more fixed and rigid ideas, as well as adolescents experiencing autistic spectrum disorders, where fixed and inflexible ideas are quite often a hallmark of the condition.

and this aids in the process of treatment and change. Finally, with specific respect to sexual offending, juveniles experience far less deviancy in their sexual activities and arousal patterns and are far more motivated by experimentation, even if abusive and sometimes heinous in nature.

Although it is likely that many adult sex offenders began their histories of sexually abusive behaviour as adolescents, every study, despite weaknesses in the research, tells us that many, if not most, treated juvenile sexual offenders will not become adult sexual offenders (Epperson *et al.*, 2006; Letourneau & Miner, 2005; Parks & Bard, 2006; Reitzel & Carbonel, 2006; Zimring, 2004). Nevertheless, the possibility of emerging adult sexual offending speaks to its adolescent counterpart as an 'at risk' condition. This highlights the importance of providing treatment to sexually abusive children and adolescents, and, given the relatively low incidence of the behaviour persisting into adulthood, the strong possibility that intervention helps prevent the development of the fixed interests and behaviours that lead or contribute to later adult sexual offending (Association for the Treatment of Sexual Abusers, 2000).

Nevertheless, as adolescents age their interests clearly develop, and their behaviours are likely to incrementally become more fixed. Accordingly, the line between adult and adolescent offenders becomes increasingly blurred as the age of majority is neared, assuming that age 18 marks adulthood, or at least 'adultolescence' as it is sometimes called. One question, then, is when do juvenile sexual offenders become adult sexual offenders? This is a question to be pondered, but has no clear answer. In fact, there is not even a clear legal answer because, although, for instance, the age of majority is age 18 in the United States and United Kingdom, juveniles can be tried and held responsible as adults in many jurisdictions for certain crimes from age 14 on (and even younger). Aside from assuming that a juvenile sexual offender can be considered to be an adult sexual offender upon his 18th birthday, what does this mean for young adults who engaged in sexually abusive behaviour prior to age 18? This particular question seems to be answered by some adult risk assessment tools that conclude that these instruments can be used to assess risk for sexual reoffence in individuals from age 16 on. However, in the 2003 revised coding rules for one of these instruments, the Static-99 (Harris *et al.*, 2003), we are advised that juvenile evaluations must be interpreted with caution because it is not clear whether juvenile sexual offending is the same phenomena as adult sexual offending with respect to the underlying dynamics of the behaviour, noting that the research literature leads us to believe that adolescent sexual offenders are not necessarily 'younger versions' of adult sexual offenders.

Because of this blurry line between sexual offending behaviour in older adolescents and young adults, we have reason to be become more concerned when we see older adolescents engaging in new or continued sexually abusive behaviour, holding beliefs that seem supportive of sexual aggression, or experiencing sexual ideation that appears, or can be assessed as, deviant. Although we tie our hands if we define a rigid line that differentiates between adolescent and adult offenders, recognising that for some the line is blurry, we must nevertheless assume a position of some kind if we are to act decisively. Accordingly, in concert with long-standing social and psychological opinions about children and adolescents, we continue to assume that sexually abusive adolescents, aged 17 and younger, are at a different developmental point in their lives than adults, that we must view and evaluate their behaviours and their motivations from a different perspective than that which we use to assess adult behaviour, and that assessment and treatment for this population should be philosophically different than its adult counterpart (Association for the Treatment of Sexual Abusers, 2000; Center for Sex Offender Management, 1999; Chaffin *et al.*, 2006; Letourneau & Miner, 2005; Steinberg & Scott, 2003).

THE DEVELOPMENT OF ADULT BEHAVIOUR: PSYCHOPATHY AND PERSONALITY DISORDER

We recognise, of course, that 'adult' behaviour does not simply pop into existence at age 18. It is developmental, which is precisely one of the reasons that it is important to understand that the roots of such behaviour are established in adolescence, and even in childhood, and recognise and treat the precursors to seriously troubled adult behaviour *before* adulthood is reached. The Diagnostic and Statistical Manual of Mental Disorder-Fourth Edition (American Psychiatric Association, 2000) diagnosis of antisocial personality disorder, for example, cannot be made in individuals before age 18 but also requires that a diagnosis of conduct disorder has been carried for at least 3 years, with onset before age 15. However, recognising that the aetiology of adult behaviour is developmental, we must nevertheless be careful how we view troubled behaviours in children and adolescents, and the conclusions we draw. In fact, antisocial personality disorder offers a good example of this, because of its suggestion of psychopathy in at least some adults diagnosed with this disorder.

Forth, Kosson and Hare (2003) describe psychopathy as a stable personality disorder that is first evident in childhood, possibly by genetic disposition. Although they are careful to acknowledge that the youth version of the Hare Psychopathy Checklist-Youth Version (PCL-YV) cannot be used to diagnose psychopathy in adolescents, Forth *et al.* nevertheless conclude that psychopathic traits are observable in adolescents (and children). Although they acknowledge that personality change can occur during adolescence, they nonetheless assert that elements of adult psychopathy can be observed and accurately measured in juveniles. Paul Frick (Frick *et al.*, 2003a, 2003b) also believes that characteristics of adult psychopathy, and particularly callous unemotionality, can be measured in children who exhibit severe forms of conduct disorder prior to adolescence, and that these characteristics mark a path towards adult psychopathy. Like Forth, Frick also warns against labelling children and adolescents as psychopaths, but clearly believes that traits of psychopathy can be measured in children as young as age six. The *Antisocial Process Screening Device*, formerly known as the *Psychopathy Screening Device*, was developed specifically for this purpose (Frick & Hare, 2002).

The value of such a perspective is that we can recognise developmental precedents to later serious antisocial personality and behavioural problems. However, the risk is that we may come to assume that the appearance of attitudes, emotional experiences, and behaviours that may contribute or lead to the later development of psychopathy are mistaken for psychopathy. Here, we may mistake the appearance of these earlier phenomena as not just early developmental concerns that can be corrected, but as earlier and less-defined versions of behaviour that is destined to blossom in adulthood in its more complete form. For this reason, Seagrave and Grisso (2002) warn against assessing children and juveniles as fledgling psychopaths.

Further, the thinking behind a model that not only seeks the roots of psychopathy prior to adulthood, but believes that psychopathy *already* exists in early childhood and adolescence is a distinctly non-developmental model. That is, it assumes that life course is established in childhood and is more likely than not to emerge in later adolescence or adulthood; in fact, in the case of the psychopathy model described, the underlying assumption is that there is a genetic component that is a more powerful determinant than environmental (or developmental) conditions. This offers an example of a model that concludes a single powerful factor is mostly responsible for later personality and behaviour, rather than the myriad of forces that come together and act upon the developmental pathway to produce later personality, attitudes, emotional resources, social relationships, and behaviours.

However, from a developmental perspective, early antisocial behaviours that resemble psychopathy (and may even become psychopathic as the juvenile approaches and enters adulthood) stem from early childhood experiences that create developmental vulnerabilities. In turn, these are fuelled by ongoing social experiences that continue to stress and exacerbate early vulnerabilities, and are further formed and hardened into personality by a combination of internal and environmental forces that act within and upon the individual (Marshall & Eccles, 1993; Rich, 2006). With respect to the development of psychopathy, this suggests that the behaviour is developmental, shaped by the environment, and not a necessary outcome, even if early signs are evident in the child or adolescent.

This particular debate offers an excellent example of two different perspectives. On the one hand, later behaviour is considered, not merely shaped, but pre-determined by earlier behaviour (and even genetics). On the other lies a belief that early developmental experiences create the potential for later emotional experiences, attitudes and behaviours, but themselves represent only one step along a developmental pathway in which many forces interact and come to bear on the development of personality and behaviour. Development, then, distinguishes adults from children, and becomes the material with which we work if we are to change developmental trajectories.

THINKING CRITICALLY ABOUT ADOLESCENT SEXUAL BEHAVIOUR

The ideas in this chapter are informed broadly by an understanding of adolescent development in the family and social environment, an understanding of social psychology and its influence, an understanding of criminogenic factors and forensics, and a psychiatric/mental health orientation which focuses on the continuum of mental well-being. These ideas recognise the developmental-learning environment in which children grow into adolescence and then adulthood; the manner in which attitudes, ideas, emotions and behaviours develop; and the myriad influences that coalesce to produce, interact with, and catalyse ideas and transform them into behaviour. The approach emphasises the need to understand and treat adolescents in a holistic manner, recognising and understanding each adolescent as an individual who is more complex than his or her behaviours alone, and whose behaviours must be understood in the entire context of his or her life as an individual.

This approach also stresses the necessity of treating juvenile sexual offenders with an integrated approach that does not emphasise one treatment mode or set of techniques above another. Such an approach instead combines cognitive behavioural, psychoeducational, and psychodynamic treatment with appropriate adjunctive therapies, such as expressive, recreational, and play therapy, into an integrated model that utilises individual, group and family therapy. The overarching framework that binds the integrated model is itself a synthesis of both forensic and clinical psychology, offering a forensic mental health approach to treatment. This also highlights the importance of reviewing and considering what we think we know about aetiology and treatment, seeking to avoid a dogmatic mindset in which we risk believing that we know what works, when, in fact, little is actually known.

Applying a level of critical thinking about our work will also focus our attention away from research alone and onto the development of clinical insight and skills in the practitioner, informed and directed by research but not swept away by it. To this end, we are discussing a clinical approach to treatment that builds upon skills and practices common to all forms of effective mental health treatment, with children, adolescents and adults. We thus avoid a one-size-fits-all approach, which may fail to recognise or treat the complexities inherent in each individual. The success of individual treatment for juvenile sexual offenders likely rests on the ability to understand each juvenile sexual offender as a unique individual, in the context of characteristics common to many juvenile sexual offenders, and the ability of the practitioner to bring critical thinking and clinical skills to every case.

THE LIFE COURSE OF ADOLESCENT SEXUAL OFFENDING

The label 'juvenile sexual offender' raises concern for the community, in part based upon legitimate concerns about what harm may be caused by the adolescent and what type of adult he might grow into if his behaviours remain sexually abusive. This fear is not without merit, and many sexual crimes against children and adults (but mostly younger children) are committed by adolescent boys aged between 12–18 (Rich, in press). According to Federal Bureau of Investigation uniform crime reports, the percentage of juveniles (under the age of 18) arrested for sexual crimes actually increased between 1998 and 2003, despite a lowering of juvenile arrests for other violent crimes (US Department of Justice, 1995, 1996, 1998, 2003, 2005).

However, despite a sometimes blurred line as adolescence meets adulthood, and our general belief that many adult sexual offenders begin to engage in sexually inappropriate and abusive behaviour as juveniles, it appears that the sexual behaviours of many, if not most, sexually abusive youth do not persist into adulthood. That is, most juvenile sexual offenders do not become adult sexual offenders. It is commonly believed that between 30% and 60% of adult sexual offenders engage in sexually inappropriate or abusive behaviour as adolescents (e.g., Abel, Osborn & Twigg, 1993; Burton, 2000; National Task Force on Juvenile Sexual Offending, 1993). This is certainly cause to consider juvenile sexual offenders at risk for engaging in sexually abusive behaviour as adults. However, although it is quite possible that many adult sexual offenders began as juvenile sexual offenders, it nevertheless seems that most juvenile sexual offenders do not continue as adult sexual offenders.

Cited rates of sexual recidivism for juvenile sexual offenders typically fall somewhere between 7–15% (Alexander, 1999; Caldwell, 2002; Epperson & Ralston, 2005; Nisbet, Wilson & Smallbone, 2004; Reitzel & Carbonel, 2006; Zimring, 2004). That is, whether some, many, or most adult sexual offenders began as juvenile sexual offenders, it seems that most juvenile sexual offenders do not continue as adult sexual offenders. In fact, various studies of recidivism among sexually abusive youth make it clear that most juvenile sexual offenders are at far greater risk for re-engaging in non-sexual criminal behaviour than sexual offences, a finding reported by Letourneau and Miner (2005) as consistent across nearly all studies of juvenile sexual offender recidivism. Put another way, somewhere between 75–98% of sexually abusive youth do not engage in further sexual offences once apprehended and treated.

DIFFERENCES BETWEEN ADOLESCENT AND ADULT OFFENDERS

Adolescents are not adults, even as they near that blurry line between late adolescence and adulthood. However, the things they do and their experience of life certainly shape and influence not just their personality and behaviour, but the sort of adults they are likely to become. Not surprisingly, adolescent and adult sexual offender share many similar life experiences and resulting behaviours and characteristics. These experiences often include variants of disrupted and unstable childhood experiences, broken or unstable family environments, the presence of domestic violence, and abuse, neglect, and other forms of maltreatment, as well as insecurely developed attachment relationships to parents.

Nevertheless, despite these commonalities, it is important that we do not confuse adult behaviours, motivations, and pathways to offending with those of adolescents, even if they appear similar. Adult patterns of and motivations for sexual offending behaviours differ from those of adolescents who engage in similar behaviours. Although difficult to empirically prove, it is likely that juveniles engage in sexually abusive behaviour for entirely different reasons than their adult counterparts, and travel along pathways that may or may not lead them further into sexual offending. In large part, this is because, despite seemingly common developmental pathways, the experience of each individual along that pathway is shaped by the context of that individual's life. In the case of the sexually abusive youth, that context is adolescence.

In fact, adolescents live in a very different world from that of adults, embedded as children within family and community systems and subject to a different set of rules, expectations and obligations from adults. They are also substantially different in the development of their bodies, in their cognitive and personality development, in their formation of attitudes and acquisition of information, and in their emotional and behavioural maturity. Adolescents experience the world in ways that are significantly different from adults; they are stimulated, pleased, influenced and motivated by different things, and are more experimental, with fewer fixed ideas than adults and fewer fixed personality characteristics. Their interests are still developing, and ideas, attitudes, emotions and behaviours that may be considered outlandish, inappropriate, hostile, antisocial, or even deviant in adults, may not represent any of these things in adolescents.

Adolescents are not adults. This is not just because they are at a different point in the development of their emotional lives, the gathering of life experience, and the experience of their daily lives, but also because they are at a different point in the development of their neurological lives and cognitive skills.

THE ADOLESCENT BRAIN

In addition to multiple behavioural, emotional and social changes that occur during adolescence, Spear (2000) describes significant and ongoing physical, cognitive and neurological development. Similarly, Giedd (2002) describes continuing neural development beginning during early adolescence and continuing through until about age 16, involving a thickening of grey matter in the prefrontal cortex, or the further development of neural cells and their axons and dendrites. This development involves the extension of cognitive skills, including the capacity for increased abstraction, insight and judgement, attention and freedom from distractibility, and decision-making skills, all functions involved in the development of executive functioning. Spear (2003) also describes greater emotionality in adolescents compared to adults, including a greater sensitivity to negative emotions and depressed mood. Similarly, Deborah Yurgelun-Todd (2002) reports that adolescents experience more emotional responses than adults, but have not yet developed the prefrontal capacity to accurately identify or process emotions. She writes also that adolescents are more susceptible than children or adults to neurological reward systems that drive and reward certain types of risk taking and exploratory behaviour. In general, just as the adolescent is socially and physically in transition between childhood and adulthood, not surprisingly the adolescent brain in is transition also, described by Spear as differing anatomically and neurochemically from the adult brain.

In describing the capacity of adolescents to be held fully (or legally) responsible for their behavioural choices, Laurence Steinberg (2003), also describes the critical role of brain maturation, with a particular focus on regions of the prefrontal cortex implicated in planning and impulse control (dorsolateral region) and the ability to both learn from experience and balance rewards against risks in decision making (ventromedial). He asserts that it not a matter of whether adolescents can distinguish right from wrong, but the fact that they are distinguished from adults in their neural (and, hence, cognitive) capacity to form decisions that take into account the possible consequences of their behaviours, the way they weigh rewards against risks, their foresight and ability to plan ahead, and their ability to recognise and control impulse.

THE ADOLESCENT CAPACITY

Remaining with the idea that adolescents are not adults, we recognise other differences also, both in terms of maturing developmental capacity and the impact of early developmental experiences on cognitive development. This is particularly relevant in trying to understand attitudes and behaviours, which victimise others. Fonagy and colleagues (Fonagy *et al.*, 1997a) assert that the basis for moral social behaviour rests upon the capacity to recognise and understand another person's perspective, and that only through secure early attachment experiences between child and caregiver(s) can the individual develop such skills, referred to by Fonagy as 'mentalising'.

Mentalisation, or metacognition, involves the capacity to recognise and, in effect, 'think about' thinking and reflect upon emotion rather than simply experiencing such states in self and others. Through this process we come to develop a higher awareness of self and others, and a clearer sense of our own capacities and responsibilities, as well as greater skills in forming and maintaining social relationships. Fonagy (2001) describes mentalisation as crucial to the ability of children to both explore the meaning behind the actions of others and their ability to label and find meaning in their own experience. Although innate to human development, Fonagy nevertheless considers that the capacity for adequate mentalisation evolves out of early attachment experiences, and that severe deprivation undermines the acquisition of mentalisation.

Fonagy *et al.* (1997a, 1997b) propose that juvenile crimes are committed by adolescents with inadequate mentalising capacities who engage in pathological attempts to adapt to a social environment in which mentalisation is essential. First, because mentalisation is intrinsically connected to self-awareness and the formation of personal identity, those with limited reflective skills and a reduced ability to envision the mental states of others will also have a less well-established sense of their own identity. This reduces their capacity to recognise and be in touch with their own thoughts, and therefore accept responsibility for their behaviours, genuinely lacking a sense of personal responsibility, or self-agency. Second, a reduced capacity for mentalisation may lead to a failure to anticipate or appreciate the consequences of personal behaviour to the victims of such behaviours. Third, reduced capacity for mentalisation may contribute or lead to devaluing or dehumanising potential or actual victims.

Finally, limited metacognitive skills may lead to easy deconstruction and reinterpretation of social representations, including ideals and values, and allow antisocial behaviour to be experienced in a self-serving manner by the adolescent as appropriate and acceptable. We can easily apply these ideas to the behaviours of juveniles who engage in the sexual abuse of others.

The capacity for mentalisation is related to the development and experience of empathy. From a different but related perspective, D'Orazio (2002) finds additional evidence of differences between adolescents and adults. In studying empathy, D'Orazio found no significant differences in empathy among groups of adult sexual offenders, non-sexual criminal offenders, and non-offenders. However, she found juveniles in her study to be generally less empathic than adults, regardless of their status as sexual offenders, non-sexual delinquents, or non-offenders. She concluded that empathy is an age-related construct that grows over time and with maturity, and that reduced capacity for empathy in adolescents, compared to adults, is normative. Hence, it is a mistake to transpose ideas about empathy deficits in adults onto adolescents and children.

ON EMPATHY AND MORALITY

Arne Johan Vetlesen (1994) describes empathy as the basic human emotional faculty that predisposes people to develop concern for others, always being other-directed rather than self-concerned. Martin Hoffman (2000), too, describes empathy as an emotional response that is "more appropriate to another's situation than one's own" (p. 4). On a broader and more connective note, Carol Rogers (1980) describes empathy 'dissolving alienation', and connecting the individual to others.

Recalling D'Orazio's conclusion that adolescents are generally less empathic than adults, we can nevertheless recognise empathy as a sense of social understanding and social connection. From this perspective, a lack of empathy reflects a lack of social relatedness rather than a lack of sympathy and concern for others. However, it is useful to understand empathy as multi-dimensional, constructed in stages, rather than a unidimensional experience. Mark Davis (1996) describes three interrelated elements of empathy involving the capacity to assume the perspective of another person, concern for the other, and a sense of personal distress that results in a helping action, mediated by the capacity to imagine the state of another person. In his four-stage model of empathy, Marshall (Marshall, 2002; Marshall et al., 2006) adds a fourth element, 'decision response', or a decision to help the other person.

Similarly, Hoffman (2000) considers the key to empathy to be 'empathic distress', or the sympathetic component of empathy, as this is the aspect that results in action. This requires psychological processes that connect one individual to another, allowing helpers to experience feelings that are more congruent with the other person's situation than their own. Here, he describes empathic distress built upon the metacognitive ability to become aware of and understand another, as well as a mentalised image of acting to help the other. This conceptualisation of empathy is thus tied to Fonagy's conception of the troubled adolescent as impoverished in the skills of mentalisation, and thus able to act without empathic regard for the other. Add to this D'Orazio's conclusion that adolescents are generally less empathic than adults, anyway.

Hoffman describes the cognitive aspects of empathy not only serving to control the emotional experience of empathy, but also allowing empathic concerns for others to serve as the base for a moral code. Similarly, Vetlesen (1994) writes that empathy is a precondition for moral decision making, and that perceptions of morality are built on the experience of empathy for others. Thus empathy and morality begin to merge, in that empathy builds the groundwork from which moral identity emerges, and morality becomes the attitudinal and behavioural equivalent of empathy.

Just as empathy is both multi-staged and requires cognitive development, so too is morality both multi-dimensional and contingent upon emotional *and* cognitive development, involving intertwined elements that mature in stages. These come together to form Barbara Stilwell's domain of 'conscience conceptualisation'. She and her colleagues (Stilwell *et al.*, 1998) describe moral development incorporating social values and integrating emotional, cognitive and behavioural systems into a dynamic mental model of conscience. Her model largely involves the transformation of early attachment and social experiences into the values, attitudes and beliefs that underlie relationships and behaviours, resulting in a moral conscience. Linking to neurological maturation, Stilwell writes that neural development provides the substrate for moral development. Consequently, although substantially the result of social experience, moral development is nonetheless built on neural and cognitive development. However, even under normative conditions morality must be nurtured, which Stilwell reports first occurs during early attachment relationships, and includes expanding relationships with other family members, adults and friends, and within the social organisations and institutions in which children are raised and grow to adulthood.

Kagan (1984) describes both empathy and morality as essential ingredients in the socialisation of behaviour. Similar to Fonagy's ideas about mentalisation, Kagan considers the child's acquisition of standards to be facilitated by the recognition of feelings and thoughts in self and others, mediated through the development of empathy. He thus makes moral development contingent upon the development of empathy. Again we see that morality can be conceptualised as the operational counterpart of empathy, in which empathy is expressed through the effects of decisions and behaviours on others.

ON EMPATHY AND TREATMENT

We recognise empathy, then, as a requirement for socially connected human experience in which one is seen, understood and cared for by others and, in turn, is able to see, understand and care about others. Developed throughout life, empathy initially unfolds through the attuned relationship between infant and mother, and later develops further through the broader experience of family life. As the child develops, the capacity for a more mature empathy is shaped by emotional experience and facilitated by cognitive development. The development of empathy is fuelled not only by the experience of being understood and cared about by others, but also linked to metacognition and the ability to recognise and experience the cognitive and emotional states of self and others. Limitations in metacognition and limitations in empathy are thus related, and central to Fonagy's model in which lack of metacognition allows, and even fosters, antisocial behaviour.

With respect to treatment, Rogers (1980) writes that empathy dissolves alienation, allowing those who experience empathy for others to feel like "part of the human race" (p. 151), and that people learn to become empathic by being with and learning from empathic people. This means having the experience of being understood by another person, allowing those who experience empathic understanding to feel valued, cared for and accepted. Of course, these are the very qualities that we wish to develop and instil in sexually abusive youth, and they are also the same qualities that our clients must experience from others in their environment, whether in their own homes, in the therapeutic relationship, or in the larger treatment milieu of the residential programme. Accordingly, we recognise that being the *subject* of empathy is the first step in the development of the capacity to be empathic.

Warner (1997) describes empathic understanding as crucial in therapy with clients whose ability to contain and process their own experiences has been weakened due to empathic failures in their early development. In this respect, the clinician's ability to be empathic is curative, developing and strengthen the client's own capacity to relate to others. In fact, it is generally believed that the capacity of treatment staff to recognise and empathically respond to distress in the client influences the development of empathy. In teaching empathy, then, it is the therapist and treatment staff who must demonstrate empathy, described by Fernandez and Serran (2002) as integral to the therapeutic relationship.

BUILDING TREATMENT PROGRAMMES

We recognise that juvenile sexual offenders are no more and no less than a variant of the troubled child, especially troubling perhaps because of the particular form of their troubling behaviour and the risk it poses to others. However, even though the likelihood is relatively low, adolescent sexual offenders are nonetheless at risk of becoming adult sexual offenders. Hence, early and timely evaluation and interventions are critical if we are to prevent this possible outcome, recognising also that these adolescents are still our children and we, as adults and as a society, are responsible for who they are now, and often for who they will become.

However, I have hopefully by now succeeded in portraying juvenile sexual offenders as more than just adolescents who engage in sexually abusive behaviour. These are complex individuals moving along a life path that may take them towards or away from continued sexual offences, influenced by many factors, but most of all by a necessary and inevitable interaction between cognitive development and life experience. Moreover, although most sexually abusive youth will not develop into adult sexual offenders, many will continue to experience non-sexual difficulties with their emotions, behaviours and relationships. With help, though, even these other, more likely, problems may be addressed and remediated.

As described, most sexually abusive adolescents are travelling along very different paths and are at considerably different points in their lives from adult sexual offenders. They are also motivated by many different current factors and experiences. Not only are they less likely to have deviant motivations and patterns of sexual arousal than adult sexual offenders, but their sexual interests and behaviours are far less likely to be driven by fixed attitudes, ideas, beliefs and emotional needs.[2] This does not lessen the very real impact of juvenile sexual crimes on their victims and society. But it does mean that we can intervene and treat sexually abusive juveniles with hope and often success, and often in ways that are not successful with adults.

However, although at substantially different points in their development and in their current lives, as noted the roots of sexually abusive behaviour are very much the same in juveniles as in adult sexual offenders. Adolescent offenders experience many of the same early childhood experiences as do their adult counterparts and the early childhood experiences of many sexually abusive youth are marked with abuse, neglect, maltreatment and disruption. Nonetheless, it would be a mistake to think that these experiences alone produce antisocial behaviours. In fact, the development of sexually abusive behaviour is a complex process that takes multiple pathways and involves multiple risk factors that combine to produce such behaviour in adolescents (Rich, 2003, 2006). Aside from many developmental vulnerabilities and negative experiences, including the possibility of their own history of sexual or physical abuse, the co-existence of a mental health disorder is common in juvenile sexual offenders. It is increasingly well recognised, for instance, that juvenile delinquents in general experience substantially higher rates of mental health disorders than youth in the general public (Bilchik, 1998; Cocozza & Skowyra, 2000; Grisso *et al.*, 2001), and most children in the juvenile justice system meet the criteria for at least one diagnosis. Among juvenile sexual offenders, attention deficit, anxiety and depressive disorders are commonly diagnosed. In addition, there is an increasing focus on the role of attachment deficits in adolescent sexual abusers, or the disruption or lack of affectional bonding that is typically formed in the relationship between young children and their primary caregivers (i.e., their parents).[3]

However, despite these frequent contributing factors, these children are still very much in the developmental and experimental stages of their lives, with few truly fixed patterns of behaviour, attitudes and relationships. On the contrary, they are developmentally open to and capable of change. They are thus often very responsive to treatment interventions that aim at mental health, rehabilitation and change, especially when delivered with structure, understanding, and genuine support and caring.

---

[2]Again, it is to be recognised that this is not necessarily true for cognitively impaired adolescents, who may experience more fixed ideas and rudimentary emotional needs than other developing adolescents.

[3]To learn more about the relevance and value of attachment theory to the treatment of sexually abusive youth, see Rich (2006, 2007).

HOLISTIC AND COMPREHENSIVE TREATMENT

If we understand the depth and complexity of the issues and factors that drive sexually abusive and other antisocial and self-destructive behaviour, then we start to see sexually abusive youth as 'whole' people in need of layers of treatment, rather than a uni-dimensional and narrow model of 'sex offender specific' treatment. This requires not just the development of clinical skills in the practitioner, but the development of treatment programmes able to recognise and treat multiple factors.

What does a holistic model look like? First, it must take into account the nature of each client as an individual whose emotions, cognitions, behaviours and relationships are driven by multiple factors, many of which are unique to that individual. The first step, then, is learning about that client. Regardless of the intention and outcome of risk assessment, in which the primary goal is to predict the possibility or likelihood of a future sexual offence, we learn about the youth through a careful and thorough psychosocial assessment in which the primary purpose is to develop an understanding of the youth. If risk assessment looks into the future, then the psychosocial assessment peers into the past, helping us to understand how this child *became* this child and what perhaps motivates and drives him or her.

A comprehensive psychosocial assessment allows us to build a formulation of the case, and create a clinical theory of who the child is, and provides the material from which to draw for the assessment of future possible risk (Rich, 2003). If we complete the risk assessment based only on file material, or depend on such material for our understanding of the youth, we are destined not to fully understand the client or have a meaningful foundation upon which to build treatment, base goals and measure progress over time.

A holistic model of treatment is 'holistic' for two primary reasons. Perhaps first and foremost, it is holistic because it recognises and responds to the client as a whole person, rather than defining, measuring and responding to clients by some of their behaviours alone (e.g., sexually abusive behaviour). Second, a holistic approach recognises that sexually abusive youth bring into treatment with them all of the myriad developmental experiences that have shaped them and the personal characteristics which define them, some or many of which will need to be addressed and become targets for treatment.

Driven by this belief in the 'whole' child and recognition of a range of treatment issues, holistic treatment is thus multi-dimensional, bringing together many elements of treatment. It is aimed at multiple treatment targets; it is multi-modal, providing different forms of treatment and types of treatment interventions (such as individual, group, family, and experiential therapy, as well as psychiatry); and it is *pantheoretical*, weaving together ideas from different theoretical backgrounds, and most notably cognitive behavioural and psychodynamic therapy, but increasingly ideas from neurology.

However, the use of the term 'holistic' is more of an expression about how the treatment programme recognises and responds to the nature of the client. With respect to their approach, programmes like this can be thought of as integrated models of treatment that bring together disparate, multiple and complex elements of treatment, including assessment and re-assessment over time, as well as interweaving different theoretical approaches to treatment into a single model. Because of their awareness and use of multiple models and approaches to treatment, integrated programmes are thus able to both customise treatment for individual clients and be flexible with respect to the 'what, when, and how' of treatment, with respect to what treatment interventions are provided, and when and how they are provided, in each case reflecting the pacing of treatment and geared to the needs of each client.

Nevertheless, treatment remains sex offender specific, despite a holistic approach and integrated model. That is, we recognise that the client is entering treatment primarily and specifically because of his or her sexually abusive behaviour, and not because of other co-existing conditions that we may recognise and also treat. Thus, in sex offender specific the holistic approach is directed specifically towards resolving and rehabilitating the sexually abusive behaviour that brought the client into treatment.

INTEGRATED MODELS

In an integrated model of treatment, we recognise that one-size-fits-all models of treatment, driven largely by psychoeducational technique and practice, are not likely to meet the complex needs of individuals, nor necessarily recognise those needs. Such models have often used psychoeducation as a primary means to instruct clients and deliver treatment, concentrated on simplistic cognitive behavioural techniques and ideas, been driven by relapse prevention models that are quite limited and often do not truly reflect the dynamic factors at play for individual clients, and have been partially dependent on workbook-style materials and exercises for the delivery and completion of treatment.

Happily, such models seem to be decreasing, and we have seen a steady expansion of treatment ideas and practices over the past 3–5 years, reflected in a study of outpatient and residential programmes treating adult and juvenile sexual offenders in the United States (McGrath, Cumming & Burchard, 2003). Between 75–97% of surveyed adolescent programmes provide treatment in intimacy and relationship skills, social skills training, and victim empathy; 81% provide a focus on the juvenile's own history of victimisation; 80% provide relaxation or stress management; 40% art therapy; and 16% drama therapy. In the treatment of juvenile sexual offenders, then, we are seeing programmes that treat far more than simply sexually abusive behaviours and provide far more than cognitive behavioural and psychoeducational treatment alone, thereby recognising that their clients are in need of a range of treatment services.

In the integrated treatment programme, then, we incorporate a range of treatment techniques, including aspects of the psychoeducationally-driven programme. But, by blending different treatments we create a multifaceted model of treatment in which no single theory predominates. These programmes consolidate elements from single theory models of treatment, weaving together strands of different therapies into a new and coherent whole, as opposed to eclecticism, which can be idiosyncratic, and without theory (Holmes & Bateman, 2002).

Hence, the integrated treatment programme uses cognitive behavioural therapy to re-structure thinking and related behaviours that contribute to sexually abusive behaviour, and psychodynamic therapy to build relationships and develop insights that help clients link current behaviours, attitudes, relationships and emotional experiences with root causes and psychological needs. Through family therapy, we explore and re-construct family relationships and support systems, and by including expressive and experiential therapies we allow for non-verbal learning and expression. The use of psychoeducation provides an effective means by which to deliver ideas and teach concepts common to all clients in treatment, and helps build a common language that can be spoken and understood by clinicians and other treatment staff, clients, parents, and other related parties, such as probation officers and social service workers. In an integrated model, relapse prevention planning serves not as the pinnacle of treatment but as a means by which we help teach sexually abusive youth and their family about triggers and risks that contribute to sexualised and antisocial behaviour, and establish a means for self-monitoring, help seeking, and harm avoidance. Finally, through the use of individual, group, and family therapy, as well as psychopharmacology and psychoeducation, we utilise multiple methods for delivering treatment.

THE INTEGRATED CLINICIAN

It is not enough to treat complex clients in complex and integrated programmes without also having treatment providers who are integrated in their approach to treatment. In describing differences, and actually underlying elements common to all effective treatment, J. Stuart Ablon and Enrico Jones (1998) described the prototypical characteristics of both the cognitive behavioural and the psychodynamic therapist, recognising essential differences between the two approaches to treatment. In combining both sets of characteristics, we produce a combined prototype for treatment that integrates both cognitive behavioural and psychodynamic therapy, and thus describe the 'integrated' clinician, not merely borrowing techniques from either discipline but operating on principles common to each model, bringing together and using techniques and clinical attributes in a single integrated model. This clinician is prepared to work within the expanding and increasingly more comprehensive model of treatment demanded by an integrated treatment that recognises the wholeness and broad needs of juvenile sexual offenders.

The integrated clinician is versatile and flexible, capable of recognising and meeting the needs of different clients under different circumstances and at different points in their treatment, and able to combine supportive therapy with a content-oriented approach to treatment. In each of five areas that define therapy, the integrated clinician pulls on and demonstrates the attributes and approaches of both cognitive behavioural and psychodynamic therapy, providing a supportive, exploratory, insight-oriented therapy and a content-driven, structured, directive and instructive form of treatment.

Involving interactive style, use of therapy, therapeutic focus, executive function, and approach to facilitation (with 31 individual attributes grouped into these five categories), clinicians working within an integrated treatment model display attributes that are accepting of the client, demonstrate a belief in the client's capacity, and are empathic, sensitive, encouraging, and emotionally responsive (Rich, 2003).

These clinicians are engaging and communicative, clear in their communication, directive and challenging, while remaining non-judgemental, open and authentic, and respectful. In this model, "the first pre-requisite for doing therapy is not a theory ... but a way of being with persons that is facilitative" (Rogers & Wood, 1974, p. 213). In the interpersonally driven and functional therapy provided by the integrated clinician, the therapist demonstrates and uses behaviours that structure, define and direct therapy, and also offers clear support and encouragement for the client, creates favourable expectancies, and, perhaps above all, creates a therapeutic climate that is facilitative and in which a belief is demonstrated in the client's capacities. This is a therapy high in interaction between clinician and client, and also in the use of therapy as a tool for practical discoveries about self, others, behaviours and relationships.

THE TREATMENT ENVIRONMENT

In the facilitative climate, treatment growth is recognised, partially at least, as a product of the environment itself and the therapeutic relationship that exists within it. However, we must always recognise those elements brought into the environment by the client, *independent* of treatment. For sexually abusive youth and other troubled adolescents and children, these personal elements often include attachment needs and difficulties, deficits in a range of critical social skills, poor self-regulation, a poorly-developed base for the development of either empathy or moral decision making, and other experiences of self and others related to early and ongoing childhood development.

In more fully describing an integrated model of treatment, then, we describe it operating within a treatment environment that focuses on the development of important social skills, recognises the therapeutic relationship, and fosters social connection and the development of attached relationships. In an environment informed by ideas about attachment and social relatedness, treatment occurs in a caring and supportive manner, through an 'attachment-friendly' environment in which relationships are genuine, respectful and supportive, while at the same time being structured and challenging, and in which the message that comes through is one of care, concern, understanding and attunement. This sort of environment may be especially important in the treatment of sexually abusive youth, who have been described by Michael Miner (Miner & Crimmins, 1997; Miner & Munns, 2005) as frequently more socially isolated and *normless* than other adolescents (including non-sexual juvenile delinquents), possibly expecting adult and peer rejection.

In this treatment environment, sexually abusive youth are recognised and treated as individuals, rather than 'sexual offenders' who all share the same backgrounds and behaviours. Despite commonalities, the needs of each client are assessed and interpreted on an individual basis, through the process of formulating each case. Of course, now conventional and well developed psychoeducational/cognitive behavioural elements of sex offender specific treatment are provided in this treatment environment, including a focus on dysfunctional behavioural cycles, thinking errors, cognitive restructuring, and relapse prevention plans. However, it is recognised that these are but elements of treatment among a larger array of treatment services that individualise treatment and avoid the one-size-fits-all model of sex offender specific treatment for sexually abusive youth.

All treatment components are thus embedded within and delivered through a treatment environment that is attuned to and responsive to clients, and in which they are recognised and understood. In this environment, opportunities are available for taking responsibility, realising potential and experiencing success, and thus building self-efficacy, self-regulation and self-agency, while also building social skills that include perspective taking, values clarification and moral decision making, social connection, and relationship building.

CONCLUSIONS: UNDERSTANDING THE CLIENT

Unless we simply wish to treat the sexually abusive behaviour apart from the totality of the youth engaging in those behaviours, or believe we can treat those behaviours in isolation from the youth's other experiences of self and others, we must find ways to treat the whole child. This means recognising the personal and social needs of each adolescent and the context of that adolescent's life, within which the sexually abusive behaviour developed and occurred. Most of all, we hope to change the trajectory along which the sexually abusive youth may be heading, knowing that although most juvenile sexual offenders do not develop into adult sexual offenders, nevertheless some will.

We can teach simplistic concepts and methods to our clients, which have represented a good part of the sex offender specific model until recently, but these are unlikely to engender the changes we seek or transmit ideas about social connection and relatedness. It is through a multi-dimensional and multi-theoretical approach that we are most likely to accomplish goals of social skill development, social competence and social rehabilitation. The qualities that we wish to effectuate in sexually abusive youth, not only of behavioural restraint, appropriate social and sexual boundaries, and belongingness, but also empathy and concern for and the valuing of others, are exactly those qualities that juvenile sexual offenders must themselves experience from others in their environment, including those who provide treatment.

Through the warmth, concern, support, safety, and structure provided in the empathic and attuned treatment environment, sexually abusive youth are experienced as children with many complex needs, including the need to be recognised and understood by others. Perhaps more to the point, they must experience themselves as being seen and understood by others. Through this experience, they are enabled to see and explore themselves in a different light; in turn, they are able to see and experience other people in a different light. Through therapy and the therapeutic relationship, these are the changes for which we aim. In the words of Urie Bronfenbrenner (1990), "human development occurs in the context of an escalating ping-pong game between two people" in which the child experiences someone caring about him or her (p. 31). Despite the label of juvenile sexual offender, our clients are first children and adolescents with the need to feel good about themselves, cared about, and engaged in social relationships. The changes in sexual attitude and behaviour we want come *after* these experiences.

REFERENCES

Abel, G.G., Osborn, C.A. & Twigg, D.A. (1993). Sexual assault through the life span: Adult offenders with juvenile histories. In H.E. Barbaree, W.L. Marshall & S.M. Hudson (Eds), *The juvenile sex offender* (pp. 104–117). New York: Guilford Press.

Ablon, J.S. & Jones, E.E. (1998). How expert clinicians' prototypes of an ideal treatment correlate with outcome in psychodynamic and cognitive-behavioral therapy. *Psychotherapy Research, 8*, 71–83.

Alexander, M.A. (1999). Sexual offender treatment efficacy revisited. *Sexual Abuse: A Journal of Research and Treatment, 11*, 101–116.

American Psychiatric Association (2000). *Diagnostic and Statistical Manual of Mental Disorders* (4th edn, text revision). Washington, DC: Author.

Association for the Treatment of Sexual Abusers. (2000, March). *The effective legal management of juvenile sexual offenders* (Position paper). Beaverton, OR: Author.

Bilchik, S. (1998). Mental health disorders and substance abuse problems among juveniles. *OJJDP Fact Sheet, 82*. Washington, DC: US Department of Justice, Office of Juvenile Justice and Delinquency Prevention.

Bronfenbrenner, U. (1990). *Rebuilding the nest: A new commitment to the American family*. Milwaukee, WI: Family Service America.

Burton, D.L. (2000). Were adolescent sexual offenders children with sexual behavior problems? *Sexual Abuse: A Journal of Research and Treatment, 12*, 37–48.

Caldwell, M.F. (2002). What we do not know about juvenile sexual reoffense risk. *Child Maltreatment, 7*, 291–302.

Center for Sex Offender Management (1999). *Understanding juvenile sexual offending behavior: Emerging research, treatment approaches and management practices*. Silver Spring, MD: Author.

Chaffin, M., Berliner, L., Block, R. *et al.* (2006). *Association for the Treatment of Sexual Abusers Task Force Report on children with sexual behavior problems*. Beaverton, OR: ATSA.

Cocozza, J.J. & Skowyra, K.R. (2000). Youth with mental health disorders: Issues and emerging responses. *Juvenile Justice, 7*, 3–13.

D'Orazio, D. (2002). *A comparative analysis of empathy in sexually offending and non-offending juvenile and adult males*. Unpublished doctoral dissertation. California School of Professional Psychology at Alliant University, Fresno, CA.

Davis, M.H. (1996). *Empathy: A social psychological approach*. Boulder, CO: Westview Press.

Epperson, D.L. & Ralston, R.A. (2005). *Optimal predictors of juvenile sexual recidivism in a large scale study of Utah adolescents who have offended sexually*. Seminar presented at the 20th Annual Conference of the National Adolescent Perpetration Network, Denver, CO, February 2005.

Epperson, D.L., Ralston, C.A., Fowers, D. *et al.* (2006). Actuarial risk assessment with juveniles who sexually offend: Development of the Juvenile Sexual Offense Recidivism Risk Assessment Tool-II (JSORRAT-II-II). In D.S. Prescott (Ed.), *Risk assessment of youth who have sexually abused* (pp. 118–169). Oklahoma City, OK: Wood 'n' Barnes.

Fernandez, Y.M. & Serran, G. (2002). Empathy training for therapists and clients. In Y. Fernandez (Ed.), *In their shoes* (pp. 110–131). Oklahoma City, OK: Wood 'n' Barnes.

Fonagy, P. (2001). *Attachment theory and psychoanalysis.* New York: Other Press.

Fonagy, P., Target, M., Steele, M. *et al.* (1997a). Morality, disruptive behavior, borderline personality disorder, crime, and their relationships to security of attachment. In L. Atkinson & K.J. Zucker (Eds), *Attachment and psychopathology* (pp. 223–274). New York: Guilford.

Fonagy, P., Target, M., Steele, M. & Steele, H. (1997b). The development of violence and crime as it relates to security of attachment. In J.D. Osofsky (Ed.), *Children in a violent society* (pp. 150–177). New York: Guilford.

Forth, A.E., Kosson, D.S. & Hare, R.D. (2003). *Hare PCL-Youth Version. Technical Manual.* North Tonawanda, NY: Multi-Health Systems, Inc.

Frick, P.J. & Hare, R.D. (2002). *Antisocial Process Screening Device.* North Tonawanda, NY: Multi-Health Systems, Inc.

Frick, P.J., Cornell, A.H., Barry, C.T. *et al.* (2003a). Callous-unemotional traits and conduct problems in the prediction of conduct severity, aggression, and self-report of delinquency. *Journal of Abnormal Child Development, 31,* 457–470.

Frick, P.J., Cornell, A.H., Bodin, S.D. *et al.* (2003b). Callous-unemotional traits and developmental pathways to severe aggressive and antisocial behavior. *Developmental Psychology, 39,* 246–260.

Giedd, J.N. (2002). *Inside the teenage brain.* Retrieved December 2004 from: http://www.pbs.org/wgbh/pages/frontline/shows/teenbrain/interviews/

Grisso, T., Barnum, R., Fletcher, K.E. *et al.* (2001). Massachusetts Youth Screening Instrument for Mental Health Needs of Juvenile Justice Youths. *Journal of the American Academy of Child and Adolescent Psychiatry, 40,* 541–548.

Harris, A., Phenix, A., Hanson, R.K. & Thornton, D. (2003). *Static-99 Coding Rules Revised – 2003.* Ottawa, Canada: Department of the Solicitor General of Canada.

Hoffman, M.L. (2000). *Empathy and moral development: Implications for caring and justice.* Cambridge, England: Cambridge University Press.

Holmes, J. & Bateman, A. (2002). *Integration in psychotherapy: Models and methods.* Oxford, England: Oxford University Press.

Kagan, J. (1984). *The nature of the child.* New York: Basic Books.

Letourneau, E.J. & Miner, M.H. (2005). Juvenile sex offenders: A case against the legal and clinical status quo. *Sexual Abuse: A Journal of Research and Treatment, 17,* 293–312.

Marshall, L. (2002). The development of empathy. In Y. Fernandez (Ed.), *In their shoes* (pp. 36–52). Oklahoma City, OK: Wood 'n' Barnes.

Marshall, W.L. & Eccles, A. (1993). Pavlovian conditioning processes in adolescent sex offenders. In H.E. Barbaree, W.L. Marshall & S.M. Hudson (Eds), *The juvenile sex offender* (pp. 118–142). New York: Guilford.

Marshall, W.L., Marshall, L.E., Serran, G.A. & Fernandez, Y.M. (2006). *Treating sexual offenders: An integrated approach.* New York: Routledge.

McGrath, R.J., Cumming, G.F. & Burchard, B.L. (2003). *Current practices and trends in sexual abuser management: The Safer Society 2002 Nationwide Survey.* Brandon, VT: Safer Society Press.

Miner, M.H. & Crimmins, C.L.S. (1997). Adolescent sex offenders: Issues of etiology and risk factors. In B.K. Schwartz & H.R. Cellini (Eds.), *The sex offender: Corrections, treatment and legal practice* (pp. 9.1–9.15) Kingston, NJ: Civic Research Institute.

Miner, M.H. & Munns, R. (2005). Isolation and normlessness: Attitudinal comparisons of adolescent sex offenders, juvenile offenders, and non-delinquents. *International Journal of Offender Therapy and Comparative Criminology, 49,* 491–504.

National Task Force on Juvenile Sexual Offending (1993). The Revised Report on Juvenile Sexual Offending (1993) of the National Adolescent Perpetration Network. *Juvenile and Family Court Journal, 44*, 1–120.

Nisbet, I.A., Wilson, P.H. & Smallbone, S.W. (2004). A prospective longitudinal study of sexual recidivism among adolescent sex offenders. *Sexual Abuse: A Journal of Research and Treatment, 16*, 223–234.

Parks, G.A. & Bard, D.E. (2006). Rick factors for adolescent sexual offender recidivism: Evaluation of predictive factors and comparison of three groups based on victim type. *Sexual Abuse: A Journal of Research and Treatment, 18*, 319–342.

Reitzel, L.R. & Carbonel, J.L. (2006). The effectiveness of sexual offender treatment for juveniles as measured by recidivism: A meta-analysis. *Sexual Abuse, 18*, 401–421.

Rich, P. (2003). *Understanding, assessing, and rehabilitating juvenile sexual offenders*. Hoboken, NJ: John Wiley & Sons, Inc.

Rich, P. (2006). *Attachment and sexual offending: Understanding and applying attachment theory to the treatment of juvenile sexual offenders*. Chichester, UK: John Wiley & Sons, Ltd.

Rich, P. (2007). The implications of attachment theory in the treatment of sexually abusive youth. In M.C. Calder (Ed.), *Children and young people who sexually abuse: Taking the field forward* (pp. 186–201). Dorset, England: Russell House Publishing.

Rich, P. (in press). The etiology and treatment of juvenile offending behavior: The complex task of understanding complexity in sexually abusive youth. In J.T. Andrade (Ed.), *Handbook of violence risk assessment and treatment for forensic social workers*. NY: Springer.

Rogers, C.R. (1980). *A way of being*. Boston, MA: Houghton Mifflin.

Rogers, C.R. & Wood, J.K. (1974). Client-centered therapy. In A. Burton (Ed.), *Operational theories of personality* (pp. 211–258). New York: Bruner/Mazel.

Seagrave, D. & Grisso, T. (2002). Adolescent development and the measurement of juvenile psychopathy. *Law and Human Behavior, 26*, 219–239.

Spear, L.P. (2000). The adolescent brain and age-related behavioral manifestations. *Neuroscience and Biobehavioral Reviews, 24*, 417–463.

Spear, L.P. (2003). *The psychobiology of adolescence*. (Working Paper 76-11.) New York: Institute for American Values.

Steinberg, L. (2003). *Less guilty by reason of adolescence: A developmental perspective on adolescence and the law*. Invited Master Lecture, biennial meetings of the Society for Research in Child, Development, Tampa, FL. April 2003.

Steinberg, L. & Scott, E.S. (2003). Less guilty by reason of adolescence. *American Psychologist, 58*, 1009–1018.

Stilwell, B.M., Galvin, M.R., Kopta, S.M. & Padgett, R.J. (1998). Moral volition: the fifth and final domain leading to an integrated theory of conscience understanding. *Journal of the American Academy of Child and Adolescent Psychiatry, 37*, 202–210.

US Department of Health and Human Services (2001). *Youth Violence: A report of the Surgeon General*. Rockville, MD: US Department of Health and Human Services.

US Department of Justice (1995). *Uniform Crime Reports for the United States, 1995*. Washington, DC: US Department of Justice.

US Department of Justice (1996). *Uniform Crime Reports for the United States, 1996*. Washington, DC: US Department of Justice.

US Department of Justice (1998). *Crime in the United States, 1998: Uniform Crime Reports*. Washington, DC: US Government Printing Office.

US Department of Justice (2003). *Crime in the United States, 2003: Uniform Crime Reports*. Washington, DC: US Government Printing Office.

US Department of Justice (2005). *Crime in the United States, 2005*. Washington, DC: US Department of Justice.

Vetlesen, A.J. (1994). *Perception, empathy, and judgment: An inquiry into the preconditions of moral performance*. University Park, PA: Pennsylvania University Press.

Warner, M.S. (1997). Does empathy cure? A theoretical consideration of empathy, processing, and personal narrative. In A.C. Bohart & L.S. Greenberg (Eds), *Empathy reconsidered: New directions in psychotherapy* (pp. 125–140). Washington, DC: American Psychological Association.

Yurgelun-Todd, D. (2002). *Inside the Teenage Brain*. Retrieved December 2004 from: http://www.pbs.org/wgbh/pages/frontline/shows/teenbrain/interviews

Zimring, F.E. (2004). *An American travesty: legal responses to adolescent sexual offending*. Chicago, IL: University of Chicago Press.

24

Multisystemic Therapy for Youth with Problem Sexual Behaviors

ELIZABETH J. LETOURNEAU

CHARLES M. BORDUIN

CINDY M. SCHAEFFER

INTRODUCTION

Many policy makers and legal and mental health professionals have the inaccurate perception that juvenile sex offenders are different from other juvenile offenders. More specifically, many professionals believe that juvenile sex offenders: (1) are at exceptionally high risk of reoffending; (2) share more characteristics with adult sex offenders than with other juvenile delinquents; and (3) exist in epidemic numbers. These beliefs have led to aggressive legal interventions such as community notification, sex offender registration, and civil commitment (Caldwell, 2002; Letourneau & Miner, 2004; Swenson & Letourneau, 2005) and to the development of restrictive, long-term, sex-offender-specific treatment programs for juvenile sex offenders and (increasingly) for younger children and adolescents with non-criminal sexual behavior problems (Carpentier, Silovsky & Chaffin, 2006).

The principal goal of these restrictive legal and clinical interventions is presumably to alter the progression of events that begin with child sexual behavior problems, progress to juvenile sexual offending, and culminate in a career of criminal sexual aggression. Yet, empirical evidence argues against any such progression. Children who display early sexual behavior problems rarely commit sexual offenses in adolescence (Carpentier *et al.*, 2006; Letourneau, Chapman & Schoenwald, 2008) and adolescents charged with sexual offenses rarely reoffend in adulthood (Alexander, 1999; Caldwell, 2002). Thus, restrictive legal and clinical interventions represent the misapplication of limited resources to many of these youths.

Assessment and Treatment of Sex Offenders: A Handbook. Edited by Anthony Beech, Leam Craig and Kevin Browne. © John Wiley & Sons Ltd, 2009.

The present chapter presents an alternative, ecologically-based intervention for youth with criminal and non-criminal sexual behavior problems and explains why, in our opinion, treatment is most effective when empirically validated (versus assumed) correlates of sexual misbehavior are addressed. A growing base of rigorous outcome research supports the efficacy of family and ecologically-focused treatments that specifically target the known correlates of sexual behavior problems (Borduin *et al.*, 1990; Borduin & Schaeffer, 2001; Hunter *et al.*, 2004). Before reviewing the treatment outcome literature, we present an overview of the correlates of problem sexual behavior in youths. The term 'problem sexual behaviors' (PSB) will be used when describing the treatment of youth who engage in serious non-normative sexual behaviors, whether formally adjudicated or not, that either victimize others or place others at risk of victimization. The range of deviant sexual behavior encompassed by this term includes non-aggressive sexual acts against others such as the fondling of a younger child in the context of an ongoing relationship, and aggressive sexual acts against others such as the violent rape of a peer. Under this definition other non-normative sexual behaviors, such as excessive or public masturbation, would not be considered a PSB unless it did or had the potential to victimize others, or was part of a larger pattern of behaviors involving sexual victimization of others. We feel that use of the term 'problem sexual behavior' is less stigmatizing and incendiary than the term 'sexual offender'. However, in light of the fact that the term 'juvenile sexual offender' (JSO) abounds in the empirical literature, we will use the acronym JSO when citing specific studies which defined their samples in this way (as do most of the studies on correlates of sexual offending).

CORRELATES OF JUVENILE SEXUAL OFFENDING

The vast majority of studies that have examined the correlates of juvenile sexual offending are characterized by relatively serious methodological limitations (see Becker, 1998; Davis & Leitenberg, 1987). For example, there is almost a complete absence of studies that have used appropriate comparison groups (e.g., juvenile offenders who have not committed sexual offenses); without such control groups, it is difficult to determine whether observed results are linked with sexual offending in particular or with delinquency in general. In addition, most studies have combined subgroups of sexual offenders (e.g., combining youth with younger versus older victims; combining youth with no versus multiple prior arrests) into a single group and may have obscured potentially important psychosocial differences between subgroups. Furthermore, the data in many of the extant studies were derived from clinical impressions and non-standardized assessment instruments, and youth self-reports are often the primary source of information. Notwithstanding these methodological limitations, the extant findings indicate that multiple characteristics of individual youths and their social systems (family, peers, school) are linked with juvenile sexual offending (Becker, 1998; Borduin & Schaeffer, 2001).

Individual Youth Factors

Juvenile sexual offenders report higher rates of emotional and behavioral problems than do non-delinquent youths but similar rates to those of non-sexually offending delinquent youths (Ronis & Borduin, 2007). In addition, despite clinical lore, there is little evidence that the majority of juvenile sexual offenders have a history of sexual abuse (Becker & Murphy, 1998); in fact, prevalence rates of self-reported abuse histories for sexual-offending youth range from approximately 20% to 50% (Becker, 1988; Kahn & Chambers, 1991; Kaufman, Hilliker & Daleiden, 1996) and are similar to those for other types of juvenile offenders (Awad & Saunders, 1991). Likewise, juvenile sexual offenders have verbal skills that are similar to those of juvenile non-sexual offenders (Lewis, Shankok & Pincus, 1981; Tarter *et al.*, 1983). Although there is some evidence that victim blaming is related to higher reoffense rates among juvenile sexual offenders (Kahn & Chambers, 1991), the prevalence of other potential cognitive distortions has not been demonstrated (e.g., Hastings, Anderson & Hemphill, 1997).

Family Characteristics

Research has indicated that, similar to families of other types of juvenile offenders, families of juvenile sexual offenders evidence lower levels of positive communication and warmth than do families of non-delinquent youths (Bischof, Stith & Whitney, 1995; Blaske *et al.*, 1989; Ronis & Borduin, 2007). In addition, consistent with findings for families of juvenile non-sexual offenders, families of juvenile sexual offenders show relatively low rates of parental monitoring (Wieckowski *et al.*, 1998) and high rates of parent – child and interparental conflict and violence (Awad & Saunders, 1989; Davis & Leitenberg, 1987; Fehrenbach *et al.*, 1986). There is also evidence that parents of juvenile sexual offenders have relatively high rates of substance abuse (Graves *et al.*, 1996; Johnson, 1989).

Peer Relations

Studies have shown that juvenile sexual offenders are more likely to be socially inept and isolated from same-age peers than are other juvenile offenders or non-delinquent youths (Awad & Saunders, 1989; Blaske *et al.*, 1989; Johnson, 1989). Perhaps as a result of isolation from their own peer group, juvenile sexual offenders often turn to younger peers for relationships that are emotionally safer and easier to control (Awad & Saunders, 1989; Fagan & Wexler, 1988; Fehrenbach *et al.*, 1986). Although there is some evidence that isolation from same-age peers and preference for younger peers are more common among juveniles who molest younger children than among juveniles who sexually assault same-age peers or adults (Awad & Saunders, 1991; Graves *et al.*, 1996), a recent study found no differences between subgroups of juvenile sexual offenders (i.e., offenders with younger vs. older victims) in maintaining close relations with same-age peers (Ronis & Borduin, 2007). Moreover, this latter study found that juvenile sexual offenders, similar to other delinquent youths, associate more extensively with deviant peers than do non-delinquent youths.

School Factors

Juvenile sexual offending has been linked with academic and behavioral difficulties in school, including low achievement, below expected grade placement (Awad & Saunders, 1989; Fehrenbach *et al.*, 1986; Johnson, 1989), behavior problems (Fehrenbach *et al.*, 1986; Tufts' New England Medical Center, Division of Child Psychiatry, 1984), suspension, and expulsion (Tufts' New England Medical Center, Division of Child Psychiatry, 1984). However, direct comparisons of sexually offending and non-sexually offending delinquents (e.g., Awad & Saunders, 1991; Ford & Linney, 1995; Ronis & Borduin, 2007) suggest that these school-related difficulties are not unique to juvenile sexual offenders.

THEORETICAL AND CLINICAL IMPLICATIONS

The findings from the correlational literature on juvenile sexual offending are consistent with a social-ecological view of behavior (Bronfenbrenner, 1979) and, for the most part, with findings from the literature on juvenile non-sexual offending. Indeed, across studies and in spite of considerable variation in research methods and measurement (e.g., correlational vs. more sophisticated causal modeling studies), investigators have shown that non-sexual offending is determined by the reciprocal interplay of characteristics of the individual youth and the key social systems (family, peers, school, neighborhood) in which youths are embedded. Table 24.1 lists the correlates that have consistently emerged in the literature on serious antisocial behavior (i.e., non-sexual offending), whether the examined antisocial behavior is conduct disorder (Kazdin, 1995; McMahon, Wells & Kotler, 2006) or criminal activity (Borduin & Schaeffer, 1998; Loeber, Farrington & Waschbusch, 1998).

The extant literature cited above and a recent report from a prospective, longitudinal study (van Wijk *et al.*, 2005) support the view that developmental pathways for sexual offending are similar to those for non-sexual offending. Juvenile sexual offending is multi-determined and treatment approaches must have the flexibility to address the known correlates of such offending. We believe that the major limitation of current specialized treatment programs for youth with serious problem sexual behaviors is that they address only a limited subset of relevant factors in the youth's social ecology, and that effective treatments must have the capacity to intervene comprehensively, at individual, family, peer, school, and possibly even neighborhood levels.

SPECIALIZED TREATMENTS FOR JUVENILES WHO ENGAGE IN PROBLEM SEXUAL BEHAVIORS

Specialized treatments for juveniles with PSBs have been widely available since 1985 (Knopp, Rosenberg & Stevenson, 1986) and remain prevalent. For example, 937

Table 24.1 Correlates of serious antisocial behavior

Individual Youth Characteristics
_ Cognitive bias to attribute hostile intentions to others
_ Favorable attitudes toward antisocial behavior
_ Low verbal skills
_ Psychiatric symptomatology

Family Characteristics
_ Lax and ineffective parental discipline
_ Poor parental monitoring
_ Low affection and cohesion
_ High conflict and hostility
_ Parental difficulties such as drug abuse, psychiatric conditions, and criminality

Peer Relations
_ Poor social skills
_ Association with deviant peers
_ Low association with prosocial peers

School Factors
_ Poor academic performance
_ Low commitment to education
_ Drop-out
_ Poor academic quality and weak structure of school

Neighborhood and Community Characteristics
_ Low social support available from church, neighbors, and the like
_ Low organizational participation among residents
_ Criminal subculture (e.g., drug dealing, prostitution)
_ High mobility

programs responded to a 2001 Safer Society survey of sex offender treatment programs, reporting that they treated more than 21,000 adolescents that year (McGrath, Cumming & Burchard, 2003). Although these programs differed on numerous characteristics, nearly all programs identified cognitive behavioral theory as best describing the program's orientation. There also was broad convergence across programs regarding core treatment targets, most of which focus on remediating individual level deficits or achieving goals such as having the offender take responsibility for the sexual offense, eliminate deviant cognitions, learn important social skills (including intimacy), develop victim awareness and empathy, and engage in behaviors and thoughts that prevent relapse (McGrath *et al.*, 2003). Consistent with the cognitive emphases of the prevailing treatment models, services are typically delivered in institutional settings ranging from outpatient clinics to long-term residential treatment centers (McGrath *et al.*, 2003). Treatment in these settings is often highly structured and sex offender specific and lasts anywhere from 6 to 36 months (McGrath *et al.*, 2003). The bulk of the treatment is delivered via group meetings that last 30 to 90 minutes. Family members, peers, and others from the youth's natural environment (e.g., teachers) are typically under-involved in these interventions. Thus, for example, in outpatient settings, youth spent an average of 359 minutes in group treatment per month, 53 minutes in individual treatment per month (15% of the time spent in group) and

58 minutes in family treatment per month (16% of the time spent in group; see Table 10.2 in McGrath *et al.*, 2003, p. 49). More recently, programs that better reflect differences between adolescent and adult offenders (e.g., Hunter *et al.*, 2004; Worling, 1998) have been developed. The majority of adolescent treatment programs, however, continue to follow from adult-oriented cognitive behavioral models and focus almost exclusively on influencing individual adolescent characteristics (e.g., cognitive strategies, attitudes) as the primary mechanism of change (Becker & Hunter, 1997; Graham, Richardson & Bhate, 1998; Worling, 1998).

Although cognitive behavioral group treatment represents the standard of care for youth with PSBs in the United States (Letourneau, 2004), limited research provides, at best, tentative support for such treatment. For example, in a recent meta-analysis of sexual offender treatment outcome studies, Hanson and colleagues (Hanson *et al.*, 2002) identified only three juvenile-focused treatment studies that included the key criteria of comparison groups and measures of sexual recidivism. Furthermore, just two of these studies examined specialized treatment for juvenile sex offenders (Guarino-Ghezzi & Kimball, 1998; Worling & Curwen, 1998), and neither included random assignment to treatment groups, a serious methodological limitation in outcome research. The two studies reported positive effects for the active treatments. However, treatment group differences in the Guarino-Ghezzi and Kimball study were based on just one youth reoffending in the comparison group, versus no youths reoffending in the specialized treatment group over a one-year follow-up. Treatment group differences for the Worling and Curwen study approached non-significance when intent-to-treat analyses were employed (e.g., when treatment drop-outs were included in the active treatment group – see Hanson *et al.*, 2002). Combined, these two studies provide limited evidence for the effectiveness of specialized treatment for youth with PSBs. Of note, specialized treatment in residential settings (which is much more costly and more restrictive) has completely escaped empirical investigation. It is disappointing that so few outcome studies have focused on the effectiveness of specialized treatment programs.

Based largely on their success in treating adult sexual offenders, cognitive behavioral approaches have proliferated in the treatment of juvenile sexual offenders. Although data provide some support for these programs, there are several good reasons why these approaches may have limited effectiveness for juvenile sexual offenders. First, as noted previously, youth with PSBs possess few of the cognitive biases and deficits that are the foci of adult sex offender treatments. Second, the cognitive behavioral model delivered in clinic and institutional settings provides little consideration of the real world contexts in which adolescents develop. In fact, treatments that are effective in the areas of delinquency (Elliott, 1998) and adolescent substance abuse (National Institute on Drug Abuse, 1999) use interventions that target risk factors across youths' natural ecologies (i.e., family, peers, school). Third, an extensive literature in the area of delinquency prevention and treatment suggests that group-based interventions have harmful side effects under some conditions (see Dishion & Dodge, 2005, for a review). This is an important consideration in light of the aforementioned findings that youth with PSBs share many characteristics with other delinquent juveniles. Alternative treatments for youth with PSBs should take these limitations into consideration.

TREATMENT THEORY, CLINICAL FEATURES AND PRINCIPLES OF MULTISYSTEMIC THERAPY (MST)

The theoretical foundation of MST draws upon the identified correlates/causes of serious antisocial behavior and Bronfenbrenner's (1979) social-ecological theory of behavior. Social-ecological theory views the youth and family's school, work, peers and community as interconnected systems with dynamic and reciprocal influences on the behavior of family members. Problem behavior can be maintained by problematic transactions within and/or between any one or combination of these systems. Thus, consistent with both the empirically established correlates/causes of youth criminality and with social-ecological theory, MST interventions target identified youth and family problems within and between the multiple systems in which family members are embedded.

The provision of MST to youth with PSBs is consistent with the family preservation model of service delivery (Nelson & Landsman, 1992). Family preservation is based on the philosophy that the most effective and ethical route to helping youth is through helping their families. Thus, families are seen as valuable resources, even when they are characterized by serious and multiple needs. A critical characteristic of the family preservation model is that interventions are delivered in the family's natural environment (home, school, neighborhood) to optimize ecological validity. Delivering interventions in the natural environment also greatly decreases barriers to service access in a population (i.e., families of adolescents presenting serious antisocial behavior) that has very high 'no-show' and drop-out rates from traditional institution-based services (for a discussion of this issue, see Snell-Johns, Mendez & Smith, 2004). Indeed, working with families on their own 'turf' sends a message of therapist commitment and respect that can greatly facilitate family engagement and the development of a therapeutic alliance – prerequisites for achieving desired outcomes.

MST for youth with PSBs is usually delivered by a masters level therapist with a caseload of four to five families. The MST therapist is a generalist who directly provides most mental health services and coordinates access to other important services (e.g., medical, educational, recreational), always monitoring quality control. Although the therapist is available to the family 24 hours a day, 7 days a week, therapeutic intensity is titrated to clinical need; thus, the range of direct contact hours per family can vary considerably. In general, therapists spend more time with families in the initial weeks of therapy (daily, if indicated) and gradually taper off (as infrequently as once a week) during a five- to seven-month course of treatment.

MST does not follow a rigid protocol in which therapists conduct sets of predetermined tasks in an invariant sequence. Indeed, because MST is typically used with complex cases that present serious and diverse problems and that also evidence a wide variety of possible strengths, fully detailing treatment parameters for each possible combination of situations would be an impossible task. Nevertheless, in the absence of strong specification, the value of MST would be greatly diminished. Thus, rather than providing session by session breakdowns of recommended clinical procedures, we have developed treatment principles to guide therapists' case conceptualizations, prioritization of interventions, and implementation of intervention strategies in MST.

The nine treatment principles enumerated below serve as general guidelines for designing multisystemic interventions. Detailed descriptions of these principles, and examples that illustrate the translation of these principles into specific intervention strategies, are provided in a clinical volume (Henggeler & Borduin, 1990) and a treatment manual (Henggeler *et al.*, 1998). MST therapists and supervisors often refer to the principles while planning interventions, and treatment fidelity can be evaluated by measuring therapist adherence to the principles.

1. The primary purpose of assessment is to understand the 'fit' between the identified problems and their broader systemic context.
2. Therapeutic contacts emphasize the positive and use systemic strengths as levers for change.
3. Interventions are designed to promote responsible behavior and decrease irresponsible behavior among family members.
4. Interventions are present-focused and action-oriented, targeting specific and well-defined problems.
5. Interventions target sequences of behavior within and between multiple systems that maintain the identified problems.
6. Interventions are developmentally appropriate and fit the developmental needs of the youth.
7. Interventions are designed to require daily or weekly effort by family members.
8. Intervention effectiveness is evaluated continuously from multiple perspectives with providers assuming accountability for overcoming barriers to successful outcomes.
9. Interventions are designed to promote treatment generalization and long-term maintenance of therapeutic change by empowering caregivers to address family members' needs across multiple systemic contexts.

The overriding goals of MST are to empower parents with the skills and resources needed to independently address the inevitable difficulties that arise in raising adolescents and to empower adolescents to cope with familial and extra-familial problems. Using well-validated treatment strategies derived from strategic family therapy, structural family therapy, behavioral parent training, and cognitive behavioral therapy, MST directly addresses intra-personal (e.g., cognitive), familial, and extra-familial (i.e., peer, school, neighborhood) factors that are known to be linked with youth serious antisocial behavior, including sexual offending. Biological contributors to identified problems (e.g., major depression, attention deficit hyperactivity disorder) in family members are also identified, and, when appropriate, psychopharmacological treatment is integrated with psychosocial treatment. Because different contributing factors are relevant for different youths and families, MST interventions are individualized and highly flexible.

Although the exact nature and sequence of interventions in MST can vary widely from family to family, several types of interventions are commonly used with sexually delinquent juveniles and their parents. At the family level, MST interventions generally aim to remove barriers to effective parenting (e.g., parental drug abuse, parental psychopathology, low social support, high stress, marital conflict), to enhance parenting knowledge (e.g., regarding the effectiveness of rewards and the importance of consistent, immediate consequences), and to promote affection and communication among family members; moreover, conjoint work with family members and other appropriate persons in the offender's social ecology (e.g., teachers, extended family members) is essential in the development of plans for risk reduction, relapse prevention and victim safety. At the peer level, interventions frequently target youth social skill and problem-solving deficits in order to promote the development of friendships and peer dating; in other cases, interventions are designed to decrease affiliation with delinquent and drug using peers and to increase affiliation with prosocial peers (e.g., through church youth groups, organized athletics, afterschool activities). Peer relations interventions are optimally conducted by the youth's parents, with the guidance of the therapist, and often consist of active support and encouragement of relationship skills and associations with non-problem peers (e.g., providing transportation, increased privileges), as well as substantive discouragement of associations with deviant peers (e.g., applying significant sanctions). Likewise, under the guidance of the therapist, the parents often develop strategies to monitor and promote the youth's school performance and/or vocational functioning; interventions in this domain typically focus on establishing positive communication lines between parents and teachers and on restructuring after-school hours to promote academic efforts. Finally, in some cases, individual interventions are used with a youth or parent to modify the individual's social perspective-taking skills, belief system, or attitudes that contribute to offending; intra-familial victims of the offender may also receive individual treatment for difficulties related to the sexual assault, although the parent or caregiver is reinforced as the change agent and is directly involved with the intervention.

Treatment fidelity in MST is maintained by weekly group supervision meetings involving three to four therapists and a doctoral level clinical supervisor (usually a child psychologist). During these meetings, the treatment team (i.e., therapists, supervisor, and, as needed, a consulting psychiatrist) reviews the goals and progress of each case to ensure the multisystemic focus of therapists' intervention strategies and to identify obstacles to success. Importantly, the treatment team accepts responsibility for engaging families in treatment and for effecting therapeutic change. Thus, when obstacles to successful engagement or to therapeutic change are identified, the team develops strategies to address those obstacles and to promote success. Fidelity is measured as part of a built-in rigorous quality assurance system. Specifically, caregivers are contacted monthly to complete a standardized measure of therapist adherence to the MST model, and numerous research studies have supported the link between this measure of therapist adherence and youth outcomes (Schoenwald, Sheidow & Letourneau, 2004; Schoenwald *et al.*, 2003).

The clinical supervisor plays a critical role in the MST treatment process. The primary focus of the MST clinical supervisor is on the therapist's thinking, behavior and interactions with the family and with the systems in which the family is embedded. Clinical supervisors ensure that therapists adhere to the nine principles of MST in all aspects of treatment (i.e., engagement and alignment, conceptualization of the causes of referral problems, design and implementation of interventions, overcoming barriers to intervention effectiveness, and assessment of outcomes). In addition, supervisors must be able to assess and promote the development of therapists' MST-like conceptualization and intervention skills across cases (generalization). To facilitate therapists' implementation of MST and the attainment of favorable family outcomes, supervisors reinforce critical thinking about all aspects of treatment.

ADAPTATION OF MST FOR YOUTH WITH PROBLEM SEXUAL BEHAVIORS

As noted earlier, MST interventions for adolescent antisocial behavior are specified in a clinical volume (Henggeler & Borduin, 1990) and a treatment manual (Henggeler *et al.*, 1998) that describe the empirical, conceptual and philosophical bases of MST and delineate the process by which youth and family problems are prioritized and targeted for change. To more fully account for clinical issues relevant to youth with PSBs, investigators have adapted MST for use with this population, specified the adaptation in a supplemental therapist training manual (Borduin et al., in press), and developed a training program for therapists and supervisors. Importantly, MST for youth with PSBs is identical to standard MST in its broad focus on the many correlates associated with juvenile offending generally, but goes beyond standard MST by specifically focusing on aspects of the youth's ecology that are functionally related to the youth's sexual delinquency. Specifically, the adaptations to MST include creating a safety plan to minimize the youth's access to potential victims, addressing youth and caregiver denial about the severity of the offense, and improving youth's peer relations so that more age-appropriate and normative sexual experiences can occur with peers. To address these concerns, the adapted MST model includes a greater emphasis on structural and strategic family therapy interventions than does standard MST.

CLINICAL TRIALS OF MST FOR YOUTH WITH PROBLEM SEXUAL BEHAVIORS

To date, two completed studies have examined the efficacy of MST in addressing sexual offending by juveniles and an ongoing study is examining the effectiveness of MST with this population. Although modest in scope and size (N = 16), Borduin and colleagues (1990) published the first randomized trial with juvenile sexual offenders. Youths and their families were randomly assigned to treatment conditions: home-based MST delivered by doctoral students in clinical psychology versus outpatient individual therapy (i.e., an eclectic blend of psychodynamic, humanistic and behavioral approaches) delivered by community-based mental health professionals. Recidivism results at three-year follow-up were encouraging. Significantly fewer youths in the MST condition were rearrested for sexual crimes (12.5% vs. 75.0%), and the mean frequency of sexual rearrests was considerably lower in the MST condition (0.12 vs. 1.62). Furthermore, the mean frequency of rearrests for non-sexual crimes was lower for the youths who received MST (.62) than for counterparts who received outpatient therapy (2.25). The favorable effects of MST supported the viability of conducting a second evaluation of MST with juvenile sexual offenders.

In a recently completed clinical trial, Borduin and colleagues (Borduin & Schaeffer, 2001; Borduin, Schaeffer & Heiblum, in press) used a multi-agent, multi-method assessment battery to evaluate instrumental (i.e., theory driven) and ultimate (i.e., common to all treatments of juvenile sexual offenders) outcomes in aggressive (i.e., sexual assault, rape) and non-aggressive (i.e., molestation of younger children) juvenile sexual offenders (N = 48) who were randomly assigned to MST or usual services (a combination of cognitive behavioral group and individual treatment administered in a juvenile court setting). Compared to youths who received usual services, youths who received MST showed improvements on a range of instrumental outcomes immediately following treatment, including fewer behavioral problems, less delinquent behavior (self-reported), improved peer relations (i.e., more emotional bonding with peers, less involvement with deviant peers), improved family relations (i.e., more warmth, less conflict), and better grades in school. A nine-year post-treatment follow-up of ultimate outcomes (Borduin & Schaeffer, 2001) revealed that MST participants were significantly less likely than their usual services counterparts to be rearrested for sexual (12.5% vs. 41.7%) and non-sexual (29.2% vs. 62.5%) offenses. In terms of frequency of rearrests, MST participants had 83% fewer rearrests for sexual crimes (average 0.13 vs. 0.79 arrests) and 70% fewer rearrests for other crimes (average 1.46 vs. 4.88 arrests) than did those receiving usual services. MST youth also spent on average 75% fewer days in youth (22.50 vs. 97.50 days) and 80% fewer days in adult (365.00 vs. 1842.50 days) detention facilities. Importantly, these outcomes did not vary on the basis of youth and family background variables (i.e., age, race, gender, socioeconomic status) or pre-treatment arrest characteristics (i.e., number of arrests at baseline, arrests for aggressive vs. non-aggressive sexual offenses).

A third randomized clinical trial involving 127 participants and comparing MST to a specialized outpatient sex offender treatment program is currently underway. The results of this trial will extend the findings of previous studies by including a larger, more diverse sample of youths with PSBs; the supplemental treatment manual that specifies additional treatment components for youths with PSBs in addition to standard MST; and more frequent assessments of youth and family functioning (i.e., instrumental outcome measurement at 6 months, 12 months, 18 months, and

24 months post-recruitment; recidivism data collected at 24 months post-recruitment). In addition, this trial uses therapists in community practice settings and thus is the first effectiveness (rather than efficacy) trial of MST for PSB. Effectiveness studies (e.g., studies completed in real-world practice settings) help determine whether effects found in efficacy studies (e.g., university-based controlled clinical trials) can be replicated in less-controlled settings (Silverman, Kurtines & Hoagwood, 2004). Preliminary results from this trial thus far are consistent with those of the smaller outcome studies. It is from this ongoing clinical trial that the following case example stems.

Case Example

'Tony' was referred for treatment at age 15 after having been adjudicated for aggravated criminal sexual assault, a felony offense in his state. Nine months prior to the start of treatment (at the age of 14), Tony and two other friends physically and sexually assaulted an 8-year-old boy who was their neighbor. The crime was recorded on one of the youth's cell phone digital recorders, and the recording shows Tony forcing a stick up the victim's anus as the victim struggled to escape. Several months after the sexual assault (and before treatment started), Tony was charged with a second crime of defacing property, a misdemeanor offense. At the time of referral, Tony resided with his mother, father, three siblings (ages 23, 22 and 7), maternal grandparents, and 1-year-old niece.

At the start of treatment, initial strengths and needs were identified across several systems (see Table 24.2), and treatment goals were obtained from relevant stakeholders. Tony indicated a desire to "not have any more problems with the police or probation office", "get into programs for my art", and "get a job". Tony's mother said that she wanted her son to "not have any more problems", and for Tony to "focus on his education". Tony's grandmother wanted him to "continue doing well". Tony's grandfather wanted to see Tony "do something productive with his artistic interests", "focus on school", and "get a job". Tony's probation officer wanted Tony to "not have any more sexual aggression cases", "stay compliant with the rules of his probation", and "be compliant at home and school". The therapist's goals were for Tony to eliminate all inappropriate sexual behaviors, get involved in prosocial activities with prosocial peers, and follow household and school rules. Tony's father initially refused to meet with the therapist, after explaining that his son could not possibly have committed the sex crime and therefore did not need any treatment.

After examining strengths and needs, and obtaining desired goals from most key stakeholders, the MST therapist developed overarching treatment goals, including:

1. Elimination of all inappropriate sexual behaviors, as evidenced by youth and caregiver reports and no additional legal charges;
2. Compliance with all terms of probation as evidenced by probation officer report for four consecutive weeks;

3. Demonstration of success in school as evidenced by no unexcused absences and no inappropriate or disruptive behaviors for four consecutive weeks, completion of assignments, and no suspensions; and
4. Engagement in prosocial activities with prosocial friends as evidenced by therapist observation, and youth and caregiver reports.

The therapist met with Tony, his parents and grandmother to conduct a functional analysis of the sexual assault. Although all family members, including Tony, initially denied his involvement in the offense, they also provided information useful to the

Table 24.2 Tony's system, strengths and needs

System	Strengths	Needs/Weaknesses
Individual	• Does well at drawing • Likes soccer	• Physically and sexually assaulted a younger boy • Poor decision-making skills • Low impulse control • Admits trying marijuana and alcohol
Family	• Dad works full-time • Large family network • Mom remains home specifically to provide more supervision for Tony and the other children	• Dad drinks 12-pack/day • Home is excessively cramped, with numerous extended family members using home for full- or part-time residence • Neither parent believes the incident took place despite incontrovertible evidence
School	• Tony receives passing grades • Tony takes several mainstream classes	• Tony is in an alternative school setting that he dislikes • Non-mainstream classes are not challenging to Tony
Peers	• Mom states that Tony has one friend (outside of the family) but that he mostly remains home	• Tony still spends time with the other two co-offenders
Community	• There are stores, activities and religious institutions within walking distance of the home	• The co-defendants reside in the same apartment building • The referral incident took place at the entrance to the apartment • The family is not involved in any of the available community activities • There is a gang presence in the neighborhood • Drugs and alcohol are easily accessible

Figure 24.1 Drivers for Tony's sexual assault behavior

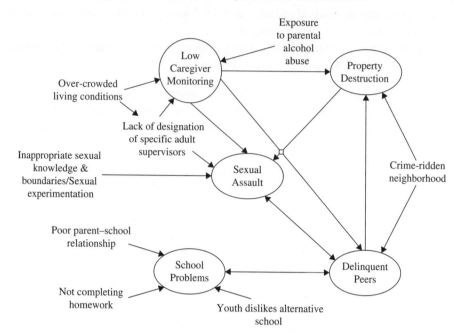

functional analysis of this event. Tony's mother stated that the victim frequently was left unsupervised by his parents for lengthy periods of time. The boy regularly visited her home, appearing dirty and hungry. Tony's mother had, on occasion, fed the boy and had been concerned for his welfare. Tony's grandmother stated that Tony had been getting into trouble with his friends for some period of time prior to the offense. Tony acknowledged having "hung out with" the 8-year-old victim and further acknowledged that he and his friends had gotten into trouble when playing together (though he specifically denied the sexual offense). From the information provided, it appeared that (a) Tony and his friends engaged in several types of delinquent behavior and such was the norm for their neighborhood; (b) Tony and his friends were largely unmonitored by their own parents, who all knew one another and believed that their children were safe so long as they played together in one of the apartment buildings where they all lived; and (c) the victim provided a relatively easy target for assault due to his own apparent neglect by his parents, his hunger for attention from the older boys, and his youthfulness.

The MST therapist also worked with Tony and his caregivers to further determine the drivers or 'fit factors' for his sexual offense, as well as for the destruction of property incident. As can be seen in Figure 24.1, the drivers for these behavior problems were shared (e.g., low caregiver monitoring and involvement with antisocial peers drove both the sexual and property offenses) or mediated by other problems (e.g., school problems were indirectly linked to both problem behaviors by increasing Tony's risk for associating with delinquent peers).

Prioritized drivers were then targeted in weekly treatment sessions. In Tony's case, the initial treatment goals included establishing a safety plan that involved eliminating contact with the other youth involved in the sexual assault, increasing (and better specifying) adult supervision during after-school hours, and changing house rules to ensure that Tony's seven-year-old sister was not at risk from victimization. Additionally, rules regarding other ways of reducing risk were established, such as prohibiting Tony from babysitting young children or being in the presence of younger children (including his sister) without adult supervision.

Although all family members initially denied the offense, the adults were willing to make changes to ensure that Tony was not at risk from being 'falsely accused' in the future. The therapist also worked with the family to raise their concern about Tony's long-term criminal trajectory (based on the property offense that everyone acknowledged had taken place) and his high likelihood of ending up in jail. The family agreed with the therapist that school and safety plans were needed to prevent Tony from continuing on his current pathway and to help him to become more involved in productive, prosocial activities. Indeed, prior to treatment, Tony's mother had quit her job primarily so she could provide better supervision for Tony and his younger sister. The grandparents were also amenable to providing more supervision to Tony, and mother agreed that Tony would have to stop interacting with his co-defendants.

Although implementation of the safety plan was progressing, the therapist remained concerned that caregiver denial might ultimately interfere with making necessary changes to increase safety. After several meetings with the family, the therapist proposed several possible fit factors for their denial. These included: (1) Tony's denial of the offense; (2) the parents' intense embarrassment at the thought of their son engaging in a sexual act; (3) the parents' belief that sex offenders were 'monsters' and their knowledge that Tony was not a monster; (4) the victim's lack of credibility (due to being young, neglected and needy).

During a session in which the therapist reviewed these fit factors, the victim's police statement, and the evidence found on the cell phone, Tony admitted the offense to the therapist and his mother. He had been feeling guilty about lying regarding his involvement in the offense and decided to 'come clean'. Faced with this admission, Tony's mother broke down and acknowledged that this 'mistake' had changed their lives. Tony's acknowledgement occurred about two months into treatment and thereafter, Tony accepted responsibility for his involvement in the offense, expressed remorse, and was able to discuss how the event changed his and his family's lives. His mother's minimization of the event declined and she and Tony also helped Tony's father acknowledge the sexual assault.

With guidance from the MST therapist, Tony's caregivers established a reasonable curfew and rules regarding appropriate and inappropriate peers. Clear consequences (e.g., setting an earlier curfew) were established in the event Tony was seen associating with an inappropriate peer. At the same time, Tony's mother and father worked to make their home inviting to prosocial peers (e.g., they provided pizza when Tony brought home new friends from school). Tony complied with these new rules, driven by a desire to stay in high school and eventually attend art school and not be held back by his delinquent friends.

Because of Tony's sexual offense, and because he expressed an interest in girls and dating, an ongoing focus of treatment involved developing and conveying rules for appropriate romantic and sexual behaviors. Tony's father was instrumental in this process and, with guidance from the MST therapist, spoke with Tony about the need to respect girls and women, which included always asking permission for each romantic or sexual behavior (e.g., "is it okay if I kiss you?"). Tony was not yet sexually active with peers, but discussion also focused on the importance of safe sex and the proper use of condoms in the future.

With safety planning in place, another focus of treatment was Tony's schooling. There was no identifiable reason for Tony's placement in an alternative school program, and the therapist hypothesized that such placement might have been due to Tony's minority status and the fact that his parents spoke only Spanish and thus were limited in their ability to advocate for their son with school staff. To improve communication with the school, the therapist helped Tony's parents locate a Spanish-speaking school-based resource aid (one was provided by the county). The therapist also (1) used instruction and role plays to help Tony's mother improve her communication skills (i.e., so as to appear calm and concerned rather than overtly angry at school staff); (2) attended initial meetings with mother and teachers; and (3) talked through mother's and father's anxieties about meeting with school staff (based on their failure to earn high school diplomas). The bilingual therapist attended initial meetings with school staff to ensure proper communication and to ensure that caregivers were given copies of evaluation materials used in determining Tony's school placement. Fortunately, several of Tony's teachers recognized his ability and joined with Tony's parents in their request to have Tony placed in mainstream classes. The high school in which Tony would be enrolled the following year initially balked at his admission, due to his sexual offense. However, high-school staff were willing to meet with Tony and his parents over the summer to work out a plan for communication and supervision, and the school staff became impressed with the parents' level of commitment to their son's education and ultimately admitted Tony to the school.

Prior to enrolling in the new school, Tony's family moved to a new address. His parents indicated their desire to get away from the other youth with whom Tony had gotten into trouble as well as the gang violence and drug crime that surrounded the neighborhood. Additionally, the family's new house was more modern and larger than the old house and was also less crowded because the parents allowed only immediate family members to move into the new home with them (a long-standing goal of the parents). At this point in treatment, Tony was abiding by curfew, associating with prosocial peers who shared his interest in art, playing on a soccer team and on track for admission into mainstream classes. He had complied with probation requirements from the start of probation. Additionally, Tony's mother reported that her husband had reduced his alcohol consumption. Following several meetings between the therapist and both parents during which concerns about the father's drinking were addressed, the father agreed to attend an outpatient alcohol treatment program. The mother developed clear contingencies (e.g., separation) if the drinking continued and the father sincerely wanted to avoid such contingencies. The mother also reinforced her husband as a competent parent and marital partner once the drinking stopped. In addition to specific contingencies, the recent reductions in economic and psychological stress (e.g., home no longer over-crowded with poor relatives; nicer neighborhood with no obvious crime problems) facilitated father's success in significantly reducing his alcohol consumption.

Over time, Tony demonstrated sustained improvements in several areas. Foremost, there was no evidence of inappropriate sexual behaviors. On the contrary, Tony acknowledged the wrongful nature of his offense. He was able to convey to the therapist and his parents appropriate dating, romantic and sexual behaviors after having several discussions with his father about these matters. Tony's grades improved and he had several consecutive weeks at school with no behavior problems. On his first report card following mainstream placement, Tony received all As and Bs. Tony's new friends had all been thoroughly vetted by his caregivers, he adhered to supervision and curfew rules and had no probation violations. Treatment was successfully concluded after each overarching goal had been achieved, a process that lasted five months.

As with drivers or fit factors for problem behaviors, MST therapists also identify fit factors for improved behaviors. Hypothesized fit factors for Tony's improved behaviors included (a) increased and consistent supervision by parents; (b) Tony's improved understanding of sexual boundaries and rules; (c) strictly enforced rules by parents regarding appropriate and inappropriate friends for Tony; (d) Tony's genuine desire to make something of himself and the related desire to avoid any future contact with the law; (e) improved communication between caregivers and school staff; (f) school staff's willingness to give Tony a chance despite his criminal record.

CONCLUSIONS

To decrease the risk for future victimization of children and to keep families together, effective treatments must be applied to the problem of serious PSBs. Indeed, there is limited empirical support for the most common type of treatment (cognitive behavioral, group-based) for this population. This lack of support does not necessarily equate to poor outcomes; rather, additional research is badly needed (see Letourneau, 2004). Although there has been an increased societal acknowledgement of the deleterious effects of sexual victimization, there has not been a concomitant increase in research regarding how to remediate sexual offenders.

Multisystemic therapy is an ecologically-focused family- and community-based treatment, with services delivered in the home. The effectiveness of MST has already been demonstrated in the treatment of serious juvenile offenders, and preliminary outcomes of MST are also promising in the treatment of youths with PSBs. In addition to two extant efficacy trials, a larger randomized clinical trial is under way that compares MST with a state-of-the-art cognitive behavioral treatment program. This study will help shed light on the relative effectiveness of two disparate interventions implemented in real-life settings with a larger sample of youth and their families. Preliminary findings are promising, in part, because this intervention addresses factors across youths' ecologies. As illustrated through the case example provided, the MST therapist is flexible both with time and structure of sessions, while maintaining the use of empirically supported treatment strategies that are individualized to meet the needs of families. The MST protocol may be particularly effective in working with juveniles who have serious PSBs and their families, as these systems require vigilant monitoring and structured intervention strategies.

REFERENCES

Alexander, M.A. (1999). Sexual offender treatment efficacy revisited. *Sexual Abuse: A Journal of Research and Treatment, 11*, 101–116.

Awad, G.A. & Saunders, E.B. (1989). Adolescent child molesters: Clinical observations. *Child Psychiatry and Human Development, 19*, 195–206.

Awad, G.A. & Saunders, E.B. (1991). Male adolescent sexual assaulters: Clinical observations. *Journal of Interpersonal Violence, 6*, 446–460.

Becker, J.V. (1988). Effects of child sexual abuse on adolescent sexual offenders. In G.E. Wyatt & G.J. Powell (Eds), *Lasting effects of child sexual abuse* (pp. 193–207). Newbury Park, CA: Sage.

Becker, J.V. (1998). What we know about the characteristics and treatment of adolescents who have committed sexual offenses. *Child Maltreatment, 3*, 317–329.

Becker, J.V. & Hunter, J. A. (1997). Understanding and treating child and adolescent sexual offenders. *Advances in Clinical Child Psychology, 19*, 177–197.

Becker, J.V. & Murphy, W.D. (1998). What we know and do not know about assessing and treating sex offenders. *Psychology, Public Policy, and Law, 4*, 116–137.

Bischof, G.P., Stith, S.M. & Whitney, M.L. (1995). Family environments of adolescent sex offenders and other juvenile delinquents. *Adolescence, 30*, 157–170.

Blaske, D.M., Borduin, C.M., Henggeler, S.W. & Mann, B.J. (1989). Individual, family, and peer characteristics of adolescent sex offenders and assaultive offenders. *Developmental Psychology, 25*, 846–855.

Borduin, C.M., Henggeler, S.W., Blaske, D.M. & Stein, R. (1990). Multisystemic treatment of adolescent sexual offenders. *International Journal of Offender Therapy and Comparative Criminology, 34*, 105–113.

Borduin, C.M., Letourneau, E.J., Henggeler, S.W., Swenson, C.C., & Saldana, L. (in press). *Treatment Manual for Multisystemic Therapy with Juvenile Sexual Offenders and Their Families.* Charleston, SC: Family Services Research Center.

Borduin, C.M., Schaeffer, C.M. & Heiblum, N. (in press). A randomized clinical trial of multisystemic therapy with juvenile sexual offenders: Effects on youth social ecology and criminal activity. *Journal of Consulting and Clinical Psychology.*

Borduin, C.M. & Schaeffer, C.M. (1998). Violent offending in adolescence: Epidemiology, correlates, outcomes, and treatment. In T.P. Gullotta, G.R. Adams & R. Montemayor (Eds), *Delinquent violent youth: Theory and interventions* (pp. 144–174). Newbury Park, CA: Sage.

Borduin, C.M. & Schaeffer, C.M. (2001). Multisystemic treatment of juvenile sexual offenders: A progress report. *Journal of Psychology and Human Sexuality, 13*, 25–42.

Bronfenbrenner, U. (1979). *The ecology of human development: Experiments by nature and design.* Cambridge, MA: Harvard University Press.

Caldwell, M.F. (2002). What we do not know about juvenile sexual reoffense risk. *Child Maltreatment, 7*, 291–302.

Carpentier, M.Y., Silovsky, J.F. & Chaffin, M. (2006). Randomized trial of treatment for children with sexual behavior problems: Ten-year follow-up. *Journal of Consulting and Clinical Psychology, 74*, 482–488.

Davis, G.E. & Leitenberg, H. (1987). Adolescent sex offenders. *Psychological Bulletin, 101*, 417–427.

Dishion, T.J. & Dodge, K.A. (2005). Peer contagion in interventions for children and adolescents: Moving towards an understanding of the ecology and dynamics of change. *Journal of Abnormal Child Psychology, 33*, 395–400.

Elliott, D.S. (1998) (Series Ed.). *Blueprints for violence prevention*. University of Colorado, Center for the Study and Prevention of Violence. Boulder, CO: Blueprints Publications.

Fagan, J. & Wexler, S. (1988). Explanations of sexual assault among violent delinquents. *Journal of Adolescent Research, 3*, 363–385.

Fehrenbach, P.A., Smith, W., Monastersky, C. & Deisher, R.W. (1986). Adolescent sexual offenders: Offender and offense characteristics. *American Journal of Orthopsychiatry, 56*, 225–233.

Ford, M.E. & Linney, J.E. (1995). Comparative analysis of juvenile sexual offenders, violent nonsexual offenders, and status offenders. *Journal of Interpersonal Violence, 10*, 56–70.

Graham, F., Richardson, G. & Bhate, S.R. (1998). Development of a service for sexually abusive adolescents in the Northeast of England. In W.L. Marshall, Y.M. Fernandez, S.M. Hudson & T. Ward (Eds), *Sourcebook of treatment programs for sexual offenders* (pp. 367–384). New York: Plenum.

Graves, R.B., Openshaw, D.K., Ascione, F.R. & Ericksen, S.L. (1996). Demographic and parental characteristics of youthful sexual offenders. *International Journal of Offender Therapy and Comparative Criminology, 40*, 300–317.

Guarino-Ghezzi, S. & Kimball, L.M. (1998). Juvenile sex offenders in treatment. *Corrections Management Quarterly, 2*(1), 45–54.

Hanson, R.K., Gordon, A., Harris, A.J.R. *et al.* (2002). First report of the collaborative outcome data project on the effectiveness of psychological treatment for sex offenders. *Sexual Abuse: A Journal of Research and Treatment, 14*, 169–194.

Hastings, T., Anderson, S.J. & Hemphill, P. (1997). Comparisons of daily stress, coping, problem behavior, and cognitive distortions in adolescent sexual offenders and conduct-disordered youth. *Sexual Abuse: A Journal of Research and Treatment, 9*, 29–42.

Henggeler, S.W. & Borduin, C.M. (1990). *Family therapy and beyond: A multisystemic approach to treating the behavior problems of children and adolescents*. Pacific Grove, CA: Brooks/Cole.

Henggeler, S.W., Schoenwald, S.K., Borduin, C.M. *et al.* (1998). *Multisystemic treatment of antisocial behavior in children and adolescents*. New York: Guilford.

Hunter, J.A., Gilbertson, S.A., Vedros, D. & Morton, M. (2004). Strengthening community-based programming for juvenile sexual offenders: Key concepts and paradigm shifts. *Child Maltreatment, 9*, 177–189.

Johnson, T.C. (1989). Female child perpetrators: Children who molest other children. *Child Abuse and Neglect, 13*, 571–585.

Kahn, T.J. & Chambers, H.J. (1991). Assessing reoffense risk with juvenile sexual offenders. *Child Welfare, 70*, 333–345.

Kaufman, K.L., Hilliker, D.R. & Daleiden, E.L. (1996). Subgroup difference in the modus operandi of adolescent sexual offenders. *Child Maltreatment, 1*, 17–24.

Kazdin, A.E. (1995). *Conduct disorders in childhood and adolescence* (2nd edn). Thousand Oaks, CA: Sage.

Knopp, F.H., Rosenberg, J. & Stevenson, W. (1986). *Report on nationwide survey of juvenile and adult sex offender treatment programs and providers*. New York: Safer Society Press.

Letourneau, E.J. (2004). Commentary on the First Report. *Sexual Abuse: A Journal of Research and Treatment, 16*, 77–81.

Letourneau, E.J., Chapman, J. & Schoenwald, S.K. (2008). Treatment outcome and future offending by youth with sexual behavior problems. *Child Maltreatment, 13*, 133–144.

Letourneau, E.J. & Miner, M.H. (2005). Juvenile sex offenders: A case against the legal and clinical status quo. *Sexual Abuse: A Journal of Research and Treatment, 17*, 313–331.

Lewis, D.O., Shankok, S.S. & Pincus, J.H. (1981). Juvenile male sexual assaulters: Psychiatric, neurological, psychoeducational, and abuse factors. In D.O. Lewis (Ed.), *Vulnerabilities to delinquency* (pp. 89–105). Jamaica, NY: Spectrum Publications.

Loeber, R., Farrington, D.P. & Waschbusch, D.A. (1998). Serious and violent juvenile offenders. In R. Loeber & D.P. Farrington (Eds), *Serious and violent juvenile offenders: Risk factors and successful interventions* (pp. 13–29). Thousand Oaks, CA: Sage.

McGrath, R.J., Cumming, G.F. & Burchard, B.L. (2003). *Current practices and trends in sexual abuser management: The Safer Society 2002 nationwide survey.* Brandon, VT: Safer Society Press.

McMahon, R.J., Wells, K.C. & Kotler, J.S. (2006). Conduct problems. In E.J. Mash & R.A. Barkley (Eds), *Treatment of childhood disorders* (3rd edn) (pp. 137–268). New York: Guilford.

National Institute on Drug Abuse (1999). *Principles of drug addiction treatment: A research-based guide.* NIH Publication No. 99-4180. Available at: http://www.nida.nih.gov/PODAT/PODAT4.html Accessed September 10, 2007.

Nelson, K.E. & Landsman, M.J. (1992). *Alternative models of family preservation: Family-based services in context.* Springfield, IL: Charles C. Thomas.

Ronis, S.T. & Borduin, C.M. (2007). Individual, family, peer, and academic characteristics of male juvenile sexual offenders. *Journal of Abnormal Child Psychology, 35*, 153–163.

Silverman, W.K., Kurtines, W.M. & Hoagwood, K. (2004). Research progress on effectiveness, transportability, and dissemination of empirically supported treatments: Integrating theory and research. *Clinical Psychology: Science and Practice, 11*, 295–299.

Schoenwald, S.K., Sheidow, A.J. & Letourneau, E.J. (2004). Toward effective quality assurance in evidence-based practice: Links between expert consultation, therapist fidelity, and child outcomes. *Journal of Clinical Child and Adolescent Psychology, 33*, 94–104.

Schoenwald, S.K., Sheidow, A.J., Letourneau, E.J. & Liao, J.G. (2003). Transportability of Multisystemic Therapy: Evidence for multi-level influences. *Mental Health Services Research, 4*, 223–239.

Snell-Johns, J., Mendez, J.L. & Smith, B.L. (2004). Evidence-based solutions for overcoming access barriers, decreasing attrition, and promoting change with underserved families. *Journal of Family Psychology, 18*, 19–35.

Swenson, C.C. & Letourneau, E.J. (2005). Multisystemic therapy with juvenile sex offenders. In B. Schwartz (Ed.), *The sex offender* Vol. 5. New York: Civic Research Institute.

Tarter, R.E., Hegedus, A.M., Alterman, A.I. & Katz-Garris, L. (1983). Cognitive capacities of juvenile violent, nonviolent, and sexual offenders. *Journal of Nervous and Mental Disease, 171*, 564–567.

Tufts' New England Medical Center, Division of Child Psychiatry (1984). *Sexually exploited children: Service and research project.* Final report for the Office of Juvenile Justice and Delinquency Prevention, US Department of Justice, Washington, DC.

van Wijk, A., Loeber, R., Vermeiren, R. *et al.* (2005). Violent juvenile sex offenders compared with violent juvenile non-sex offenders: Explorative findings from the Pittsburgh Youth Study. *Sexual Abuse: A Journal of Research and Treatment, 17*, 335–352.

Wieckowski, E., Hartsoe, P., Mayer, A. & Shortz, J. (1998). Deviant sexual behavior in children and young adolescents: Frequency and patterns. *Sexual Abuse: A Journal of Research and Treatment, 10*, 293–303.

Worling, J.R. (1998). Adolescent sexual offender treatment at the SAFE-T program. In W.L. Marshall, Y.M. Fernandez, S.M. Hudson & T. Ward (Eds), *Sourcebook of treatment programs for sexual offenders* (pp. 353–366). New York: Plenum.

Worling, J.R. & Curwen, T. (1998). *The adolescent sexual offender project: A 10-year follow-up study. SAFE-T Program (Sexual Abuse: Family Education & Treatment).* Toronto, ON: Thistletown Regional Centre for Children and Adolescents & Probation and Community Services, Ontario Ministry of Community and Social Services.

25

Female Sex Offenders: Issues and Considerations in Working with this Population

HANNAH J. FORD

INTRODUCTION

In the past, sexually deviant or offending behaviour was primarily viewed as something committed by males, which women (with the possible exceptions of prostitution or promiscuity) were neither motivated nor physically able to do. In considering the possibility of women sexually abusing children, Mathis (1972), for example, stated "that she might seduce a helpless child into sexplay is unthinkable, and even if she did so, what harm can be done without a penis?" (p. 12). Victim reports of sexual assaults by females have sometimes been greeted with denial, shock or disbelief, even from professionals (Denov, 2003), potentially leading victims to withhold disclosure of their experiences and enabling perpetrators to continue with their behaviour.

Although acceptance and belief about female sexual offending has increased considerably, research continues to point to discrepancies in how male and female offenders are viewed, both by the general population and by professionals, whether the offence has been committed against adult or child victims (Davies & Rogers, 2006). Davies, Pollard and Archer (2006), for example, found that while male and female university students reported similarly negative views about the male perpetrator in a hypothetical sexual assault vignette, male students viewed a female perpetrator more favourably, even though she had committed the same sexually abusive act.

Similar findings have been reported among professional groups. Hetherton and Beardsall (1998) found that male social workers believed social service involvement and investigation to be more appropriate for cases in which the perpetrator was male rather than female. Furthermore, all the participants in their sample of social workers and police officers stated that incidents were more appropriately registered as cases

Assessment and Treatment of Sex Offenders: A Handbook. Edited by Anthony Beech, Leam Craig and Kevin Browne. © John Wiley & Sons Ltd, 2009.

of child sexual abuse when the abuser was male rather than female. Similarly, while a study of Australian police officers found that all abuse scenarios were perceived as serious and as impacting on the victim, the vignette describing male-perpetrated abuse was rated as significantly more serious, in need of more serious action, and impacting more greatly on the victim, than when the vignette described a female perpetrator (Kite & Tyson, 2004). Although responses to hypothetical scenarios may not predict behaviour in real situations, these differential attitudes to male and female offenders persist, despite findings that victims are often equally harmed by abuse, whether the person who assaulted them was male or female (e.g., Denov, 2004; Dube *et al.*, 2005).

Although researchers and clinicians have increasingly turned their attention to the issue of sexual offending by females, our knowledge and understanding of these offenders remains more scant than for their male counterparts. This is somewhat inevitable, given the slower pace of recognition of female sexual offending, some reasons for which have been documented elsewhere (see Ford, 2006, for a review). Although female-perpetrated abuse is now more readily recognised and acknowledged, the comparatively small numbers of female sex offenders in prison or probation settings frequently render specific treatment programmes logistically difficult, even before we begin to consider what such programmes should include, how they should be structured and delivered, or how the biases described above may influence the process of dealing with female sexual offenders.

This chapter outlines some considerations in working with adult female sex offenders, focusing particularly on the assessment of risk and identification of treatment needs and some of the concomitant difficulties. It does not aim to offer a comprehensive 'how to' guide to the assessment of female sex offenders, as detailed discussions of key assessment areas and approaches have been provided elsewhere (e.g., Ford & Cortoni, 2008; Grayston & De Luca, 1999; Saradjian, 1996). Instead, it aims to outline some of the potentially broad-ranging needs of these women and question whether directly applying assessment procedures for male offenders to females is appropriate, as other researchers have done (e.g., Nathan & Ward, 2002; Saradjian, 1996). Throughout the chapter, suggestions are made for further areas of research to inform our understanding in this developing field and the chapter concludes by reflecting on some of the potential responses to working with female sex offenders and how these may play out in work with groups of sexual offenders.

ASSESSING RISK

While a great deal of research attention has been given to identifying the static (historic) and dynamic (psychological) factors (see Chapters 3, 4 & 5) which predict sexual reoffending in males and incorporating these into risk assessment tools, the applicability of such tools to other sex offender populations, including females, has been questioned (Beech, Fisher & Thornton, 2003). Evidence from the general offending field suggests some difficulties in directly applying risk assessment measures developed and normed on male offenders to females. Blanchette and Brown (2006) reviewed some of the risk assessment instruments frequently used in general offender populations, which have been well researched with males, but found less evidence to support their use with the female offender population. Even when measures developed for male offenders show acceptable validity and predictive accuracy when used with women, Blanchette and Brown (2006) suggest that some evidence indicates that using assessments designed specifically for women provides better prediction of risk.

It is important to identify the variables most strongly associated with sexual reoffending in females but, at present, little is known about these (Cortoni & Hanson, 2005; Oliver, 2007) or the extent to which they may overlap with risk factors for males. While the static variable of previous offending history is an important risk factor in males, for example, it is unclear whether this has a similar level of importance for female offenders, given that fewer females have such histories (Nathan & Ward, 2001). The relevance of other dynamic risk factors identified in male sex offenders, such as deviant sexual interests, is also unknown for female sex offenders. When compared with the volume of work addressing this issue in males, there has been very limited consideration of deviant sexual interest in female sex offenders (Ford, 2006). In part, this is perhaps because assessment of such interests is already problematic with male offenders and may be even more so with females (see Ford & Cortoni, 2008, for a discussion). However, it could also reflect our traditional sexual scripts, which view women as less interested in sex and more motivated by commitment (Byers & O'Sullivan, 1998), and therefore also less likely to be interested in deviant sex. The potential role of deviant sexual interest in female sexual offending requires further investigation before its contribution to the prediction of recidivism can be assessed.

A contextual factor to consider in the assessment of risk, and one which may be specific to women, is whether or not the female offended alone, as female sexual offending has often been suggested to occur either in the context of coercion from another, or in the company of a co-offender, although the actual proportions reported vary considerably (Johansson-Love & Fremouw, 2006; Vandiver, 2006). Although this factor is discussed again later in this chapter, it is important here to consider its contribution to the risk of reoffending. Although based on a small sample, Williams and Nicholaichuk (2001) found that this factor differentiated women who had and had not sexually reoffended, with the two recidivists having previously abused alone, without a co-offender. Findings based on two women are clearly not conclusive and may not take account of women who begin offending under coercion but progress to acting alone. However, as so little is presently known about risk factors in female sexual reoffending, this potential difference may benefit from additional research with larger samples. If women have been coerced into offending by others, any assessment of risk should include consideration of their ability to resist such coercion in the future, particularly if women are hoping to rejoin their own children (Beech *et al.*, 2003).

A related issue is the extent to which sexual abuse against children overlaps with other types of child maltreatment. Although sexual abuse is both physically and emotionally abusive in its nature, some researchers have noted other types of child maltreatment, alongside sexual abuse, in some women who sexually offend against children (see Ford, 2006, for further discussion). Grayston and De Luca (1999) suggest that this may be more likely when the abuser occupies a primary caregiving role, while Tardif *et al.* (2005) found that physical abuse more commonly accompanied sexual abuse when offences were committed against younger victims. Any assessment of risk for sexual reoffending should therefore also consider the possibility of other forms of child maltreatment, again particularly if family reunification is to be attempted.

Although there is very little data on recidivism rates in female sex offenders, Cortoni and Hanson (2005) reviewed the available studies and found a very low recidivism rate of just one percent across all studies during an average five-year follow-up period. This was much lower than the recidivism rate for male offenders, leading these authors to suggest that risk assessment tools developed for male sex offenders are unlikely to be applicable to females. These lower rates could also reflect different rates of detection/reporting of further sexual offending by females or different responses to male and female sexual offending by criminal justice system agencies. Whatever the reason, however, this very low sexual recidivism rate creates a further difficulty for the development of risk assessment tools for females, as very large sample sizes will consequently be needed (Cortoni & Hanson, 2005). Given the comparatively small numbers of female sex offenders in prison or community settings internationally, the development of risk assessment measures specifically for this group seem a long way off. This has potential ramifications for those agencies responsible for allocating female sex offenders to treatment or managing them in the community. In the UK, for example, a survey of Multi-Agency Public Protection Arrangements (MAPPA) highlighted that the absence of risk assessment instruments for female offenders impacted negatively on the management plans developed and sometimes resulted in these women's risk being downgraded (Bunting, 2005). It is perhaps on account of difficulties such as these that Aylward *et al.* (2002) note that actuarial risk assessment tools developed and validated for male offenders are being used to make assessments of women's recidivism risk. In view of the above discussion, however, this does not seem to be a satisfactory course of action.

However, while sexual recidivism was low, the rate of non-sexual recidivism among female sex offenders was much higher, with a rate of 6.3% for violent (including sexual) offences and 20.2% for any recidivism (including violent and sexual offences) (Cortoni & Hanson, 2005). While this was still lower than the expected recidivism rates for male offenders, these authors suggested that the higher rates of general recidivism in female sex offenders indicate that this is perhaps a greater area of concern for this population and that assessments of risk should therefore include factors related to general recidivism. Previous histories of offending and an earlier age of first offence were significantly related to reconviction in a general UK female prison sample, as well as disruptions in care during childhood, lack of formal educational qualifications and drug abuse (Clark & Howden-Windall, 2000). Although results have not always been consistent, other factors potentially related to general recidivism in females include employment difficulties, antisocial attitudes, poor self-esteem, relationship problems and impaired emotion regulation (Blanchette & Brown, 2006; Denov & Cortoni,

2006) and should therefore be considered for inclusion in assessments of reoffending risk.

Finally, research should perhaps move beyond solely identifying risk factors for reoffending to also consider factors which might protect women from further sexual offending and incorporate these into risk assessment models (Blanchette & Brown, 2006). These authors suggest that identification of protective factors or strengths may be particularly pertinent for female offenders, given that research has tended to report lower recidivism rates among female than male offenders. Clearly, however, the difficulties of small sample sizes remain.

IDENTIFYING NEEDS

As with the assessment of risk, the comparatively early stage of female sexual offender research means that our understanding and assessment of treatment needs in this group is less well developed than with male offenders. Those working with male offenders have offered different views about whether interventions should target primarily those criminogenic needs which may be expected to reduce the likelihood of sexual reoffending (e.g., Ogloff & Davis, 2004) or more global human needs (e.g., Ward & Brown, 2004), although detailed discussion of these is beyond the scope of this chapter. Criminogenic needs are suggested to be primarily identified from empirical literature on recidivism and the opinion of experienced clinicians (Hollin & Palmer, 2006). However, this raises difficulties in identifying these for female sex offending as there is little research on female sexual recidivism and their comparatively smaller numbers are likely to result in fewer practitioners regularly encountering this group. Furthermore, as Blanchette and Brown (2006) suggest, a strengths-based approach may be more applicable with women. The next part of this chapter, therefore, discusses potential areas of need more generally, rather than focusing solely on those that could be labelled criminogenic.

The sexual offending behaviours committed by females and the processes through which they achieve them are not necessarily reported to differ considerably from abusive acts committed by males (Kaufman *et al.*, 1995; Nathan & Ward, 2001), including both contact and non-contact offences and penetrative and non-penetrative acts. However, it should not immediately be assumed that similar offending behaviours between male and female abusers constitute similar treatment needs. Even if common areas of need are identified, the association between that particular need and offending may not be the same for both genders (Hollin & Palmer, 2006).

Work with female sex offenders has clearly identified a number of treatment needs that overlap with those of males, including denial, minimisation, or distorted cognitions about their sexual offending, limited understanding of the impact of their offending on victims, socio-affective and interpersonal difficulties and, in some cases, work on specific factors such as deviant sexual arousal (Eldridge & Saradjian, 2000; Grayston & De Luca, 1999; Nathan & Ward, 2002). However, the relative importance of these similar needs may vary for male and female offenders. Researchers have presented contrasting findings regarding the extent of denial among female offenders, for example, with Matthews (1993) suggesting that women are less likely to initially deny their abuse and more willing to accept primary responsibility for it, even when their offences were the result of coercion from others (Matthews, Mathews & Speltz, 1991). Rather than minimise their role in the offence, these authors note, some coerced women further commented that they should have done more to try and prevent the abuse from occurring. Allen (1991), meanwhile, stated that women offenders were more reluctant than men to admit abusing children, with only 27% of women acknowledging their guilt, compared with almost half the men, and female offenders were significantly more likely than males to report that they had been wrongly accused.

There may be some interpersonal difficulties for women offenders that differentiate them from men, particularly in terms of dependency and excessive reliance on their partners (Eldridge & Saradjian, 2000), sometimes even placing these relationships above those with their child victims (Saradjian, 1996). As stated previously, sexual arousal has been less thoroughly examined in female offending compared with that committed by males. Whether this represents an actual difference in the importance of sexual motivations between males and females, or just differences in the extent to which researchers and clinicians can accept the idea of women being aroused by deviant sexual behaviour, remains an area for further study. A proportion of the women in Nathan and Ward's (2002) sample reported being motivated at least in part by deviant sexual arousal, and this may be more important for subgroups of female offenders, such as those abusing alone who select victims according to their own preferences rather than those of a co-offender, or those abusing adolescents, who may select victims according to their own sexual orientation and treat them as surrogate partners (Saradjian, 1996).

Not all of these needs are likely to apply equally to all female sex offenders. Potential differences between women who abuse independently or under the coercion of others may benefit from further investigation, particularly as, in one of the few extant recidivism studies, the women who sexually reoffended were those who had abused alone (Williams & Nicholaichuk, 2001). Vandiver (2006) compared female sexual offenders who had acted alone with those who had offended with another individual. She found a number of differences between these two offender types in terms of offence characteristics, with co-offenders having significantly more victims and also more female victims. Women offending alone were more likely to offend against males, meanwhile, perhaps suggesting that they are choosing the gender of the victim, while in the predominantly male-coerced cases, perhaps the male co-offender chose a female victim. This could have implications in terms of whether women are selecting victims according to their own motivation, or that of the co-offender, and therefore the extent to which factors like sexual arousal could be important.

Although at an early stage of research and development, typologies of female sexual offenders are emerging. Earlier classifications identified three main offender types among women who sexually abused children. Matthews *et al.* (1991) described the teacher/lover (who falls in love with her adolescent, usually male victim, seeing him as an equal and believing he wants sexual contact), the intergenerationally predisposed offender (motivated by the emotional distress of her own extensive abuse history), and the male-coerced offender. Saradjian (1996), meanwhile, classified offenders into those who abused young children, those who abused adolescents and those coerced into abuse by men, although she noted that some women did not fit into any of these categories. Most recently, Vandiver and Kercher (2004) analysed a significantly larger sample of women offenders, including those who had abused adult victims, and identified six different offender types. Different motives or needs are suggested to drive the offending of women in the different typologies, therefore suggesting different treatment foci. Women who have offended under coercion from others, for example, may have different needs to those who have abused independently. The former may need to develop their ability to assertively resist such coercion, increase their self-esteem and develop skills to form new relationships, while women who have offended alone may need to address offending-related beliefs, such as that their victim was like an adult partner who wished for the sexual contact, in the case of women who have abused adolescents (Ford, 2006). One of Vandiver and Kercher's (2004) categories – the homosexual criminal – contained women whose offences often consisted of 'forcing' behaviours, such as forcing female victims into prostitution, leading these authors to suggest that the motivation for these offenders may centre more on economic gain than on any sexual motivation. Although there may be some overlapping areas of need, such as victim empathy work, this type of offender may require a different treatment focus to a woman offending owing to a deviant sexual preference.

With the exception of clinical interviewing, assessment of offence-supportive attitudes and beliefs remains difficult. There is a dearth of psychometric measures developed specifically for the female sex offender population but, given their small numbers, development and validation of such measures is problematic (see Ford & Cortoni, 2008, for discussion). As with risk assessment, practitioners may find themselves having to choose between using measures designed for and standardised on males, and being unsure of the relevance of their outcomes for females, or relying on the information from clinical interview alone. In the UK, researchers such as Beckett (2005), and Ring (2005), have begun to compare female and male sex offenders on a number of psychometric measures and have found areas of similarity between males and females, and some differences between women abusing alone versus those abusing with others, which further indicates a need to examine these offender types more carefully. While clearly a useful first step, this research is still based on measures originally developed for male offenders, which may omit important female-specific characteristics. Further work is needed to develop gender-specific measures, including the gathering of female non-offender comparison data.

While attitudes and beliefs supporting their offending behaviour have been identified in female sex offenders and should be targeted as part of treatment, other factors have also been suggested which may impact more indirectly on offence-related cognitions, or beliefs about oneself and one's situation. Blanchette and Brown (2006) argue that women offenders are likely to be disadvantaged in a number of ways and state that interventions should therefore additionally focus on identifying and addressing these other relevant issues, whether or not they are criminogenic in the strict sense. Some of these are briefly outlined now.

Past Victimisation Experiences

High rates of sexual, physical or emotional abuse, or a combination of all three, have been reported in the backgrounds of women who sexually offend (e.g. Lewis & Stanley, 2000; Saradjian, 1996; Tardif *et al.*, 2005). While it is not suggested that this is a direct causal factor in these women's offending behaviour, the high levels of abuse frequently reported suggest that this may be an area of need for many abusive women. Addressing offending women's own experiences of victimisation may be important as a history of abuse may have impacted on the ability to regulate emotions and influenced patterns of coping, both of which may limit the ability to cope effectively with life stressors. Past abuse experiences are also likely to have impacted on the woman's developing sexuality and potentially contributed to beliefs about abuse and the harm caused, originally to themselves and now to their victims, although some women may be aware of the harm they are causing and intend to hurt victims in order to 'avenge' their own abuse (Saradjian, 1996). Both the abuse experience itself and the response (if any) made to it, is likely to have influenced the woman's developing self-identity and self-concept and her expectations about how others will respond to her. Saradjian (1996), for example, found that the female abusers in her study were more likely than non-offending women to have been physically abused in childhood and unless their injuries were very serious, fewer than half received appropriate treatment for them. Such experiences may have produced feelings of low self-worth and beliefs that others are abusive and uncaring.

If offenders' own abusive experiences are not addressed, this could influence their ability to benefit from any intervention, particularly if women struggle to regulate the emotions raised during treatment. Craissati (2003) (cited in Beech & Ward, 2004) examined the impact of experiencing certain childhood difficulties (including but not exclusively abuse) on engagement in treatment. Experiencing two or more childhood difficulties and having never cohabited correctly identified 87% of those whose treatment attendance was poor, while childhood difficulties alongside contact with adult mental health services correctly identified 83% of those who did not comply with treatment. Although the difficulties experienced in childhood were not exclusively abuse experiences and this research was not specifically considering the impact on women's engagement in treatment, it does highlight the potential for past experiences to negatively influence treatment and may therefore warrant further investigation in relation to women sex offenders. However, it is important to ensure that the past abusive experiences of female sex offenders do not overshadow or take precedence over their sexual offending behaviour (Denov & Cortoni, 2006). Over-focusing on past experiences could hinder women in understanding how they reached the decision to sexually offend and may limit the extent to which they feel responsible for their offending or the degree to which they feel able to change or control it in the future (Ford & Cortoni, 2008).

Relationships, Social Supports and Coping

The literature suggests that women who have sexually offended against children have a history of poor family relationships (e.g., Green & Kaplan, 1994; Saradjian, 1996) and that these poor early relationship patterns tend to be repeated in adult sexual relationships, which are themselves often abusive (e.g., Lewis & Stanley, 2000; Saradjian, 1996). When asked about what sex meant to them, Saradjian (1996) found that all the female offenders in her study endorsed at least one negative statement about their sexual experiences with adult partners, which distinguished them from the comparison group of women, and most offenders described adult sexual experiences very negatively. Childhood peer relationships also tended to be poor, with many offenders reporting isolation from other children and bullying at school. These early difficulties also continued in adulthood; a major difference between offending and non-offending women was that none of the offenders could name anyone who was a friend at the time they were abusing children (Saradjian, 1996). Thought about in terms of the 'Good Lives Model' (Ward & Brown, 2004), this suggests that some important human 'goods' are lacking for these women, such as relatedness to others, sexual satisfaction in life (at least through an appropriate outlet) and also, perhaps, happiness. Whether arising from skills deficits, or deeper underlying attachment disruptions and negative models of self, these difficulties are obstacles which prevent women offenders from meeting their most fundamental needs. Identifying ways of overcoming these obstacles in order to attain basic needs through non-abusive means should be a goal of any intervention programme (Sorbello et al., 2002).

The limited social support networks of many female sexual offenders may also impact on engagement with treatment. The treatment process may raise a number of difficult emotions for female offenders such as shame or guilt which, given their potential difficulties with emotion regulation, may require external emotional support – something which is often absent for these women. Such emotions may be more problematic for female offenders; Matthews (1993) believes that women sex offenders continue to experience feelings of shame for longer than male offenders and tend to forgive themselves less quickly. Travin, Cullen and Protter (1990) suggest that there may be a high drop-out rate among female abusers, particularly when they openly acknowledge their offences and are overwhelmed by shame and guilt, perhaps because such feelings are too difficult to deal with, particularly if they have limited external support. Saradjian (1996) therefore suggests that it may be important to ensure the availability of support to women when they enter treatment and to maintain this until they develop the skills and confidence to begin building social networks by themselves.

Assessment of coping patterns is also important, particularly as many difficulties are reported in the earlier years of abusive women's lives and these women may have had few or no external sources of assistance and support either at the time of these difficulties or subsequently. Saradjian (1996) reported that women who sexually abused children rated themselves as experiencing more stress, but having fewer internal or external resources to cope with this than the non-offending comparison group. She additionally noted that it was when women were not sexually offending against children that many reported self-harm, depression, anxiety or other indications of psychological distress, leading to suggestions that women might use sexual abuse as a way of coping with a variety of negative feelings (Eldridge & Saradjian, 2000). There is evidence of male sex offenders using sex as a means of coping. Cortoni and Marshall (2001) found that men who had sexually offended reported making extensive use of both deviant and non-deviant sexual activities as a way of coping with stressful situations or negative emotional states. Higher levels of emotional loneliness and low ratings of intimate engagement with others were both associated with increased use of sexual activity as a way of relieving the negative feelings evoked by these difficulties. The extent to which this may be true for female offenders requires closer investigation, particularly as Saradjian (1996) found that many female offenders viewed their adult sexual experiences as generally negative. However, she also found that almost all female offenders endorsed at least one statement about increased feelings of power and control when they sexually abused children. Perhaps female offenders, unlike males, could find deviant sexual activities more useful in coping with negative emotions or stress than more normative sexual activities, at least based on their own negative adult sexual experiences. While this is speculation only, the potential use of sex as a coping mechanism in female offenders should be assessed, as well as a more general examination of women's patterns of coping across a variety of situations.

Current Life Situation

The general life situations of sexually offending women may give rise to additional needs. Factors such as education or employment difficulties, which have been linked to recidivism in general male offenders, are less clearly associated with female offenders (Blanchette & Brown, 2006), and female sex offenders specifically, although Hollin and Palmer (2006) maintain that difficulties in these areas are likely to be criminogenic for both genders, even though they may differ in their level of relative importance. Some studies have suggested that female sexual offenders tend to be of lower socioeconomic status (e.g., Grayston & De Luca, 1999; Nathan & Ward, 2002), poorly educated, often unemployed or, if working, employed in unskilled/low-paid jobs or traditional female occupations (e.g., Allen, 1991; Nathan & Ward, 2002; Saradjian, 1996). Such findings may partly reflect greater scrutiny of the behaviour of some members of society than others, and Saradjian's (1996) sample of female child abusers certainly contained women of higher socio-economic status. However, social disadvantage seems a reality for some female sexual offenders, which may compound their other difficulties such as lack of support networks and negatively impact on their self-esteem or ability to cope with other stresses. Economic and/or social disadvantage for women coerced into sexual offending may leave them heavily dependent on the coercer for financial support, for example, and may therefore make it even harder to resist the coercion (Vandiver, 2006). Some of these difficulties may be further compounded if others find out that a woman has sexually offended. Tewksbury (2004) surveyed females registered on the Sex Offender Registries in Indiana and Kentucky in the USA. While the very low response rates cast doubt on the overall representativeness of the results, the findings are nonetheless interesting. More than 40% of the 40 female sex offenders who responded had lost a job and over 30% had lost or been denied a place to live or been harassed after their offending became public knowledge, while almost 40% had lost a friend, perhaps a particularly hard consequence when social support is already very limited. The proportion of women reporting these negative consequences increased as time on the registry also increased. While the study offers no information as to how these experiences compare with those of registered male offenders, such experiences are unlikely to be beneficial to women who may already be experiencing a number of social disadvantages and who may be relying on limited coping skills and support to avoid reoffending in the future.

The theme of power pervades the typologies developed for women who have sexually abused children (Ford, 2006), perhaps because offending women rate themselves as powerless and lacking any real control in any aspect of their life (Saradjian, 1996), supported by Ring's (2005) finding that women offenders had a significantly more external locus of control than a comparison group of non-offending women. Feelings of powerlessness may arise from past or current abuse experiences, be exacerbated by the stereotypical role of women in society (Eldridge & Saradjian, 2000), or be reinforced by experiences such as those described by Tewksbury (2004), over which women have very little control. Ward and Brown (2004) describe autonomy and self-directedness as primary human goods, alongside experiences of mastery at work or play, and the evidence suggests that these basic goods may be lacking for female sex offenders in many or all aspects of their lives. This further suggests a need to bolster women offender's skills, self-esteem and coping abilities in order to reassert some feelings of control in her life and a belief that she is able to exert control over her offending behaviour.

Mental Health Issues

While mental health issues have been raised as an area of concern for female offenders, it is not clear whether this is a criminogenic need in the strict sense (Blanchette & Brown, 2006; Hollin & Palmer, 2006). Nonetheless, assessment of mental health needs is important, to determine whether these made any contribution to the sexual offending, or whether current difficulties may impact on a woman's ability to participate in treatment. If mental health needs are identified, these may have to be managed before any treatment takes place; if these issues are not addressed, the likelihood of the woman being able to benefit from treatment for her sexual offending is considerably reduced (Ford & Cortoni, 2008). Although clearly requiring individual assessment, the research literature presents mixed findings regarding the level of mental health difficulties in female sex offenders, with some studies reporting high levels of such needs (e.g., Green & Kaplan, 1994), while others, such as Saradjian (1996) identified lower levels of mental health difficulties. However, variations in methodology and definition may account for some of the differences between studies and individualised assessment of mental health needs is strongly recommended.

Substance abuse is a stronger predictor of recidivism among general samples of female offenders (Hollin & Palmer, 2006), drug use more so than alcohol (Clark & Howden-Windall, 2000). Women with substance abuse problems may also require help in some of the areas described previously, including employment and relationships (Blanchette & Brown, 2006). The evidence tends to suggest that this is an area of need for some female sex offenders, as it is for some female non-sexual offenders, with Aylward *et al.* (2002) reporting over half the abusive women in their sample to have substance abuse problems and Grayston and De Luca (1999) summarising a number of studies indicating substance abuse problems to be common in women who sexually abused children. However, Saradjian (1996) found that rates of substance abuse did not differ between offending and non-offending women and there was a trend for the non-offenders to be the heavier users. Nonetheless, this appears to be an area of need for some female sex offenders and should be fully assessed, as it may impact directly on their offending behaviour, perhaps by disinhibiting themselves or their victims, or on many other areas of their lives, as well as potentially influencing their current ability to engage in and benefit from treatment.

CONCLUSIONS

This chapter has made clear that although our knowledge about female sex offenders is steadily increasing, there is much that remains speculative and uncertain when working with this group. This continues to cause difficulties for the agencies and practitioners who are required to manage and care for these offenders, both in assessing the level of risk posed by sexually offending women and being able to allocate appropriate and effective treatment provision. With a limited research base upon which to draw, it is perhaps not surprising that the more extensive literatures for male sex offenders and female non-sex offenders have been accessed in order to guide and direct the assessment methods and treatment procedures used with female sexual offenders. As there are broad overlapping areas of need between female sex offenders and both male sex offenders and female non-sexual offenders, this is not entirely inappropriate, particularly given the small number of sexually offending women available for study, and may provide a useful starting point in guiding our thinking about this offender group. As it is hoped this chapter has demonstrated, however, there are also important areas of difference, and uncertainty about the relative importance of some of the similarities reported. It is therefore essential that work continues to further develop our understanding of the particular needs and issues for this group of offenders, to develop means of assessing these without having to rely solely on measures designed for males and to ascertain important factors in sexual recidivism in women. While treating sexual offending behaviour in women clearly necessitates a focus on the offending behaviour and the factors contributing to it, this chapter has outlined a number of other factors which may impact on the lives of these women and indirectly contribute to their offending, and has attempted to indicate the importance of expanding our interventions to identify and address those factors which may be hindering women from leading more fulfilling lives (Ward & Brown, 2004).

There are other issues to consider in working with this offender population, particularly as, in the UK at least, the comparatively small numbers of such women make group treatment programmes a less likely option. Although there are some advantages to working individually with women offenders, in that there can be increased flexibility in approach and greater tailoring of treatment to individual offence motivations and needs, such work can also leave women feeling isolated and 'bizarre' (Eldridge & Saradjian, 2000), thereby reinforcing their general sense of alienation and difference from others. Such work could also prove isolating for the therapist who, without the contributions from other group members, and with potentially very limited external support for the woman, may find him or herself the only source of support for the woman in dealing with the difficult feelings potentially raised in treatment.

As the opening section of this chapter described, professionals may share some of the general population views about female sexual offenders and it is important to question our own beliefs and consider whether they focus our attention towards certain aspects and away from others. It may be particularly important to be aware of this during the assessment phase as the information gathered here guides later work with the women. We may have particular expectations about female sex offenders; Matthews (1998) candidly admits that when she first met a female abuser, she had expected to meet "a hostile, unrepentant monster", but the individual she instead saw was "a tiny woman curled in the corner of a large leather sofa" (p. 259). Eldridge and Saradjian (2000) suggest that because sexual abuse by women so strongly transgresses expectations of female behaviour, researchers have tended to examine these women's life histories, relationships, beliefs and motivations in greater depth than much of the research carried out with male offenders, perhaps in an effort to understand how *women* could act in this way. However, this focus has left a number of other potentially important factors largely unexamined. Alternatively, the unusualness of female sexual offending may result in professionals focusing primarily on the deviant behaviour itself and neglecting other, equally important aspects of the woman's life (Ford & Cortoni, 2008). This chapter has hopefully emphasised that in working with female offenders, we should endeavour to address all these factors.

It is also important to be aware of personal feelings raised for us in working with this group of offenders and how these may impact on our responses to them, whether or not we work with women abusers on a regular basis. These may include negative feelings towards a woman who has sexually offended, particularly if the victim is a child, potentially resulting in angry or punitive responses to the woman and further exacerbating her feelings of isolation, shame and powerlessness (Saradjian, 1996). Another common response, Saradjian suggests, is over-identification with the woman's own victimisation experiences, leading to protective responses towards her and minimisation of her offending behaviour. Awareness of one's own feelings and responses may be even more important when work is taking place on an individual basis and the dynamics are not observable to other group members or leaders.

Finally, it may be important to consider whether certain features of treatment programmes can potentially repeat negative aspects of women offender's lives and how this may be attended to. As previously suggested, the potential isolation of individual work may reinforce feelings of loneliness or highlight the unavailability of support from others and so attempting to make provision for some social support before commencing treatment may be important (Saradjian, 1996). As treatment is often a requirement once sexual offending becomes known, this may feel like an undertaking that the woman has been pressured into, rather than one she wants to complete. Perhaps particularly for those coerced into abuse, but for all women offenders who report feeling powerless, entering assessment or treatment may seem like another coerced activity in which they again have to take a subordinate role. Saradjian (1996) therefore emphasises the importance of taking a collaborative stance with women, in an effort to develop feelings of involvement and control in the process, as well as perhaps a sense of shared responsibility. This may not be specific to women; Drapeau (2005) found that male child molesters in a prison treatment programme expressed a wish for greater 'mastery', including increased independence and the ability to make some decisions for themselves, and tended to react negatively when this was denied or they felt coerced by staff. Whether this wish is stronger among women offenders, who feel powerless in many or all aspects of their lives, however, is an interesting area for further study, with potentially important implications for our future work with these women.

REFERENCES

Allen, C.M. (1991). *Women and men who sexually abuse children: A comparative analysis*. Brandon, VT: The Safer Society Press.

Aylward, A., Christopher, M., Newell, R.M. & Gordon, A. (2002). What about women who commit sex offences? Paper presented at the 22nd Annual Research and Treatment Conference, Association for the Treatment of Sexual Abusers, Montréal, Canada. October, 2002.

Beckett, R.C. (2005). What are the characteristics of female sex offenders? *NOTA News, 51*, 6–7.

Beech, A.R., Fisher, D. & Thornton, D. (2003). Risk assessment of sex offenders. *Professional Psychology: Research and Practice, 34*, 339–352.

Beech, A.R. & Ward, T. (2004). The integration of etiology and risk in sexual offenders: a theoretical framework. *Aggression and Violent Behavior, 10*, 31–63.

Blanchette, K. & Brown, S.L. (2006). *The assessment and treatment of women offenders*. Chichester: John Wiley & Sons, Ltd.

Bunting, L. (2005). *Executive summary: Females who sexually offend against children: Responses of the child protection and criminal justice systems*. Retrieved January 3, 2006 from the World Wide Web: http://www.nspcc.org.uk/Inform/Research/Findings/FemalesWhoSexuallyOffend_ifega27751.html

Byers, E.S. & O'Sullivan, L.F. (1998). Similar but different: men's and women's experiences of sexual coercion. In P.B. Anderson & C. Struckman-Johnson (Eds), *Sexually aggressive women: Current perspectives and controversies* (pp. 144–168). New York: Guilford Press.

Clark, D. & Howden-Windall, J. (2000). *A retrospective study of criminogenic factors in the female prison population*. London: Her Majesty's Prison Service.

Cortoni, F. & Hanson, R.K. (2005). *A review of the recidivism rates of adult female sexual offenders.* Research Report R-169. Ottawa, ON: Correctional Service Canada.

Cortoni, F. & Marshall, W.L. (2001). Sex as a coping strategy and its relationship to juvenile sexual history and intimacy in sexual offenders. *Sexual Abuse: A Journal of Research and Treatment, 13*, 27–43.

Craissati, J. (2003). Risk, reconviction and their relationship to key developmental variables in a complete urban sample of child molesters and rapists. Unpublished PhD Thesis, University of Birmingham, U.K.

Davies, M., Pollard, P. & Archer, J. (2006). Effects of perpetrator gender and victim sexuality on blame towards male victims of sexual assault. *The Journal of Social Psychology, 146*, 275–291.

Davies, M. & Rogers, P. (2006). Perceptions of male victims in depicted sexual assaults: A review of the literature. *Aggression and Violent Behavior, 11*, 367–377.

Denov, M.S. (2003). To a safer place? Victims of sexual abuse by females and their disclosures to professionals. *Child Abuse and Neglect, 27*, 47–61.

Denov, M.S. (2004). The long-term effects of child sexual abuse by female perpetrators: A qualitative study of male and female victims. *Journal of Interpersonal Violence, 19*, 1137–1156.

Denov, M.S. & Cortoni, F. (2006). Adult female sexual offenders. In C. Hilarski & J. Wodarski (Eds), *Comprehensive mental health practices with sex offenders and their families* (pp. 71–99). New York: Haworth Press.

Drapeau, M. (2005). Research on the processes involved in treating sexual offenders. *Sexual Abuse: A Journal of Research and Treatment, 17*, 117–125.

Dube, S.R., Anda, R.F., Whitfield, C.L. *et al.* (2005). Long-term consequences of childhood sexual abuse by gender of victim. *American Journal of Preventative Medicine, 28*, 430–438.

Eldridge, H.J. & Saradjian, J. (2000). Replacing the function of abusive behaviours for the offender: Remaking relapse prevention in working with women who sexually abuse children. In D.R. Laws, S.M. Hudson & T. Ward (Eds), *Remaking Relapse Prevention With Sex Offenders: A Sourcebook* (pp. 402–426). Thousand Oaks, CA: Sage Publications.

Ford, H. (2006). *Women who sexually abuse children*. Chichester: John Wiley & Sons, Ltd.

Ford, H.J. & Cortoni, F. (2008). Assessment and treatment of sexual deviance in females. In D.R. Laws & W. O'Donohue (Eds), *Sexual deviance* (2nd edn). New York: Guilford Press.

Grayston, A.D. & De Luca, R.V. (1999). Female perpetrators of child sexual abuse: A review of the clinical and empirical literature. *Aggression and Violent Behavior, 4*, 93–106.

Green, A.H. & Kaplan, M.S. (1994). Psychiatric impairment and childhood victimization experiences in female child molesters. *Journal of the American Academy of Child and Adolescent Psychiatry, 33*, 954–961.

Hetherton, J. & Beardsall, L. (1998). Decisions and attitudes concerning child sexual abuse: does the gender of the perpetrator make a difference to child protection professionals? *Child Abuse and Neglect, 22*, 1265–1283.

Hollin, C.R. & Palmer, E.J. (2006). Criminogenic need and women offenders: A critique of the literature. *Legal and Criminological Psychology, 11*, 179–195.

Johansson-Love, J. & Fremouw, W. (2006). A critique of the female sexual perpetrator research. *Aggression and Violent Behavior, 11*, 12–26.

Kaufman, K.L., Wallace, A.M., Johnson, C.E. & Reeder, M.L. (1995). Comparing male and female perpetrators' modus operandi: Victims' reports of sexual abuse. *Journal of Interpersonal Violence, 10*, 322–333.

Kite, D. & Tyson, G.A. (2004). The impact of perpetrator gender on male and female police officers' perceptions of child sexual abuse. *Psychiatry, Psychology and Law, 11*, 308–318.

Lewis, C.F. & Stanley, C.R. (2000). Women accused of sexual offences. *Behavioral Sciences and the Law, 18*, 73–81.

Mathis, J.L. (1972). *Clear thinking about sexual deviations: A new look at an old problem*. Chicago: Nelson-Hall.

Matthews, J.K. (1993). Working with female sexual abusers. In M. Elliot (Ed.), *Female sexual abuse of children* (pp. 57–73). New York: Guilford Press.

Matthews, J.K. (1998). An 11-year perspective of working with female sexual offenders. In W.L. Marshall, Y.M. Fernandez, S.M. Hudson & T. Ward (Eds), *Sourcebook of treatment programs for sexual offenders* (pp. 259–272). New York: Plenum Press.

Matthews, J.K., Mathews, R. & Speltz, K. (1991). Female sexual offenders: A typology. In M.Q. Patton. (Ed.), *Family sexual abuse: Frontline research and evaluation* (pp. 199–219). Newbury Park, CA: Sage.

Nathan, P. & Ward, T. (2001). Females who sexually abuse children: Assessment and treatment issues. *Psychiatry, Psychology and Law*, *8*, 44–55.

Nathan, P. & Ward, T. (2002). Female sex offenders: clinical and demographic features. *The Journal of Sexual Aggression*, *8*, 5–21.

Ogloff, J.R.P. & Davis, M.R. (2004). Advances in offender assessment and rehabilitation: contributions of the risk-need-responsivity approach. *Psychology, Crime and Law*, *10*, 229–242.

Oliver, B.E. (2007). Preventing female-perpetrated sexual abuse. *Trauma, Violence and Abuse*, *8*, 19–32.

Ring, L. (2005). Psychometric profiles of female sexual abusers: A preliminary analysis into the differences between sexually abusive and non-offending females. Unpublished MSc thesis, University of Birmingham, UK.

Saradjian, J. (1996). *Women who sexually abuse children: From research to clinical practice.* Chichester: John Wiley & Sons, Ltd.

Sorbello, L., Eccleston, L., Ward, T. & Jones, R. (2002). Treatment needs of female offenders: A review. *Australian Psychologist*, *37*, 198–205.

Tardif, M., Auclair, N., Jacob, M. & Carpentier, J. (2005). Sexual abuse perpetrated by adult and juvenile females: an ultimate attempt to resolve a conflict associated with maternal identity. *Child Abuse and Neglect*, *29*, 153–167.

Tewksbury, R. (2004). Experiences and attitudes of registered female sex offenders. *Federal Probation*, *68*, 30–33.

Travin, S., Cullen, K. & Protter, B. (1990). Female sex offenders: Severe victims and victimisers. *Journal of Forensic Sciences*, *35*, 140–150.

Vandiver, D.M. (2006). Female sex offenders: A comparison of solo offenders and co-offenders. *Violence and Victims*, *21*, 339–354.

Vandiver, D.M. & Kercher, G. (2004). Offender and victim characteristics of registered female sex offenders in Texas: A proposed typology of female sexual offenders. *Sexual Abuse: A Journal of Research and Treatment*, *16*, 121–137.

Ward, T. & Brown, M. (2004). The Good Lives Model and conceptual issues in offender rehabilitation. *Psychology, Crime and Law*, *10*, 243–257.

Williams, S.M. & Nicholaichuk, T. (2001). *Assessing static risk factors in adult female sex offenders under federal jurisdiction in Canada.* Paper presented at the 20th Research and Treatment Conference, Association for the Treatment of Sexual Abusers, San Antonio, Texas. November, 2001.

Policy and Practice

PART SIX

Policy and Practice

26

Working to Prevent Sexual Abuse in the Family

KEVIN D. BROWNE

INTRODUCTION

The sexual assault of women and children continues to be an abhorrent and pervasive problem in most societies around the world (World Health Organization, 2002). In the past 20 years, there has been a greater awareness of sexual abuse in the family, and how it can be handled sensitively and carefully by all involved (Pinheiro, 2006). The aim of this chapter is to consider the extent, identification, assessment and management of sexual offences committed in the family home and ways to prevent it.

SOCIAL POLICY AND LEGISLATION

In the UK, a multi-sector, inter-disciplinary approach is seen as the most effective way of working together to provide protection to women and children in domestic settings (Home Office, 2005). Indeed, guidelines have been published by Her Majesty's Government (2006) on how a range of agencies and their professionals can work together to safeguard children, with the establishment of *Local Safeguarding Children Boards*, under the Children Act 2004 (Department for Education and Skills, 2007). Similarly, there has been coordinated action against spouse abuse with monthly meetings of Multi-Agency Risk Assessment Conferences (MARACs) for domestic violence in most areas, as recommended by the Domestic Violence, Crime and Victims Act (2004). The objective is to prevent spouse abuse by better sharing of information and risk assessment (Douglas *et al.*, 2004). The Home Office (2005) defines domestic violence as:

Assessment and Treatment of Sex Offenders: A Handbook. Edited by Anthony Beech, Leam Craig and Kevin Browne. © John Wiley & Sons Ltd, 2009.

Any incident of threatening behaviour, violence or abuse (psychological, physical, sexual, financial or emotional) between adults who are, or have been, intimate partners or family members, regardless of gender or sexuality (p. 7).

This definition concerns adults (any person aged 18 years or over) who are family members such as mother, father, son, daughter, brother, sister and grandparents, whether directly related, in-laws or stepfamily. It now encompasses rape in marital or intimate relationships, forced marriage, so-called 'honour crimes', and female genital mutilation, which have caused increasing concerns in communities throughout the UK.

In 2006, the police recorded 1,344 incest or familial sexual offences compared to 966 the year before. The 39% increase was thought to have been influenced by the Sex Offences Act 2003 (Nicholas, Kershaw & Walker, 2007). The Sex Offences Act (2003) replaces the 1956 Act and redefines rape to include penetration of the mouth or anus and a new offence of sexual assault by penetration covers acts involving the insertion of objects or body parts other than the penis. This includes 'marital rape' between cohabiting or separated intimate partners. Any sexual intercourse with a child aged 12 or younger will now be treated as rape. The offence of 'adult sexual activities with a child' covers any sexual act that takes place between an adult and a child under the age of 16 regardless of whether it appears to be consensual or not. This also covers non-contact sexual activities such as inducing children to remove their clothes for adult sexual pleasure, filming or photography. Sexual activities with victims who were abducted subjected to threats or fear of serious harm will be classed as non-consensual. Similarly, victims who are unable to consent due to a learning disability, mental disorder, being drugged or rendered unconscious will also be classified as non-consensual sex. The crime of incest has been replaced with the offence 'familial sexual abuse' to cover sexual offences by cohabitees not related to the child, foster and adoptive parents. Furthermore, the 2003 act covers sexual abuse by acquaintances and extended family members with the new offence of 'abuse of position of trust'.

THE EXTENT OF SEXUAL OFFENCES AGAINST CHILDREN

The World Health Organization defines child sexual abuse as *"the involvement of a child in sexual activity, by either adults or other children who are in a position of responsibility, trust or power over that child, that he or she does not fully comprehend, is unable to give informed consent to, or for which the child is not developmentally prepared, or else that violates the laws or social taboos of society"* (Butchart *et al.*, 2006, p. 10).

An early prevalence study of sexual abuse as a child, retrospectively reported by British adults (Baker & Duncan, 1985), found that 12% of women and 8% of men recall sexually abusive experiences in their childhood. More recent prevalence studies of over 3,000 adults who also gave retrospective self-reports about their childhood in England (Cawson *et al.*, 2000) and Ireland (McGee *et al.*, 2002) showed that contact

Table 26.1 Prevalence of self-reported sexual victimisation and the perpetrators of the sexual abuse in Ireland* (Adapted from McGee et al., 2002)

Characteristic	Female Child (16 yrs or younger)	Male Child (16 yrs or younger)	Female Adult (17 yrs or older)	Male Adult (17 yrs or older)
Contact Sexual Abuse (of which % Penetration)	20.4% (5.6%)	16.2% (2.7%)	20.4% (6.1%)	9.7% (0.9%)
Non-Contact Sexual Abuse only	10%	7.2%	5.1%	2.7%
No Sexual Abuse reported	69.6%	76.6%	74.5%	87.6%
Family Perpetrator	24%	14%	28% (23.6% partner or ex-partner)	1.4%
Acquaintance Perpetrator	52%	66%	42%	60.6%
Stranger as Perpetrator	24%	20%	30%	38%

*Anonymous telephone survey of 3,120 adults, selected at random

sexual abuse had been experienced by 11% of English children and 18.3% of Irish children (see Table 26.1).

Similarly, the prevalence of child sexual abuse has been estimated in the USA by David Finkelhor and his colleagues (1990). They interviewed 1,481 women and 1,145 men by telephone and found that 15% of women and 9.5% of men were found to have been victims of sexual intercourse during childhood. In addition, 20% of women and 5% of men admitted to being touched, grabbed or kissed as a child. An international comparison of 21 countries, around the same time, showed that the prevalence of child sexual abuse ranged from 7% to 36% for women and 3% to 29% for men (Finkelhor, 1994). According to these studies, girls were between 1.5 and 3 times more likely to be sexually abused than boys. Up to 56% of the girls and 25% of the boys were sexually abused within the family environment perpetrated by blood relatives, step-parents, foster carers and adoptive parents. In Ireland, 24% of women and 14% of men reported being sexually abused as children by a member of their family (see Table 26.1). In Romania, when young teenagers (aged 13 to 14 years) were surveyed about maltreatment in the family home (Browne et al., 2002), 9% claimed to have been sexually abused by a family member.

Evidence from victim surveys and prevalence studies consistently indicate that the number of people that anonymously report abuse in childhood is much more than the detected incidence rate (Creighton, 2002). For example, in England on the day of 31st March 2007, 25 children per 10,000 (0–17 years) were on child protection registers for actual or highly suspected abuse and/or neglect. Of these 27,900 children on the register, 2,500 were registered for sexual abuse, which represents 7% of cases. Nevertheless, a further 3,200 (10%) children were registered under mixed abuse, some of which included sexual abuse (Department for Children, Schools and Families, 2007). In comparison to prevalence rates, the incidence figures indicate that there is a significant 'dark figure' of unreported sexual crime on children, as only two children in every 10,000 are identified as victims of sexual abuse, 60% of these are girls and 40% are boys. One reason for this discrepancy is that only a quarter of English adults, who had unwanted sexual experiences or sex with someone five years older or more as a child, chose to disclose the event. This disclosure was usually to a friend, less often to a family member and rarely to the police (Cawson *et al.*, 2000). In cases of child sexual abuse, only 5% are disclosed and 2% reported to the police, half of which are prosecuted (Kelly, Regan & Burton, 1991). The same small proportion (2%) of cases reported to the police has also been found in the USA (Russell, 1983, 1986). Generally, studies (e.g., Davenport, Browne & Palmer, 1994) show that proximity in the relationship between victim and offender influences the disclosure of sexual abuse. Close relationships are less likely to be disclosed than those that are more distant or involving a stranger.

Finkelhor (1986) observed that most USA sexual abuse victims outside the family (60%) described a single unpleasant experience. Consequently, they avoided the perpetrator or told a parent/guardian, who helped them to prevent it happening again. However, victims of sexual abuse by family members or friends and associates of the family described sexual assaults on an episodic or regular basis. The average duration for female victims of sexual abuse within the family was 31 weeks. Similarly in Ireland, 60% of cases experienced a single abusive event, for those 40% of cases who experienced ongoing sexual abuse (58% of girl victims and 42% of boy victims) the duration was over one year and was more likely to be perpetrated by a family member or friend of the family. Four out of five victims reported they knew their offender prior to the sexual assault and 67% of girl victims and 62% of boy victims reported that the sexual abuse took place before they reached 12 years of age. Over a third (36%) of those who had experienced sexual abuse as a child believed that their abuser was also sexually assaulting other children at the same time (McGee *et al.*, 2002).

SEX OFFENDERS WHO ABUSE CHILDREN IN THE FAMILY

Frequently a distinction is made between incestuous and non-incestuous offenders (e.g., Herman & Hirschman, 1981). This is a false dichotomy to some extent because research shows that one in two incestuous fathers also abuse children outside the family (Weinrott & Saylor, 1991) and up to one in five admit to raping adult women (Conte, 1985; Elliott, Browne & Kilcoyne, 1995). Obviously incestuous parents and step-parents find children sexually arousing and perhaps children within their own family are those most easily available? Indeed, interviews with sex offenders convicted for sexually assaulting children outside their family have found that a third of them confess to sexually abusing their own children (Weinrott & Saylor, 1991). Therefore, it is suggested that 33% to 50% of 'incest' offenders could be regarded as 'true' paedophiles with a primary 'fixated' sexual interest in children and not merely 'situational' sex offenders as suggested by Howells (1981).

In all contexts, the vast majority of sex offenders (80–95%) are male (Finkelhor, 1986; Jehu, 1988; McGee *et al.*, 2002). Nevertheless, a meta-analysis of eight victim surveys found that on average 2.5% of female victims and 21.3% of male victims report that they were abused by female perpetrators (Fergusson & Mullen, 1999). In Ireland, 89% of the perpetrators of sexual abuse of children were men acting alone, 7% of children were abused by one female perpetrator and in 4% of cases there was more than one abuser involved in the same incident (McGee *et al.*, 2002).

According to the American Humane Association (McDonald *et al.*, 2005), cases of child sexual abuse also represented 7% of all child maltreatment referrals in 2003. Biological parents were alleged perpetrators in only 3% of these cases. The parents' male partners were thought to be responsible for 11% of cases, other relatives (grandparent, siblings, cousins, uncles) accounted for 30% of cases. Hence, 44% of sexual abuse cases were perpetrated in the family. People in a position of trust, not related to the child, accounted for 40% of cases as: child caregivers in institutional and day care settings 23%, teachers 11% and foster carers 6%. In the other cases (16%), the perpetrators were unknown, many of which involved a sex offender who was a stranger to the child victim.

A review of cases in the UK, Mrazek, Lynch and Bentovim (1981) found that biological fathers were responsible in 20% of cases, stepfathers 12% and biological mothers 2%. Other relatives and acquaintances were responsible for the abuse in 41% of cases and 25% of the time the abuse was perpetrated by strangers. By comparison, a child sex offender survey by Elliott *et al.* (1995) found that approximately one-third of convicted offenders were intra-familial, one-third were extra-familial acquaintances known to the child, and one-third were strangers. A recent review of research on violence against children by the UN Secretary General's Study on Violence against Children also estimates that between 21% and 34% of sexual assaults on children are committed by strangers (Pinheiro, 2006). What is clear is that majority of child sexual abuse is perpetrated by caregivers or someone in a position of trust.

Step-parent or cohabitee in the family is often considered to be a risk factor, although the figures (around 11–12% of cases) would suggest step-parents are somewhat maligned considering their relative contribution to the child sexual abuse. When the maternal caregiver is unavailable, disabled or ill and where the child victim has a poor relationship with the mother, the situation may enhance the possibility of child sexual abuse (Browne, 1994). Usually children sexually abused within the family are victims of other forms of abuse such as physical and emotional abuse. These forms coexist with child sexual abuse or have a previous history. Research shows that one-third of all sexually abused children have been physically abused under five (Finkelhor & Baron, 1986). Other types of family violence such as wife abuse are also highly associated with child physical and sexual abuse, so that when the mother is present in the home and recognises there is a problem the perpetrator's response is usually violence (Browne, 1993; Browne & Herbert, 1997).

A further difficulty with the intra-familial/extra-familial dichotomy arises from child sex offenders outside the family targeting single parent families and separated/divorced families where there has been marital discord. They regard children from these families to be more vulnerable than those from intact families because of their lack of confidence and low self-esteem. The children are unsure of themselves and as a consequence are more compliant to the approaches of teenage or adult perpetrators, whether previously known or unknown (Browne, 1994).

Grooming Strategies

The relationship between perpetrator and victim will affect the frequency and duration of the abuse and strategies used to engage the victim in the abuse (Faller, 1990). For example, those that are family or acquainted with the victim are more likely to employ psychological strategies such as coercion and bribery, whereas strangers are more likely to rely on physical force and surprise as a means of overcoming their victims, which increases their chance of being discovered. Indeed, Kirby (1995) found that in 30 of the 53 offences in which physical force was used the offender was a stranger to the child. Intra-familial abusers also have fewer victims partly because the '*grooming process*' is coercive by nature.

'*Grooming*' was a term originally used by Christiansen and Blake (1990) to describe the processes by which fathers perpetrated incestuous relationships with their daughters. However, the term has been generalised since to describe the processes and strategies that all sexual offenders use to initiate and perpetuate the sexual abuse of children. The strategies are employed by the offender to: target particular children and/or parents; create opportunities to engage and interact with child victims in a sexual way; encourage secrecy about the contact; maintain the victims in their victim role and the abusive situation; and further, to prevent disclosure both during the abuse and once the sexual relationship has ceased.

According to the sex offender survey carried out by Elliott et al. (1995), a third of sex offenders work on becoming welcome in the child's home and just under half the offenders (46%) felt that a 'special relationship' with the child was vital. Half of all sex offenders of children have previously isolated their victims through babysitting. On these occasions, the offenders start by talking about sex (27%) offering to bath or dress the child (20%) and/or using coercion by misrepresenting the abuse as having a different purpose (21%). For example, the offender might say 'it would be good for you to do this for your education' or 'this is what people do who love each other'. Other offenders (61%) used passive methods of control such as stopping the abuse and then coercing and persuading once again.

SEXUAL MALTREATMENT BY SIBLINGS

In the UK, teenage male perpetrators aged 20 and younger account for about one-third of all allegations of sexual abuse (Glasgow et al., 1994; Watkins & Bentovim, 1992) and approximately a quarter of those convicted of a sexual offence (Masson & Erooga, 1999). This was confirmed by the Irish prevalence study, which found that victims of sexual abuse claimed the perpetrator was a child (under 17 years) in one out of four cases (McGee *et al.*, 2002). With regard to the family context, the sexual maltreatment of brothers and sisters by their siblings is much more common than once thought. To a certain extent this has been the result of a reappraisal of what was once considered sexual exploration between brothers and sisters, which has been more appropriately described as exploitation where the age difference between the siblings is greater than five years (De Jong, 1989; Finkelhor, 1980), although it has been observed that adolescent incest offenders were less likely to be court ordered for treatment than non-incest offenders (O'Brian, 1991).

In a study of family conflict, 2% of English undergraduate students reported being sexually maltreated by a sibling on at least one occasion (Browne & Hamilton, 1998). Often this sexual maltreatment was associated with physical abuse and bullying, a fact that has been confirmed by a number of American studies for both boys and girls (De Jong, 1989; Johnson, 1988, 1989). Similar to physical and sexual assaults by adults, it is in the context of caregiving or 'child minding' that many of these attacks by adolescent and teenage perpetrators takes place (Margolin, 1990).

Indeed, most child sexual offenders begin to take advantage of younger children during their teenage years, with the majority (57%) having been physically and/or sexually assaulted themselves by other teenagers and adults (Elliott *et al.*, 1995). Nevertheless, sibling maltreatment of both a physical and sexual nature has been observed in young children (Cantwell, 1988). For example, Johnson (1988) noted that 46% of a sample of 47 sexually abusive boys was involved in the abuse of their siblings. Similarly, Pierce and Pierce (1987) reported in their study that of the 59 sex offences that had been committed by 37 juvenile offenders, 40% were against sisters and 20% were against brothers. The study of physical and sexual maltreatment by brothers and sisters is limited and prevention is only just beginning. It requires a great deal more research given its prevalence and consequences (Laviola, 1989; Mueller & Silverman, 1989).

INTIMATE PARTNER RAPE

In line with the Sex Offences Act 2003 rape is defined as an assault upon an individual with the intent to commit penetrative sexual acts without the victim's permission (Fisher & Beech, 2004). The British Crime Survey (2000) using a narrower definition of 'forced sexual intercourse (vaginal or anal penetration)' showed that 1 in 20 adult women, over the age of sexual consent of 16 years or more, claimed that they had been raped but only a minority (20% of rape victims) had reported it to the police. Twice as many (1 in 10) adult women claimed that they had suffered some form of sexual victimisation (Myhill & Allen, 2002). Similar to the risk to children, adult women are more likely to be sexually assaulted by someone they know rather than a stranger. The SAVI report (McGee *et al.*, 2002) found that, unlike men (1%), almost a quarter (24%) of perpetrators of sexual violence against women as adults were intimate partners or ex-partners, which were the vast majority (28%) of family perpetrators to women.

Most women (42%) were assaulted by an acquaintance as were men (61%). The risk of sexual assault by a stranger was higher for adults (30% for women and 38% for men) than for children (see Table 26.1).

Sexual assaults by strangers are those most often reported to the police and this gives a distorted picture of the prevalence of rape by someone known to the victim. Date rape, acquaintance and marital rape are much less likely to be reported to the police but according to prevalence studies, appear to be more common. In a recent review of marital rape, Martin, Taft and Resick (2007) estimated that 10% to 14% of married women have experienced forced sex by their intimate partner and as many as 40% to 50% of battered women are raped within their physically abusive relationship. In an earlier study, Russell (1991) interviewed 930 women in San Francisco, 644 of who were married. It was found that 4% had experienced 'marital rape' but no other physical violence, 14% had been raped and battered, and 12% had been battered but not raped. Likewise, Finkelhor and Yllo (1985) previously estimated that 1 in 10 women in Boston had experienced forced sex by their intimate partner. In 82% of the cases, this occurred after they had separated. They categorised 'marital rape' into three types, based on Groth's (1977, 1979) previous work:

- In 10% of the cases, the intimate partner was forced to engage in bizarre and perverse sexual activities without their consent (e.g., bondage). Such activities had an obsessive element and were likened to Groth's *'sadistic rapists'*.
- In 40% of the cases, violence was used only to obtain sex from the spouse and rarely occurred at other times. This control and authority over intimate partners was associated with Groth's *'power rapists'*.
- In 50% of cases, the forced sex is a part of the general domestic violence suffered by the woman and used as another way of humiliating and degrading them. This was associated with Groth's *'anger rapists'*.

The nature of sexual violence in intimate relationships, whether married or non-married, is not limited to heterosexual couples and occurs to a similar extent between homosexual and lesbian relationships (Renzetti, 1992). Furthermore, the occurrence of physical and sexual violence is not restricted to cohabiting couples or those who previously lived together. Acquaintance and date rape is just as common and surveys of college students in the USA revealed that 15% reported having unwanted sexual advances (Levine & Kanin, 1987) and 7 to 9% reported being raped during a date (Mufson & Kranz, 1993; Pirog-Good, 1992).

Prevalence studies of sexual violence by intimate partners or ex-partners reported in different countries (WHO, 2002) indicate that between 6% and 46% of women in relationships experience attempted or actual forced sex at some time in their lives. In London, it was estimated that 23% of women had had such experiences associated with domestic violence (Morley & Mullender, 1994). Female spouses are especially reluctant to disclose violence in the family as they recognise that this is one of the reasons why social services would intervene in family life and prioritise interventions to prevent emotional and psychological harm to children in the family. This may result in the children being taken into public care with the mother accused of 'failing to protect the child(ren)'. This social service response is not helpful to women who are victims of physical and sexual violence by their intimate partners. These women are not in a position to protect their children without help. Therefore, women in this position sometimes report the violence to the police and social services only to retract it later.

LINKS BETWEEN SPOUSE ABUSE AND CHILD ABUSE

The importance of the links between spouse abuse and child maltreatment has been recognised for family protection work for some time (Browne & Hamilton, 1999; Dietz and Craft, 1980; Jaffe, Wolfe & Wilson, 1990). In the vast majority of cases this involves the father/stepfather seriously assaulting the mother as well as the children. An Australian study by Goddard and Hiller (1993) found that child sexual abuse was evident in 40% of families with intimate partner violence. Truesdell, McNeil and Deschner (1986) also claimed that domestic violence was more common than expected in North American incestuous families with nearly three-quarters (73%) of mothers from incestuous families experiencing at least one incident of domestic violence, a third of whom were threatened or injured with a knife or a gun.

Mental Health Factors

Where spouse abuse and child maltreatment are occurring together in the family, mental health problems, alcohol and drug dependency appear to be the most significant risk factors for violence (Browne & Hamilton, 1999). In the USA, surveys of battered women typically show that 60% of their partners have an alcohol problem and 21% have a drug problem (Roberts, 1987) and the majority of female victims suffer from mental health problems as a result. Some authors propose that these are the major causes of family violence (Pernanen, 1991). However, it is more likely that alcohol and drug dependency relieves the man of the responsibility of his behaviour and gives the wife justification for remaining in the relationship in the hope that he will control his addiction and end his abuse. It is true that alcohol and drugs appear to exacerbate pre-existing emotional problems, which increases the likelihood of violent and sexual assault. This relationship is also associated with the sexual abuse of elderly relatives in the family by partners, ex-partners or adult children (Campbell-Reay & Browne, 2008). However, the majority of individuals who abuse drugs and alcohol admit they have been violent to their dependants while not under the influence of alcohol and drugs (Sonkin, Martin & Walker, 1985).

Indeed, mental health problems, alcohol and drug dependency are not the causes of family violence but rather conditions that co-exist with it, along with many other factors. Nevertheless, they are often used as excuses for sexual and violent abuse – personally, socially and legally. Renzetti (1992) found physical and sexual violence in USA lesbian and homosexual relationships to be highly associated with alcohol consumption in both victims and offenders. The SAVI report (McGee *et al.*, 2002) observed that alcohol was involved in almost half of the cases of sexual assault that occurred to an adult. Of those who reported that alcohol was involved, both parties were drinking in 57% of cases concerning sexual assault of women, and in 63% of cases concerning sexual assault of men. Where only one party was drinking, the perpetrator was the one drinking in the majority of cases (84% of female and 70% of male assault cases). It has been suggested that sex offenders may sometimes deliberately use alcohol and drugs as a part of their 'modus operandi' (Craig, Browne & Beech, 2008) or use it as a way of denying, minimising and distorting their behaviour (Allam & Browne, 1998; Allam, Middleton & Browne, 1997). Therefore, interventions aimed at the protection of women and children must first address these associated factors, as individuals addicted to alcohol and drugs or suffering from mental illness can rarely benefit from interventions.

Inter-agency cooperation between probation, social services, community psychiatric and primary health care is a necessary prerequisite when there is evidence of spouse or child abuse and mental health problems in the family. The psychological disturbances shown by sex offenders of children in domestic settings have been reported by Conte (1985) and Overholser and Beck (1986) to be: alcohol and drug abuse, depression, poor self-concept, low self-esteem, relationship problems, poor impulse control, poor anger management, fear of negative evaluation and highly stereotypic views of sex roles and behaviour. However, adult mental health services are considered by Reder and Duncan (1997) as a missing link in the child/family protection system, since their staff rarely contribute to the work of safeguarding women and children.

LONG-TERM EFFECTS OF SEXUAL ABUSE IN THE FAMILY

It is now well established that sexual abuse causes serious harm to women and children and has negative consequences for their health and development, both in the short and long term (see Briere, 1992; Felitti, 1998). The severity of harm is mediated by a number of factors (Davenport, Browne & Palmer, 1994; Watkins & Bentovim, 1992). These are:

- The type and form of the abusive and/or neglectful act (contact or non-contact);
- The child's age and developmental stage at the time of the maltreatment;
- The duration and frequency of the maltreatment;
- The method used to overcome victim resistance (eg; coercion or physical restraint);
- The relationship of the child to the perpetrator (abuse of trust in close relationships);
- The response to the child's disclosure of abuse and neglect (acceptance or denial);
- The support the child receives after being maltreated (helpful or unhelpful).

All forms of abuse and neglect will have both physical and psychological consequences for the victim, some of which may present as symptoms of the maltreatment. These include attachment disorders, post-traumatic stress, somatic symptoms, sexual dysfunctions, emotional disorders, mental illness, self-harm, alcohol and drug abuse, antisocial personality, aggressive behaviour, and sexual assault on others (i.e., victim to offender, see Falshaw, Browne & Hollin, 1996; Widom, 1989). Taking into account the serious consequences that sexual abuse has on women and children, the necessity of interventions and psychotherapeutic treatment is obvious. Undetected and untreated abuse yield devastating results for both the individual and the community (Briere, 1992). Research has demonstrated that three-quarters of young criminals in prison have a childhood history of abuse and neglect (Falshaw & Browne, 1997, 1999; Hamilton, Falshaw & Browne, 2002). However, only a minority (12.5%) of sexually abused boys commit sexual offences later and this minority were more likely to have also experienced family violence and/or neglect (Salter *et al.*, 2003). Sexually victimised girls are more likely to commit violent offences later (Widom & Ames, 1994). Therefore immediate reporting, intervention and treatment of abused and neglected children is an essential priority of public and social policy to prevent further victimisation.

Trauma of Recurrent Abuse

Abusive behaviour towards women and children in the family must be considered, within context, as a process not an event. For most victims abuse and sexual assault occurs on more than one occasion, with the same perpetrator or with different perpetrators. In a review of 45 studies, De Panfilis and Zuravin (1998) report repeat victimisation rates of up to 50% in families followed up over a five-year period and up to 85% for families followed for up to 10 years. Furthermore, the SAVI report (McGee *et al.*, 2002) which found for those disclosing sexual abuse that 28% of women and 19.5% of men were abused by different perpetrators as both children and adults (i.e., revictimised). It is generally considered that repeat or revictimisation will lead to more severe trauma (Briere, 1992; Browne & Hamilton, 1997; Hamilton & Browne, 1998, 1999) and that some memory of these events may be lost from conscious memory, while those victimised outside the family and who experience a single event may be less traumatised and details of the incident will be remembered (Terr, 1991; Whitfield, 1995). This may be because memories from different abusive incidents become confused, particularly when the same perpetrator is involved and the incidents occur frequently. Furthermore, denial, repression and disassociation may be more associated with repeated victimisation and revictimisation, whereas single incidents are more likely to be recollected and talked about freely, particularly if the victim experiences a supportive and understanding environment (Whitfield, 1995). These facts need to be taken into account when interviewing or assessing the needs of victims in relation to the sexual abuse they have suffered.

PREVENTION

Prevention is traditionally classified into three levels: primary prevention (universal services aimed at the whole population); secondary prevention (targeted services for families identified as in need of further support); and tertiary prevention (services offered once difficulties have occurred). However, interventions for sexual abuse of women and children in the family are most often '*reactive*' once difficulties have occurred (*Tertiary prevention*). Proactive strategies to prevent sexual victimisation are emerging (see Chapters 27 and 28 of this book) but most of these are based on intervening with those most at risk of offending (*Secondary prevention*). *Primary preventions* that do exist are usually limited to public awareness (zero tolerance) campaigns or to educational approaches with children (Briggs & Hawkins, 1997). These prevent bullying and inform children about 'good' secrets and 'bad' secrets in the family and 'stranger danger', through sexual abuse prevention programmes in schools (Collins & Elliott, 1994). However, educational approaches to prevention are limited in their effectiveness. Indeed, increasing individual self-esteem through therapy, parenting programmes or school initiatives have proved to be a more effective way to empower women and children to protect themselves and disclose any risk of sexual abuse to others (Briggs, 2000; Browne, 1995; Sanders & Cann, 2002).

Targeting Risk Factors in the Family

Taking a multifaceted approach, Milner (1986) developed the Child Abuse Potential (CAP) Inventory based on characteristics associated with child maltreatment in USA domestic settings. Indeed, the CAP Inventory is one of the few self-report questionnaires (160 items) that has been evaluated in terms of its reliability (internal consistency and temporal stability) and construct validity. In addition, it has been applied to spouse abusers (Milner & Gold, 1986). However, the relevance of such checklists and inventories for the prediction of child sexual abuse remains questionable, especially when the epidemiological differences between sexual and physical abuse are considered (Browne *et al.*, 2006; Jason *et al.*, 1982). Nevertheless, certain family risk factors are the same for all forms of child and spouse abuse (Browne, 1993, 1994; Finkelhor, 1980b, 1986; Finkelhor & Baron, 1986; Russell, 1983), such as:

- adult or child learning difficulties;
- adult or child physical health problems or disabilities;
- financial hardship and/or unemployment;
- poor relationships within family;
- marital conflict and/or family breakdown;
- single, separated or divorced family;
- step-parent or cohabitee in family;
- family emotional and social isolation with social support deficits;
- adult or child victim of abuse and/or neglect in the past;
- adult or child alcohol and drug abuse;
- adult or child mental illness;
- adult antisocial behaviour or child conduct disorder;
- adult or child criminal convictions;
- adult or child with a history of violent or sexual offending.

For secondary prevention, it is important to target families with the above risk factors (prior to abuse) and place them in priority for health and social support services. The aim is to reduce the chances of spouse and child abuse by ameliorating the effects of adverse family characteristics that influence the personality and behaviour of family members. Women and children from disruptive/violent homes may become socially withdrawn, shy and unsure of themselves, with feelings of low self-esteem and a poor sense of self-worth. These women and children are especially vulnerable to the initial advances of a child sex offender inside or outside the family. Indeed, sex offenders report these behaviour components of a 'submissive personality' make women and children vulnerable and attractive to potential sex offenders and act as a signal for possible recruitment (Elliot *et al.*, 1995).

Targeting Offender Risk Factors

A criminal lifestyle in general is a good predictor of sexual recidivism in those individuals convicted of a sexual offence (Hanson & Harris, 2000). Indeed Browne, Foreman and Middleton (1998) found that previous involvement with the police and convictions for violent offences were predictive of the 37% of sex offenders who drop-out of community treatment programmes. Owen and Steele (1991) looked at recidivism rates in incest offenders and found that 6.8% of those who completed treatment reoffended compared to 25% who did not complete treatment. They identified four further factors that predicted reoffending: (1) living in a different household from the victim; (2) chemical dependency problems; (3) offending against multiple victims; (4) being introverted.

Men who do not complete treatment still pose a significant risk to women and children (Abel *et al.*, 1988). For those convicted offenders who complete treatment, North American studies (Hanson & Bussière, 1998) show a reconviction rate for sexual offences of 13%, with incest offenders lower (4%) than boy victim paedophiles (21%). Beech (1998) found that highly deviant men were more likely to have committed offences against boys, or both boys and girls, and to have committed both extra- and intra-familial offences. They were also less likely to respond to treatment.

Challenges for Risk Assessment and Prevention

The usual response to sexual abuse in the family and home environment is to take the children into public care and sometimes to offer shelter to the mother (the non-abusive carer in the vast majority of cases). This is to prevent 'repeat victimisation' by the same offender. Nevertheless, without victim support and therapeutic help for these women and children, the victims remain at a higher risk of 'revictimisation' by a different offender (Coid *et al.*, 2001; Hamilton & Browne, 1998, 1999).

The conviction and imprisonment of the sex offender only occurs in a minority of cases (6% to 10%), when there is sufficient evidence to prove a sex crime 'beyond all reasonable doubt'. More often the alleged perpetrator of sexual abuse is banned from contacting or approaching the victim by order of a family court (e.g., exclusion and/or occupation orders) working with the principle 'on the balance of probability'. The alleged sex offender may only then be convicted and imprisoned for breach of the order and contempt of court. However, he is at liberty to 'befriend' other women and children and hence, single parent families are at considerable risk (Browne & Herbert, 1997). Furthermore, the majority of convicted incest offenders attempt to return to their families. For example, Owen and Steele (1991) followed up 43 incest offenders a year after they had been released from a prison treatment programme, of those offenders who were married, 34% returned to live with their partners and 28% were living with partners and children.

WORKING WITH FAMILIES TO PREVENT SEXUAL ABUSE

The prevention of further sexual abuse once it has occurred in the family (tertiary prevention) is the most common approach to working with families. Views range from the necessity of working with a family together from the earliest point of detection/disclosure, to the view that work has to be focused on members of the family separately. For example, Berliner and Wheeler (1978) suggested that the sexually abused victim should be separated from the offender in the family, and the two treated independently, together with the non-abusing family member. Conjoint family work is seen only as a final step in suitable families. Nevertheless, it is possible to integrate work with individuals, couples and the family as a group and create a favourable context to assist victims while working with offenders and other family members and to prevent re-abuse.

There are four basic stages of treatment with families when sexual abuse has occurred (Bentovim, 1991). These are:

1. Family assessment and the stage of disclosure – the period of crisis around the discovery of abuse;
2. The stage of separation;
3. The stage of family rehabilitation;
4. Placement in a new family – when rehabilitation has failed and it is not possible for the child to live with either the non-abusive parent or the offender.

It is important to recognise that the final placement of children is affected more by the quality of treatment and therapeutic care offered by professionals, the family attitude and offender's responsibility for the abuse, than by the extent of the abuse itself (Bentovim et al., 1988).

Family Assessment and the Stage of Disclosure

All members of the family need to be assessed in order to obtain a clear prognosis for change in the offender and determine the safety of the victim(s) and the level of protection required. Members of the family are assessed separately at this stage in case the allegations are denied, or the offender refuses to take any responsibility for his behaviours. Denial from the offender or the victim may arise because of fear of family break-up, rejection and suicide. Similarly, non-abusive family members may not believe the victim because of fear of marital breakdown or of their own guilt and mental stability, after not being available for the victim.

Once the perpetrator accepts full responsibility, it may be possible for family members to be seen together, with the exception of young children. Acknowledgement of responsibility is essential for victims and non-abusing family members to hear, because it frees them from an overwhelming sense of guilt and confusion. Nevertheless, only supervised and cautious family repatriation should be conducted in the early stages. This is because, with a formal acknowledgement of responsibility, the perpetrator may be facing prosecution, loss and separation and may feel too victimised himself to empathise with the child he has harmed and hurt.

It is important to assess the stance of non-abusing family members (both adults and children) to find how genuinely sympathetic they are to the victim, as opposed to how much they are scapegoating and blaming the child. For example, what is the likelihood of the mother taking the father back and rejecting the child who has been sexually abused? This will determine whether the child can live with the non-abusing parent, or if he or she needs to be fostered.

Family Separation

Bentovim (1991, 2002) describes three assessment categories of families, which he labels as 'hopeful', 'doubtful' and 'hopeless', with regard to the possibility of successful rehabilitation or the need for permanent separation (see Table 26.2).

It can be seen from Table 26.2 that of 120 families treated, and followed up at Great Ormond Street Hospital, only 15% of the families were categorised as 'hopeful' and were able to engage completely in treatment and achieve full rehabilitation. Another 30% were categorised as 'doubtful' and the children were only allowed to live with their mothers. In 25% cases, the circumstances were considered 'hopeless' and the children were placed outside the family because they were unable to return to either parent, due to rejection and the difficulty of putting children's needs before those of adults.

Family Rehabilitation

There is little research on when it is safe and appropriate to reunite a child, or woman, with a prior sex offender in the family home. The key question is whether the family members want the offender to return and what is the risk of further abuse. There may be competing demands and conflict between what family members want and what professionals believe to be in their best interests. Offenders tend to deny distorted thinking and behaviours and frequently respond by denying and minimising

Table 26.2 Categories of prognosis for rehabilitation of families in cases of incest (Adapted from Bentovim, 1991, 2002)

1. Families who are hopeful (15%)

- initially child and mother together;
- subsequently the father joins after appropriate treatment, when the father fully and unequivocally takes responsibility for the abuse;
- the mother believes the child;
- both parents are able to appreciate that the child's needs come first;
- there is a degree of flexibility and potential for change;
- atmosphere of cooperation and trust with professionals;
- appropriate availability of therapeutic resources;
- collaboration between child care, criminal justice agencies and therapeutic agencies.

In the above rare circumstances (15%), there was a hopeful prognosis for family rehabilitation.

2. Families who are doubtful for rehabilitation (30%)

- insufficient information to be either hopeful or hopeless;
- father is doubtful about the amount of responsibility that he is willing to take for the abusive behaviours described by the child;
- mother accepts that the abuse has happened but does not accept she was unavailable to her child;
- mother partially blames the child;
- parents partially resistant to changes in their attitudes and perceptions;
- child's needs are not seen as a first priority;
- mother not able to manage alone;
- family disorganised and chaotic in its functioning;
- relationship problems between mother and child;
- partial resentment, anger and difficulties in cooperation with professionals.

With doubtful families (30%), it was essential to have either a contract of work, which includes failure clauses or a care order.

3. Families who are hopeless (25%)

- absolute rejection of responsibility for the abuse;
- mother totally blames the child;
- parents completely resistant to changes in their attitudes and perceptions;
- choice of opting for the marriage and rejecting the child;
- the abused child is seen as bad, promiscuous and provocative;
- professionals are seen as interfering with inappropriate physical and psychological assessments;
- failure to recognise other longstanding problems of psychiatric illness, addiction or major marital conflict in the family.

With hopeless cases (25%), the children had to be permanently placed outside the family. A further 30% of older children were living independently on follow-up.

the severity of their abusive behaviour and placing the blame elsewhere (Salter, 1988). Denial, minimisation and blaming may not just be a feature of the offender but of other family members as well (Fisher & Beech, 1998). The assessment of families in terms of the danger of repeated physical and/or sexual assault to the child requires a comprehensive assessment using psychological methods and risk factors for reoffending as emphasised by Fisher and Beech (1998). They list 13 preconditions for a sex offender

Table 26.3 Goals that an offender would be expected to achieve in treatment for reconstituting families (Adapted from Fisher and Beech, 1998)

---

1. Admit the full extent of the abuse
2. Take full responsibility for the offending rather than attempting to place the blame elsewhere
3. Demonstrate genuine empathy for the victim
4. Demonstrate remorse for the offence
5. Recognise and be able to challenge cognitive distortions
6. Demonstrate an understanding of their motivation to offend
7. Be able to admit to deviant thoughts and fantasies and to have developed appropriate control strategies
8. To be able to describe the situations that would pose a risk in the future
9. To have developed appropriate relapse prevention strategies
10. Acknowledge risk of reoffending
11. Improve communication skills
12. Discuss the offending with appropriate family members
13. Develop a support network

---

to accomplish before they consider the risk to be potentially small enough for the man to be considered for reunification with his family (see Table 26.3).

When attempts are made to rehabilitate an incest offender with his family, decisions need to be taken in terms of placement of children, timing of rehabilitation and assessment of change and a clear care plan devised for the child. In addition to offender work, it is essential to work with the child victim to help with his or her traumatic responses and the (non-abusive) mother – child relationship. The mother requires help to deal with her own stress and feelings about the father's abusive behaviour and later couple work may be necessary for marital and sexual counselling and to increase the mother's authority in the family. There may be a need to work with other members of the family including the prevention of potential sibling abuse (see Deblinger & Heflin, 1996).

Placement in a New Family

New families are required for abused children where the offender is unable to take responsibility for the abuse and to change appropriately or when rehabilitation has failed and it is not possible for the child to live with either the non-abusive parent or the offender. Under these circumstances, long-term alternative care is needed, preferably with a foster family and adoption if necessary. The child requires preparation for fostering or adoption, addressing feelings of loss, guilt, failure, anger and let down. Foster and adoptive parents also require counselling to feel confident in dealing with potential behaviour problems, such as inappropriate sexualised behaviour. The child needs to be helped to re-learn safe boundaries, but only a minority of victims of sexual abuse and those placed in long-term care are given any practical help to deal with their abusive experiences (Prior, Glaser & Lynch, 1997). Hence, children fostered by relatives do better in all aspects of physical and emotional recovery and are more likely to remain in touch with their siblings and non-abusive family members (Rowe *et al.*, 1984). The costs of going into public care for the child should not be ignored; these may include: feelings of stigmatisation, bewilderment and abandonment; diminished contact with original family members with a change of family, school, friends and social community; potential for foster home breakdown and the risk of further abuse and a lack continuity of care (Falshaw & Browne, 1997, 1999).

TREATMENT OF SEX OFFENDERS

The treatment of offenders is perhaps the most effective way of protecting children on a long-term basis. Without treatment, offenders are more likely to reoffend and place other women and children at risk, as well as previous victims (Browne *et al.*, 2002). Given that sex offenders may have a range of deficits (cognitive distortions, low self-esteem, poor assertion and social skills, little empathy for others, sexuality problems and sexual fantasies, inappropriate and antisocial behaviour), the model presented in Figure 26.1 attempts to illustrate how the various deficits that may be found in sex offenders relate to their assessment and treatment needs.

In an evaluation of the UK Prison Sex Offender Treatment Programme (Beech *et al.*, 1998), it was found that 67% of men attending showed a treatment effect with significant changes in some or all of the main themes targeted. Long-term treatment (160 hours) was more effective than short-term treatment (80 hours) in creating change, especially for those offenders who showed high deviancy. Similarly, an audit of a English community treatment programme in the West Midlands (Browne, Foreman & Middleton, 1998) showed that 81% of sex offenders showed some improvement with all those completing a programme (63%) showing significant changes (Allam, Middleton & Browne, 1997). A review of seven other community treatment programmes in the UK (Beech *et al.*, 1996) demonstrates that the above findings are typical.

CONCLUSIONS

It is important to point out that the treatment programmes described above are limited to North America, Western Europe and Australasia. Few examples of such programmes exist elsewhere. Indeed, in Eastern Europe they are more likely to institutionalise the child than prosecute or treat the offender. In North America, Western Europe and Australasia, professionals concerned with the safety and protection of women, children and other vulnerable adults were the first to develop initiatives beyond that of separating the offender from the victim. It was realised that responding to the needs of individuals who commit sex offences is a more effective way of protecting vulnerable individuals in the community. Therefore, comprehensive risk assessment and interventions are necessary to assess who can remain in the community for treatment and supervision and who cannot because of the danger they pose to individuals and families in the community. Sexual offenders who are assessed as low risk of reoffending may be treated and

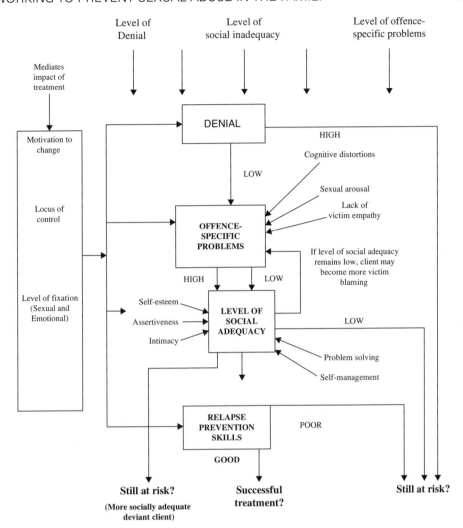

Figure 26.1 Model of cognitive behavioural treatment (from Fisher & Beech, 2002; p. 342, reprinted by kind permission of John Wiley & Sons, Ltd)

managed in the community, enhancing the chances of their rehabilitation. Individuals who are at high risk of violent and/or sexual offences require interventions while they are incarcerated in secure environments, such as young offender institutions, prisons and special hospitals. This dual track approach is likely to meet with more success in safeguarding women, children and vulnerable adults on a long-term basis.

REFERENCES

Abel., G., Mittelman, M., Becker, J. *et al.* (1988). Predicting child molesters' response to treatment. *Annals of the New York Academy of Sciences*, *528*, 223–234.

Allam, J. & Browne, K.D. (1998). Evaluating community-based treatment programmes for sexual abusers of children. *Child Abuse Review, 7*, 13–29.

Allam, J., Middleton, D. & Browne, K.D. (1997). Different clients, different needs? Practice issues in community-based treatment for sex offenders. *Criminal Behaviour and Mental Health, 7*, 69–84.

Baker, A.W. & Duncan, S.P. (1985). Child sexual abuse: a study of prevalence in Britain. *Child Abuse and Neglect, 8*, 457–467.

Beech, A.R. (1998). A psychometric typology of child abusers. *International Journal of Offender Therapy and Comparative Criminology, 42*, 319–339.

Beech, A., Fisher, D., Beckett, R. & Fordham, A. (1996). Treating sex offenders in the community. *Home Office Research and Statistics Directorate Research Bulletin, 38*, 21–25.

Beech, A., Fisher, D., Beckett, R. & Scott-Fordham, A. (1998). An evaluation of the prison sex offender treatment programme *Home Office Research and Statistics Directorate Research Findings 79*, 1–4. London: Home Office.

Bentovim, A. (1991). Clinical work with families in which sexual abuse has occurred. In C.R. Hollin & K. Howells (Eds), *Clinical approaches to sex offenders and their victims* (pp. 179–208). Chichester: John Wiley & Sons, Ltd.

Bentovim, A. (2002). Preventing the victim to offender cycle: Risk and protective factors, and the implication for therapeutic intervention. In K.D. Browne, H. Hanks, P. Stratton & C.E. Hamilton (Eds), *Early prediction and prevention of child abuse: A handbook* (pp. 283–299). Chichester: John Wiley & Sons, Ltd.

Bentovim, A., Elton, A., Hildebrand, J. *et al.* (1988). *Child sexual abuse within the family: Assessment and Treatment*. London: Wright.

Berliner, L. & Wheeler, J.R. (1978). Treating the effects of sexual abuse on children. *Journal of Interpersonal Violence, 2*, 415–434.

Briere, J. (1992). *Child abuse trauma*. Beverley Hills, CA: Sage.

Briggs, F. (2000). *Teaching children to protect themselves*. Sydney: Allen & Unwin.

Briggs, F. & Hawkins, R. (1997). *Child protection: A guide for teachers and early childhood professionals*. Sydney: Allen & Unwin.

Browne, K.D. (1993). Violence in the family and its links to child abuse. *Bailliere's Clinical Paediatrics, 1*, 149–164.

Browne, K.D. (1994). Child sexual abuse. In J. Archer (Ed.), *Male violence* (pp. 210–230). London: Routledge.

Browne, K.D. (1995). Alleviating spouse relationship difficulties. *Counselling Psychology Quarterly, 8*, 109–122.

Browne, K.D., Cartana, C., Momeu, L. *et al.* (2002). *Child abuse and neglect in Romanian families: A national prevalence study*. Copenhagen, Denmark: WHO Regional Office for Europe.

Browne, K.D., Douglas, J., Hamilton-Giachritsis, C.E. & Hegarty, J. (2006) *A Community Health Approach to the Assessment of Infants and their Parents: The CARE programme*. Chichester: John Wiley & Sons, Ltd.

Browne, K.D., Foreman, L. & Middleton, D. (1998). Predicting treatment drop-out in sex offenders. *Child Abuse Review, 7*, 410–428.

Browne, K.D. & Hamilton, C.E. (1997). The repeat and revictimisation of children: Possible influences on recollections for trauma. In D. Read & S. Lindsay (Eds), *Recollections of trauma* (pp. 425–433). New York: Plenum Press.

Browne, K.D. & Hamilton, C.E. (1998). Physical violence between young adults and their parents: Associations with a history of child maltreatment. *Journal of Family Violence, 13*, 59–79.

Browne, K.D. & Hamilton C.E. (1999). Police recognition of links between spouse abuse and child abuse. *Child Maltreatment, 4*, 136–147.

Browne, K.D., Hanks, H., Stratton, P. & Hamilton, C.E. (Eds) (2002). *Early prediction and prevention of child abuse: A handbook*. Chichester: John Wiley & Sons, Ltd.

Browne, K.D. & Herbert, M. (1997). *Preventing family violence*. Chichester: John Wiley & Sons, Ltd.

Butchart, A., Harvey, A.P., Mian, M. & Furniss, T. (2006). *Preventing child maltreatment: A guide to taking action and generating evidence*. Geneva, Switzerland: World Health Organization and International Society for Prevention of Child Abuse and Neglect.

Campbell-Reay, A.M. & Browne, K.D. (2008). Elder abuse or neglect. In R. Woods & L. Clare (Eds), *Handbook of clinical psychology of ageing* (2nd edn) (pp. 311–322). Chichester: John Wiley & Sons, Ltd.

Cantwell, H.B. (1988). Child sexual abuse: Very young perpetrators. *Child Abuse and Neglect, 12*, 579–582.

Cawson, P., Wattam, C., Brooker, S. & Kelly, G. (2000). *Child maltreatment in the United Kingdom: A study of prevalence of child abuse and neglect*. London: NSPCC.

Christiansen, J. & Blake, R. (1990). The grooming process in father–daughter incest. In A. Horton, B.L. Johnson, L.M. Raundy & D. Williams (Eds), *The incest perpetrator* (pp. 88–98). Beverly Hill, CA: Sage.

Collins, P. & Elliott, M. (1994). *Keeping safe*. London: Jessica Kingsley Publications.

Coid, J., Petruckevitch, A., Feder, G. *et al.* (2001). Relation between childhood sexual and physical abuse and risk of revictimisation in women: A cross-sectional survey. *Lancet 358*: 450–454.

Conte, J. (1985). Clinical dimensions of adult sexual interest in children. *Behavioral Sciences and the Law, 3*, 341–354.

Craig, L., Browne, K.D. & Beech, T. (2008). *Assessing risk in sex offenders: A practitioner's guide*. Chichester: John Wiley & Sons, Ltd.

Creighton, S.J. (2002). Recognising changes in incidence and prevalence. In K.D. Browne, H. Hanks, P. Stratton & C.E. Hamilton (Eds), *Early prediction and prevention of child abuse: A handbook* (pp. 5–22). Chichester: John Wiley & Sons, Ltd.

Davenport, C.F., Browne, K.D. & Palmer, R. (1994). Opinions on the traumatizing effects of child sexual abuse: Evidence for consensus. *Child Abuse and Neglect, 18*, 725–73.

Deblinger, E. & Heflin, A.H. (1996). *Treating sexually abused children and their non-offending parents: A cognitive behavioral approach*. Beverley Hills, CA: Sage.

De Jong, A.R. (1989). Sexual interactions among siblings and cousins: Experimentation or exploitation? *Child Abuse and Neglect, 13*, 271–279.

De Panfilis, D. & Zuravin, S.J. (1998). Rates, patterns, and frequency of child maltreatment recurrences among public CPS families. *Child Maltreatment, 3*, 27–42.

Department for Children, Schools and Families (2007). *Referrals, assessments and children and young people who are the subject of a child protection plan or are on child protection registers, England – year ending 31 March* 2007. London: National Statistics.

Department for Education and Skills (2007). *Local Safeguarding Children's Boards: A Review of Progress*. London: Department for Education and Skills Publications.

Dietz, C.A. & Craft, J.L. (1980). Family dynamics of incest: A new perspective. *Social Case Work, 61*, 602–609.

Douglas, N., Lilley, S., Kooper, L. & Diamond, A. (2004). Safety and justice: Sharing personal information in the context of domestic violence – an overview. *Development and Practice Report, 30*. London: Home Office.

Elliott, M., Browne, K.D. & Kilcoyne, J. (1995). Child sexual abuse: What offenders tell us. *Child Abuse and Neglect, 19*, 579–594.

Faller, K.C. (1990). *Understanding child sexual maltreatment*. Beverley Hills, CA: Sage.

Falshaw, L. & Browne, K.D. (1997). Adverse childhood experiences and violent acts of young people in secure accommodation. *Journal of Mental Health, 6*, 443–456.

Falshaw, L. & Browne, K.D. (1999). A young man referred to specialist secure accommodation: A Case Study. *Child Abuse Review, 8*, 419–432.

Falshaw, L., Browne, K.D. & Hollin, C.R. (1996). Victim to offender: A review. *Aggression and Violent Behavior, 1*, 389–404.

Felitti, V. (1998). Relationship of childhood abuse and household dysfunction to many of the leading causes of death in adults: The Adverse Childhood Experience (ACE) study. *American Journal of Preventive Medicine, 14*, 245–258.

Fergusson, D.M. & Mullen, P.E. (1999). *Child Sexual Abuse: An Evidence-Based Perspective*. Thousand Oaks, CA: Sage Publications.

Finkelhor, D. (1980a). Sex among siblings: A survey on prevalence, variety and effects. *Archives of Sexual Behavior, 9*, 171–194.

Finkelhor, D. (1980b). Risk factors in the sexual victimization of children. *Child Abuse and Neglect, 4*, 265–273.

Finkelhor, D. (1986). *A source book on child sexual abuse*. Beverly Hills, CA: Sage.

Finkelhor D. (1994). The international epidemiology of child sexual abuse. *Child Abuse and Neglect, 18*, 409–418.

Finkelhor, D. & Baron, L. (1986). Risk factors for child sexual abuse. *Journal of Interpersonal Violence, 1*, 43–71.

Finkelhor, D., Hotaling, G., Lewis, I.A. & Smith, C. (1990). Sexual abuse in a national survey of adult men and women: Prevalence, characteristics and risk factors. *Child Abuse and Neglect, 14*, 19–28.

Finkelhor, D. & Yllo, K. (1985). *License to rape: Sexual abuse of wives*. New York: Holt, Rinehart & Winston.

Fisher, D. & Beech, A. (1998). Reconstituting families after sexual abuse: The offender perspective. *Child Abuse Review, 7*, 420–434.

Fisher, D. & Beech, A.R. (2002). Treating adult sex offenders. In K.D. Browne, C. Davies, P. Stratton & C.E. Hamilton (Eds), *Early prediction and prevention of child abuse: A handbook* (pp. 337–353). Chichester: John Wiley & Sons, Ltd.

Fisher, D. & Beech, A.R. (2004). Adult male sexual offenders. In H. Kemshall & G. McIvor (Eds), *Research highlights in social work: Sex offenders: Managing the risk* (pp. 25–48). London: Jessica Kingsley Publications.

Glasgow, D., Horne, L., Calam, R. & Cox. A. (1994). Evidence, incidence, gender and age in sexual abuse of children perpetrated by children: Towards a developmental analysis of child sexual abuse. *Child Abuse Review, 3*, 196–210.

Goddard, C. & Hiller, P. (1993). Child sexual abuse: assault in a violent context. *Australian Journal of Social Issues, 28*, 20–33.

Groth, A.N. (1979). *Men who rape: the psychology of the offender*. New York: Plenum.

Groth, A.N., Burgess, A.W. & Holmstrom, L.L. (1977). Rape, power, anger and sexuality. *American Journal of Psychiatry, 134*, 1239–1248.

Hamilton, C.E. & Browne, K.D. (1998). The repeat victimisation of children: should the concept be revised? *Aggression and Violent Behavior, 3*, 47–60.

Hamilton C.E. & Browne, K.D. (1999). Recurrent abuse during childhood: A survey of referrals to police child protection units. *Child Maltreatment, 4*, 275–286.

Hamilton, C.E., Falshaw, L. & Browne, K.D. (2002). The link between recurrent maltreatment and offending behaviour. *International Journal of Offender Therapy and Comparative Criminology, 46*, 75–94.

Hanson, R.K. & Bussière, M. (1998). Predicting relapse: A meta-analysis of sexual offender recidivism studies. *Journal of Consulting and Clinical Psychology, 66*, 348–362.

Hanson. R.K. & Harris, A.J.R. (2000). Where should we intervene? Dynamic predictors of sexual offense recidivism. *Criminal Justice and Behavior, 27*, 6–35.

Herman, J. & Hirschman, L. (1981). Families at risk for father–daughter incest. *American Journal of Psychiatry, 138*, 967–970.

HM Government (2006). *Working together to safeguard children: A guide to inter-agency working to safeguard and promote the welfare of children*. London: The Stationery Office.

Home Office (2005). *Domestic Violence: A National Report*. London: Home Office.

Howells, K. (1981). Adult sexual interest in children: Considerations relevant to theories of aetiology. In M. Cook & K. Howells (Eds), *Adult sexual interest in children* (pp. 55–94). London: Academic Press.

Jaffe, P.G., Wolfe, D.A. & Wilson, S.K. (1990). *Children of battered women*. Beverley Hills, CA: Sage.

Jason, J., Williams, S., Burton, A. & Rochat, R. (1982). Epidemiologic differences between sexual and physical child abuse. *Journal of the American Medical Association, 247*, 3344–3348.

Jehu, D. (1988). *Beyond sexual abuse: Therapy with women who were childhood victims*. Chichester: John Wiley & Sons, Ltd.

Johnson, T. (1988). Child perpetrators – Children who molest other children: Preliminary findings. *Child Abuse and Neglect, 12*, 219–229.

Johnson, T. (1989). Female Child Perpetrators: Children who molest other children. *Child Abuse and Neglect, 13*, 571–585.

Kelly, L., Regan, L. & Burton, S. (1991). *An exploratory study of the prevalence of sexual abuse in a sample of 16 to 21 year olds*. London Polytechnic of North London: Child Abuse Studies Unit.

Kirby, S. (1993). The child molester: Separating myth from reality. Unpublished doctoral dissertation, University of Surrey, Surrey, UK.

Laviola, M. (1989). Effects of older brother – younger sister incest: a review of four cases. *Journal of Family Violence, 4*, 259–274.

Levine, E.M. & Kanin, E.J. (1987). Sexual violence among dates and acquaintances: Trends and their implications for marriage and family. *Journal of Family Violence, 2*, 55–65.

Margolin, L. (1990). Child abuse by adolescents caregivers. *Child Abuse and Neglect, 14*, 365–373.

Martin, E.K., Taft, C.T. & Resick, P.A. (2007). A review of marital rape. *Aggression and Violent Behavior, 12*, 329–347.

Masson, H. & Erooga, M. (1999). *Children and young people who sexually abuse others*. London: Routledge.

McDonald, W.R. & Associates (2005). *Child maltreatment 2003: Reports from the States to the National Child Abuse and Neglect Data System*. Washington, DC: US Department of Health and Human Services, Children's Bureau.

McGee, H., Garavan, R., De Barra, M. *et al.* (2002). *The sexual abuse and violence in Ireland (SAVI) report*. Dublin: Dublin Rape Crises Centre and Liffey Press.

Milner, J.S. (1986). *The Child Abuse Potential Inventory Manual* (2nd edn). De Kalb, IL: Psytec.

Milner, J.S. & Gold, R.G. (1986). Screening spouse abusers for child abuse potential. *Journal of Clinical Psychology, 42*, 169–172.

Morley, R. & Mullender, A. (1994). Preventing domestic violence to women. *Police Research Group – Crime Prevention Series 48*. London: Home Office.

Mrazek, P., Lynch, M. & Bentovim, A. (1981). Sexual abuse of children in the United Kingdom. *Child Abuse and Neglect, 7*, 147–153.

Mueller, E. & Silverman, N. (1989). Peer relations in maltreated children. In D. Cicchetti & V. Carlson (Eds), *Child Maltreatment: Theory and research on the causes and consequences of child abuse and neglect* (pp. 529–578). Cambridge: Cambridge University Press.

Mufson, S. & Kranz, R. (1993). *Straight talk about date rape*. New York: Facts on File.

Myhill, A. & Allen, J. (2002). Rape and sexual assault of women: The extent of the problem. *Home Office Study 237*. London: Home Office.

Nicholas, S., Kershaw, C. & Walker, A. (Eds) (2007). *Crime in England and Wales 2006/07*. London: Home Office.

O'Brian, M. (1991). Taking sibling incest seriously. In M. Parton (Ed.), *Family sexual abuse* (pp. 75–92) London: Sage.

Overholser, J. & Beck, S. (1986). Multi-method assessment of rapists, child molesters and three control groups on behavioral and psychological measures. *Journal of Consulting and Clinical Psychology, 54*, 682–687.

Owen, G. & Steele, N. (1991). Incest offenders after treatment. In M. Parton (Ed.), *Family sexual abuse* (pp. 178–198). London: Sage.

Pernanen, K. (1991). *Alcohol in human violence*. London: Guilford Press.

Pierce, L.H. & Pierce, R.L. (1987). Incestuous victimization by juvenile sex offenders. *Journal of Family Violence, 2*, 351–364.

Pinheiro P.S.(Ed.) (2006). *World Report on Violence against Children: Secretary General's Study on Violence against Children*. New York: United Nations.

Pirog-Good, M. (1992). Sexual abuse in dating relationships. In E.C. Viano (Ed.), *Intimate violence: Interdisciplinary perspectives* (pp. 101–109). Washington, DC: Taylor & Francis.

Prior, V., Glaser, D. & Lynch, M.A. (1997). Responding to child sexual abuse: The criminal justice system. *Child Abuse Review, 6*, 128–140.

Reder, P. & Duncan, S. (1997). Adult psychiatry – a missing link in the Child Protection network. *Child Abuse Review, 6*, 35–40.

Renzetti, C.M. (1992). *Violent betrayal: Partner abuse in lesbian relationships*. London: Sage.

Roberts, A.R. (1987). Psychosocial characteristics of batterers: A study of 234 men charged with domestic violence offences. *Journal of Family Violence, 2*, 81–94.

Rowe, J., Cain, H., Hundleby, M. & Keane, A. (1984). *Long-term foster care*. London: Batsford.

Russell, D.E.H. (1983). The incidence and prevalence of intrafamilial and extrafamilial sexual abuse of female children. *Child Abuse and Neglect, 7*, 133–146.

Russell, D.E.H. (1986). *The secret trauma: Incest in the lives of girls and women*. New York: Basic Books.

Russell, D.E.H. (1991). Wife rape. In A. Parrot & L. Bechofer (Eds), *Acquaintance rape: The hidden crime* (pp. 129–139). New York: John Wiley & Sons, Inc.

Salter, A. (1988). *Treating child sex offenders and victims*. London: Sage.

Salter, D., McMillan, D., Richards, M. *et al.* (2003). Development of sexually abusive behaviour in sexually victimised males: A longitudinal study. *Lancet 361*: 471–476.

Sanders, M. & Cann, W. (2002). Promoting positive parenting as an abuse prevention strategy. In K.D. Browne, H. Hanks, P. Stratton & C.E. Hamilton (Eds), *Early prediction and prevention of child abuse: A handbook* (pp. 145–164). Chichester: John Wiley & Sons, Ltd.

Sonkin, D., Martin, D. & Walker, L. (1985). *The male batterer: A treatment approach*. New York: Springer.

Terr, L.C. (1991). Childhood traumas: An outline and overview. *American Journal of Psychiatry, 148*, 10–20.

Truesdell, D., McNeil, J. & Deschner, J. (1986). Incidence of wife abuse in incestuous families. *Social Work, 31*, 138–140.

Watkins, B. & Bentovim, A. (1992). The sexual abuse of male children and adolescents: A review of current research. *Journal of Child Psychology and Psychiatry, 33*, 197–248.

Weinrott, M.R. & Saylor, M. (1991). Self-report of crimes committed by sex offenders. *Journal of Interpersonal Violence, 6*, 286–300.

Whitfield, C.L. (1995). *Memory and abuse: Remembering and healing the effects of trauma*. Dearfield Beach, FL: Health Communications Inc.

Widom, C.S. (1989). Does violence beget violence? A critical examination of the literature. *Psychological Bulletin, 106*, 3–28.

Widom, C.S. & Ames, M.A. (1994). Criminal consequences of childhood sexual victimization. *Child Abuse and Neglect, 18*, 303–318.

World Health Organization (2002). *World report on violence and health*. Geneva: WHO.

27

Police Work with Sex Offenders: Detection, Management and Assessment

KEVIN D. BROWNE

INTRODUCTION

Reports to the police of sexual assault have more than doubled over the last 20 years, and the latest Home Office figures show that the police recorded 43,755 serious sexual offences for 2006/07 (Jansson, Povey & Kaiza, 2007). These included rape, sexual assault and sexual activity with children. Therefore, sex offences currently account for about 8 in 1,000 crimes, which is approximately 1% of all recorded crimes.

Nearly a third of recorded sex crimes involve rape and 13,780 rapes were reported in 2006/7 (92% to female victims and 8% to male victims). However, the conviction rate for adult rape is only a fraction of the number reported to the police. One-third of reported cases failed to proceed past the investigation stage due to lack of evidence or victim credibility. Another third are lost as a result of victims not wishing to proceed due to fear of the emotional consequences and not being believed in court. Furthermore, many cases of sexual assault are associated with alcohol use in the victim as well as the offender and the majority of perpetrators are known to their victims. These facts complicate successful conviction of sexual offenders, with 9% regarded as false allegations and only 14% of reported cases leading to trial (Kelly, Lovett & Regan, 2005).

Home Office statistics on the sexual abuse of children are recorded as a subset of 'serious sexual offences'; unlawful sexual intercourse, incest and gross indecency. Research findings from the Home Office estimated that at least 110,000 men (7 in every 1000) in the 1993 population of England and Wales had a conviction for an offence against a child (Marshall, 1997). Most of these men were convicted for an offence with a girl victim (6 in 1000) rather than with a boy victim (1 in 1000). Overall,

Assessment and Treatment of Sex Offenders: A Handbook. Edited by Anthony Beech, Leam Craig and Kevin Browne. © John Wiley & Sons Ltd, 2009.

sexual abuse of children made up the majority of serious sexual offences committed by men under 40 years of age, with at least a third having committed a sexual offence before the age of 18 (Marshall, 1997).

At least two-thirds of sex offenders know their child victim personally, at the time the sex offence is committed (Grubin, 1998). Hence, the Sex Offences Act 2003 has introduced a new offence of '*abuse of a position of trust*' prohibiting contact between adults and children under 18 in schools, colleges and residential care. Nevertheless, due to the secretive nature of sexual assaults on children and the problems of obtaining reliable evidence, many child sexual assaults go unreported and only a small minority of cases come to the attention of the police. An even smaller number of cases (approximately 1 in 3) result in the perpetrator being charged and approximately 1 in 10 are convicted. For example, 2 independent studies carried out 10 years ago (Browne & Afzal, 1998; Prior, Glaser & Lynch, 1997) showed similar findings. Of those cases that came to the attention of the police, only 35 to 38% of the sex offenders were charged, 5 to 9% received a caution and for 56–59% of cases, there was no further action. These findings may be related to the observation that convicted male sex offenders, on average, claim six years of undetected offending prior to their first arrest for a sexual assault on a child (Elliott, Browne & Kilcoyne, 1995).

The large number of referrals which led to 'no further action' by the police service is likely to reflect the factors influencing decisions to bring charges such as the interests of the child, insufficient evidence and the decision of the Crown Prosecution Service (Browne & Hamilton, 1999). However, the findings of the study by Hamilton and Browne (1999) suggest that the actions taken during a child protection joint investigation by police and social services are not effective in preventing a re-referral for recurrent abuse (within 27 months) for at least a quarter of those children initially referred for child maltreatment. This may reflect increased vulnerability or alternatively vigorous monitoring by Child Protection Agencies.

Such findings in England and Wales demonstrate the need to develop more effective police strategies to prevent and detect the sexual victimisation and repeat victimisation of women and children. There are obvious limitations to the Register of Sex Offenders, introduced by the Sex Offender Act (1997) and modified by the Sex Offences Act (2003). The laws compel all offenders who have been cautioned or convicted of a sexual offence (after 1996) to register their names and addresses with the police to help manage and prevent further sex offences. However, as only a minority of individual who commit sex crimes are detected and convicted, the Register is of limited value in terms of prevention (Wyre, 1997). Thus, there is a necessity to collect and maintain intelligence on alleged sex offenders as well those cautioned or convicted.

Recent legislation has attempted to cast the net wider, it is now an offence to make or possess indecent photographs of children and use the Internet to download such images (see Craig, Browne & Beech, 2008). With regard to the Internet, a new offence of '*sexual grooming*' identifies the crime of befriending a child personally or on the Internet with the intention of sexual activity. The offence of '*adult sexual activities with a child*' covers any sexual act that takes place between an adult and a child under the age of 16 regardless of whether it appears to be consensual or not. This would also cover non-contact sexual activities such as inducing children to remove their clothes for adult sexual pleasure, filming or photography. Furthermore, the Sex Offences Act (2003) has introduced a number of new offences and tough penalties to deal with those who abuse and exploit children (up to age 18) through prostitution. These new offences include: causing or inciting child prostitution, controlling a child prostitute, arranging or facilitating child prostitution, paying for the sexual services of a child. The police services now regard children and young adults who prostitute themselves as victims rather than individuals who have committed an offence. It is the *punter* who 'purchases' the sex and the *pimp* who manages the 'service' that the police regard as sex offenders.

POLICING SEXUAL ASSAULT

The role of the police in cases of child maltreatment and sexual assault is the same as that of police in society generally, which is the protection of life (and property), the prevention and detection of crime and the prosecution of offenders against the peace (Ainsworth 1995, 2002; Gregory & Lees, 1999; Thomas, 1994). The investigative role of the police is to establish whether an offence to a child or adult has occurred and attempt to identify the perpetrator of the offence. When an investigation has resulted in the alleged perpetrator being charged with an offence, the police have a responsibility to report the investigation to the Crown Prosecution Service (CPS) who decides on whether court proceedings should follow.

Changes in the way police deal with rape and sexual assault over the last two decades may have contributed to the dramatic increase in reported cases. Victims are treated now in a more caring manner by police officers, who are usually specially trained in how to sensitively interview and gain information from victims of rape and child sexual abuse. The environment for victim disclosure has also improved with the establishment of sexual assault referral centres, SARC (Cybulska, 2007; Matravers, 2003). Nevertheless, the majority of sexual offences still go unreported, which can be determined by the prevalence of sexual offending (as reported in the British Crime Survey) in comparison to reports to the police within the same time period. The British Crime Survey of households (2005/06) shows that approximately 3% of women and 1% of men self-report experiencing a sexual assault in the previous 12 months, but only 62,081 were reported to the police in 2005/6, which represents approximately 1 in 10 victimisations.

Similarly, British community surveys of young adults have found that 11 to 12% retrospectively report 'contact sexual abuse as children' (Baker & Duncan, 1985; Cawson *et al.*, 2000) but only two to three children in every 10,000 are identified as victims of sexual abuse and placed on the child protection register by police and social services, of which 60% are girls and 40% are boys (Department for Children, Schools and Families, 2007). At best, this suggests that for every child who is identified as sexually abused, there are approximately 400 other child victims who are undetected.

Sexual assault by strangers and acquaintances is usually dealt with by Criminal Investigation Departments (CID), whereas sexual assault within the home by parents and relatives or partners and ex-partners is first investigated by police Child Protection Units (CPUs) or Domestic Violence Units (DVUs), respectively. In some police forces, the domestic violence units are part of Community Safety Units which also tackle racist and hate crime. In other police forces, they are housed with Child Protection Units to form 'Family Protection Units'. The latter recognises the link between spouse abuse and child maltreatment. Indeed, the link between domestic violence and sexual abuse of children in the family has been well established for over 25 years (Dietz & Craft, 1980; Goddard & Hiller, 1993). For example, a study of West Midlands Child Protection Units showed that 46% of child protection files indicated the presence of domestic violence in the family home, yet the rate of overlap of families with files also held by the DVUs was 22% (Browne & Hamilton, 1999). Greater collaboration through the establishment of Family Protection Units has the potential to reduce the discrepancy. The same study also found that the severity of maltreatment was greater among families where spousal abuse and child abuse co-occurred. Therefore, the way in which police services structure the units may be important for the detection of crime.

In a study conducted by Plotnikoff and Woolfson (1995), it was found that practical factors can also influence whether a case of child sexual assault is dealt with by the police service CPU or the CID; for example, the time of day that an offence was reported or the relationship of the victim to the offender. This has implications for the successful investigation and prosecution of a case. The UK Government guidelines in the Memorandum of Good Practice (Home Office, 1992), state that only those officers who have received appropriate training may conduct videotaped interviews with a child.

The complexity of structures in the large urban police services may sometimes interfere with intelligence gathering, providing evidence and the successful prosecution of violent and sexual offences. For example, in the Metropolitan Police, the investigation and prosecution of a recently released high risk child molester who had allegedly murdered his ex-partner and abducted her child involved information from the following police units (Browne & Afzal, 1998):

- Joint Public Protection Panel: manages risk of offenders released into the community with the probation services;
- Prison Intelligence Unit: manages the flow of information from prison to the police;
- Community Safety (and Domestic Violence) Unit: investigates domestic violence and hate crimes;
- Major Investigation Team: investigates homicides;
- Paedophile Unit: investigates child sex offenders and child pornography;
- High-Tech Crime Unit: provides technical computer support for Internet offences;
- Safeguarding Children and Development (Child Protection) Unit: investigates child maltreatment;

- Ports Safeguarding Team: works on child trafficking, abduction and protection issues with immigration officers;
- Surveillance Team: responds to life-threatening situations;
- Technical Support Unit: deploys specialist technical equipment to assist in investigations;
- Authorities Office: manages sensitive and complex surveillance;
- Covert Source Management Unit: manages and handles informant information;
- Cover Operations Group: controls undercover operations;
- Facial Imaging Team: compiles an E-FIT or Artist's Composite's of alleged offenders.

It is commonly accepted that child sexual abuse is a complex problem that requires the efforts and co-ordination of multiple agencies and disciplines. Within this context, police officers interact with a variety of professionals and agencies during the investigation process. Nevertheless, the police officer is focused more on admissible evidence of '*what*' happened than on an emotional belief or assumption that '*something*' happened (Lanning, 1996). The neutral and objective role of a police officer investigating a case of adult sexual assault or the sexual abuse of a child is to listen to, assess and evaluate the victim's statement and then attempt to corroborate some or all of what the victim has said. Ideally, it is in the best interest of the victim to avoid testifying in court and for the police to build a case where the evidence is so strong that the offender pleads guilty.

Allegations involving an adult victim are always investigated when the victim discloses, to the police, details of a sexual assault or rape. But it is at the discretion of the police to make enquiries following a third party allegation, if the victim is not cooperative. In cases of child sexual abuse (CSA), social services and the police have a statutory duty to jointly investigate all allegations, regardless of a testimony from the child. Lanning (1996) identifies a disclosure continuum in child witness statements. From children who have made voluntary and full disclosures to one or more people, to those children where CSA is only suspected. In between, there are children who have decided to disclose but have made only incomplete disclosures, and children where CSA has been discovered, but they have yet to disclose.

Factors surrounding the circumstances of the sexual offence distort the traumatic memory of the child and can influence the victim's account of what happened (Browne & Hamilton, 1997). As a part of the sexual abuse the child may have been introduced to alcohol, drugs, pornography, bribes, games and rituals. These 'methods' are sometimes used deliberately by the offender to cause misperception and confusion in the victim and make their statements inaccurate and unreliable without necessarily making them a 'lie' (Elliott, Browne & Kilcoyne, 1995; Lanning, 1992a,b). In fact, children rarely lie about their own sexual assault but traumatic memories combined with childhood fears and fantasies and/or a suggestive style of interviewing can make the victim's testimony inadmissible as evidence (Lanning, 1996).

False Allegations

Mandatory reporting laws in the United States and other countries demand that all those who have professional contact with children must report any suspicions of abuse or neglect to the relevant authorities. Understandably, professionals err on the side of caution and a number of unsubstantiated allegations emerge. Indeed, as much as 65% of child abuse and neglect allegations in the USA have been claimed to be unfounded (Besharov, 1985). This figure represents child abuse allegations *in general* and does not distinguish between allegations arising from children and those arising from adults. By contrast, clinical research about false allegations arising from children quotes figures of between 1% and 6%. For example, Peters (1988) reported only four false accusations from a total of 64 children brought to a hospital emergency room for suspected sexual abuse. Goodwin, Sahd and Rada (1978) also discovered that only 3 out of 46 sexual abuse cases reported to a child abuse agency were based upon false allegations. Thus, in both studies, only 6% of reported cases of child sexual abuse could not be substantiated.

Jones and McGraw (1987) reviewed 576 reports of child sexual abuse made to the Denver Department of Social Services during 1983. They found that 49% of reports were reliable accounts of child sexual abuse, and action by social services and the police followed. In 24% of reports, there was insufficient information to continue with any health, social or legal intervention. For 17% of the reports there was not enough evidence but unsubstantiated suspicions remained, while 4% of the time the children recanted their allegation and nothing could be done. Only 5% of reports from adults were proven to be fictitious, and only 1% of reports by children were proven to be fictitious. The fictitious reports were again found to be 6% of cases and frequently lacked detail.

The 1% of children initiating false allegations demonstrated little or no accompanying emotion while describing the abuse. Descriptions of threats were absent from their accounts. Most of the mothers who made false allegations were involved in custody/visitation disputes. Larger scale studies (Everson & Boat, 1989) have confirmed these as representative figures. There is little doubt that unfounded allegations for child sexual abuse occur when parents are involved in custody and/or visitation disputes over a child and one in two allegations from adults are claimed to be false. Hence, the most important question of an investigation into alleged sexual abuse of a child is 'where did the allegation originate from?' If the allegation originates from the child, then ninety-nine times out of a hundred it is true.

Corroboration of the Victim's Statement

Corroboration of the victim's statement can be helped by descriptions and documentation from a variety of sources:

- The victim's patterns of behaviour, especially behavioural symptoms as a consequence of child sexual abuse (Briere, 1992);

- The offender's patterns of behaviour (Elliott, Browne & Kilcoyne, 1995);
- Statements by other victims and adult witnesses and suspects.
- Medical and physical evidence.
- The presence of child pornography and erotic material relating to children, that serves a sexual purpose for a given individual, which may sometimes be found in scrapbooks of magazine cuttings and photographs or on computers and videotapes (Lanning, 1992).

The evidence obtained by the police in cases of child maltreatment and adult sexual assault is often insufficient for criminal proceedings as the 'burden of proof' in a criminal court is 'beyond reasonable doubt'. Nevertheless, the same evidence may be of crucial importance in civil and family court proceedings where judgements are made on the 'balance of probability' in relation to the care of the child. In relation to the probability that a child may suffer 'significant harm', the provisions of the Children Act (1989, 2004) allow the police, health and social services to remove a child (a person under 18 years of age) to a place of safety for their protection and well-being. In addition, the police and social services have a duty to investigate in all cases where a violent or sex crime involving a child is suspected.

Child Protection Referrals to the Police

Any person who has knowledge or suspicion of a child suffering some form of significant harm can refer their concerns to the police or social services. Although there is no legal mandate to report British cases of child abuse and neglect to the police and social services, there is a clear expectation that doctors "must refer these concerns to the statutory agencies" (Department of Health, British Medical Association, Conference of Medical Royal Colleges, 1994, p. 5). Indeed, it could be argued that withholding information about ongoing child maltreatment, even on the basis of patient confidentiality, is professional malpractice. The National Health Service Executive has stated that "all health service staff have a duty to protect children" (Department of Health, 1996, p. 15).

Referrals may come from any person involved with the child (e.g., doctors, health visitors, teachers, nursery workers, neighbours, babysitters), an agency involved with the family (e.g., community health, probation, housing, etc.) or even the child in question. Therefore, either the police or social services may be the first statutory agency to receive the referral but information is then shared between them. The division of responsibility is that social services are ultimately responsible for child-care decisions whilst the police are responsible for criminal issues and proceedings.

Under the auspices of Local Safeguarding Children Boards (formally Area Child Protection Committees – ACPCs), who lay down multi-disciplinary procedures at a local level, Child Protection Case Conferences are held, these conferences aim to make informed decisions about what actions are needed to safeguard the child in question and to promote his or her welfare. Those representatives attending the Case Conference, who may be social workers, health professionals, teachers, police officers, local authority lawyers, parents and substitute carers, formulate proposals for a Care Plan and whether the child should be placed on the Child Protection Register. In doing so they may ask a court to issue a Child Assessment Order or an Exclusion Order (for the alleged offender).

It has been estimated that 1.5% of the 11 million children in England are subject to a child protection (Section 47) enquiry each year. Of these 160,000 referrals: 75% receive a family visit during a joint investigation and 1% experiences an emergency separation. A quarter of the children referred are the subject of a case conference, 15% are placed on the child protection register and 2% are taken into public care (Department of Health, 1995).

The Police Act 1997 extended access to criminal records to relevant agencies (e.g., social services) and the release of relevant information on individuals who have, or will have, unsupervised access to children. Police officers from Child Protection Units have the responsibility for the dissemination of confidential information to other agencies involved in child protection. The officers participate in multi-agency child protection case conferences and the Local Safeguarding Children Boards that have the statutory responsibility to oversee child protection activities (Department for Education and Skills, 2007). The officers may represent other parts of the police service with which they maintain regular contact, such as police officers from other specialist units dealing with paedophiles, domestic violence and community safety.

CHILD PROTECTION UNITS

UK police forces nationwide have established 'Child Protection Units' (CPUs). These units usually deal with all cases of child maltreatment and sexual abuse within the family. The purpose of these units is to investigate the majority of allegations or suspicions of child abuse and neglect, jointly with the relevant social services departments and with representatives of other caring agencies (e.g., the National Society for the Protection of Cruelty to Children – NSPCC). The police officers and social workers associated with these units are specially trained to interview and deal with child witnesses (Thomas, 1994), although sexual assaults perpetrated by strangers are usually dealt with by police Criminal Investigation Departments (CID).

An in-depth study of 121 referrals for child sexual abuse (CSA) made in November 1994 (Hamilton, 1997) demonstrated the difficulty of police work with child sexual abuse cases. The sample was approximately 6% of the total number (2,100 in 1994) of CSA referrals to CPUs in the West Midlands Police Area per annum. The study found that in 9 out of 10 referrals there was true cause for concern. Nearly a quarter (24%) of the cases allegedly involved actual or attempted penetration, vaginal and/or anal; 7% involved oral sexual abuse; 60% involved contact abuse, manipulation and fondling of the child's and/or the offender's genitals; and 9% concerned non-contact abuse exhibitionism, or obscene photography and video film. However, for 75% of the 108 CSA concern cases there was no further action on behalf of the police, and only 17% resulted in a caution or charge of the suspected perpetrator. Eight percent of these cases were pending further investigations. Over a quarter (27%) of the suspects were already known to the police and had been subject to prior investigations. Eight percent of perpetrators had been subject to 'no further action' in a prior referral, 4% had been 'cautioned' or 'convicted' and 10% were 'Schedule 1 offenders' (a person who has been identified as a '*risk to children*' with the potential for harm).

Lloyd and Burman (1996) examined CPUs in Scotland, with particular reference to the 'Working Together' initiative (Home Office, Departments of Health, Education and Science, Welsh Office, 1991). They found that in many cases allegations of child abuse were not actually passed between agencies and that guidelines governing which cases required a joint investigation were unclear. Waterhouse and Carnie (1990) outlined the barriers to good collaboration, these included: competing aims and objectives; difficulties in decision making; and delay in disseminating information. As summarised by Ainsworth (1995) inter-agency collaboration can be classified into three forms: '*Minimalist*', where only basic information is shared formally; '*Collaborative*', where there is an informal and often personal free exchange of information; and '*Integrated*', involving joint interviewing, investigation and appraisal of cases from a multi-disciplinary perspective and common agenda.

Thomas (1994) believes that truly integrated ways of working have been inhibited by the Criminal Justice Act 1991, which gave the police a greater role in child abuse cases and shifted the focus away from protecting the child to obtaining good evidence for court proceedings. The different approaches to child protection work adopted by various police services is exemplified by the varying rates of arrests, charges and cautions across the UK. For example, Hamilton (1997) found in her study of CPUs within one police force, that the police response of 'charging' or 'cautioning' the offender ranged from 5% to 30% of referrals depending on the CPU involved.

Government inter-agency guidelines on 'Working Together to Safeguard Children' (HM Government 2006; Home Office, Departments of Health, Education and Science, Welsh Office, 1991) have enlarged the role of the police in terms of child protection and all investigations into child maltreatment are carried out jointly with social services. Thus, the police make decisions to refer cases of child maltreatment to the CPS in consultation with social services. They consider whether the prosecution is both possible and desirable in terms of the available evidence, whether it is in the best interests of the child, and whether it is in the best interests of the public. Nevertheless, the principal role of the police for the prevention and detection of sexual assaults to children and adults remains that of primary investigator and intelligence gatherer and proactive approaches are essential.

PROACTIVE INTELLIGENCE GATHERING

The work of family and child protection units is, by its very nature, dependent on referrals in which the alleged offender is usually known to the victim(s). These domestic violence and child abuse referrals therefore come under the umbrella of reactive policing and are victim-focused rather than offender-focused (Browne & Afzal, 1998). This is reflected in the databases and information held by these units, which sometimes do not even record details of the alleged offender(s).

The 'Powers of Arrest' granted under the Police and Criminal Evidence Act (PACE, 1984) have been quoted as sufficient for facilitating searches relating to investigations involving child abuse (Home Office, 1988). When evaluated (Browne & Afzal, 1998), it was found that searches were rarely undertaken under such powers. The relevance of conducting searches whilst investigating intra-familial child abuse cases was overshadowed by the myth that paedophiles are usually strangers to the child.

Search Warrants

Searches serve as an evidence-gathering exercise, resulting in the identification of crime, possible victims and associate offenders. Under the Criminal Justice and Police Act 2001, computer equipment can be taken away for further investigation to explore the possible production, possession or distribution of child pornography. Search warrants are also used to obtain corroborative evidence and incriminating evidence against a suspect such as details in a written or electronic diary. The difficulty in sexual assault cases is that search warrants may not be obtained soon enough. Evidence can be moved or destroyed by an alleged offender relatively quickly (Browne & Afzal, 1998). Physical evidence such as bed sheets, articles of clothing, sexual aids, magazines and ornaments described by a woman or child can be disposed of, or hidden, if the alleged offender is aware of a report to social services or to the police. The opportunity for matching a DNA sample is then lost. Crime and Punishment Act 1997 introduced new powers for police to take DNA samples from offenders convicted of sexual and violent offences.

Active Intelligence Seeking

Actively seeking intelligence, for example, asking a community safety officer to note down the movements of a suspect on a certain day or note down what vehicles are being used by a suspect, can provide invaluable information for detection, management and risk assessment of suspects and offenders. Neighbours can also provide useful information on the movements and habits of an alleged or known offender. They may know who has been seen visiting the suspect's premises. Furthermore, closed-circuit TV recordings of premises such as clubs, schools and sports centres may be available. This intelligence can be used to justify resources for surveillance activities as part of an ongoing investigation or as a proactive intelligence-gathering operation.

Tracking and Surveillance

Tracking and surveillance can be either static or mobile and both options are very expensive on police time and resources; hence they are usually reserved for very high-risk offenders. A request for the use of surveillance teams to watch a suspect or high-risk offender is usually assessed by senior police officers in relation to other policing demands, although surveillance might involve the use of covert cameras or auditory devices being installed at less cost. Satellite tracking and tagging systems to monitor offenders on licence and enforce curfews are controversial but an effective way of managing sex offenders in the community. Undercover operations and covert body recorders may be used with the consent of the senior investigating officer but run the risk of 'entrapment' accusations by the defence lawyers. It should be recognised that in most cases, information on the behaviour and compliance of sex offenders in the community comes from the probation service.

PAEDOPHILE UNITS

The large urban police services (e.g., Metropolitan Police, Manchester Police, West Midlands Police) have set up specialist Paedophile Units to investigate all paedophile activities, allegations, organisations, Internet activity and circulating child pornography. However, they vary in terms of reference. Smaller police services have dedicated 'Paedophile Intelligence Officers' to facilitate information flow from other local units and police services. The Paedophile Intelligence Officers establish working links with agencies such as the National Child Exploitation and Online Protection (CEOP) Centre, the National Criminal Intelligence Service (NCIS), Probation, Social Services and Customs. These specialist 'Paedophile Units' do have terms of reference which include proactive targeting of sex offenders and national information gathering (e.g., NCIS packages of intelligence). The Paedophile Units also provide training for the investigation of child pornography on the Internet.

At national level, the Child Exploitation and Online Protection (CEOP) Centre works across the UK and maximises links to tackle child sex abuse both nationally and internationally. Part of the Centre's work is to provide Internet safety advice for parents and carers. The CEOP website also provides a 'virtual police station' online for people to report child abuse, child pornography and information that may be of help in tracking down and apprehending 'missing child sex offenders'. The 'most wanted' list on the CEOP home page includes face photos (mugshots) of high-risk sex offenders who have been placed on the Sex Offenders Register but not complied and are in 'breach of notification requirements' (see Case Study A).

CEOP Past Case (Case Study A)

AD – aged 34, was charged and convicted of unlawful sex with a 13-year-old girl and indecent assault of another 13-year-old girl in July 2001. He pleaded guilty and was sentenced to six months in prison for the first charge and a further three months in prison for the latter, to run consecutively. He was put on the Sex Offenders Register for 10 years and classed as a 'risk to children' by Social Services. At the time the offences were committed, he was working as the entertainments manager at a caravan park in North Wales where the two 13-year-old girls were on holiday with their families. After being released from prison, AD went on the run in October 2002 and was featured on TV's Crimewatch because the police wanted to talk to him about another incident similar to his previous sex offences and a separate allegation of child rape. Between October 2002 and December 2006, he was spotted several times in Ireland working as a DJ under five different names. Eventually, AD handed himself in to the police in the Republic of Ireland. Since then he's been required to sign on once a week and is at liberty. He could have been imprisoned for up to five years for 'breach of notification requirements' under the Sex Offences Act 2003.

MANAGING THE RISK OF SEX OFFENDERS IN THE COMMUNITY

Multi-Agency Public Protection Arrangements (MAPPA) have been set up across 42 areas of England and Wales in line with the police services, following the implementation of measures contained in the Criminal Justice and Court Services Act (2000) to protect the public from harm. Three categories of offender fall under MAPPA: those who have committed violent and sexual offences, those offenders who are listed on the Sex Offenders Register and other offenders considered by the police and probation services to pose a serious risk to the public and others. Bryan and Doyle (2003) estimated that there were 18,513 registered sex offenders dealt with by MAPPA between 2001 and 2002. This represented 39% of the 47,209 other violent and sex offenders reviewed under MAPPA. It was observed that 682 (3.7%) registered sex offenders were in breach of their *notification* requirements and 81 (0.4%) were issued *Sex Offender Orders* because the offender's behaviour in the community had given cause for concern (following the Crime and Disorder Act, 1998). For the most dangerous offenders, other measures were included such as new sentences to prevent their release from secure environments if they remain at risk of harming others or themselves (Crime Sentences Act, 1998).

The core of the MAPPA is the joint public protection unit (JPPU) run by the probation and police service in each area. This 'responsible authority' coordinates information and intelligence-gathering activities to ensure the effective monitoring and supervision of high-risk violent and/or sexual offenders, who were approximately 6% of those convicted of violent and sexual crimes throughout England and Wales ('the critical few'). Furthermore, the public protection unit has a 'duty to cooperate' with a wide range of organisations and agencies associated with education, health, housing, job centres, prisons, social services and youth offending teams to ensure that high-risk offenders are managed appropriately in the community. In order to facilitate this, Multi-Agency Public Protection Panels (MAPPPs) meet on a regular basis with a broad range of representatives from the cooperating agencies with specific management tasks (see Table 27.1).

Table 27.1 The work of Multi-Agency Public Protection Panels – MAPPPs (Adapted from Craig *et al.*, 2008 and Lieb, 2003)

A) How does the panel manage risk:
- share information on highest risk offenders and determine risk
- recommend actions to manage risk
- monitor and implement agreed actions
- review decisions when circumstances change
- manage resources.

B) What conditions does the panel place on offenders:
- requirement to live at a specific address and obey a curfew (electronically monitored)
- prohibition from entering certain localities and making contact with certain people (victims)
- restrictions on type of employment.

C) How does the panel reduce risk to the community:
- informing professionals
- informing schools and associations
- informing the victim
- restricting the individual's employment
- rehousing the person
- visiting the person
- prompting follow-up in the event of failed visits to the probation officer
- setting treatment requirements.

D) What information is referred to the panel:
- treatment outcomes from prison programmes
- assessment of risk from prison psychology departments
- assessment of risk from probation
- assessment of risk from Regional Secure Units
- treatment outcomes from Regional Secure Units
- information from the police
- information from probation.

E) How is information on an offender used and how does it influence the assessment of risk:
- risk assessment tools used
- personnel carrying out the assessments
- decision-making process
- weighting of clinical judgement and risk assessment tools in decision making
- quality of risk assessments used.

F) What factors are considered to assess risk:
- the nature and pattern of previous offences
- compliance with previous sentences or court orders
- the probability that a further offence will be committed
- harm that such behaviour will cause
- any behaviour that may indicate a likelihood that the perpetrator will reoffend
- potential objects of harm e.g., children
- potential consequences of disclosure to offender and their family
- potential consequences of disclosure in a wider context e.g., Law and Order.

Risk Assessment

The potential risk of a sex offender committing another offence may be informed by information on nature and pattern of previous offences, compliance with previous sentences or court orders, avoidance of contexts where a further offence could be committed and any behaviour that may indicate a likelihood that the perpetrator will reoffend (Craig *et al.*, 2008). Hence, risk assessments by police and probation services can direct decisions about the management of offenders and those who should be prioritised for tracking, surveillance or supervision. The quality of risk assessment depends on the quality of information on which it is based, which can only be achieved if case information is explicit and well documented (Dalgleish, 2003).

Guidelines for the implementation of The Sex Offender Act (1997) from the Home Office (HOC 39/1997) recommended that a number of risk factors (see Table 27.1, Section F) be considered for offenders reviewed by inter-agency meetings and developed a risk assessment approach to the targeting of known sex offenders. Since these guidelines were published, the UK National Offender Management Service (NOMS) has standardised the Offender Assessment System (OASys; Office for Criminal Justice Reform, 2007) for adult offenders. While, the Youth Justice Board uses ASSET for children and young people under 18 years. These have been developed as tools to assess risk and identify those offenders who present the greatest danger to the community. Where there is cause for concern, more detailed risk assessments using an actuarial approach are implemented by police and probation officers working in the public protection units using Risk Matrix 2000 (RM2000; Thornton, 2002; Thornton *et al.*, 2003). Using RM2000 offenders are categorised as very high, high, medium or low risk and these assessments are reviewed when there are changes in circumstances or patterns of behaviour or new information has been provided relevant to risk management (e.g., response to treatment).

Management Strategies

MAPPPs are chaired by a senior member of the police service and provide a forum for risk assessment of offenders who have been put on probation and/or just released from prison, and for agencies to share information in order to assess and manage the risk posed by registered sex offenders and other offenders who are considered to be potentially dangerous. Multi-agency arrangements for public protection often apply a four-tier system for dealing with offenders (see Table 27.2) to help devise a management strategy. An example of an offender dealt with under the MAPPA is given in Case Study 2.

Case Study Two

A man convicted of a number of rapes on women was due to be released at the very end of his prison sentence. He was visited in prison by the local police offender manager,

Table 27.2 Multi-Agency arrangements for Public Protection Panel's management of offenders

Offender Level of risk	Management strategy
Low risk	• Dealt with by one agency, usually police or probation, and offender has no current factors to suggest a risk of harm.
Medium risk	• Jointly managed by police and probation, supported by information provided by other agencies to develop a risk action plan. • Some identifiable risk factors for harm and the potential to cause harm. • Judged unlikely to do harm unless there is a change in circumstances, e.g., drug or alcohol misuse or failure to take medication.
High risk	• Assessed, managed and reviewed by all agencies represented on the panel. • Identifiable risk factors for serious harm, and the potential to reoffend is high.
Very high risk	• Placed in the highest priority. • Assessed, managed and reviewed by all agencies represented on the panel. • Identifiable risk factors that place them at imminent risk of serious harm and are very likely to reoffend at any time.

and his probation officer, in order to assess his risk prior to release and to agree a risk management plan. This included placing him in the most appropriate accommodation where he could best be supervised, monitored and helped to find his own suitable accommodation in the community – in this case a probation hostel. At the hostel, he is continuously monitored and is on a curfew which only allows him outside the hostel for specific short periods of time. The local police are aware of these times and are able to monitor him during these periods (West Midlands Police, 2003).

Recent legislation (the Sex Offences Act, 2003) has helped the police and probation services to manage sexual and/or violent offenders in English and Welsh communities. The police can apply to a magistrate's court for a Sexual Offences Prevention Order (SOPO) in relation to a convicted offender. For example, a SOPO may prohibit a known sex offender from loitering near schools or playgrounds and from visiting swimming pools or beaches. Indeed, any behaviour that the court considers would put children at risk of harm. The SOPO runs in parallel to any Sex Offenders Register notification requirements and other orders in place and any breach is a criminal offence, with a maximum penalty of five years in prison.

Similarly by making an application to civil court for a 'Risk of Sexual Harm Order' (RSHO), the police can protect children from the risks posed by individuals without convictions for sexual and/or violent offences but who have 'on at least two occasions engaged in sexually explicit conduct or communication with a child'. For example, a RHSO can be used to prohibit an individual from using the Internet because there is evidence that it is being used to communicate with children in a sexually explicit way through Internet chat rooms. The RSHO also makes the offender subject to the Sex Offenders Register's notification requirements and also carries a maximum penalty of five years in prison if breached.

Disclosure and Community Notification

Information shared between the agencies is confidential and most professionals working with sex offenders recognise the negative impact of personal details being unintentionally 'leaked' or intentionally disclosed to people in the community. Most professionals working with sex offenders are against the principle of 'Sarah's Law' (or Megan's Law, as it is referred to in the USA). This proposes that the local community should be informed of all sex offenders who reside in their locality. Besides placing the convicted offender at personal risk of retaliation, revenge and vigilante activities, such disclosures will interfere with a reintegration of the offender into society and drive them underground. This makes it difficult for police and probation services to monitor the offender and places them at risk to the public at large. However, for those high-risk sex offenders who do not follow the notification requirements of their registration and 'go on the run', the CEOP website does place their names, profiles and photos on the Internet for the public to view.

Using public disclosure and the threat of a prison sentence (up to five years) as a deterrent to non-compliance, the notification requirements of the Sex Offenders Register seems to work very well. The Home Office (2002) claimed a national compliance rate of 96% of sex offenders in the community. These individuals initially registered their names and addresses with police and probation and reported any change of address, which helped the joint public protection units to keep track of them.

This level of compliance is significantly higher than that observed in a US survey of agencies dealing with sex offenders; on average nearly a quarter of sex offenders could not be accounted for and only 76% had been registered on the appropriate database (Matravers, 2003). This may be a consequence of Megan's Law, whereby federal legislation mandates the release of information about high-risk sex offenders to the community where they reside. This law followed the sexual assault and murder of seven-year-old Megan Kanka. The sexual murder of Sarah Payne had a number of similarities to the case of Megan, including the call for the same law in the UK. Nevertheless, the current arrangements to protect the public in the UK seem to be working better without such a law.

In some circumstances, it is necessary to disclose information about the offender's presence in a household or neighbourhood in order to protect victims, families and the public at large. Decisions to disclose information are carefully considered case by case at a MAPPP meeting. The panel considers the nature of the risk and if all agencies agree, a recommendation is made to the senior officer responsible in the police service who makes the final decision. Under the Children Act (1999, 2004) social services are also at liberty to disclose information on offenders who are a 'risk to children' (previously referred to as a Schedule 1 offender). Social services may inform the offender's risk status to relatives, families and those caring for specific children, if there is a possibility of the offender coming into unsupervised contact with those specific children. Normally, this is carried out in collaboration with police and probation services.

CONCLUSIONS

Thus, public warning systems form part of the overall strategy for managing risk and positive steps being taken to track and control the activities of sex offenders. The limitations of current policies are that they focus selectively on known or convicted sex offenders. It is evident that there are a larger group of sex offenders whose behaviour is hidden or suspected but not subject to criminal or civil court proceedings.

There is a necessity to collect and maintain intelligence on alleged sex offenders as well as those cautioned or convicted for the prevention and detection of sexual assaults on children and adults. The principal role of the police as primary investigator and intelligence gatherer must be adequately supported both in terms of human and financial resources so that essential proactive approaches are always applied in the detection, management and assessment of sex offenders. In the UK, a lot has been achieved in police work with sex offenders and their victims. However, to make the prevention of sexual offences a reality there is a lot of work yet to be done.

REFERENCES

Ainsworth, P.B. (1995). *Psychology and policing in a changing world*. Chichester: John Wiley & Sons, Ltd.

Ainsworth, P.B. (2002). *Psychology and policing*. Cullompton, Devon: Willan Publishing.

Baker, A.W. & Duncan, S.P. (1985). Child sexual abuse: a study of prevalence in Britain. *Child Abuse and Neglect*, 8, 457–467.

Besharov, E. (1985). Doing something about child abuse: The need to narrow the grounds for state intervention. *Harvard Journal of Law and Public Policy*, 8, 539–589.

Briere, J. (1992). *Child abuse trauma*. Beverley Hills, CA: Sage.

Browne, K.D. & Afzal, S. (1998). *Police operations against child sexual abuse: Prevention and detection*. Report to the Home Office Crime Detection and Prevention Series. London: Home Office (Police Research Group).

Browne, K.D. & Hamilton, C.E. (1997). The repeat and revictimisation of children: Possible influences on recollections for trauma. In D. Read & S. Lindsay (Eds), *Recollections of trauma* (pp. 425–433). New York: Plenum Press.

Browne, K.D. & Hamilton, C.E. (1999). Police recognition of links between spouse abuse and child abuse. *Child Maltreatment*, 4, 136–147.

Bryan, T. & Doyle, P. (2003). Developing multi-agency public protection arrangements. In A. Matravers (Ed.), *Sex offenders in the community: Managing and reducing the risks* (pp. 189–206). Cullompton, Devon: Willan.

Cawson P., Wattam C., Brooker S. & Kelly G. (2000). *Child maltreatment in the United Kingdom: A study of prevalence of child abuse and neglect.* London: NSPCC.

Craig, L., Browne, K.D. & Beech, A.R. (2008). *Assessing risk in sex offenders: A practitioner's guide.* Chichester: John Wiley & Sons, Ltd.

Cybulska, B. (2007). Sexual assault: Key issues. *Journal of the Royal Society of Medicine, 100,* 1–4.

Dalgleish, L.I. (2003). Risk, needs, and consequences. In M.C. Calder (Ed.), *Assessments in child care: A comprehensive guide to frameworks and their use.* (pp. 86–99). Lyme Regis, Dorset: Russell House Publishing.

Department for Children, Schools and Families (2007). *Referrals, assessments and children and young people who are the subject of a child protection plan or are on child protection registers, England – Year ending 31 March 2007.* London: Office for National Statistics.

Department for Education and Skills (2007). *Local Safeguarding Children Board: A review of progress.* London: The Stationery Office.

Department of Health (1995). *Child protection: Messages from research.* London: HMSO.

Department of Health (1996). *Child health in the community: A guide to good practice.* London: National Health Service Executive.

Department of Health, British Medical Association, Conference of Medical Royal Colleges (1994). *Child protection: Medical responsibilities (Addendum to working together under the Children Act 1989).* London: Department of Health.

Dietz, C.A. & Craft, J.L. (1980). Family dynamics of incest: A new perspective. *Social Case Work, 61,* 602–609.

Elliott, M., Browne, K.D. & Kilcoyne, J. (1995). Child sexual abuse prevention: What offenders tell us. *Child Abuse and Neglect, 19,* 579–594.

Everson, M.D. & Boat, B.W. (1989). False allegations of sexual abuse by children and adolescents. *Journal of the American Academy of Child and Adolescent Psychiatry, 28,* 230–235.

Goddard, C. & Hiller, P. (1993). Child sexual abuse: assault in a violent context. *Australian Journal of Social Issues, 28,* 20–33.

Goodwin, J., Sahd, D. & Rada, R. (1978). Incest hoax: False accusations, false denials. *Bulletin of the American Academy Psychiatry and Law, 6,* 269–276.

Gregory, J. & Lees, S. (1999). *Policing sexual assault.* London: Routledge.

Grubin, D. (1998). Sex offending against children: Understanding the risk. *Police Research Series Paper, 99.* London: Home Office Research, Development and Statistics Directorate.

Hamilton, C.E. (1997). *Repeat victimisation of children.* Unpublished PhD thesis. Birmingham: School of Psychology, University of Birmingham.

Hamilton C.E. & Browne, K.D. (1999). Recurrent abuse during childhood: A survey of referrals to police child protection units. *Child Maltreatment, 4,* 275–286.

HM Government (2006). *Working together to safeguard children: A guide to inter-agency working to safeguard and promote the welfare of children.* London: The Stationery Office.

Home Office (1988). *The investigation of child abuse.* Circular 52/1988. London: Home Office.

Home Office (1992). *Memorandum of good practice on video interviewing of child witnesses.* London: HMSO.

Home Office, Departments of Health, Education and Science, Welsh Office (1991). *Working together under the Children Act 1989: A guide to arrangements for interagency co-operation for the protection of children from abuse.* London: HMSO.

Jansson, K., Povey, D. & Kaiza, P. (2007). Violent and sexual crime. In S. Nicholas, C. Kershaw & A. Walker (Eds), *Crime in England and Wales 2006/07* (4th edn) (pp. 49–65). London: Home Office Statistical Bulletin. Available from: www.homeoffice.gov.uk/rds/pdfs07/hosb1107.pdf

Jones, D.P.H. & McGraw, J.M. (1987). Reliable and fictitious accounts of sexual abuse in children. *Journal of Interpersonal Violence, 2,* 27–45.

Kelly, L., Lovett, J. & Regan, L.A. (2005). *A gap or a chasm: Attrition in reported rape cases. Home Office Research Study, 293.* London: Home Office.

Lanning, K. (1992a). *Child molesters: A behavioral analysis.* Arlington, VA: National Center for Missing and Exploited Children.

Lanning, K. (1992b). *Child sex rings: A behavioral analysis.* Arlington, VA: National Center for Missing and Exploited Children.

Lanning, K. (1996). Criminal investigation of sexual victimisation of children. In J.N. Briere, L. Berliner, J. Bulkley, C. Jenny & T. Reid (Eds), *The APSAC Handbook on Child Maltreatment, American Professional Society on the Abuse of Children* (pp. 247–264). Beverley Hills, CA: Sage.

Lieb, R. (2003). Joined-up worrying: the Multi-Agency Public Protection Panels. In A. Matravers (Ed.), *Sex offenders in the community: Managing and reducing the risks* (pp. 207–218). Cullompton, Devon: Willan.

Lloyd, S. & Burman, M. (1996). Specialist police units and the joint investigation of child abuse. *Child Abuse Review, 5,* 4–17.

Marshall, P. (1997). The prevalence of convictions for sexual offending. *Home Office Research and Statistics Directorate Research Findings, 55.* London: Home Office.

Matravers, A. (2003). Setting some boundaries: Rethinking responses to sex offenders. In A. Matravers (Ed.), *Sex offenders in the community: Managing and reducing the risks* (pp. 1–29). Cullompton, Devon: Willan Publishing.

Office for Criminal Justice Reform (2007) – see www.ocjt.gov.uk

Peters, S.D. (1988). Child sexual abuse and later psychological problems. In G. Wyatt & G. Powell (Eds), *Lasting effects of child sexual abuse* (pp. 101–118). Beverly Hills, CA: Sage.

Plotnikoff, J. & Woolfson, R. (1995). *Prosecuting child abuse: An evaluation of the Government's speedy progress policy.* London: Blackstone Press.

Prior, V., Glaser, D. & Lynch, M.A. (1997). Responding to child sexual abuse: The criminal justice system. *Child Abuse Review, 6,* 128–140.

Thomas, T. (1994). *The Police and Social Workers* (2nd edn). Aldershot, Hants: Ashgate Publishing.

Thornton, D. (2002). Constructing and testing a framework for dynamic risk assessment. *Sexual Abuse: A Journal of Research and Treatment, 14,* 137–151.

Thornton, D., Mann, R., Webster, S. *et al.* (2003). Distinguishing and combining risks for sexual and violent recidivism. In R. Prentky, E. Janus, M. Seto & A.W. Burgess (Eds), *Understanding and managing sexually coercive behavior.* Annals of the New York Academy of Sciences, *989,* 225–235.

Waterhouse, L. & Carnie, J. (1990). Investigating child sexual abuse: Towards inter-agency co-operation. *Adoption and Fostering, 14,* 7–12.

West Midlands Police (2003). *Keeping communities safe: West Midlands Multi-Agency Public Protection Arrangements Annual Report 2002–03.* Birmingham: West Midlands Police. (p. 15).

Wyre, R. (1997). A matter of conviction. *Community Care, 30,* October 4th, 2–3.

28

Community Strategies for Managing High-Risk Offenders: The Contribution of Multi-Agency Public Protection Arrangements

HAZEL KEMSHALL

JASON WOOD

INTRODUCTION

High-risk offenders have attracted much media and political interest in recent times (Kitzinger, 2004; Thomas, 2005), not least due to high-profile failures to effectively manage them in the community. Cases such as the murder of John Monckton by Damien Hanson whilst subject to parole supervision have placed both agency procedures and multi-agency arrangements under the spotlight (see, for example, the HMIP inquiry report: HMIP, 2006). Other inspection reports have raised concerns about the effective management of sex offenders in the community (HMIP, 2005), drawing attention to [until comparatively recently]: the lack of accredited treatment programmes in the community and the resultant long delays for some sex offenders; the limited availability of surveillance and the necessity to balance its use against other competing demands; the lack of specific training for staff working with sex offenders; the fact that Multi-Agency Public Protection Arrangements (MAPPA) processes for managing sex offenders varied across the country; and that good practice tended to be based on personal experience and anecdotal data rather than research evidence (pp. 9–11).

This has resulted in increased policy and practice concern with high-risk offenders, and most notably sex offenders, followed by a raft of legislation to deal more

Assessment and Treatment of Sex Offenders: A Handbook. Edited by Anthony Beech, Leam Craig and Kevin Browne. © John Wiley & Sons Ltd, 2009.

proactively with those deemed to present the highest risk of harm (Kemshall, 2003a).

Such cases have also resulted in a perception of system and organisational failure in the management of high-risk offenders (the Chief Inspector of Probation termed this a "collective failure" in respect of Hanson), and attendant media coverage such as the 'File on Four' investigation (8 February 2006) has eroded public trust.

Work with high-risk offenders, or public protection as it came to be known, was given added impetus throughout the 1990s into the 21st century by a number of key factors. Most notable was the 'discovery' of the predatory paedophile (Kitzinger, 1999a,b) and various studies that established the extent of the problem nationally and internationally (Cobley, 2000; Grubin, 1998). The prevalence of child sexual abuse has continued to attract concern (Kitzinger, 1999a,b) with research estimates that one in six children will be the victims of such abuse (Cawson, Wattam & Kelly 2000), leading to calls for a UK version of 'Megan's Law' (Sarah's Law) following the murder of Sarah Payne in 2000[1]. These cases have resulted in what some commentators have described as a 'moral panic' about organised abuse and paedophile rings (Kitzinger, 1999a,b; Thompson, 1998). As a result, public and media pressure grew for more restrictive and effective measures for the management of such offenders particularly post-release from prison, resulting in a 'community protection model' (Connelly & Williamson, 2000) in which legislation prioritises public protection, partly through provisions for mandatory, indeterminate and preventative sentencing, and through intensive supervision methods in the community.

LEGISLATION AND PUBLIC PROTECTION

Most notable has been legislation covering the surveillance and monitoring of sex offenders, in particular the creation of the Sex Offenders Register by the Sex Offender Act 1997 and the provision of the Sex Offender Order in the Crime and Disorder Act 1998. Registration requirements have been strengthened by the Sexual Offences Act 2003 which also created three new orders: 'sexual offences prevention orders' (SOPOs), 'foreign travel orders' and 'risk of sexual harm orders' and repealed the previous legislation above (see Shute, 2004, for a full review; Criminal Justice System, 2004). Public protection panels were created by Sections 67 and 68 of the Criminal Justice and Court Services Act 2000, with the Criminal Justice Act 2003 adding the Prison Service to Police and Probation as 'Responsible Authorities'. These acts in effect formalised the community management of high-risk offenders, and placed a duty on a range of agencies to cooperate in their assessment and management. Multi-Agency

---

[1]Megan's Law (named after 7-year-old Megan Kanka murdered in the USA by a known paedophile) allows the 'community notification' of details of sex offenders to members of the public; this can include the use of posters, distribution of flyers, and access to sex offenders registers via the Internet (Kanka, 2000; Power, 2003).

Public Protection Arrangements (MAPPA) have been strengthened by subsequent Home Office guidance (Home Office, 2003, 2004) and circulars on best practice (PC 39/2005; PC 49/2005; PC 88/2005; see also Kemshall *et al.*, 2005). MAPPA have a statutory duty to identify high-risk offenders, carry out risk assessments and ensure that such offenders are appropriately managed within the community (Home Office, 2004; CJCS Act 2000; CJA, 2003).

The Criminal Justice Act 2003 also established 'public protection sentences', in effect reinforcing the use of selective custody (including mandatory life sentences) for those deemed to pose a high risk of serious harm to the public (NPS, 2005).

PROTECTION THROUGH PARTNERSHIP

As the public protection agenda grew during the 1990s, so did the notion of 'partnership' and the use of multi-agency arrangements to increase the effectiveness of risk assessment and management of high-risk offenders (Home Office, 2003, 2004). Following an evaluation of arrangements by Maguire *et al.* (2001) a number of recommendations to strengthen partnerships and give legislative force to MAPPA were implemented (see Kemshall, 2003a, for a full review). A further evaluation was conducted in 2004 (Kemshall *et al.*, 2005), with a focus on effective community management strategies as well as partnership arrangements. Whilst this report found many improvements since the original evaluation report (Maguire *et al.*, 2001), a number of key issues still required further attention. In brief, these were the need for greater effectiveness and appropriateness in the allocation of offenders to the appropriate level of risk management; the full completion of risk assessment tools in all cases; clearer mechanisms for recording risk assessments and risk management decisions, particularly in the case of panel minutes; the need for a case review system that is matched to the risk management plans: and, appropriate, dedicated resources for the coordination and administration of MAPPA (Kemshall *et al.*, 2005).

A number of these issues were reiterated by the Inspectorate report on the community management of sex offenders, and in particular:

- Lack of clarity and consistency about the level of MAPPA management for individual sex offender cases;
- Lack of completion of OASys risk of harm sections;
- Lack of clear recording in case files;
- Lack of home visiting and monitoring of sex offenders;
- Lack of appropriate resourcing for police visits to sex offenders;
- Risk management plans not always implemented;
- Poor minute taking and actions not clear;
- Lack of reviews, and no follow-up on failed actions;
- Lack of appropriate and dedicated resources for MAPPA (HMIP, 2005).

Table 28.1

% Above the line (Excellent/Sufficient)	SOTI[a]	ESI
(For high/very high risk of harm cases only)		
Has a good quality risk management plan been produced under MAPPA or other inter-agency arrangement?	50%	58%
Is this risk management plan being executed appropriately, with effective liaison between the agencies, particularly police and probation, including on accommodation issues?	42%	66%
Has the risk management plan been appropriately reviewed?	50%	66%
(For child protection cases only)		
Has there been probation and police involvement in child protection arrangements – e.g., core group or case conference and liaison between agencies to reduce the risk to the child(ren)?	59%	80%

Source: HMIP, 2005: 39, Table 5.

[a] SOTI stands for Sex Offender Treatment Inspection, and ESI stands for Effective Supervision Inspection.

The effectiveness of risk management planning, delivery and review continues to warrant questioning. Kemshall *et al.* (2005) found that risk management plans were comprehensive in many cases but poorly documented and prone to poor review mechanisms, reflected in the HMIP report. Table 28.1 summarises the HMIP findings:

However, despite these difficulties, Kemshall *et al.* (2005) found that MAPPA made a significant contribution to the effective management of high-risk offenders (and in particular sex offenders) in a number of key areas. These will now be reviewed.

Identification and Assessment of High-Risk Offenders

The appropriate identification of high-risk offenders is crucial to the effective operation of MAPPA, in essence, are the 'critical few' targeted for detailed risk assessment and for the deployment of additional multi-agency resources? The official guidance identifies this group as very high-risk offenders (as defined by the Offender Assessment System (OASys), the standard risk assessment tool used by MAPPA) and those requiring very intensive risk management at Level 3 of MAPPA.[2]

This group can include:

> *[those] although not assessed as high or very high risk, the case is exceptional because the likelihood of media scrutiny and/or public interest in the management of the case is very high and there is a need to ensure that public confidence in the criminal justice system is sustained.*
> *An offender on discharge from detention under a hospital order.*
> *An offender returning from overseas (whether immediately following their release from custody or not).*

---

[2] Level 1 management is carried out by a single agency; Level 2 management is through local interagency arrangements but does not usually require the intensive management of the formal MAPPA procedures.

An offender having been managed as medium or even a low risk in the community . . .
comes to present a high or very high risk as the result of a significant change of
circumstances.
(Home Office, 2004: paragraphs 116–117, p. 36).

However, the issue is somewhat more complex in practice. For example, presenting index offences can be misleading about risk levels due to plea bargaining, and those offenders categorised as medium risk are in fact the most likely to commit a 'Further Serious Offence', that is to commit a serious offence of harm whilst the subject of probation/parole supervision (Public Protection and Licence Recall Unit, 2005). This currently runs at 80% of all SFOs (PC 82/2005; HMIP, 2006). This issue is exacerbated by the poor completion of formal actuarial risk tools (both OASys and Risk Matrix 2000 (Thornton *et al.*, 2003), see Kemshall *et al.*, 2005; and HMIP, 2005, p. 38) which potentially leads to the misclassification of high-risk offenders as low or medium risk. In some instances formal risk assessments do not necessarily influence subsequent case management decisions. In the case of Hanson, he was risk assessed as a 91% risk of reconviction for a violent offence, and yet on release was classified and managed as a medium risk case – one of the key contributing factors to the subsequent risk management failure (HMIP, 2006).

This means that the identification and referral of offenders to MAPPA is critical, and crucially dependent upon the quality of information and internal risk assessments done by the referring agency. The national survey indicated that there was a more consistent use of the OASys (Offender Assessment System) risk tool, although the full risk of harm assessments were incomplete in about two-thirds of the probation cases examined. (This was supported by the findings of the subsequent HMIP report 2005.) Good practice in the identification and subsequent risk assessment of offenders was seen as dependent upon:

- A full risk assessment by the referring agency using a reliable risk assessment tool;
- Presentation of the key characteristics of the offender including any 'local knowledge' about the offender;
- Prison information (if relevant and available) such as discipline record, response to treatment programmes, contacts, visits;
- Previous convictions and previous responses to supervision;
- Relevant victim information (ages and gender of children, for example);
- Previous targeting and victim grooming behaviours, modus operandi.
  (Adapted from Kemshall *et al.*, 2005, p. 13).

This information enabled more thorough panel preparation and discussion, leading to more in-depth risk assessments and risk management planning. Proactive, competent chairs made a significant contribution to the quality of panel risk assessments, and chairs were essential to ensuring that decisions were defensible and grounded in the evidence presented. This process depended upon well-structured agendas, and an evidential rather than anecdotal approach to information sharing.

Risk Management Planning

A key function of multi-agency public protection panels is to decide both the level of risk presented by the offender, and the risk management plan required to effectively manage that offender in the community. The response to the national survey indicated a generally positive picture on risk management planning, with plans matching risks in individual cases, plans identifying actions and activities, and plans having 'high' or 'very high' impact on harmful behaviours. A number of factors contributed to effective planning:

- A systematic review of the risk factors and plans well matched to them;
- A review of the factors likely to lead to escalating risk or deteriorating behaviour and how to reduce them;
- Clear summaries from panel chairs as to what is required to manage the case;
- Clear records and minutes to enable case tracking and accountability over time;
- Clear actions, with roles and responsibilities properly attributed and recorded, with clear timescales;
- Contingency plans in case of breakdown or risk escalation.
    (Adapted from Kemshall *et al.*, 2005, p. 14).

Intervention programmes should also:

- Take into account the 'readiness to change' of the offender/prisoner;
- Be delivered as intended;
- Be enforced;
- Have a relapse prevention plan.

HMIP (2005) plotted the range of interventions used for sex offenders (with more than one intervention sometimes used), and these are reproduced in Table 28.2 below:

Most notable in the HMIP findings is the lack of accredited sex offender programmes, difficulties in finding approved accommodation, and the long treatment waiting times in the community. Of further note is the use of a wide range of restrictive conditions, possibly indicating an imbalance between treatment and restriction in some cases. The inquiry also noted that: "In the 100 cases we inspected interventions and their level of intensity were not proportionate to the assessed risk of harm in 35% of cases which indicates either more or less input was required in those cases to manage risk of harm" (p. 27). Whilst developments since the CJCS Act (2000) have enabled a pyramid structure of risk management levels to develop in areas, particularly in the matching of 'resources to risk', there are difficulties in establishing and maintaining risk management thresholds (Kemshall *et al.*, 2005).

These findings also indicate that case managers (whether in police or probation) are central to effective risk management, either because they are directly delivering sessions, treatment or interventions, or because they have a crucial role in the effective coordination of risk management plans (HMIP, 2006). Case managers/practitioners

Table 28.2 Types of intervention commonly used with sex offenders by police and probation staff

Interventions	%
Residing at approved premises	33
Accredited sex offender programme: Planned (23%), currently attending (22%) or finished (11%)	55
Office-based supervision sessions	91
Monitoring of movements	47
Restrictions on associations	51
Restrictions on residence	48
Restrictions on movement – Prohibited areas	26
Restrictions on movement – Curfew	14
Restrictions on activities and possessions	11
Electronic monitoring	4
Surveillance	1

Source: HMIP, 2005: 27, Table 2.

attend panels and need to be prepared to participate in panel discussions to answer questions (e.g., about previous victims); to clarify issues (e.g., response to any treatment programme); to update information on motivations, attitude and behaviours; and to provide information on networks and peer associates. Case managers should also consider what they believe to be necessary to safely manage the offender in the community, for example, does the case require supervised accommodation, police surveillance, or specialised treatment services? If the offender is being released on parole licence are there any licence conditions that will require monitoring and enforcing (e.g., a curfew, exclusion from certain areas, etc.)? What other agencies will need to be involved in ensuring that these conditions are met?

Restrictive Conditions Versus Internal Controls

Restrictive conditions are those conditions attached to supervision orders or licences which restrict where an offender can go, live, what they can or cannot do, who they must not approach or contact. For example, a sex offender may have a restriction against using certain leisure facilities (e.g., swimming pools), approaching local schools, and may have a condition to reside in a certain place (e.g., a probation hostel). Offenders can also be made the subject of a curfew to restrict their activities at certain times of the day or night when they are known to be more risky (e.g., when children either enter or leave school). These conditions restrict the opportunity to commit offences and to 'groom' victims. Restrictive conditions are specific to individual offenders, and it is important that they are well matched to the assessed risk factors, are proportionate, justified and workable in practice. It is also important that they are monitored and enforced if breached. Monitoring, surveillance and control procedures are those which provide a 'watching eye' over the offender, usually used to monitor compliance with restrictive conditions, to monitor grooming activities and to gain further information on networks and criminal activities. These procedures can include electronic or satellite tracking, CCTV and police observation.

However, restrictive conditions can sometimes have an adverse affect. The HMIP thematic report on sex offenders (HMIP, 2005) noted sex offenders subject to restrictions prohibiting living in proximity to schools and parks resulted in social isolation, distance from their own families and support networks, and lack of reintegration. In addition, this type of policy can result in sex offenders being accommodated together in a small geographical area, inadvertently fuelling paedophile networks (Levenson & Cotter, 2005).

Whilst some high risk, unmotivated offenders may require the exclusive use of restrictive conditions, they can prove resource hungry and if they breakdown or fail then any external constraint on offenders' behaviour is removed. Risk management plans should also take account of the offender's capacity to exercise (or acquire) internal controls. Internal controls are strategies that focus more on developing the offender's own ability to avoid and manage risk situations and will include accredited programmes. Self-risk management is promoted through programmes of intervention that seek to address the offender's readiness to change and to help them develop skills and strategies for:

- Avoidance – e.g., of specific triggers for offending behaviour
- Involvement in other activities to 'divert' away from offending
- Cognitive skills – understanding consequences of behaviour, identifying reasons not to offend or cause serious harm.

The development of internal controls can be a very effective way to reduce risk but it is hard to achieve and hard to measure with certainty. It will often require the use of intensive cognitive behavioural programmes and attention to relapse prevention techniques. External controls are therefore the primary way agencies deliver risk management but opportunities to develop internal controls are also very important.

As well as identifying risk factors, it is important to identify protective factors that can counteract negative influences. Interventions should aim to strengthen and develop these protective factors alongside other measures to promote external and internal controls. These protective factors include:

- Individual factors, e.g., education/employment achievements, constructive leisure activities, friends who are not involved in offending, sense of self-efficacy, having goals or ambitions, resilience, opportunities for turning points, a willingness to discuss problems, willingness to engage with interventions;
- Family factors, e.g., positive and stable relationships, family members who model prosocial behaviour;
- Community factors, e.g., receiving professional help/support, strong stable relationship with prosocial others outside the family home, involvement in community activities.

A case example:

Mike was sentenced to 36 months imprisonment for indecent assault on a 4-year-old boy (the son of his partner). The risk management plan for his release contained a condition not to approach his previous partner or her child, to attend a sex offender programme (when available), and to reside with his mother.

Mike was released on licence and went to live with his mother. Mike and his mother had a difficult time, and Mike blamed her for the abuse he suffered from his own stepfather. Very shortly after release Mike began to contact his previous partner. The local police reported to the probation officer that they had been called to an incident at the home of Mike's previous partner. Mike had apparently begun a relationship with her again, and had gained access to, and abused, her son aged 7.

The risk management plan included the following **external control**: a licence condition not to contact his previous partner or her child. The lack of a sex offender programme meant very little focus on **internal controls**. An attempt was made to utilise and strengthen **protective factors** by encouraging Mike to reside with his mother, but this in itself became a source of further difficulty and hence risk.

Risk Management

Risk management packages developed by MAPPA, particularly for the highest risk offenders were often intensive, tailored to the individual offender, and delivered by agencies working together (most notably police and probation, and increasingly prisons and probation under the new National Offender Management Service).

From the MAPPA national survey the following were found to be the key components of effective risk management:

Proactive planning – before release from prison enables appropriate licence/parole conditions to be made, accommodation to be secured, victim protection and support work to take place, and surveillance and reporting requirements to be set up.

Police intelligence – this helps to monitor grooming and targeting activities, and to identify offender networks.

Boundaries and swift enforcement – written contracts with offenders can reinforce such conditions and hold offenders to account for programme attendance and compliance with conditions.[3]

Targeted surveillance – to establish key contacts and offender movements, to provide evidence of further offending, evidence to justify rapid recall.

Supervised accommodation – can be crucial for effective risk management. It provides stability, and can be combined with curfews, intensive treatment-based work, CCTV surveillance, electronic monitoring, and high levels of staff contact.

---

[3]Whilst not legally binding, such contracts may engender a stronger commitment by the offender and can be used in conjunction with a clear warning system and swift enforcement, including rapid parole recall.

Accredited programmes – these can be used with positive effect with some offenders (see Kemshall, 2001). However, programme selection and work must be done with care and as part of a wider risk management strategy. Offenders can present false compliance and on occasion a false reassurance to workers that risk is falling. In some cases offenders will have experienced similar programmes in prison or under earlier supervision and have 'learnt the responses'.

Victim protection – this can include providing information, personal alarms, rapid response police numbers, restraining orders, conditions on licences or supervision orders.

Addressing criminogenic and welfare needs – On release from custody, for example, a failure to meet the basic needs of the offender (e.g., benefit claims or accommodation) can undermine the risk management plan. However, these should not be the sole focus of the risk management plan.

In addition, sometimes offenders are unmotivated to change their risky behaviours.

In such cases risk management is almost entirely about containment in the community, restriction of opportunities to reoffend, and protection of known or likely victims. Surveillance and police intelligence are usually the key components of such plans, along with rapid recall procedures.

A package of interventions for an individual offender would depend upon the risk factors assessed and the level of intervention(s) required to effectively manage the risk is shown as an example in Table 28.3.

In addition, PC 10/2005, *Public Protection Framework, Risk of Harm and MAPPA Thresholds,* requires risk management plans in probation to address the following:

1. **Other agencies involved**
   Provide brief outline of the activity of each agency that can be shared with the offender. Cross-reference should be made to any supporting risk management framework used, e.g., child protection procedures.
2. **Existing support/controls**
   In place or can be reactivated if offender is being released into community.
3. **Added measures for specific risks**
   Reference to work with Victim Contact Unit where appropriate.
4. **Who will undertake the actions and by when**
   Cross-reference to any recent or planned MAPPA meeting.
5. **Additional conditions/requirements to manage the specific risks**

Table 28.3 Typical risk management plan for a known paedophile on release from custody

- Electronic tagging
- Supervised accommodation
- Restriction of access to school locations
- Identification and intensive one-to-one work on key triggers, e.g., mood change, attitudes to and the sexualisation of children
- Use of local police intelligence about offending networks and surveillance on key movements

6. **Level of contact**

> *Including frequency of home visits.*
>
> *Risk management plans by their purpose should be managed robustly and reviewed on a regular basis, especially when significant new information or events arise. The above headings will assist offender managers in the preparation of release plans for those on licence.*
>
> *(PC 10/2005,* Public Protection Framework, Risk of Harm and MAPPA Thresholds, *p. 6).*

The effective implementation of risk management plans depends upon well delivered, appropriate and timely day-to-day case management. Minutes of panel meetings should detail clear action plans for agencies to respond to, which are both appropriate to the risk level and measurable in terms of delivery and impact.

Effective Case Management

Features of case management that have been shown to be effective both in custody and in the community are:

- Regular contact and monitoring to note changes, and to take action on individual and situational factors that result in harmful offending. **What is changing and what does it mean? Is risk escalating? What action do I need to take and how quickly?**
- Offenders should be assisted to gain insight into high-risk situations and into their own grooming/targeting behaviours and to develop techniques for self-risk management. **What situations of risk does this offender seek out, when and why? How can they develop risk avoidance strategies?**
- Case management *responsibility* should be vested with one person/agency. This does not mean that one person or one agency will do everything or act alone. **But it does mean that one worker and one agency has overall responsibility for coordinating and ensuring the appropriate delivery of the risk management plan.**
- There should be continuity of risk management, both in terms of personnel and intervention strategies. **Personnel should be clear about who is doing what and by when and provide a consistent risk management message. Interventions should be delivered as specified and on time.**
- There should be speedy access to support services for the offender and contingency plans in case of risk management breakdown or relapse. **What does the offender need to promote risk management (e.g., drug interventions, accommodation), and what needs to happen if parts of the risk management plan begin to fail?**
- There should be appropriate power and authority to limit risky behaviours and to enforce requirements that reduce risk. **For example, the proper use of conditions, the use of warnings and sanctions, the use of parole recall and licence/order breach.**

- Appropriate recording of decisions and actions. **Have I provided sufficient evidence that the risk management plan is well matched to the risk factors identified? Will the plan provide victim protection, public protection and staff protection? Is there a clear record of the defensibility of my actions?**
- Appropriate pre-release planning. **Is there a clear and realistic plan for release? Have the relevant agencies and personnel been informed (including victim support)? Have the appropriate conditions been imposed?**
- Effective case transfer, where possible early and timely with the appropriate exchange of information enabling proper risk management planning within the receiving area to avoid 'risk dumping'. **Why is the case being transferred and is it appropriate and timely? What are the procedures governing transfer and are they being applied (e.g., MAPPA guidance)? What information should be disclosed and to whom?** (See PC 20/2004, *National scheme for transfer of public protection cases*; and PC 52/2004, *Case transfer instructions*. London: NPS.)

WHAT DOES MAPPA CONTRIBUTE TO THE COMMUNITY MANAGEMENT OF HIGH-RISK OFFENDERS?

Risk management can be divided into two basic approaches: the coercive and the integrative. The coercive relies upon the 'community protection model': conditions, restrictions, sanctions, enforcement and intrusive community measures (Connelly & Williamson, 2000). MAPPA is almost exclusively concerned with the effective delivery of the 'community protection model' and the strength of its contribution lies in its ability to deliver additional, multi-agency resources at short notice, and to combine surveillance with programmes targeted at behavioural change. MAPPA can be particularly effective in securing important resources such as supervised accommodation, and in enforcing licence conditions such as curfews, exclusion zones, and intensive monitoring in the community. These techniques are all central to managing high-risk, 'low motivation to change' offenders in the community (Kemshall *et al.*, 2005).

However, MAPPA risk management is resource intensive and it is imperative to be able to evaluate the outcomes of such plans. Panel meetings are costly in themselves, without the additional delivery of costly services such as police surveillance, monitoring, intensive probation programmes or hostel placements. Whilst the potential prevention of a serious crime, or the protection of one victim is morally justified, senior managers must also be concerned with costs, particularly as resources are finite and there are competing demands on agency resources.

MAPPA is also operating in a climate of acute political, public and media blame, in which one case failure can quickly plunge the whole system into disrepute (File on Four, 8 February 2006). In these circumstances, evaluating the impact of risk management is imperative for the sake of public, political and professional confidence in the system to effectively manage high-risk offenders.

The absence of disaster is not enough as an evaluation strategy for success, and while some MAPPA have already begun to monitor their work in order to meet the requirements of the annual report (Home Office, 2005), it is important that this monitoring is extended into genuine evaluations of risk management work. This issue has been recognised by the NPS and PC 49/05 which addresses both quality issues in risk assessment and how to monitor risk assessments and subsequent case reviews.

The HMIP inspection report (2005) noted the difficulty in establishing whether risk management reduces risk, and concluded that some offenders will remain a high risk whatever constructive interventions are provided. However, the report concluded that there was anecdotal evidence that MAPPA did contribute to the effective community management of sex offenders.

When annual reports are published by the Home Office, information about the offenders managed by such arrangements is also made available to the public. The most recent figures, from 2004/2005, show that 44,592 offenders in England and Wales were covered by MAPPA arrangements (Home Office, 2005). Of this, 1,478 'critical few' offenders were managed at Level 3 MAPPPs. For the Home Office, this 'indicates a better understanding of the level of management required for different offenders' (Home Office, 2005).

However, key performance indicators for MAPPA are still embryonic. The following may assist:

- The level of reoffending from the 'critical few' offenders considered by MAPPA.
- The number of Serious Further Offences committed by those subject to MAPPA supervision.

Both measures may indicate some level of impact of MAPPA at its most resource intensive interventions, those targeted at the 'critical few'.

In addition, interim and 'softer' measures could also be used. For example, the proportion of cases meeting the SMART criteria, that is plans should be:

Specific.
Measurable.
Achievable.
Realistic.
Targeted (and timely)
    (Kemshall, 2001, 2003b).

These criteria could be supported by the headings from PC 10/2005 to establish the quality of subsequent case management. This would enable the identification of 'drift', and ensure that the objectives set in individual cases are met (a key concern of the probation inspectorate (HMIP, 2006)). Audits by panel personnel of say 10% of cases each year would assist reviews of practice standards, encourage consistency, and help to identify system failures and resource gaps early (Kemshall et al., 2005). Corrective action could then be taken as a matter of course, integrated within the quality assurance function of MAPPA Strategic Management Boards. The HMIP inspection, for example, found that planned unannounced visits to the homes of sex offenders actually took place 10% less than originally planned (HMIP, 2005, p. 41). This is important quality assurance information and can reveal issues in resource shortfall, lack of integrity in risk management, and conflicting priorities (in this case in policing priorities).

The inspection on the community management of sex offenders also asked the important question 'what does MAPPA contribute to the work of frontline staff?' and found that staff and managers found MAPPA to be generally supportive and helpful. In particular MAPPA was seen as helpful for sharing information, responsibility, and garnering additional scarce resources such as accommodation or surveillance (HMIP, 2005, p. 40). Interestingly, some staff were unaware of MAPPA, and some felt that "MAPPA was taking away the ability of case managers to make decisions on their own, until approval could be obtained at a MAPPA meeting" (HMIP, 2005, p. 40). There are also examples of case managers and local areas not using MAPPA appropriately for relevant cases, hence reducing both the effectiveness of risk management and the defensibility of the decisions subsequently made (the case of Hanson, for example, HMIP, 2006). The inspection report also noted that a lack of resources was diminishing the impact of MAPPA (particularly on surveillance and police home visits to sex offenders).

MAPPA – FUTURE DEVELOPMENTS AND IMPROVEMENTS

Probation Circular 49/05 outlines a 'risk of harm improvement plan' and improvements to MAPPA should be seen within the overall concern to improve practice standards in risk of harm work. The in-depth evaluations of 2004–05 (Kemshall *et al.*, 2005; HMIP, 2006) indicate that attention should be paid to at least the following:

- Joint training for police and probation case managers on the main indicators of risk of harm, risk assessment tools, and risk management interventions.
- Strengthening the powers and accountability of Strategic Management Boards – to facilitate quality assurance and to ensure integrity of delivery of risk plans.
- Attention to the risk of harm in ALL cases, with appropriate training and case attention to escalation of risk and deterioration of behaviour.
- Minimum standards for risk management, including of home visiting, case review, and contact levels commensurate with risk levels.
- Appropriate resources for MAPPA, and for public protection work – public protection work is not resource neutral and it is time to agree a formula funding system for MAPPA and implement it.
- Evaluation of MAPPA impact and value for money.

MAPPA promises much in the way of risk management and has shown to be an effective arrangement for partnership working across agencies that have not traditionally held such formal arrangements. The national consistency envisaged as a result of the Criminal Justice and Court Services Act (2000), the subsequent MAPPA guidance and the Criminal Justice Act (2003), is somewhat realised. However, MAPPA must respond to the challenges of ensuring its risk management systems are well planned, implemented and can be systematically monitored and evaluated. Only in doing this, will MAPPA be able to evidence its contribution to the community management of high-risk offenders.

ACKNOWLEDGEMENTS

Our thanks to Gill Mackenzie, Roy Bailey and Joe Yates who worked with us on the MAPPA evaluation. Thanks are also extended to Bernadette Wilkinson of KWP Trainers for material on self-risk management. The views expressed here are entirely the responsibility of the authors.

REFERENCES

Cawson, P., Wattam, S. & Kelly, G. (2000). *Child maltreatment in the United Kingdom: A study of the prevalence of child abuse and neglect.* London: NSPCC.

CJA (2003). *Criminal Justice Act (2003).* London: Home Office.

CJCS Act (2000). *Criminal Justice and Court Services Act (2000).* London: Home Office.

Cobley, C. (2000). *Sex offenders: Law, policy and practice.* Bristol: Jordans.

Connelly, C. & Williamson, S. (2000). *Review of the research literature on serious violent and sexual offenders.* Edinburgh: Scottish Executive Central Research Unit.

Criminal Justice System (2004). *Protecting the public from sexual crime.* London: Home Office Communications Directorate.

File on Four (2006). BBC Radio 4, 8 February 2006.

Grubin, D. (1998). *Sex offending against children: Understanding the risk.* London: Home Office. Available from: www.homeoffice.gov.uk/rds

Her Majesty's Inspectorate of Probation (HMIP) (2005). *Managing sex offenders in the community: A joint inspection on sex offenders.* London: Home Office. Available from: http://inspectorates.homeoffice.gov.uk/hmiprobation/

Her Majesty's Inspectorate of Probation (HMIP) (2006). *An independent review of a serious further offence: Damien Hanson and Elliot White.* London: Home Office. Available from: http://inspectorates.homeoffice.gov.uk/hmiprobation/

Home Office (2003). *MAPPA guidance: protection through partnership.* London: Home Office.

Home Office (2004). *MAPPA guidance: protection through partnership (Version 1.2).* London: Home Office. Available from: www.probation.homeoffice.gov.uk/files/pdf/MAPPAGuidanceUpdate202004.pdf

Home Office (2005). MAPPA Annual Reports press release. Retrieved from: http://www.probation.homeoffice.gov.uk/output/Page306.asp

Kanka, M. (2000). 'How Megan's death changed us all: The personal story of a mother and anti-crime advocate'. The Megan Nicole Kanka Foundation. Online: www.apbnews.com/safetycenter/family/kanka/sooo/03/28/kanka0328_01.htm Retrieved 3rd March 2006.

Kemshall, H. (2001). *Risk assessment and management of known sexual and violent offenders: A review of current issues.* London: Home Office. Available from: www.homeoffice.gov.uk/rds

Kemshall, H. (2003a). *Understanding risk in criminal justice.* Buckingham: Open University.

Kemshall, H. (2003b). Community management of high-risk offenders – a review of best practice for MAPPA. *Prison Service Journal, 146,* 2–5.

Kemshall, H., Mackenzie, G., Wood, J. *et al.* (2005). *Strengthening multi-agency public protection arrangements,* London: Home Office. Available from: www.homeoffice.gov.uk/rds

Kitzinger, J. (1999a). Researching risk and the media. *Health, Risk and Society, 1,* 55–70.

Kitzinger, J. (1999b). The ultimate neighbour from hell: Media framing of paedophiles. In B. Franklin (Ed.), *Social policy, media and misrepresentation.* (pp. 207–221). London: Routledge.

Kitzinger, J. (2004). *Framing abuse: Media influence and public understanding of sexual violence against children.* London: Pluto Press.

Levenson, J.S. & Cotter, L.P. (2005). The impact of the sex offender residence restrictions: 1,000 feet from danger or one step from the absurd? *International Journal of Offender Therapy and Comparative Criminology, 49,* 168–178.

Maguire, M., Kemshall, H., Noaks, L. & Wincup, E. (2001). *Risk management of sexual and violent offenders: The work of public protection panels.* London: Home Office, Police Research Series, 139. Available from: www.homeoffice.gov.uk/rds

National Probation Service (NPS) (2005). *National guide for the new Criminal Justice Act 2003 sentences for public protection.* London: Home Office.

Probation Circular PC 10/2005. *Public Protection Framework, Risk of Harm and MAPPA Thresholds.* London: National Probation Service.

Probation Circular PC 20/2004. *National scheme for transfer of public protection cases.* London: National Probation Service.

Probation Circular PC 39/2005. *MAPPA Consultation Paper.* London: National Probation Service.

Probation Circular PC 49/2005. *Monitoring the risk of harm.* London: National Probation Service.

Probation Circular PC 52/2004. *Case transfer instructions.* London: National Probation Service.

Probation Circular PC 82/2005. *Monitoring of risk of harm.* London: National Probation Service.

Probation Circular PC 88/2005. *The MAPPA national business plan.* London: National Probation Service.

Power, H. (2003). Disclosing information on sex offenders: the human rights implications. In A. Matravers (Ed.), *Sex offenders in the community: managing and reducing the risk* (pp. 72–101). Cullompton: Willan.

Public Protection and Licence Recall Unit (2005). *Learning points from further serious offences.* London: NPS.

Sex Offender Act (1997). London: Home Office.

Sexual Offences Act (2003). London: Home Office.

Shute, S. (2004). The Sexual Offences Act 2003.The new civil preventative orders: Sexual offences prevention orders; foreign travel orders; risk of sexual harm orders. *Criminal Law Review, 4,* 417–440.

Thomas, T. (2005). *Sex crime: Sex offending and society.* Cullompton: Willan.

Thompson, K. (1998). *Moral panics.* London: Routledge.

Thornton, D., Mann, R., Webster, S., Blud, L., Travers, R, Friendship, C. & Erikson, M. (2003). Distinguishing and combining risks for sexual and violent recidivism. In R. Prentky, E. Janus, M. Seto & A.W. Burgess (Eds.), Understanding and managing sexually coercive behavior. *Annals of the New York Academy of Sciences, 989,* 225–235.

29

Actuarial Risk Assessments in USA Courtrooms[1]

DENNIS M. DOREN

INTRODUCTION

> By nature we like the familiar and dislike the strange.
>
> Maimonides

The amount we pay for insurance is determined by identifying us as members of groups with a few shared characteristics. This is common knowledge. The idea that actuarial information is used to establish how much we pay for premiums is something we, as a society, seem to have become accustomed to a long time ago.

Courtroom determinations are different, however. Decisions are made concerning the individual supposedly without reference to any characteristics the person shares with others. A defendant is found guilty because of that person's criminal actions. A person is involuntarily hospitalized because of a mental illness that makes the person dangerous. Evidentiary rules typically preclude testimony concerning characteristics of groups to which the individual might belong. While insurance payments reflect our various relevant group memberships, courtroom evidence is not typically of this kind.

Arguably, there are good reasons for things being the way they are. Insurance companies concentrate on profits, like any other business. Insurance profits occur as a bottom line across the complete set of customers, not as reflected by how much is paid out to a single individual. In contrast, justice can be viewed as reflected in how each individual is processed, not simply how people are treated on average. The more accurate insurance actuaries are in their assessments of risk of classifications of people, the more financially sound will be the insurance company. In contrast, the

---

[1] Dennis M. Doren, PhD is the Evaluation Director at the Sand Ridge Secure Treatment Center in Mauston, Wisconsin, USA. All opinions expressed herein are those of the author and do not necessarily reflect those of the State of Wisconsin Department of Health Services.

Assessment and Treatment of Sex Offenders: A Handbook. Edited by Anthony Beech, Leam Craig and Kevin Browne. © John Wiley & Sons Ltd, 2009.

'accuracy' of a court system may be better thought of as counted one person at a time.

Within this context, it may come as a surprise that actuarial-type risk assessments have moved into courtrooms. The recent inclusion of actuarial information into court considerations has been with its detractors, but has occurred nevertheless.

This chapter describes how actuarial risk assessment information has been incorporated into USA courtrooms. Initially, some description of relevant actuarial risk assessment instruments is given. Circumstances in which actuarial risk assessments are at least sometimes considered of relevance to the courts are delineated. Issues that have been raised about the judicial consideration of actuarial information are then discussed in detail. Finally, some comments are offered concerning apparent future trends. It is hoped that the reader of this chapter will obtain an understanding of how actuarial risk assessment instrumentation is currently used in the US courtrooms, the arguments made about this process, and where the future utility of actuarial information for the courts may lie.

ACTUARIAL RISK ASSESSMENT INSTRUMENTATION

The race is not always to the swift, nor the battle to the strong – but that's the way to bet.

Damon Runyon

The development of an actuarial instrument starts with the determination of characteristics which statistically differentiate an undesired outcome from a desired outcome. In the world of offenders, the undesired outcome is a recidivist criminal act while the desired outcome is the lack thereof. The characteristics found to be associated with recidivism are called risk factors. Characteristics associated with the decreased likelihood of recidivism are called protective factors.

Actuarial instrument developers use a set of the relevant risk and protective factors, typically chosen from existing professional literature, to form their instrument. Subsets of the most relevant characteristics are then studied in combination. If the combined set of factors is found sufficiently related to the outcome of interest (recidivism and the lack thereof), then the combined set of factors is viewed as an actuarial scale.

Invariable among current commonly used actuarial risk assessment instruments is the determination of differing levels of risk. In other words, no scale simply results in a prediction of recidivism or the lack of recidivism. The outcomes from all current scales involve categories for different proportions of recidivism risk. For instance, one scale (Rapid Risk Assessment for Sexual Offense Recidivism [RRASOR]; Hanson, 1997) results in six different levels of sexual recidivism risk ranging from 7% to 73%, while another (Violence Risk Appraisal Guide [VRAG]; Webster *et al.*, 1994) results in nine different levels of violent recidivism risk across the full range from 0% to 100%.

To score any offender, the person's relevant characteristics are quantified according to the coding rules of the instrument for the specific risk and protective characteristics included in the instrument. The offender's total score then is interpreted as placing the person in a category of people who collectively showed a certain recidivism rate over a specified time period.

There are a variety of actuarial risk assessment instruments currently available. Concentrating on those that have been tested many times with samples of offenders beyond their development sample, and therefore the instruments most commonly used, the following set are highlighted here:

(a) Level of Service Inventory-Revised (LSI-R) (Andrews & Bonta, 2001)
(b) Minnesota Sex Offender Screening Tool-Revised (MnSOST-R) (Epperson *et al.*, 1999)
(c) RRASOR
(d) Sex Offender Risk Appraisal Guide (SORAG) (Quinsey *et al.*, 1998)
(e) Static-99 (Hanson & Thornton, 2000)
(f) VRAG

There are certainly many other actuarial risk assessment instruments currently available, but these have typically been tested far fewer times. Other such instruments that are sometimes used, and may become more frequently tested in the near future include the STABLE (Hanson, 2006), and the Vermont Assessment of Sex Offender Risk (VASOR; McGrath & Hoke, 2001). Using these latter instruments currently in courtroom proceedings, however, leaves open an easy counter-argument about how these instruments have been only rarely tested for reliability and validity. The instruments in the enumeration above are less open to such an argument being effective, though at least in some locales some would argue the MnSOST-R is open to that criticism as well. (The fact the MnSOST-R was developed and cross-validated with USA samples, and hence, involves less extrapolation from foreign samples can be argued to counterbalance the 'generalizability from fewer samples' concern.)

The proper choice of instrument used typically depends on the type or types of recidivism risk of interest. The LSI-R indicates the risk for general criminal and specifically violent recidivism over a year or two post-release from incarceration. The SORAG and VRAG assess interpersonal violence risk and sexual recidivism risk up to a decade post-release. The MnSOST-R, RRASOR, and Static-99 assess sexual recidivism risk, though the Static-99 also assesses risk for violence of any type as well. All of these latter tools assess risk over at least 5 years post-release, with the Static-99 offering risk assessment information for as far out as 15 years. An evaluator interested in assessing an offender's violent recidivism risk over the next decade might therefore choose to use the SORAG, Static-99, and/or VRAG (though the use of both the VRAG and SORAG would be essentially redundant, as these instrument share so many items).

As indicated above, these instruments do not offer predictions of recidivism or lack of recidivism. They place individuals into groups with some degree of empirically based recidivism risk. This placement simultaneously accomplishes two things.

One of those things is to indicate the person is in a category that is higher risk than some other people (or is in the lowest risk category) and lower risk than other people (or is in the highest risk category). This rank ordering of risk can be very useful under certain circumstances, such as in determining relative community supervisory resource allocations or when notification to a community of impending prison release is warranted more than in other cases.

The second potential utility of placing offenders into different risk categories is to facilitate determining if the person appears to be a member of an offender group who represents risk beyond a specified threshold. For instance, a judge may believe it is appropriate to place certain offenders on probation if their risk is low enough, but to place them in prison if their reoffense risk is higher than a 'comfortable' threshold. Likewise, sex offender civil commitment laws in the USA are all premised on the idea that an important determination is whether or not the offender's risk is above or below a statutorily specified threshold.

A common misconceptualization of the utility for placing offenders into risk categories is to determine an offender's exact degree of risk. Even if it were true that every offender who falls into a certain risk category had exactly the same degree of recidivism risk (which is not currently true), there is no current courtroom-related purpose for which exact risk percentages are needed.

CIRCUMSTANCES UNDER WHICH ACTUARIAL RISK ASSESSMENTS ARE RELEVANT TO COURTS

What men really want is not knowledge, but certainty.

Bertrand Russell

The assessment of a person's recidivism risk is of relevance to USA courts under a variety of circumstances. These circumstances fall into both the criminal and civil realms.

Within the criminal realm, risk assessments can become of concern as soon as a defendant has been found guilty of a crime. A growing tendency is for Courts to order pre-sentence risk assessments along with the usual pre-sentence investigations (PSIs). While PSIs often include the writer's overall recommendation for sentencing including whether probation and/or a term of incarceration is warranted, the newer pre-sentence risk assessments offer the Courts a relatively wide variety of risk-related information quite typically including actuarial risk estimates (as well as information related to the potential for managing the defendant's risk). So, for instance, in using the actuarial instruments enumerated above, a risk evaluator for a pre-sentence assessment could offer the Court descriptive statements about the defendant's risk for general criminal recidivism (using the LSI-R), general interpersonal violence risk (using the LSI-R, Static-99, and/or VRAG or SORAG), and sexual recidivism risk (using the MnSOST-R, RRASOR, and/or Static-99). The STABLE and VASOR or other such instruments will someday likely fill in the gap to inform the Court about defendants' potential failure on probation as well. Virtually all kinds of potential harm to others can be covered by a report based solely on the results of actuarials. (For instance, there is even an actuarial instrument designed for assessing the risk for domestic violence (the Ontario Domestic Assault Risk Assessment [ODARA]; Hilton *et al.*, 2004) though it is not yet widely used.) This kind of risk assessment information is used by Courts in deciding what sentence to give to a defendant, for instance, prison or probation, though of course other (non-risk) considerations are of relevance as well (such as to punish the offender, and to deter future potential offenders). Even when giving a prison sentence, a Court can utilize a pre-sentence risk assessment through the consideration of also imposing a short versus long period of post-incarceration probation.

A second circumstance in which actuarial information has been used to assist the Courts within criminal proceedings occurs when a defendant might be placed into a forensic psychiatric hospital. This can occur either when: (a) a defendant is found not competent to proceed to trial and in need of treatment to 'restore' that competency, or (b) a defendant has been adjudicated not guilty by reason of 'insanity' (described with different terms in different States) and still dangerous to self and/or others.

Competency to proceed to trial is a mental and behavioral status presumed to be true of all criminal defendants in the USA until the issue is raised at any point in the criminal proceedings. Typically, once the issue is raised, the Court orders an evaluation of the defendant. If the Court ultimately adjudicates the defendant incompetent (and likely to be able to have competency restored), then the defendant is ordered into treatment for that purpose. At least in certain jurisdictions, that treatment can occur either on an inpatient or outpatient basis. The choice between those two options is made by the Court. It is here that a risk assessment can be informative to the Court, although does not appear to be commonly used under the circumstance.

The use of actuarial risk assessment instrumentation to assist in the determination of when an insanity acquittee can be released from a forensic hospitalization to the community is far more common. Instruments related to a patient's violence potential are used here, such as the LSI-R and VRAG. Risk assessment reports are submitted to courts describing the degree to which the outside community is viewed as at risk if the patient is granted outpatient status or discharged from the commitment altogether. Although this writer does not have empirical data in this regard, his impression is that this use of actuarial risk assessment instrumentation for Court consideration is currently the second most common among all possibilities. (The most common appears to be within sex offender civil commitment assessments, as described below.)

Within civil commitment (versus criminal) proceedings, the legal issues include whether the person has a certain type of mental status and whether the person's mental status causes the person to be dangerous beyond a specified threshold and in certain ways. In theory, actuarial risk assessment instruments can help address the latter aspect of commitment criteria.

In practice, traditional mental health civil commitment evaluations do not seem to use actuarial risk assessments on any regular basis. One reason for this is straightforward. Within traditional civil commitments, the time period of relevance for the person's dangerousness is typically short term, such as the next six months and sometimes much shorter. Current actuarial risk instrumentation has not typically been tested for such short time periods, with the LSI-R being a major exception. The LSI-R, however, was designed for use with convicted criminals, not with psychiatric patients who may never have been charged with a criminal offense. The unavailability of a proper actuarial instrument easily explains why such tools are not commonly found in traditional civil commitment evaluation reports.

In contrast, probably the most common time the courts receive and accept actuarial risk assessment evidence occurs during sex offender civil commitment hearings. (The reader may be more familiar with the phrase 'sexual predator' to describe this type of commitment. This phrase was not used here, however, both because some laws in the USA pertaining to these commitments never use the phrase and because some laws that use the phrase do not pertain to civil commitment procedures.) Like traditional civil commitments, sex offender civil commitments involve determinations related to a person's mental status and his dangerousness of a certain type. Unlike traditional civil commitments, however, the requisite mental status for sex offender commitments must be related to the person's sexual offending, and the dangerousness related to that requisite mental status must specifically pertain to sexual offending risk. Additionally, the reoffense risk requirement for sexual offending involves a time period that is anything but short term, instead typically thought of as the subject's remaining lifetime.

This latter factor seems to have opened the door for evaluators to use actuarial risk assessment tools. Just like with very short-term dangerousness, there are no currently available actuarial instruments that measure risk of any kind over people's remaining lifetime. On the other hand, long-term risk (such as over 10 years post-incarceration) is what is commonly found among current actuarial instruments. If a subject's relevant risk is found to exceed the statutory threshold for commitment within such a time period, then the person's risk clearly exceeds that same threshold over his or her remaining lifetime. It is that type of argument that has brought actuarial data into courtrooms in 20 jurisdictions in the USA (Arizona, California, Florida, Illinois, Iowa, Kansas, Massachusetts, Minnesota, Missouri, New Hampshire, New Jersey, New York, North Dakota, Pennsylvania, South Carolina, Texas, Virginia, Washington, Wisconsin, and the Federal Government).

These types of commitment hearings are highly contested nationally, often going days and even weeks including with expert testimony solicited by both sides. Within that context, it should not be surprising that what serves as a common piece of evidence by the prosecution also serves as a common focus of attack by the defense. These are the roles actuarial risk assessments play in sex offender civil commitments, though mostly during the initial commitment hearings. While regular (typically annual) re-examinations of committed persons are mandated by virtually all of the relevant statutes, re-examination hearings (for the purpose of determining the person's readiness for outpatient placement or complete discharge from the commitment) typically focus far more on the subject's potential benefit from treatment than his historically-based actuarial assessment. (The day will likely come when actuarial instruments take treatment benefit into significant and detailed consideration. When that happens, the instruments will likely become the focus of re-examination proceedings as well.)

ARGUMENTS FOR AND AGAINST COURTROOM USE OF ACTUARIAL INSTRUMENTATION

> He uses statistics the way a drunkard uses lamp posts – for support, not illumination.
>
> Andrew Lang

There have been a wide variety of arguments made against the use of actuarial evidence in the courtrooms, and essentially only one argument specifically in their favor. To the latter first, that one argument is that (the empirically-based) actuarial instruments represent the most accurate risk assessment procedure evaluators currently available (and implicitly they are accurate enough for the application). There are, of course, multiple ways of offering this one argument without saying it explicitly. For instance, expert witnesses can state that the use of certain actuarial instruments represents the standard procedure in the relevant field for the specific risk assessment at hand. This statement indicates the same idea as the first.

The arguments against the use of actuarial evidence are far more varied. There are essentially four types of such arguments:

(a) they do not meet evidentiary admissibility standards for the courts,
(b) they may be the 'best' thing available, but they still are not good enough,
(c) they may be useful generally, but not specifically as applied to this person, and
(d) a large set of arguments that are inherently inaccurate (from a factual, statistical, and/or conceptual perspective).

Each of these four types of arguments is described below.

Actuarials Do Not Meet Evidentiary Admissibility Standards

The entry of actuarial risk assessment information into the courts largely seemed to coincide with the increase in numbers of states with sex offender civil commitment laws. This was not coincidental, as the actuarial data were commonly brought as testimony in those specific hearings (cf. Doren, 2002). Simultaneously, the argument was made that actuarial risk assessment data should not be allowed into evidence as they do not meet courtroom evidentiary standards for admissibility.

There are actually different evidentiary admissibility standards across the States with sex offender civil commitment laws. Most of these States (e.g., Arizona, Kansas, Missouri) use a variant of the Frye standard (*Frye* v. *United States*, 54 App. D.C. 46, 47, 293 F. 1013, 1014 (1923)) which essentially translates to the concept that the procedure or information is generally accepted in the relevant field. Texas uses the Daubert standard (*Daubert* v. *Merrel Dow Pharmaceuticals* (92[102], 509 U. S. 579 (1993)]), a more complicated and inclusive standard involving multiple components. Wisconsin uses a relevancy standard, meaning that the information simply needs to be found relevant for the judge or jury if there is one.

Despite these differences in evidentiary standards, the argument stating the actuarial instruments fail to meet such standards has been litigated dozens of times, but ultimately found not accepted by appellate level courts. (See the ruling in 2004 WL 2902452 (Ill.) – *Illinois* v. *Stephen E. Simons*, Docket No. 97026 – Agenda 7 – December 16, 2004 both for a specific appellate ruling in Illinois and a summary of rulings from other States.) Actuarial risk assessment evidence is now accepted quite regularly in sex offender civil commitment hearings throughout the country with the exception of literally only a couple of local jurisdictions (i.e., in certain Florida counties).

Actuarial Instruments Are Not Good Enough

A second argument against the use of actuarial risk assessment information in the courtroom also does not necessarily dispute the idea that actuarial procedures are the most accurate available for current day evaluators. Instead, the argument is made that, despite this potential acknowledgement, the accuracy of the current actuarial instruments is still not 'good enough' to be used to address questions of law (i.e., questions with very serious outcomes). This concept of 'good enough' reflects any of three different ways of defining the relevant threshold.

One way in which the concept of 'not good enough' can be applied is an argument that will always have to be correct to a degree. No actuarial instrument is perfect in its accuracy, no matter how one defines the accuracy of relevance. Such is likely always to be the case. If one puts the proverbial bar high enough for what defines 'good enough', then this argument will always apply, accurately. The only counter-argument will be that the bar has been set too high.

A second way the 'not good enough' argument has been made involves specific statistical analyses of an instrument's accuracy, with results suggesting inadequate performance under specific circumstances. The third approach uses more generic analyses to portray the idea that the use of actuarial risk instrumentation in the courtroom represents a professional ethical violation.

Concerning specific statistical analyses, the arguments almost always pertain to the degree of accuracy of the risk percentages associated with actuarial instrument scores. In general, the argument made is that the risk percentages originally derived for each instrument are not stable enough to be generalized to sex offenders from other jurisdictions, from other times, and with other characteristics. Methods for attempting to demonstrate the accuracy of this argument have varied, including the use of Bayes' (1764) theorem (Wollert, 2006), re-computations of confidence intervals (Hart, Michie & Cooke, 2007), and Campbell's (2004) use of predictive accuracy measures such as sensitivity and specificity. All of these types of analyses have been brought into courtroom testimony. At the same time, the accuracy of all of these types of analyses has been disputed (Doren, 2006b; R. Karl Hanson, personal communication, May 2006; Doren, 2006a; respectively).

Campbell (2004) seems to be the main proponent of the third 'generically not good enough so they are professionally unethical to use' argument. After making certain assumptions of high relevance (and very questionable accuracy, from this writer's view; see Doren, 2006a), general statistical arguments are made that ultimately state no current instrument's results should be allowed into courtroom testimony. Notably, these arguments are often the same that had been used for a previously described issue (of not meeting evidentiary standards for admissibility). The only difference is that more recent testimony arguing the instruments are not good enough has been given to counter other professionals' testimony involving actuarial data, as opposed to the argument being made for the purpose of trying to get actuarial data excluded from all testimony before a jury or judge even hears it. Additionally, Campbell (2004) has argued that the use of actuarial risk assessment instrumentation in at least sex offender civil commitment assessments is professionally unethical.

In contrast to the arguments made in this section, the personal experience of this author is that the argument that the instruments are not good enough rarely convinces jurors or judges.

Actuarial Instruments Do Not Apply to This Person

This type of argument may be the most viable, at least currently, among all arguments used against actuarial risk assessment instrumentation. The acknowledgement is implicitly made that actuarial assessments are the best assessment technique available in a generic sense, but explicitly the argument is made that there is an important characteristic or set of characteristics that makes the application of actuarial instrumentation at least problematic in the specific case. There are empirical reasons to support this argument under some circumstances. As might be expected, the argument is sometimes also extended beyond what current research would support.

Conceptually, the argument against the case-specific application of actuarial risk instrument results begins with an acknowledgement (or at least no fight against the idea) that the actuarial instruments can be useful and appropriate. All actuarial instruments have some degree of shortcoming, however, including that there can be subpopulations of offenders who show different results from the more typical as measured by an actuarial instrument. Different results mean that the risk percentages typically associated with actuarial scores may be incorrect when applied to one of the cases of the different type.

As mentioned, there are findings in the empirical literature from which this argument gains support. To exemplify, see the following enumeration:

(a) There is a current debate about the effect of older age on recidivism rates of actuarially assessed higher risk sexual offenders, with different studies showing significantly different results (cf. Doren, 2006c). There clearly are some pieces of research that would support the argument the current actuarials might not maintain their accuracy with at least certain older sex offenders.

(b) On the other side of the age spectrum are people who have been known to commit sexual offenses solely while they were still of juvenile age. There is current debate about whether or not 'juvenile-only' sex offenders even have the same risk factors as adult sex offenders, such that the adult-based actuarial instruments may not accurately measure the recidivism risk of juvenile-only offenders (cf. Caldwell, 2002).

(c) The degree to which treatment completion lowers an offender's risk compared to at least some current actuarial instrument findings is not clearly known, but the idea that some risk has been reduced has its support (e.g., McGrath *et al.*, 2003).

(d) Probably at least correlated to that previous finding is the research that shows that changes in dynamic (changeable over time by willful effort) risk factors also may be associated with lower risk than the current more static-oriented actuarial instruments show (Beech, Fisher & Beckett, 1999; Beech *et al.*, 2002).

(e) The recent advent of very long-term mandated community supervision, including what has been termed lifetime probation, likely lowers recidivism rates compared to what the actuarials would indicate (given they were developed and typically cross-validated on samples of offenders without such supervision), though this is an untested hypothesis.

(f) Contrary to many of the above considerations that suggest lower risk estimates may be appropriate compared to current actuarial findings, the combination of two characteristics, a high degree of psychopathy coupled with sexual deviance, may represent higher recidivism risk than our current actuarial instruments are capable of assessing (Harris *et al.*, 2003; Hildebrand, deRuiter & deVogel, 2004; Rice & Harris, 1997).

(g) There is some reason to believe that sexual sadists, especially those who have murdered have a relatively unique set of risk factors (cf. Doren, 2002), such that the application of current actuarial instruments to such people may not be on target.

Some day, it is reasonable to believe that updated actuarial instruments will include the above (and potentially other not yet known) considerations to the extent appropriate. At that time, the argument will no longer be scientifically viable that there are categories of sexual offenders to whom the actuarials do not accurately apply. Until that day, however, this type of argument will frequently be found in courtrooms, and at least to some degree, appropriately so.

That does not mean that any 'special' characteristic for a particular person represents an exclusionary consideration. In this author's experience alone, courtroom arguments have been made to discount actuarial findings due to the person's having 'found religion', being of an understudied race, being from an understudied jurisdiction, having one or more of various physical disorders or disabilities, being developmentally disabled, having lower intelligence, having higher intelligence, having a supportive family, having been imprisoned for a long time, not having a paraphiliac disorder, and others. The empirical support is minimal to non-existent for these alleged reasons to discount current actuarial risk assessment findings.

Inherently Inaccurate Arguments

In this section, a review is made of arguments involving faulty underlying (and typically unstated) assumptions. These will be referred to as the inherently inaccurate arguments (as opposed to arguments of potential viability but found wanting empirically). By definition, none of the arguments included in this section are thought to be credible from an analytic perspective, though their viability in courtrooms still depends on the skill of expert witnesses both in the presentation of the arguments and in the presentation of their flaws.

While not meant to represent a comprehensive enumeration, the following list provides examples of inherently inaccurate arguments to be discussed herein:

(a) Flawed instrument developmental procedures equate to meaningless outcomes;
(b) Actuarial instruments are only good for screening purposes;
(c) His category has 50% likelihood, but which half is he in? and
(d) Equating prediction and risk assessment.

To be clear, other inherently inaccurate arguments also exist, though these are typically of a more technical nature. For illustration, arguments are made that the risk percentages associated with actuarial scores are not exact enough, while ignoring the courtroom application of the actuarial information that only necessitates the far simpler determination that a person's risk is above or below a specific threshold.

(a) Flawed instrument developmental procedures equate to meaningless outcomes

The argument here points out that the developmental procedures for an actuarial instrument were not up to some standard, with the implication being drawn that anything that comes from a flawed process must itself represent error. This is a common argument used in an attempt to discount the MnSOST-R, but it might as well be applied to virtually all other actuarial instruments as well. None of them was perfect in its development. The issue with this argument, however, is that the implication itself represents flawed logic.

By way of metaphor, penicillin was discovered by accident. There was no systematic, scientifically specified process by which penicillin was derived involving months or years of toil. On the other hand, penicillin was found to work for a specific purpose, and quite regularly has been found to work for that same purpose by other researchers. The fact that penicillin works over and over again is what makes it valuable. The fact that it was developed in a non-standard way does not detract from its value.

The same is true for actuarial instruments. Their method of development simply facilitates the likelihood that a researcher will find something valuable through typical scientific efforts. At the same time, failure to follow typical procedures does not guarantee a flawed product. As the saying goes, the proof is in the pudding – the issue is whether the instrument works over and over again, not how it was developed. Arguments about how an instrument was developed simply represent distractions from the real issue: how well does the instrument work for the purpose to which it is being applied?

(b) Actuarial instruments are only good for screening purposes

The argument made here is that actuarial instruments only put people into groups involving averaged degrees of risk, but that individualized risk assessments must go beyond placing people into groups by assessing individual characteristics. This argument can sound proper when stated by an articulate expert witness, but it ultimately misrepresents the nature of empirically-based assessments.

Again by way of metaphor, physicians conduct assessments of individuals multiple every day. They do this by conducting blood tests, getting biopsies, listening to heart beats, and gathering data in various other ways. After gathering data, they then compare the results to what research has told them are important differentiating factors between healthy and unhealthy findings. For instance, a cholesterol number of 300 has no inherent meaning until it is compared to research (i.e., group) results which show this number is in the unhealthy (i.e., higher risk) range. Likewise, a biopsy finding has no inherent meaning until the type of tissue is compared to what research has shown to be either healthy or unhealthy cells. In fact, for all of the data used by physicians in assessing our health, the comparison is made between the individual and groups of individuals as studied in research. We are all compared to groups for each such assessment. We are then categorized as to which groups we belong. Our 'individualized' health assessment is derived from this set of categorizations. There is no medical assessment that avoids comparing an individual's characteristics with a larger view of what is normal (or healthy) and what is not.

The same is true of any risk assessment, including for recidivism among offenders. There is no individualized assessment beyond comparisons to what is believed to be the norm and what is believed to be beyond the norm. These are all group comparisons and categorizations.

Actuarial instruments are clearly not yet comprehensive in including everything that potentially matters (as was illustrated in the previous section). At the same time, to say that actuarial risk assessments 'only' represent group data, with risk evaluations needing to be more individualized is an inherently inaccurate argument.

(c) His category has 50% likelihood, but which half is he in?

Putting this argument into different words, it essentially says that the person may fall into a certain risk category, but is he (or she) really going to reoffend? This argument actually does not discount an actuarial finding per se, as it assumes that a risk percentage derived from an instrument, such as 50%, can be accurate as far as it goes. The problem with this argument is that it changes the typical courtroom task involving risk assessment to one of predicting recidivism.

There is no courtroom circumstance in the USA that requires, or even asks an expert witness to opine about whether or not the assessment subject will reoffend (i.e., a prediction task). The input requested in courtrooms is an assessment of the degree of risk someone represents for certain undesired outcomes (i.e., a risk assessment task). Equating the two tasks represents an error. Discounting actuarial information based on this error is inherently improper.

(d) Equating prediction and risk assessment

The prior issue only represents one of many inherently faulty arguments equating recidivism prediction with risk assessment that are used to attempt to discount actuarial findings in courtrooms. To exemplify, arguments are made that:

(a) an instrument's sensitivity (i.e., ability to detect recidivists) is too low;
(b) the predictive accuracy of an instrument is at best moderate;
(c) any actuarial risk finding represents a prediction of recidivism (which is seriously inaccurate) (cf. Campbell, 2004, relative to this and the previous two examples); and
(d) each instrument has a consistent sensitivity and specificity across all risk levels (cf. Wollert, 2006).

Once again, a metaphor serves to illustrate the inherent flaw in these types of arguments. When people consider buying insurance, home owners' insurance, for example, they view the degree to which the cost of insurance premiums outweighs the risk they face without the insurance. The purchase of insurance does not typically occur because people predict their homes will catch on fire or the like, but because people recognize a degree of risk. They buy insurance to lower the degree to which the risk will hurt them if eventually actualized. A risk assessment is made, and risk management steps are enacted. No prediction is ever made, however. Risk assessments and predictions are not the same things. Arguments involving the contrary assumption contain an inherent flaw.

WHAT THE FUTURE HOLDS

> You've got to be careful if you don't know where you're going, 'cause you might not get there.
>
> Yogi Berra

Actuarial risk assessment findings have made it into USA courtroom testimony to a growing degree over the past decade. Despite various arguments made against such evidence, there is no reason to believe that actuarial risk assessment information testimony will go away in the near future.

To the contrary, with a growing acceptance of such evidence in certain court proceedings (such as sex offender civil commitments and pre-sentence risk assessments), there would seem to be reason to believe there will be an expansion in this regard in the future. For instance, traditional mental health civil commitments necessarily involve 'dangerousness' assessments. When a validated actuarial instrument exists that directly pertains to the relevant type of risk (short-term violence potential, potentially including against self), it seems likely that the courts will soon hear and accept testimony based on that actuarial finding. Arguments about court testimony involving actuarial information will probably concentrate more on the appropriateness of application to the individual subject than on the generic accuracy of the data themselves.

The future of actuarial risk assessment instrumentation can already be seen based on currently ongoing research. While most of today's instruments involve solely static, historical data input, instruments are being developed concentrating on dynamic factors (e.g., the STABLE, Hanson, 2006). The attempt to integrate these two types of data will very likely soon follow.

Testing existing and future instruments with a greater variety of offender samples will almost certainly occur. In this process, we will learn more about the degree to which treatment completion lowers risk, community supervision status matters, how and when to adjust risk assessments based on age of the offender, etc. While we can always expect new questions to arise (as they do in all science), it also seems reasonable to believe that our current areas of concern will largely be addressed.

At some point, actuarial risk assessment instruments will become far more comprehensive than they currently are. We have already seen this type of transition over the past 25 years in the successive updates in the series of instruments stemming from the Level of Service Inventory (see Andrews & Bonta, 2001).

Courts will face issues not previously of concern as this happens. For instance, actuarial risk assessment instruments may come not to require specialized disciplinary training for their proper use. As the instruments become more comprehensive, and specialized 'clinical' knowledge becomes of lesser utility, the courts may need to reconsider who is allowed to give opinion testimony based on actuarial instrumentation findings. Currently, giving such testimony is substantially the purview of psychologists, psychiatrists and some social workers. The future may find prison case workers, probation officers, occupational therapists, and even people who solely specialize in risk assessments (within a job classification that currently does not exist) being allowed to give opinion testimony to the court related to risk assessments, with psychiatrists and psychologists being relegated to giving testimony only when diagnostic and/or treatment issues need to be addressed. Maybe this is how it should be.

Finally, the day will likely come when risk assessment information based on actuarial instruments will be considered obsolete except under special circumstances. There are other statistically more sophisticated methods for evaluating risk that already exist. For instance, the use of a 'neural net' has been proposed and tested (Edward Dow, personal communication, 2002) where a subject's data are entered for comparison to those from thousands of other individuals, the best statistical (weighted) matches are made statistically both per piece of data and in their combination, and an estimate of risk is produced based on all of the information entered. Actuarial procedures may not be found as useful as such a more sophisticated risk assessment method. Scientific development rarely stops with something that simply works, such that an older methodology is often left behind.

REFERENCES

Andrews, D.A. & Bonta J.L. (2001). *The Level of Service Inventory-Revised user's manual.* North Tonawanda, NY: Multi-Health Systems.

Bayes, T. (1764). An essay toward solving a problem in the doctrine of chances. *Philosophical Transactions of the Royal Society of London, 53*, 370–418.

Beech, A., Fisher, D. & Beckett, R. (1999). *STEP 3: An Evaluation of the Prison Sex Offender Treatment Programme.* Home Office Information Publications Group, Research and Statistics Directorate, Room 201, Queen Anne's Gate, London, SW1H 9AT, England. Available electronically from: www.homeoffice.gov.uk/rds/pdfs/occ-step3.pdf

Beech, A., Friendship, C., Erikson, M. & Hanson, R.K. (2002). The relationship between static and dynamic risk factors and reconviction in a sample of UK child abusers. *Sexual Abuse: A Journal of Research and Treatment, 14*, 155–168.

Caldwell, M.F. (2002). What we do not know about juvenile sexual reoffense risk. *Child Maltreatment, 7*, 291–302.

Campbell, T.W. (2004). *Assessing sex offenders: Problems and pitfalls.* Springfield, IL: Charles C. Thomas.

Doren, D.M. (2002). *Evaluating sex offenders: A manual for civil commitments and beyond.* Thousand Oaks, California: Sage.

Doren, D.M. (2006a). Inaccurate arguments in sex offender civil commitment proceedings. In A. Schlank,(Ed.), *The sexual predator – Volume III*, Chapter 3. Kingston, NJ: Civic Research Institute.

Doren, D.M. (2006b). Battling with Bayes: When statistical analyses just won't do. *Sex Offender Law Report, 7*, 49–50 & 60–61.

Doren, D.M. (2006c). What do we know about the effect of aging on recidivism risk for sexual offenders? *Sexual Abuse: A Journal of Research and Treatment, 18*(1), 137–158.

Epperson, D.L., Kaul, J.D., Huot, S.J. *et al.* (1999). Minnesota Sex Offender Screening Tool-Revised (MnSOST-R): Development, performance, and recommended risk level cut scores. Available at: http://www.psychology.iastate.edu/faculty/epperson/mnsost_download.htm

Hanson, R.K. (1997). The development of a brief actuarial risk scale for sexual offense recidivism. Department of the Solicitor General of Canada, Ottawa, Ontario. Available at: http://www.psepc.gc.ca/publications/corrections/199704_e.pdf

Hanson, R.K. (2006). The latest meta-analytic research and research on dynamic risk assessment. Presentation at the Second Annual Wisconsin ATSA Spring Conference, Madison, Wisconsin, May 2006.

Hanson, R.K. & Thornton, D. (2000). Improving risk assessments for sex offenders: A comparison of three actuarial scales. *Law and Human Behavior, 24*, 119–136.

Harris, G.T., Rice, M.E., Quinsey, V.L. *et al.* (2003). A multi-site comparison of actuarial risk instruments for sex offenders. *Psychological Assessment, 15*, 413–425.

Hart, S.D., Michie, C. & Cooke, D. (2007). Precision of actuarial risk assessment instruments. *British Journal of Psychiatry, 190*, 60–65.

Hildebrand, M., de Ruiter C. & de Vogel, V. (2004). Psychopathy and sexual deviance in treated rapists. *Sexual Abuse: A Journal of Research and Treatment, 19*, 1–24.

Hilton, N.Z., Harris, G.T., Rice, M.E. *et al.* (2004). A brief actuarial assessment for the prediction of wife assault recidivism: The Ontario Domestic Assault Risk Assessment. *Psychological Assessment, 16,* 267–275.

McGrath, R.J. & Hoke, S.E. (2001). Vermont Assessment of Sex Offender Risk Manual (Research edition). Available at: www.csom.org/pubs/VASOR.pdf

McGrath, R.J., Cumming, G., Livingston, J.A. & Hoke, S.E. (2003). Outcome of a treatment program for adult sex offenders: From prison to community. *Journal of Interpersonal Violence, 18,* 3–17.

Quinsey, V.L., Harris, G.T., Rice, M.E. & Cormier, C.A. (1998). *Violent offenders: Appraising and managing risk.* Washington, DC: American Psychological Association.

Rice, M.E. & Harris, G.T. (1997). Cross-validation and extension of the violence risk appraisal guide for child molesters and rapists. *Law and Human Behavior, 21,* 231–241.

Webster, C.D., Harris, G.T., Rice, M.E. *et al.* (1994). *The violence prediction scheme: Assessing dangerousness in high risk men.* Toronto: University of Toronto, Centre of Criminology.

Wollert, R. (2006). Low base rates limit expert certainty when current actuarials are used to identify sexually violent predators: An application of Bayes's theorem. *Psychology, Public Policy, and Law, 12,* 56–85.

Index

AAI (Adult Attachment Interview) 17–19, 24, 25
AASI (Abel Assessment for Sexual Interest) 119, 125
Abel and Becker Cognition Scale 227
Abel, G.G. 132, 311
Ablon, J.S. 448
Abracen, J. 422
Abrams, S. 145
Abstinence Violation Effect (AVE) 79
accountability scales, in psychometric assessment 90–1
active intelligence seeking 524, 562
actuarial risk assessment 5, 53, 54–61, 69, 70
    and female offenders 476
    and functional offence risk analysis 85
    instrumentation 552–4
    of intellectually disabled (ID) offenders 219–20, 221
    and psychometric assessment 102–3
    and public protection 539
    in USA courtrooms 10, 551–65
acute dynamic risk factors 66, 67, 69, 82
    and Internet sex offenders 210–11
    and personality disorder 245
    and sexual recidivism 48–9
ACUTE-2000 system 68, 211
Adams, H.E. 111–12, 113, 131
admissibility standards, and actuarial risk assessment in
        USA courtrooms 557–8
adolescent attachment 21, 26, 27, 28
adolescent offenders 2, 7, 8–9, 9, 431–49
    and adolescent sexual behaviour 435–6
    and adult sex offenders 432–4, 437–8
    and attachment 23, 26
    attention-based measuring of 119–210
    and brain development 438–9
    and empathy 440–2
    life course of 436–7
    mentalisation 439–40
    post-conviction polygraph testing 149–50
    predicting risk of recidivism 265–84
    psychopathy and personality disorder 434–5
    risk of recidivism 49

subpopulations of 432
treatment programmes for 340, 442–9
see also juvenile offenders
adult romantic attachment 17–19, 22, 24
aetiological pathways model of child sexual abuse
        200–4
aetiological rehabilitation theories 296, 297–8
age of offenders
    and actuarial risk assessments 559–60
    and attention-based measures of sexual interest 124
    juvenile offenders 271, 274, 560
    and risk of sexual recidivism 40
    sexual aggressors of women 187–8
Ageton, S.S. 268
aggression, psychometric assessment of 94, 95
aggression replacement training 342
Ahlmeyer, S. 150, 409, 411
Ainsworth, M. 15–16
alcohol abuse/addiction
    and juvenile offenders 268
    and relapse prevention 78
    and risk of sexual recidivism 40, 48
    and sexual abuse in families 499–500
    and sexual addiction 166–7
    and sexual aggressors of women 186, 192
Alder, L. 224
Alexander, R. 221–2
Allam, J. 421
Allen, C.M. 478
American Psychiatric Association, Diagnostic and
        Statistical Manual 434
American Psychological Association 172
ammonia aversion 316–17
anamnestic approach to risk assessment 55
Anderson, D. 317, 332, 378
Andrews, D.A. 295, 302, 421
anger
    angry sexual aggressors of women 181, 185–6,
        190–2, 193–4, 498
    as a dynamic risk factor 82

anger (*Continued*)
    and intellectually disabled (ID) offenders 223–5
antisocial attitudes/behaviour
    and attachment 26–8
    and child sexual abuse 201, 203
    and functional offence risk analysis 83–4
    and intellectually disabled (ID) offenders 219, 222, 223
    and juvenile offenders 267–8, 271, 282, 456, 457
    personality disorder 410, 412, 418
    psychometric assessment of 93
    and risk of sexual recidivism 40, 41, 47–8
    and the SOTSEC-ID treatment model 378
antisocial personality disorder (APD) 282, 434
anxiety
    and adolescent offenders 443
    and female offenders 482
    and intellectually disabled (ID) offenders 225
    psychometric assessment of 94, 99
    and risk of recidivism 39, 44, 48, 82
APD (antisocial personality disorder) 282, 434
approach goals 80
approach-automatic self-regulation 80
approach-explicit self-regulation 80
Apsche, J. 321
Area Under the Curve *see* AUC (Area Under the Curve)
Arkowitz, S. 412
ASAP (Assessment for Safe and Appropriate Placement), and juvenile offenders 272–5
ASOTP (adapted sex offenders treatment programme) 373, 374, 381–2
Asperger's syndrome 311
assertiveness training 356–7
assessment approaches 5–7
    measuring attachment 23–6
    psychometric assessment 89–103
    see also risk assessment
assisted covert sensitisation 320
Astell, A. 218–19, 223
ATSA (Association for the Treatment of Sexual Abusers) 137
attachment 13–32
    and adolescent offenders 447
    and antisocial behaviour 26–8
    and experiences of abuse and trauma 22–3
    measuring 23–6
    and mentalisation 439
    in sexual offenders 28–30
    theory 4–5, 14–22
        psychobiological processes 16–20
        stability over the lifespan 20–2
    and treatment programmes 30–2, 342, 356
attention-based measures of sexual interest 109–25
    cautions when using 124
    choice reaction time (CRT) 110–14
    clinical applicability of 124–5
    Emotional Stroop studies 114–16, 124–5

    implicit association tests (IATs) 116–17, 123, 124
    rapid serial visual presentation (RSVP) 12, 117–18, 124, 125
    startle probe reflex 121–3
    viewing time (VT) 118–21
attitudes supportive of sexual offending *see* pro-offending attitudes
attrition prevention planning 414–15
Auburn, T. 402
AUC (Area Under the Curve) 54, 56, 58, 68, 92, 99–100, 118, 278
audiotapes, use of in penile plethysmograph (PPG) 132–3
autistic spectrum disorder 387, 411
AVE (Abstinence Violation Effect) 79
aversion techniques, for modifying sexual preferences 314, 315–19, 324
avoidance goals 80
avoidant-active self-regulation 80
avoidant-passive self-regulation 80
Axelrod, S. 321
Aylward, A. 484

Baldwin, M.W. 117
Barbaree, H.E. 132, 137, 149, 200, 265
Bartholomew, K. 17–19, 26
Bartosh, D.L. 65
Baumeister, R.F. 417, 418
BDHI (Buss-Durkee Hostility Inventory) 93
Beauregard, E. 412–13
Beck Anxiety Inventory 225
Beck, A.T. 418
Beck Depression Inventory 225
Becker, J.V. 268, 282
Beckett, R. 338, 359, 423, 479
Beech, A.R. 31, 45, 48, 69, 89, 148, 206, 331
    actuarial risk assessment 58, 59, 66, 102–3
    dynamic risk factors 81–2, 210–11
    family rehabilitation 506–7, 509
    Group Environment Scale (GES) 336–7
    integrated theory of risk assessment 101–2
    personality disorder offenders 411, 416, 422
    RSVP method 118
    sexual homicide typology 413
    STEP test battery 95–7
    treatment programmes 338, 355, 363
behaviour modification
    modifying sexual preferences 314–23, 339
    and polygraph testing 150–2
    and rehabilitation theory 296
    treatment programmes 339–40, 359–60
Behavioural Activating System 419–20
Bell, J. 238
Bentovim, A. 495, 504, 505
Berner, W. 410
bipolar disorder 394, 405
Blackburn, R. 94, 95, 222, 240, 410, 419

Blair, R.J. 417
Blairy, S. 417
Blake, R. 496
Blanchard, E.B. 311
Blanchard, E.G. 132
Blanchard, R. 206, 230
Blanchette, K. 475, 477, 479–80
Boer, A. 227
Boer, D.P. 60, 227
Bogaerts, S. 410, 411–12
Boies, S.C. 172
Bond, I.K. 311
Bonner, B. 265
Bonta, J. 295, 302, 421
Book, A. 220, 223, 231
Borduin, C.M. 462–3
Boster, F.J. 397
Bowlby, J. 15, 27, 29
BPS (British Psychological Society), and PSCOT
        (post-conviction polygraph testing) 158
brain development
    in adolescence 438–9
    and childhood abuse and neglect 363
    and juvenile offenders 270–1
Briken, P. 410
Bronfenbrenner, U. 449
Brown, L.S. 21
Brown, M. 483
Brown, S.L. 475, 477, 479–80
Brown, S.M. 172
Browne, K.D. 55, 59, 61, 89, 421
Bryan, T. 526
Bumby Rape and Molest Scales 227
Burchard, B.L. 314, 445
Burman, M. 523
Buschman, J. 424
Buss-Durkee Hostility Inventory (BDHI) 93
Bussière, M.T. 39, 40, 41, 44, 47, 266, 314
Butcher, J. 93

California Sex Offender Treatment Evaluation Project
        (SOTEP) 334–5
Campbell, T.W. 559
Cantor, J.M. 206, 230
CAP (Child Abuse Potential) Inventory 502
carers, of intellectually disabled (ID) offenders 386
Carlisle, J.M. 311
Carnes, P. 164, 165–6, 170, 171, 172
Carr, L. 169
Castell, D.A. 322
Castonguay, L.G. 134, 317
CAT (Child and Adolescent Taxon) 220
CAT (Cognitive Analytic Therapy) 241, 244, 248, 412
catastrophe theory 283
Cattell, R.B. 189
Cautela, J.R. 319, 320
CBT *see* cognitive behaviour therapy

CEOP (Child Exploitation and Online Protection)
        Centre 525–6
Chaffin, M. 265
Chantry, K. 93
Chapple, C.L. 27
Check, J.V.P. 205–6
chemical castration 424
Chesterman, P. 395
child abuse
    adolescent offenders 2
    and attachment 13
    extent of child sexual abuse 494–4
    in the family 494–508
    Four Preconditions descriptive theory of 330
    maltreatment 475–6, 495
    policing 517–31
    policy and practice 9
    sex offenders as victims of 363–4, 370, 386, 420–1
Child Abuse Potential (CAP) Inventory 502
Child and Adolescent Taxon (CAT) 220
Child Exploitation and Online Protection Centre
        (CEOP) 525–6
child molesters/abusers
    and attachment 23, 25, 28–9
    aversion techniques 316, 317, 318
    changing sexual interests 313
    cognitive distortions 332
    contact abuse and Internet offending 200–5
    convictions 515–16
    and covert sensitisation 321–2
    denial by 149
    dynamic risk factors for 67
    feelings of powerlessness 486
    grooming of victims 496, 516
    and personality disorder 411–12
    phallometric assessment of 136–7, 138, 139, 311
    risk of recidivism 42, 46, 67
    and Sexual Risk Behaviours factors 58
    STEP test battery assessment of 96–7
    treatment programmes for 339
    see also incest offenders
child pornography *see* Internet
child prostitution 517
child protection
    and domestic violence 518
    police referrals 521–2
    and the Wolvercote treatment programme 360–1
Child Protection Case Conferences 521–2
Child Protection Register 517, 522
Child Protection Units (CPUs) 518, 522–3
child sexual victimisation, and attachment 23
children
    and implicit association tests (IATs) 116–17
    and Internet pornography 3, 172
    and intimate partner violence 498–9
    offender contact with, and polygraph testing 150, 151
    and phallometric assessment 131–2, 136

children (*Continued*)
  in residential programmes 315
  sexually reactive 431
choice reaction time (CRT) 110–14
Christiansen, J. 496
Cicchetti, D. 282
CID (Criminal Investigation Departments) 518
Circles of Support and Accountability 357–8, 362, 364
civil commitments, and actuarial risk assessment in
    USA courtrooms 555–6, 564
Clarke, D.A. 420
clinical judgement, and risk assessment 53, 54, 55, 66
clinically adjusted actuarial approach, to risk
    assessment 55
clinicians, integrated 446–7
Cochran, W. 79
Cognitive Analytic Therapy (CAT) 241, 244, 248, 412
cognitive behaviour therapy (CBT) 351
  and family rehabilitation 509
  and intellectually disabled (ID) offenders 373–4,
    386–7
  and juvenile offenders 457, 458
  and mentally ill offenders 400–1
  and personal disorder 419–20
cognitive deconstruction theory 333
Cognitive Dissonance Theory 398
cognitive distortions
  and intellectually disabled (ID) offenders 223, 225–8,
    373, 380–1, 386, 387
  offence-supportive cognitions 341
  and risk of recidivism 44–5
  treating incarcerated offenders 329, 330–2
Cohen, L. 182
Coldwell, J. 219
collecting behaviour, and Internet pornography use
    211–12
community management, of high-risk offenders 546–8
community notification, and registered sex offenders
    530–1
Community Rehabilitation Orders 370, 396
Community Safety Units 518
community-based interventions 7–8
comparison studies, and post-conviction polygraph
    testing 152–3
compassionate mind training 363–4, 417, 421
compensatory sexual aggressors of women 181, 187,
    192–3
Conley, R.W. 218
convicted sex offenders 1
  choice reaction time (CRT) 112–13
  Internet-related sexual offences (ISOs) 199, 206
  and Internet-related sexual offences (ISOs) 205–7
  and sexual abuse in the family 503–4
  see also reconvicted offenders
Cooper, A. 169–70, 172
Cooray, S. 221–2
Copes, H. 330–1

coping strategies
  female offenders 481–2
  sexual addiction 167–8
  and sexual preoccupation 44, 48
CORIs (Criminal Offender Record Information) 275
corrosion, and sexual aggressors of women 184
cortisol levels, and attachment 20
Cortoni, F. 167, 476
counterfeit deviance 226
covert sensitisation/association 319–22
CPS (Crown Prosecution Service) 517
CPUs (Child Protection Units) 518, 522–3
Craft, Ann 369–70
Craig, L.A. 53, 55, 59, 61, 65, 82, 92, 100, 101, 386
Craig, R.J. 93
Craissati, J. 23, 25, 58, 81–2, 205, 395–6, 419, 422, 480
criminal associates, and risk of recidivism 45–6
criminal justice system
  and intellectually disabled (ID) offenders 370, 372
  and intellectually disabled offenders 217–18
CRT (choice reaction time) 110–14
Cullen, K. 481
Cumming, G.F. 314, 445
Curnoe, S. 93
Curwen, T. 268, 458
custodial sentences 1–2

dangerous world implicit theory 418
Daniels, M. 341
DAST (Drug Abuse Screening Test) 166
Davis, M. 440
DBRS (Daily Behaviour Rating Scale) 255
DBT (Dialectical Behaviour Therapy) 31, 241, 248,
    249, 254–5
  and personal disorder 413, 414
De Luca, R.V. 476, 484
De Panfilis, D. 501
Deane, K. 229
Decety, J. 417
Declercq, F. 410
denial
  and female offenders 478
  and risk of recidivism 45
  and sexual abuse in families 505
denial training phase, and mentally ill offenders 402–3
depression
  and adolescent offenders 443
  and female offenders 482
  and functional behaviour analysis 82–3
  and functional offence risk analysis 84
  and Internet sex offenders 205
  and online sexual compulsivity 170
  psychometric assessment of 94, 99
  and risk of recidivism 39, 44, 48, 82
Desmet, J. 411–12
deterrence-based treatment 294
deviance domains, predictive accuracy of 99–102

deviant fantasies
    and drug therapy 363
    and Internet sex offenders 207
    and polygraph testing 149, 150
    and sexual addiction 167
    and sexual aggressors of women 192–3
    and the Wolvercote treatment programme 351, 356
deviant sexual interests
    and adolescent offenders 433
    assessment of the construct of deviancy 95–9
    and child sexual abuse 201, 202, 203
    criteria for identifying 312
    decreasing 323, 339–41
    and female offenders 482
    and functional offence risk analysis 84
    and juvenile offenders 269
    and phallometry 311–12, 339
    psychometric assessment of 89–103
    and risk of recidivism 41, 43–4, 56, 57
Devilly, G.J. 116–17
DeWaal, F.B.M. 417
DeWall, C.N. 417
Dhaliwal, G.K. 422
Dialectical Behaviour Therapy see DBT (Dialectical
        Behaviour Therapy)
diary keeping 254, 335
disclosure
    and mentally ill offenders 403
    and registered sex offenders 520–1
    and sexual abuse in families 504–5
distorted attitudes/beliefs see cognitive distortions
DNA samples, and police work 524
Domestic Violence Units (DVUs) 518
D'Orazio, D. 440, 441
Dowset, J. 419
Doyle, P. 526
Drake, D.R. 419
Drapeau, M. 486
drop-out prevention plans 252–3
drug abuse/addiction
    and juvenile offenders 268
    and risk of sexual recidivism 40, 48
    and SARN 250
    and sexual abuse in families 499–500
    and sexual addiction 166–7
    and sexual aggressors of women 186, 192
drug therapy 32, 312, 340–1, 363
DSM III-R 163
DSM-IV-TR 420
DSPD (Dangerous and Severe Personality Disorder)
        Programme 237–8, 243, 245–6, 247–8
    Planning and Delivery Guide 238
    and SARN 250
Dutton, W.A. 149–50
dynamic risk factors 31, 66–8, 69–70, 77
    assessing intellectually disabled (ID) offenders
        223–30, 231

and female offenders 475
and FORA (functional offence risk analysis) 84
and Internet sex offenders 199, 210–11
and juvenile offenders 280–1
and personality disorder 245
rehabilitation theories 300, 301, 302, 304, 305
and severe personality disorder 244
and sexual recidivism 41–8, 81–2
and treatment programmes 338
Dynamic Supervision Project 48–9

Earls, C.M. 134, 317
Eccles, A. 135, 314
ECR (Experiences in Close Relationships) 26
Eke, A.W. 209
elbow criterion, and MCA (multiple correspondence
        analysis) 189–90
Eldridge, H.J. 355, 485
Elliot, S.F. 218–19, 223
Elliott, M. 495, 496
Emerick, R.L. 149–50
emotional management training 342
emotional states
    and child sexual abuse 201, 203
    and Internet sex offenders 204, 204–5
    psychometric assessment of 99, 100
    and risk of recidivism 48, 99
    and SARN 250
Emotional Stroop studies 114–16, 124–5
empathy, and adolescent offenders 440–2
empathy formulation
    and personality disorder 416–17
    see also victim awareness/empathy
English, K. 146, 148, 152
epistemological assumptions, of rehabilitation theories
        297
Epperson, D.L. 60
ethical issues
    PSCOT (post-conviction polygraph testing) 157–9
    use of nude photographs of children 131–2
ethnicity, and mentally ill offenders 395–6
eugenics, and intellectually disabled (ID) offenders
        369
Evans, D.R. 311
exhibitionism 4
    aversion techniques 317, 320
Extended Sex Offender Treatment Programme 31

false allegations, of child sexual abuse 520
false disclosures, and PSCOT (post-conviction
        polygraph testing) 158–9
false negatives, in risk assessment scales 61
false positives
    in attention-based measures 120
    and juvenile offenders 283
    in risk assessment scales 61
Falshaw, L. 65

families of sex offenders
  and MST 459–62
  and treatment programmes 351, 360
families, sexual abuse in 491–509
  child sexual abuse 492–4
  intimate partner rape 492, 497–9
  long-term effects of 500–1
  mental health factors in 499–500
  placement in a new family 507–8
  prevention 501–4, 504–8
  risk assessment 503–4
  siblings 496–7
  social policy and legislation 491–2
  targeting risk factors 502–3
fantasies *see* deviant fantasies
Farley, F. 271
Felson, M. 182
female genital mutilation 492
female offenders 2, 9, 473–86, 495
  attitudes to 473–4
  and child maltreatment 475–6
  current life situation 482–3
  juvenile 431–2
  risk assessment 49, 474–7
  treatment needs 474, 477–84
  typologies of 478–9
female sex offenders 420
Fernandez, Y.M. 133, 136, 311, 317, 332, 378, 442
fetishism, and risk of recidivism 43–4
Fincknaeuer, J. 294
Finkelhor, D. 330, 381, 493–4, 498
Firestone, P. 117
Fisher, D. 66, 89, 338, 506
Fisher, M.J. 420
Fonagy, P. 16, 27, 439, 440–1, 442
FORA (functional offence risk analysis) 83–5, 86
Ford, H. 359–60
Fordham, A. 31, 336, 337, 355
Forensic Psychiatric Centre (FPC), Veldzicht 424
formulation driven interventions, and personality
    disorder offenders 419–20
Forth, A.E. 434
Frenzel, R.R. 136
Frothingham, S. 320
functional behaviour analysis 82–3, 86
functional offence risk analysis (FORA) 83–5, 86

Gangadajran, S.K. 222
GAS (Goal Attainment Scaling) 255, 256–7, 259
Geer, T.M. 91–2
gender
  and attention-based measures of sexual interest
      111–13, 122–3
  see also female offenders; women
GES (Group Environment Scale) 336–7
gestalt therapy 418
Giargiari, T.D. 122

Gibson, C.L. 184
Giedd, J.N. 438
Gilbert, P. 363–4, 417, 418, 421
Giotakis, O. 112–13
Glaser, W. 226, 229
Goal Attainment Scaling (GAS) 255, 256–7, 259
Good Lives Model (GLM) of rehabilitation 244, 294,
    296, 303–8, 335, 338
  aetological assumptions 306
  and changing sexual interests 313
  and female offenders 481
  and primary goods 303–4, 305
  and treatment programmes 335, 338, 362
Goodwin, D.W. 314
Goodwin, J. 520
Gordon, J.R. 78
GPSPP (General Personality and Social Psychology
    Perspective on Criminal conduct) 300
Gray, N.S. 116
Gray, S.R. 319
Grayston, A.D. 476, 484
Greenwald, A.G. 258
Grendon Therapeutic Community 423
Gress, C.L. 113, 120–1, 124
Gretton, H.M. 268
grievance motivated offenders 411
Griffiths, D. 226
Griffiths, E. 318
Grisso, T. 435
Groth, A.N. 498
Group Environment Scale (GES) 336–7
group therapy, for incarcerated offenders 336–7
Grubin, D. 151, 157
Guay, J.P. 412
Gudjonsson, G.H. 93
Guloien, T.H. 205–6

Haag, A.M. 58
Hall, G.C.N. 201
Hamilton, C.E. 229, 523
Hanson, Damien 535, 536, 539
Hanson, R.K. 39, 40, 41, 44–5, 46, 47, 48, 67, 70, 81,
    266, 314, 342
  actuarial risk scales 57–8
  Dynamic Supervision Project 48–9
  female offender studies 476
  juvenile offender treatment studies 458
  reconviction rates 337
  STABLE/ACUTE 2000 system 68, 211
Hare Psychopathy Checklist-Youth Version (PCL-YV)
    434
Harris, A. 44–5, 46, 47, 48, 67
  STABLE/ACUTE 2000 system 68, 211
Harris, A.J.R. 220, 231, 337
Harris, G.T. 133, 134–5
Hastings, R. 219
Hayes Ability Screening Index 218

Hayes, S. 371
HCR (Historical Clinical Risk Management) 238
Hecker, J.E. 122
Henry, F. 360–1
Hesselton, D. 60
Hildebran, D. 333
Hill, A. 410–11
Hingsburger, D. 226
Hirschman, R. 201
history of offending
    and deviant sexual interests 312
    intellectually disabled (ID) offenders 371–2
    and Internet sex offenders 209–10
    and juvenile offenders 268
    and post-conviction polygraph testing 147, 149–50,
        153
    and risk of recidivism 40–1, 56
history of sexual victimisation, and juvenile offenders
    269–70
HMPS Revised Psychometric Assessment Battery
    Manual 253–4
Hodes, P. 395
Hodge, J. 394
Hoffman, M. 440, 441
Hogue, T.E. 240–1
holistic treatment, of adolescent offenders 444–5
Holland, A.J. 217
Hollin, C.R. 482
Holmen, M.L. 314, 318
homicide *see* sexual murders
homosexuality
    and attention-based measures of sexual interest 111,
        112, 113
    and intimate partner violence 498
Horowitz, H.M. 17–19, 26
hostility, as a dynamic risk factor 82
Howes, R.J. 133–4, 137, 138
Hubble, M.A. 401
Hudson, S.M. 265, 333, 341
Hughes, R.C. 283–4
Hunter, J.A. 268, 283, 314
Hutchinson, R. 65
hypersexual behaviour 163

IATs (implicit association tests) 116–17, 123, 124, 258
ID *see* intellectually disabled (ID) offenders
IDA (Initial Deviance Assessment) 67–8, 95, 210
idiographic risk factors 66
implicit association tests (IATs) 116–17, 123, 124, 258
implicit theories 418
impulsivity 81
    and intellectually disabled (ID) offenders 229
    and Internet sex offenders 204
    and juvenile offenders 276
    psychometric assessment of 94, 95
    and rehabilitation models 306
    and treatment programmes 342

incarcerated offenders
    mental illness in 394
    risk assessment scales 61
    sexual addiction in 165, 168
    treatment of 329–43
incest offenders 494–6
    actuarial risk assessment of 65
    attachment problems 13
    convicted 504
    phallometric testing of 311–12
    psychometric assessment of 96
    and risk of recidivism 41
individual intervention, and personality disorder
        offenders 419
infant attachment 15–16, 17–19, 20–1, 22
Initial Deviance Assessment (IDA) 67–8, 95, 210
insecure attachment 15–16, 17–19, 20–1, 22, 27,
        28, 31
integrated models of treatment, for adolescent offenders
        445–7
Integrated Theory of Sexual Offending 419
intellectually disabled (ID) offenders 2–3, 8, 217–31,
        369–88
    assessment of personality disorder 221–3
    carers of 386
    characteristics of 371–3
    definition problems 217–18
    distorted attitudes/beliefs 223, 225–8
    and eugenics 369
    polygraph testing of 159
    prevalence of sexually abuse behaviour 370–1
    risk assessment of 61, 65
    sexual preference and sexual drive 229–30
    socio-affective functioning 223–5
    treatment for 373–88
    and victim empathy 377, 382–4, 386–7
    see also SOTSEC-ID treatment model
intelligence, and attention-based measures of sexual
        interest 124
intensive supervision 149
Internet
    CEOP (Child Exploitation and Online Protection)
        Centre 525–6
    child pornography sites 171, 173
        blockage of 199
    legislation on photographs of children 516
    sex offenders 1, 3, 6–7, 199–212
        and contact sexual offences 205–7
        convictions 199, 209–10
        dual offenders 206–7
        dynamic risk factors 199, 210–11
        level of sexual preoccupation 211–12
        psychometric assessment of 200–5
        and RSHOs (Risk of Sexual Harm Orders) 529–30
        sentencing guidelines for 207–8
        and the Stop it Now! campaign 361
    and sexual addiction 169–72

Internet Sex Offender Treatment Programme (i-SOTP) 211
intervention implications, of rehabilitation theories 296, 298–9
intimacy difficulties
  and child sexual abuse 201, 202, 203
  and dynamic risk factors 46, 81–2, 84
  and Emotional Stroop studies 115
  and Internet sex offenders 204–5
  and the Wolvercote treatment programme 350
IPPA (Inventory of Parent and Peer Attachment) 26
IPT (Imaginal Provocation Test) 224, 225
IQ measurement
  intellectually disabled offenders 218, 226–7, 230
  juvenile offenders 274–5

J-SOAP-II (Juvenile Sex Offender Assessment Protocol) 266, 272–82, 284
Jackson, P.L. 417
Jackson, R.L. 412
Jellicoe, D. 422
Jensen, S. 319
Johnson, G.J. 420
Johnson, T. 497
Johnston, P. 324
Jones, D.P.H. 520
Jones, E. 446
Jones, L. 241, 252, 409–10, 413, 415, 420, 422–3
juvenile offenders 453–70
  complexities and needs of 431–49
  family characteristics 454, 457
  individual factors 454, 457
  multisystemic therapy for 9, 459–69
  peer relations 455–6, 457
  PSBs (problem sexual behaviours) 454, 456–9, 462–9
  risk assessment of 265–84
  sexual maltreatment of siblings 496–7
  subgroups of 454
  treatment programmes 294
  see also adolescent offenders

Kagan, J. 441
Kaul, J.D. 60
Keen, S. 205
Keltner, A. 318
Kemshall, H. 538
Kennedy, P. 412
Kenney, D.T. 268
Keogh, T. 268
Kercher, G. 479
Kibblewhite, K. 402
King, M.W. 122
Kirby, S. 496
Kirsch, L.G. 282
Knight, R.A. 187, 412
Koerner, K. 414–15
Kohlenberg, R.J. 414–15

Kokish, R. 157, 158
Kolton, D.J.C. 227
Korenreich, C. 417
Koukounas, E. 122

Lab, S. 293
Lalumière, M.L. 133, 134–5
Lambrick, F. 226
Lang, R.A. 136
Langevin, R. 93, 131, 409, 421
Langström, N. 267
Langton, C.M. 58, 85
Lanning, K. 519
Laws, D.R. 130, 132, 314, 318, 323, 334
Le Blanc 26–7
Lea, S. 402
learning disabilities, offenders with see intellectually disabled (ID) offenders
Lee, D.A. 418
Letourneau, E.J. 119, 120, 137, 437
Lie, D. 83
life course, of adolescent sexual offending 436–7
Lindsay, W.R. 217, 218–19, 220–1, 222, 223, 224, 225, 226, 230, 231, 373–4, 386–7
Linehan, M. 413, 414, 415
Lippens, K. 323
Lipsey, M. 294
Livesley, W.J. 240, 241, 243, 409, 414
Lloyd, S. 523
Local Safeguarding Children Boards 521–2
Longo, R.E. 172
Looman, J. 422
low self-esteem
  and personality disorder 413
  psychometric assessment of 99
  and treatment programmes 342
LSI-R (Level of Service Inventory-Revised) 553, 554, 555, 556, 564
Lucy Faithfull Foundation, Wolvercote residential clinic 349–64
Luiselli, J.K. 226
Lunsky, Y. 226
Lussier, P. 47
Lynch, M. 495

MAC (minimal arousal conditioning) 319
McAnulty, R.D. 131
McCabe, M.P. 122
McCabe, S. 371
McCarthy, M. 369
McConaghy, N. 130, 314
McCormack, J. 341
McDougall, C. 420
McGhee, J.L. 258
McGrath, R.J. 314, 315, 321, 445
McGraw, J.M. 520
McGuire, R.J. 311

McMillan, D. 219
Madsen, L. 157, 158–9
Maguire, M. 537
male victims
    and juvenile offenders 270
    and risk of recidivism 41
Maletzky, B.M. 149, 230, 314, 322
Mann, R.E. 45, 331, 341
MAPPA *see* Multi-Agency Public Protection
    Arrangements (MAPPA)
MARA (Multiaxial Risk Appraisal) 66
MARACs (Multi-Agency Risk Assessment
    Conferences) 491
marital status, and risk of sexual recidivism 40
Marlatt, G.A. 78
Marquis, J.N. 322
Marshall, L.E. 166
Marshall, W.L. 31, 46, 85, 133, 135, 136, 137, 139, 166,
    167, 200, 206, 311, 314, 317, 318, 320
    covert association 321–2
    empathy model 440
    personality disorders 411, 412
    satiation therapy 323
    treatment programmes 332, 333, 336–7, 339, 340,
    378
Martin, E.K. 498
Maruna, S. 295, 330–1
MAST (Michigan Alcoholism Screening Test) 166
Masters, W.H. 322
masturbation
    and Internet sex offenders 206, 211
    modifying sexual preferences 314, 319, 322–3, 324,
    340
    and sexual addiction 167, 171, 172–3
    and sexual self-regulation 43, 44
Mathis, J.L. 473
Matthews, J.K. 478–9, 485
MCA (multiple correspondence analysis), of data on
    sexual aggressors of women 189–90
MCMI (Millon Clinical Multiaxial Inventory) 412
media representations of sex offenders, and treatment
    programmes 360
medications 32, 312, 340–1, 363
Megan's Law 530, 536
Mental Health Acts 370, 393–4
    and victim empathy 405
mental health civil commitments, and actuarial risk
    assessment in USA courtrooms 555–6, 564
mental health factors
    and female offenders 480, 483–4
    and sexual abuse in families 499–500
mentalisation 439–40
mentally ill offenders 2, 8, 393–406
    and adolescent offenders 443
    and cognitive behaviour therapy (CBT) 400–1
    confronting 397–8
    denial training phase 402–3

disclosure phase 403
group interventions 398–402
prevalence of 394–6
and readiness 400–1
and relapse prevention 405–6
and sexual recidivism 39
treatment issues 396–7
metacognition 439–40, 442
metaphysical assumptions, of rehabilitation theories 297
Meyer, J. 314, 318
MI (Motivational Interviewing) 336
Michie, A.M. 227
Middleton, D. 421
Milhailides, S. 116–17
Milloy, C.D. 268
Miner, M.H. 119, 120, 437, 447
minimal arousal conditioning (MAC) 319
Minnesota Multiphasic Personality Inventory (MMPI)
    91–2, 93–5
Minnesota Sex Offender Screening Tool-Revised
    (MnSOST-R) 60, 553, 561
Mitchell, I.J. 363
MMPI (Minnesota Multiphasic Personality Inventory)
    91–2, 93–5
MnSOST-R (Minnesota Sex Offender Screening
    Tool-Revised) 60, 65, 553, 561
modifying sexual preferences 311–24
    behavioural procedures 314–23
    and future life plans 312–13
    medication 312
    treatment programmes 338–41
Mokros, A. 113
Molinder, I. 90
Mongeau, P. 397
Morahan-Martin, J. 205
Morey, L.C. 222
Morton-Bourgon, K.E. 40, 44, 46, 47, 58, 342
Mossman, D. 278, 280
motivational interviewing (MI) 336
Mrazek, P. 495
MSI (Multiphasic Sex Inventory) 85, 90, 91–2, 101, 119
MST (Multisystemic Therapy) 9, 459–69
    case study 464–9
Multi-Agency Public Protection Arrangements
    (MAPPA) 10, 30, 358, 476, 526–31, 535–49
    community management 546–8
    future developments and improvements 548–9
    risk management packages 543–5
    Strategic Management Boards 548
    see also public protection
Multiphasic Sex Inventory (MSI) 85, 90, 91–2, 101, 119
multiple correspondence analysis *see* MCA (multiple
    correspondence analysis)
multiple dysfunctional mechanisms, and child sexual
    abuse 201, 202
multiple victims, juvenile offenders and reoffending
    269, 270

multisystemic therapy (MST) 459–69
    case study 464–9
Muran, J.C. 414
murder *see* sexual murders
Murphy, C. 412

Naik, B.I. 222
narrative identity/agency, and rehabilitation models 303,
    305
narrative therapies 416
NAS (Novaco Anger Scale) 224, 225
Nathan, P. 478
National Probation Service, psychometric tests 201–2,
    203
NCSAC (National Council on Sexual Addiction and
    Compulsivity) 169–70
need principle, and the RNR model of rehabilitation
    300, 301
needs assessment, of juvenile offenders 284
neutralisation theory 330–1
Nicholaichuk, T. 475
Nichols, H.R. 90
Nika, E. 410
Nisbet, I.A. 283
Noble, J.H. 218
NOMS (National Offender Management Service) 528
normative rehabilitation theories 296
Noutch, T. 238
Novaco, R.W. 224
Nowicki-Strickland Internal-External Locus of Control
    Scale 89
Nunes, K.L. 117
Nussbaum, D. 229

OASys (Offender Assessment System) 538–9
O'Brien, M.D. 209–10
Obsessive Compulsive Disorder 212
ODARA (Ontario Domestic Assault Risk Assessment)
    555
O'Donohue, W. 137
offence disclosure work, and personality disorder 415
offence paralleling behaviour (OPB) 418, 420
offence-supportive cognitions 341
Ogard, E. 145
olfactory aversion 317–19
OPB (offence paralleling behaviour) 418, 420
opportunistic sexual aggressors of women 181, 186,
    191, 192
Orcutt, D.P. 172
Over, R. 122
overarching rehabilitation theories 296

PAI (Personality Assessment Inventory) 204–5
paraphilias
    dynamic risk factors for 67
    and personality disorder 413
    psychometric assessment of 91

and risk of recidivism 43–4
and sexual preoccupation 211
Parker, R. 415
Parry, C. 230
Pathways Model (Ward and Siegert) 200–4, 243, 416
PBI (Parental Bonding Instrument) 23, 25–6
PCC (Psychology of Criminal Conduct Perspective) 300
PCL-R (Psychopathy Checklist-Revised) 84–5, 93, 238,
    239, 399, 412, 422
PD *see* personality disorder (PD)
the Peaks (Dangerous and Severe Personality Disorders
    Unit) 237–60
    approach to treatment 239–40
    assessment process 245–6, 247–58
    assessment reporting 259
    clinical strategy 240–4
    drop-out prevention plan 252–3
    goal attainment scaling 255, 256–7
    phallometric assessment 246, 255–8
    population characteristics 238–9
    self-report measures 253–4
    Sex Offender Groups 248, 249–50, 251, 258, 259
    treatment suitability 246–9
    ward behaviour 254–5
peer relations
    female offenders 481
    juvenile offenders 455–6
penile plethysmograph (PPG) 67, 109, 119, 129–39
    assessing severe personality disorder 246, 255–8
    audiotapes 132–3
    and deviant sexual interests 311–12, 339
    European Court ruling on 158
    faking during 137–8
    future of 138–9
    and juvenile offenders 268
    measuring devices 130–1, 137
    and minimal arousal conditioning (MAC) 319
    offender/non-offender subject differences 136
    and satiation therapy 323
    scoring methods 133–6
    standardisation in 136–8
    stimulus differences 131–2
perception-action model of empathy 417
Perkins, D. 419
personality, and risk of sexual recidivism 40
Personality Assessment Inventory (PAI) 204–5
personality disorder (PD) 409–25
    and adolescent offenders 434–5
    APD (antisocial personality disorder) 282, 434
    assessments of 221–3
    child abusers 411–12
    interventions with offenders 413–23
    outcome studies 423–4
    and psychopathy 412
    rape offenders 410
    sadistic offenders 411, 412–13, 424
    severe and dangerous 237–60

sexual homicide and 410–11
see also the Peaks (Dangerous and Severe Personality Disorders Unit)
personality traits, psychometric assessment of 92–5
Peters, S.D. 520
Peterson-Quay-Cameron Psychopathy (PQC) scale 93
Petrosino, A. 294
phallometry *see* penile plethysmograph (PPG)
Philippot, P. 417
Pierce, L.H. 497
Pierce, R.L. 497
PIG (Problem of Immediate Gratification) 79
Piquero, A.R. 184
Pithers, W.D. 79, 333
Plotnikoff, J. 518
Polaschek, D.L.L. 416
police work 10, 515–31
    and intellectually disabled (ID) offenders 387
    legislation on sexual offences 516–17
    paedophile units 525
    proactive intelligence gathering 523–5
    recorded sex crimes 515
    Register of Sex Offences 30, 516
    reported sex crimes 1, 498, 516
    and sexual assault 517–22
Pollak, S.D. 417
polygraph testing
    background to 146–7
    see also PSCOT (post-conviction polygraph testing)
pornography, child pornography and Internet sex offenders 171, 173, 199–212
Porter, S. 410, 412
post-conviction polygraph testing *see* PSCOT (post-conviction polygraph testing)
power, and female offenders 483
PPG *see* penile plethysmograph (PPG)
PQC (Peterson-Quay-Cameron Psychopathy) scale 93
predictive accuracy
    of psychometric assessment 99–102
    of risk assessment 53–70
Prentky, R.A. 187
Price, S. 115
Prison Service
    ASOTP (adapted sex offenders treatment programme) 373, 381–2
    Grendon Therapeutic Community 423
    Sex Offender Treatment Programme (SOPT) 336–7, 373, 399, 508
    and the Wolvercote programme 350, 359
pro-offending attitudes
    psychometric assessment of 95, 97–8, 100
    and risk of recidivism 44–5, 82, 84
probation orders 2
Problem of Immediate Gratification (PIG) 79
professional discretion, and the RNR model of rehabilitation 300
prostitution 517

Protter, B. 481
Proulx, J. 410, 412–13
PSCOT (post-conviction polygraph testing) 145–59
    accuracy of 156–7
    and behaviour modification 150–2
    comparison studies 152–3
    containment approach to 148
    disclosures regarding current behaviour 153–4
    ethics of 157–9
    false disclosures 158–9
    maintenance testing 147, 153
    monitoring test 148
    rationale for 148–9
    risk assessment and intervention 154–5
    seriousness of disclosures 154
    sex history disclosure testing 147, 149–50, 153
    specific issue offence test 147–8
    and treatment programmes 152, 155–6
psychological functioning in sex offenders, psychometric assessment of 90–2
psychometric assessment 89–103
    of the construct of sexual deviancy 95–9
    of female offenders 479
    of Internet sex offenders 201–5
    of personality traits 92–5
    predictive accuracy of 99–102
    of psychological functioning 90–2
    standardisation of 89
    and the Wolvercote treatment programme 350, 352–3
psychopathy
    and adolescent offenders 434–5
    PCL-R (Psychopathy Checklist-Revised) 84–5, 93, 238, 239, 399, 412, 422
    and personality disorder 221, 412
    psychometric assessment of 93
    and risk of recidivism 43, 56, 57
    and sexual addiction 168
    and sexual aggressors of women 184, 194
Psychopathy Checklist-Revised (PCL-R) 84–5, 93
public protection 10, 30, 358, 476, 526–31, 535–49
    effective case management 545–6
    identification and assessment of high-risk offenders 538–9
    and legislation 526–7
    and risk management planning 540–1

QACSO (Questionnaire on Attitudes Consistent with Sexual Offences) 227–8
Quayle, E. 200
Questionnaire on Attitudes Consistent with Sexual Offences (QACSO) 227–8
Quinsey, V.L. 59, 134, 137, 220, 223, 226, 231

Rada, R. 520
Rampton Hospital *see* the Peaks (Dangerous and Severe Personality Disorders Unit)

rape offenders 1, 3
  actuarial risk assessment of 58
  adolescents 2
  and attachment 23, 25
  denial by 149
  dynamic risk factors 67
  intimate partner rape 492, 497–9
  and mental illness 395
  and penile plethysmograph (PPG) 136
  personality disorder 410
  rape kits 183, 185
  recorded 515
  typologies of 181–95
  see also sexual aggressors of women
rapid serial visual presentation (RSVP) 117–18, 124, 125
rational choice perspective, on sexual aggressors of women 182–7
Raymond, N.C. 411
readiness, and mentally ill offenders 400–1
recidivism
  actuarial risk assessment approach to 10, 54–66, 552, 562–3
  and age of offenders 559–60
  and cognitive distortions 331
  dynamic risk factors in 41–8, 81–2
  factors associated with 39–49, 67, 68, 70
  and female offenders 49, 475, 476–7, 485
  and FORA (functional offence risk analysis) 83–5
  intellectually disabled (ID) offenders 3, 219, 222, 223, 377
  and Internet sex offenders 211
  and juvenile offenders 364, 458
  and modification of sexual preferences 314–15
  and phallometric assessment 139, 258
  and polygraphy 145
  predicting risk of in juveniles 265–84
  psychometric assessment of 92, 98
  and relapse prevention 334–5
  and the RNR rehabilitation model 302
  and self-regulation 43–4, 47–8, 80–1, 99, 102
  and sexual addiction 171, 173
  and sexual deviance 7
  static risk factors in 40–1, 53, 81–2
  and treatment planning 337–8
  and treatment programmes 294, 343
  and victim empathy 332
reconvicted offenders 1–2
  actuarial risk assessment of 65
  ID sex offenders 3
  Internet offences 209–10
  psychometric assessment of 99, 103
  reconviction rates and treatment programmes 337–8, 359–60
  see also recidivism
Register of Sex Offenders 30, 516, 530, 536
rehabilitation, and sexual abuse in families 505–7

rehabilitation theories 293–308
  aetiological assumptions 296, 297–8
  evaluation 299
  general principles 296, 297
  intervention implications 296, 298–9
  nature of 295
  RNR (Risk-Need-Responsivity) model 294, 296, 299–303, 307–8
  and treatment programmes 307–8
  see also Good Lives Model (GLM) of rehabilitation; treatment programmes
reintegration, and rehabilitation theory 295
relapse prevention (RP) 78–9, 80
  intellectually disabled (ID) offenders 384–5
  and mentally ill offenders 405–6
  treating incarcerated offenders 329, 334–5
  Wolvercote treatment programme 354, 357, 362
relationship skills, and treatment programmes 341–2, 356, 461
Renwick, S.J. 384
Renzetti, C.M. 499
repertory grids 254
research-guided clinical judgement 55
Resick, P.A. 498
responsivity principle
  and personality disorder interventions 421
  and the RNR model of rehabilitation 300, 301, 303
Reyna, V.F. 271
Rich, P. 267
Richards, H.J. 412
Riggan, M. 320
rights
  of people with intellectual disabilities 370
  and rehabilitation theories 298
  and treatment programmes 294
Ring, L. 479, 483
risk assessment 5–6, 7
  clinical judgement 53, 54
  and clinical judgement 53, 54, 55
  defining 39–49
  factors associated with recidivism 39–49
  female offenders 49, 474–7
  functional offence risk analysis 83–5
  of intellectually disabled (ID) offenders 7, 218–31
  of juvenile offenders 265–84
  and personality disorder 244–5
  and police work 528
  and post-conviction polygraph testing 154–5
  predictive accuracy of 53–70
    limitations of current scales 61–6
  sexual abuse in families 503–4
  and treatment planning of incarcerated offenders 337–8
  see also actuarial risk assessment; dynamic risk factors; static risk factors
risk management planning, and public protection 540–1
risk taking, and juvenile offenders 271

risk-adversity, and juvenile offenders 271
risk-based case formulation 77–86
  functional behaviour analysis 82–3, 86
  functional offence risk analysis (FORA) 83–5, 86
  relapse prevention (RP) 78–9, 80
  self-regulation model of 79–81
Risk-Need-Responsivity *see* RNR
  (Risk-Need-Responsivity) model of
  rehabilitation
RM2000 (Risk Matrix 2000) 59, 61, 63
  and intellectually disabled offenders 220–1, 231
  and Internet sex offenders 209
  and severe personality disorder 238
RNR (Risk-Need-Responsivity) model of rehabilitation
  294, 296, 299–303, 307–8
  aetiological assumptions of 300–1
  need principle 300, 301
  responsivity principle 300, 301, 303
ROC (Receiver Operating Characteristic) analysis 54,
  56, 58, 68, 92, 99–100, 118, 278
  juvenile offenders 278–81
Rogers, C.R. 442
Rogers, R.W. 397
Rogosch, F.A. 282
romantic attachment 17–19, 22, 24, 29–30
Rose, J. 387
Rowe, W.E. 268
RP *see* relapse prevention (RP)
RRASOR (Rapid Risk Assessment for Sexual Offence
  Recidivism) 41, 57, 58, 61, 62, 65, 220, 221,
  231, 552, 553
RSHO (Risk of Sexual Harm Order) 529–30
RSQ (Relationships Questionnaire) 24–5
RSVP (rapid serial visual presentation) 117–18, 124,
  125
Rubin, H.B. 131
Rycus, J.S. 283–4
Ryle, A. 403

SACJ-Min (Structured Anchored Clinical Judgement),
  predictive accuracy of 57, 58, 61, 62
sadistic offenders
  actuarial risk assessment of 560
  aversion techniques 318
  and personality disorder 411, 412–13, 424
  sexual aggressors of women 181, 185, 190, 191, 193,
  194, 498
Safran, J.D. 414
Sahd, D. 520
Sahota, K. 395
Salter, A.C. 330, 332, 336
Samenow, S.E. 184
Santtila, P. 113
Saradjian, J. 420, 479, 482, 484, 485–6
Sarah's Law 526, 530
SARN (Structured Risk Assessment of Risk and Need)
  97, 244, 250, 258, 259

SAST (Sexual Addiction Screening Test) 165–6, 168
satiation therapy 323, 340, 351
scared straight programmes 294
schema therapy 417–18
schizophrenia 394, 395, 397
Schmidt, E. 322
Schneider, J.P. 170–1
schools, and juvenile offenders 456, 457
Schouten, P.G.W. 132, 135
Schram, D.D. 268
Schumacher, P. 205
Schwartz, J.L. 258
Scoular, R.J. 122
screening, and active intelligence seeking 562
SDI-R (Sexual Dependence Inventory-Revised) 165,
  166
Seager, J.A. 422
Seagrave, D. 435
search warrants 524
secure attachment 15–16, 17–19, 20–1, 22, 27
Seidler, K. 268
self-efficacy training 356–7
self-harm, and severe personality disorder 239
self-management
  and intellectually disabled (ID) offenders 223,
  228–9
  and personality disorder 416
  psychometric assessment of 99, 100, 101
  and relapse prevention 335
  severe personality disorder offenders 241–2
  and treatment programmes 342
self-regulation
  and FORA (functional offence risk analysis) 84
  and intellectually disabled (ID) offenders 228–9
  model for conceptualising sex offences 79–81
  and risk of recidivism 43–4, 47–8, 80–1, 82
self-report measures
  deviant sexual interests 312
  of Internet sex offenders 206
  and penile plethysmograph (PPG) 133
  and severe personality disorder assessment 253–4
  of sexual abuse 493
  of sexual addiction 163, 168
  of sexual assaults 517
  of sexual deviance 109–25
  victim empathy 333
sentences 1–2
Sentencing Guidelines Council (SGC), and Internet sex
  offenders 207–8
Serber, M. 315–16
serotonin 363
Serran, G.A. 137, 139, 442
Seto, M.C. 206, 209, 265
sex education, and the SOTSEC-ID treatment model
  379–80
Sex Knowledge and Beliefs Scale 91
Sex Offences Act (2003) 516, 517

Sex Offender Treatment Evaluation Project (STEP)
95–7
Sex Offender Treatment Groups 248, 249–50, 251, 258,
259
Sex Offender Treatment Programme *see* SOPT (Sex
Offender Treatment Programme)
Sex Offenders Act (1997) 30
sexual addiction 163–73
behaviour of 167
and co-morbid addictions 166–7
coping strategies 167–8
Internet users 169–72
measures of 165–6
medications for 341
prevalence of 166
and psychopathy 168
and recidivism 171
research review of 164–5
in sexual offenders 173
treatment programmes 163
Sexual Addiction Screening Test (SAST) 165–6, 168
sexual aggressors of women 181–95
angry 181, 185–6, 190–2, 193–4, 498
compensatory 181, 187, 192–3
crime scripts 182, 183–4, 189, 192, 193–4, 194–5
data analysis of 189–90
opportunistic 181, 186, 191, 192
rational choice perspective on 182–7
research subjects 187–8
sadistic 181, 185, 190, 191, 193, 194, 498
situational factors in 189, 194–5
see also rape offenders; sexual murders
sexual deviance scales, in psychometric assessment 91
Sexual Dysfunction Scales 91
sexual interest
attention-based measures of 110–23
and SARN 250
sexual murders 3, 181
angry 185, 186
opportunistic 186
and personality disorder 410–11, 413
research subjects 187–8
sadistic 185, 193, 413
Sexual Offences Prevention Orders (SOPOs) 529
sexual preferences, modifying 311–24
sexual preoccupation
and Internet offenders 211–12
and juvenile offenders 276
and risk of recidivism 43–4
Sexual Risk Behaviours factors 58
Sexual Violence Risk-20 54, 85
sexually compulsive behaviour 163
online 170–1
sexually excessive behaviour 163
sexually impulsive behaviour 163
sexually motivated offenders 411
shame aversion 315–16, 320

SHAPS (Special Hospitals Assessment of Personality
and Socialisation) 93–5, 101
siblings, sexual maltreatment by 496–7
Siegert, R.J. 200–4, 243
Significant Other Scale 225
Sigurdsson, J.F. 93
Simkins, L. 92
Sinclair, N. 375
Singer, B. 111
Singleton, N. 394
Sizmar, S. 238
Skilling, T.A. 220, 223, 231
skills development
and treatment programmes 341–2, 351–2
adolescent offenders 445, 448
Skinner, B.F. 314
Smallbone, S.W. 29, 268
Smith, A.W.H. 373–4, 387
Smith, P. 115
social exclusion 329, 417
social influences, and risk of recidivism 45–6, 82
Social Knowledge & Attitudes Assessment Tool
(SSKAART-R) 226
social services, and disclosure of sex offenders 530–1
social support, and female offenders 481–2
socio-affective functioning, intellectually disabled (ID)
offenders 223–5
solution-focused offence work 415–16
SONAR (Sex Offender Need Assessment Rating)
68
SOPOs (Sexual Offences Prevention Orders) 529
SOPT (Sex Offender Treatment Programme) 336–7,
373, 399, 508
SORAG (Sex Offender Risk Appraisal Guide) 41, 59,
63, 65, 220, 553, 554
SOTEP (California Sex Offender Treatment Evaluation
Project) 334–5, 382
SOTSEC-ID treatment model 8, 374–88
assessment measures 376–7
cognitive model 380–1
definitions 375
human relations and sex education 379–80
limitations of 387–8
purpose 374–5
relapse prevention 384–5
social and therapeutic framework 278–9
and victim empathy 383
Spaccarelli, S. 268
Spear, L.P. 438
Special Hospitals Assessment of Personality and
Socialisation (SHAPS) 93–5
Sperry, L. 240
Spitzer, C. 420
SPJ (structured professional judgement) 85, 86
SRA (Structured Risk Assessment) model 67, 69, 95,
97–9
and Internet sex offenders 210

SSKAAT-R (Social-Sexual Knowledge & Attitudes Assessment Tool) 226, 227
SSRIs (selective serotonin re-uptake inhibitors) 32, 340–1, 363
stable dynamic risk factors 66, 67, 69
  and Internet sex offenders 210
  and personality disorder 245
  and sexual recidivism 43–8, 81–2
STABLE-2000 system 68, 211
startle probe reflex 121–3
State-Trait Anger Expression Inventory (STAXI) 224
static risk factors 31
  and actuarial risk assessment 53, 54–66
  assessing intellectually disabled (ID) offenders 7, 218–21
  and Internet sex offenders 199
  and juvenile offenders 280–1
  and sexual recidivism 40–1, 53, 81
  and treatment programmes 338
Static-99 41, 57–8, 61, 62–3, 65, 85, 99–100, 101, 102, 433, 553
Static-2002 58
statistically fallacy, and risk assessment scales 61
STAXI (State-Trait Anger Expression Inventory) 224
Steinberg, L. 271, 439
STEP (Sex Offender Treatment Evaluation Project) 95–7
Steptoe, L. 225
Stewart, C.A. 303
Stilwell, B. 441
Stirpe, T. 342
Stop it Now! campaign 360–1
Strange Situation behaviour 15–16, 17–19, 22
stress, and risk of recidivism 48
Stringer, I. 55, 61
structured clinical judgement 55
structured professional judgement (SPJ) 85, 86
Structured Risk Assessment see SRA (Structured Risk Assessment) model
Structured Risk Assessment of Risk and Need (SARN) 97, 244, 250
substance abuse
  and female offenders 484
  and juvenile offenders 455, 458
  and relapse prevention 78
  and risk of recidivism 48, 82
SUDS (seemingly unimportant decisions), and relapse prevention 79
suicide, and severe personality disorder 239
Sullivan, J. 206
supervision
  cooperation with, and risk of recidivism 47–8
  intensive 149
surveillance of high-risk offenders 524–5, 541–3
SVR (Sexual Violence Risk-20) 60–1, 64, 66

Taft, C.T. 498
tagging offenders 149
Tasse, M.J. 83
Taylor, J.L. 224
Tesser, A. 79
Tewksbury, R. 483
theory of mind 411
therapeutic alliance 298
  and the RNR rehabilitation model 303
therapeutic communities, and mentally ill offenders 398–400
therapists, and victim empathy 333–4
Thom, R. 283
Thomas, T. 523
Thornton, D. 99, 423
  actuarial risk assessment 57, 58, 59, 66
  domains of dynamic risk factors 223–30
  Structured Risk Assessment 67–8, 95, 97–8, 210
Thorpe, J.G. 322
Tibbets, S.G. 184
TIBs (therapy interfering behaviours) 251, 252
TILs (therapy interfering limitations) 251, 252
Tough, S. 220, 231
tracking high-risk offenders 524–5
Travin, S. 481
treatment drop-out, and personality disorder interventions 421, 422–3
treatment programmes
  deterrence-based 294
  and the effects of childhood abuse 363–4
  incarcerated offenders 329–43
  for intellectually disabled (ID) offenders 369–88
  juvenile offenders 294, 456–70
  modifying sexual preferences 311–24
  and polygraph testing 152, 155–6
  and rehabilitation theories 307–8
  risk-based case formulation 77–86
  sexual abuse in families 508
  Wolvercote residential clinic 349–64
Tsai, M. 414
Turpin-Petrosino, C. 294
types of sexual offenders 1–4

unguided clinical judgement 55
United Nations, Declaration and Convention on people with intellectual disabilities 370
United States
  actuarial risk assessment in USA courtrooms 10, 551–65
  actuarial risk assessments in US courtrooms 10
  polygraph testing 146, 148

validity scales, in psychometric assessment 90
values, and rehabilitation theories 297, 299
van Beek, D.J. 424
Vandiver, D.M. 478, 479
Vanheule, S. 410, 411

Vess, J. 412
Vetlesen, A.J. 440, 441
vicarious sensitisation 320
victim awareness/empathy
  and adolescent offenders 445
  and female offenders 479
  and intellectually disabled (ID) offenders 377, 382–4,
    386–7
  and juvenile offenders 269
  and mentally ill offenders 405
  treating incarcerated offenders 329, 332–4, 343
  and the Wolvercote treatment programme 255
victim injury, and sexual recidivism 39
victimisation
  and attachment 23
  and female offenders 480–1, 485–6
  and juvenile offenders 269–70, 282, 454
  sex offenders as victims of abuse 363–4, 370, 386,
    420–1
  and sexual abuse in families 501, 503
victims
  and attachment problems 13
  female victims of sexual aggression 188–9
  of juvenile offenders 282–3
  male 41, 270
  rights of, and rehabilitation theories 298
  and sexual offenders with learning disabilities 61
viewing time (VT) 118–21
Viljanen, K. 113
VIM (violence inhibition mechanism) 417
violence inhibition mechanism (VIM) 417
Violence Risk Appraisal Guide (VRAG) 220, 221, 231,
  552
violent offenders
  and Internet sex offenders 209
  juveniles 268
  personality traits compared with sex offenders 93
  see also sexual aggressors of women
Vivian-Byrne, S.E. 420
VRAG (Violence Risk Appraisal Guide) 220, 221, 231,
  552, 553, 554, 555
VRS (Violence Risk Scale) 238
VT (viewing time) 118–21

Wald, D. 283
Wald statistical tests 277–8
Walker, N. 371
Walter, T.S. 132, 135
Ward, T. 29, 48, 69, 79, 101, 116–17, 148, 483
  cognitive deconstruction theory 333

formulation-based interventions 419
  Pathways Model 200–4, 243, 416
  rehabilitation theories 295, 303, 304, 335
  relationship skills 341
  schema therapy 417–18
Warner, M.S. 442
WARS (Ward Anger Rating Scale) 224
Waterman, M. 115
Webb, L. 205
Webster, S.D. 209–10
Wechsler Adult Intelligence Scale 218
Weinrott, M. 320
Wheeler, D. 131
Whitehead, J. 293
Wilcox, D. 206
Williams, F. 374
Williams, S.M. 475
Wilson, P.H. 268
Wolak, J. 206, 207
Wolfensberger, W. 369
Wolvercote treatment programme 349–64
  assessment 352–3
  Circles of Support and Accountability 357–8, 362,
    364
  effectiveness of 358–60
  intervention 352, 354–7
  pre-intervention 352, 353–4
  programme enhancement 361–4
  and the Stop it Now! campaign 360–1
women
  and Internet pornography 172
  sexual aggressors of 181–95
  see also female offenders
Woolfson, R. 518
Woolverton, M. 283
Worling, J.R. 120, 267, 268, 269, 272, 458
Wright, J. 21
Wright, L.W. 111–12, 113

Yates, P. 137, 139, 412
Yllo, K. 498
Yochelson, S. 184
Young, B.G. 311
Young, J. 418
young offenders see adolescent offenders; juvenile
  offenders
Yurgelun-Todd, D. 438

Zuravin, S.J. 501
Zwicke, L. 171